-La-
Cuisine

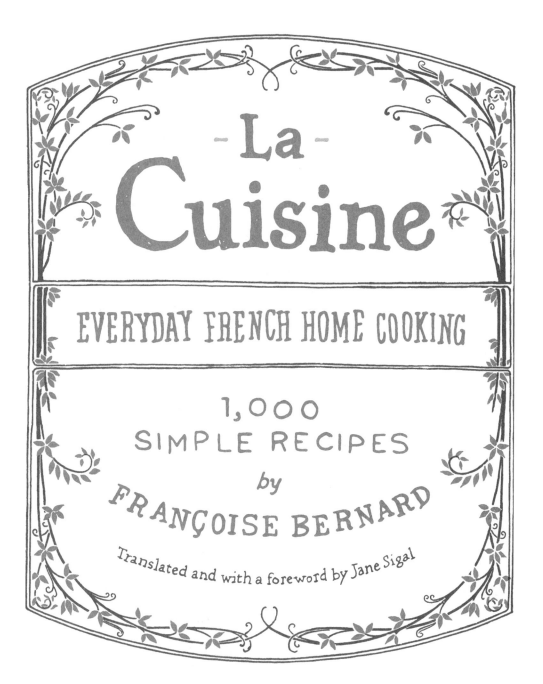

-La- Cuisine

EVERYDAY FRENCH HOME COOKING

1,000 SIMPLE RECIPES

by

FRANÇOISE BERNARD

Translated and with a foreword by Jane Sigal

RIZZOLI
NEW YORK

New York · Paris · London · Milan

First published in the English language
by RIZZOLI INTERNATIONAL PUBLICATIONS, INC.
300 PARK AVENUE SOUTH, NEW YORK, NY 10010

www.rizzoliusa.com

Originally published in the French language as *Cuisine 1000 Recettes*,
© 2008 HACHETTE LIVRE (Hachette Pratique)

© 2010 RIZZOLI INTERNATIONAL PUBLICATIONS, INC.

2010 2011 2012 2013 / 10 9 8 7 6 5 4 3 2 1

Distributed in the U.S. trade by Random House, New York

Printed in the United States of America

Translator: JANE SIGAL
Typesetter: TINA HENDERSON
Designer: ERICA HEITMAN-FORD *for* MUCCA DESIGN
Copy editor: LEDA SCHEINTAUB
Editor: CHRISTOPHER STEIGHNER
Proofreader: RACHEL SELEKMAN
Indexer: CATHY DORSEY
Production manager: KAIJA MARKOE
Editorial coordination, French edition: CATHERINE VIALARD-RUCHON *and* STÉPHAN LAGORCE

ISBN-13: 978-0-8478-3501-0

Library of Congress Control Number: 2010930504

TABLE OF CONTENTS

❖ ❖ ❖ ❖ ❖

FOREWORD
- Jane Sigal -

❖ ❖ ❖ ❖ ❖

In 1946, Françoise Bernard answered an ad in the French daily *Le Figaro* for a secretarial job at Unilever. This young, engaging Parisian, the daughter of dry cleaners, was quickly tapped to promote the company's latest product—margarine—by creating recipes, testing products, and answering customers' letters. (One housewife wrote to say that her eggs had exploded; she had put them in a saucepan to cook without water.) Eventually, Françoise's face appeared on billboards and commercials across France.

Françoise went on to dispense advice to generations of French home cooks in a career spanning almost sixty years. She cooked live on a TV series that lasted for three hundred episodes. She organized cooking competitions. And she wrote more than twenty cookbooks, including the iconic *Recettes Faciles (Easy Recipes)*, which has sold more than a million copies since the first edition was published in 1963 and has regularly been revised over the past forty years.

La Cuisine is the culmination of Françoise Bernard's work. It is a comprehensive volume of one thousand of her best recipes, interwoven with thousands of chatty hand-holding tips. (Her secret to weaving a lattice top on a tart? Alternate the direction of the dough strips as they are laid across the filling, arranging one lengthwise, then one crosswise, and so forth. Also, adding a little crème fraîche seems to make any dish noticeably better.)

In developing recipes for leaflets, cards, and other Unilever giveaways, and, later, for her own books, Françoise was a passionate defender of *la cuisine familiale*—uncomplicated, traditional French home cooking. But foreign dishes have quietly been absorbed into the French repertoire, too. So *La Cuisine* includes recipes for North African Couscous and Italian Osso Buco as well as Boeuf Bourguignon.

Françoise's other major cause was economy. As a young woman during the Occupation in the 1940s and the postwar years, she was familiar with scarcity and making do. As a result, each recipe in *La Cuisine* indicates not only how long it takes to prepare and the degree of difficulty, but also the cost. This thriftiness, the idea that food is precious, seems relevant today, feeding our current interest in eating responsibly. Françoise's ideas for not letting anything go to waste are interesting. Why throw out the cooking water when asparagus is simmered? She makes an asparagus soup with the tasty liquid. Radish greens and watercress stems, usually tossed, are transformed into delicious soups. And Françoise buys (and uses up every part of) whole chickens; there are few recipes for boneless chicken breasts.

Even though Françoise's mission has always been to guide the cook in the kitchen, *La Cuisine* lacks the methodical precision of most contemporary cookbooks. Some instructions may feel loosey-goosey or liberating, depending on your sensibility and confidence. Amounts of chopped parsley leaves (and thyme, cloves, and peppercorns) are not always listed, since it is understood that herbs and spices will be added to taste. Sizes of cookware, cooking temperatures, and times may be open-ended because it all depends: Do you have one very large skillet to sear four hefty steaks? Two smaller ones work fine. The temperature and how long it takes to cook something can vary according to the taste and the habit of the cook.

Françoise doesn't always specify the kind of oil, butter, vinegar, and other pantry items she uses either. Until recently, a neutral oil like peanut was the standard cooking oil in French homes; olive oil used to be found only in Provence. Butter in France is traditionally unsalted; salted butter still remains largely a regional specialty from the north of France. Vinegar is typically red wine vinegar, though in some rare instances it could also be white wine vinegar to avoid adding color to other ingredients. The salt added to season cooking water for boiling pasta, lobsters, and vegetables is typically *gros sel*; kosher salt, with its larger crystal size, is a fine substitute.

Like any mother, Françoise deals often with food likes and dislikes: She counsels to add water or broth to a stew if you're out of wine. If you don't like kirsch in a dessert, try rum or Cognac. The recipes are endlessly variable.

Most of her dishes are familiar and sweetly old-fashioned, like Clafoutis, Classic Crêpes, and Pot-au-Feu. Several of these cozy recipes—for example, Croque-Mignon (Baked Eggs in Brioches) and the Croquefort, a croque-monsieur made with Roquefort cheese—are terrific discoveries. Some items, like Pieds de Veau à la Poulette, have become so rare they can be found only in a few time-honored bistros in France.

Françoise's repertoire includes ingredients that are common in France and now available elsewhere as our tastes have broadened. For instance, vanilla sugar, called for in many of the dessert recipes, can be found at many supermarkets. Françoise also gives a half-dozen recipes for *poule* (hen). To make them, you will have to find an old laying hen, which may require chatting up an egg farmer at the farmers' market. But then you'll know how to poach it, stew it, and stuff it. I don't think I've ever seen conger eel at my local markets, however, and several varieties of fish are not on lists of sustainable seafood.

Naturally, over decades of cooking, Françoise changed her methods of preparing such basics

as rice, vinaigrette, and mayonnaise. When recipes from different eras are placed side by side, inconsistencies sometimes emerge. The order of adding ingredients to make a vinaigrette may vary, but you will still end up with the perfect French dressing.

La Cuisine offers a portrait of the way the French were eating in the second half of the twentieth century. Françoise prefers subtlety: shallots over garlic, onions soaked in water to soften the pungency, and amounts and varieties of spices that may seem limited to today's palates. Vegetables are wildly overcooked by many current standards (twenty minutes for asparagus).

Occasionally, Françoise's efforts to encourage novices in the kitchen lead to a few oddball recipes. In one instance, luxurious beef tenderloin steaks are served with a garnish of canned artichoke bottoms stuffed with canned peas. "It's expensive but it's fast and impressive," she tells inexperienced hostesses. "Serve with potato chips and a green salad, and your menu is done." This advice has a certain value as a relic of a particular time and place.

Her recipes for dishes made to look like other things took me back to cooking school. One trompe l'oeil salad consisting of hard-cooked eggs, tomatoes, mayonnaise, and watercress is concocted to resemble . . . toadstools in a forest! But for drama, nothing beats Françoise's Langouste en Bellevue—the whole spiny lobster, boiled then chilled, with its tail meat sliced and arrayed down the shell, a decorative skewer planted between its eyes.

Françoise's fondness for butter, eggs (and raw egg yolks), crème fraîche, and mayonnaise—sometimes all in the same recipe—may give pause. But I like to think of it as *La Cuisine*'s bona fides as a bible of classic French cooking. Leeks vinaigrette, soufflés, quiches, golden gratins, chocolate mousse, and crème caramel are eternally seductive. With the one thousand old-fashioned standbys in *La Cuisine*, you can linger in Françoise's company, reading about everything you probably never would have learned from your grandmother.

PREFACE
- Françoise Bernard -

❖ ❖ ❖ ❖ ❖

For many years I have tried to be a guiding presence for all those who want to master the cooking that I love and grew up with.

It's for this reason that I decided to gather together all my easy recipes—the ones of which I am especially proud and which have stood the test of time. I've tried not to fiddle with them too much, but I have made certain changes to bring them more in line with our current lifestyle.

One thousand recipes, each more enticing than the other: This is my most complete work to date.

For each recipe, you will find my simple, clear, and precise directions, as well as tricks for making them work every time.

Now it's your move!

SOUPS

RADISH GREEN SOUP WITH BUTTERY CROUTONS
- *Potage aux fanes de radis* -

❖ VERY EASY   ❖ INEXPENSIVE   ❖ 50 MINUTES   ❖ SERVES 4

4 tablespoons (½ stick) butter
Green tops from 1 bunch of radishes, chopped
2 onions, chopped

1 large potato, peeled and chopped
Salt and pepper
4 slices day-old country bread

❖ ❖ ❖ ❖ ❖

1. In a large saucepan, melt 2 tablespoons of the butter over medium-low heat. Add the radish greens, onions, and potato and cook, stirring occasionally, until the onions are soft, about 5 minutes. Add 6 cups of water and season with salt and pepper. Increase the heat to medium-high, cover, and bring to a boil, then reduce the heat to low and simmer for 30 to 40 minutes.

2. Meanwhile, in a large skillet, melt the remaining 2 tablespoons butter over medium heat. Add the bread slices and cook until golden on both sides. Transfer the croutons to a soup tureen.

3. Puree the soup using a food mill or blender. Return the soup to the pan and heat gently, then pour over the croutons in the tureen and serve.

From Françoise:
• A little crème fraîche stirred in at the last moment will make a noticeable difference in the taste of the soup.

SIMPLE TOMATO SOUP
- *Potage portugais* -

❖ VERY EASY   ❖ INEXPENSIVE   ❖ 40 MINUTES   ❖ SERVES 4

4 tomatoes, chopped
4 potatoes, peeled and chopped

Salt and pepper
Chopped chervil or parsley leaves for serving

❖ ❖ ❖ ❖ ❖

1. In a large saucepan, combine the tomatoes and potatoes with 6 cups of water. Season with salt and pepper. Cover and bring to a boil over medium-high heat, then reduce the heat to low and simmer for 30 minutes.

2. Puree the soup using a food mill or blender. Return the soup to the pan and heat gently, then pour into a tureen, sprinkle with chervil or parsley, and serve.

From Françoise:

• To give store-bought tomato soup a fresh flavor, add a peeled, finely diced tomato to the soup and cook for 5 minutes before serving.

• For a more elegant presentation, sauté cubes of crustless white sandwich bread in butter until golden and pass them at the table along with the soup.

WATERCRESS SOUP

- *Potage au cresson* -

❖ VERY EASY   ❖ INEXPENSIVE   ❖ 50 MINUTES   ❖ SERVES 4

Salt

1 bunch of watercress, leaves reserved

4 potatoes, peeled and quartered

1 to 2 tablespoons tapioca, to taste

2 tablespoons butter

❖ ❖ ❖ ❖ ❖

1. In a large saucepan, bring 6 cups of salted water to a boil over high heat. Add the watercress stems and potatoes, reduce the heat to low, and simmer for 30 minutes.

2. Puree the soup using a food mill or blender. Return the soup to the pan and bring to a simmer over low heat. Add the tapioca and cook, stirring often, until slightly thickened, 10 to 15 minutes.

3. Finely chop some of the reserved watercress leaves. Add the butter to the soup and stir until it melts creamily. Pour the soup into a tureen or bowls, garnish with the chopped watercress leaves, and serve.

From Françoise:

• Don't overdo the tapioca, because it puffs up and thickens dramatically with cooking. Stir the soup frequently after adding the tapioca to discourage lumps from forming.

• Vermicelli can replace the tapioca; the cooking time will be quicker—7 minutes at most.

• The reserved watercress leaves are especially good (and superhealthy) in a salad or as a garnish for meat—roast beef, steak, or chicken. They are also delicious with buttery croutons.

• The advantage of using watercress stems, in addition to not letting anything go to waste, is that they keep their bright green color when cooked.

continued

- Green radish tops can be substituted for the watercress stems. They'll need at least 30 minutes of cooking.

- Adding a little crème fraîche will make it even better.

VEGETABLE JULIENNE SOUP
- *Potage aux légumes julienne* -

❖ EASY ❖ INEXPENSIVE ❖ 45 MINUTES ❖ SERVES 4

2 tablespoons butter

2 carrots, peeled and cut into julienne strips

1 turnip, peeled and cut into julienne strips

1 small celery root, thickly peeled and cut into julienne strips

5 tender inner cabbage leaves, cut into julienne strips

1 onion, cut into julienne strips

3 medium potatoes, peeled and cut into julienne strips

2 leeks, white and light green parts only, cut into julienne strips

Salt and pepper

❖ ❖ ❖ ❖ ❖

1. In a large saucepan, melt the butter over medium-low heat. Add the vegetables and cook, stirring occasionally, until softened, 5 to 10 minutes. Add 5 cups of water and season with salt and pepper. Cover, increase the heat, and bring to a boil, then reduce the heat to low and simmer for 20 minutes. Remove from the heat and serve as is.

From Françoise:

• One advantage of this soup is how quickly it cooks. By cutting the vegetables into julienne strips, I've taken liberties with this classic recipe, which typically calls for cutting them in small dice, which would make the preparation and cooking times longer.

BLACK MUSHROOM SOUP WITH VERMICELLI

- Potage chinois au vermicelli -

❖ EASY   ❖ MODERATE   ❖ 2 HOURS   ❖ SERVES 4

BROTH

Neck, wings, and giblets from 1 or 2 chickens

1 carrot, peeled and sliced crosswise

1 onion stuck with 2 cloves

1 garlic clove

1 bouquet garni made with parsley, thyme,
   and bay leaf

Salt and pepper, to taste

GARNISH

1 ounce dried black mushrooms

2 ½ ounces rice vermicelli

4 large eggs

Salt and pepper

2 tablespoons butter

2 Boston lettuce leaves, sliced into thin strips

❖ ❖ ❖ ❖ ❖

1. In a large saucepan, combine the broth ingredients with 8 cups of water. Bring to a boil over medium-high heat, then reduce the heat to low and simmer for 1 ½ hours.

2. Meanwhile, soak the mushrooms in warm water to cover for 30 minutes; drain.

3. Strain the broth, reserving the chicken parts, and return it to the pan. Bring to a boil over medium-high heat, add the mushrooms and vermicelli, then reduce the heat to low and simmer for 10 to 15 minutes.

4. Remove the meat from the neck and wings and finely chop with the giblets. Add the meat to the broth and remove the pan from the heat. Cover and let stand for 5 minutes.

5. In a medium bowl, lightly beat the eggs with salt, pepper, and 1 tablespoon cold water. (You want 2 very thin omelets.) In a large skillet, melt 1 tablespoon of the butter over medium heat. Add half the beaten eggs and cook, stirring gently, until set, then transfer to a work surface. Repeat with the remaining butter and eggs. Roll up the omelets and slice crosswise into thin strips.

6. Ladle the soup into bowls, garnish with the omelet and lettuce strips, and serve.

From Françoise:

• You can substitute 4 cups of prepared broth, from a can or carton, if you need to save time. Likewise, you could substitute white mushrooms for the black mushrooms. It's okay to work with what you have at hand.

• Dried black mushrooms and rice vermicelli can be found at grocers specializing in Asian products.

CHICKEN SOUP WITH PARMESAN, BREAD CRUMBS, AND EGG
- *Potage mille-fanti* -

❖ EASY ❖ MODERATE ❖ 25 MINUTES ❖ SERVES 4

5 cups chicken broth

2 large eggs

½ cup grated Parmesan cheese
  (about 1 ½ ounces)

1 ½ cups fresh bread crumbs (about 2 ½ ounces)

Freshly grated nutmeg

❖ ❖ ❖ ❖ ❖

1. In a large saucepan, bring the chicken broth to a simmer over medium heat.

2. In a bowl, lightly whisk the eggs. Whisk in the cheese and bread crumbs and season with nutmeg to taste.

3. Whisk the egg mixture into the simmering chicken broth, then reduce the heat to low, cover, and simmer for 5 minutes. Whisk again just before serving.

From Françoise:

• To make bread crumbs quickly, grind crustless bread in a food processor.

• This soup has a grainy texture, which is completely normal.

• For a garnish, you can add small basil leaves to each bowl just before serving.

VEGETABLE SOUP WITH TOMATO PASTE
- *Potage au concentré de tomates* -

❖ EASY ❖ INEXPENSIVE ❖ 45 MINUTES ❖ SERVES 4

2 tablespoons butter

2 medium onions, finely chopped

1 rounded tablespoon all-purpose flour

1 carrot, peeled and cut into ¼-inch dice

1 garlic clove, crushed

3 tablespoons tomato paste (about 2 ½ ounces)

1 bouquet garni made with parsley, thyme,
  and ¼ bay leaf

Salt and pepper

1. In a large saucepan, melt the butter over medium heat. Add the onions and cook, stirring occasionally, until lightly browned, 5 to 6 minutes. Sprinkle in the flour and cook, stirring, until lightly browned.

2. Add the carrot, garlic, tomato paste, bouquet garni, and 6 cups of water. Season with salt and pepper. Cover and bring to a boil, then reduce the heat to low and simmer, partially covered, for 30 minutes. Remove the bouquet garni before serving.

From Françoise:
• Here's a small detail that will considerably improve this soup: Peel a tomato, finely chop the flesh, and add it to the soup a few minutes before serving.

• Don't add too much bay leaf or thyme to your bouquet garni. Parsley is essential, though, and, if you have it, a little celery is nice.

VELVETY AVOCADO SOUP
- *Potage velouté d'avocat* -

❖ VERY EASY   ❖ MODERATE   ❖ 15 MINUTES   ❖ SERVES 4

4 cups chicken broth
1 avocado, peeled, seeded, and diced
A few tarragon leaves

Pepper and a little salt
1 tablespoon crème fraîche
2 large egg yolks

❖ ❖ ❖ ❖ ❖

1. In a small saucepan, heat the chicken broth until very hot. In a blender or food processor, combine the avocado with the tarragon, and season with pepper and salt. Add enough chicken broth to cover and pulse 2 or 3 times. Gradually add the remaining chicken broth, pulsing to blend. Add the crème fraîche and egg yolks and puree until smooth. Serve immediately in a soup tureen or bowls.

From Françoise:
• Sauté diced crustless white sandwich bread in butter to make croutons and use them to garnish the soup.

• Chives or chervil can be used instead of tarragon.

• For a bolder flavor, add ¼ garlic clove, no more.

FRENCH GAZPACHO

- Potage froid andalou -

❖ EASY   ❖ INEXPENSIVE   ❖ 20 MINUTES, PLUS 2 TO 3 HOURS CHILLING   ❖ SERVES 4

1 small cucumber, peeled and thinly sliced
Salt
2 pounds ripe tomatoes, peeled, seeded, and
  coarsely chopped
Pepper

2 small spring onions, finely chopped
A small handful of finely chopped parsley, chervil,
  and chives
Juice of 1 lemon

❖ ❖ ❖ ❖ ❖

1. In a colander, sprinkle the cucumber slices with salt and let drain for 1 hour in the refrigerator. Squeeze out as much water as possible from the cucumber slices and pat dry with paper towels.

2. Puree the tomatoes using a food mill or food processor. Season with salt and pepper.

3. In a bowl, combine the tomatoes with the cucumber, onions, herbs, and lemon juice. Season with salt and pepper. Cover and refrigerate until cold, 2 to 3 hours. Serve chilled.

From Françoise:
• If the tomatoes don't release enough liquid, you can add a little cold water or tomato juice and adjust the seasoning.

• The proportions of vegetables and herbs can vary according to your taste and availability. If you don't have enough fresh tomatoes, use tomato juice.

RUSTIC LETTUCE SOUP

- Potage de laitue -

❖ EASY   ❖ MODERATE   ❖ 50 MINUTES   ❖ SERVES 4

4 tablespoons (½ stick) butter
1 head Boston lettuce, sliced into thin strips
Salt and pepper

4 slices day-old country bread
1 cup milk
2 tablespoons potato starch

1. In a large saucepan, melt 2 tablespoons of the butter over medium-low heat. Add the lettuce and cook, stirring occasionally, for 5 minutes. Add 4 cups of water and season with salt and pepper. Cover, increase the heat to medium-high, and bring to a boil, then reduce the heat to low and simmer for 30 minutes.

2. Meanwhile, in a large skillet, melt the remaining 2 tablespoons butter over medium heat. Add the bread slices and cook until golden, about 3 minutes per side. Transfer the croutons to soup plates.

3. In a cup, gradually stir the milk into the potato starch. Whisk this mixture into the simmering soup and cook briefly until slightly thickened. Ladle the soup over the croutons and serve.

From Françoise:

• To improve a soup—of any kind—you can always blend in 1 or 2 tablespoons of crème fraîche just before serving.

• To easily slice the lettuce, stack several leaves on a work surface, then roll them up and cut crosswise into thin strips.

• For a deeper flavor, a chicken bouillon cube can be added to this soup with the water in Step 1. Or replace part or all of the water with chicken broth.

CREAMY MUSSEL SOUP

- *Velouté aux moules* -

❖ EASY   ❖ MODERATE   ❖ 45 MINUTES   ❖ SERVES 4

2 pounds mussels, scrubbed and
  debearded
2 tablespoons butter
1 tablespoon all-purpose flour
2 ounces white mushrooms, finely chopped

1 small leek, white and light green parts only,
  finely chopped
Salt and pepper
1 large egg yolk
1 tablespoon crème fraîche

❖ ❖ ❖ ❖ ❖

1. Add the mussels to a pot, cover, and cook over high heat, stirring once or twice, just until they open, 3 to 5 minutes. Remove the pot from the heat. Remove the mussel meat from the shells and reserve. Discard the shells and any unopened mussels. Strain the mussel broth using a fine strainer.

2. In a large saucepan, melt the butter over low heat. Stir in the flour, then gradually whisk in the mussel broth, 2 cups of cold water, the mushrooms, and leek. Season lightly with salt and pepper. Increase the heat to medium-high

continued

and bring to a boil, whisking constantly, then reduce the heat to low and simmer for 30 minutes. Add the reserved mussels just before serving.

3. In a soup tureen, whisk the egg yolk with the crème fraîche. Gradually blend in the soup and serve immediately.

From Françoise:

• Remove the mussels from the heat as soon as they open; they toughen when cooked too long.

• If your strainer isn't very fine, line it with a double layer of moistened cheesecloth. Pour in the mussel broth; the cheesecloth will catch the tiniest grains of sand. This method will also perfectly degrease a fatty broth.

ASPARAGUS SOUP
- *Velouté d'asperges* -

❖ VERY EASY ❖ INEXPENSIVE ❖ 15 MINUTES ❖ SERVES 4

5 cups asparagus cooking water
2 tablespoons tapioca
Salt and pepper

1 large egg yolk
1 or 2 tablespoons crème fraîche, to taste

❖ ❖ ❖ ❖ ❖

1. In a large saucepan, bring the asparagus cooking water to a boil over medium-high heat. Add the tapioca, season with salt and pepper, then reduce the heat to low and simmer, stirring occasionally, until slightly thickened, 7 to 10 minutes.

2. In a soup tureen, whisk the egg yolk with the crème fraîche. Gradually blend in the soup and serve immediately.

From Françoise:

• To prepare this easy soup, save the water you use to cook spears of asparagus for a starter or side dish.

• A few croutons—diced crustless white sandwich bread that has been sautéed in butter or tossed with melted butter and toasted in the oven—add a refined note to all soups of this type. So they remain crisp, pass them separately or add them at the last minute.

SILKY CELERY ROOT SOUP

- *Velouté de céleri* -

❖ EASY   ❖ INEXPENSIVE   ❖ 45 MINUTES   ❖ SERVES 4

1 small celery root, thickly peeled and thinly sliced
Salt and pepper

2 heaping tablespoons rice flour
1 large egg yolk

❖ ❖ ❖ ❖ ❖

1. In a large saucepan, bring 5 cups of water to a boil over medium-high heat. Add the celery root and season with salt and pepper. Reduce the heat to low and simmer for 30 minutes.

2. Puree the soup in a food mill or blender. Return the soup to the pan and bring to a simmer. In a cup, gradually stir 1 cup of water into the rice flour. Whisk this mixture into the simmering soup and cook until slightly thickened, about 5 minutes.

3. In a soup tureen, gradually whisk the soup into the egg yolk. Taste for seasoning and serve immediately.

From Françoise:

• You may not like wasting an egg white, but that's often what happens when a soup or sauce is enriched with the yolk. As an alternative, use a whole egg, lightly beaten. It may be a little less refined, and the white may cook into strings, but it will still be good and nothing is wasted.

• You can add a chicken bouillon cube with the water in Step 1. In this case, you may not need to salt the soup. Or replace part or all of the water with chicken broth.

FRENCH LEAFY GREENS SOUP

- Velouté aux herbes du jardin -

❖ VERY EASY   ❖ MODERATE   ❖ 1 HOUR   ❖ SERVES 6

2 tablespoons butter

1 small head Boston lettuce, chopped

2 small bunches of sorrel, large stems removed, chopped

2 small bunches of spinach, large stems removed, chopped

1 small bunch of chervil or parsley, stems removed, chopped

1 small bunch of watercress, chopped with stems, half the leaves reserved

1 celery rib, chopped

Salt and pepper

2 cups milk

¼ cup rice

1 large egg yolk

1 tablespoon crème fraîche

❖ ❖ ❖ ❖ ❖

1. In a large saucepan, melt the butter over low heat. Add the lettuce, sorrel, spinach, chervil or parsley, watercress, and celery and cook, stirring occasionally, until the celery is soft, about 10 minutes. Add 4 cups of water and season with salt and pepper. Cover and bring to a boil, then simmer over low heat for 30 minutes.

2. Puree the soup using a food mill or blender. Return the soup to the pan and add the milk. Bring to a boil, add the rice, and cook until tender, 15 to 20 minutes.

3. In a soup tureen, whisk the egg yolk with the crème fraîche. Gradually blend in the soup and serve immediately.

From Françoise:

• This recipe puts to use whatever you have growing in the garden or any leftover herbs and leafy greens in the refrigerator. With a handful or this and a bit of that, you have a very good soup.

• Save the nicest watercress leaves to make a salad.

FRESH SHELL BEAN SOUP WITH PISTOU

- *Soupe au pistou* -

❖ INTERMEDIATE ❖ MODERATE ❖ 2 HOURS ❖ SERVES 4

Salt

1 ½ pounds fresh shell beans, shelled (1 ½ cups)

1 zucchini, cut into ¼-inch dice

¼ pound green beans, sliced crosswise
   ¼ inch thick

¼ pound leeks, white and light green parts only,
   finely chopped

¼ pound carrots, peeled and cut into ¼-inch dice

¼ pound turnips, peeled and cut into ¼-inch dice

¼ pound celery root, thickly peeled and cut into
   ¼-inch dice

2 tomatoes, peeled and cut into ¼-inch dice

2 ounces spaghetti, broken into pieces

PISTOU

2 or 3 bulbs green garlic, root and green parts
   trimmed, outer layer removed, or 2 or 3
   mature garlic cloves

2 teaspoons salt

1 or 2 bunches of basil, stems removed

¼ cup olive oil

½ cup freshly grated Parmesan cheese
   (about 1 ½ ounces)

❖ ❖ ❖ ❖ ❖

1. In a large saucepan, bring 8 cups of salted water to a boil over medium-high heat. Add the shell beans, zucchini, green beans, leeks, carrots, turnips, celery root, and tomatoes. Cover, reduce the heat to low, and simmer for 1 hour. Add the spaghetti and cook for 15 minutes.

2. Meanwhile, make the pistou: In a mortar, crush the garlic. Season with the salt and gradually add the basil leaves, working the ingredients to a paste. Gradually blend in the olive oil as for a mayonnaise, then the cheese.

3. Pour the soup into a tureen, blend in some of the pistou, and serve very hot. Pass the remaining pistou separately.

From Françoise:
• A mix of grated Gouda and Gruyère cheeses is delicious in the soup. Pass some in a bowl at the table.

PUMPKIN SOUP WITH RICE

- *Soupe au potiron* -

❖ VERY EASY ❖ INEXPENSIVE ❖ 1 HOUR ❖ SERVES 4

2 tablespoons butter
2 pounds pumpkin, peeled and cut into 1- or
  2-inch pieces

4 cups milk
¼ cup rice
Salt and pepper

❖ ❖ ❖ ❖ ❖

1. In a large saucepan, melt the butter over medium heat. Add the pumpkin and ½ cup water. Cover and bring to a boil, then reduce the heat to low and cook for 30 minutes.

2. Mash the pumpkin. Stir in the milk and rice and season with salt and pepper. Simmer over low heat for 20 minutes. Pour the soup into a tureen or bowls and serve.

From Françoise:
• Once the milk has been added, do not cover the pan or the soup will easily boil over.

• If you don't especially like rice (which thickens the soup), add 2 or 3 peeled, diced potatoes instead and cook along with the pumpkin in Step 1.

• Sprinkle a few pinches of chopped parsley on the soup just before serving.

PUREED POTATO AND CELERY ROOT SOUP WITH GARLIC

- *Soupe des Flandres* -

❖ VERY EASY ❖ INEXPENSIVE ❖ 1 HOUR, 15 MINUTES ❖ SERVES 4

1 pound potatoes, peeled and chopped
¼ pound celery root, thickly peeled and chopped
2 onions, chopped
1 garlic clove
1 tablespoon tomato paste

1 thyme sprig
Salt and pepper
2 tablespoons butter
Chopped chervil or parsley leaves for serving
  (optional)

1. In a large saucepan, combine the potatoes, celery root, onions, garlic, tomato paste, and thyme with 6 cups of water. Season with salt and pepper. Cover and bring to a boil over medium-high heat, then reduce the heat to low and simmer for 1 hour.

2. Puree the soup in a food mill or blender. Return the soup to the pan and heat gently.

Add the butter and stir until it melts creamily. Pour the soup into a tureen, sprinkle with chervil or parsley if desired, and serve.

From Françoise:
• If you add a little crème fraîche or even a bit of milk to this soup, you will be cooking in the Flemish tradition, and it's very good!

GRATINÉED ONION SOUP
- *Soupe à l'oignon* -

❖ EASY   ❖ MODERATE   ❖ 45 MINUTES   ❖ SERVES 4

4 tablespoons (½ stick) butter
3 large onions, thinly sliced
1 tablespoon all-purpose flour
Salt and pepper

4 slices country bread, each cut into 4 pieces
½ cup shredded Gruyère cheese (about 1 ½ ounces)

❖ ❖ ❖ ❖ ❖

1. In a large saucepan, melt 2 tablespoons of the butter over medium heat. Add the onions and cook until lightly browned, about 20 minutes. Sprinkle in the flour and cook, stirring, until lightly browned. Stir in 6 cups of water and season with salt and pepper. Bring to a boil, then reduce the heat to low and simmer for 20 minutes.

2. In a large skillet, melt the remaining 2 tablespoons butter over medium heat. Add the bread and cook until golden, about 3 minutes per side.

3. Preheat the broiler. Ladle the soup into a deep baking dish or ovenproof bowls and set on a baking sheet. Float the croutons in the soup and sprinkle with the cheese. Broil

8 inches from the heat for about 2 minutes, or until melted and golden. Serve right away.

From Françoise:
• To prevent the onions from sticking to the pan, stir in 1 or 2 tablespoons of cold water once they are lightly browned. Cover and simmer gently.

• You can add a half cup or so of dry white wine or ¼ cup of port and reduce it slightly before adding the water in Step 1.

• To save time, you can serve the soup without the cheese croutons, or use plain toast instead. Alternatively, top bowls of store-bought onion soup with homemade cheese croutons and broil until melted and golden.

GOLDEN LEEK AND POTATO SOUP.
WITH CANTAL CHEESE

- *Soupe auvergnate* -

❖ VERY EASY   ❖ MODERATE   ❖ 1 HOUR, 30 MINUTES   ❖ SERVES 6

Salt

3 leeks, white and light green parts only,
  finely chopped

4 potatoes, peeled and thinly sliced

½ cup milk

3 garlic cloves

1 ¾ cups shredded Cantal or Cheddar cheese
  (about 7 ounces)

6 thin slices country bread

1 tablespoon crème fraîche

Pepper

❖ ❖ ❖ ❖ ❖

1. In a large saucepan, bring 8 cups of salted water to a boil over medium-high heat. Add the leeks and potatoes, reduce the heat to low, and simmer for 45 minutes.

2. Preheat the broiler. In a small saucepan, heat the milk. Rub a deep baking dish with the garlic and add ¾ cup of the cheese, the bread, crème fraîche, and hot milk. Season with salt and pepper. Ladle in the soup and sprinkle the remaining 1 cup of cheese on top. Transfer to a baking sheet and broil 8 inches from the heat for about 2 minutes, or until the cheese is melted and golden. Serve right away.

From Françoise:

• If you're in a hurry, use a store-bought leek and potato soup as the base for this recipe. That will save you half an hour, which isn't inconsiderable.

• The Cantal cheese, a pressed, uncooked cheese aged for 3 to 6 months in the mountains of central France, gives this soup its Auvergnat accent.

PROVENÇAL FISH SOUP

- *Soupe de poisson provençale* -

❖ EASY　　　❖ EXPENSIVE　　　❖ 1 HOUR　　　❖ SERVES 4

¼ cup olive oil

1 large onion, chopped

2 tomatoes, chopped

Fronds and trimmings from 1 fennel bulb, chopped

½ bay leaf

2 to 2 ½ pounds mixed whole white fish, cleaned
　and cut into steaks, heads reserved

1 tablespoon tomato paste

4 garlic cloves

Pinch of saffron threads

2 whole cloves

Salt and pepper

3 tablespoons vermicelli (optional)

4 slices bread, toasted

Shredded Gruyère or grated Parmesan cheese
　for serving

❖　❖　❖　❖　❖

1. In a large saucepan, heat the olive oil over medium-low heat. Add the onion and cook, stirring occasionally, until soft, about 5 minutes. Add the tomatoes, fennel, bay leaf, fish steaks and heads and cook, stirring to break up the fish, for 10 minutes. Add the tomato paste, 3 of the garlic cloves, 6 cups of water, the saffron, and whole cloves and season with salt and pepper. Raise the heat to medium-high, bring to a boil, then reduce the heat to low and simmer for 25 minutes.

2. Work the soup through a food mill. Return the soup to the pan and bring to a simmer over low heat. Add the vermicelli, if using, and cook for 7 to 10 minutes.

3. Rub the toasts with the remaining garlic clove. Serve the soup in a tureen or bowls and pass the cheese and garlic toasts at the table.

From Françoise:

• Select a variety of whole fish, such as grouper, tilefish, red snapper, tilapia, porgy, whiting, perch, black sea bass, and hogfish. You can also add a few blue crabs.

• This is a good way to use up fennel trimmings, but the bulb will also do or, in a pinch, a tablespoon of pastis.

CHUNKY LEEK AND POTATO SOUP

- *Soupe bonne femme* -

❖ VERY EASY   ❖ INEXPENSIVE   ❖ 1 HOUR   ❖ SERVES 4

3 tablespoons butter
3 leeks, white and light green parts only,
  finely chopped

½ pound potatoes, peeled and sliced into rounds
Salt and pepper
4 slices day-old country bread

❖ ❖ ❖ ❖ ❖

1. In a large saucepan, melt 2 tablespoons of the butter over low heat. Stir in the leeks, then add 1 tablespoon of water. Cover and cook until soft, about 5 minutes. Add the potatoes and 6 cups of water. Season with salt and pepper. Increase the heat to medium-high, cover, and bring to a boil, then reduce the heat to low and simmer for 45 minutes.

2. Spread the remaining tablespoon of butter on the bread slices and add them to a soup tureen. Pour the soup over them and serve.

From Françoise:
• You can replace half of the water with milk.

• Be sure to avoid allowing the leeks to brown or they will taste bitter.

CREAM OF SORREL SOUP

- *Crème à l'oseille* -

❖ EASY   ❖ MODERATE   ❖ 45 MINUTES   ❖ SERVES 4

Salt
1 pound potatoes, peeled and chopped
2 tablespoons butter

½ pound sorrel, large stems trimmed, chopped
1 or 2 tablespoons crème fraîche, to taste

❖ ❖ ❖ ❖ ❖

1. In a large saucepan, bring 5 cups of salted water to a boil over medium-high heat. Add the potatoes, reduce the heat to low, cover, and simmer for 30 minutes.

2. Meanwhile, in a medium saucepan, melt the butter over low heat. Add the sorrel and cook, stirring occasionally, for 5 minutes; drain if needed. Add to the potatoes.

3. Puree the soup in a food mill or blender. Return the soup to the pan and heat gently. Stir in the crème fraîche and serve.

From Françoise:

• Sorrel tends to stick to the bottom of the pan, so be sure to stir it while cooking.

• Don't add the sorrel to the potatoes without cooking it first because it can give the soup an unpleasantly acidic flavor.

FRENCH MINESTRONE

- Soupe minestrone -

❖ EASY   ❖ MODERATE   ❖ 1 HOUR, 45 MINUTES   ❖ SERVES 4

Salt

¼ pound green beans, sliced crosswise
  ¼ inch thick

¼ pound leeks, white and light green parts only,
  finely chopped

¼ pound carrots, peeled and cut into ¼-inch dice

¼ pound turnips, peeled and cut into ¼-inch dice

¼ pound celery root, thickly peeled and cut into
  ¼-inch dice

¼ pound tomatoes, peeled and cut into
  ¼-inch dice

2 garlic cloves, finely chopped

Pepper

1½ ounces spaghetti, broken into pieces

2 tablespoons butter

1 teaspoon chopped basil

½ cup grated Parmesan or shredded Gruyère
  cheese (about 1½ ounces)

❖ ❖ ❖ ❖ ❖

1. In a large saucepan, bring 8 cups of salted water to a boil over medium-high heat. Add the vegetables and season with pepper. Reduce the heat to low, cover, and simmer for 50 minutes. Add the spaghetti and cook for 20 minutes. Just before serving, stir in the butter and basil and sprinkle with the cheese.

From Françoise:

• This soup is delicious, but it takes a long time to prepare. There are some very good store-bought minestrone soups, which you could simply heat, spruce up with some diced cooked vegetables that you may have on hand, then serve in a soup tureen, passing the cheese at the table.

CHICKEN SOUP WITH GIBLETS
- *Consommé aux abattis de volaille* -

❖ VERY EASY   ❖ INEXPENSIVE   ❖ 1 HOUR   ❖ SERVES 4

1 carrot, peeled and chopped

2 leeks, white and light green parts only, chopped

1 celery rib, chopped

1 bouquet garni made with parsley, thyme, and
  bay leaf

1 onion stuck with 2 whole cloves

Salt and pepper

Neck, wings, and giblets from 1 or 2 chickens

2 tablespoons tapioca

❖ ❖ ❖ ❖ ❖

1. In a large saucepan, combine the carrot, leeks, celery, bouquet garni, and onion with 6 cups of water. Season with salt and pepper and bring to a boil over medium-high heat.

2. Add the chicken neck, wings, and giblets, reduce the heat to low, cover, and simmer for 45 minutes.

3. Strain the broth. Return the broth to the pan and bring to a simmer. Add the tapioca and cook, stirring, 10 minutes, until thickened.

From Françoise:

• Much of the appeal of this soup is putting leftover chicken giblets to good use, so I don't recommend buying the giblets just for this recipe.

• If you would like a more deeply flavored soup, by all means simmer it longer.

CHICKEN SOUP WITH ANGEL HAIR PASTA
- *Consommé aux cheveux d'ange* -

❖ VERY EASY   ❖ INEXPENSIVE   ❖ 15 MINUTES   ❖ SERVES 4

5 cups beef broth

¾ pound skinless, boneless chicken cutlets,
  thinly sliced

½ cup crème fraiche

4 ounces angel hair pasta

⅓ cup Madeira

2 Boston lettuce leaves, thinly sliced

1. In a large saucepan, bring the beef broth to a boil over medium-high heat. Add the chicken and crème fraîche, reduce the heat to low, and simmer for 3 minutes. Add the pasta and cook, stirring, for 2 minutes. Stir in the Madeira and pour the soup into a tureen or bowls. Garnish with the lettuce and serve.

From Françoise:

• Angel hair pasta is a long and extremely fine kind of vermicelli, so the cooking time is very fast. Any delicate strands of pasta can be substituted.

BEEF BROTH WITH SHALLOTS AND GARLIC

- *Consommé Bordelais* -

❖ VERY EASY   ❖ INEXPENSIVE   ❖ 30 MINUTES   ❖ SERVES 4

2 tablespoons butter
3 shallots, finely chopped
2 garlic cloves, finely chopped

4 cups beef broth
1 rounded tablespoon potato starch

❖ ❖ ❖ ❖ ❖

1. In a large saucepan, melt the butter over medium-low heat. Add the shallots and garlic and cook, stirring occasionally, until soft, 2 to 3 minutes. Add the beef broth, raise the heat to medium-high, and bring to a boil, then reduce the heat to low and simmer for 15 minutes.

2. In a cup, gradually stir ½ cup cold water into the potato starch. Add to the simmering broth and cook, stirring, until slightly thickened, about 5 minutes.

From Françoise:

• Don't let the shallots and garlic color or they will become bitter.

• Season with salt and pepper to taste, depending on the saltiness of the broth.

GRATINÉED BEEF BROTH

- Croûte au pot gratinée -

❖ VERY EASY   ❖ INEXPENSIVE   ❖ 15 MINUTES   ❖ SERVES 4

4 cups beef broth
Salt and pepper
4 slices day-old country bread or toast

½ cup shredded Gruyère cheese (about
1½ ounces)
2 tablespoons butter

❖ ❖ ❖ ❖ ❖

1. Preheat the broiler. In a small saucepan, bring the beef broth to a boil over medium-high heat. Season with salt and pepper. Pour the broth into a deep baking dish. Add the slices of bread, sprinkle with the cheese, and dot with the butter. Transfer to a baking sheet and broil 8 inches from the heat for about 2 minutes, or until melted and golden. Serve right away.

From Françoise:
• This is an excellent soup to prepare for unexpected guests.

• You can improve the flavor by lightly browning some thinly sliced onion in butter before adding the broth. Also, you can stir ¼ cup of port into the broth just before broiling.

CREAMY BREAD SOUP

- Panade fine -

❖ VERY EASY   ❖ INEXPENSIVE   ❖ 50 MINUTES   ❖ SERVES 4

¼ pound leftover bread, cut into cubes
2 cups milk
Salt and pepper

2 tablespoons butter
1 to 2 tablespoons crème fraîche, to taste

❖ ❖ ❖ ❖ ❖

1. In a large saucepan, combine the bread with the milk and 3 cups of water. Season with salt and pepper. Bring to a boil over medium-high heat, then reduce the heat to low and simmer, stirring often, for 40 minutes. Puree the soup in a food mill or blender. Return the soup to the pan and heat gently. Stir in the butter and crème fraîche and serve.

From Françoise:

• This is not haute gastronomy, but if the soup is well prepared, it is good and a bargain, since you can use up the ends of bread you otherwise wouldn't know what to do with.

• I sometimes add a little freshly grated nutmeg or even an egg, lightly beaten and stirred in at the same time as the crème fraîche. It's a bread soup for a gourmet!

CHICKEN NOODLE SOUP WITH GRUYÈRE CHEESE
- *Consommé milanais* -

❖ VERY EASY   ❖ INEXPENSIVE   ❖ 10 MINUTES   ❖ SERVES 4

4 cups chicken broth
1 tablespoon tomato paste
Salt and pepper

1 ounce vermicelli
½ cup shredded Gruyère or grated Parmesan
  cheese (about 2 ounces)

❖ ❖ ❖ ❖ ❖

1. In a large saucepan, gradually stir the chicken broth into the tomato paste and bring to a boil over medium-high heat. Season with salt and pepper. Add the vermicelli, reduce the heat to low, cover partially, and simmer for 5 to 7 minutes. Serve the soup and pass the cheese at the table.

From Françoise:

• A mix of shredded cheeses would be nice here—for instance, a blend of Gouda and Gruyère, Gruyère and Cantal, or Gruyère and Parmesan. This bit of creativity isn't likely to shock anyone; instead it's likely to delight your diners.

CREAM OF ONION SOUP

- *Thourins* -

❖ EASY   ❖ MODERATE   ❖ 25 MINUTES   ❖ SERVES 4

5 cups milk

2 tablespoons butter

3 onions, thinly sliced

1 tablespoon all-purpose flour

Salt and pepper

2 large egg yolks

1 tablespoon crème fraîche

12 thin slices baguette

❖   ❖   ❖   ❖   ❖

1. In a medium saucepan, bring the milk to a simmer over medium-high heat, then remove from the heat. In a large saucepan, melt the butter over medium heat. Add the onions and cook, stirring occasionally, until lightly browned, about 5 minutes. Add the flour and cook, stirring, until lightly browned.

2. Add the milk and season with salt and pepper. Bring to a simmer and cook over low heat for 15 minutes.

3. In a soup tureen, blend the egg yolks with the crème fraîche. Gradually add the soup, stirring constantly. Add 3 baguette slices to each bowl. Ladle the soup into the bowls and serve.

From Françoise:

• This soup, called *thourins*, *tourin*, and even *tourain*, is mostly found on tables south of the Loire Valley. There are many variations, so in Bordeaux water replaces the milk. In the Southwest, it's also made with water, but diced tomato is added, too.

• Once the soup is added to the egg yolks, do not reheat it.

• You can lightly toast the baguette slices in the oven if you like.

PROVENÇAL EGG SOUP WITH SAFFRON

- *Bouillabaisse d'oeufs* -

❖ INTERMEDIATE   ❖ MODERATE   ❖ 50 MINUTES   ❖ SERVES 4

2 tablespoons olive oil

1 large onion, finely chopped

3 leeks, white and light green parts only, finely chopped

2 tomatoes, peeled and cut into ¼-inch dice

3 potatoes, peeled and cut into ¼-inch dice

½ small fennel bulb, cut into ¼-inch dice

4 garlic cloves

1 strip of orange zest

Pinch of saffron threads

Salt and pepper

4 slices toast

4 or 8 large eggs

❖ ❖ ❖ ❖ ❖

1. In a large saucepan, heat the olive oil over medium-low heat. Add the onion and leeks and cook, stirring occasionally, until soft, about 5 minutes. Add the tomatoes, potatoes, fennel, 2 of the garlic cloves, orange zest, 6 cups of water, and saffron. Season with salt and pepper. Increase the heat to medium-high, bring to a boil, then reduce the heat to low and simmer for 30 minutes.

2. Rub the toasts with the remaining 2 garlic cloves.

3. Strain the soup. Transfer the vegetables to a serving bowl and keep warm. Return the broth to the pan and bring to a boil. Break the eggs into the pan, reduce the heat to a simmer, and poach the eggs until the whites are set but the yolks are still soft, 3 to 4 minutes. Using a slotted spoon, set the eggs on the reserved vegetables.

4. Pour the broth into a soup tureen and add the garlic toasts. Serve with the poached eggs and vegetables.

From Françoise:

• Saffron is one of the most expensive spices. It is available at specialty food shops in small quantities.

• At the table, let guests help themselves to broth, vegetables, and 1 or 2 poached eggs.

• Here's a simpler recipe: Heat store-bought potato and leek soup and season it with tomato paste, saffron, and 1 or 2 pinches of fennel seed. I poach the eggs directly in the soup, which takes no more than 10 minutes.

COLD STARTERS

LANGOUSTINE PASTA SALAD WITH SPICY MAYONNAISE

- Hors d'oeuvre de langoustines à la rouille -

❖ EASY   ❖ EXPENSIVE   ❖ 30 MINUTES   ❖ SERVES 4

1 bouquet garni made with parsley, thyme, and
    bay leaf
Salt and pepper
12 langoustines or colossal shrimp in the shell
2 cups short pasta, such as macaroni, farfalle,
    or gemelli
1 tablespoon olive oil
Boston lettuce leaves for garnishing
4 small tomatoes, quartered lengthwise
12 black olives
1 tender celery heart, quartered lengthwise
Toasted bread slices for serving

ROUILLE
2 or 3 garlic cloves
1 small red chile or cayenne pepper, to taste
1 large egg yolk
Salt
1 teaspoon tomato paste
1 cup olive oil
1 teaspoon water

❖ ❖ ❖ ❖ ❖

1. Bring a large saucepan of water to a boil
with the bouquet garni and season generously
with salt and pepper. Add the langoustines or
shrimp, reduce the heat to low, and simmer
for 3 to 5 minutes. Drain and discard the
bouquet garni.

2. In another large saucepan, cook the pasta in
boiling salted water, stirring occasionally, until
al dente. Drain and toss with the olive oil.

3. Make the rouille: Using a mortar or small
food processor, grind the garlic and chile,
if using, to a paste. Add the egg yolk, salt,
cayenne pepper, if using, and tomato paste and
puree. Blend in the olive oil a few drops at a
time to begin, then in a steady stream. Mix in
the water to stabilize the rouille.

4. Add some of the rouille to the pasta and toss
to coat. Line a platter with the lettuce. Mound
the pasta in the center. Arrange the langoustines or shrimp around the pasta along with the
tomatoes, olives, and celery. Serve, passing the
toasts and remaining rouille separately.

From Françoise:

• Not all food processors can make a successful mayonnaise—or a similar sauce such as a
rouille—using just an egg yolk. Sometimes a
whole egg is necessary.

• Please note that the finished dish contains
raw egg.

BEET AND CELERY ROOT SALAD WITH WALNUTS
- *Salade Belle Hortense* -

❖ EASY   ❖ MODERATE   ❖ 15 MINUTES, PLUS 2 HOURS CHILLING   ❖ SERVES 4

½ pound celery root
½ cup mayonnaise
1 teaspoon Dijon mustard
1 teaspoon vinegar
1 tablespoon oil

Salt and pepper
1 small cooked red beet, peeled and sliced
  crosswise
16 walnut halves

❖　❖　❖　❖　❖

1. Two hours before serving, thickly peel the celery root and cut it into julienne strips. In a medium bowl, blend the mayonnaise with the mustard. Fold in the celery root. Cover and refrigerate for 2 hours.

2. In a medium bowl, whisk the vinegar with the oil and season with salt and pepper. Add the beet and toss to coat. Mound the celery root in a wide salad bowl or on a platter and ar-range the beets around it. Sprinkle the walnuts on top and serve.

From Françoise:
• Tossing the julienned celery root with lemon juice will keep it from browning.

• The beet will bleed into the celery root if left too long.

GRUYÈRE AND ONION SALAD
WITH CREAMY VINAIGRETTE
- *Salade au fromage* -

❖ VERY EASY   ❖ MODERATE   ❖ 15 MINUTES   ❖ SERVES 4

1 tablespoon vinegar
1 teaspoon Dijon mustard
1 tablespoon oil
2 tablespoons crème fraîche
Salt and pepper
½ pound Gruyère or Emmenthal cheese,
  cut into sticks

1 celery rib, cut into ¼-inch dice
1 small spring onion or sweet onion,
  finely chopped
1 garlic clove, finely chopped
Snipped chives for sprinkling

continued

1. In a salad bowl, whisk the vinegar with the mustard. Blend in the oil and crème fraîche and season with salt and pepper. Add the cheese, celery, onion, and garlic and toss to coat. Sprinkle with chives and serve.

From Françoise:

• You can kick up the flavor of this salad with a little prepared horseradish. Or add thin slices of black or red radish.

• Instead of crème fraîche, a little mayonnaise can be blended into the vinaigrette.

SALMON TERRINE SALAD

- *Mousse froide de saumon* -

❖ INTERMEDIATE   ❖ INEXPENSIVE   ❖ 1 HOUR, 45 MINUTES, PLUS OVERNIGHT   ❖ SERVES 6 TO 8

BÉCHAMEL SAUCE
2 tablespoons butter
2 tablespoons all-purpose flour
1 cup milk
Salt and pepper

SALMON
1½ pounds salmon, filleted, skin removed
Salt
Pinch of cayenne pepper

SALAD
Boston lettuce leaves for garnishing
8 small tomatoes, sliced crosswise
4 hard-boiled eggs, sliced crosswise
1 cucumber, peeled and sliced crosswise
16 black and green olives
Vinaigrette for drizzling
Mayonnaise for serving

❖ ❖ ❖ ❖ ❖

1. Preheat the oven to 400 degrees. Butter a 9-by-5-inch loaf pan.

2. Make the béchamel: In a small saucepan, melt the butter over medium heat. Whisk in the flour until it starts foaming. Whisk in the milk. Season with salt and pepper. Bring to a boil, whisking, then remove from the heat. The sauce will be thick.

3. In a food processor, blend the salmon with the béchamel. Season with salt and cayenne pepper.

4. Scrape the salmon into the prepared loaf pan and transfer to a roasting pan. Fill the roasting pan with hot water to come halfway up the sides of the loaf pan. Bake in the oven for 40 minutes. Let cool slightly, then cover and refrigerate overnight.

5. Run a knife around the salmon. Invert a platter over the loaf pan. Holding the pan and platter together, quickly invert the salmon onto the platter. Slice the salmon. Line another platter with the lettuce and arrange the salmon on it. Surround the salmon with the tomatoes, eggs, cucumber, and olives. Drizzle the vinaigrette over the top and serve. Pass the mayonnaise separately.

FISH SALAD IN SCALLOP SHELLS

- *Coquilles de poisson mayonnaise* -

❖ EASY   ❖ MODERATE   ❖ 25 MINUTES   ❖ SERVES 4

MAYONNAISE

1 large egg yolk

1 teaspoon Dijon mustard

¾ cup oil

1 tablespoon vinegar

Salt and pepper

½ pound cooked skinless fish fillets,
** flaked or cut into bite-size pieces**

Boston lettuce leaves for garnishing

2 hard-boiled eggs, halved lengthwise

Chopped parsley leaves for sprinkling

❖ ❖ ❖ ❖ ❖

1. Make the mayonnaise: In a small bowl, whisk the egg yolk with the mustard. Blend in the oil a few drops at a time to begin, then in a steady stream. Beat in the vinegar and season with salt and pepper.

2. In a medium bowl, fold the fish into ½ cup of the mayonnaise. Line scallop shells or salad plates with the lettuce. Mound the fish salad on top, decorate with the hard-boiled eggs, and sprinkle with parsley. Pass the remaining mayonnaise separately.

From Françoise:

• This recipe is extremely easy if you use prepared mayonnaise (¾ cup). It can be thinned with 1 or 2 tablespoons of cold water.

• Canned fish packed in water would work in this recipe, too.

• You can also decorate the salad with quartered tomatoes and cornichons.

• Please note that the finished dish contains raw egg.

CRAB AND RICE SALAD WITH FINES HERBES

- *Riz au crabe en timbales* -

❖ VERY EASY   ❖ MODERATE   ❖ 40 MINUTES, PLUS 1 HOUR CHILLING   ❖ SERVES 4

Salt

¾ cup white rice

2 tablespoons vinegar

6 tablespoons oil

Pepper

6 ounces crabmeat

¼ cup mixed chopped parsley, chives,
  and chervil leaves

Mayonnaise for decorating

4 olives

❖ ❖ ❖ ❖ ❖

1. Bring a medium saucepan of salted water to a boil. Rinse the rice in a colander under cold running water. Add the rice to the boiling water and cook until tender, 15 to 17 minutes. Drain and let cool.

2. In a medium bowl, whisk the vinegar with the oil and season with salt and pepper. Add the rice, crab, and herbs and toss to coat.

3. Pack the crab salad into ramekins. Cover and chill the ramekins in the refrigerator for 1 hour. Unmold onto plates, decorate with the mayonnaise and olives, and serve.

From Françoise:

• Use prepared mayonnaise for this salad since you don't need much. If you can find mayonnaise in a tube, it makes the decorating so much easier.

• The crabmeat can be replaced by flaked, oil-packed tuna. Use the oil from the can in the vinaigrette.

• After boiling the rice, rinse it in cold running water to stop the cooking and cool it down quickly.

• You might line the plates with lettuce leaves before unmolding the crab salad.

FISH SALAD WITH SHALLOTS
AND CREAMY VINAIGRETTE

- Salade de poisson aux fines herbes -

❖ VERY EASY   ❖ INEXPENSIVE   ❖ 30 MINUTES   ❖ SERVES 4

1 pound skinless fish fillets

2 tablespoons vinegar

Salt

1 tablespoon lemon juice or vinegar

3 tablespoons heavy cream

Pepper

1 shallot, finely chopped

Mixed chopped parsley, chives, and
  chervil leaves for sprinkling

❖ ❖ ❖ ❖ ❖

1. In a medium saucepan of water, combine the fish with the 2 tablespoons of vinegar and season with salt. Slowly bring to a boil, then remove the pan from the heat and let cool. Drain and break up the fish into large flakes.

2. In a salad bowl, whisk the lemon juice or vinegar with the heavy cream and season with salt and pepper. Add the fish and shallot and stir to coat. Sprinkle with the herbs and serve.

From Françoise:

• If you have some leftover cooked fish, but not quite enough to make this salad, stretch what's there with a little steamed rice.

• For a variation, make a vinaigrette thickened with a tablespoon of mayonnaise and add a few cornichons, sliced into rounds, or capers.

• This salad can be made with any kind of fish—mackerel is especially good—or with canned fish packed in water.

• A spring onion or scallion could replace the shallot.

HERRING AND APPLE SALAD WITH
TANGY MUSTARD VINAIGRETTE

- Salade aux harengs fumés et aux pommes -

❖ VERY EASY   ❖ INEXPENSIVE   ❖ 30 MINUTES   ❖ SERVES 4

Salt
½ cup rice
1 apple
1 tablespoon lemon juice
½ tablespoon vinegar

1 tablespoon Dijon mustard
⅓ cup oil
Pepper
6 smoked herring fillets, cut into ¼-inch dice

❖ ❖ ❖ ❖ ❖

1. Bring a medium saucepan of salted water to a boil. Rinse the rice in a colander under cold running water. Add the rice to the boiling water and cook until tender, 15 to 17 minutes. Drain and rinse in cold running water, then drain well. Pat dry with paper towels.

2. Peel the apple and cut it into ¼-inch dice. In a small bowl, toss the apple with the lemon juice.

3. In a salad bowl, whisk the vinegar with the mustard. Blend in the oil and season with salt and pepper. Add the rice, herring, and apple and toss to mix. Refrigerate before serving.

From Françoise:
• Vacuum-packed smoked herring isn't especially salty, which typically makes it ready to serve. If that isn't the case, soak the fish in water or milk for an hour, turning it several times.

• You can also prepare this recipe with smoked haddock.

CLASSIC SEAFOOD AND RICE SALAD WITH HERBS
- *Salade de riz aux fruits de mer* -

❖ EASY   ❖ MODERATE   ❖ 30 MINUTES   ❖ SERVES 4

Salt

½ cup long-grain rice

2 pounds mussels, scrubbed and debearded

1 onion, finely chopped

½ tablespoon vinegar

⅓ cup oil

Pepper

8 cooked, shelled shrimp, sliced lengthwise

Mixed chopped parsley, chives, and chervil leaves

2 tomatoes, quartered lengthwise

❖　❖　❖　❖　❖

1. Bring a medium saucepan of salted water to a boil. Rinse the rice in a colander under cold running water. Add the rice to the boiling water and cook until tender, 15 to 17 minutes. Drain and rinse in cold running water, then drain well. Let cool completely.

2. Add the mussels and onion to a pot, cover, and cook over high heat, stirring once or twice, just until the mussels open, 3 to 5 minutes. Remove the pot from the heat. When the mussels are cool enough to handle, remove the mussel meat from the shells and reserve. Discard the shells and any unopened mussels. Reserve the mussel broth for another use.

3. In a salad bowl, whisk the vinegar with the oil and season with salt and pepper. Add the rice, mussels, shrimp, and herbs and toss to coat. Garnish with the tomatoes and serve.

From Françoise:

• This salad is also delicious with sweet, delicate cockles. Prepare them in the same way as the mussels.

• To make a one-dish meal out of this for a summer evening or a lunch in the countryside, increase the amount of mussels and shrimp and, if needed, add hard-boiled eggs.

RICE SALAD WITH SMOKED HERRING AND ANCHOVY VINAIGRETTE

- *Salade de riz aux harengs, sauce aux anchois* -

❖ VERY EASY   ❖ INEXPENSIVE   ❖ 45 MINUTES   ❖ SERVES 4

Salt

1 cup rice

1 carrot, peeled and cut into julienne strips

1 small spring onion or sweet onion, cut into
  julienne strips

½ red bell pepper, cut into julienne strips

½ green bell pepper, cut into julienne strips

4 smoked herring fillets, cut into ¼-inch dice

¾ cup pitted black olives

2 hard-boiled eggs, sliced crosswise

ANCHOVY VINAIGRETTE

1 hard-boiled egg, white chopped and reserved

8 oil-packed anchovies

1 tablespoon Dijon mustard

1 cup oil

Salt and pepper

❖ ❖ ❖ ❖ ❖

1. Bring a medium saucepan of salted water to a boil. Add the rice and cook until tender, 15 to 17 minutes. Drain in a colander and rinse under cold running water, then drain well. Let cool completely.

2. Make the vinaigrette: In a mortar or food processor, grind the egg yolk and anchovies to a paste. Blend in the mustard, then the oil a few drops at a time to begin, then in a steady stream. Season lightly with salt and generously with pepper.

3. Spread the rice on a platter or in a wide bowl. Arrange the carrot, onion, bell peppers, herring, olives, and chopped egg white on top. Drizzle some of the vinaigrette over the salad. Garnish with the egg slices and serve.

From Françoise:

• Look for vacuum-packed smoked herring; it isn't overly salty and is therefore ready to use. Still, be careful when seasoning the vinaigrette with salt.

SALT-PACKED ANCHOVIES
WITH PARSLEY AND CAPERS
- *Persillade d'anchois* -

❖ VERY EASY   ❖ MODERATE   ❖ 25 MINUTES   ❖ SERVES 8

20 salt-packed anchovies

4 hard-boiled eggs, sliced crosswise

1 large bunch of parsley, stems removed,
  leaves chopped

1 tablespoon capers or 4 cornichons,
  sliced into rounds

6 tablespoons olive oil

Juice of 1 lemon

❖ ❖ ❖ ❖ ❖

1. Remove the anchovy bones and discard.
Soak the fillets in cold water for 20 minutes.

2. Pat the anchovies dry. Lay them in a criss-
cross pattern on a platter. Arrange the egg
slices around them and sprinkle with the
parsley and capers or cornichons. Drizzle with
the olive oil and lemon juice.

From Françoise:

• Anchovies packed in salt are easy to use and,
to my taste, better than oil-packed anchovies.
The fillets separate easily from the bones,
which can simply be pulled out with your
fingers.

ZUCCHINI STUFFED WITH LEMONY RICE
AND VEGETABLE SALAD
- *Courgettes farcies au riz* -

❖ EASY   ❖ INEXPENSIVE   ❖ 40 MINUTES, PLUS 1 HOUR CHILLING   ❖ SERVES 4

Salt

4 small zucchini

¼ cup rice

¼ pound white mushrooms, thinly sliced

1 tablespoon plus 1 teaspoon lemon juice

1 tablespoon vinegar

3 tablespoons oil

Pepper

2 tomatoes, peeled, seeded, and cut into
  ¼-inch dice

continued

1. In a large saucepan of boiling salted water, cook the zucchini until just tender, about 20 minutes. Remove the zucchini and rinse in a colander under cold running water. Cut them in half lengthwise, then scoop out the seeds.

2. Add the rice to the boiling water and cook until tender, 15 to 17 minutes. Drain in a colander and rinse under cold running water, then drain well. Let cool completely.

3. In a medium bowl, toss the mushrooms with the 1 tablespoon of lemon juice.

4. In another bowl, whisk the vinegar and remaining 1 teaspoon of lemon juice with the oil and season with salt and pepper. Add the rice, mushrooms, and tomatoes. Spoon the rice mixture in the zucchini halves. Refrigerate at least 1 hour before serving.

From Françoise:

• To remove the skin from the tomatoes easily, cut a shallow cross in the bottoms and add them to the boiling water briefly until the skin begins to peel. Using a slotted spoon, transfer them to a work surface.

• Try adding a little mayonnaise to the vinaigrette to thicken it slightly.

LIGHT SHRIMP SALAD WITH VEGETABLES AND GRUYÈRE

- *Salade de crevettes et crudités* -

❖ VERY EASY ❖ EXPENSIVE ❖ 30 MINUTES ❖ SERVES 4 TO 6

1 tablespoon plus 1 teaspoon lemon juice
⅓ cup plus 1 tablespoon oil
Salt and pepper
½ pound cooked, shelled shrimp
½ tablespoon vinegar
¼ pound white mushrooms, thinly sliced
Boston lettuce leaves, sliced into thin strips
   for garnishing

1 cucumber, peeled and cut into ¼-inch dice
3 small tomatoes, peeled, seeded, and cut into
   ¼-inch dice
¼ pound Gruyère cheese, cut into ¼-inch dice
Mixed chopped herbs, such as parsley, chives,
   chervil, dill, and fennel fronds, for sprinkling

❖ ❖ ❖ ❖ ❖

1. In a medium bowl, whisk 1 teaspoon of the lemon juice with 1 tablespoon of the oil and season with salt and pepper. Add the shrimp and toss to coat.

2. In a small bowl, whisk the vinegar with the remaining ⅓ cup of oil and season with salt and pepper.

3. In another bowl, toss the mushrooms with the remaining 1 tablespoon of lemon juice.

4. In individual bowls, mound the lettuce. Layer the vegetables, cheese, and shrimp on top. Refrigerate until chilled. Sprinkle with the herbs, drizzle the vinaigrette over the salads, and serve.

From Françoise:
• To serve this salad family style, spread the lettuce on a platter or in a wide salad bowl and layer the vegetables, cheese, and shrimp on top.

• Select the firmest mushrooms—the ones with caps tightly attached to the stems.

ENDIVE, BEET, APPLE, AND HAM SALAD WITH DIJON VINAIGRETTE
- *Salade Beaucaire* -

❖ EASY   ❖ MODERATE   ❖ 20 MINUTES, PLUS 2 HOURS MARINATING   ❖ SERVES 4

1 tablespoon vinegar

2 teaspoons Dijon mustard

3 tablespoons oil

Salt and pepper

2 or 3 tender inner celery ribs, sliced crosswise 1 inch thick

½ pound celery root, thickly peeled and cut into julienne strips

2 endives, sliced crosswise

2 apples, peeled and cut into 1-inch pieces

1 or 2 tablespoons mayonnaise

1 slice ham, sliced into strips

Mixed chopped herbs, such as parsley, chives, chervil, and tarragon, for sprinkling

2 boiled potatoes, peeled and sliced crosswise

1 small cooked red beet, peeled and sliced crosswise

❖ ❖ ❖ ❖ ❖

1. Two hours before serving, in a salad bowl, whisk the vinegar with 1 teaspoon of the mustard. Blend in the oil and season with salt and pepper. Add the celery, celery root, endives, and apples and toss to coat. Let mixture marinate in the refrigerator.

2. In a small bowl, stir the mayonnaise with the remaining 1 teaspoon of mustard. Add the ham and toss to coat. Fold into the salad.

3. Mound the salad on a platter and sprinkle with the herbs. Arrange the potatoes and beet around it and serve.

From Françoise:
• To keep the julienned celery root white, toss it with a little lemon juice.

• Try using lemon juice in the vinaigrette instead of vinegar to vary the flavor.

MACARONI, ARTICHOKE, AND HAM SALAD WITH FINES HERBES

- *Salade de coquillettes au jambon* -

❖ VERY EASY   ❖ MODERATE   ❖ 30 MINUTES   ❖ SERVES 4

Salt

½ pound macaroni

1 tablespoon oil

¾ cup mayonnaise

1 teaspoon paprika

1 teaspoon ketchup

4 cooked artichoke bottoms or marinated
artichoke hearts, chopped

A few cornichons, chopped

A few radishes, chopped

20 pitted green olives, chopped

Mixed chopped herbs, such as parsley, chives,
chervil, and tarragon

2 slices ham, diced

4 hard-boiled eggs, quartered lengthwise

3 small tomatoes, quartered lengthwise

❖ ❖ ❖ ❖ ❖

1. In a medium pan of boiling salted water, cook the macaroni, stirring occasionally, until al dente. Drain and toss with the oil.

2. In a large bowl, thin the mayonnaise with a little cold water or vinegar. Stir in the paprika and ketchup. Fold in the macaroni, artichokes, cornichons, radishes, olives, and herbs.

3. Mound the salad on a platter or in a wide salad bowl. Decorate with the ham, eggs, and tomatoes and serve.

From Françoise:

• If you're making a pasta salad (not a pasta dish to serve hot), you can rinse the cooked pasta in a colander under cold running water to stop the cooking. Drain it thoroughly.

• This is a recipe to play with. Try adding chicken breast, shellfish, crab, shrimp, langoustines, or vegetables such as corn, hearts of palm, cucumber, and so on.

• Short pasta like shells, gemelli, and macaroni are best suited to this salad because they keep their shape when folded into the dressing.

GREEN SALAD WITH POTATOES, EGGS, APPLE, AND GRUYÈRE
- *Salade Mireille* -

❖ VERY EASY   ❖ MODERATE   ❖ 20 MINUTES   ❖ SERVES 4

½ tablespoon vinegar

1 teaspoon Dijon mustard

¼ cup oil

Salt and pepper

1 small head Boston lettuce, leaves separated

4 large boiled potatoes, peeled and sliced
  crosswise

4 hard-boiled eggs, quartered lengthwise

1 apple, peeled, quartered, and thinly sliced
  lengthwise

¼ pound Gruyère cheese, cut into sticks

10 olives

❖ ❖ ❖ ❖ ❖

1. In a salad bowl, whisk the vinegar with the mustard. Blend in the oil and season with salt and pepper. Add the lettuce, potatoes, eggs, apple, and cheese and gently toss to coat. Decorate with the olives and serve.

DAISY SALAD
- *Salade Marguerite* -

❖ EASY   ❖ INEXPENSIVE   ❖ 50 MINUTES   ❖ SERVES 4

1 tablespoon vinegar

3 tablespoons oil

Salt and pepper

2 boiled potatoes, peeled and sliced crosswise

¾ pound cooked green beans

2 hard-boiled eggs, quartered lengthwise

Mayonnaise for decorating

❖ ❖ ❖ ❖ ❖

1. In a small bowl, whisk the vinegar with the oil and season with salt and pepper. In separate bowls, toss the potatoes and green beans with the vinaigrette.

2. In a salad bowl, layer the potatoes, then the green beans. Arrange the eggs like the petals

continued

41

of a daisy around a mayonnaise center. Pipe mayonnaise rosettes between the egg petals.

From Françoise:

From Françoise:
• The amount of mayonnaise needed here is very little, so it's fine to use mayonnaise from a squeeze-bottle for convenience.

MUSHROOMS WITH LEMON AND HERBS
- *Champignons citronette* -

❖ VERY EASY ❖ INEXPENSIVE ❖ 15 MINUTES ❖ SERVES 4

½ pound white mushrooms, thinly sliced
1 tablespoon lemon juice
3 tablespoons oil

Salt and pepper
Mixed chopped herbs, such as parsley, chives, or chervil, for sprinkling

❖ ❖ ❖ ❖ ❖

1. In a salad bowl, toss the mushrooms with the lemon juice. Add the oil, season with salt and pepper, and toss to coat. Just before serving, sprinkle with the herbs.

From Françoise:
• This mushroom salad is best when prepared at the last minute.

• The quality of the mushrooms is especially important in this recipe because they're eaten raw. Select the freshest, smallest, whitest, firmest ones you can find.

• Another option: Simply toss the thinly sliced mushrooms with crème fraîche.

LOOKS-LIKE-A-MUSHROOM SALAD
- *Champignons-surprise* -

❖ VERY EASY ❖ INEXPENSIVE ❖ 30 MINUTES ❖ SERVES 4

½ tablespoon vinegar
2 tablespoons oil
Salt and pepper
½ bunch of watercress, tough stems removed

4 hard-boiled eggs
2 small tomatoes, halved and partially scooped out
¾ cup mayonnaise

1. In a small bowl, whisk the vinegar with the oil and season with salt and pepper.

2. Spread the watercress sprigs on a platter. Remove a thin slice from both ends of each egg so it stands upright. Arrange the eggs on the watercress and set a tomato half on each like a hat. Dot the tomatoes with mayonnaise to look like, well, toadstools. Drizzle the watercress with the vinaigrette and serve. Pass the remaining mayonnaise separately.

From Françoise:
• You can prepare this salad with even the youngest cook at home.

• Try using cooked green beans or haricots verts instead of the watercress.

• Save the egg trimmings to make a little salad. Finely chop them and mix with a tablespoon or so of mayonnaise.

GREEN SALAD WITH ORANGES AND NUTS
- *Salade des lords* -

❖ VERY EASY   ❖ MODERATE   ❖ 20 MINUTES   ❖ SERVES 4

1 orange
Juice of ½ lemon
2 tablespoons crème fraîche
Salt and pepper

5 walnut halves, chopped
6 or 8 almonds, chopped
1 head Boston lettuce, leaves separated

❖ ❖ ❖ ❖ ❖

1. Using a vegetable peeler, remove the zest from the orange in strips. Cut it into fine julienne. Using a sharp knife, peel the orange, removing all the white pith. Thinly slice it crosswise, removing any seeds.

2. In a salad bowl, whisk the lemon juice with the crème fraîche and season with salt and

pepper. Add the orange zest, walnuts, and almonds and toss to coat. Add the lettuce and arrange the orange slices around the bowl. Toss the salad at the table.

From Françoise:
• Try to remove only the orange zest to make the julienne; the white pith is bitter.

CHICKEN SALAD WITH VEGETABLE JULIENNE
- *Salade de poulet* -

❖ EASY   ❖ MODERATE   ❖ 45 MINUTES   ❖ SERVES 8

Salt

½ cup rice

¾ cup mayonnaise

½ teaspoon paprika

2 pinches of cayenne pepper

1 tablespoon lemon juice, vinegar, or water

1 roasted chicken, meat cut into ¼-inch dice

3 tender inner celery ribs, cut into
  julienne strips

1 fennel bulb, cut into julienne strips

½ red bell pepper, cut into julienne strips

½ green bell pepper, cut into julienne strips

Mixed chopped parsley, chives, and chervil leaves

Boston lettuce leaves for garnishing

3 tomatoes, quartered lengthwise

5 hard-boiled eggs, quartered lengthwise

Sliced radishes for garnishing

Olives for garnishing

❖ ❖ ❖ ❖ ❖

1. In a medium saucepan of boiling salted water, cook the rice until tender, 15 to 17 minutes. Drain in a colander and rinse under cold running water, then drain well. Let cool completely.

2. In a small bowl, blend the mayonnaise with the paprika and cayenne pepper. Thin it with the lemon juice, vinegar, or water. In one bowl, mix half the mayonnaise with the diced chicken. In another bowl, mix the remaining mayonnaise with the celery, fennel, bell peppers, rice, and herbs and season with salt. Cover both salads and refrigerate.

3. Just before serving, fold the chicken salad into the vegetables. Line individual bowls or salad plates with the lettuce. Mound the chicken salad on top and garnish with the tomatoes, eggs, radishes, and olives.

From Françoise:

• You can buy a rotisserie chicken and prepared mayonnaise to make this. They're very practical, especially when you're cooking in a vacation rental.

FRENCH CHEF'S SALAD
- *Salade du chef* -

❖ EASY   ❖ MODERATE   ❖ 40 MINUTES   ❖ SERVES 4 TO 6

1 small cucumber

Salt

½ pound cooked skinless, boneless chicken breast

½ pound cooked ham

½ pound Gruyère cheese

1 heart of Boston lettuce, leaves separated

Several leaves of romaine lettuce, torn into pieces

1 celery heart, quartered lengthwise

2 small tomatoes, quartered

2 hard-boiled eggs, quartered lengthwise

VINAIGRETTE

1 teaspoon Dijon mustard

4 tablespoons oil

Salt and pepper

1 tablespoon vinegar

❖ ❖ ❖ ❖ ❖

1. Peel the cucumber and slice it thinly. In a colander, toss it with 1 teaspoon of salt and let it drain.

2. Make the vinaigrette: In a large salad bowl, using a whisk, mix the mustard with the oil, then the salt, pepper, and the vinegar. The vinaigrette should be light and creamy.

3. Cut the chicken, ham, and cheese into small sticks, about 1 inch long. Add to the vinaigrette and let marinate for about 30 minutes, tossing from time to time.

4. Arrange the Boston and romaine lettuce leaves in 4 or 6 individual salad bowls. Rinse the salt from the cucumber, pat dry, and divide the slices among the bowls. Top each serving with some of the meat-vinaigrette mixture. Garnish with the tomatoes and eggs. Serve immediately and let each diner toss at the table.

From Françoise:

• This salad is a complete meal in itself. Everything is there, even the cheese. All you need is a generous dessert to finish it off well.

CONFETTI CORN SALAD WITH BELL PEPPERS

- Salade de maïs aux couleurs de l'été -

❖ VERY EASY   ❖ INEXPENSIVE   ❖ 15 MINUTES   ❖ SERVES 4

1 tablespoon vinegar

3 tablespoons oil

½ teaspoon paprika

Salt and pepper

2 cups canned corn, drained and patted dry

2 mixed bell peppers, cut into julienne strips

Boston lettuce leaves for garnishing

3 tomatoes, quartered

8 pimiento-stuffed olives, sliced crosswise

❖   ❖   ❖   ❖   ❖

1. In a salad bowl, whisk the vinegar with the oil and season with the paprika, salt, and pepper. Add the corn and bell peppers and toss to coat. Cover and refrigerate.

2. Just before serving, line a platter with the lettuce. Gently fold the tomatoes and olives into the corn salad. Mound the salad on the lettuce and serve.

CANNELLINI BEAN SALAD WITH PARSLEY VINAIGRETTE AND ANCHOVY TOASTS

- Salade canaille -

❖ VERY EASY   ❖ MODERATE   ❖ 30 MINUTES   ❖ SERVES 4 TO 6

1 ½ tablespoons vinegar

⅓ cup oil

1 shallot, finely chopped

3 garlic cloves, 1 finely chopped

Chopped parsley leaves

Salt and pepper

½ cup canned cannellini beans, rinsed and drained

Pitted green olives

A few radishes, sliced

A few cornichons, sliced into rounds

⅓ cup roasted red bell peppers, cut into ¼-inch dice

4 or 6 slices crustless white sandwich bread

2 tablespoons olive oil

12 oil-packed anchovies, drained and crushed

Boston lettuce leaves for garnishing

4 or 6 hard-boiled eggs, quartered lengthwise

2 or 3 tomatoes, quartered lengthwise

⅓ cup oil-packed sardines, drained

1. In a salad bowl, whisk the vinegar with the oil, shallot, chopped garlic, and parsley and season with salt and pepper. Add the cannellini beans, olives, radishes, cornichons, and bell peppers and toss to coat. Cover and refrigerate.

2. Toast the bread. Rub both sides with the whole garlic cloves. While still warm, brush

with the olive oil. Cut each slice into 2 triangles. Spread with the crushed anchovies.

3. Line a wide salad bowl or a platter with the lettuce. Mound the bean salad in the center. Arrange the eggs, tomatoes, sardines, and anchovy toasts in a star pattern around the salad and serve.

GREEN BEAN, TUNA, AND BELL PEPPER SALAD
- *Salade niçoise* -

❖ VERY EASY   ❖ MODERATE   ❖ 15 MINUTES   ❖ SERVES 4

1 tablespoon vinegar
1 teaspoon Dijon mustard
3 tablespoons olive oil
Salt and pepper
2 boiled potatoes, peeled and sliced crosswise
½ pound cooked green beans
2 tomatoes, quartered lengthwise
2 hard-boiled eggs, quartered lengthwise

1 (3-ounce) can oil-packed tuna, separated
   into large flakes, with oil
1 bell pepper, cut into julienne strips
½ cucumber, peeled and sliced crosswise
1 small spring onion or sweet onion, sliced
   crosswise and separated into rings
8 to 10 oil-packed anchovies
10 black olives

❖ ❖ ❖ ❖ ❖

1. In a small bowl, whisk the vinegar with the mustard. Blend in the olive oil and season with salt and pepper.

2. In a wide salad bowl or on a platter, mound the potatoes and arrange the green beans around them. Decorate with the tomatoes, eggs, tuna, bell pepper, cucumber, onion, anchovies, and olives. Drizzle with the vinaigrette and serve.

From Françoise:

• If you like garlic, toast several slices of baguette and rub them with garlic cloves. Drizzle with olive oil and add these garlic toasts to the bowl.

• Serve this salad as a starter, a summer lunch entrée, or a one-dish meal, or take it to a picnic. If making it into a meal-in-one dish, cook 1 egg per person and increase the tuna, potatoes, and vinaigrette accordingly.

LETTUCE, ORANGE, AND BANANA SALAD WITH CITRUS VINAIGRETTE

- *Salade mimosa* -

❖ VERY EASY   ❖ MODERATE   ❖ 15 MINUTES   ❖ SERVES 4

1 orange

1 tablespoon lemon juice

3 tablespoons crème fraîche

Salt and pepper

1 head Boston lettuce, leaves separated

1 banana, sliced

❖ ❖ ❖ ❖ ❖

1. Using a sharp knife, peel the orange, removing all the white pith. Thinly slice it crosswise and remove any seeds.

2. In a salad bowl, whisk the lemon juice with the crème fraîche and season with salt and pepper. Taste the dressing and add more lemon juice if you like. Add the lettuce and decorate with the orange and banana. Toss at the table just before serving.

From Françoise:

• Cross your salad servers in the bowl over the vinaigrette and lay the remaining ingredients on top so the lettuce won't wilt before serving.

• If the crème fraîche is too thick, thin it with a little cold water.

• This is the true recipe for salad mimosa. Still, the name is more often used to mean a green salad sprinkled with finely chopped hard-boiled egg whites and yolks.

POTATO SALAD WITH APPLES AND COMTÉ CHEESE

- *Salade de pommes de terre, pommes et Comté* -

❖ VERY EASY   ❖ MODERATE   ❖ 30 MINUTES   ❖ SERVES 4

½ tablespoon vinegar

1 teaspoon Dijon mustard

⅓ cup oil

Salt and pepper

Boston lettuce leaves for garnishing

4 boiled potatoes, peeled and sliced crosswise

4 hard-boiled eggs, sliced crosswise

1 apple, peeled, quartered, and thinly sliced lengthwise

½ pound Comté cheese, cut into sticks

Chopped parsley leaves for sprinkling

Paprika for dusting

1. In a small bowl, whisk the vinegar with the mustard. Blend in the oil and season with salt and pepper.

2. Line a platter with the lettuce. Layer the potatoes, eggs, apple, and cheese on top. Drizzle with some of the vinaigrette. Sprinkle the parsley over the potatoes, dust the cheese with the paprika, and serve. Pass the remaining vinaigrette separately.

From Françoise:

• Toss the apple with a little lemon juice to keep it from turning brown.

• To emulsify the vinaigrette, beat it energetically—using a whisk, food processor, blender, or electric mixer.

CLASSIC GREEN SALAD WITH VINAIGRETTE
- *Salade verte* -

❖ VERY EASY   ❖ INEXPENSIVE   ❖ 15 MINUTES   ❖ SERVES 4

1 tablespoon vinegar
3 tablespoons oil

Salt and pepper
1 head Boston lettuce, leaves separated

❖ ❖ ❖ ❖ ❖

1. In a salad bowl, whisk the vinegar with the oil and season with salt and pepper. Cross the salad servers over the vinaigrette and add the lettuce. Toss the salad just before serving.

From Françoise:

• Never toss the salad ahead of time. The vinegar "cooks" it, and the lettuce quickly wilts. You can, however, make the vinaigrette in advance. Crossing the salad servers over the vinaigrette and adding the lettuce on top of them keeps the dressing and lettuce separate until you're ready to toss and serve the salad.

• Dry the lettuce very well so the water doesn't dilute the vinaigrette.

MÂCHE SALAD WITH CELERY ROOT AND BEETS
- *Salade M.C.B.* -

❖ VERY EASY   ❖ INEXPENSIVE   ❖ 20 MINUTES   ❖ SERVES 4

¼ pound celery root, thickly peeled and
  cut into julienne strips
Juice of ½ lemon
1 tablespoon vinegar
3 tablespoons oil

Salt and pepper
1 small cooked red beet, peeled and sliced
  crosswise or cut into ¼-inch dice
¼ pound mâche greens
1 shallot, finely chopped
Chopped parsley leaves for sprinkling

❖ ❖ ❖ ❖ ❖

1. In a medium bowl, toss the celery root with the lemon juice.

2. In a salad bowl, whisk the vinegar with the oil and season with salt and pepper. Add the celery root, beet, mâche, and shallot and toss to mix. Sprinkle with the parsley and serve.

From Françoise:
• M.C.B. stands for mâche, celery root, and beet.

• If the mâche isn't prewashed, swish it around in several changes of water because these greens tend to be gritty.

• You can vary a beet-based salad with the addition of thinly sliced apples, walnut halves, celery or fennel sticks, watercress sprigs, green beans, or haricots verts, or—it goes without saying—boiled potatoes.

TOMATO SALAD WITH SHALLOTS AND HERBS
- *Salade de tomates* -

❖ VERY EASY   ❖ INEXPENSIVE   ❖ 15 MINUTES   ❖ SERVES 4

1 pound tomatoes
1 tablespoon vinegar
3 tablespoons oil
Salt and pepper

1 shallot, finely chopped
Finely chopped parsley leaves or chives
  for sprinkling

1. Bring a large saucepan of water to a boil. Core the tomatoes and make a shallow cross in the bottom of each. Add the tomatoes briefly to the boiling water. Using a slotted spoon, remove them as soon as the skins begin to peel. Peel and slice them.

2. In a small bowl, whisk the vinegar with the oil and season with salt and pepper.

3. Arrange the tomatoes on a platter, slightly overlapping. Drizzle the vinaigrette over them, sprinkle with the shallot and parsley or chives, and serve.

From Françoise:

• Out-of-season tomatoes can be watery. To draw out the water, I sprinkle the slices with salt for 30 minutes, then pat them dry and proceed with the recipe. It's a good precaution.

• Add a little mayonnaise or crème fraîche to the vinaigrette to make it creamy.

• Tomato salad is good with so many things— boiled potatoes, sliced cucumbers, olives, anchovies, hard-boiled eggs, and bell peppers, to name a few.

SIMPLE WATERCRESS SALAD
- Cresson en salade -

❖ VERY EASY ❖ INEXPENSIVE ❖ 15 MINUTES ❖ SERVES 4

1 tablespoon vinegar
3 tablespoons oil

Salt and pepper
1 bunch of watercress, large stems removed

❖ ❖ ❖ ❖ ❖

1. In a salad bowl, whisk the vinegar with the oil and season with salt and pepper. Cross the salad servers over the vinaigrette and add the watercress sprigs. Toss the salad just before serving.

From Françoise:
• Choose watercress that has a nice green color. If some of the leaves are yellow or limp, it's not fresh.

• To store watercress, wrap it in paper towels and refrigerate.

• Stems and leaves that are less than perfect can be used to make soup.

• You can vary this basic salad by adding hard-boiled eggs, sliced or quartered lengthwise; boiled potatoes; garlic toasts; or a finely chopped shallot.

CUCUMBER, BELL PEPPER, AND TOMATO SALAD WITH MINT

- Salade de concombre et poivron à la menthe -

❖ VERY EASY ❖ INEXPENSIVE ❖ 30 MINUTES ❖ SERVES 5

1 small cucumber, peeled and thinly sliced
  crosswise
Salt
1 tablespoon vinegar
¼ cup oil
2 or 3 pinches of paprika
Pepper

1 bell pepper, cut into julienne strips
1 shallot, finely chopped
4 mint leaves, finely chopped
Finely chopped parsley
4 small tomatoes, quartered lengthwise
2 slices crustless sandwich bread,
  cut into ½-inch cubes

❖ ❖ ❖ ❖ ❖

1. In a colander, sprinkle the cucumber with salt for 30 minutes, if time allows, then pat dry with paper towels.

2. In a small bowl, whisk the vinegar with the oil and season with paprika, salt, and pepper.

3. In a salad bowl, combine the cucumber with the bell pepper, shallot, mint, parsley, and to-matoes. Add the bread cubes, drizzle with the vinaigrette, and serve.

From Françoise:

• If the cucumber has a lot of seeds, scoop them out before slicing. It's easy to do with the tip of a vegetable peeler or a small spoon.

• It's up to you whether you prefer to toast the bread before cubing it and tossing with the salad.

FENNEL SALAD WITH VINAIGRETTE

- Fenouil en salade -

❖ EASY ❖ INEXPENSIVE ❖ 50 MINUTES ❖ SERVES 4

2 fennel bulbs, trimmed, fronds reserved
1 tablespoon vinegar

3 tablespoons oil
Salt and pepper

1. In a large saucepan of boiling water, cook the fennel until tender, about 30 minutes. Drain in a colander and rinse under cold running water, then drain well. Let cool completely.

2. In a small bowl, whisk the vinegar with the oil and season with salt and pepper.

3. Cut the fennel into matchstick strips. Arrange on a platter or add to a salad bowl. Drizzle with the vinaigrette and serve.

From Françoise:
• It would be a shame to cook the fennel fronds. They are so tender they're better served raw and finely chopped along with some vinaigrette.

• Instead of a vinaigrette, you might drizzle the fennel with ¼ cup of crème fraîche thinned with a tablespoon of wine vinegar or lemon juice and seasoned with salt and pepper.

RAW ARTICHOKE SALAD WITH DIJON VINAIGRETTE
- *Salade fraîche aux artichauts crus* -

❖ INTERMEDIATE   ❖ MODERATE   ❖ 30 MINUTES   ❖ SERVES 4

2 tablespoons vinegar
3 medium artichokes
1 tablespoon lemon juice or vinegar
1 teaspoon Dijon mustard
3 tablespoons oil
Salt and pepper

20 radishes, sliced
2 small spring onions or sweet onions,
    sliced crosswise
2 tender celery ribs, cut into sticks
4 small tomatoes, quartered lengthwise
2 tablespoons black olives

❖ ❖ ❖ ❖ ❖

1. Add the 2 tablespoons of vinegar to a bowl of cold water. Working with 1 artichoke at a time, cut off the stem using a very sharp knife. Slice off all the leaves level with the top of the artichoke bottom. Trim the bottom. Scrape out the hairy choke with a small spoon, then drop the artichoke bottom into the vinegar water.

2. In a salad bowl, whisk the lemon juice or vinegar with the mustard. Blend in the oil and season with salt and pepper.

3. Thinly slice the artichoke bottoms. Add to the vinaigrette with the radishes, onions, celery, and tomatoes and toss to coat. Decorate with the olives.

From Françoise:
• Instead of using vinegar in the water to keep the cut artichokes from darkening, you can squeeze in the juice from 2 lemon halves. Rub the artichoke bottoms with the lemons before dropping them in the water.

• The salad can be refrigerated for 1 to 2 hours.

LENTIL SALAD WITH SHALLOT VINAIGRETTE

- Lentilles en salade -

❖ VERY EASY   ❖ INEXPENSIVE   ❖ 15 MINUTES   ❖ SERVES 4

1 tablespoon vinegar

1 teaspoon Dijon mustard

3 tablespoons oil

Salt and pepper

2 cups cooked green lentils

2 hard-boiled eggs, quartered lengthwise

2 tomatoes, diced

1 shallot, finely chopped

Finely chopped parsley leaves

❖ ❖ ❖ ❖ ❖

1. In a salad bowl, whisk the vinegar with the mustard. Blend in the oil and season with salt and pepper. Add the lentils, eggs, tomatoes, shallot, and parsley and gently toss to coat.

From Françoise:

• To turn this into a summery salad, add finely diced bell peppers, cucumbers, and fines herbes (parsley, chives, chervil, tarragon).

• You can add this salad to a platter of crudités.

MIXED VEGETABLES WITH DIJON MAYONNAISE

- Salade russe -

❖ EASY   ❖ MODERATE   ❖ 15 TO 30 MINUTES, PLUS 1 HOUR CHILLING   ❖ SERVES 6

¾ cup mayonnaise

1 teaspoon Dijon mustard

1 cup canned mixed diced vegetables,
   drained and patted dry

½ cup diced canned mushrooms,
   drained and patted dry

½ cup diced canned artichoke bottoms or
   hearts, drained and patted dry

A few cornichons, sliced into rounds

1 slice of ham, sliced into strips

Boston lettuce leaves for garnishing

3 hard-boiled eggs, quartered lengthwise

2 tomatoes, diced

1 small cooked red beet, peeled
   and diced

❖ ❖ ❖ ❖ ❖

1. In a medium bowl, blend the mayonnaise with the mustard. Fold in the diced vegetables, cornichons, and ham. Pack into a soufflé mold or other deep dish and refrigerate for at least 1 hour.

2. Line a platter with the lettuce. Unmold the vegetable salad in the center. Surround it with the eggs, tomatoes, and beet and serve.

From Françoise:
• It's important to dry the diced vegetables very well, or the mixture won't keep its shape when unmolded.

LEMONY MIXED VEGETABLE GELÉES
- *Aspics de légumes* -

❖ INTERMEDIATE   ❖ INEXPENSIVE   ❖ 30 MINUTES, PLUS 1 HOUR CHILLING   ❖ SERVES 4 TO 6

2 cups frozen or canned mixed diced vegetables
1 envelope (1 tablespoon) unflavored powdered
  gelatin
1 tablespoon lemon juice

Salt and pepper
Boston lettuce leaves or watercress sprigs
  for garnishing
Oil for drizzling

❖   ❖   ❖   ❖   ❖

1. In a large saucepan of boiling water, cook the frozen vegetables until tender. Drain in a colander and rinse under cold running water, then drain well. Pat the diced vegetables dry with paper towels.

2. In a small saucepan, sprinkle the gelatin over ¼ cup of water. Let stand until spongy, about 3 minutes. Set the saucepan over medium heat until the water is warm and the gelatin melts, about 1 minute. Stir in 1 ¾ cups of water and the lemon juice and season with salt and pepper.

3. Pour ¼ inch of the gelatin mixture into ramekins, turning to coat the sides, and refrigerate for 5 minutes. Spoon the vegetables into the ramekins and cover with more of the gelatin. Refrigerate until firm, about 1 hour. The gelées can be made up to a day ahead.

4. Line salad plates with the lettuce or watercress and drizzle lightly with oil. Unmold the gelées on top and serve.

From Françoise:
• For a more luxe version, add crabmeat or diced, cooked shrimp to the diced vegetables.

• Spice up the gelées with a few drops of hot sauce or a pinch of cayenne pepper.

• The gelées will slip out of the ramekins more easily if you dip the bottoms in hot water for 3 or 4 seconds. Any longer, though, and the aspic will start to melt.

• The gelées can be unmolded ahead of time, but keep them in the refrigerator until ready to serve, or they will soften and collapse. Drizzle with the oil at the last minute.

ARTICHOKES WITH VINAIGRETTE

- *Artichauts vinaigrette* -

❖ VERY EASY ❖ INEXPENSIVE ❖ 1 HOUR ❖ SERVES 4

Salt

4 artichokes

3 tablespoons vinegar

½ cup plus 1 tablespoon oil

Salt and pepper

❖ ❖ ❖ ❖ ❖

1. Bring a large pot of salted water to a boil. Meanwhile, break off the artichoke stems. Pull off any tough, stringy outer leaves. Rinse the artichokes under cold running water, spreading the leaves apart to dislodge any dirt.

2. Add the artichokes to the boiling water, reduce the heat to medium, cover, and simmer until you can easily remove a leaf, 30 to 45 minutes. Drain in a colander, leaves pointing down.

3. In a small bowl, whisk the vinegar with the oil and season with salt and pepper. Serve the artichokes, passing the vinaigrette separately.

From Françoise:
• If you find any bugs in your artichokes, soak them, leaves pointing down, in a large bowl of vinegar water for 5 minutes before rinsing.

• I like to eat artichokes while they're still warm—I find them more flavorful.

• Typically, artichokes are served with a simple oil-and-vinegar vinaigrette. I prefer to prepare a more unctuous dressing at the table, crushing a hard-boiled egg on my plate and blending in the vinaigrette.

• No red wine with artichokes. Pour a white wine instead or even . . . water. Artichokes are tough to match with wine because they contain a chemical called cynarin, which for most people makes wines taste overly sweet.

• You can add these artichokes to a platter of crudités.

ARTICHOKE BOTTOMS STUFFED WITH MIXED VEGETABLES

- *Artichauts à la macédoine (fonds d')* -

❖ INTERMEDIATE   ❖ MODERATE   ❖ 50 MINUTES   ❖ SERVES 4

Salt

2 tablespoons vinegar

4 artichokes

1½ cups frozen or canned mixed diced vegetables

2 tablespoons mayonnaise

Boston lettuce leaves for garnishing

4 radish roses or olives

❖ ❖ ❖ ❖ ❖

1. Bring a large saucepan of salted water to a boil. Meanwhile, add the vinegar to a bowl of cold water. Working with 1 artichoke at a time, cut off the stem using a very sharp knife. Slice off all the leaves level with the top of the artichoke bottom. Trim the bottoms. Scrape out the hairy chokes with a small spoon, then drop the artichoke bottoms into the vinegar water.

2. Cook the artichoke bottoms in the boiling water until tender, about 12 minutes. Using a slotted spoon, transfer the artichokes to a colander and rinse under cold running water, then drain well.

3. Add the frozen vegetables to the boiling water and cook until tender. Drain in a colander and rinse under cold running water, then drain well. Pat the diced vegetables dry with paper towels.

4. In a medium bowl, stir the mayonnaise into the diced vegetables. Mound the vegetables on the artichoke bottoms. Line a platter with the lettuce, arrange the artichokes on top, and garnish with the radishes or olives.

From Françoise:

• You can also prepare artichoke bottoms in the same way as whole artichokes (see Artichokes with Vinaigrette, page 56). Once they're cooked, slice off all the leaves, trim the bottoms, and scrape out the hairy choke.

• Artichokes tend to bob in boiling water. Keep them submerged during cooking by putting a plate that fits inside the saucepan on top.

ARTICHOKES STUFFED WITH ROSY ROQUEFORT SAUCE

- *Artichauts sauce rose au Roquefort* -

❖ VERY EASY   ❖ MODERATE   ❖ 40 MINUTES, PLUS COOLING   ❖ SERVES 4

Salt

4 artichokes

1 tablespoon vinegar or lemon juice

2 tablespoons crème fraîche

¾ cup crumbled Roquefort cheese
  (about 3 ½ ounces)

2 or 3 tablespoons ketchup

Dash of hot sauce

1 teaspoon Cognac

Salt and pepper

❖   ❖   ❖   ❖   ❖

1. Bring a large pot of salted water to a boil. Meanwhile, break off the artichoke stems. Pull off any tough, stringy outer leaves. With a small, sharp knife, slice ½ inch off the top and peel the base. Using a melon baller, scoop out some of the choke to form a cup. Rinse the artichokes under cold running water, spreading the leaves apart to dislodge any dirt. Tie each artichoke with kitchen string.

2. Add the artichokes to the boiling water, cover, reduce the heat to medium, and simmer until you can easily remove a leaf, about 30 minutes. Drain in a colander, leaves pointing down, and let cool.

3. In a small bowl, whisk the vinegar or lemon juice with the crème fraîche, cheese, ketchup, hot sauce, and Cognac. Season with salt and pepper.

4. Discard the string. Using a small spoon, fill the cooled artichokes with some of the Roquefort sauce. Arrange on a platter and serve, passing the remaining sauce separately.

From Françoise:

• The trick to getting tightly closed artichokes after they've cooked—so the leaves don't flop open as they sometimes do when they're overcooked—is to tie them with kitchen string before boiling. Remove the string once they're completely cooled.

• The Roquefort sauce would also be a tasty accompaniment to hard-boiled eggs, tomatoes, celery, and asparagus.

WHITE ASPARAGUS WITH VINAIGRETTE
- *Asperges vinaigrette* -

❖ VERY EASY   ❖ EXPENSIVE   ❖ 40 MINUTES   ❖ SERVES 4

Salt

2 pounds thick white asparagus

3 tablespoons vinegar

½ cup plus 1 tablespoon oil

Salt and pepper

❖　❖　❖　❖　❖

1. Bring a large pot of salted water to a boil. Meanwhile, break about an inch off the bottoms of the asparagus spears. Peel the stems. Rinse the asparagus under cold running water. Tie them in bundles of 5 or 6 with string. Add to the boiling water and cook until tender, about 20 minutes. Drain and discard the string. Pat dry with paper towels and transfer to a platter.

2. In a small bowl, whisk the vinegar with the oil and season with salt and pepper.

3. Serve the asparagus warm or at room temperature, passing the vinaigrette separately.

From Françoise:
• Asparagus bottoms don't need to be trimmed using a knife because they naturally break where they stop being tender; the same goes for green asparagus.

• Be careful not to boil asparagus for too long. It is cooked when the bottoms are easily pierced with a fork.

• Drain asparagus quickly or it will get soggy.

• Asparagus tastes better when it is warm rather than at room temperature, and it's not so flavorful when it just comes out of the fridge.

• Sometimes I like to enrich the vinaigrette with a mashed hard-boiled egg yolk or a little mayonnaise.

• Instead of vinaigrette, you can blend crème fraîche with a little lemon juice or vinegar and season with salt and pepper.

• If you cook extra asparagus or have any left over, you can transform it into another dish. For example, spread the spears in a gratin pan, sprinkle the tips with grated Parmesan cheese, and slide under the broiler until the cheese melts.

AVOCADO AND GRAPEFRUIT SALAD WITH CITRUS DRESSING

- *Panaché d'avocat pamplemousse* -

❖ VERY EASY   ❖ MODERATE   ❖ 20 MINUTES   ❖ SERVES 4

2 tablespoons lemon juice
2 to 3 tablespoons oil
1 garlic clove, crushed
Salt and pepper
1 grapefruit

2 avocados, peeled, pit removed, and thinly
  sliced lengthwise
1 tomato, peeled and thinly sliced
Boston lettuce leaves for garnishing

❖ ❖ ❖ ❖ ❖

1. In a small bowl, whisk 1 tablespoon of the lemon juice with the oil and garlic and season with salt and pepper.

2. Using a sharp knife, peel the grapefruit, removing all the white pith. Cut in between the membranes to release the sections.

3. In a bowl, combine the avocados and tomato with the remaining 1 tablespoon of lemon juice.

4. Line a platter with the lettuce. Arrange the avocados, grapefruit, and tomato slightly overlapping on the platter. Drizzle with some of the dressing. Remove the garlic and serve the remaining dressing with the salad.

From Françoise:
• The secret to a salad that's dressed but not limp is to refrigerate it without mixing it. Toss right before serving.

BRIOCHES STUFFED WITH ROQUEFORT CREAM

- *Croque-mousseline* -

❖ EASY   ❖ MODERATE   ❖ 15 MINUTES   ❖ SERVES 6

6 small brioches
¾ cup Roquefort cheese (about 3 ½ ounces)
¼ cup fromage blanc
2 tablespoons milk

Pinch of cayenne pepper
Black pepper
½ cup heavy cream

1. Cut a small "hat" out of each brioche, then carefully cut out much of the crumb, leaving a sturdy shell.

2. In a small bowl, mash the cheese with the fromage blanc and milk until smooth. Season with the cayenne and black pepper.

3. Whip the cream until soft peaks form. Spoon a little into each brioche and top with some of the cheese mixture. Cover with their "hats" and serve.

From Françoise:
• Heavy cream whips best when it's beaten in a cold metal bowl with a cold whisk or beaters.

ROQUEFORT AND AVOCADO CANAPÉS
- Canapés au Roquefort -

❖ VERY EASY	❖ MODERATE	❖ 30 MINUTES	❖ MAKES 10 OR 20 PIECES

6 tablespoons crumbled Roquefort cheese
  (about 1 ½ ounces)
1 avocado, peeled and pit removed
1 tablespoon lemon juice

Salt and pepper
5 slices crustless white sandwich bread, each cut
  into 2 or 4 pieces

❖ ❖ ❖ ❖ ❖

1. In a small bowl, mash the cheese with the avocado and lemon juice. Season with salt and pepper.

2. Spread the cheese mixture on the bread and serve.

From Françoise:
• The key to making canapés is to work fast at the last minute so they stay fresh. For instance, instead of cutting the bread into individual pieces first, you could spread the topping on large slices of bread—even cutting an unsliced loaf lengthwise—then cut the bread into triangles, rectangles, or squares of the desired size.

PROVENÇAL GUACAMOLE CANAPÉS
- Canapés d'avocat à la niçoise -

❖ VERY EASY   ❖ MODERATE   ❖ 30 MINUTES   ❖ MAKES 10 OR 20 PIECES

1 avocado, peeled and pit removed
1 shallot, finely chopped
1 tablespoon lemon juice
Salt and cayenne pepper

5 slices crustless white sandwich bread,
   each cut into 2 or 4 pieces
Sliced black olives for garnishing
Sliced tomatoes for garnishing

❖ ❖ ❖ ❖ ❖

1. In a small bowl, mash the avocado. Stir in the shallot and lemon juice and season with salt and cayenne pepper.

2. Spread the avocado mixture on the bread, garnish with the olives and tomatoes, and serve.

AVOCADO AND ONION CANAPÉS
- Canapés d'avocat à l'oignon -

❖ VERY EASY   ❖ MODERATE   ❖ 30 MINUTES   ❖ MAKES 10 OR 20 PIECES

1 avocado, peeled and pit removed
1 small onion, minced
1 teaspoon lemon juice

Salt and pepper
5 slices crustless white sandwich bread,
   each cut into 2 or 4 pieces

❖ ❖ ❖ ❖ ❖

1. In a small bowl, mash the avocado with the onion and lemon juice and season with salt and pepper.

2. Spread the avocado mixture on the bread and serve.

AVOCADOS STUFFED WITH SPICY VEGETABLES

- *Avocats "diabolic"* -

❖ EASY   ❖ MODERATE   ❖ 30 MINUTES   ❖ SERVES 4

¼ red bell pepper, cut into ¼-inch dice

Salt

2 avocados, halved and pits removed

1 lemon, halved

2 tomatoes, peeled and seeded

1 small spring onion or sweet onion, finely chopped

1 teaspoon capers

1 tablespoon fromage blanc

Pepper

Dash of hot sauce

3 tablespoons oil

❖ ❖ ❖ ❖ ❖

1. In a small bowl, sprinkle the bell pepper with salt.

2. Using a soup spoon, scoop the avocado flesh out of the shells. Drizzle the shells with lemon juice and refrigerate. Cut the avocado flesh into ¼-inch dice and add to a medium bowl. Squeeze in the remaining lemon juice.

3. Cut the tomatoes into ¼-inch dice and pat dry with paper towels. Pat dry the bell pepper. Add the tomatoes, bell pepper, onion, capers, and fromage blanc to the avocado. Season with salt and pepper, add the hot sauce and oil, and toss to coat. Refrigerate for 15 minutes.

4. Spoon the salad mixture into the avocado shells and serve immediately.

From Françoise:

• A few diced, cooked shrimp could be added to the vegetable filling.

• Tossing cut avocado with lemon juice keeps it from turning brown.

• Rock-hard avocados can ripen at home at room temperature.

• Like a pear, a ripe avocado is firm yet yields to the touch.

• When ripe, avocados can be stored in the refrigerator for a few days, but after that the flesh starts to darken inside.

• Avocados have the most flavor when served at room temperature.

LOBSTER-STUFFED AVOCADOS

- *Avocats farcis* -

❖ INTERMEDIATE   ❖ EXPENSIVE   ❖ 45 MINUTES, PLUS 1 HOUR COOLING   ❖ SERVES 4

1 frozen spiny or regular lobster tail

1 onion, thinly sliced

1 carrot, thinly sliced

1 whole clove

1 teaspoon vinegar

1 bouquet garni made with parsely, thyme, and
  bay leaf

4 peppercorns

Salt

¾ cup mayonnaise

Dash of hot sauce or pinch of cayenne pepper

Mixed chopped herbs, such as parsley, chives,
  chervil, and tarragon

½ roasted bell pepper, cut into ¼-inch dice

1 tablespoon capers

1 tablespoon lemon juice, plus 4 lemon slices

Salt and pepper

2 avocados

Boston lettuce leaves for garnishing

❖ ❖ ❖ ❖ ❖

1. In a large saucepan, combine the lobster tail with 2 cups of water and the onion, carrot, clove, vinegar, bouquet garni, peppercorns, and salt. Slowly bring to a boil over medium heat, then reduce the heat to low and cook gently for 5 to 7 minutes. Remove the pan from the heat and let cool for 1 hour. Drain and discard all but the lobster.

2. In a medium bowl, blend the mayonnaise with the hot sauce or cayenne pepper, herbs, bell pepper, capers, and lemon juice. Season with salt and pepper.

3. Using scissors, slit the tail shell and remove the meat. Remove the dark intestinal vein. Cut 4 thin slices from the thickest end of the tail. Cut the remaining meat into ¼-inch pieces and fold into the mayonnaise.

4. Just before serving, halve the avocados and remove the pits. Line with the lettuce. Mound the lobster salad on top and decorate with the lobster and lemon slices.

From Françoise:

• Slowly cooking frozen lobster tails in a court bouillon and then letting them cool in the seasoned water makes them much more flavorful.

• This dish can be made through Step 3 and refrigerated for several hours or overnight.

• You might try cutting each lemon slice almost in half and twisting it, then setting it on an artichoke half for decoration.

CELERY ROOT JULIENNE IN MUSTARD MAYONNAISE

- *Céleri rémoulade* -

❖ EASY   ❖ MODERATE   ❖ 20 MINUTES   ❖ SERVES 4

1 pound celery root, thickly peeled and cut into
   julienne strips
Juice of ½ lemon
1 large egg yolk

1 tablespoon Dijon mustard
1 cup oil
1 tablespoon vinegar
Salt and pepper

❖ ❖ ❖ ❖ ❖

1. In a medium bowl, toss the celery root with the lemon juice.

2. In a small bowl, whisk the egg yolk with the mustard. Blend in the oil a few drops at a time to begin, then in a steady stream. Beat in the vinegar and season with salt and pepper.

3. Fold the mayonnaise into the celery root just before serving.

From Françoise:
• Thump the celery root before buying it; it should feel "full." Or lift it; it should feel heavy for its size.

• It's easier to peel the celery root if you quarter it lengthwise first.

• You can soften the flavor of celery root, which some people like to do, by cooking the julienned strips in boiling water for 1 minute.

Drain in a colander and rinse under cold running water, then pat dry before tossing with the lemon juice.

• Conversely, you can develop the flavor of this salad by letting it stand for an hour or two.

• Have all the ingredients for the mayonnaise at room temperature to keep it from separating as you make it.

• I recommend using sunflower oil to make mayonnaise because the sauce is less likely to curdle in the refrigerator.

• To simplify things, you can replace the homemade mayonnaise in this recipe with 1 cup of store-bought mayonnaise.

• Please note that the finished dish contains raw egg.

TANGY MARINATED MUSHROOMS

- *Champignons à la grecque* -

❖ EASY   ❖ MODERATE   ❖ 30 MINUTES, PLUS 2 TO 3 HOURS CHILLING   ❖ SERVES 4

⅓ cup dry white wine

Juice from 2 lemons

1 fennel rib

1 celery rib

12 coriander seeds

1 bay leaf

1 thyme sprig

10 peppercorns

2 teaspoons sugar

Salt

1 pound small white mushrooms

10 pearl onions, peeled

⅓ cup oil

❖　❖　❖　❖　❖

1. In a large saucepan, combine 1 cup of water with the white wine, lemon juice, fennel, celery, coriander, bay leaf, thyme, peppercorns, and sugar. Season with salt. Bring to a boil over medium-high heat, then reduce the heat to low and simmer for about 10 minutes.

2. Add the mushrooms, onions, and oil to the pan, cover, and continue to simmer over low heat for 6 to 8 minutes. Remove from the heat, let cool, then refrigerate until cold, 2 to 3 hours. Serve chilled.

From Françoise:

• If you don't like to pick out the aromatic seasonings on your plate, tie up the coriander seeds, bay leaf, thyme, and peppercorns in a piece of cheesecloth before adding them to the pan. Remove the bundle before serving.

• The sugar mellows the slightly sharp flavor of the lemony marinade.

• If the mushrooms and onions are large, quarter them lengthwise. It's not as appealing, but it is more practical.

SHREDDED CARROTS WITH LEMONY VINAIGRETTE

- *Carottes râpées* -

❖ VERY EASY   ❖ INEXPENSIVE   ❖ 15 MINUTES   ❖ SERVES 4

1 tablespoon lemon juice

3 tablespoons oil

Salt and pepper

½ pound carrots, peeled and shredded

Boston lettuce leaves for garnishing (optional)

Chopped parsley leaves for garnishing (optional)

❖ ❖ ❖ ❖ ❖

1. In a salad bowl, whisk the lemon juice with the oil. Season with salt and pepper. Add the carrots and toss to coat.

2. If desired, line a platter or wide bowl with the lettuce. Mound the carrot salad on top and sprinkle with the parsley, if using.

From Françoise:

• You can embellish this salad to your heart's content with such tasty additions as quartered hard-boiled eggs, black and green olives, and fines herbes (parsley, chives, chervil, tarragon). Anything really that encourages you to eat more of this delicious, inexpensive, and vitamin-rich salad will work.

• If you want to deepen the flavor of this salad, or if you're using older carrots instead of tender young ones, let the carrots marinate in the lemon-oil dressing for 2 to 3 hours.

• Vinegar can replace the lemon juice in the vinaigrette.

BEETS WITH SHALLOT VINAIGRETTE

- *Betterave vinaigrette* -

❖ VERY EASY   ❖ INEXPENSIVE   ❖ 10 MINUTES   ❖ SERVES 4

1 large cooked red beet, peeled and sliced
   crosswise or diced

½ teaspoon sugar (optional)

1 tablespoon vinegar

3 tablespoons oil

Salt and pepper

1 shallot, finely chopped

Finely chopped parsley leaves

continued

1. In a medium bowl, toss the beet with the sugar, if using.

2. In a small bowl, whisk the vinegar with the oil and season with salt and pepper. Blend in the shallot and parsley. Pour over the beet and toss to coat.

From Françoise:

• Some finely chopped hard-boiled egg whites would make a nice complement.

• Other possible additions include thinly sliced apples, walnut halves, celery sticks, watercress sprigs, or haricots verts.

• These beets could also be added to a platter of crudités.

CLASSIC ENDIVE SALAD WITH VINAIGRETTE
- *Endives vinaigrette* -

❖ VERY EASY ❖ MODERATE ❖ 10 MINUTES ❖ SERVES 4

1 tablespoon vinegar
3 tablespoons oil

Salt and pepper
1 pound endives, cored and sliced crosswise

❖ ❖ ❖ ❖ ❖

1. In a salad bowl, whisk the vinegar with the oil and season with salt and pepper. Cross the salad servers over the vinaigrette and add the endives. Toss the salad at the table.

From Françoise:

• The vinaigrette can be sharpened with a teaspoon of Dijon mustard, flavored or not.

• Discard any limp endive leaves.

• Don't soak the endives too long in water when you're cleaning them, or they may water down the vinaigrette.

• With your endive salad, try other accompaniments, such as walnut halves, sliced apples, sliced or diced beets, potatoes, or garlic croutons.

CABBAGE SALAD WITH VINAIGRETTE
- Chou vinaigrette -

❖ VERY EASY   ❖ INEXPENSIVE   ❖ 15 MINUTES   ❖ SERVES 4

1 tablespoon vinegar
3 tablespoons oil
Salt and pepper

1 small red or green cabbage, shredded
1 or 2 small onions, thinly sliced crosswise

❖ ❖ ❖ ❖ ❖

1. In a salad bowl, whisk the vinegar with the oil. Season with salt and pepper.

2. Add the cabbage and toss to coat. Garnish with the onion and serve.

From Françoise:
• It's easier to handle the cabbage if you quarter it lengthwise.

• Slice out the core once the cabbage is quartered.

• You can use a knife, a food processor with the slicing disk, or a box grater to shred the cabbage.

• This cabbage salad can also be refrigerated for up to 12 hours before serving—it will be tastier but not as crunchy.

• Another option is to toss the shredded cabbage with boiling vinegar, which softens it.

• To vary the recipe, try adding thinly sliced apple; the two make good partners. Or mix green and red cabbages. The red cabbage will bleed into the green; if that bothers you, toss them together just before serving.

• You can add this cabbage salad to a platter of crudités.

CUCUMBERS WITH VINAIGRETTE
- *Concombre vinaigrette* -

❖ VERY EASY ❖ INEXPENSIVE ❖ 15 MINUTES, PLUS 1 HOUR SALTING ❖ SERVES 4

½ pound cucumbers, peeled and sliced crosswise
Salt
1 tablespoon vinegar

3 tablespoons oil
Pepper
Chopped parsley leaves for sprinkling

❖ ❖ ❖ ❖ ❖

1. In a colander, sprinkle the cucumbers with salt and, if time allows, refrigerate for 1 hour. Pat dry with paper towels.

2. In a salad bowl, whisk the vinegar with the oil. Season with salt and pepper. Add the cucumbers and toss to coat. Sprinkle with the parsley and serve.

From Françoise:

• To vary the recipe, toss the cucumbers with crème fraîche or a blend of half crème fraîche, half mayonnaise.

• If the cucumbers are full of seeds, scoop them out before slicing with the tip of a vegetable peeler or a small spoon.

• Salting the cucumbers to draw out the water makes them more digestible. Press handfuls between your palms to remove as much water as possible.

ICY MELONS WITH BANYULS
- *Melons glacés au Banyuls* -

❖ EASY ❖ MODERATE ❖ 30 MINUTES, PLUS 2 TO 3 HOURS CHILLING ❖ SERVES 4

4 small melons

1 cup Banyuls

❖ ❖ ❖ ❖ ❖

1. Cut a small "hat" out of the top of each melon; reserve the hats. Discard the seeds. Then scoop out the flesh and add to a bowl. Add the Banyuls and chill for 2 to 3 hours.

2. Replace the flesh in the melons, set the hats on top, and serve.

From Françoise:

• Banyuls is a sweet wine that comes from the southwest of France. It may be served as an aperitif, or it is sometimes used to heighten the flavors in fruit salads like this one. I sometimes add port or another fortified or sweet wine like Maury or Muscat de Beaumes de Venise to the melon. They're just as delicious.

• If I have the time, I use a melon baller to scoop out the flesh, in which case you can call this dish "melon pearls with Banyuls."

• You might want to buy an extra melon to amply fill the 4 melons used as serving bowls.

• Instead of small, one-per-person melons, which can be hard to find, you can buy a couple of larger melons and slice them in half crosswise.

• If you're rushing, simply cut out the "hat" and discard the seeds, then pour the wine directly into the melon. The flesh won't be as perfumy, but it's quicker.

• To speed up the macerating, toss the melon and wine with 1 or 2 tablespoons of sugar.

GRAPEFRUIT SALAD WITH CREAMY CRABMEAT
- *Pamplemousse au crabe* -

❖ VERY EASY   ❖ EXPENSIVE   ❖ 45 MINUTES   ❖ SERVES 4

Salt

¼ cup rice

1 large egg yolk

1 teaspoon Dijon mustard

Pinch of cayenne pepper (optional)

¾ cup oil

1 teaspoon vinegar

Salt and pepper

2 grapefruits

7 ounces crabmeat

16 green or black olives, chopped

❖   ❖   ❖   ❖   ❖

1. Bring a small saucepan of salted water to a boil. Add the rice and cook until tender, 15 to 17 minutes. Drain in a colander, then rinse in cold running water and drain well. Pat dry with paper towels.

2. In a small bowl, whisk the egg yolk with the mustard and, if desired, the cayenne. Blend in the oil a few drops at a time to begin, then in a steady stream. Beat in the vinegar and season with salt and pepper.

3. Cut the grapefruits in half crosswise. Cut out the grapefruit segments from between the membranes and reserve. Remove the membranes to make grapefruit shells.

4. In a large bowl, combine the grapefruit segments with the crab, rice, and olives and fold in the mayonnaise. Mound the salad in the grapefruit shells and serve.

continued

From Françoise:
- The rice, mayonnaise, and grapefruit can be refrigerated, separately. Fold them together just before serving.

- You could, of course, use ¾ cup store-bought mayonnaise instead of making your own.

- Please note that the finished dish contains raw egg.

CHILLED GRAPEFRUIT HALVES
- *Pamplemousses rafraîchis* -

❖ VERY EASY   ❖ INEXPENSIVE   ❖ 15 MINUTES, PLUS 1 HOUR CHILLING   ❖ SERVES 4

2 grapefruits

Sugar for sprinkling

❖ ❖ ❖ ❖ ❖

1. Cut the grapefruits in half crosswise. Cut out the segments from between the membranes. Refrigerate the grapefruit halves until cold, about 1 hour.

2. Transfer the grapefruits to plates and serve. Pass the sugar separately.

From Françoise:
- If you refrigerate the cut grapefruits, wrap them in plastic.

- This grapefruit can be served as either a starter or a dessert.

- The best tool for cutting out the grapefruit segments is, naturally, a grapefruit knife, which has a curved blade with a serrated edge.

CRUDITÉS WITH VINAIGRETTE
- *Crudités vinaigrette* -

❖ VERY EASY   ❖ MODERATE   ❖ 10 MINUTES   ❖ SERVES 4

½ cucumber, halved lengthwise
Salt
3 carrots, peeled and shredded
Juice of 1 lemon
6 tablespoons oil

Pepper
1 tablespoon vinegar
½ pound white mushrooms, thinly sliced
2 endives, cored and sliced crosswise
1 bunch of watercress, tough stems removed

1. If the cucumber has a lot of seeds, scoop them out. Thinly slice the cucumber crosswise. If time allows, in a colander, sprinkle the cucumber with salt and refrigerate for 1 hour. Pat dry with paper towels.

2. In a bowl, toss the carrots with half the lemon juice and 3 tablespoons of the oil and season with salt and pepper.

3. In a small bowl, whisk the vinegar with the remaining 3 tablespoons of oil and season with salt and pepper.

4. In bowl, toss the mushrooms with the remaining lemon juice. Arrange the cucumber, endives, and watercress sprigs in separate bowls. Drizzle some of the vinaigrette over the salads (except the carrots, which are already dressed) and toss to coat. Mound the salads in piles on a platter and serve.

From Françoise:
• With your endive salad, try other accompaniments, such as walnut halves, sliced apples, sliced or diced beets, potatoes, or garlic croutons.

• You can vary the watercress salad by adding hard-boiled eggs, sliced or quartered lengthwise; boiled potatoes; garlic toasts; or finely chopped shallot.

• Don't bother to peel the cucumber, especially if you are salting it (strictly a matter of taste). Instead of using a vinaigrette, you can toss the cucumbers with crème fraîche or a blend of half crème fraîche, half mayonnaise.

• You might add quartered hard-boiled eggs, black and green olives, or fines herbes (parsley, chives, chervil, tarragon) to the carrots.

• The quality of the mushrooms is especially important in this recipe because they're eaten raw. Select the freshest, smallest, whitest, firmest ones you can find. You can replace the vinaigrette with crème fraîche.

• The vinaigrette can be accented with Dijon mustard, flavored or not.

• If you want to intensify the taste of your crudités, refrigerate them for an hour or so.

• To fill out the assortment of crudités, you can add Beets with Shallot Vinaigrette (page 67), Cabbage Salad with Vinaigrette (page 69), and Artichokes with Vinaigrette (page 56).

RABBIT AND HAM PÂTÉ
- Pâté de lapin -

❖ INTERMEDIATE   ❖ EXPENSIVE   ❖ 3 HOURS ACTIVE TIME   ❖ SERVES 10 TO 12

MARINADE

2 cups dry white wine

¼ cup Cognac

1 tablespoon oil

1 large onion, thinly sliced

2 shallots, thinly sliced

1 carrot, peeled and thinly sliced

2 garlic cloves, crushed

2 whole cloves

Parsley sprigs

Tarragon sprigs

Thyme sprigs

1 bay leaf

1 ½ tablespoons salt

10 peppercorns

1 (4 ½- to 5-pound) rabbit

¼ pound ham, cut into ½-inch strips

¼ pound shoulder end boneless pork loin

½ pound pork fat

½ pound sliced barding fat or bacon

Salt and pepper

❖ ❖ ❖ ❖ ❖

1. For the marinade: In a large bowl, combine all the ingredients.

2. Cut and slice the rabbit meat off the bones. Reserve the rabbit kidneys and liver. Cut the back meat into ½-inch strips. Add all the rabbit meat to the marinade with the kidneys, liver, ham, pork, and pork fat. Cover and refrigerate overnight.

3. Remove the meat and fat from the marinade. Discard the marinade. Pat the meats and fat dry with paper towels. Reserve the ham and several rabbit strips. Coarsely grind the remaining meats and fat. Beat with a wooden spoon. Cook a piece of the ground meat in a skillet and taste. Add salt and pepper to the remaining meat if necessary.

4. Preheat the oven to 400 degrees. Line a terrine with the barding fat or bacon, reserving some for the top. Spread one-third of the ground meat in the terrine, then lay in half the ham and rabbit strips lengthwise. Repeat with the ground meat and ham and rabbit strips, then cover with the remaining ground meat. Lay the remaining barding fat or bacon on top and cover with the lid.

5. Set the terrine in a roasting pan and fill the pan with hot water to come halfway up the terrine. Bake for about 1 hour and 15 minutes. Uncover and bake for 15 minutes more.

6. Remove from the oven and let cool for 30 minutes. Press the pâté with a weight until cooled. Cover and refrigerate for at least 2 days before serving.

From Françoise:
• I don't throw out the rabbit bones. I make a little broth with them, simmering them over low heat with a cup of water, a bouquet garni (parsley, thyme, and bay leaf), onion, garlic,

and so on while the pâté bakes. This broth is very concentrated by the end of cooking. I strain it and pour it over the pâté when it comes out of the oven. When it's chilled, what was "a little broth" becomes a beautiful and delicious gelée.

• Don't add too much salt and pepper to the pâté because the seasoning develops with cooking.

• When the pâté is done, a skewer inserted in the pâté will be hot to the touch.

• Set another loaf pan weighted down with canned goods directly on the warm terrine.

RABBIT AND PORK PÂTÉ
- *Pâté de lapin à la façon du Nord (avec os)* -

❖ INTERMEDIATE   ❖ EXPENSIVE   ❖ 2 HOURS ACTIVE TIME   ❖ SERVES 10 TO 12

MARINADE
2 cups dry white wine
1 tablespoon oil
1 onion, quartered
1 garlic clove, crushed
4 whole cloves
Parsley sprigs
Thyme sprigs
1 bay leaf
10 peppercorns

2 ½ pounds rabbit backs and thighs,
  cut into pieces
1 ½ pounds lean ground pork
¼ pound ground pork fat
Salt and pepper
½ pound sliced barding fat or bacon

❖ ❖ ❖ ❖ ❖

1. For the marinade: In a large bowl, combine all the ingredients. Add the rabbit, cover, and refrigerate overnight. Drain and reserve the rabbit. Discard the vegetables and herbs.

2. In a bowl, beat the pork and pork fat with a wooden spoon. Season with salt and pepper. Cook a piece of the ground meat in a skillet and taste. Add salt and pepper to the remaining meat if necessary.

3. Preheat the oven to 350 degrees. Line a terrine with the barding fat or bacon, reserving some for the top. Spread one-half of the ground meat in the terrine, then lay in the rabbit pieces and cover with the remaining ground meat. Lay the remaining barding fat or bacon on top and cover with the lid.

continued

4. Set the terrine in a roasting pan and fill the pan with hot water to come halfway up the terrine. Bake for about 1 hour and 30 minutes.

5. Remove from the oven and let cool for 30 minutes. Remove the lid and press the pâté with a weight until cooled. Cover and refrigerate for at least 1 day before serving.

From Françoise:

• Season this pâté generously.

• Don't use too heavy a weight to press this pâté, or the fat will rise to the surface and the meat will be dry.

• When serving this pâté, let your guests know it has bones!

RUSTIC CHICKEN LIVER PÂTÉ
- Pâté de foies de volaille -

❖ INTERMEDIATE ❖ MODERATE ❖ 30 MINUTES ACTIVE TIME ❖ SERVES 6 TO 8

½ pound chicken livers
¼ cup Cognac
Thyme sprigs
1 bay leaf
Pepper

7 ounces lean ground pork
7 ounces ground veal shoulder
¼ pound ground pork fat
Salt
½ pound sliced barding fat or bacon

❖ ❖ ❖ ❖ ❖

1. In a medium bowl, combine the livers with the Cognac, thyme, bay leaf, and pepper. Cover and refrigerate for 2 to 3 hours. Drain, reserving the Cognac.

2. Cut 2 of the livers into large pieces and chop the rest. In a bowl, beat the pork, veal, pork fat, chopped livers, and reserved Cognac with a wooden spoon. Season with salt and pepper. Cook a piece of the ground meat in a skillet and taste. Add salt and pepper to the remaining meat if necessary.

3. Preheat the oven to 350 degrees. Line a terrine with the barding fat or bacon, reserving some for the top. Spread one-half of the ground meat in the terrine, then lay in the large pieces of liver and cover with the

remaining ground meat. Lay the remaining barding fat or bacon on top and cover with the lid.

4. Set the terrine in a roasting pan and fill the pan with hot water to come halfway up the terrine. Bake for about 1 hour.

5. Remove from the oven and let cool for 30 minutes. Remove the lid and press the pâté with a weight until cooled. Cover and refrigerate for 1 or 2 days before serving.

From Françoise:
• You could chop all the chicken livers, but I prefer to keep 1 or 2 in largish pieces so you can see them when the pâté is sliced. Also, their unctuous texture reminds me of foie gras.

COUNTRY PORK PÂTÉ

- *Pâté de campagne* -

❖ INTERMEDIATE ❖ MODERATE ❖ 30 MINUTES ACTIVE TIME ❖ SERVES 6 TO 8

1 ½ pounds lean ground pork

¼ pound pork liver, finely chopped

¼ pound ground pork fat

1 large egg

¼ cup Cognac

2 pinches of allspice

Salt and pepper

½ pound sliced barding fat or bacon

4 thyme sprigs

❖ ❖ ❖ ❖ ❖

1. In a medium bowl, beat the pork, liver, fat, egg, and Cognac with a wooden spoon. Season with the allspice and salt and pepper. Cook a piece of the ground meat in a skillet and taste. Season more if necessary.

2. Preheat the oven to 400 degrees. Line a terrine with the barding fat or bacon, reserving some for the top. Spread the ground meat in the terrine. Lay the remaining barding fat or bacon and the thyme on top and cover.

3. Set the terrine in a roasting pan and fill the pan with hot water to come halfway up the terrine. Bake for about 1 hour and 15 minutes. Remove the lid and bake for 15 minutes.

4. Remove from the oven and let cool for 30 minutes. Press the pâté with a weight until cooled. Cover and refrigerate for at least 1 day before serving.

From Françoise:

• Don't use too heavy a weight to press this pâté. Packing it down too much makes the fat rise to the surface when it should be mixed throughout the meat, keeping it moist.

FROMAGE BLANC WITH RED RADISHES

- *Fromage blanc aux radis roses* -

❖ VERY EASY ❖ INEXPENSIVE ❖ 10 MINUTES ❖ SERVES 4

1 pound fromage blanc

1 tablespoon crème fraîche

12 red radishes, very thinly sliced, several slices
  reserved for garnishing

1 tablespoon chopped parsley, chives, chervil,
  and tarragon leaves

Salt and pepper

Thin slices of toasted country bread

continued

1. In a bowl, whisk the fromage blanc with the crème fraîche, radishes, and herbs and season with salt and pepper.

2. Transfer to a serving bowl, decorate with the reserved radishes, and serve very cold. Pass the toasts separately.

From Françoise:
• Fromage blanc, like fromage frais or crème fraîche, is an extremely soft, fresh cream cheese with the consistency of sour cream and a similar tang. The fat content, however, is significantly lower.

FROMAGE BLANC WITH ONIONS, PAPRIKA, AND CUMIN
- *Fromage rose aux oignons blancs* -

❖ VERY EASY   ❖ INEXPENSIVE   ❖ 10 MINUTES   ❖ SERVES 4

1 pound fromage blanc
1 tablespoon crème fraîche
1 or 2 small spring onions or sweet onions
½ to 1 teaspoon paprika

1 teaspoon cumin seeds
Salt and pepper
Thin slices of toasted country bread

❖ ❖ ❖ ❖ ❖

1. In a bowl, whisk the fromage blanc with the crème fraîche, onions, paprika, and cumin and season with salt and pepper.

2. Transfer to a serving bowl and serve very cold. Pass the toasts separately.

OLIVE AND PARMESAN BREAD
- *Cake salé aux olives et au parmesan* -

❖ EASY   ❖ MODERATE   ❖ 1 HOUR, 15 MINUTES   ❖ SERVES 4

10 tablespoons butter, melted, plus more
  for brushing
2 cups all-purpose flour
½ tablespoon baking powder
5 large eggs

¼ cup dry white wine
6 ounces pitted black olives, sliced
1 cup grated Parmesan cheese
Pinch of salt and pepper

1. Preheat the oven to 400 degrees. Lightly brush a loaf pan with butter. In a medium bowl, whisk the flour with the baking powder. Beat in the eggs. Using a wooden spoon, stir in the melted butter and white wine just until mixed. Fold in the olives, cheese, salt, and pepper. Scrape the batter into the loaf pan.

2. Transfer to the oven and bake for 15 minutes, then reduce the oven temperature to 325 degrees and bake until the bread is firm and golden, about 45 minutes. Run a knife around the pan and unmold the bread. Remove from the oven and let cool completely on a rack. Slice or cut into cubes and serve.

From Françoise:
• This savory loaf is especially good cut into cubes and served with drinks. Or pack it for a picnic.

• You can add a little turmeric to the flour to give the bread a golden color.

• Choose olives that aren't too salty.

TUNA, TOMATO, AND EGG TART
- *Quiche froide au thon* -

❖ EASY   ❖ MODERATE   ❖ 45 MINUTES   ❖ SERVES 4

Pâte Brisée (page 92)
1 (6-ounce) can oil-packed tuna, drained and flaked
3 tomatoes, sliced crosswise
Salt

½ lemon
2 hard-boiled eggs, thickly sliced crosswise
10 olives
10 oil-packed anchovies

❖ ❖ ❖ ❖ ❖

1. On a lightly floured work surface, roll the dough (Pâte Brisée) into a round about ⅛ inch thick. Wrap the dough around the rolling pin and fit it into an 8-inch tart pan with a removable bottom. Trim off any excess. Use the scraps to patch any cracks. Prick holes all over the bottom of the tart shell with a fork. Wrap and refrigerate until firm, 15 to 20 minutes.

2. Preheat the oven to 400 degrees. Cut a round of foil slightly larger than the tart pan and roll up the edge. Fit it inside the tart shell; it will help the shell keep its shape during baking. Bake until the crust is lightly browned and cooked through, 15 to 20 minutes. Transfer to a rack to cool completely, then unmold.

3. Spread the tuna in the tart shell. Arrange the tomatoes on top, slightly overlapping. Lightly season with salt and sprinkle with lemon juice. Decorate with the eggs, olives, and anchovies and serve.

From Françoise:
• You can definitely use a store-bought rolled pie crust here.

• Add the tuna and tomatoes to the cooked tart shell at the last minute, or the pastry will get soggy.

• Arrange the tomato slices, overlapping, in concentric circles; it's prettier that way.

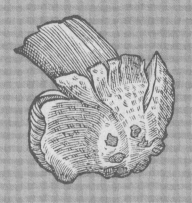

WARM STARTERS

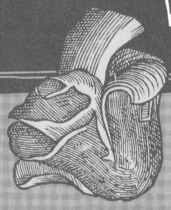

CREAMY BABY ARTICHOKE HEARTS

- *Artichauts à la crème (fond d')* -

❖ INTERMEDIATE   ❖ MODERATE   ❖ 50 MINUTES   ❖ SERVES 4

8 baby artichokes
1 lemon, halved
2 tablespoons butter

Salt and pepper
¼ cup crème fraîche

❖ ❖ ❖ ❖ ❖

1. Have ready a bowl of water. Working with 1 artichoke at a time, snap off all of the dark green leaves. Using a sharp knife, slice off the top half of the leaves. Peel and trim the stem. Cut the artichoke in half lengthwise and scrape out the hairy choke. Rub with 1 lemon half and add to the water.

2. In a large saucepan, melt the butter over low heat. Drain the artichokes. Add them to the saucepan and squeeze in the juice from the remaining lemon half. Season with salt and pepper. Cover and cook until tender, about 30 minutes. Add the crème fraîche, raise the heat and bring to a boil, then serve.

From Françoise:
• It takes some effort to trim the artichokes for cooking, but it's worth it because, prepared this way, these little artichokes keep all their flavor. The crème fraîche only adds to their delicate taste.

GRATIN OF ARTICHOKE BOTTOMS STUFFED WITH MUSHROOM DUXELLES

- *Artichauts à la duxelles (fonds d')* -

❖ EASY   ❖ MODERATE   ❖ 50 MINUTES   ❖ SERVES 4

1 pound white mushrooms, finely chopped,
**   4 small mushroom caps reserved**
4 tablespoons (½ stick) butter
1 tablespoon lemon juice
1 shallot, finely chopped
Salt and pepper
4 cooked artichoke bottoms

BÉCHAMEL SAUCE
1 tablespoon butter
1 tablespoon all-purpose flour
¼ cup milk
Salt and pepper

1. Preheat the oven to 425 degrees. In a small saucepan, combine the mushroom caps with 1 tablespoon of the butter, the lemon juice, and water to cover. Bring to a boil over medium-high heat, then reduce the heat to low and simmer until tender, about 5 minutes. Drain, reserving the juice.

2. In a large skillet, melt 2 tablespoons of the butter over low heat. Add the chopped mushrooms and shallot and season with salt and pepper. Cook, stirring occasionally, until the liquid evaporates.

3. Make the béchamel sauce: In a small saucepan, melt the butter over medium heat. Whisk in the flour until it starts foaming. Whisk in the milk and ¼ cup reserved mushroom juice. Season with salt and pepper. Bring to a boil, whisking, then reduce the heat to very low and cook for 10 minutes. The sauce will be thick. Stir in the mushroom duxelles.

4. Arrange the artichoke bottoms in a gratin dish. Spread some of the mushroom mixture over each artichoke. Set a mushroom cap on top of each and dot with the remaining 1 tablespoon of butter. Bake on the top shelf of the oven until golden and heated through, about 10 minutes, and serve.

From Françoise:
• Classically, duxelles is a blend of finely chopped mushrooms and shallots, sometimes with a little minced garlic.

• You can make the béchamel even better by adding some crème fraîche and a pinch of freshly grated nutmeg.

• Canned, frozen, or fresh artichoke bottoms may be used. To prepare and cook fresh artichoke bottoms, see Artichoke Bottoms Stuffed with Mixed Vegetables, page 57.

ARTICHOKES WITH BÉARNAISE SAUCE
- *Artichauts béarnaise (fonds d')* -

❖ ADVANCED   ❖ EXPENSIVE   ❖ 1 HOUR   ❖ SERVES 4

Salt
4 large or 8 small artichokes
1 lemon, halved

1 tablespoon all-purpose flour
Béarnaise Sauce (page 138)

❖   ❖   ❖   ❖   ❖

1. Bring a large saucepan of salted water to a boil. Meanwhile, have ready a bowl of water. Working with 1 artichoke at a time, cut off the stem using a very sharp knife. Slice off all the leaves level with the top of the artichoke bottom. Trim the bottom. Rub with a lemon half and add to the bowl of water.

2. In a small cup, stir a little cold water into the flour, then stir into the boiling water. Drain the artichokes, add them to the boiling water, and cook until tender, 25 to 30 minutes.

continued

3. Drain the artichokes and pat dry with paper towels. Scrape out the hairy choke with a small spoon. Serve with the béarnaise sauce.

From Françoise:
• Everything possible has been done to keep the artichokes from darkening: The bottoms are rubbed with lemon halves and added to water, and a flour-and-water paste is stirred into the cooking water.

• Artichoke bottoms are tender when a knife can easily be inserted. When testing for doneness, be careful not to break the bottoms apart.

• You can also serve whole warm artichokes with béarnaise sauce.

GOLDEN GRATINÉED ARTICHOKES WITH MORNAY SAUCE
- *Artichauts gratinés (fonds d')* -

❖ EASY　　　❖ MODERATE　　　❖ 25 MINUTES　　　❖ SERVES 4

MORNAY SAUCE
2 tablespoons butter
2 tablespoons all-purpose flour
1 ½ cups milk
Salt and pepper
½ cup shredded Gruyère cheese

2 tablespoons butter, plus more for
　brushing
4 large or 8 small cooked
　artichoke bottoms

❖　❖　❖　❖　❖

1. Make the Mornay sauce: In a small saucepan, melt the butter over medium heat. Whisk in the flour until it starts foaming. Whisk in the milk. Season with salt and pepper. Bring to a boil, whisking, then reduce the heat to low and cook for 10 minutes. Remove the pan from the heat and whisk in ¼ cup of the cheese.

2. Preheat the oven to 425 degrees. Lightly brush a gratin dish with butter. Set the artichokes in the dish and spoon the Mornay sauce into the bottoms. Sprinkle the remaining ¼ cup of cheese over the tops and dot with the 2 tablespoons of butter. Bake on the top shelf of the oven until melted and golden, about 10 minutes, and serve.

From Françoise:
• I like to add any leftovers I have on hand into the Mornay sauce, such as chopped, hard-boiled eggs; cooked shrimp, mussels, fish, or meat; or sautéed mushrooms.

• Canned, frozen, or fresh artichoke bottoms may be used. To prepare and cook fresh artichoke bottoms, see page 83.

• The proportions in this Mornay make a sauce that is thicker than usual, but that makes it less likely to spill over.

• Instead of baking the artichokes, you can also broil them for a couple of minutes.

WHITE ASPARAGUS WITH CREAMY BUTTER SAUCE
- *Asperges sauce mousseline* -

❖ ADVANCED   ❖ EXPENSIVE   ❖ 45 MINUTES   ❖ SERVES 4

Salt

2 pounds thick white asparagus

MOUSSELINE SAUCE

3 large egg yolks

Salt and pepper

10 tablespoons butter, cut into pieces

2 tablespoons crème fraîche

❖ ❖ ❖ ❖ ❖

1. Bring a large pot of salted water to a boil. Meanwhile, break about an inch off the bottoms of the asparagus spears. Peel the stems. Rinse the asparagus under cold running water. Tie them in bundles of 5 or 6. Add to the boiling water and cook until tender, about 20 minutes. Drain and discard the string. Pat dry with paper towels and transfer to a platter; keep warm.

2. Make the mousseline sauce: In a small, heavy saucepan, whisk the egg yolks with 3 tablespoons of water until light, about 30 seconds. Season with salt and pepper. Set the pan over very low heat and whisk constantly until the mixture thickens and becomes fluffy. Remove the pan from the heat and gradually add the butter, whisking so it melts creamily. Keep the sauce warm in a water bath. Just before serving, whisk in the crème fraîche.

3. Serve the asparagus with the mousseline sauce.

From Françoise:

• Make sure the saucepan never gets too hot when you are whisking the egg yolks over the heat or they will scramble.

• Mousseline sauce is basically hollandaise sauce with the addition of cream. Also called Chantilly sauce, it sometimes has whipped cream folded in instead of crème fraîche.

• For a more savory sauce, reserve a little of the flavorful asparagus cooking water and whisk it—cooled—into the egg yolks in the mousseline sauce instead of water.

• Green asparagus could of course be used here, in which case peeling the stems would be a matter of personal taste.

• For this dish, you could reheat the asparagus briefly in hot water, then pat dry with paper towels.

GARLIC-AND-HERB-STUFFED MUSHROOMS
- *Champignons farcis* -

❖ VERY EASY   ❖ MODERATE   ❖ 1 HOUR, 15 MINUTES   ❖ SERVES 4

16 large white mushrooms (1 to 1 ½ pounds total),
  stems and caps separated, stems and gills
  finely chopped
5 garlic cloves, finely chopped
1 large bunch of parsley, stems removed,
  leaves chopped, or chives

¼ cup milk
2 slices of toast
Pinch of cayenne pepper
Salt and pepper
2 tablespoons butter, plus more for brushing

❖ ❖ ❖ ❖ ❖

1. In a bowl, combine the chopped mushrooms with the garlic and parsley or chives.

2. In a small saucepan, warm the milk. Remove the pan from the heat. Crumble in the toast and stir to absorb the milk. Squeeze the bread crumbs dry and beat into the mushroom stuffing. Season with the cayenne, salt, and pepper.

3. Preheat the oven to 350 degrees. Lightly brush a baking sheet with butter. Spoon the stuffing into the mushroom caps, mounding it slightly, and transfer to the baking sheet. Dot the tops with the 2 tablespoons of butter and bake for 30 to 45 minutes.

From Françoise:
• To make it easier to stuff the caps, remove the mushroom stems and scrape out the gills.

• If you have any leftover meat or chicken, you can chop it and add it to the stuffing. The meat alone, however, would make too dense a stuffing.

ROASTED VEAL-STUFFED ONIONS
- *Oignons farcis* -

❖ EASY   ❖ MODERATE   ❖ 1 HOUR, 40 MINUTES   ❖ SERVES 4

Salt
8 large onions, peeled
2 tablespoons butter, plus more for brushing
5 ounces ground veal
3 ounces ground pork fat
1 large egg

1 garlic clove, finely chopped
1 bunch of parsley, stems removed,
  leaves chopped
Salt and pepper
Bread crumbs for sprinkling

1. Bring a large saucepan of salted water to a boil over medium-high heat. Add the onions, reduce the heat to low, and simmer for 15 minutes. Drain well and pat dry. Cut a thin slice off the top of each onion. Using a melon baller or small spoon, remove the center of each onion, leaving a two-layer shell. Coarsely chop the centers and tops. Trim the root ends so the onions stand upright.

2. Preheat the oven to 350 degrees. Lightly brush a large gratin dish with butter. In a bowl, mix the veal with the pork fat, egg, garlic, and parsley. Season with salt and pepper.

Spoon the stuffing into the onions, mounding it slightly, and transfer to the gratin dish. Sprinkle the tops with the bread crumbs, dot with the 2 tablespoons of butter, and bake for 1 hour.

From Françoise:
• The best season to make these stuffed onions is in the summer and fall, using mild, sweet fresh onions. Winter storage onions can be strong and bitter.

• It's easier to hollow out the onions if they are simply cut in half.

SEAFOOD AND BACON SKEWERS
- *Brochettes de fruits de mer* -

❖ EASY   ❖ EXPENSIVE   ❖ 20 MINUTES   ❖ MAKES 4 SKEWERS

12 langoustine tails or colossal shrimp in the shell
8 scallops
8 pancetta or bacon cubes

1 lemon, cut into 8 half slices
Oil for brushing
Salt and pepper

❖ ❖ ❖ ❖ ❖

1. On each of 4 long metal skewers, thread 1 langoustine or shrimp lengthwise, 1 scallop, 1 pancetta or bacon cube, and 1 lemon slice, then repeat; finish the skewer with another langoustine or shrimp.

2. Heat the broiler. Transfer the skewers to a large baking sheet, brush with oil, and season with salt and pepper. Broil on the top shelf of the oven, turning once, for 2 to 3 minutes on each side.

From Françoise:
• Use the bacon rather than the pancetta if you want a smoky flavor.

FROGS' LEGS WITH GARLIC AND SHALLOT BUTTER

- *Cuisses de grenouilles sautées aux fines herbes* -

❖ EASY   ❖ EXPENSIVE   ❖ 25 MINUTES   ❖ SERVES 4

3 tablespoons butter

4 pairs frogs' legs, separated

Salt and pepper

1 shallot, finely chopped

1 garlic clove, finely chopped

Pinch of cayenne pepper

Chopped parsley for sprinkling

Lemon wedges for serving

❖ ❖ ❖ ❖ ❖

1. In a large skillet, melt the butter over high heat. Add the frogs' legs, season with salt and pepper, and lightly brown. Reduce the heat to medium and cook for 10 minutes. Stir in the shallot, garlic, and cayenne, reduce the heat to low, and cook for 5 minutes.

2. Transfer the frogs' legs to a platter. Sprinkle with the parsley and serve with the lemon wedges.

From Françoise:

• Frogs' legs are generally sold frozen, in pairs.

• If your skillet is too small to hold all the frogs' legs without crowding them, cook them in 2 batches, adding 2 tablespoons of butter to each.

• Don't lose a drop of this fragrant sauce: Stir dry bread crumbs into the skillet after the frogs' legs have come out, then sprinkle over the frogs' legs.

SNAILS IN THE SHELL WITH GARLICKY HERB BUTTER

- *Escargots en coquilles* -

❖ VERY EASY   ❖ MODERATE   ❖ 45 MINUTES   ❖ SERVES 4

GARLICKY HERB BUTTER

1 cup (2 sticks) butter, softened

1 medium shallot, finely chopped

1 garlic clove, finely chopped

1 bunch of parsley, stems removed, leaves
  finely chopped

2 tablespoons dry white wine

Salt and pepper

4 dozen canned snails, rinsed and drained,
  with shells

¾ cup dry white wine

1. Make the garlicky herb butter: In a medium bowl, beat the butter with the shallot, garlic, parsley, and white wine and season with salt and pepper.

2. In a large saucepan, combine the snails and ¾ cup white wine and warm over low heat for 5 minutes.

3. Preheat the oven to 300 degrees. Using a spoon, stuff each snail shell with a little flavored butter, a snail, and more flavored butter; pack well. Transfer the snails to a shallow baking dish. Pour into each shell a little of the white wine used to warm the snails. Bake until

the stuffing is hot and melted, 5 to 10 minutes, and serve.

From Françoise:

• Canned snails are fast, easy to use, and very tasty. Select those sold with their shells. Rinse canned snails in cold water before cooking them.

• You can also sauté the snails in a skillet with the flavored butter, then spoon them into the shells and serve.

• The flavored butter can be tightly wrapped and refrigerated or frozen.

WARM OYSTER-MUSHROOM SALAD WITH CONFIT GIZZARDS

- *Salade de pleurotes et de gésiers confits* -

❖ VERY EASY   ❖ EXPENSIVE   ❖ 20 MINUTES   ❖ SERVES 4

1 tablespoon vinegar

3 tablespoons oil

Salt and pepper

3 ounces mesclun salad

3 or 4 canned confit duck or goose gizzards, sliced, with 2 tablespoons fat from the can

¾ pound oyster mushrooms, sliced if large

1 small shallot, finely chopped

❖ ❖ ❖ ❖ ❖

1. In a small bowl, whisk the vinegar with the oil and season with salt and pepper. Line salad plates with the mesclun.

2. In a large skillet, melt the fat over medium-high heat. Add the mushrooms, season with salt and pepper, and cook, stirring occasionally, until lightly browned, about 5 minutes. Reduce the heat to medium, stir in the shallot, and cook for 1 minute. Transfer to the salad plates.

3. In the same skillet, spread the gizzards, season with pepper, and cook over medium heat, turning them once, until heated through. Add the gizzards to the plates. Sprinkle the vinaigrette over the salads and serve right away.

continued

From Françoise:

• The freshest oyster mushrooms are white bordering on beige, with a pleasant, slightly floury smell. They are dry to the touch, but the edges are not dried out.

• It is not necessary to wash oyster mushrooms. Once they are cooked, they will have a better flavor than mushrooms that have been washed; even the most carefully dried ones get a little soggy.

• Still, if the mushrooms are dirty and must be washed, it is essential to dry them well in a kitchen towel, twisting both ends. Then add them to the hot duck fat.

• Here's how to get organized: Make the vinaigrette, slice the gizzards, line the plates with the mesclun, clean the oyster mushrooms, chop the shallots, and refrigerate everything. Then, just before sitting down to eat, the cooking can be done in 5 minutes.

CRISPY GRUYÈRE-STUFFED CRÊPES
- Crêpes fourrées sauce Mornay -

❖ INTERMEDIATE   ❖ INEXPENSIVE   ❖ 1 HOUR, PLUS 1 HOUR RESTING   ❖ SERVES 4

CRÊPES
1 cup all-purpose flour
1½ cups milk
2 large eggs, lightly beaten
3 tablespoons butter, 2 melted, plus more
  for brushing
Salt

MORNAY SAUCE
3 tablespoons butter
3 tablespoons all-purpose flour
2 cups milk
Salt and pepper
½ cup shredded Gruyère cheese

❖ ❖ ❖ ❖ ❖

1. Make the crêpes: In a medium bowl, whisk the flour with the milk, eggs, 2 tablespoons of the melted butter, and ½ teaspoon salt. Cover and let stand at least 1 hour.

2. Meanwhile, make the Mornay sauce: In a small saucepan, melt the butter over medium heat. Whisk in the flour until it starts foaming. Whisk in the milk. Season with salt and pepper. Bring to a boil, whisking, then reduce the heat to very low and cook for 10 minutes. Remove the pan from the heat and whisk in ¼ cup of the cheese.

3. Lightly brush a 7-inch skillet with melted butter and heat over medium heat. Whisk the batter and add about 2 tablespoons to the skillet, swirling to coat the bottom. Cook until the edge begins to brown, about 30 seconds. Flip using a thin-bladed spatula and cook for 20 seconds. Slide onto a plate and repeat with the remaining batter, stacking the crêpes as they're cooked.

4. Preheat the oven to 400 degrees. Lightly brush the bottom of a large gratin dish with butter. Spread about 1 tablespoon of filling over each crêpe and roll up. Arrange the crêpes

in the gratin dish. Sprinkle with the remaining ¼ cup of cheese and dot the top with the remaining 1 tablespoon of butter. Bake until the filling is hot and the cheese melts, 15 to 20 minutes. Serve right away.

From Françoise:
• This batter makes about 16 crêpes. Any left over can be wrapped in plastic and refrigerated for 2 or 3 days.

• The amount of milk may vary according to the flour and the eggs. The batter should have the consistency of heavy cream.

• To turn these first-course crêpes into a main dish, add a slice of ham to each one before rolling it up.

• These crêpes can be assembled ahead of time and then baked in the oven just before serving.

PROVENÇAL ONION TART WITH ANCHOVIES
- *Pissaladière niçoise* -

❖ INTERMEDIATE   ❖ INEXPENSIVE   ❖ 1 HOUR   ❖ SERVES 4 TO 6

PÂTE BRISÉE
1 ¼ cups all-purpose flour
½ teaspoon salt
5 tablespoons unsalted butter,
  cut into pieces

FILLING
2 tablespoons butter
¾ pound onions, thinly sliced
Salt and pepper
2 tomatoes, sliced
10 oil-cured anchovy fillets
Black olives

❖   ❖   ❖   ❖   ❖

1. Make the pâte brisée: In a bowl, combine the flour with the salt and butter. Rub the butter into the flour between your palms. Sprinkle over ¼ cup of water and knead briefly until large crumbs form. Press into a disk. On a lightly floured surface, scrape the dough away from you with the heel of your hand in a long sliding motion, then press into a disk; repeat 3 times. Wrap and refrigerate until firm, 15 to 20 minutes.

2. Meanwhile, make the filling: In a large skillet, melt the butter over medium heat. Add the onions and cook over medium heat until lightly browned. Add 1 tablespoon of water

and season with salt and pepper. Reduce the heat to low, cover, and cook for 15 minutes.

3. Preheat the oven to 400 degrees. On a lightly floured work surface, roll the dough into a round about ⅛ inch thick. Wrap the dough around the rolling pin and fit it into an 8-inch tart pan with a removable bottom. Trim off any excess. Use the scraps to patch any cracks. Prick holes all over the bottom of the tart shell with a fork.

continued

4. Spread the onions in the tart shell. Arrange the tomato slices on top and decorate with the anchovies and black olives. Transfer to the oven and bake for 35 to 40 minutes. Serve the tart hot, warm, or at room temperature.

From Françoise:
• If, like me, you don't like a strong onion taste, use sweet onions or spring onions instead of yellow onions. Alternatively, cook yellow onions in boiling water for a few minutes to soften the flavor.

• Adding a tablespoon of water to the onions in Step 2 helps keep them from sticking.

• If you use salt-cured anchovies, soak them first in water for a few minutes to remove the salt. Oil-cured anchovies can be used as is.

• If you're in a rush, you can use a store-bought rolled pie crust.

CREAMY ONION AND BACON TART
- *Tarte aux oignons* -

❖ INTERMEDIATE   ❖ INEXPENSIVE   ❖ 1 HOUR, 30 MINUTES   ❖ SERVES 4

PÂTE BRISÉE
1 ¼ cups all-purpose flour
½ teaspoon salt
5 tablespoons unsalted butter,
   cut into pieces

FILLING
3 ½ tablespoons butter
½ pound onions, thinly sliced
Salt and pepper
¼ pound thick-sliced bacon, cut crosswise into
   ¼-inch-thick strips
1 ½ tablespoons all-purpose flour
1 cup milk

❖ ❖ ❖ ❖ ❖

1. Make the pâte brisée: In a bowl, combine the flour with the salt and butter. Rub the butter into the flour between your palms. Sprinkle over ¼ cup of water and knead briefly until large crumbs form. Press into a disk. On a lightly floured surface, scrape the dough away from you with the heel of your hand in a long sliding motion, then press into a disk; repeat 3 times. Wrap and refrigerate until firm, 15 to 20 minutes.

2. Meanwhile, make the filling: In a large skillet, melt 2 tablespoons of the butter over

medium heat. Add the onions, season with salt and pepper, and cook until lightly browned. Reduce the heat to low, cover, and cook for 15 minutes.

3. Bring a small saucepan of water to a boil. Add the bacon and cook for 3 minutes; drain.

4. In a large saucepan, melt the remaining 1 ½ tablespoons of butter over medium heat. Whisk in the flour until it starts foaming. Whisk in the milk and season with salt and

pepper. Bring to a boil, whisking, then reduce the heat to low and cook until it thickens. Remove the pan from the heat and stir in the onions.

5. Preheat the oven to 400 degrees. On a lightly floured work surface, roll the dough into a round about ⅛ inch thick. Wrap the dough around the rolling pin and fit it into an 8-inch tart pan with a removable bottom. Trim off any excess. Use the scraps to patch any cracks. Prick holes all over the bottom of the tart shell with a fork.

6. Scatter the bacon in the tart shell. Spread the onion filling on top. Bake for 20 minutes, then reduce the oven temperature to 350 degrees and bake for 20 to 30 minutes. Serve the tart hot, warm, or at room temperature.

From Françoise:

• I often make this tart in advance. Then, at dinnertime, I have only to reheat it in a low oven for 15 minutes. With a soup to start, a side salad, and fruit for dessert, it's the perfect Sunday night supper after a long walk.

• This tart is especially good with spring onions and large sweet onions.

• You could substitute leeks for the onions. Coarsely chop them and cook them in the same way as the onions.

• To keep the onions from sticking to the skillet, add a tablespoon of water.

• Briefly boiling the bacon in water removes some of the salt and smokiness.

ZUCCHINI FRITTERS
- *Beignets de courgettes* -

❖ INTERMEDIATE   ❖ MODERATE   ❖ 30 MINUTES, PLUS 1 HOUR RESTING   ❖ SERVES 4

FRITTER BATTER
1 cup all-purpose flour
1 teaspoon salt
1 large whole egg, plus 2 large egg whites
1 tablespoon oil
½ cup beer or water

4 zucchini (1 ½ pounds total), sliced crosswise
 ¼ inch thick
Salt and pepper
3 tablespoons all-purpose flour
4 cups oil for frying

❖ ❖ ❖ ❖ ❖

1. Make the fritter batter: In a large bowl, whisk the flour with the salt, whole egg, egg whites, and oil. Gradually whisk in the beer or water. The batter should be slightly thicker than heavy cream. Use a little more beer or water if you prefer a lighter batter coating. Cover and let stand for 1 hour.

2. In a bowl, sprinkle the zucchini with salt and pepper, then toss with the flour, discarding the excess.

continued

3. In a large skillet, heat the oil to 375 degrees. Using a fork, dip the zucchini slices one at a time in the batter. Gently drop them into the oil without crowding. Fry the zucchini, turning them once, until golden, 1 to 3 minutes total. Using a slotted spoon, transfer the fritters to paper towels to drain. Keep warm in a medium oven while frying the remaining zucchini. Season with salt and serve very hot.

From Françoise:

• For this recipe, it's not necessary to beat the whites to make the fritter batter.

• Flouring the zucchini slices helps the fritter batter stick to them.

• Don't crowd the zucchini slices when frying them; they should have plenty of room in the skillet.

CREAMY SWEETBREADS AND CHICKEN IN PUFF PASTRY SHELLS

- Bouchées à la reine -

❖ INTERMEDIATE   ❖ EXPENSIVE   ❖ 1 HOUR, PLUS 2 TO 3 HOURS SOAKING   ❖ SERVES 4

Vinegar

1 pound veal sweetbreads

4 tablespoons (½ stick) butter

1 small carrot, peeled and cut in ¼-inch dice

1 onion, cut in ¼-inch dice

¼ cup dry white wine

3 thyme sprigs

1 bay leaf

Salt and pepper

¼ pound white mushrooms, thinly sliced

1 tablespoon lemon juice

1 tablespoon all-purpose flour

¼ pound diced, cooked chicken

Freshly grated nutmeg

4 baked puff pastry shells

❖ ❖ ❖ ❖ ❖

1. In a large bowl of cold water and a little vinegar, soak the sweetbreads in the refrigerator for 2 to 3 hours.

2. Drain the sweetbreads and transfer to a large saucepan. Cover with cold water by 1 inch. Slowly bring to a boil, then cook for 2 minutes. Drain in a colander, then rinse under cold running water and drain again. Cut away any fat and pull away as much membrane and connective tissue as possible with a small paring knife.

3. In the same saucepan, melt 2 tablespoons of the butter over medium-low heat. Add the carrot and onion and cook, stirring occasionally, until soft, about 5 minutes. Add the sweetbreads, wine, thyme, and bay leaf and season with salt and pepper. Reduce the heat to low, cover, and cook for 20 minutes.

4. Meanwhile, in a medium saucepan, melt 1 tablespoon of the remaining butter over medium-high heat. Add the mushrooms and lemon juice and season with salt and pepper.

Barely cover with water and bring to a boil, then reduce the heat to low and cook for 5 minutes.

5. In another large saucepan, melt the remaining 1 tablespoon of butter over medium heat. Whisk in the flour until it starts foaming. Whisk in 6 tablespoons of the mushroom cooking liquid and 6 tablespoons of the sweetbread cooking liquid. Season with salt and pepper. Bring to a boil, whisking, then reduce the heat to very low and cook for 8 minutes.

6. Preheat the oven to 300 degrees. Set the puff pastry shells on a baking sheet and warm in the oven. Dice the sweetbreads and add them to the sauce with the mushrooms and chicken and season with nutmeg. Spoon the filling into the pastry shells and serve.

From Françoise:

• To simplify the recipe, you can substitute chopped ham for the sweetbreads.

• Chicken quenelles, either homemade or prepared, can replace the chicken in this recipe.

PORTUGUESE SALT COD AND POTATO FRITTERS
- *Beignets de morue à la portugaise* -

❖ INTERMEDIATE   ❖ INEXPENSIVE   ❖ 30 MINUTES, PLUS 12 HOURS SOAKING   ❖ SERVES 4

½ **pound skinless salt cod fillet**
¼ **pound potatoes, peeled**
1 small bunch of parsley, leaves chopped

Salt and pepper
1 large egg, separated
4 cups oil for frying

❖ ❖ ❖ ❖ ❖

1. In a bowl, soak the salt cod in plenty of cold water at room temperature for 12 hours, changing the water at least 3 times.

2. Bring a medium saucepan of water to a boil. Add the potatoes and cook until tender, 25 to 30 minutes. Using a slotted spoon, remove the potatoes to a large bowl. Mash or rice the potatoes or work them through a food mill.

3. Drain the salt cod. In the same saucepan of water, cook the salt cod at a bare simmer for 15 minutes. Drain the cod well. Flake the fish, removing any bones.

4. Beat the mashed potatoes with the salt cod and parsley. Season with pepper. Taste and add salt if needed. Beat in the egg yolk. The mixture should not be too soft.

5. In another bowl, beat the egg white with a pinch of salt until it holds a stiff peak. Carefully fold the beaten egg white into the salt cod mixture.

6. In a large skillet, heat the oil to 375 degrees. Using 2 small spoons, form the mixture into

continued

small egg shapes. Gently drop them into the oil without crowding and fry, turning them once, until puffed and golden, 1 to 3 minutes total. Using a slotted spoon, transfer the fritters to paper towels to drain. Keep warm in a low oven while frying the remaining mixture. Season with salt and pepper and serve very hot.

From Françoise:
• To shape the fritters more easily, dip the spoons in the hot oil.

• If the mixture is a little too stiff before you've added the whipped egg white, beat in a whole egg.

CREAMY HAM-STUFFED CROISSANTS
- *Croissant au jambon* -

❖ EASY   ❖ MODERATE   ❖ 30 MINUTES   ❖ SERVES 4

1 ½ tablespoons butter
1 ½ tablespoons all–purpose flour
1 cup milk

Salt and pepper
2 slices of ham, diced
4 croissants

❖   ❖   ❖   ❖   ❖

1. Preheat the oven to 400 degrees. In a small saucepan, melt the butter over medium heat. Whisk in the flour until it starts foaming. Whisk in the milk and season with salt and pepper. Bring to a boil, whisking, then reduce the heat to very low and cook for 10 minutes. Remove the pan from the heat and stir in the ham.

2. Slice the croissants horizontally almost in half. Sandwich with the ham filling. Transfer to a baking sheet and heat in the oven. Serve hot.

From Françoise:
• To make this a vegetarian dish, you can replace the ham with sliced, sautéed mushrooms. A mushroom filling will need a little more seasoning.

CREAMY ROQUEFORT CHEESE TOASTS
- *Croqueforts* -

❖ EASY   ❖ MODERATE   ❖ 30 MINUTES   ❖ SERVES 4

3 tablespoons butter

1 tablespoon all-purpose flour

¾ cup milk

Salt and pepper

2 tablespoons crème fraîche

¾ cup crumbled Roquefort cheese (about 3 ½ ounces)

4 slices of white sandwich or country bread

❖ ❖ ❖ ❖ ❖

1. In a small saucepan, melt 1 tablespoon of the butter over medium heat. Whisk in the flour until it starts foaming. Whisk in the milk and season lightly with salt and pepper. Bring to a boil, whisking, then add the crème fraîche, reduce the heat to low, and cook for 2 to 3 minutes. Remove the pan from the heat and stir in the cheese.

2. In a large skillet, melt the remaining 2 tablespoons of butter over medium heat. Add the bread slices and cook until golden. Spread the bread slices with the cheese sauce and serve.

From Françoise:

• You might cover these Roquefort cheese toasts with thinly sliced Cantal or cheddar cheese and broil them on a baking sheet until melted.

• Croqueforts are a variation of the popular grilled cheese sandwich croque-monsieur. I recommend them especially to vegetarians and Roquefort lovers.

BAKED EGGS IN BRIOCHES
- *Croque-mignon* -

❖ VERY EASY   ❖ MODERATE   ❖ 30 MINUTES   ❖ SERVES 4

4 small brioches

2 tablespoons butter, softened

4 small eggs

Salt and pepper

4 teaspoons shredded Gruyère cheese

continued

1. Preheat the oven to 350 degrees. Cut a small "hat" out of each brioche, then carefully cut out much of the crumb, leaving a sturdy shell. Brush the insides with the butter. Transfer to a baking sheet and toast for 5 minutes. Increase the oven temperature to 400 degrees.

2. Break an egg into each brioche. Season with salt and pepper and sprinkle with the cheese. Return to the oven and bake until the whites are set but the yolks are still soft, 10 to 12 minutes. Serve the brioches with their "hats."

From Françoise:

• Try to buy wide brioches and use the smallest eggs you can find, or the whites may spill out.

• Toast the hollowed-out brioches before breaking in the eggs. The eggs will cook much faster.

• Watch the brioches carefully in the oven because these buttery buns tend to burn quickly. You may need to cover them with a piece of foil toward the end of baking.

BRIOCHES STUFFED WITH CURRIED CHICKEN
- Brioches farcies d'effilochés de volaille -

❖ VERY EASY   ❖ INEXPENSIVE   ❖ 30 MINUTES   ❖ SERVES 4 TO 6

4 small brioches
2 tablespoons butter, softened

FILLING
1 ½ tablespoons butter
1 ½ tablespoons all-purpose flour

1 ⅓ cups milk
1 tablespoon crème fraîche
1 teaspoon curry powder
Salt and pepper
1 ½ cups diced, cooked chicken
1 large egg yolk

❖ ❖ ❖ ❖ ❖

1. Preheat the oven to 350 degrees. Cut a small "hat" out of each brioche, then carefully cut out much of the crumb, leaving a sturdy shell. Brush the insides with the butter. Transfer to a baking sheet and toast for 5 minutes. Increase the oven temperature to 400 degrees.

2. Meanwhile, make the filling: In a large saucepan, melt the butter over medium heat. Whisk in the flour until it starts foaming. Whisk in the milk and crème fraîche and season with the curry powder, salt, and pepper. Bring to a boil, whisking. Whisk in the chicken. Remove the pan from the heat and whisk in the egg yolk.

3. Spoon the chicken into the warm brioches, top with their "hats," and serve.

From Françoise:

• This lovely recipe is great for using up any roast chicken scraps you may have around. But it's so good you might want to poach a couple of chicken breasts just to make this dish. Then you can use the chicken poaching liquid to make the sauce instead of milk.

HAM-STUFFED ÉCLAIRS

- *Éclairs au jambon* -

❖ ADVANCED   ❖ MODERATE   ❖ 1 HOUR   ❖ MAKES 18 TO 20 PIECES

CHOUX PASTRY

5 tablespoons (½ stick plus 1 tablespoon) butter, diced

½ teaspoon salt

⅔ cup all-purpose flour

3 large eggs

FILLING

1½ tablespoons butter, plus more for brushing

1½ tablespoons all-purpose flour

1 cup milk

Salt and pepper

2 thin slices of ham, chopped

❖ ❖ ❖ ❖ ❖

1. Preheat the oven to 400 degrees. Position 2 racks in the upper and lower third of the oven. Lightly brush 2 baking sheets with butter.

2. Make the choux pastry: In a saucepan, bring ⅔ cup of water, the butter, and salt to a boil. Remove the pan from the heat, add all the flour at once, and beat well using a wooden spoon. Return the pan to low heat and beat until the dough is smooth and pulls away from the pan to form a ball. Off the heat, add the eggs, 1 at a time, beating well after each addition.

3. Using a pastry bag or 2 spoons, pipe or spoon 9 or 10 éclairs well apart on each baking sheet. Bake for 20 minutes, shifting the pans halfway through, until the éclairs are risen and golden. Transfer to a rack and let cool.

4. Meanwhile, make the filling: In a small saucepan, melt the butter over medium heat.

Whisk in the flour until it starts foaming. Whisk in the milk. Season with salt and pepper. Bring to a boil, whisking, then reduce the heat to very low and cook for 10 minutes. Remove the pan from the heat and whisk in the ham.

5. Cut a thin slice off the top of each éclair, keeping it attached. Carefully pipe or spoon some of the filling into each éclair, then close. Serve warm or at room temperature.

From Françoise:

• To make a vegetarian dish, I transform my ham éclairs into mushroom éclairs. I chop the mushrooms and sauté them in butter before adding them to the sauce. I also prefer to season them more generously and serve them warm.

• Before removing your éclairs from the oven, test for doneness by tapping them; they should be firm.

CLASSIC CHEESE PUFFS

- *Gougères bourguignonnes* -

❖ INTERMEDIATE   ❖ INEXPENSIVE   ❖ 1 HOUR, 20 MINUTES   ❖ SERVES 6

Butter for brushing

1½ ounces Gruyère cheese, cut into ¼-inch dice

CHOUX PASTRY

5 tablespoons butter, diced

½ teaspoon salt

⅔ cup all-purpose flour

3 large eggs

1½ cups shredded Gruyère cheese

Pepper

❖ ❖ ❖ ❖ ❖

1. Preheat the oven to 400 degrees. Brush 2 baking sheets with butter.

2. Make the choux pastry: In a saucepan, bring ⅔ cup of water, the butter, and salt to a boil. When the butter melts, remove the pan from the heat, add all the flour at once, and beat well using a wooden spoon. Return the pan to low heat and beat until the dough is smooth and pulls away from the pan to form a ball. Off the heat, add the eggs, 1 at a time, beating well after each addition. Beat in the shredded cheese and pepper.

3. Drop tablespoons of the batter onto the baking sheets and dot with the cheese dice. Transfer to the oven and bake until puffed and golden, about 45 minutes, reducing the oven temperature to 350 degrees after 20 minutes. Transfer to a rack to cool slightly. Serve warm.

From Françoise:

• The baked gougères should feel firm when you touch them. If not, return to a 225-degree oven for a few minutes.

• These cheese puffs can be served warm or at room temperature but, frankly, they are better warm when the insides are still a little creamy.

MUSHROOM TARTS

- Tartelettes aux champignons -

PÂTE BRISÉE

1 ¼ cups all-purpose flour

½ teaspoon salt

5 tablespoons unsalted butter,
   cut into pieces

FILLING

3 ½ tablespoons butter

½ pound white mushrooms, thinly sliced

1 tablespoon lemon juice

Salt and pepper

1 ½ tablespoons all-purpose flour

½ cup milk

❖ ❖ ❖ ❖ ❖

1. Make the pâte brisée: In a bowl, combine the flour with the salt and butter. Rub the butter into the flour between your palms. Sprinkle over ¼ cup of water and knead briefly until large crumbs form. Press into a disk. On a lightly floured surface, scrape the dough away from you with the heel of your hand in a long sliding motion, then press into a disk; repeat 3 times. Wrap and refrigerate until firm, 15 to 20 minutes.

2. Preheat the oven to 400 degrees. On a lightly floured work surface, roll the dough into a round about ⅛ inch thick and line 8 tartlet pans. Trim off any excess. Use the scraps to patch any cracks. Prick holes all over the bottom of the tartlet shells with a fork. Transfer to a baking sheet and bake in the oven until crisp and brown, 15 to 20 minutes. Transfer the tartlets to a rack to cool completely.

3. Meanwhile, make the filling: In a medium saucepan, melt 2 tablespoons of the butter over medium heat. Add the mushrooms and lemon juice and season with salt and pepper. Barely cover with water and bring to a boil, then reduce the heat to low and simmer for 5 minutes.

4. In a large saucepan, melt the remaining 1 ½ tablespoons of butter over medium heat. Whisk in the flour until it starts foaming. Whisk in the milk and ½ cup of the mushroom cooking liquid and season with salt and pepper. Bring to a boil, whisking, then reduce the heat to very low and cook for 10 minutes. Remove the pan from the heat and stir in the mushrooms.

5. Spread the filling in the tartlet shells and serve.

From Françoise:

• For a more refined presentation, reserve some of the cooked mushrooms and arrange them on top of the tartlets before serving.

FRENCH GRILLED HAM-AND-CHEESE SANDWICHES

- Croque-monsieur -

❖ VERY EASY ❖ MODERATE ❖ 15 MINUTES ❖ SERVES 4

8 slices of white sandwich bread
8 thin slices of Gruyère cheese

4 thin slices of ham
6 tablespoons butter

❖ ❖ ❖ ❖ ❖

1. On each of 4 slices of bread, layer 1 slice of cheese, 1 slice of ham, and 1 slice of cheese. Cover with the remaining slices of bread.

2. In a large skillet, melt 3 tablespoons of the butter over medium heat. Add the sandwiches and cook until golden on the bottom. Add the remaining 3 tablespoons of butter, turn the sandwiches, and cook until golden on the second side. Transfer to paper towels to drain. Serve at once.

From Françoise:

• If you spread the outside of the sandwiches with softened butter and bake them in the oven instead of frying them in butter, they will be less greasy. Transfer the buttered sandwiches to a baking sheet and bake on the top shelf of a 400-degree oven until browned on both sides, turning once.

• A soup, a croque-monsieur, a green salad, and a piece of fruit and, voilà, dinner.

GRATIN OF ROQUEFORT-STUFFED CRÊPES

- Coussinets au roquefort -

❖ INTERMEDIATE ❖ INEXPENSIVE ❖ 45 MINUTES, PLUS 1 HOUR RESTING ❖ SERVES 4

CRÊPES
1 cup all-purpose flour
1½ cups milk
2 large eggs, lightly beaten
3 tablespoons butter, 2 melted, plus more
  for brushing
Salt

FILLING
1½ tablespoons butter
1½ tablespoons all-purpose flour
1 cup milk
Pepper
¾ cup crumbled Roquefort cheese (about
  3½ ounces)
2 tablespoons crème fraîche
¼ cup shredded Gruyère cheese

1. Make the crêpes: In a medium bowl, whisk the flour with the milk, eggs, melted butter, and ½ teaspoon salt. Cover and let stand at least 1 hour.

2. Meanwhile, make the Roquefort filling: In a small saucepan, melt the butter over medium heat. Whisk in the flour until it starts foaming. Whisk in the milk. Season with pepper. Bring to a boil, whisking, then reduce the heat to very low and cook for 5 to 7 minutes. Remove the pan from the heat and whisk in the Roquefort and crème fraîche.

3. Lightly brush a skillet with melted butter and heat over medium heat. Whisk the batter and add 2 or 3 tablespoons to the skillet, swirling to coat the bottom. Cook until the edge begins to brown, about 30 seconds. Flip using a thin-bladed spatula and cook 20 seconds. Slide onto a plate and repeat with the remaining batter, stacking the crêpes as they're cooked.

4. Heat the broiler. Lightly brush the bottom of a large gratin dish with butter. Spread about 1 tablespoon of filling over each crêpe. Roll up, folding in the ends as you go. Arrange the crêpes in the gratin dish. Spoon any remaining Roquefort sauce over them. Sprinkle with the Gruyère and dot the top with the remaining 1 tablespoon of butter. Broil until the filling is hot and the cheese melts. Serve right away.

From Françoise:
• The number of crêpes depends on the size of your skillet and the thickness of your crêpe batter.

• If you are a big crêpe fan, I recommend buying a special crêpe pan in steel, stainless steel, or nonstick.

GRUYÈRE CHEESE TARTS
- *Tartelettes au fromage* -

❖ INTERMEDIATE   ❖ INEXPENSIVE   ❖ 50 MINUTES   ❖ MAKES 8 TARTLETS

PÂTE BRISÉE
1 ¼ cups all-purpose flour
½ teaspoon salt
5 tablespoons unsalted butter, cut into pieces

FILLING
1 ½ tablespoons butter
1 ½ tablespoons all-purpose flour
1 cup milk
Salt and pepper
1 cup shredded Gruyère cheese
1 large egg, lightly beaten

❖ ❖ ❖ ❖ ❖

1. Make the pâte brisée: In a bowl, combine the flour with the salt and butter. Rub the butter into the flour between your palms. Sprinkle over ¼ cup of water and knead briefly until large crumbs form. Press into a disk. On a lightly floured surface, scrape the dough away

continued

from you with the heel of your hand in a long sliding motion, then press into a disk; repeat 3 times. Wrap and refrigerate until firm, 15 to 20 minutes.

2. Meanwhile, make the filling: In a medium saucepan, melt the butter over medium heat. Whisk in the flour until it starts foaming. Whisk in the milk and season with salt and pepper. Bring to a boil, whisking, then reduce the heat to low and cook until it thickens. Remove the pan from the heat and stir in the cheese and egg.

3. Preheat the oven to 400 degrees. On a lightly floured work surface, roll the dough into a round about ⅛ inch thick and line 8 tartlet

pans. Trim off any excess. Use the scraps to patch any cracks. Prick holes all over the bottom of the tartlet shells with a fork.

4. Spread the filling in the tartlet shells. Transfer to a baking sheet and bake in the oven until lightly browned, about 25 minutes. Serve the tarts hot, warm, or at room temperature.

From Françoise:
• These tarts can be prepared and baked an hour or two ahead of time and reheated just before serving. So it's a very practical recipe for when you have guests coming for lunch or dinner. And for a buffet, these tarts—warm— are easy to serve and eat out of hand while standing.

SEAFOOD QUICHE
- Quiche aux fruits de mer -

❖ INTERMEDIATE ❖ MODERATE ❖ 1 HOUR ❖ SERVES 4

PÂTE BRISÉE
1 ¼ cups all-purpose flour
½ teaspoon salt
5 tablespoons unsalted butter,
  cut into pieces

FILLING
2 tablespoons butter
1 shallot, finely chopped

½ cup dry white wine
4 scallops
½ pound cockles, scrubbed
½ pound mussels, scrubbed and bearded
4 langoustines or colossal shrimp in the shell
4 large eggs
½ cup heavy cream
Chopped parsley leaves
Salt and pepper

❖ ❖ ❖ ❖ ❖

1. Make the pâte brisée: In a bowl, combine the flour with the salt and butter. Rub the butter into the flour between your palms. Sprinkle over ¼ cup of water and knead briefly until large crumbs form. Press into a disk. On a lightly floured surface, scrape the dough away from you with the heel of your hand in a long

sliding motion, then press into a disk; repeat 3 times. Wrap and refrigerate until firm, 15 to 20 minutes.

2. Meanwhile, make the filling: In a large skillet, melt the 2 tablespoons of butter over medium-low heat. Add the shallot and cook until soft,

2 to 3 minutes. Add the wine and cook until it evaporates. Add the scallops and cook until opaque. Transfer the scallops to a plate.

3. Add the cockles, mussels, and langoustines or shrimp to the skillet, increase the heat to high, cover, and cook, stirring once or twice, just until the cockles and mussels open, 3 to 5 minutes. Remove the skillet from the heat. When the seafood is cool enough to handle, remove the meat from the shells and reserve. Discard the shells and any unopened shellfish. Strain the broth using a fine strainer and reserve.

4. Preheat the oven to 400 degrees. On a lightly floured work surface, roll the dough into a round about ⅛ inch thick. Wrap the dough around the rolling pin and fit it into an 8-inch tart pan with a removable bottom. Trim off any excess. Use the scraps to patch any cracks. Prick holes all over the bottom of the tart shell with a fork.

5. In a bowl, whisk the eggs with the cream, ¾ cup of the reserved shellfish broth, and the parsley and season lightly with salt and pepper. Scatter all the seafood in the tart shell. Pour in the custard and bake until the custard is set and the top is puffed and browned, 30 to 35 minutes. Serve the tart hot, warm, or at room temperature.

From Françoise:
• Line a strainer with a moistened paper towel, then pour in the shellfish broth; the paper towel will catch the tiniest grains of sand.

• Shellfish broth is often salty, so taste it before seasoning the custard.

• For a less expensive recipe, shrimp can be substituted for the langoustines, and calico scallops can replace the sea scallops.

• Instead of making the dough, you can, of course, buy a rolled pie crust.

QUICHE LORRAINE
- *Quiche lorraine* -

❖ INTERMEDIATE ❖ MODERATE ❖ 1 HOUR ❖ SERVES 4

PÂTE BRISÉE
1 ¼ cups all-purpose flour
½ teaspoon salt
5 tablespoons unsalted butter,
  cut into pieces

FILLING
¼ pound thick-sliced bacon, cut crosswise
  into ¼-inch-thick strips
3 large eggs
1 ½ cups milk or heavy cream
Salt and pepper

❖ ❖ ❖ ❖ ❖

1. Make the pâte brisée: In a bowl, combine the flour with the salt and butter. Rub the butter into the flour between your palms. Sprinkle over ¼ cup of water and knead briefly until large

crumbs form. Press into a disk. On a lightly floured surface, scrape the dough away from

continued

you with the heel of your hand in a long sliding motion, then press into a disk; repeat 3 times.

2. On a lightly floured work surface, roll the dough into a round about ⅛ inch thick. Wrap the dough around the rolling pin and fit it into an 8-inch tart pan with a removable bottom. Trim off any excess. Use the scraps to patch any cracks. Prick holes all over the bottom of the tart shell with a fork. Wrap and refrigerate until firm, 15 to 20 minutes.

3. Preheat the oven to 400 degrees. Bring a small saucepan of water to a boil. Add the bacon and when the water returns to a boil, drain.

4. In a bowl, whisk the eggs with the milk or cream and season with salt and pepper. Scatter the bacon in the tart shell. Pour in the custard. Bake for 15 minutes, then reduce the oven temperature to 350 degrees and bake until

the custard is set and the top is puffed and browned, 15 to 20 minutes. Serve the tart hot, warm, or at room temperature.

From Françoise:

• My friends from Lorraine prepare their quiche with crème fraîche, but to save money, they sometimes blend the cream with milk. Try it both ways and see what you prefer. Me, I vote for the version with crème fraîche.

• The bacon can be replaced with smoked or baked ham. To remove some of the salt and smokiness in any cured meat, boil it as for the bacon.

• You can be prepared and bake this tart ahead of time and eat it at room temperature or re-heated. It won't be beautifully puffed like it is when it just comes out of the oven, but it will still be delicious.

ROQUEFORT QUICHE
- *Quiche au roquefort* -

❖ INTERMEDIATE　　❖ MODERATE　　❖ 1 HOUR　　❖ SERVES 4

PÂTE BRISÉE
1 ¼ cups all-purpose flour
½ teaspoon salt
5 tablespoons unsalted butter,
　cut into pieces

FILLING
3 large eggs
¼ cup crème fraîche
Pepper
1 cup crumbled Roquefort cheese (about
　4 ½ ounces)

❖　❖　❖　❖　❖

1. Make the pâte brisée: In a bowl, combine the flour with the salt and butter. Rub the butter into the flour between your palms. Sprinkle over ¼ cup of water and knead briefly until large

crumbs form. Press into a disk. On a lightly floured surface, scrape the dough away from you with the heel of your hand in a long sliding motion, then press into a disk; repeat 3 times.

2. On a lightly floured work surface, roll the dough into a round about ⅛ inch thick. Wrap the dough around the rolling pin and fit it into a 9-inch tart pan with a removable bottom. Trim off any excess. Use the scraps to patch any cracks. Prick holes all over the bottom of the tart shell with a fork. Wrap and refrigerate until firm, 15 to 20 minutes.

3. Preheat the oven to 400 degrees. In a bowl, whisk the eggs with the crème fraîche and season with pepper. Scatter the cheese in the tart shell. Pour in the custard and bake until the custard is set and the top is puffed and browned, about 30 minutes. Serve the tart hot, warm, or at room temperature.

From Françoise:

• If the quiche starts to brown in the oven before the custard is set, cover it with a piece of foil.

• I don't add salt to this custard because Roquefort cheese is salty enough.

QUICHE WITH WALNUTS AND FROMAGE BLANC
- *Quiche aux noix et fromage blanc* -

❖ INTERMEDIATE   ❖ MODERATE   ❖ 1 HOUR   ❖ SERVES 4

1 rolled pie crust

1 ¼ cups fromage blanc

1 ½ tablespoons all-purpose flour

3 large eggs, separated

½ cup walnut halves

1 teaspoon salt

❖   ❖   ❖   ❖   ❖

1. Preheat the oven to 400 degrees. Fit the dough into a 9-inch tart pan with a removable bottom and refrigerate.

2. In a bowl, whisk the fromage blanc with the flour, egg yolks, walnuts, and salt. In another bowl, beat the egg whites until they hold firm peaks. Gently fold into the custard.

3. Spread the custard in the tart shell. Bake until the custard is set and the top is puffed and browned, 35 to 40 minutes. Serve the tart hot, warm, or at room temperature.

From Françoise:

• If you have the time, drain the fromage blanc in a strainer lined with paper towels or a double layer of cheesecloth to firm it up slightly.

• To make the custard creamier, try adding a tablespoon of mascarpone.

• I deepen the flavor of the walnuts by sautéing them in butter for 2 or 3 minutes until toasted.

FRENCH-STYLE PIZZA WITH TOMATOES AND ANCHOVIES

- *Pizza aux tomates et anchois* -

❖ EASY   ❖ INEXPENSIVE   ❖ 30 MINUTES   ❖ SERVES 4 TO 6

¼ cup extra-virgin olive oil, plus more for brushing

1 pound prepared bread dough

1 black olive

1 small jar (about 4 ounces) anchovy fillets in oil

2 or 3 small tomatoes, thinly sliced

1 cup pitted green olives, roughly chopped

Marjoram or thyme leaves

Pepper

❖ ❖ ❖ ❖ ❖

1. Preheat the oven to 500 degrees. Brush a baking sheet with oil.

2. In a bowl, sprinkle the dough with 1 tablespoon of the oil. Work the oil into the dough by kneading for a minute or two. On a lightly floured work surface, roll out the dough to a round about ⅛ inch thick. Place the dough on the baking sheet. Sprinkle it again with 1 tablespoon of the oil. Roll up the edges to form a border all around.

3. Place the olive in the center of the dough. Arrange the anchovies in a star pattern around the olive. Arrange the tomato slices between the anchovies. Distribute the green olives among the areas in between the anchovies. Sprinkle the majoram and pepper over the pizza. Do not add salt, since the anchovies and olives will provide enough saltiness on their own.

4. Sprinkle everything again with the remaining 2 tablespoons of the oil. Bake until the dough is golden and crisp, about 8 minutes. Serve hot (or reheat later).

From Françoise:

• If you are not an experienced at making bread dough, just buy ready-made bread (or pizza) dough at the supermarket, or, better yet, ask your local bakery if you can buy some dough.

• If you use anchovies preserved in salt instead of those preserved in oil, then you should be sure to rinse them briefly under running cold water in order to remove some of the salt.

SALAD WITH WARM GOAT CHEESE TOASTS

- *Crottin chaud en salade* -

1 small head Boston lettuce, leaves separated

1 tablespoon vinegar

1 teaspoon Dijon mustard

2 tablespoons oil, plus more for brushing

Salt and pepper

2 (3 ½ ounce) round goat cheeses, such as
   Crottin de Chavignol, halved horizontally

4 slices of country bread

❖ ❖ ❖ ❖ ❖

1. Mound the lettuce on salad plates. In a bowl, whisk the vinegar with the mustard and oil and season with salt and pepper.

2. Heat the broiler. Brush the goat cheese halves with oil and set each on a slice of bread. Transfer the cheese toasts to a baking sheet and broil on the top shelf of the oven until the cheese is warmed and soft.

3. Drizzle the lettuce with the vinaigrette and set a cheese toast on top. Serve at once.

From Françoise:

• Try adding raisins and thinly sliced apples to the salad.

• You can also whisk a dash of Cognac into the vinaigrette.

GOLDEN SEARED GRUYÈRE SLICES
- *Escalopes de gruyère panés* -

❖ EASY   ❖ MODERATE   ❖ 15 MINUTES   ❖ SERVES 4

1 large egg

Salt and pepper

¼ cup dry bread crumbs

7 ounces Gruyère cheese, sliced ½ inch thick

Dijon mustard for brushing

3 tablespoons butter

❖ ❖ ❖ ❖ ❖

1. In a soup plate, beat the egg with 1 teaspoon of cold water and season with salt and pepper. In another soup plate, spread the bread crumbs.

2. Brush each slice of cheese with the mustard. Dip it in the egg, then dredge in the bread crumbs, patting to make them adhere.

3. In a large skillet, melt the butter over low heat. Add the cheese slices and cook just until golden, about 1 minute per side. Serve immediately.

From Françoise:

• This recipe is a showstopper at winter dinner parties. Serve it with a green salad of Boston lettuce, escarole, or frisée and pass garlic toasts alongside.

• Use plenty of bread crumbs; the slices of cheese must be entirely coated with them or the cheese will melt in the skillet.

• You can make your own bread crumbs by grinding stale or toasted bread in the food processor.

CLASSIC CHEESE FONDUE
- *Fondue savoyarde* -

❖ EASY   ❖ EXPENSIVE   ❖ 15 MINUTES   ❖ SERVES 4

2 garlic cloves

2 ¼ cups dry white wine

1 ½ pounds Gruyère cheese, thinly sliced

½ cup Kirsch

2 pinches of baking soda

1 teaspoon potato starch or cornstarch

2 pinches of freshly grated nutmeg

Salt and pepper

Crusty bread cubes

❖ ❖ ❖ ❖ ❖

1. Rub the inside of a cheese fondue pot or medium flameproof casserole with the garlic; add the garlic. Pour in the wine and bring to a simmer over medium heat. Gradually add the cheese, stirring constantly with a wooden spoon, just until the cheese is melted and smooth. Stir in the Kirsch, baking soda, and potato starch or cornstarch and season with nutmeg, salt, and pepper.

2. Set the pot on a hot plate on the table and pass a basket of bread. Let guests spear their own bread cubes and twirl them in the warm melted cheese.

From Françoise:

• A fondue supper doesn't require a first course, but if you would like to serve one, pick something simple like crudités (page 72) or a light soup (see the Soups chapter). To finish the meal, choose a fruit dessert or, better yet, ice cream. For a beverage, pour a dry white wine from Switzerland, preferably, or Alsace.

• You might also like to set out boiled new potatoes, salami, and cornichons for serving.

• Make the fondue with two different kinds of cheeses, say half Gruyère, half Emmentaler. Or try two different Gruyères.

• The potato starch or cornstarch helps keep the fondue from separating. If it does separate, try rescuing it with a splash of vinegar.

EGGS

EGG FLAN WITH TOMATO SAUCE

- *Flan d'oeufs à la tomate* -

❖ ADVANCED   ❖ MODERATE   ❖ 50 MINUTES   ❖ SERVES 4

Butter for brushing
2 cups milk
5 large eggs
Freshly grated nutmeg
Salt and pepper

TOMATO SAUCE
3 tablespoons butter
1 onion, finely chopped
3 tablespoons all-purpose flour
3 tablespoons tomato paste (about 2 ½ ounces)
1 garlic clove, crushed
1 bouquet garni made with parsley, thyme, and
   bay leaf
Salt and pepper

❖   ❖   ❖   ❖   ❖

1. Preheat the oven to 400 degrees. Generously brush a soufflé dish with butter.

2. In a small saucepan, bring the milk to a bare simmer. Remove the pan from the heat. In a bowl, whisk the eggs to mix and season with nutmeg, salt, and pepper. Gradually whisk in the hot milk.

3. Pour this custard into the soufflé dish and set in a roasting pan. Fill the roasting pan with hot water to come halfway up the sides of the dish. Transfer to the oven and bake until a knife inserted in the center comes out clean, about 20 minutes.

4. Meanwhile, make the tomato sauce: In a medium saucepan, melt the butter over medium-low heat. Add the onion and cook, stirring, until soft, about 5 minutes. Stir in one at the time the flour, tomato paste, and, gradually, 2 cups of water. Add the garlic and bouquet garni and season with salt and pepper.

Bring to a simmer, then reduce the heat to low and cook for 15 minutes. Discard the bouquet garni and garlic.

5. Run a knife around the flan. Invert a round platter over the dish. Holding the dish and platter together, quickly invert the flan onto the platter. Spoon some of the sauce over and around the flan and serve, passing the remaining tomato sauce separately.

From Françoise:
• When I'm making a quick tomato sauce from tomato paste, I like to add a little peeled and diced fresh tomato 5 minutes before the end of cooking. You can see the pieces of tomato on the plate when it's served. This little touch, which isn't a lot of trouble, changes the taste and the appearance of my sauce.

• This recipe could be called "savory egg custard" because it's prepared like a dessert custard but without the addition of sugar.

SOFT-BOILED EGGS

- Oeufs à la coque -

❖ VERY EASY ❖ INEXPENSIVE ❖ 10 MINUTES ❖ SERVES 4

4 large eggs
Salt and pepper

Butter for frying
Slices of bread cut into rectangles

❖ ❖ ❖ ❖ ❖

1. In a small saucepan, combine the eggs with cold salted water to cover. Bring to a boil over medium heat, then immediately remove the eggs. The egg whites will be barely set. Serve the eggs in the shell, passing salt and pepper at the table.

2. If you prefer to have the whites lightly set, remove the saucepan from the heat when the water comes to a boil and leave the eggs in the water for 1 minute before serving.

3. Meanwhile, melt some butter in a skillet and fry the bread until golden to have buttery soldiers to dip into the soft yolks.

From Françoise:
• To prevent the eggshells from breaking in the pan, remove the eggs from the refrigerator at least 10 minutes before cooking. Also, adding salt to the water keeps the shells from cracking.

• A perfectly cooked soft-boiled egg has a lightly set white and a warm, soft yolk.

MOLLET EGGS

- Oeufs mollets -

❖ VERY EASY ❖ INEXPENSIVE ❖ 10 MINUTES ❖ SERVES 4

4 large eggs

Salt and pepper

❖ ❖ ❖ ❖ ❖

1. In a small saucepan, combine the eggs with cold salted water to cover. Bring to a boil over medium heat, then immediately remove the pan from the heat and leave the eggs in the water for 3 minutes before removing. Serve the eggs in the shell, passing salt and pepper at the table.

From Françoise:
• A mollet egg is midway between soft-boiled and hard-boiled.

• Be especially careful when peeling mollet eggs because the yolks are soft.

SHIRRED EGGS ON BACON AND CHEESE
- Oeufs à la lorraine -

❖ VERY EASY ❖ INEXPENSIVE ❖ 10 MINUTES ❖ SERVES 4

2 tablespoons butter

4 bacon slices

4 thin slices of Gruyère cheese cut to
the same size as the bacon

4 large eggs

Salt and pepper

❖ ❖ ❖ ❖ ❖

1. In a large heatproof gratin pan or skillet, melt the butter over medium heat. Add the bacon and cook until lightly browned on the bottom. Turn the bacon and lay the cheese slices on top. When they begin to melt, break the eggs into the skillet. Cover and cook until the whites are set and the yolks are still soft. Add pepper, and, if necessary, salt to taste (the bacon often provides enough salt on its own). Serve immediately.

From Françoise:
• You can finish cooking this dish in the oven instead of on the stovetop. Transfer the fried bacon and cheese to a gratin dish, break the eggs on top, and bake in a 425 degree oven.

FRIED-EGG BURGERS
- Oeufs à cheval -

❖ VERY EASY ❖ INEXPENSIVE ❖ 15 MINUTES ❖ SERVES 4

1 pound ground beef chuck

1 tablespoon Dijon mustard

1 tablespoon chopped parsley leaves

Salt and pepper

3 tablespoons butter

1 tablespoon oil

All-purpose flour for dusting

4 large eggs

❖ ❖ ❖ ❖ ❖

1. In a bowl, lightly mix the beef with the mustard and parsley and season with salt and pepper. Shape into 4 patties.

2. In a large skillet, melt 1 tablespoon of the butter in the oil over medium-high heat. Dust the burgers with the flour. Add to the skillet and cook for 3 minutes per side. Transfer to plates.

3. Wipe out the skillet and in it melt the remaining 2 tablespoons of butter over medium heat. Break in the eggs and cook until the whites are set and the yolks are still soft. Season with salt and pepper. Set 1 fried egg on each burger and serve.

From Françoise:
• To get perfectly round fried eggs, stamp them out in the skillet with a cookie cutter. Or using a saucer as a pattern, trim away the ragged whites.

HARD-BOILED EGGS WITH CREAMY ONIONS
- Oeufs à la tripe -

❖ EASY   ❖ INEXPENSIVE   ❖ 15 MINUTES   ❖ SERVES 4

6 large eggs
Salt
3 tablespoons butter
2 onions, halved and thinly sliced

3 tablespoons all-purpose flour
2 cups milk
Pepper
Chopped parsley leaves for sprinkling

❖ ❖ ❖ ❖ ❖

1. In a small saucepan, cover the eggs with cold salted water. Bring to a boil, then cook the eggs at a gentle boil for 10 minutes. Drain and run cold water into the pan to make the eggs easier to peel.

2. In a medium saucepan, melt the butter over low heat. Add the onions, cover, and cook until soft, about 10 minutes. Stir in the flour. Add the milk, season with salt and pepper, and bring to a boil, whisking. Reduce the heat to very low and cook for 5 minutes.

3. Peel the eggs and slice them crosswise. Arrange them on a platter and spoon the creamy onions on top. Sprinkle with the parsley and serve.

From Françoise:
• This is a good way to use up hard-boiled eggs left over in the refrigerator.

• To spruce up this homey dish, add a few triangles of bread, sautéed in butter, to the plate.

• Add a teaspoon of water to the onions, if needed, so they don't stick to the pan.

SHIRRED EGGS ON A BED OF CREAMY SPINACH

- Oeufs aux épinards marius à la crème -

❖ EASY   ❖ MODERATE   ❖ 1 HOUR, 30 MINUTES   ❖ SERVES 4

3 pounds spinach, tough stems removed

4 tablespoons (½ stick) butter

2 onions, finely chopped

1½ pounds potatoes, peeled and thinly sliced
  crosswise

2 garlic cloves, finely chopped

Pinch of saffron

Salt and pepper

4 large eggs

4 slices of bread

❖ ❖ ❖ ❖ ❖

1. In a large pot of boiling salted water, cook the spinach for 5 minutes. Drain and squeeze out as much of the water as possible. Coarsely chop the spinach.

2. In a large heatproof gratin pan or skillet, melt 2 tablespoons of the butter over medium heat. Add the onions and cook until lightly browned. Add the potatoes, spinach, garlic, 1 cup of water, and the saffron and season with salt and pepper. Reduce the heat to low, cover, and cook, stirring occasionally, for 40 minutes.

3. Make 4 indentations in the spinach and break an egg into each. Cover and cook for 10 minutes.

4. In a large skillet, melt the remaining 2 tablespoons of butter over medium heat. Add the bread and cook until golden on both sides. Serve the eggs in the pan garnished with the bread.

From Françoise:

• Using frozen chopped spinach will save you some time. Don't bother to defrost it first, but do add a little less water in Step 2.

BAKED EGGS IN MASHED POTATOES

- Oeufs au nid -

❖ EASY   ❖ INEXPENSIVE   ❖ 45 MINUTES   ❖ SERVES 4

2 pounds potatoes, peeled

2 tablespoons butter, plus more for brushing

1½ cups milk

Salt and pepper

8 large eggs

2 tablespoons dry bread crumbs

1. In a large pot of boiling salted water, cook the potatoes for 25 to 30 minutes; drain. Mash the potatoes. Gradually beat in the butter and milk using a wooden spoon. Season with salt and pepper.

2. Preheat the oven to 400 degrees. Brush a large gratin dish with butter. Spread the mashed potatoes in the dish and make 8 indentations in them. Transfer the dish to the upper third of the oven for a few minutes until the potatoes are very hot. Break an egg into each indentation. Sprinkle with the bread crumbs and bake until the egg whites are set and the yolks are still soft, 6 to 8 minutes. Season with salt and pepper and serve immediately.

From Françoise:
• If you're using leftover mashed potatoes to make this dish, it's very important that you reheat the potatoes before adding the eggs. Otherwise, the eggs will be hard-cooked before the potatoes are hot, and that's not the intent.

SHIRRED EGGS ON CANADIAN BACON
- *Oeufs au bacon* -

❖ VERY EASY   ❖ INEXPENSIVE   ❖ 10 MINUTES   ❖ SERVES 4

2 tablespoons butter
4 thin slices of Canadian bacon

8 large eggs
Pepper

❖   ❖   ❖   ❖   ❖

1. In a large heatproof gratin pan or skillet, melt the butter over medium heat. Add the bacon and cook until lightly browned on the bottom, 1 to 2 minutes. Turn the bacon and break the eggs into the skillet. Cook until the whites are set and the yolks are still soft. Season with pepper but do not salt. Serve immediately.

From Françoise:
• If you have 4 small heatproof gratin pans, cook the eggs and serve them directly in the pans to avoid transferring them to another dish at serving time.

• If your heatproof gratin pan or skillet isn't large enough to cook all the eggs at once, cook them in 2 batches. They won't be as attractive, but they will be just as good.

SHIRRED EGGS ON ROQUEFORT TOAST
- Oeufs au plat en roquefortaise -

❖ EASY   ❖ MODERATE   ❖ 20 MINUTES   ❖ SERVES 4

3 tablespoons butter, plus more for brushing
4 slices of white sandwich or country bread
1 cup crumbled Roquefort cheese (about
   4 ½ ounces)

½ cup crème fraîche
Pepper
8 large eggs

❖ ❖ ❖ ❖ ❖

1. In a large skillet, melt 3 tablespoons of the butter over low heat. Add the bread and cook until golden on both sides.

2. In a bowl, mash the cheese with the crème fraîche. Season with pepper but do not salt.

3. Brush 4 small heatproof gratin pans with butter. Add a crouton to each and spread with some of the cheese. Set over low heat briefly, then break in the eggs, cover, and cook until

the whites are set and the yolks are still soft. Serve immediately.

From Françoise:
• When making shirred eggs, use very fresh eggs. You can tell they're fresh—when you break them—by the yolk, which doesn't spread out and keeps its plump shape on the white.

• Organic, cage-free eggs are a good choice.

SOFTLY SCRAMBLED EGGS
- Oeufs brouillés -

❖ ADVANCED   ❖ INEXPENSIVE   ❖ 15 MINUTES   ❖ SERVES 4

8 large eggs
Salt and pepper

3 tablespoons butter, cut into
   small pieces

❖ ❖ ❖ ❖ ❖

1. In the top of a double boiler or in a bowl or saucepan, preferably with a rounded bottom, lightly whisk the eggs with salt, pepper, and the butter.

2. Set the pan or bowl in a larger saucepan or skillet of barely simmering water and cook the eggs, stirring continuously with a wooden spoon, until they thicken creamily. The rather long cooking time is 8 to 10 minutes. Serve immediately.

From Françoise:

• What makes eggs brouillés a flop? (When they're more like an omelet—not saucy or creamy.) They were cooked in a saucepan over direct heat. They were overcooked. Maybe the pan wasn't heavy enough. Or they were stirred with a whisk instead of a wooden spoon.

• To rescue eggs that are cooking too quickly, add a teaspoon of cold water. Or dip the bottom of the pan in very cold water to stop the cooking.

• Dot the eggs with butter toward the end of cooking. They will be creamier.

• Other possibilities: When the eggs are almost done, stir in shredded Gruyère cheese; chopped, cooked mushrooms; chicken livers, diced and sautéed in butter; fines herbes (parsley, chives, chervil, tarragon); strips of smoked salmon; and so on.

• If you're preparing a larger quantity of eggs, cook them in batches.

SOFTLY SCRAMBLED EGGS WITH FINES HERBES
- *Oeufs brouillés aux fines herbes* -

❖ ADVANCED   ❖ INEXPENSIVE   ❖ 15 MINUTES   ❖ SERVES 4

4 slices of bread
3 tablespoons butter, cut into small pieces,
  plus more for spreading
8 large eggs

Salt and pepper
Chopped fines herbes (parsley, chives, chervil,
  tarragon)

❖ ❖ ❖ ❖ ❖

1. Preheat the broiler. Spread the bread on both sides with the butter and set the slices on a baking sheet. Toast on the top shelf of the oven until lightly browned, about 1 minute per side.

2. In the top of a double boiler or in a bowl or saucepan, preferably with a rounded bottom, lightly whisk the eggs with salt and pepper. Add the pieces of butter.

3. Set the pan or bowl in a larger saucepan or skillet of barely simmering water and cook the eggs, stirring continuously with a wooden spoon, until they thicken slightly, 5 to 6 minutes. Add the fines herbes and cook, stirring, until the eggs thicken creamily, 1 or 2 minutes

longer. Spoon the eggs on the toasts and serve immediately.

From Françoise:

• If you are not very experienced, don't scramble more than 4 eggs at a time. If you're serving more than 2 people, as in this recipe, cook the eggs in 2 or 3 batches. Keep the scrambled eggs warm in a pan or bowl set above—not in—a pan of hot water until all the eggs are cooked.

• You can sauté the bread in a skillet—1 minute per side—with a good amount of butter. Add plenty of butter at the beginning because the bread absorbs it quickly.

SOFTLY SCRAMBLED EGGS WITH GRUYÈRE
- Oeufs brouillés au fromage -

❖ ADVANCED　　　❖ INEXPENSIVE　　　❖ 15 MINUTES　　　❖ SERVES 4

7 large eggs
Salt and pepper
2 tablespoons butter, cut into small pieces

½ cup shredded Gruyère cheese
1 tablespoon crème fraîche

❖ ❖ ❖ ❖ ❖

1. In the top of a double boiler or in a bowl or saucepan, preferably with a rounded bottom, lightly whisk the eggs with salt, pepper, and the butter.

2. Set the pan or bowl in a larger saucepan or skillet of barely simmering water and cook the eggs, stirring continuously with a wooden spoon, until they thicken slightly, about 4 minutes. Add the cheese and cook, stirring, until it melts. Stir in the crème fraîche and serve immediately.

From Françoise:

• Crème fraîche does make these scrambled eggs tastier, but it's not indispensable in a dish already enriched with Gruyère cheese.

• Instead of Gruyère, try some Cantal or cheddar, or a mix.

• Use a heavy saucepan for cooking the eggs. To be on the safe side, remove the pan from the heat a little before the eggs are done and continue stirring them until they are perfect.

• You can wait to stir in the last raw egg until just before serving—that will make the eggs even creamier.

SOFTLY SCRAMBLED EGGS WITH MUSHROOMS
- Oeufs brouillés aux champignons -

❖ ADVANCED　　　❖ INEXPENSIVE　　　❖ 20 MINUTES　　　❖ SERVES 4

¼ pound small white mushrooms, quartered
Lemon juice for sprinkling
Salt and pepper

3 tablespoons butter, 2 tablespoons cut into
　small pieces
7 large eggs

1. In a medium saucepan, add the mushrooms, sprinkle with the lemon juice, and season with salt and pepper. Add 1 tablespoon of the butter and 6 tablespoons of cold water. Cook over medium heat until tender, about 5 minutes, then drain.

2. In the top of a double boiler or in a bowl or saucepan, preferably with a rounded bottom, lightly whisk the eggs with salt, pepper, and the pieces of butter.

3. Set the pan or bowl in a larger saucepan or skillet of barely simmering water and cook the eggs, stirring continuously with a wooden spoon, until they thicken slightly, about 4 minutes. Add the mushrooms and cook, stirring, until the eggs thicken creamily. Serve immediately.

From Françoise:
• By the second time you make eggs brouillés, you'll have mastered them.

• More variations: Spooned into baked tartlet or puffed pastry shells, these eggs make an elegant first course. Warm the pastry shells in the oven before stuffing them.

SOFTLY SCRAMBLED EGGS WITH MOREL MUSHROOMS
- Oeufs brouillés aux morilles -

❖ ADVANCED   ❖ EXPENSIVE   ❖ 20 MINUTES, PLUS 1 HOUR SOAKING   ❖ SERVES 4

¼ pound small dried morel mushrooms
4 tablespoons (½ stick) butter, 2 tablespoons
  cut into small pieces

Salt and pepper
8 large eggs
1 or 2 tablespoons crème fraîche

❖ ❖ ❖ ❖ ❖

1. In a bowl, cover the mushrooms with warm water and let soak for 1 hour. Drain and pat dry.

2. In a skillet, melt 2 tablespoons of the butter over high heat. Add the mushrooms, season, and cook about 5 minutes, stirring occasionally.

3. In the top of a double boiler or in a bowl or saucepan, preferably with a rounded bottom, lightly whisk the eggs with salt, pepper, and the pieces of butter.

4. Set the pan or bowl in a larger saucepan or skillet of barely simmering water, and cook the eggs, stirring continuously with a wooden spoon, until they thicken creamily, 7 to 8 minutes. Just before serving, stir in the crème fraîche.

5. Spoon the eggs into individual gratin dishes, top with the morels, and serve immediately.

From Françoise:
• Morels hide a lot of grit in their crevices, and you want to remove every speck before adding to your eggs. Once the morels soften in the warm water, swish them around. Let stand until all the grit falls to the bottom, then carefully remove the mushrooms, leaving the grit behind.

• Save the morel soaking liquid, carefully strained, for another recipe. It has a lot of flavor.

SOFTLY SCRAMBLED EGGS WITH CHICKEN LIVERS

- *Oeufs brouillés aux foies de volaille* -

❖ ADVANCED   ❖ INEXPENSIVE   ❖ 25 MINUTES   ❖ SERVES 4

4 tablespoons (½ stick) butter, 2 tablespoons
  cut into small pieces
2 chicken livers, diced
Salt and pepper

¼ pound white mushrooms, diced
Lemon juice for sprinkling
7 large eggs

❖   ❖   ❖   ❖   ❖

1. In a medium skillet, melt 2 tablespoons
of the butter over medium-low heat. Add the
chicken livers, season with salt and pepper,
and cook over medium-high heat for about
3 minutes, stirring. Transfer to a plate.

2. In the same skillet, add the mushrooms,
sprinkle with the lemon juice, and season with
salt and pepper. Increase the heat to high and
cook for 3 to 4 minutes.

3. In the top of a double boiler or in a bowl or
saucepan, preferably with a rounded bottom,
lightly whisk the eggs with salt, pepper, and
the pieces of butter.

4. Set the pan or bowl in a larger saucepan
or skillet of barely simmering water and
cook the eggs, stirring continuously with a
wooden spoon, until they thicken creamily,
7 to 8 minutes.

5. Spoon the eggs into a serving dish, arrange
the livers and mushrooms on top, and serve
immediately.

From Françoise:
• This is an excellent recipe for using up 2 or
3 chicken livers lurking in the fridge.

• Duck liver is even more delectable.

• The chicken livers should not be seared,
but rather gently simmered, otherwise they
get dry and bitter.

EGGS BAKED IN RAMEKINS WITH CRÈME FRAÎCHE
- *Oeufs cocotte* -

❖ VERY EASY   ❖ INEXPENSIVE   ❖ 15 MINUTES   ❖ SERVES 4

Butter for brushing
Salt and pepper

4 large eggs
4 teaspoons crème fraiche

❖ ❖ ❖ ❖ ❖

1. Preheat the oven to 475 degrees. Brush
4 ramekins with butter and season with salt
and pepper.

2. Break an egg into each ramekin. Set the
ramekins in a roasting pan and fill it with
boiling water to come halfway up the sides of
the ramekins. Cover the pan with foil, transfer
to the oven, and bake until the egg whites are
set and the yolks are still soft, 6 to 8 minutes.
Remove the ramekins from the water bath,
add a teaspoon of crème fraîche to each,
and serve.

From Françoise:
• I call any dish "egg cocotte" that has an
egg baked in an individual heatproof cup—
ramekin, mold, etc.—or an egg baked in an
edible cup, such as a scooped-out brioche,
tomato, potato, or cucumber; as well as
rice, mashed potatoes, creamed spinach, or
other food bed with a depression for holding
an egg.

• Vary the flavorings. Sautéed mushrooms,
diced ham, chorizo, salmon eggs, and crumbled Roquefort are all delicious in the bottom
of a ramekin with a baked egg on top.

EGGS BAKED IN RAMEKINS WITH MUSHROOMS
- *Oeufs cocotte aux champignons* -

❖ EASY   ❖ INEXPENSIVE   ❖ 20 MINUTES   ❖ SERVES 4

1 tablespoon butter, plus more for brushing
Salt and pepper
¼ pound white mushrooms, finely chopped

Chopped parsley leaves
Lemon juice for sprinkling
4 large eggs

continued

1. Preheat the oven to 500 degrees. Brush 4 ramekins with butter and season with salt and pepper.

2. In a skillet, melt the 1 tablespoon of butter over high heat. Add the mushrooms and parsley, sprinkle with lemon juice, and season with salt and pepper. Cook for 4 or 5 minutes.

3. Spoon some of the mushroom mixture into each ramekin. Break an egg into each ramekin. Set the ramekins in a roasting pan and fill it with boiling water to come halfway up the sides of the ramekins. Cover the pan with foil, transfer to the oven, and bake until the egg

whites are set and the yolks are still soft, 6 to 8 minutes. Remove the ramekins from the water bath and serve.

From Françoise:
• Eggs en cocotte can also be cooked in a water bath on the stovetop. The cooking time will be slightly longer, more like 12 minutes.

• Don't forget to cover the roasting pan with foil before cooking the eggs.

• Ramekins are small, cuplike baking dishes. They can be made of glass, porcelain, or earthenware.

EGGS BAKED IN RAMEKINS WITH FINES HERBES
- *Oeufs cocotte aux fines herbes* -

❖ EASY   ❖ INEXPENSIVE   ❖ 15 MINUTES   ❖ SERVES 4

Butter for brushing
Salt and pepper

Chopped fines herbes (parsley, chives, chervil, tarragon)
4 large eggs

❖ ❖ ❖ ❖ ❖

1. Preheat the oven to 500 degrees. Brush 4 ramekins with butter and season with salt and pepper.

2. Add some fines herbes to each ramekin. Break an egg into each. Set the ramekins in a roasting pan and fill it with boiling water to come halfway up the sides of the ramekins. Cover the pan with foil, transfer to the oven,

and bake until the egg whites are set and the yolks are still soft, 6 to 8 minutes. Remove the ramekins from the water bath and serve.

From Françoise:
• This dish is more evenly seasoned if you sprinkle the buttered ramekins with salt and pepper before adding the eggs.

NORTH AFRICAN VEGETABLE STEW WITH SOFT EGGS
- *Chouchouka* -

❖ EASY   ❖ INEXPENSIVE   ❖ 1 HOUR   ❖ SERVES 4

6 tablespoons oil

½ pound sweet onions, chopped

1 ½ pounds tomatoes, peeled, seeded, and
   chopped

2 bell peppers, cut into thin strips

2 small eggplants, cut into ½-inch dice

2 garlic cloves, crushed

Salt and pepper

4 or 8 large eggs

Chopped parsley leaves for sprinkling

❖   ❖   ❖   ❖   ❖

1. In a large skillet, heat the oil over medium-low heat. Add the onions and cook over medium-low heat until softened. Stir in the tomatoes, bell peppers, eggplants, and garlic. Season with salt and pepper. Reduce the heat to low and cook, uncovered, for 45 minutes. If the liquid evaporates too quickly, cover the skillet.

2. Preheat the oven to 450 degrees. Remove the garlic cloves. Spread the vegetables in a large gratin dish and make 4 or 8 indentations in them. Break an egg into each indentation.

Transfer the dish to the top rack of the oven and bake until the egg whites are set and the yolks are still soft, about 5 minutes. Sprinkle with the parsley and serve.

From Françoise:

• To peel tomatoes easily, score the bottoms and drop them in boiling water until the skin begins to curl, about 1 minute.

• It is not necessary to turn on the oven to make this recipe. You can cover the skillet and cook the eggs on top of the stove.

GRATIN OF HARD-BOILED EGGS WITH GRUYÈRE
- *Oeufs durs au gratin* -

❖ EASY   ❖ INEXPENSIVE   ❖ 25 MINUTES   ❖ SERVES 4

4 large eggs

3 tablespoons butter

3 tablespoons all-purpose flour

2 cups milk

Salt and pepper

½ cup shredded Gruyère cheese

continued

1. In a small saucepan, cover the eggs with cold water. Bring to a boil, then cook the eggs at a gentle boil for 10 minutes. Drain and run cold water into the pan to make the eggs easier to peel.

2. Meanwhile, in a small saucepan, melt the butter over medium heat. Whisk in the flour until it starts foaming. Whisk in the milk. Season with salt and pepper. Bring to a boil, whisking, then reduce the heat and cook for 10 minutes.

3. Preheat the broiler. Peel the eggs and halve them lengthwise. Spread half of the sauce in a gratin dish. Arrange the eggs on top and spoon the remaining sauce over them. Sprinkle with the cheese. Broil the eggs on the top shelf of the oven until lightly browned, then serve.

From Françoise:
• Add a smidgen of freshly grated nutmeg to the sauce—it's delicious.

• If you're pressed for time, serve the dish without broiling it.

• You can bake the gratin in a hot oven if you don't have a broiler. But not for too long, or the sauce will curdle.

HARD-BOILED EGGS
- *Oeufs durs* -

❖ EASY ❖ INEXPENSIVE ❖ 10 MINUTES ❖ SERVES 2

4 large eggs **Salt**

❖ ❖ ❖ ❖ ❖

1. In a small saucepan, cover the eggs with cold salted water. Bring to a boil, then cook the eggs at a gentle boil for 10 minutes. Drain and run cold water into the pan to make the eggs easier to peel.

From Françoise:
• To get perfectly hard-boiled yolks, cook the eggs for precisely the prescribed time (10 minutes). The yolks of overcooked eggs develop an unappetizing outer layer of gray-green.

• To discourage the eggshells from cracking when they're being boiled, take the eggs out of the refrigerator as much as a half hour before cooking them. Alternatively, add the eggs to a bowl of hot water to warm them up. Or cook them in salted water. Finally, you can pierce the two ends with a pin.

• Hard-boiled eggs are easier to shell if you run cold water into the pan and peel them in it.

CREAMY STUFFED HARD-BOILED EGGS
- Oeufs mimosa -

❖ INTERMEDIATE ❖ INEXPENSIVE ❖ 20 MINUTES ❖ SERVES 4

4 large eggs
Salt
Finely chopped parsley leaves
Boston lettuce leaves for garnishing

MAYONNAISE
1 large egg yolk
1 teaspoon Dijon mustard
¾ cup oil
1 tablespoon vinegar
Salt and pepper

❖ ❖ ❖ ❖ ❖

1. In a small saucepan, cover the eggs with cold salted water. Bring to a boil, then cook the eggs at a gentle boil for 10 minutes. Drain and run cold water into the pan to make the eggs easier to peel.

2. Meanwhile, make the mayonnaise: In a small bowl, whisk the egg yolk with the mustard. Blend in the oil a few drops at a time to begin, then in a steady stream. Beat in the vinegar and season with salt and pepper.

3. Peel the eggs and halve them lengthwise. Carefully add 3 of the yolks to the mayonnaise. Transfer the remaining yolk to another bowl. Mash the yolks with the mayonnaise and parsley until smooth.

4. Carefully mound the filling in the egg white halves. Grate the remaining yolk over them. Line a platter with the lettuce, arrange the eggs on top, and serve.

From Françoise:
• Have all the ingredients for the mayonnaise at room temperature.

• You can, of course, use store-bought mayonnaise to make eggs mimosa.

• This dish is best when prepared just before serving.

• The hard-boiled egg yolk grated over the stuffed eggs resembles the wispy flowers of a mimosa tree.

MUSTARDY STUFFED HARD-BOILED EGGS
- Oeufs durs farcis à la moutarde -

❖ VERY EASY ❖ INEXPENSIVE ❖ 20 MINUTES ❖ SERVES 4

4 large eggs

Salt

1 tablespoon Dijon mustard

2 or 3 cornichons, chopped

3 tablespoons butter, softened

Pepper

Lemon juice to taste

Boston lettuce leaves for garnishing

❖ ❖ ❖ ❖ ❖

1. In a small saucepan, cover the eggs with cold salted water. Bring to a boil, then cook the eggs at a gentle boil for 10 minutes. Drain and run cold water into the pan to make the eggs easier to peel.

2. Peel the eggs and halve them lengthwise. Carefully add the yolks to a bowl and mash with the mustard, cornichons, and butter. Season with salt, pepper, and lemon juice.

3. Carefully mound the filling in the egg white halves. Line a platter with the lettuce, arrange the eggs on top, and serve.

GOLDEN ROQUEFORT-STUFFED HARD-BOILED EGGS
- Oeufs durs gratinés farcis au roquefort -

❖ EASY ❖ INEXPENSIVE ❖ 30 MINUTES ❖ SERVES 4

6 large eggs

¾ cup crumbled Roquefort cheese
  (about 3 ½ ounces)

2 tablespoons butter, softened

SAUCE

1 ½ tablespoons butter

1 ½ tablespoons all-purpose flour

1 cup milk

Salt and pepper

½ cup crème fraîche

¼ cup shredded Gruyère cheese

1. In a small saucepan, cover the eggs with cold salted water. Bring to a boil, then cook the eggs at a gentle boil for 10 minutes. Drain and run cold water into the pan to make the eggs easier to peel.

2. Meanwhile, make the sauce: In a small saucepan, melt the butter over medium heat. Whisk in the flour until it starts foaming. Whisk in the milk. Season with salt and pepper. Bring to a boil, whisking, then reduce the heat to very low and cook for 2 minutes. Remove the pan from the heat and stir in the crème fraîche and Gruyère.

3. Preheat the broiler. Peel the eggs and halve them lengthwise. Carefully add the yolks to a bowl and mash with the Roquefort and butter.

4. Carefully mound the filling in the egg white halves. Arrange the egg halves in a gratin dish. Spoon the sauce over them. Broil them on the top shelf of the oven until lightly browned, then serve.

From Françoise:
• Go easy on the seasoning in the sauce because both Gruyère and Roquefort are salty.

CHIVE-STUFFED HARD-BOILED EGGS
- *Oeufs durs froids farcis à la ciboulette* -

❖ EASY   ❖ INEXPENSIVE   ❖ 15 MINUTES   ❖ SERVES 4

6 large eggs
Salt
2 tablespoons chopped chives
3 tablespoons butter, softened

Pepper
Pinch of cayenne pepper
12 radishes
Boston lettuce leaves for garnishing

❖ ❖ ❖ ❖ ❖

1. In a small saucepan, cover the eggs with cold salted water. Bring to a boil, then cook the eggs at a gentle boil for 10 minutes. Drain and run cold water into the pan to make the eggs easier to peel.

2. Peel the eggs and halve them lengthwise. Carefully add the yolks to a bowl and mash with the chives and butter. Season with salt, pepper, and cayenne.

3. Carefully mound the filling in the egg white halves. Set a radish on top of each. Line a platter with the lettuce, arrange the eggs on top, and serve.

GRATIN OF HARD-BOILED EGGS
WITH CREAMY SPINACH

- Oeufs durs aux épinards -

❖ EASY   ❖ INEXPENSIVE   ❖ 45 MINUTES   ❖ SERVES 4

3 pounds spinach, tough stems removed

5 tablespoons butter

1 garlic clove, chopped

Salt and pepper

6 large eggs

3 tablespoons all-purpose flour

2 cups milk

½ cup shredded Gruyère cheese

❖ ❖ ❖ ❖ ❖

1. In a large pot of boiling salted water, cook the spinach for 5 minutes. Drain and squeeze out as much of the water as possible. Coarsely chop the spinach.

2. In a saucepan, melt 2 tablespoons of the butter over very low heat. Add the spinach and garlic and season with salt and pepper. Cook for 30 minutes.

3. Meanwhile, in a small saucepan, cover the eggs with cold salted water. Bring to a boil, then cook the eggs at a gentle boil for 10 minutes. Drain and run cold water into the pan to make the eggs easier to peel.

4. In a medium saucepan, melt the remaining 3 tablespoons of butter over medium heat. Whisk in the flour until it starts foaming. Whisk in the milk and season with salt and pepper. Bring to a boil, whisking. Cook over low heat, whisking, until it thickens.

5. Preheat the broiler. Peel the eggs and halve them lengthwise. Stir half of the sauce into the spinach and spread in a gratin dish. Arrange the egg halves in the dish and cover with the remaining sauce. Sprinkle with the cheese. Broil on the top shelf of the oven until lightly browned, then serve.

From Françoise:

• This is one of my favorite make-ahead dishes. You can assemble the gratin and refrigerate it, then just before serving, slide it under the broiler.

• One of my secrets: Grate a little nutmeg into the spinach. It's exquisite.

ANCHOVY-STUFFED HARD-BOILED EGGS

- *Oeufs farcis aux anchois* -

❖ VERY EASY   ❖ INEXPENSIVE   ❖ 25 MINUTES   ❖ SERVES 4

6 large eggs

Salt

2 tablespoons crème d'anchois (anchovy cream)
  in a tube

3 tablespoons butter, softened

Pepper

Boston lettuce leaves for garnishing

Mayonnaise for decorating (optional)

Tomato or radish dice for decorating (optional)

Thin slices of lemon (optional)

❖ ❖ ❖ ❖ ❖

1. In a small saucepan, cover the eggs with cold salted water. Bring to a boil, then cook the eggs at a gentle boil for 10 minutes. Drain and run cold water into the pan to make the eggs easier to peel.

2. Peel the eggs and halve them lengthwise. Carefully add the yolks to a bowl and mash with the crème d'anchois and butter. Season with pepper.

3. Carefully mound the filling in the egg white halves. Line a platter with the lettuce and arrange the eggs on top. If desired, decorate with the mayonnaise, tomato, and/or radish and lemon. Serve.

From Françoise:

• You can make the anchovy cream yourself. Soak anchovy fillets in water to remove some of the saltiness. In a mortar, crush the anchovies with an equal amount of unsalted butter to a paste.

• There's no need to add salt to this dish. The anchovy cream is already quite salty.

FRIED EGGS ON CANADIAN BACON WITH TOMATOES

- *Oeufs frits au bacon* -

❖ INTERMEDIATE   ❖ MODERATE   ❖ 30 MINUTES   ❖ SERVES 4

¾ cup oil

4 slices Canadian or regular bacon

4 large eggs

2 small tomatoes, halved

Salt and pepper

Chopped parsley leaves for sprinkling

continued

1. Brush a medium skillet with a little of the oil, and heat over medium heat. Add the bacon and cook until lightly browned, 1 to 2 minutes per side for Canadian bacon and 3 to 4 minutes per side for regular bacon. Transfer to paper towels to drain; keep warm.

2. In a small skillet, heat the remaining oil over medium-high heat until hot but not smoking. Break 1 egg into a cup. Carefully tilt the skillet and slide the egg into the oil. Immediately reduce the heat to medium. Using a wooden spoon, coax the white around the yolk. Fry the egg until the white is set and the yolk is still soft, about 2 minutes. Using a slotted spoon, transfer the egg to paper towels and keep warm. Fry the remaining eggs.

3. Pour off the oil in the skillet. Increase the heat to high, add the tomato halves and cook until lightly browned.

4. Set each fried egg on a slice of bacon. Arrange them on a platter, alternating with the tomatoes. Season with salt and pepper. Sprinkle the parsley over the tomatoes and serve.

From Françoise:

• Fried eggs, with or without the tomatoes, make an excellent English breakfast or a brunch. Often the eggs are served on slices of toast.

• Drain the fried eggs on paper towels; they will be less greasy—and lighter.

• To turn this dish into a main course, double the quantities.

• Use only the freshest eggs to make this dish and fry only one egg at a time.

STUFFED HARD-BOILED EGGS
WITH CREAMY TOMATO SAUCE
- Oeufs farcis sauce aurore -

❖ EASY   ❖ INEXPENSIVE   ❖ 20 MINUTES   ❖ SERVES 4

6 large eggs

3 tablespoons butter

3 tablespoons all-purpose flour

2 cups milk

Salt and pepper

1 teaspoon tomato paste

Chopped parsley leaves for sprinkling

❖　❖　❖　❖　❖

1. In a small saucepan, cover the eggs with salted cold water. Bring to a boil, then cook the eggs at a gentle boil for 10 minutes. Drain and run cold water into the pan to make the eggs easier to peel.

2. Meanwhile, in a small saucepan, melt the butter over medium heat. Whisk in the flour until it starts foaming. Whisk in the milk. Season with salt and pepper. Bring to a boil, whisking. Whisk in the tomato paste, reduce

the heat to very low, and cook for 10 minutes. Keep warm.

3. Peel the eggs and halve them lengthwise. Carefully add the yolks to a bowl and mash with some of the tomato sauce. Carefully mound the filling in the egg white halves. Transfer the eggs to a serving dish. Spoon the remaining sauce over the top, sprinkle with parsley, and serve.

From Françoise:
• Try to move through this recipe in one go, without interruption, so the finished dish can be served hot.

OLIVE-STUFFED HARD-BOILED EGGS
- *Oeufs durs froids farcis aux olives* -

❖ VERY EASY   ❖ INEXPENSIVE   ❖ 20 MINUTES   ❖ SERVES 4

6 large eggs

Salt

8 or 10 black or green olives, chopped

3 tablespoons butter, softened

Pepper

12 anchovy fillets, halved crosswise

Boston lettuce leaves for decorating (optional)

Tomatoes and other crudités for decorating (optional)

❖ ❖ ❖ ❖ ❖

1. In a small saucepan, cover the eggs with cold salted water. Bring to a boil, then cook the eggs at a gentle boil for 10 minutes. Drain and run cold water into the pan to make the eggs easier to peel.

2. Peel the eggs and halve them lengthwise. Carefully add the yolks to a bowl and mash with the olives and butter. Season with salt and pepper.

3. Carefully mound the filling in the egg white halves and garnish with an anchovy half. If desired, line a platter with the lettuce, arrange the eggs on top, and decorate with tomato and other crudités. Serve.

POACHED EGGS
- Oeufs pochés -

❖ INTERMEDIATE   ❖ INEXPENSIVE   ❖ 10 MINUTES   ❖ SERVES 4

3 tablespoons white vinegar
4 large eggs

Salt and pepper

❖ ❖ ❖ ❖ ❖

1. In a sauté pan or large saucepan, bring 2 quarts of water to a boil with the vinegar. Reduce the heat to medium and keep it at a gentle boil.

2. Break 1 egg at a time into a cup. Holding the cup close to the water, carefully slide the egg into the pan. Using a spoon, coax the white around the yolk. Poach the eggs over medium heat until the white is set and the yolk is still soft, 3 to 4 minutes. Using a slotted spoon, transfer the eggs to paper towels and keep warm.

3. Serve the eggs, passing salt and pepper at the table.

From Françoise:

• What makes a poached egg a flop? You dropped it too far away from the water that was boiling too furiously. You tried to remove it from the water with a fork. You cooked too many eggs in a pan that was too small.

• All you need is a little focus. One trick to making the poaching go smoothly is to cook the eggs a few hours ahead of serving time, not at the last minute when you're frazzled. Refrigerate them in their cooking liquid. Then bring another pan of water to a boil, remove it from the heat, and add the eggs. Using a slotted spoon, lift one out and gently touch it to see if it's hot.

FRIED EGGS
- Oeufs frits -

❖ EASY   ❖ INEXPENSIVE   ❖ 3 MINUTES   ❖ SERVES 4

6 tablespoons oil
8 large eggs

Salt and pepper

1. In a small skillet, heat the oil over medium-high heat until hot but not smoking. Break 1 egg into a cup. Carefully slide the egg into the oil. Immediately reduce the heat to low. Cook the egg, basting constantly with the oil, until the white is set and the yolk is still soft, 1 to 2 minutes. Using a slotted spoon, transfer the egg to a plate and keep warm. Fry the remaining eggs.

2. Serve the eggs, passing salt and pepper at the table.

From Françoise:

• The eggs are perfectly cooked when they're covered with a milky film.

• By all means, serve these eggs with potato galettes.

POACHED EGGS WITH CHEESE SAUCE ON TOASTS
- *Oeufs pochés bohémienne* -

❖ ADVANCED ❖ INEXPENSIVE ❖ 45 MINUTES ❖ SERVES 4

MORNAY SAUCE
3 tablespoons butter
3 tablespoons all-purpose flour
2 cups milk
Salt and pepper
½ cup shredded Gruyère cheese
1 large egg yolk

2 tablespoons butter
4 slices of crustless white sandwich bread
3 tablespoons white vinegar
5 large eggs, 1 hard-boiled, white and yolk
   chopped separately
1 slice of ham, finely chopped
Salt and pepper

❖ ❖ ❖ ❖ ❖

1. Make the Mornay sauce: In a small saucepan, melt the butter over medium heat. Whisk in the flour until it starts foaming. Whisk in the milk. Season with salt and pepper. Bring to a boil, whisking, then reduce the heat to very low and cook for 10 minutes. Remove the pan from the heat and whisk in the cheese and egg yolk.

2. In a large skillet, melt the 2 tablespoons of butter over medium heat. Add the bread slices and cook until golden.

3. In a sauté pan or large saucepan, bring 2 quarts of water to a boil with the vinegar. Reduce the heat to medium and keep it at a gentle boil.

4. Break the 4 remaining eggs, 1 at a time, into a cup. Holding the cup close to the water, carefully slide the egg into the pan. Using a spoon, coax the white around the yolk. Poach the eggs over medium heat until the white is set and the yolk is still soft, 3 to 4 minutes. Using a slotted spoon, transfer the eggs to paper towels and keep warm.

5. Set each egg on a bread slice. Transfer to a platter. Spoon some of the sauce over the eggs. Garnish with the ham and egg white and yolk and serve with salt and pepper.

From Françoise:
• Trim the ragged edges of the poached eggs with a large cookie cutter or simply use a knife.

POACHED EGGS WITH BÉARNAISE SAUCE IN PUFF PASTRY SHELLS

- *Oeufs pochés en bouchées* -

❖ ADVANCED   ❖ MODERATE   ❖ 1 HOUR   ❖ SERVES 4

1 tablespoon butter

¼ pound white mushrooms, thinly sliced

Lemon juice for sprinkling

Salt and pepper

2 tablespoons crème fraîche

3 tablespoons white vinegar

4 large eggs

4 baked puff pastry shells

BÉARNAISE SAUCE

¼ cup vinegar

2 shallots, finely chopped

2 teaspoons tarragon leaves

2 large egg yolks

Salt and pepper

7 tablespoons butter, softened

❖ ❖ ❖ ❖ ❖

1. In a medium skillet, melt the 1 tablespoon of butter over medium-high heat. Add the mushrooms, sprinkle with lemon juice, and season with salt and pepper. Cook until lightly browned. Stir in the crème fraîche.

2. Make the béarnaise sauce: In a small, heavy saucepan over medium heat, simmer the vinegar with the shallots and tarragon until the liquid evaporates. Remove the pan from the heat and let cool slightly. Whisk in the egg yolks with 2 tablespoons of cold water until light, about 30 seconds. Season with salt and pepper. Set the pan over very low heat and whisk constantly until the mixture thickens and becomes fluffy. Remove the pan from the heat and gradually add the butter, whisking so it melts creamily. Keep the sauce warm in a water bath.

3. In a sauté pan or large saucepan, bring 2 quarts of water to a boil with the vinegar.

Reduce the heat to medium and keep it at a gentle boil.

4. Break 1 egg at a time into a cup. Holding the cup close to the water, carefully slide the egg into the pan. Using a spoon, coax the white around the yolk. Poach the eggs over medium heat until the white is set and the yolk is still soft, 3 to 4 minutes. Using a slotted spoon, transfer the eggs to paper towels and keep warm.

5. Meanwhile, preheat the oven to 300 degrees. Set the puff pastry shells on a baking sheet and warm in the oven. Reheat the mushrooms and spoon them into the pastry shells. Set a poached egg on top and spoon in some of the béarnaise sauce. Serve immediately, passing the remaining sauce separately.

POACHED EGGS IN TARRAGON ASPIC

- *Oeufs pochés en gelée à l'estragon* -

❖ ADVANCED   ❖ INEXPENSIVE   ❖ 30 MINUTES, PLUS 2 TO 3 HOURS CHILLING   ❖ SERVES 4

3 tablespoons white vinegar

4 large eggs

1 envelope (1 tablespoon) unflavored powdered gelatin

Salt and pepper

1 tarragon sprig, stem removed

2 slices of ham, finely chopped

Boston lettuce leaves for decorating

❖ ❖ ❖ ❖ ❖

1. In a sauté pan or large saucepan, bring 2 quarts of water to a boil with the vinegar. Reduce the heat to medium and keep it at a gentle boil.

2. Break 1 egg at a time into a cup. Holding the cup close to the water, carefully slide the egg into the pan. Using a spoon, coax the white around the yolk. Poach the eggs over medium heat until the white is set and the yolk is still soft, 3 to 4 minutes. Using a slotted spoon, transfer the eggs to paper towels. Let cool completely.

3. In a small saucepan, sprinkle the gelatin over ¼ cup of water. Let stand until spongy, about 3 minutes. Set the saucepan over medium heat and heat until the water is warm and the gelatin melts, about 1 minute. Stir in 1 ¾ cups of water and season with salt and pepper.

4. Pour ¼ inch of the gelatin mixture into ramekins or other individual molds, turning to coat the sides, and refrigerate for 15 minutes.

5. Moisten the tarragon leaves in the remaining gelatin. Arrange the leaves in a star pattern on the bottom of each ramekin. Refrigerate for 10 minutes.

6. Set 1 poached egg, yolk side down, in each ramekin. Add the ham and cover with more of the gelatin. Refrigerate until firm, 2 to 3 hours.

7. Line salad plates with the lettuce. Unmold the aspics on top and serve.

From Françoise:

• To simplify the recipe, you can replace the poached eggs with eggs mollets or hard-boiled eggs.

• You might embellish the eggs in aspic with slices of ham, cut into diamond shapes; hard-boiled egg rounds; chervil sprigs; and so on.

• If there's any gelatin left, refrigerate it until set, then crush it with a fork and decorate the plates with it.

• The aspics will slip out of the ramekins more easily if you dip the bottoms in hot water for 3 or 4 seconds.

EGGS

EGGS POACHED IN RED WINE SAUCE

- *Oeufs pochés en meurette* -

❖ INTERMEDIATE   ❖ MODERATE   ❖ 40 MINUTES   ❖ SERVES 4

3 tablespoons butter

¼ pound thick-sliced bacon, cut crosswise into
  ¼-inch-thick strips

1 onion, finely chopped

2 cups red wine

3 garlic cloves, crushed

1 bouquet garni made with parsley, thyme,
  and bay leaf

Salt and pepper

8 slices of crustless white sandwich bread,
  toasted

8 large eggs

2 tablespoons all-purpose flour

❖ ❖ ❖ ❖ ❖

1. In a sauté pan or large saucepan, melt 1 tablespoon of the butter over low heat. Add the bacon and cook until lightly browned. Using a slotted spoon, transfer the bacon to a plate. Add the onion and cook until lightly browned. Stir in the wine, 2 cups of water, 1 garlic clove, and the bouquet garni and season with salt and pepper. Bring to a boil over medium high heat, then reduce the heat to low and cook for 15 minutes. Remove the bouquet garni.

2. Rub the toasts with the remaining 2 garlic cloves and arrange in a serving dish.

3. Break 1 egg at a time into a cup. Holding the cup close to the wine, carefully slide the egg into the saucepan. Using a spoon, coax the white around the yolk. Poach the eggs over medium heat until the white is set and the yolk is still soft, 3 to 4 minutes. Using a slotted spoon, transfer the eggs to the toasts.

4. Strain the sauce. Return it to the pan with the bacon and bring to a boil. Mash the flour with the remaining 2 tablespoons of butter. Whisk in this paste and simmer for 2 minutes. Pour the sauce over the eggs and serve.

From Françoise:

• Since I don't especially like the purplish color of the sauce, I like to add a half-teaspoon of tomato paste to brighten it.

• This sauce is also good with freshwater fish, such as pike, trout, and eel.

• To serve eggs en meurette as a starter, cut the ingredients in half.

• If your bacon is very smoky, bring it to a boil in water, then drain it before starting the recipe so it won't overwhelm the sauce.

• This recipe comes from Burgundy, so pour a red Burgundy with it.

SHIRRED EGGS

- Oeuf sur le plat -

❖ VERY EASY ❖ INEXPENSIVE ❖ 5 MINUTES ❖ SERVES 1

1 tablespoon butter
Salt and pepper

2 large eggs

❖ ❖ ❖ ❖ ❖

1. In a small heatproof gratin pan or skillet, melt the butter over medium heat. Season with salt and pepper. Break the eggs into the skillet. Cook until the whites are set and the yolks are still soft. Serve immediately.

From Françoise:
• What makes shirred eggs a flop? The eggs weren't fresh enough. The yolk was broken when the egg was cracked into the pan.

They were cooked at too high a heat, so the edges got crusty before the yolk was cooked. You sprinkled salt on the yolks and white specks appeared on the surface, making it unappetizing.

• Break the eggs one by one in a ramekin before sliding them into the pan. That way you can check the freshness and you can be sure you're not adding a broken egg yolk to the pan.

EGGS

SHIRRED EGGS WITH GRUYÈRE

- Oeufs sur le plat au Gruyère -

❖ VERY EASY ❖ INEXPENSIVE ❖ 10 MINUTES ❖ SERVES 4

2 tablespoons butter
Salt and pepper

8 large eggs
½ cup shredded Gruyère cheese

❖ ❖ ❖ ❖ ❖

1. In each of 4 small heatproof gratin pans, melt ½ tablespoon of the butter over medium heat. Season with salt and pepper.

2. Break 2 eggs into each pan. Sprinkle with the cheese and cook until the whites are set and the yolks are still soft. Serve immediately.

From Françoise:
• If you don't have individual heatproof gratin pans, use a large skillet and cook 4 of the eggs at a time.

• To turn eggs "sur le plat" into eggs "miroir," slide them under the broiler briefly until shimmering with a film lightly coating the yolks.

MOLLET EGGS IN RED WINE SAUCE

- *Oeufs mollets en matelote* -

❖ EASY   ❖ INEXPENSIVE   ❖ 1 HOUR   ❖ SERVES 4

2 tablespoons butter

¼ pound thick-sliced pancetta, cut crosswise
  into ¼-inch-thick strips

¼ pound pearl onions, peeled

1 ½ tablespoons all-purpose flour

¾ cup red wine

Salt and pepper

1 shallot, finely chopped

1 garlic clove, finely chopped

¾ pound white mushrooms, quartered lengthwise

1 bouquet garni made with parsley, thyme, and
  bay leaf

1 whole clove

4 large eggs

2 slices of crustless white sandwich bread,
  toasted, each cut into 2 triangles

❖ ❖ ❖ ❖ ❖

1. In a small saucepan, melt 1 tablespoon of the butter over medium heat. Add the pancetta and onions and cook until lightly browned. Using a slotted spoon, transfer them to a plate.

2. In the same pan, melt the remaining 1 tablespoon of butter. Whisk in the flour until it starts foaming. Whisk in the wine and ¾ cup of water. Season with salt and pepper. Bring to a boil, whisking. Add the bacon, onions, shallot, garlic, mushrooms, bouquet garni, and whole clove. Cook over low heat for about 30 minutes. Remove the bouquet garni.

3. Meanwhile, in a small saucepan, combine the eggs with cold salted water to cover. Bring to a boil over medium heat, then immediately remove the pan from the heat and leave the eggs in the water for 3 minutes before removing. Carefully peel them. Add them to the sauce briefly.

4. Transfer the eggs and sauce to a serving dish, garnish with the toasts, and serve.

From Françoise:

• The sauce can be prepared ahead, which will give you a head start of at least 45 minutes. Reheat it at the same time as you cook the eggs mollets (which could be replaced with poached or hard-boiled eggs).

• Meurette and matelote sauces are related. Their base of wine, white or red, serves as the poaching liquid for eggs or firm-fleshed river fish. Like all regional specialties, meurettes and matelotes vary in the details.

• For a smoky flavor, use bacon instead of pancetta.

FLAT OMELET WITH MUSHROOMS, BACON, AND POTATOES

- *Omelette forestière* -

❖ EASY   ❖ MODERATE   ❖ 20 MINUTES   ❖ SERVES 4

3 tablespoons oil

2 ounces thick-sliced bacon, cut crosswise into
  ¼-inch-thick strips

¼ pound white mushrooms, thinly sliced

2 or 3 boiled potatoes, thinly sliced crosswise

6 large eggs

Salt and pepper

3 tablespoons chopped parsley leaves

❖ ❖ ❖ ❖ ❖

1. In a large skillet, heat the oil over medium heat. Add the bacon, mushrooms, and potatoes and cook until lightly browned, then reduce the heat to low and cook, stirring occasionally, for 5 minutes.

2. Meanwhile, in a bowl, beat the eggs with salt, pepper, and the parsley. Pour into the skillet and cook over medium heat, pulling the egg that is cooking at the sides of the pan toward the center and tipping the pan to allow the uncooked egg to flow underneath. When the bottom is browned and the top is almost firm, slide the omelet (or turn it over) onto a round platter and serve.

From Françoise:

• Adding fresh morel or cèpe mushrooms to this omelet, even if only a few, is one of the best ways of eating them. These wild mushrooms are more deeply flavored than white mushrooms.

• Note that dried morels and cèpes are very practical, if fairly expensive. They need a good half hour's soaking in warm water before they can be cooked.

• If your bacon is particularly smoky or salty, bring it to a boil in water, then drain before sautéing it in Step 1.

EGGS

CLASSIC OMELET

- Omelette -

❖ VERY EASY   ❖ INEXPENSIVE   ❖ 10 MINUTES   ❖ SERVES 4

7 large eggs
Salt and pepper

2 tablespoons butter
1 tablespoon oil

❖ ❖ ❖ ❖ ❖

1. In a bowl, beat the eggs with salt and pepper. In a large skillet, melt the butter in the oil, then beat it into the eggs.

2. Heat the skillet over medium-high heat until hot. Pour in the eggs, reduce the heat to medium, and cook, pulling the egg that is cooking at the sides of the pan toward the center and tipping the pan to allow the uncooked egg to flow underneath. When the edges are set and the center is still creamy, fold the omelet in half and slide it onto a warmed platter. Serve at once.

From Françoise:
• The simplest way to make an omelet is to use a nonstick skillet. If you don't have one, use a good, heavy skillet and keep it spotless. Even a trace of food will make your omelet stick.

• If despite everything, your omelet does stick, it's because the eggs were poured into a skillet that wasn't hot enough. Or the skillet was used to cook something else and it wasn't perfectly cleaned and dried.

• Some variations: Just before folding the omelet, add a sautéed dice of potatoes, sliced, sautéed mushrooms, chopped fines herbes (parsley, chives, chervil, tarragon), a sautéed dice of bacon, chopped baked or cured ham, tiny shrimp cooked with a little cream, and so on.

MUSHROOM OMELET

- Omelette aux champignons -

❖ EASY   ❖ INEXPENSIVE   ❖ 10 MINUTES   ❖ SERVES 4

2 tablespoons oil
5 ounces white mushrooms, thinly sliced
Salt and pepper

7 large eggs
1 tablespoon butter

1. In a small saucepan, heat 1 tablespoon of the oil over high heat. Add the mushrooms, season with salt and pepper, and cook, stirring, for 1 to 2 minutes.

2. In a bowl, beat the eggs with salt and pepper. In a large skillet, melt the butter in the remaining 1 tablespoon of oil, then beat it into the eggs.

3. Heat the skillet over medium-high heat until hot. Pour in the eggs, reduce the heat to medium, and cook, pulling the egg that is cooking at the sides of the pan toward the center and tipping the pan to allow the uncooked egg to flow underneath. When the edges are set and the center is still creamy, add half the mushrooms. Fold the omelet in half and slide it onto a warmed platter. Mound the remaining mushrooms at both ends of the omelet and serve at once.

From Françoise:

• The mushrooms or other filling must never be cooked in the skillet destined for the omelet. If you don't believe me, you're courting disaster. Your omelet will stick.

• Don't add any more fat to the skillet before pouring in the eggs. It will be amply filmed with the butter or oil you've just heated in it.

FLAT OMELET WITH DICED POTATOES
- *Omelette parmentier* -

❖ VERY EASY   ❖ MODERATE   ❖ 20 MINUTES   ❖ SERVES 4

3 tablespoons oil
2 boiled potatoes, cut into ¼-inch dice

5 large eggs
Salt and pepper

❖ ❖ ❖ ❖ ❖

1. In a large skillet, heat the oil over medium heat. Add the potatoes and cook, stirring occasionally, until golden brown.

2. Meanwhile, in a bowl, beat the eggs with salt and pepper. Pour into the skillet and cook, pulling the egg that is cooking at the sides of the pan toward the center and tipping the pan to allow the uncooked egg to flow underneath. When the edges are set and the center is still creamy, set a round platter over the skillet and invert it to turn out the omelet. Serve.

From Françoise:

• In my omelet parmentier, I like to add all the fines herbes I have around—chives, chervil, parsley. Some people like to add a little ham or sautéed bacon, and that's also good.

• You can increase the amount of potatoes or eggs, too.

OMELET WITH VELVETY RED PEPPER STEW
- *Omelette à l'andalouse* -

❖ EASY ❖ INEXPENSIVE ❖ 45 MINUTES ❖ SERVES 4

3 tablespoons butter
2 onions, finely chopped
½ pound tomatoes, peeled and chopped
1 small red bell pepper, thinly sliced

7 large eggs
Salt and pepper
1 tablespoon oil

❖ ❖ ❖ ❖ ❖

1. In a large saucepan, melt 2 tablespoons of the butter over medium heat. Add the onions and cook until lightly browned. Add the tomatoes and bell pepper, season with salt and pepper, reduce the heat to low, and cook until very soft, about 30 minutes.

2. In a bowl, beat the eggs with salt and pepper. In a large skillet, melt the remaining 1 tablespoon of butter in the oil, then beat it into the eggs.

3. Heat the skillet over medium-high heat until hot. Pour in the eggs, reduce the heat to medium, and cook, pulling the egg that is cooking at the sides of the pan toward the center and tipping the pan to allow the uncooked egg to flow underneath. When the edges are set and the center is still creamy, add half the pepper mixture. Fold the omelet in half and slide it onto a warmed platter. Mound the remaining pepper mixture at both ends of the omelet and serve at once.

From Françoise:
• Do not cook the pepper mixture in the skillet destined for the omelet or it will stick.

SOUFFLÉED OMELET
- *Omelette du Mont-Saint-Michel* -

❖ INTERMEDIATE ❖ INEXPENSIVE ❖ 15 MINUTES ❖ SERVES 4

6 large eggs, separated
2 tablespoons crème fraîche
Salt and pepper

3 tablespoons butter
Mixed chopped parsley, chervil, and tarragon,
  for sprinkling

1. In a soup plate, beat the egg yolks lightly with the crème fraîche and season with salt and pepper. In another soup plate, beat the egg whites with a little salt and pepper until frothy.

2. In a large skillet, melt the butter over medium heat. When the butter foams, pour in the yolks, then the whites, and cook, pulling the egg that is cooking at the sides of the pan toward the center and tipping the pan to allow the uncooked egg to flow underneath. When the edges are set and the center is still creamy, fold the omelet in half and slide it onto a warmed platter. Sprinkle with the herbs and serve at once.

From Françoise:

• I've chosen the easiest of the Mont-Saint-Michel omelets, because, of course, there are several variations on this piece of gastronomic history found in the restaurants on this tiny island off the Normandy coast. The egg whites should not be beaten until stiff, but only lightly, as for a regular omelet.

• I heartily recommend a nonstick skillet for this omelet.

SOUFFLÉED OMELET WITH GRUYÈRE

- Omelette soufflée au fromage -

❖ INTERMEDIATE   ❖ INEXPENSIVE   ❖ 20 MINUTES   ❖ SERVES 4

7 or 8 large eggs, separated
Salt and pepper
1 cup shredded Gruyère cheese

3 tablespoons butter
3 tablespoons crème fraîche

❖ ❖ ❖ ❖ ❖

1. Preheat the oven to 425 degrees. In a bowl, beat the yolks with salt, pepper, and a few pinches of the cheese. In another bowl, beat the egg whites until stiff. Beat a quarter of the egg whites into the yolks, then fold this lightened mixture into the remaining whites.

2. In a large heatproof skillet, melt the butter over high heat. Scrape in the eggs, reduce the heat to medium, and cook, shaking the pan so the omelet doesn't stick, until the bottom is browned and the center is still creamy. Spread the crème fraîche in the center and sprinkle the remaining cheese over the top.

3. Transfer the skillet to the hot oven and bake with the door open until the omelet is puffed and lightly browned, 3 or 4 minutes. Serve at once.

From Françoise:

• I recommend a nonstick skillet for all your omelets, and in particular when they are stuffed with Gruyère, tomatoes, and so on.

• Gruyère's sister cheese, fruity Comté, is often preferred for recipes that call for Gruyère, such as soufflés and gratins. To make fondue, Comté is often blended with other cheeses in the Gruyère family, for instance, Emmental and Beaufort.

BACON OMELET

- Omelette au lard -

❖ VERY EASY   ❖ INEXPENSIVE   ❖ 15 MINUTES   ❖ SERVES 4

3 ounces thick-sliced bacon, cut crosswise into
   ¼-inch-thick strips
6 large eggs

Salt and pepper
1 tablespoon butter
1 tablespoon oil

❖ ❖ ❖ ❖ ❖

1. In a small saucepan of water, add the bacon and bring to a boil; drain.

2. In a bowl, beat the eggs with the bacon, salt, and pepper. In a large skillet, melt the butter in the oil, then beat it into the eggs.

3. Heat the skillet over medium-high heat until hot. Pour in the eggs, reduce the heat to medium, and cook, pulling the egg that is cooking at the sides of the pan toward the center and tipping the pan to allow the uncooked egg to flow underneath. When the edges are set and the center is still creamy, fold the omelet in half and slide it onto a warmed platter. Serve at once.

From Françoise:
• When I make an omelet with a dry-cured ham or country ham, I add it to the eggs without blanching it. However, I don't salt the eggs at all, since the ham is already salty.

• Do not cook the bacon in the skillet destined for the omelet. Or if you do, clean and dry it meticulously between preparations, otherwise—I can't say this enough—the omelet will stick.

SHRIMP OMELET

- Omelette aux crevettes -

❖ VERY EASY   ❖ INEXPENSIVE   ❖ 15 MINUTES   ❖ SERVES 4

2 tablespoons butter
3 ounces very small shrimp, shelled and chopped
Pepper

7 large eggs
Salt
1 tablespoon oil

1. In a small saucepan, melt 1 tablespoon of the butter over low heat. Add the shrimp and cook until white throughout. Season with pepper

2. In a bowl, beat the eggs with salt and pepper. In a large skillet, melt the remaining 1 tablespoon of butter in the oil, then beat it into the eggs.

3. Heat the skillet over medium-high heat until hot. Pour in the eggs, reduce the heat to medium, and cook, pulling the egg that is cooking at the sides of the pan toward the center and tipping the pan to allow the uncooked egg to flow underneath. When the edges are set and the center is still creamy, add the shrimp. Fold the omelet in half and slide it onto a warmed platter. Serve at once.

From Françoise:
• If you can find *crevettes grises*, these tiny, sweet shrimp are delicious in this omelet. They are so small, they are often eaten whole, in the shell.

• Adding a tablespoon of crème fraîche at the same time as the shrimp will get you compliments.

• Shrimp are more or less salty. Take that into account when seasoning the eggs.

• You can also use shelled frozen shrimp in this recipe. One-and-a-half ounces will do it.

DRY-CURED HAM OMELET
- *Omelette fermière* -

❖ VERY EASY   ❖ INEXPENSIVE   ❖ 15 MINUTES   ❖ SERVES 4

3 tablespoons butter
1 slice of dry-cured ham, such as jambon de
   Bayonne, prosciutto, or serrano ham, diced
6 large eggs

2 tablespoons chopped fines herbes
   (parsley, chives, chervil, tarragon)
Salt and pepper

❖   ❖   ❖   ❖   ❖

1. In a small skillet, melt 1 tablespoon of the butter over medium-high heat. Add the ham and cook, turning once, until lightly browned.

2. In a bowl, beat the eggs with the ham, herbs, salt, and pepper. In a large skillet, melt the remaining 2 tablespoons of butter, then beat it into the eggs.

3. Heat the skillet over medium-high heat until hot. Pour in the eggs, reduce the heat to medium, and cook, pulling the egg that is cooking at the sides of the pan toward the center and tipping the pan to allow the uncooked egg to flow underneath. When the bottom is browned and the top is almost firm, set a round platter over the skillet and invert it to turn out the omelet. Serve.

From Françoise:
• Get the skillet very hot before adding the eggs so they don't stick. Quickly reduce the heat to medium, however, so the omelet can cook evenly.

PUFFY OMELET WITH CHEESE

- *Omelette allemande* -

❖ INTERMEDIATE   ❖ INEXPENSIVE   ❖ 20 MINUTES   ❖ SERVES 6

1 tablespoon all-purpose flour

¾ cup milk

6 large eggs, separated

⅓ cup shredded Gruyère cheese

Salt and pepper

3 tablespoons oil

❖ ❖ ❖ ❖ ❖

1. In a bowl, beat the flour with the milk, egg yolks, cheese, salt, and pepper. In another bowl, beat the egg whites until stiff. Beat a quarter of the egg whites into the yolks, then fold this lightened mixture into the remaining whites.

2. In a large skillet, heat the oil over high heat. Scrape in the eggs, reduce the heat to medium, and cook until the bottom is browned and the center is still creamy. Set a round platter over the skillet and invert the omelet on the platter. Slide the omelet back into the skillet and cook until browned on the bottom. Serve immediately in the skillet.

From Françoise:

• This unusual, economical, and substantial omelet will satisfy the heartiest appetites.

• Serve it quickly, while it's still risen, directly from the skillet.

• Instead of shredded Gruyère cheese, you can accent this omelet with chopped fines herbes (parsley, chives, chervil, tarragon).

• Always break your eggs one by one into a cup. Don't add it to the rest until you're sure of its freshness.

• Discard any egg with a yolk that's lusterless, flattened, spotted with white, or breaks easily; or an egg with a runny white; or one that smells bad.

LEFTOVER-PASTA OMELET

- *Omelette aux pâtes* -

❖ VERY EASY ❖ INEXPENSIVE ❖ 15 MINUTES ❖ SERVES 4

2 tablespoons butter

½ to 1 cup leftover pasta, chopped if large

5 large eggs

Salt and pepper

1 tablespoon oil

❖ ❖ ❖ ❖ ❖

1. In a small saucepan, melt 1 tablespoon of the butter over low heat. Add the pasta and warm it.

2. In a bowl, beat the eggs with the pasta, salt, and pepper. In a large skillet, melt the remaining 1 tablespoon of butter in the oil, then beat it into the eggs.

3. Heat the skillet over medium-high heat until hot. Pour in the eggs, reduce the heat to medium, and cook, pulling the egg that is cooking at the sides of the pan toward the center and tipping the pan to allow the uncooked egg to flow underneath. When the edges are set and the center is still creamy, fold the omelet in half and slide it onto a warmed platter. Serve at once.

From Françoise:

• When I can, I mix a little finely chopped ham or even a bit of shredded Gruyère into the eggs. It's a small thing that makes a good dish even better.

• You might add more pasta or eggs, depending upon what you have on hand.

• If there's a lot of pasta and not so much egg, you'll have a difficult time folding the omelet. In that case, simply slide the flat omelet onto the platter.

SORREL OMELET WITH HAM AND CHIVES

- *Omelette nivernaise à l'oseille* -

❖ VERY EASY ❖ INEXPENSIVE ❖ 30 MINUTES ❖ SERVES 4

3 tablespoons butter

1 handful of sorrel, large stems removed, coarsely chopped

8 large eggs

1 slice of ham, finely chopped

1 tablespoon chopped chives

Salt and pepper

continued

1. In a small saucepan, melt 1 tablespoon of the butter over low heat. Add the sorrel and cook, stirring occasionally, for 5 to 7 minutes. Drain.

2. In a bowl, beat the eggs with the sorrel, ham, chives, salt, and pepper. In a large skillet, melt the remaining 2 tablespoons of butter, then beat it into the eggs.

3. Heat the skillet over medium-high heat until hot. Pour in the eggs, reduce the heat to medium and cook, pulling the egg that is cooking at the sides of the pan toward the center and tipping the pan to allow the uncooked egg to flow underneath. When the edges are set and the center is still creamy, fold the omelet in half and slide it onto a warmed platter. Serve at once.

SOUFFLÉED OMELET WITH ROQUEFORT
- *Omelette mousseline au roquefort* -

❖ INTERMEDIATE   ❖ INEXPENSIVE   ❖ 15 MINUTES   ❖ SERVES 4

7 large eggs, separated
1 cup finely crumbled Roquefort cheese
3 tablespoons crème fraîche

Pepper
2 tablespoons butter

❖ ❖ ❖ ❖ ❖

1. Preheat the broiler. In a bowl, beat the yolks with the cheese, crème fraîche, and pepper. In another bowl, beat the egg whites until stiff. Beat a quarter of the egg whites into the yolks, then fold this lightened mixture into the remaining whites.

2. In a large skillet, melt the butter over high heat. Scrape in the eggs, reduce the heat to medium, and cook, shaking the pan so the omelet doesn't stick, until the bottom is browned and the center is still creamy.

3. Slide the skillet under the broiler and cook until the omelet is puffed and lightly browned. Serve at once.

From Françoise:
• The ideal pan for making a souffléed omelet is a nonstick oval, typically used for cooking fish. But any nonstick skillet, even round, will do. What's important is that the omelet not adhere to the pan!

EGG SOUFFLÉ RING

- Pain d'oeufs -

❖ INTERMEDIATE   ❖ INEXPENSIVE   ❖ 45 MINUTES   ❖ SERVES 4

Butter for brushing

¾ cup milk

2 slices crustless white sandwich bread, torn into pieces

2 large eggs, separated

Salt and pepper

Freshly grated nutmeg

Finely chopped parsley leaves

3 hard-boiled eggs, finely chopped

Tomato sauce for serving (optional)

❖ ❖ ❖ ❖ ❖

1. Preheat the oven to 400 degrees. Generously brush a ring mold with butter.

2. In a medium saucepan, warm the milk. Remove the pan from the heat, add the bread, and let soak. Mash with a fork, then beat in the egg yolks, salt, pepper, nutmeg, parsley, and hard-boiled eggs. In a bowl, beat the egg whites until stiff. Beat a quarter of the egg whites into the yolk mixture, then fold this lightened mixture into the remaining whites.

3. Scrape the soufflé mixture into the mold and set in a roasting pan. Fill the roasting pan with hot water to come halfway up the sides of the mold. Transfer to the oven and bake until a knife inserted in the center comes out clean, about 30 minutes.

4. Remove the mold from the water bath. Run a knife around the soufflé. Invert a round platter over the mold. Holding the mold and platter together, quickly invert the soufflé onto the platter. Serve as is or, if desired, spoon some of the tomato sauce (heated) over and around the soufflé and serve, passing more tomato sauce separately.

From Françoise:

• You can substitute a loaf pan for the ring mold.

GRATIN OF PASTA AND HARD-BOILED EGGS WITH TOMATO SAUCE

- *Pâtes aux oeufs durs gratinées* -

❖ EASY   ❖ INEXPENSIVE   ❖ 30 MINUTES   ❖ SERVES 4

Salt

½ pound short pasta

6 large eggs

1 tablespoon butter, plus more for brushing

½ cup shredded Gruyère cheese

TOMATO SAUCE

3 tablespoons butter

3 tablespoons all-purpose flour

3 tablespoons tomato paste (about 2 ½ ounces)

1 garlic clove, crushed

1 thyme sprig

1 bay leaf

Salt and pepper

❖ ❖ ❖ ❖ ❖

1. Bring a medium saucepan of salted water to a boil. Add the pasta and cook until al dente; drain.

2. Meanwhile, in a small saucepan, cover the eggs with cold salted water. Bring to a boil, then cook the eggs at a gentle boil for 10 minutes. Drain and run cold water into the pan to make the eggs easier to peel.

3. Make the tomato sauce: In a medium saucepan, melt the butter over medium heat. Whisk in the flour until it starts foaming. Whisk in the tomato paste, garlic, thyme, bay leaf, and 2 cups of water and season with salt and pepper. Bring to a boil, whisking, until it thickens, then reduce the heat to very low and cook for 10 minutes. Remove the garlic, thyme, and bay leaf.

4. Preheat the broiler. Butter a gratin dish. Peel the eggs and halve them lengthwise. Spread the pasta in the gratin dish, leaving a space in the center. Arrange the egg halves in the center. Ladle some of the tomato sauce over the top. Sprinkle with the cheese and dot with the butter. Broil on the top shelf of the oven until lightly browned. Serve, passing the remaining tomato sauce separately.

CLASSIC CHEESE SOUFFLÉ
- Soufflé au fromage -

❖ ADVANCED ❖ MODERATE ❖ 45 MINUTES ❖ SERVES 4

2 tablespoons butter, plus more for brushing
2 tablespoons all-purpose flour
1 cup milk

Salt and pepper
3 large eggs
¾ cup shredded Gruyère cheese

❖ ❖ ❖ ❖ ❖

1. In a medium saucepan, melt the butter over medium heat. Whisk in the flour until it starts foaming. Whisk in the milk. Season with salt and pepper. Bring to a boil, whisking. Reduce the heat to low and cook until it thickens. Remove the pan from the heat and whisk in the cheese.

2. Preheat the oven to 350 degrees. Generously butter a soufflé dish.

3. Break the eggs, adding the whites to a large bowl and the yolks to the saucepan with the sauce. Beat in the yolks. Beat the egg whites with a pinch of salt until stiff. Beat a quarter of the egg whites into the yolk mixture, then fold this lightened mixture into the remaining whites.

4. Scrape the soufflé mixture into the soufflé dish. Bake in the oven until risen and browned, 25 to 30 minutes. Serve immediately.

From Françoise:
• Your soufflé won't rise properly unless the egg whites are beaten to very stiff peaks.

• Before beating them, add a pinch of salt so they whip better.

• Fold together the beaten egg whites and egg yolk mixture delicately. Use a large spoon or rubber spatula—not a whisk—so the egg whites stay puffy.

• If you want your soufflé to rise more evenly, run a table knife around the edge to make a groove.

• Bake the soufflé only when your guests have arrived, not before. The 25- to 30-minute cooking time is precise. Remember that a soufflé doesn't wait, guests do.

• Using individual ramekins instead of a large soufflé dish is an attractive alternative. What's more, the soufflés don't deflate as fast, and the baking is a little shorter.

• Don't start celebrating too early! Your soufflé isn't done just because it's well risen. Wait a little. You can leave it in the oven longer than you think, and a soufflé that's cooked through doesn't fall so quickly.

• After your third or fourth try, making a soufflé will seem easy.

EGGS

MEAT & POULTRY

SAUTÉED VEAL CHOPS WITH CRÈME FRAÎCHE
- Côtes de veau à la crème -

❖ VERY EASY   ❖ EXPENSIVE   ❖ 15 MINUTES   ❖ SERVES 4

4 veal chops or cutlets
Salt and pepper
All-purpose flour for dusting

2 tablespoons butter
3 or 4 tablespoons crème fraîche

❖ ❖ ❖ ❖ ❖

1. Season the veal with salt and pepper and dust lightly with flour, patting off the excess.

2. In a large skillet, melt the butter over medium heat. Add the veal and cook, turning once, until golden brown, 4 to 5 minutes per side, depending on the thickness. Transfer to a warmed platter.

3. Add the crème fraîche to the skillet and boil, scraping up any brown bits stuck to the bottom. Pour over the veal and serve.

From Françoise:
• You may need to cook the veal chops or cutlets in 2 batches if your skillet won't hold the meat easily.

• For a decadent addition, pour 1 or 2 tablespoons of Cognac or Armagnac into the pan when the veal is nicely browned and bring it to a boil. Tilt the pan and carefully ignite the Cognac. When the flames subside, transfer the veal to a platter and continue with the recipe.

VEAL CHOPS STUFFED WITH SMOKED HAM AND GRUYÈRE
- Côtes de veau en portefeuille -

❖ EASY   ❖ EXPENSIVE   ❖ 40 MINUTES   ❖ SERVES 4

4 thick veal chops
4 thin slices of smoked ham or Canadian bacon
½ cup shredded Gruyère cheese
Pepper

3 tablespoons butter
Salt
1 lemon, halved

1. Preheat the oven to 425 degrees. Using a thin, sharp knife, cut a pocket in each veal chop, cutting horizontally to the bone. Tuck a ham or bacon slice in each and spread with 2 pinches of cheese. Season the pockets with pepper. Press on the chops to close, or seal with toothpicks.

2. In a large skillet, melt 2 tablespoons of the butter over medium heat. Cook the chops, turning once, until golden brown, about 5 minutes per side. Season with salt and pepper. Reduce the heat to low, cover, and cook for 5 to 10 minutes, depending on the thickness.

3. Transfer the chops to a gratin dish, sprinkle with the remaining cheese and dot with the remaining 1 tablespoon of butter. Roast on the top shelf of the oven for 10 minutes. Sprinkle with lemon juice and serve.

From Françoise:
• This delicious dish makes a big impression for something that's so easy to prepare. It's not for every day because it's pretty expensive, but whenever it is served it's a hit.

• You can ask your butcher to cut a pocket in the chops. He'll do it better than you can.

• Serve the stuffed chops with spaghetti or steamed rice and a light red wine from Italy (which is where this recipe comes from).

• Also, you might roast 4 whole tomatoes in the oven 5 minutes before adding the chops. They'll be ready at the same time and make a nice accompaniment.

CRISPY VEAL "CHOPS" WITH PAPRIKA
- Côtes de veau à la hongroise -

❖ EASY   ❖ MODERATE   ❖ 20 MINUTES   ❖ SERVES 4

4 slices of crustless white sandwich bread

6 tablespoons milk

10 ounces ground veal, preferably shoulder

1 large egg

1 teaspoon sweet paprika

Salt and pepper

4 to 5 tablespoons dry bread crumbs

3 tablespoons butter, plus more if needed

❖   ❖   ❖   ❖   ❖

1. In a food processor, grind the bread slices into crumbs. Soak these fresh bread crumbs in the milk, then squeeze dry.

2. In a bowl, mix the veal with the moist bread crumbs, the egg, and paprika. Season with salt and pepper. Form into rib chop–shaped patties. Dredge in the dry bread crumbs, patting off the excess.

3. In a large skillet, melt the butter over medium heat. Add the patties and cook, turning once, until golden brown, about 5 minutes per side.

4. Transfer the patties to a warmed platter and serve.

continued

• You can make the patties look more like veal chops by attaching paper frills. Wrap each frill around a piece of uncooked penne and insert it into the narrow end of your patty.

• Sweet paprika isn't fiery, but add it judiciously because not everyone likes its particular taste.

CLASSIC PAN-SEARED VEAL CHOPS
- *Côtes de veau à la poêle* -

❖ VERY EASY   ❖ EXPENSIVE   ❖ 15 MINUTES   ❖ SERVES 4

4 veal chops or cutlets
Salt and pepper

All-purpose flour for dusting
2 tablespoons butter

❖ ❖ ❖ ❖ ❖

1. Season the veal with salt and pepper and dust lightly with flour, patting off the excess.

2. In a large skillet, melt the butter over medium heat. Add the veal and cook, turning once, until golden brown, 4 to 5 minutes per side, depending on the thickness. Transfer to a warmed platter and serve.

From Françoise:

• I often sprinkle my veal chops with a few pinches of aromatic herbs, like thyme, marjoram, or even rosemary.

• Dusting the meat with flour is not crucial, but it does help the chop or cutlet to brown nicely and keeps it moist.

• Don't cover the skillet or cook at too low a temperature or the meat will lose its juiciness.

CREAMY PAN-SEARED VEAL CHOPS WITH AVOCADO

- *Côtes de veau à l'avocat* -

❖ EASY ❖ EXPENSIVE ❖ 30 MINUTES ❖ SERVES 4

2 firm, ripe avocados
3 tablespoons butter
4 veal chops or cutlets

Salt and pepper
¾ cup Banyuls wine
½ cup crème fraîche

❖ ❖ ❖ ❖ ❖

1. Halve the avocados lengthwise and remove the pit. Using a melon baller, scoop out the flesh into nice balls.

2. In a large skillet, melt 1 tablespoon of the butter. Add the avocado and cook, shaking the skillet, until warmed through. Keep the avocado warm between 2 plates set over a pan of simmering water.

3. In the same skillet, melt the remaining 2 tablespoons of butter. Add the veal and cook over medium-high heat, turning once, until golden brown. Season with salt and pepper. Reduce the heat to medium and cook through, about 10 minutes, depending on the thickness. Remove the veal to a platter.

4. Add the wine to the skillet and boil, scraping up any brown bits stuck to the bottom. Add the crème fraîche and let simmer until slightly thickened. Return the veal to the skillet and turn in the sauce to coat. Transfer the meat to a warmed platter.

5. Add the reserved avocado to the skillet and heat through briefly, then pour the avocado and sauce around the veal and serve.

From Françoise:

• Use a melon baller to scoop out the avocado flesh, if possible. With a teaspoon, the balls won't be as nice.

• If you are using veal cutlets, which are drier than chops, prick them with the point of a knife before adding them to the skillet in Step 4, so they absorb the sauce better.

• Banyuls is a sweet wine from the south of France. You could substitute port.

MEAT & POULTRY

POT-ROASTED VEAL CHOPS WITH PANCETTA, PEARL ONIONS, AND POTATOES

- Côtes de veau bonne femme -

❖ VERY EASY   ❖ EXPENSIVE   ❖ 1 HOUR, 30 MINUTES   ❖ SERVES 4

4 veal chops

Salt and pepper

All-purpose flour for dusting

4 tablespoons (½ stick) butter

¼ pound thick-sliced pancetta, cut crosswise
  into ¼-inch-thick strips

4 or 5 pearl onions, peeled

1 pound potatoes, peeled and sliced crosswise

Chopped parsley leaves for sprinkling

❖ ❖ ❖ ❖ ❖

1. Season the veal chops with salt and pepper and dust lightly with flour, patting off the excess.

2. In a large skillet, melt 2 tablespoons of the butter over medium heat. Add the chops and lightly brown them, turning once, 2 to 3 minutes per side. Transfer them to a flameproof casserole.

3. Wipe out the skillet. Melt 1 tablespoon of the butter over medium heat in it. Add the pancetta and lightly brown. Add the onions and cook until both the onions and pancetta are golden brown.

4. Add the pancetta and onions to the veal chops along with the potatoes. Season with salt and pepper and dot with the remaining 1 tablespoon of butter. Reduce the heat to very low, cover, and cook for 1 hour, stirring and turning the chops occasionally.

5. Transfer to a warmed serving dish, sprinkle with parsley, and serve.

From Françoise:

• This dish is even better if you cook it in the oven instead of on top of the stove, and there's less chance of the chops sticking to the casserole. The oven should be moderately hot, about 350 degrees.

• Thick pork chops can also be prepared in the same way.

• Bacon can replace the pancetta.

• To save time, you can add the onions and the pancetta to the casserole without browning them first.

• If the potatoes start to stick, add ¼ cup of boiling water to the casserole.

CRUSTY VEAL CUTLETS WITH LEMON

- Escalopes de veau panées -

❖ EASY   ❖ EXPENSIVE   ❖ 25 MINUTES   ❖ SERVES 4

All-purpose flour for dredging

2 large eggs, lightly beaten

4 to 5 tablespoons dry bread crumbs

Salt and pepper

4 thin veal cutlets

3 tablespoons butter, plus more if needed

1 lemon, cut lengthwise into wedges

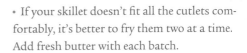

1. In separate soup plates, spread the flour, eggs, and bread crumbs. Season the eggs with salt and pepper. Season the cutlets with salt and pepper, then dredge lightly in flour and dip in the eggs, letting any excess drip back into the plate. Dredge the cutlets in the bread crumbs, pressing lightly to help the crumbs adhere.

2. In a large skillet, melt the butter over medium heat. Add the cutlets and cook, turning once, until golden brown, 4 to 5 minutes per side. Transfer to a warmed platter and serve with the lemon wedges.

From Françoise:

• From the start, melt a good chunk of butter in the skillet because the crumbs really soak it up. If there isn't enough to begin with, the cutlets tend to burn. Don't hesitate to add more butter so the cutlets have plenty to fry in.

• If your skillet doesn't fit all the cutlets comfortably, it's better to fry them two at a time. Add fresh butter with each batch.

PAN-SEARED VEAL CHOPS WITH CHANTERELLES IN PARCHMENT

- Côtes de veau aux girolles en papillotes -

❖ EASY   ❖ EXPENSIVE   ❖ 1 HOUR   ❖ SERVES 4

1 tablespoon oil

1 ¼ pounds chanterelle mushrooms

4 tablespoons (½ stick) butter

4 thin veal chops

¼ cup dry white wine

Salt and pepper

continued

1. Preheat the oven to 400 degrees. In a large skillet, heat the oil over medium heat. Add the mushrooms and cook until they release their liquid, about 5 minutes. Drain.

2. Wipe out the skillet. Melt 2 tablespoons of the butter over medium heat in it. Add the veal chops and lightly brown them, turning once, 2 to 3 minutes per side. Transfer the chops to a platter. Return the mushrooms to the skillet with the wine and season with salt and pepper. Increase the heat to high and cook, stirring occasionally, for 5 to 6 minutes.

3. Tear off 4 very large sheets of parchment or foil and fold them in half. Open each one up and on one half set a veal chop alongside the folded edge. Pile a quarter of the mushrooms on top and dot with the remaining 2 table-spoons of butter. Fold the other half of the sheet over the chops and pleat it all around to seal, if using parchment; if using foil, fold in

the edges. Transfer the papillotes to 2 baking sheets and bake for about 20 minutes.

4. Serve the veal chops in the papillotes and let guests open them at the table.

From Françoise:

• The secret to well-puffed papillotes: Tear off sheets of parchment or foil that are quite long. The meat should be loosely wrapped in its package. Take into account that the veal chop will be placed on one-half of the sheet; the other half is folded over it to make the package. But, in addition, leave a 2- or 3-inch border around each chop so the sheet won't be tightly sealed against it, allowing the package to inflate during baking.

• You can make the papillotes more attractive by cutting the sheets of parchment or foil into heart shapes before filling them.

SAUTÉED VEAL CUTLETS WITH HERBS, CRÈME FRAÎCHE, AND PORT
- *Escalopines de veau à la crème et au porto* -

❖ VERY EASY ❖ EXPENSIVE ❖ 15 MINUTES ❖ SERVES 4

4 thin veal cutlets, cut into 2-inch pieces
Salt and pepper
All-purpose flour for dusting
3 tablespoons butter

Dried sage, marjoram, or herbes de Provence
  for sprinkling
¾ cup port
3 or 4 tablespoons crème fraîche

❖ ❖ ❖ ❖ ❖

1. Season the veal with salt and pepper and dust lightly with flour, patting off the excess.

2. In a large skillet, melt the butter over medium heat. Add the veal and lightly brown,

turning once, 2 to 3 minutes per side. Sprinkle with the dried herbs and transfer to a warmed platter.

3. Add the port to the skillet and boil, scraping up any brown bits stuck to the bottom. Add the crème fraîche and simmer until slightly thickened. Pour over the veal and serve.

From Françoise:
• Serve these veal cutlets with pasta or sautéed spinach.

GOLDEN VEAL CUTLETS WITH ORANGE PAN SAUCE
- Escalopes de veau à l'orange -

❖ VERY EASY   ❖ EXPENSIVE   ❖ 20 MINUTES   ❖ SERVES 4

4 veal cutlets
Salt and pepper
All-purpose flour for dusting

3 tablespoons butter
Juice of 2 oranges

❖ ❖ ❖ ❖ ❖

1. Season the cutlets with salt and pepper and dust lightly with flour, patting off the excess.

2. In a large skillet, melt 2 tablespoons of the butter over medium heat. Add the cutlets and lightly brown, turning once, about 4 minutes per side. Add the orange juice and 2 table-spoons of water, reduce the heat to low, cover, and cook for 5 minutes. Transfer the cutlets to a warmed platter.

3. Add the remaining 1 tablespoon of butter to the skillet, raise the heat, and boil, scraping up any brown bits stuck to the bottom. Pour over the veal and serve.

From Françoise:
• Serve the veal cutlets with steamed rice.

• Try decorating the dish with finely grated orange zest; sprinkle a pinch of it over each cutlet.

• The secret to cutlets that don't curl: Make 1 or 2 snips in the edges with kitchen scissors.

PAN-SEARED VEAL CHOPS WITH TARRAGON AND CRÈME FRAÎCHE

- Côtes de veau à l'estragon -

❖ VERY EASY   ❖ EXPENSIVE   ❖ 30 MINUTES   ❖ SERVES 4

4 veal chops or cutlets
Salt and pepper
All-purpose flour for dusting
3 tablespoons butter

6 tablespoons dry white wine
1 large tarragon sprig, leaves finely chopped,
    stem reserved
¼ cup crème fraîche

❖ ❖ ❖ ❖ ❖

1. Season the veal with salt and pepper and dust lightly with flour, patting off the excess.

2. In a large skillet, melt the butter over medium heat. Add the veal and cook, turning once, until lightly browned, 3 to 4 minutes per side. Add the wine and tarragon stem, reduce the heat to low, cover, and cook for 10 to 15 minutes, depending on the thickness. Transfer the veal to a warmed platter.

3. Remove the tarragon stem. Simmer the pan juices for 1 to 2 minutes, scraping up any brown bits stuck to the bottom. Add the crème fraîche and tarragon leaves and simmer for 1 minute. Taste the sauce for seasoning. Pour over the veal and serve.

From Françoise:

• This dish can be made only with fresh tarragon, so it is seasonal.

• To lessen the risk of seeing your delicious sauce curdle, be careful to avoid bringing the sauce to a full boil after adding the crème fraîche.

PAN-FRIED VEAL CHOPS WITH MUSHROOMS

- Côtes de veau aux champignons -

❖ EASY   ❖ EXPENSIVE   ❖ 15 MINUTES   ❖ SERVES 4

4 veal chops or cutlets
Salt and pepper
All-purpose flour for dusting
3 tablespoons butter

5 ounces white mushrooms, halved or quartered
    if large
Juice of ½ lemon

1. Season the veal with salt and pepper and dust lightly with flour, patting off the excess.

2. In a large skillet, melt the butter over medium heat. Add the veal and cook until the bottom is golden, 4 to 5 minutes. Turn the veal and add the mushrooms. Season with salt and pepper and sprinkle with lemon juice. (The lemon juice prevents the mushrooms from turning brown.) Cook for 5 minutes.

3. Transfer the veal to a warmed platter, arrange the mushrooms around the meat, and pour the pan juices over the top.

From Françoise:

• It's not critical to dust the meat with flour, but I do recommend it. The flour helps the meat to brown nicely and keeps it moist.

• Cutlets cook a little more quickly than chops, which are thicker and have bones.

• I like to add 1 or 2 tablespoons of crème fraîche to the pan juices once the meat and the mushrooms have come out of the skillet. Just bring to a simmer before pouring it over the dish.

CLASSIC POT-ROASTED VEAL

- *Rôti de veau en cocotte* -

❖ VERY EASY   ❖ EXPENSIVE   ❖ 1 HOUR, 30 MINUTES   ❖ SERVES 4

2 tablespoons butter
2-pound boneless veal roast, tied
1 small carrot, peeled and cut into pieces

1 onion, cut into pieces
Salt and pepper

❖ ❖ ❖ ❖ ❖

1. In a flameproof casserole, melt the butter over medium heat. Add the veal roast and lightly brown on all sides. Add the carrot and onion and cook for 5 minutes. Season with salt and pepper. Reduce the heat to low, cover, and cook for about 1 hour, turning the meat halfway through cooking. If the meat sticks, add 1 or 2 tablespoons of boiling water.

2. Transfer the meat to a cutting board and remove the string. Cover loosely with foil and let stand for 10 minutes. Add 2 or 3 tablespoons of boiling water to the casserole and simmer, scraping up any brown bits stuck to the bottom, for a few minutes.

3. Carve the meat, transfer to a warmed platter, and serve, passing the pan juices separately in a warmed sauceboat.

From Françoise:

• Some less-expensive veal roasts you could try are shoulder, top round, rump, or sirloin.

• Warm the sauceboat by filling it with hot water, then draining it before adding the pan juices so they will stay warm longer.

• Serve the pot roast with mashed potatoes, spinach, peas, green beans, endives, cabbage, even pasta.

CLASSIC OVEN-ROASTED VEAL

- *Rôti de veau au four* -

❖ VERY EASY   ❖ EXPENSIVE   ❖ 1 HOUR, 15 MINUTES   ❖ SERVES 4

2-pound boneless veal roast, tied
2 tablespoons butter, softened

Salt and pepper

❖ ❖ ❖ ❖ ❖

1. Preheat the oven to 400 degrees. Set the veal in a roasting pan and rub with the butter. Season with salt and pepper. Transfer to the oven and roast for about 1 hour, turning the meat halfway through cooking and basting several times with the pan juices.

2. Transfer the meat to a cutting board and remove the string. Cover loosely with foil and let stand for 10 minutes. Pour a little boiling water into the roasting pan and simmer, scraping up any brown bits stuck to the bottom, for a few minutes. Carve the meat, arrange on a warmed platter, and serve, passing the pan juices in a warmed sauceboat.

From Françoise:
• The general rule for cooking roast veal is 30 to 35 minutes per pound.

• It's a good idea to buy a veal roast that's at least 2 pounds. The smaller the roast, the more it shrinks during cooking. You can use leftovers to innovate: A few slices of cold veal roast are delicious with mayonnaise. Chop the end of a roast and use to stuff crêpes or blend with sautéed onions, celery, carrots, and garlic to make a filling for shepherd's pie.

• You can make a more flavorful pan sauce by adding a halved onion and half a sliced carrot to the casserole before sliding it into the oven.

• Halfway through roasting, add a little hot water to the casserole, pouring it around, not over, the meat. Baste the roast with these simmering pan juices. If you do add water at this point, don't add any more once the meat comes out of the roasting pan, or the pan juices will be watery.

SPIT-ROASTED VEAL

- *Rôti de veau à la broche* -

❖ VERY EASY   ❖ EXPENSIVE   ❖ 1 HOUR, 15 MINUTES, PLUS OVERNIGHT MARINATING   ❖ SERVES 4

2-pound boneless veal roast, tied
Rosemary, sage, or thyme sprigs
Salt and pepper

MARINADE
1 onion, thinly sliced crosswise
4 whole cloves

Thyme
Bay leaf
¾ cup dry white wine
1 tablespoon oil
Pepper

❖   ❖   ❖   ❖   ❖

1. In a bowl, combine the veal roast with the marinade ingredients. Cover and refrigerate overnight, turning the meat several times.

2. Scrape the marinade off the meat. Tuck the herb sprigs under the string used to tie the roast. Season with salt and pepper. Spit-roast the meat until it is well browned, about 1 hour.

3. Transfer the meat to a cutting board and remove the string. Cover loosely with foil and let stand for 10 minutes. Skim any collected juices. Carve the meat, transfer to a warmed platter, and serve, passing the juices in a warmed sauceboat.

From Françoise:
• The secret to spit-roasting: Every 15 minutes, brush the roast with softened butter; it will baste the meat as the spit turns. Also, you can brush the roast with marinade for extra flavor.

POT-ROASTED VEAL WITH MUSHROOMS AND PEARL ONIONS

- *Rôti de veau bûcheronne* -

❖ EASY ❖ EXPENSIVE ❖ 1 HOUR, 30 MINUTES ❖ SERVES 4

2-pound boneless veal rib roast, tied

Salt and pepper

All-purpose flour for dusting

3 tablespoons butter

½ garlic clove, finely chopped

1 bouquet garni made with parsley, thyme, and bay leaf

15 pearl onions, peeled

½ teaspoon sugar

¼ pound white mushrooms, halved or quartered lengthwise if large

❖ ❖ ❖ ❖ ❖

1. Season the veal roast with salt and pepper and dust lightly with flour, patting off the excess.

2. In a flameproof casserole, melt 2 tablespoons of the butter over medium heat. Add the meat and lightly brown on all sides. Add the garlic, bouquet garni, and 1 cup of water. Reduce the heat to low, cover, and cook for about 1 hour, turning the meat halfway through.

3. Meanwhile, in a small saucepan, combine the onions with water to just cover. Slowly bring to a boil, then drain. Return the onions to the pan. Add the sugar and remaining 1 tablespoon of butter and cook over medium-low heat until lightly browned.

4. Add the mushrooms to the casserole and cook for 15 minutes. Transfer the meat to a cutting board and remove the string. Cover loosely with foil and let stand for 10 minutes. Boil the pan juices, scraping up any brown bits stuck to the bottom, for a few minutes.

5. Remove the bouquet garni. Carve the meat and transfer to a warmed platter. Spoon the onions, mushrooms, and pan juices on top and serve.

From Françoise:

• Instead of a pricey veal rib roast, you could use a less expensive top or bottom round roast.

• Pearl onions prepared in this way won't fall apart while pot-roasting.

• Cut mushrooms turn dark quickly, so slice them just before cooking.

• Try simmering 2 or 3 tablespoons of crème fraîche in the pan juices once the meat has come out of the casserole. Your sauce will only be tastier.

• Serve the pot roast with boiled potatoes.

GRATIN OF CREAMY ROASTED VEAL
WITH MUSHROOMS

- Rôti de veau à la royale -

❖ EASY   ❖ EXPENSIVE   ❖ 30 MINUTES   ❖ SERVES 4

BÉCHAMEL SAUCE

3 tablespoons butter

3 tablespoons all-purpose flour

2 ¼ cups milk

Salt and pepper

4 thick slices cooked veal roast

⅓ cup shredded Gruyère cheese

2 tablespoons butter

¼ pound white mushrooms, thinly sliced

1 tablespoon lemon juice

Salt

❖ ❖ ❖ ❖ ❖

1. Preheat the oven to 400 degrees. Make the béchamel sauce: In a small saucepan, melt the butter over medium heat. Whisk in the flour until it starts foaming. Whisk in the milk. Season with salt and pepper. Bring to a boil, whisking, then reduce the heat to very low and cook for 5 minutes.

2. Arrange the veal slices in a gratin dish. Spread the sauce on top. Sprinkle with the cheese and dot with 1 tablespoon of the butter. Bake on the top shelf of the oven until melted and golden, about 10 minutes.

3. Meanwhile, in a small saucepan over medium heat, cook the mushrooms with the lemon juice and remaining 1 tablespoon of butter and season with salt. Drain.

4. Serve the veal with the mushrooms.

From Françoise:

• If you'd like to make a complete meal-in-one or stretch it to serve a few more guests, spread cooked pasta or steamed rice in the gratin dish before adding the slices of veal.

BRAISED VEAL SHANKS WITH PRUNES

- *Jarret de veau aux pruneaux* -

❖ EASY ❖ EXPENSIVE ❖ 1 HOUR, 45 MINUTES, PLUS 1 HOUR SOAKING ❖ SERVES 4

½ pound prunes

⅓ cup raisins

4 pieces of veal shank, about ¾ pound each

Salt and pepper

All-purpose flour for dusting

3 tablespoons butter

2 onions, quartered

2 carrots, peeled and sliced crosswise

1 bouquet garni made with parsley, thyme,
  and bay leaf

❖ ❖ ❖ ❖ ❖

1. In a small bowl, cover the prunes and raisins with hot water and let soak for 1 hour.

2. Meanwhile, season the veal shanks with salt and pepper and dust lightly with flour, patting off the excess.

3. In a flameproof casserole, melt the butter over medium heat. Add the shanks and brown well on 2 sides. Add the onions and lightly brown. Stir in 2 cups of water, the carrots, and bouquet garni. Season with salt and pepper. Reduce the heat to low, cover, and cook for 1 hour.

4. Drain the dried fruit, add to the casserole, and cook for 30 minutes.

5. Remove the bouquet garni. Transfer the veal shanks to a warmed serving dish, spoon the sauce over the top, and serve.

From Françoise:

• This slightly sweet dish should be highly seasoned with salt and pepper.

• Add extra thyme to your bouquet garni for this braise.

• Serve the veal shanks with boiled potatoes, mashed potatoes, or steamed rice.

WINE-BRAISED VEAL SHANKS WITH OLIVES

- *Jarret de veau aux olives* -

❖ EASY ❖ EXPENSIVE ❖ 2 HOURS ❖ SERVES 4

4 pieces of veal shank, about ¾ pound each

Salt and pepper

All-purpose flour for dusting

3 tablespoons butter

1 pound tomatoes, peeled, seeded, and chopped

3 or 4 onions, chopped

2 garlic cloves, crushed

6 tablespoons dry white wine

1 bouquet garni made with parsley, thyme,
  and bay leaf

1 cup green and black olives, pitted

❖ ❖ ❖ ❖ ❖

1. Season the veal shanks with salt and pepper and dust lightly with flour, patting off the excess.

2. In a flameproof casserole, melt the butter over medium heat. Add the shanks and brown well on 2 sides. Stir in the tomatoes, onions, and garlic. Add the wine, 6 tablespoons of water, and the bouquet garni. Season with salt and pepper. Reduce the heat to low, cover, and cook for 1 hour and 15 minutes.

3. Meanwhile, in a small saucepan, cover the olives with water. Bring to a boil, then drain. Add the olives to the casserole and cook for 15 minutes. Remove the bouquet garni. Transfer the veal shanks to a warmed serving dish, spoon the sauce over the top, and serve.

From Françoise:

• If you're in a hurry, you can skip peeling the tomatoes and pitting the olives. Just warn your guests about the pits. Or buy pitted olives.

• Garlic lends more flavor to dishes when it's crushed before it's cooked.

• The white wine isn't required—feel free to use water instead.

• Serve the veal shanks with pasta, steamed rice, or a rice pilaf.

MEAT &
POULTRY

LEMONY BRAISED VEAL SHANKS WITH TOMATOES

- *Jarret de veau au citron* -

❖ EASY   ❖ EXPENSIVE   ❖ 2 HOURS   ❖ SERVES 4

4 pieces of veal shank, about ¾ pound each

Salt and pepper

All-purpose flour for dusting

4 tablespoons (½ stick) butter

2 onions, thinly sliced

2 carrots, peeled and sliced crosswise

¾ cup dry white wine

1 garlic clove, crushed

1 bouquet garni made with parsley, thyme, and bay leaf

Thinly peeled zest of ½ lemon

1 pound tomatoes, peeled, seeded, and chopped

1 tablespoon tomato paste

❖ ❖ ❖ ❖ ❖

1. Season the veal shanks with salt and pepper and dust lightly with flour, patting off the excess.

2. In a flameproof casserole, melt 2 tablespoons of the butter over medium heat. Add the shanks and brown well on 2 sides. Transfer the shanks to a plate.

3. In the same casserole, melt the remaining 2 tablespoons of butter over medium heat. Add the onions and carrots and cook until lightly browned. Return the shanks to the casserole with the wine. Bring to a boil and add the garlic, bouquet garni, lemon zest, tomatoes, and tomato paste. Season with salt and pepper. Reduce the heat to low, cover, and cook for 1 hour and 30 minutes.

4. Remove the bouquet garni and lemon zest. Transfer the veal shanks to a warmed serving dish, spoon the sauce over the top, and serve.

From Françoise:

• Serve the veal shanks with potatoes, pasta, or steamed rice.

• With a green salad and a ripe cheese, you have a complete—and completely delicious—meal.

• If you've bought some tender, young carrots to add to this braise, don't peel them. Just scrub them with a vegetable brush under running water.

BRAISED VEAL SHANKS WITH CARROTS

- Jarret de veau à la mode -

❖ EASY   ❖ EXPENSIVE   ❖ 2 HOURS   ❖ SERVES 4

4 pieces of veal shank, about ¾ pound each

Salt and pepper

All-purpose flour for dusting

3 tablespoons butter

2 onions, quartered

2 pounds carrots, peeled and sliced crosswise

1 garlic clove, crushed

¾ cup dry white wine

1 bouquet garni made with parsley, thyme, and bay leaf

Chopped parsley for sprinkling

❖ ❖ ❖ ❖ ❖

1. Season the veal shanks with salt and pepper and dust lightly with flour, patting off the excess.

2. In a flameproof casserole, melt the butter over medium heat. Add the shanks and brown well on 2 sides. Add the onions and lightly brown. Add the carrots, garlic, wine, 1 ½ cups of water, and the bouquet garni. Season with salt and pepper. Reduce the heat to low, cover, and cook for 1 hour and 30 minutes.

3. Remove the bouquet garni. Transfer the carrots, then the veal shanks, to a warmed serving dish and spoon the sauce over the top. Sprinkle with parsley and serve.

From Françoise:

• If you'd like to make this dish with lamb, have your butcher cut whole lamb shanks crosswise into pieces.

• Dusting the shanks with flour helps brown the meat nicely and gives your sauce some body.

• The wine is not indispensable here and can be replaced with the same quantity of water.

CREAMY VEAL SAUTÉ WITH TARRAGON

- *Sauté de veau à la crème et à l'estragon* -

❖ EASY ❖ MODERATE ❖ 1 HOUR, 15 MINUTES ❖ SERVES 4

3 tablespoons butter

2 onions, chopped

2 pounds boneless veal shoulder, cut into
   1½-inch pieces

3 tarragon sprigs, stems reserved

Salt and pepper

1 teaspoon all-purpose flour

3 tablespoons crème fraîche

❖ ❖ ❖ ❖ ❖

1. In a flameproof casserole, melt the butter over medium-low heat. Add the onions and cook until soft. Add the meat and tarragon stems and season with salt and pepper. Reduce the heat to low, cover, and cook for 1 hour.

2. Transfer the meat to a warmed serving dish. In a small bowl, whisk the flour with the crème fraîche and tarragon leaves. Whisk this into the pan juices, bring to a boil, and simmer for a few moments. Spoon the sauce over the meat and serve.

From Françoise:

• The meat from the veal riblets could also be used. It's fattier than shoulder meat but less expensive.

• I think it's always worthwhile to add a little crème fraîche in a pan sauce.

• Serve the sauté with boiled rice.

FRENCH OSSO BUCO

- *Osso-buco milanaise* -

❖ EASY ❖ EXPENSIVE ❖ 1 HOUR, 30 MINUTES ❖ SERVES 4

4 pieces of veal shank, about ¾ pound each

Salt and pepper

All-purpose flour for dusting

5 tablespoons butter

2 onions, finely chopped

1 tablespoon tomato paste

¾ cup dry white wine

1 bouquet garni made with parsley, thyme,
   and bay leaf

1 garlic clove, crushed

Thinly peeled zest of ½ lemon

3 small tomatoes, peeled, seeded, and chopped

½ pound spaghetti

½ cup grated Gruyère cheese

1. Season the veal shanks with salt and pepper and dust lightly with flour, patting off the excess.

2. In a flameproof casserole, melt 3 tablespoons of the butter over medium heat. Add the shanks and brown well on 2 sides. Add the onions, tomato paste, and wine. Bring to a simmer. Add 2 ¼ cups water, the bouquet garni, and garlic. Season with salt and pepper. Cover and bring to a boil, then reduce the heat to low and simmer for about 1 hour.

3. Add the lemon zest and tomatoes to the casserole and cook for about 15 minutes.

4. Meanwhile, in a large saucepan of boiling, salted water, cook the spaghetti until al dente. Drain, then transfer to a warmed bowl and toss with the remaining 2 tablespoons of butter.

5. Remove the bouquet garni and lemon zest from the stew. Transfer the veal shanks to a warmed serving dish. Spoon the sauce over the top and serve, passing the spaghetti and cheese separately.

From Françoise:

• The white wine is not absolutely necessary. You can substitute water.

• A strip of orange zest added to the stew during cooking also lends a nice flavor.

• You can replace the spaghetti with rice, rinsed and cooked in a large saucepan of boiling salted water for 15 to 17 minutes.

• Osso buco can be made with tomato paste alone, without fresh tomatoes. Still, it's better with a few ripe tomatoes added.

MEAT & POULTRY

VEAL SAUTÉ WITH PEARL ONIONS, CARROTS, AND MUSHROOMS

- Sauté de veau bourgeoise -

❖ EASY   ❖ MODERATE   ❖ 1 HOUR, 30 MINUTES   ❖ SERVES 4

3 tablespoons butter

2 pounds boneless veal shoulder, cut into
 1½-inch pieces

10 pearl onions, peeled

2 pounds carrots, peeled and sliced

¾ cup dry white wine

1 bouquet garni made with parsley, thyme,
 and bay leaf

Salt and pepper

¼ pound thick-sliced bacon, cut crosswise into
 ¼-inch-thick strips

¼ pound white mushrooms, halved or quartered
 if large

continued

1. In a flameproof casserole, melt the butter over medium heat. Add the meat and lightly brown on all sides. Add the onions, carrots, wine, and bouquet garni and season with salt and pepper. Reduce the heat to low, cover, and cook, turning the meat occasionally, for 50 minutes.

2. Meanwhile, in a small saucepan, cover the bacon with water. Bring to a boil, then drain. Add the bacon and mushrooms to the casserole and cook for 15 minutes. Remove the bouquet garni. Transfer the meat, then the vegetables, to a warmed serving dish, spoon the pan juices over the top, and serve.

From Françoise:
• If your family has a hearty appetite, boil some potatoes to serve with this dish.

• You might want to halve or quarter the onions and mushrooms if they are large.

VEAL SAUTÉ WITH TOMATOES AND GREEN OLIVES
- Sauté de veau à la mentonnaise -

❖ EASY ❖ MODERATE ❖ 1 HOUR, 15 MINUTES ❖ SERVES 4

¾ cup pitted green olives

3 tablespoons butter

2 pounds boneless veal shoulder, cut into
  1½-inch pieces

1 tablespoon all-purpose flour

1 pound tomatoes, peeled, seeded, and chopped

1 onion, thinly sliced

1 whole clove

¾ cup dry white wine

1 bouquet garni made with parsley, thyme,
  and bay leaf

Salt and pepper

Chopped parsley leaves for sprinkling

❖ ❖ ❖ ❖ ❖

1. In a small saucepan, cover the olives with water. Bring to a boil, then drain.

2. In a flameproof casserole, melt the butter over medium heat. Add the meat and lightly brown on all sides. Stir in the flour. Add the tomatoes, onion, clove, wine, and bouquet garni. Season lightly with salt and generously with pepper. Reduce the heat to low, cover, and cook, turning the meat occasionally, for 1 hour.

3. Remove the bouquet garni. Transfer the sauté to a warmed serving dish, sprinkle with parsley, and serve.

From Françoise:
• The meat from the veal riblets could also be used, but it takes longer to cook.

• The secret to a sauté simmered with tomatoes that is not swimming in liquid: ripe tomatoes that are peeled, halved, and squeezed to remove the seeds and water. If it chagrins you to throw away any part of a beautiful tomato, you can always use the trimmings to make soup.

GARLICKY VEAL STEW
- Aillade de veau -

❖ EASY ❖ MODERATE ❖ 1 HOUR, 15 MINUTES ❖ SERVES 4

2 tablespoons oil

1 ½ pounds bottom or top round veal, cut into
  2-inch pieces

1 tablespoon dry bread crumbs

10 garlic cloves, crushed

1 tablespoon tomato paste

¾ cup dry white wine

Salt and pepper

❖ ❖ ❖ ❖ ❖

1. In a flameproof casserole, heat the oil over medium heat. Add the meat and lightly brown on all sides. Stir in the bread crumbs, garlic, tomato paste, and wine and season with salt and pepper. Reduce the heat to low, cover, and cook, turning the meat occasionally, for 1 hour.

2. Transfer the stew to a warmed serving dish and serve.

From Françoise:

• This delightful dish needs a cut of meat that's a little more expensive, such as the bottom or top round. It isn't nearly as good with a lesser cut.

• Serve it with fresh tagliatelle noodles to mop up the sauce.

MEAT &
POULTRY

VEAL SIMMERED WITH TOMATOES AND RED PEPPERS
- Sauté de veau méridionale -

❖ EASY ❖ EXPENSIVE ❖ 1 HOUR, 45 MINUTES ❖ SERVES 4

3 tablespoons butter

2 pounds boneless veal shoulder, cut into
  1 ½-inch pieces

1 onion, chopped

1 tablespoon all-purpose flour

¾ cup dry white wine

2 garlic cloves, crushed

1 ½ pounds tomatoes, peeled, seeded, and
  coarsely chopped

½ pound red bell peppers, coarsely chopped

Salt and pepper

continued

1. In a flameproof casserole, melt the butter over medium heat. Add the meat and lightly brown on all sides. Stir in the onion and flour. Add the wine, ¾ cup of water, the garlic, tomatoes, and bell peppers. Season with salt and pepper. Reduce the heat to low, cover, and cook, turning the meat occasionally, for 1 hour and 30 minutes.

2. Transfer to a warmed serving dish and serve.

From Françoise:

• Serve with boiled potatoes or rice. You might stir some stewed tomatoes and bell peppers into the rice when they're in season.

• To boost the dish's southern flavor, add a few green or black olives.

• The wine is not critical here and can be replaced with the same quantity of water.

• I like to add a little tomato paste to amplify the flavor of the fresh tomato and soften any acidity. A tablespoon will do it.

DOUBLE-CRUSTED MEAT PIE

- *Tourte à la viande* -

❖ ADVANCED   ❖ MODERATE   ❖ 1 HOUR, 40 MINUTES, PLUS 12 HOURS MARINATING   ❖ SERVES 6

1 pound boneless veal shoulder, cut into
   1 ½-inch pieces
½ pound pork top loin (shoulder end of the loin),
   cut into 1 ½-inch pieces
Salt and pepper
1 large egg, lightly beaten
2 large egg yolks

MARINADE
1 cup red wine
1 carrot, chopped

1 onion, chopped
1 shallot, chopped
Parsley, thyme, and bay leaf
Salt and pepper

PÂTE BRISÉE
1 ½ cups all-purpose flour
¾ teaspoon salt
7 tablespoons unsalted butter, cut into pieces

❖   ❖   ❖   ❖   ❖

1. In a large bowl, combine the veal and pork with the marinade ingredients. Cover and refrigerate for 12 hours.

2. Make the pâte brisée: In a bowl, combine the flour with the salt and butter. Rub the butter into the flour between your palms. Sprinkle over 5 or 6 tablespoons of water and knead briefly until large crumbs form. Press into a disk. On a lightly floured surface, scrape the dough away from you with the heel of your hand in a long sliding motion, then press into a disk; repeat 3 times. Press into 2 disks, wrap, and refrigerate until firm, 15 to 20 minutes.

3. Scrape the marinade off the meat, reserving the liquid. Finely chop the meat. Season with salt and pepper.

4. Preheat the oven to 400 degrees. On a lightly floured work surface, roll 1 disk into a round. Wrap the dough around the rolling pin and fit it into an 8-inch springform pan.

5. Roll the second disk into a round. Spread the meat in the shell. Brush the edges of the rounds with water. Press the second round on top, pinching the edges together to seal. Poke a hole in the center of the pie and insert a foil "chimney" to allow steam to escape. Brush the top with the beaten egg. Set on a baking sheet, transfer to the oven, and bake for 1 hour.

6. Mix the egg yolks with 3 tablespoons of the reserved marinade. Pour into the "chimney" and bake for 5 minutes. Serve warm.

From Françoise:
• The secret to a double-crusted pie that doesn't come apart at the seams: Don't wet the edges of the bottom and top rounds too much or they'll separate instead of sticking together.

CRISPY VEAL CROQUETTES WITH LEMON
- *Croquettes de veau milanaise* -

❖ EASY ❖ MODERATE ❖ 30 MINUTES ❖ SERVES 4

1 cup finely chopped cooked veal
3 ½ ounces ham, finely chopped
1 cup cooked pasta, finely chopped
½ cup shredded Gruyère cheese
Salt and pepper
1 or 2 tablespoons crème fraîche

All-purpose flour for dredging
2 large eggs, lightly beaten
4 to 5 tablespoons dry bread crumbs
3 tablespoons butter
1 lemon, quartered lengthwise
Parsley sprigs

❖ ❖ ❖ ❖ ❖

1. In a bowl, combine the veal with the ham, pasta, and cheese. Season with pepper and, lightly, with salt. Shape the mixture into croquettes.

2. In separate soup plates, spread the flour, eggs, and bread crumbs. Dredge the croquettes lightly in flour and dip in the eggs, letting any excess drip back into the plate. Dredge the cutlets in the bread crumbs, pressing lightly to help the crumbs adhere.

3. In a large skillet, melt the butter over medium heat. Add the croquettes and brown on all sides, 8 to 10 minutes. Transfer to a warmed platter, garnish with the lemon wedges and parsley, and serve.

From Françoise:
• Serve with broccoli or a green salad.

VEAL BUNDLES WITH BACON

- *Paupiettes de veau au bacon* -

❖ INTERMEDIATE   ❖ EXPENSIVE   ❖ 1 HOUR   ❖ SERVES 4

4 thin, large veal cutlets

Salt and pepper

4 slices Canadian bacon or lightly browned
  regular bacon

4 pinches of thyme leaves

All-purpose flour for dusting

2 tablespoons butter

1 onion, chopped

6 tablespoons dry white wine

1 garlic clove, crushed

1 bouquet garni made with parsley, thyme,
  and bay leaf

❖ ❖ ❖ ❖ ❖

1. Season the cutlets with salt and pepper.
Top each with a bacon slice and a pinch of
thyme. Roll up each cutlet, tucking in the sides
as you go. Tie the bundles with kitchen string.
Dust lightly with flour, patting off the excess.

2. In a flameproof casserole, melt the butter
over medium heat. Add the veal bundles and
lightly brown. Add the onion and lightly
brown. Add the wine, 6 tablespoons of water,
the garlic, and bouquet garni. Reduce the heat
to low, cover, and cook for about 45 minutes.

3. Remove the bouquet garni and kitchen
string. Transfer the veal bundles to a warmed
platter and serve with the pan juices.

From Françoise:

• These veal bundles are even better if, halfway
through cooking, you transfer the casserole to
a moderate oven to finish the braising.

• Have your butcher pound the cutlets ⅛ inch
thick.

• You could roll thin slices of ham in the veal
cutlets.

• The wine is not essential, though it does help
flavor the pan sauce.

VEAL BUNDLES WITH HAM AND GRUYÈRE

- *Paupiettes cordon-bleu* -

❖ INTERMEDIATE ❖ EXPENSIVE ❖ 1 HOUR ❖ SERVES 4

4 veal cutlets, pounded ⅛ inch thick
Salt and pepper
2 thin slices of ham, cut in half
1 tablespoon Dijon mustard
4 thin slices of Gruyère cheese

All-purpose flour for dredging
2 large eggs, lightly beaten
4 to 5 tablespoons dry bread crumbs
3 tablespoons butter, plus more if needed

❖ ❖ ❖ ❖ ❖

1. Season the cutlets with salt and pepper. Top each with a half slice of ham, spread with mustard, and cover with a cheese slice. Roll up each cutlet, tucking in the sides as you go. Tie the bundles with kitchen string.

2. In separate soup plates, spread the flour, eggs, and bread crumbs. Dredge the cutlets lightly in flour and dip in the eggs, letting any excess drip back into the plate. Dredge the cutlets in the bread crumbs, pressing lightly to help the crumbs adhere.

3. In a flameproof casserole, melt the butter over medium heat. Add the veal bundles and brown on all sides, then reduce the heat to low, cover, and cook for 30 to 40 minutes.

4. Remove the kitchen string. Transfer the veal bundles to a warmed platter and serve.

From Françoise:

• It's even better to bake these paupiettes in a moderate oven.

• Serve simply with pasta or, more indulgently, with deep-fried Pommes Dauphine (page 585).

VEAL BUNDLES WITH OLIVES

- *Paupiettes de veau aux olives* -

❖ INTERMEDIATE   ❖ EXPENSIVE   ❖ 1 HOUR   ❖ SERVES 4

8 slices of crustless white sandwich bread
½ cup milk
¼ pound white mushrooms, chopped
Chopped parsley leaves
1 garlic clove, finely chopped

Salt and pepper
4 veal cutlets, pounded ⅛ inch thick
4 strips of barding fat (optional)
3 tablespoons butter
¾ cup green olives, pitted

❖ ❖ ❖ ❖ ❖

1. In a food processor, grind the bread slices into crumbs. Soak these fresh bread crumbs in the milk, then squeeze dry. Mix with the mushrooms, parsley, and garlic. Season lightly with salt and pepper.

2. Spread each cutlet with a quarter of the filling. Roll each up, tucking in the sides as you go. Wrap a strip of barding fat around each bundle, if using. Tie with kitchen string.

3. In a flameproof casserole, melt the butter over medium heat. Add the veal bundles and lightly brown. Season with salt and pepper. Reduce the heat to low, cover, and cook for 30 minutes.

4. Meanwhile, in a small saucepan, cover the olives with water. Bring to a boil, then drain. Add the olives to the casserole and cook for 10 to 15 minutes.

5. Remove the barding fat and kitchen string. Transfer the veal bundles and olives to a warmed platter and serve.

From Françoise:
• The cutlets should be very large and thin so you can stuff them easily.

• Try an exotic variation: Stuff the veal cutlets with small sautéed bananas, or, preferably, plantains, that have been wrapped in lightly browned bacon.

BRAISED VEAL BREAST WITH VEGETABLES

- *Poitrine de veau paysanne* -

❖ EASY   ❖ MODERATE   ❖ 2 HOURS   ❖ SERVES 4

3 pounds boneless veal breast, cut into
  2-inch pieces
½ pound pancetta
4 carrots, peeled
2 turnips, peeled
1 onion, peeled and stuck with a clove
1 garlic clove, crushed
1 bouquet garni made with parsley, thyme,
  and bay leaf

Salt and pepper
1 small green cabbage, quartered and cored
1 tablespoon butter
1 tablespoon all-purpose flour
1 large egg yolk or 1 tablespoon crème fraîche
Juice of ½ lemon
1 cornichon, sliced crosswise
Chopped parsley leaves

MEAT &
POULTRY

❖   ❖   ❖   ❖   ❖

1. In a flameproof casserole, cover the veal breast and pancetta with water. Slowly bring to a boil, then drain.

2. Return the casserole to the heat. Add the carrots, turnips, onion, garlic, and bouquet garni and season with salt and pepper. Cover one-third with boiling water. Bring to a simmer over medium heat.

3. Meanwhile, bring a large pot of water to a boil. Add the cabbage and simmer for 5 minutes. Drain and add to the veal. Reduce the heat to low, cover, and cook for 1 hour and 30 minutes.

4. In a small saucepan, melt the butter over medium heat. Whisk in the flour until it starts foaming. Whisk in 1 cup of the cooking liquid. Season with salt and pepper. Bring to a boil, whisking, then reduce the heat to very low and cook for 5 minutes. In a bowl, whisk the egg yolk or crème fraîche with the lemon juice, cornichon, and parsley. Whisk this mixture into the sauce, then remove the pan from the heat.

5. Remove the bouquet garni. Using a slotted spoon, transfer the meat and vegetables to a warmed serving dish. Serve, passing the sauce separately.

STUFFED VEAL BREAST WITH GRUYÈRE SAUCE

- *Poitrine de veau farcie et gratinée* -

❖ ADVANCED   ❖ MODERATE   ❖ 2 HOURS, 30 MINUTES   ❖ SERVES 8 OR 10

5-pound boneless veal breast

12 slices crustless white sandwich bread

¾ cup milk

1 large egg

5 ounces sweet Italian sausage, casing removed

Chopped parsley leaves

Salt and pepper

Freshly grated nutmeg

2 hard-boiled eggs

3 tablespoons butter

1 onion, quartered

1 carrot, peeled and sliced crosswise

1 bouquet garni made with parsley, thyme, and bay leaf

1 celery rib, cut into large pieces

MORNAY SAUCE

1 ½ tablespoons butter

1 ½ tablespoons all-purpose flour

1 cup milk

Salt and pepper

1 large egg yolk

½ cup shredded Gruyère cheese

❖ ❖ ❖ ❖ ❖

1. Cut a large pocket in the veal breast: Beginning at the center of the thickest side, insert a large knife horizontally and cut into the center of the veal as evenly as possible, leaving a 1-inch border on 3 sides.

2. In a food processor, grind the bread slices into crumbs. In a large bowl, mix the bread crumbs with the milk, egg, sausage, and parsley. Season with salt, pepper, and nutmeg.

3. Spread the stuffing evenly in the pocket and place the 2 hard-boiled eggs in the center. Sew the pocket closed with a carpet needle and kitchen string, or close with a skewer.

4. In a flameproof casserole, melt the butter over medium heat. Add the veal breast and brown well on 2 sides. Add the onion, carrot, bouquet garni, celery, and ¾ cup of boiling water. Season with salt and pepper. Reduce the heat to low, cover, and cook for 1 hour and 30 minutes to 2 hours.

5. Meanwhile, make the Mornay sauce: In a small saucepan, melt the butter over medium heat. Whisk in the flour until it starts foaming. Whisk in the milk. Season with salt and pepper. Bring to a boil, whisking, then reduce the heat to very low and cook for 10 minutes. Remove the pan from the heat and whisk in the egg yolk and cheese.

6. Transfer the veal breast to a cutting board. Slice the meat and transfer to a warmed serving dish. Spoon the sauce over the top and serve.

From Françoise:

• Stuffed veal breast is also good cold. It's perfect for picnics, buffets, and cold suppers. If you are serving it cold, skip the Mornay sauce and pass tart pickles and assorted flavored mustards instead.

CREAMY VEAL PAPRIKA

- *Marmite de veau* -

❖ EASY   ❖ EXPENSIVE   ❖ 20 MINUTES   ❖ SERVES 4

1 pound veal top round or tenderloin,
  cut into thin strips
All-purpose flour for dusting
3 tablespoons butter
1 tablespoon oil
1 onion, chopped

Salt and pepper
1 teaspoon sweet paprika
½ pound white mushrooms, thinly sliced
¾ cup dry white wine
½ cup crème fraîche
Chopped parsley leaves for sprinkling

❖ ❖ ❖ ❖ ❖

1. Dust the veal strips lightly with flour, patting off the excess. In a skillet, melt 1 tablespoon of the butter in the oil over medium-high heat. Add the veal and lightly brown. Add the onion and lightly brown. Season with salt, pepper, and the paprika. Using a slotted spoon, transfer the veal to a plate.

2. In the same skillet, melt the remaining 2 tablespoons of butter over medium-high heat. Add the mushrooms and cook for 2 to 3 minutes. Add the wine and crème fraîche and simmer until slightly thickened, a few minutes.

3. Return the veal to the skillet and reheat. Transfer to a serving dish, sprinkle with parsley, and serve.

From Françoise:
• Sauté the veal strips over fairly high heat. If the meat isn't well seared, it releases a grayish liquid in which it steams and toughens.

• You can bring a touch of freshness to this recipe by stirring in 2 tablespoons of snipped chives at the last moment.

VEAL WITH MUSHROOMS AND TOMATO

- *Veau marengo* -

❖ EASY   ❖ EXPENSIVE   ❖ 1 HOUR, 50 MINUTES   ❖ SERVES 4

3 tablespoons butter

2 pounds boneless veal shoulder, cut into
  1½-inch pieces

3 shallots, finely chopped

1 carrot, peeled and finely chopped

1½ tablespoons all-purpose flour

2 tablespoons tomato paste

1 cup dry white wine

2 garlic cloves, crushed

1 bouquet garni made with parsley, thyme,
  and bay leaf

Salt and pepper

¼ pound white mushrooms, thinly sliced

❖ ❖ ❖ ❖ ❖

1. In a flameproof casserole, melt the butter over medium heat. Add the veal and brown well. Add the shallots and carrot. Stir in the flour. Add the tomato paste, wine, 1 cup of water, the garlic, and bouquet garni. Season with salt and pepper. Reduce the heat to low, cover, and cook for 1 hour and 30 minutes.

2. Add the mushrooms to the casserole and cook for 15 minutes. Transfer to a warmed serving dish and serve.

From Françoise:

• The secret to a good Marengo: The sauce should be rich and concentrated. If at the end of cooking it's too thin, remove the pieces of meat and simmer the sauce until it thickens.

• When tomatoes are in season, you can add them, but always blend in a little tomato paste. It's vital for flavoring the sauce.

VEAL ROAST STUFFED WITH
CREAMY MUSHROOMS AND ONIONS
- *Veau Orloff* -

❖ ADVANCED   ❖ EXPENSIVE   ❖ 2 HOURS   ❖ SERVES 8

4- to 5-pound bottom round veal roast

4 tablespoons (½ stick) butter, softened

2 carrots, peeled and cut into ¼-inch dice

2 onions, cut into ¼-inch dice

2 veal bones, cracked

Salt and pepper

STUFFING

4 tablespoons (½ stick) butter

3 onions, chopped

1 pound white mushrooms, finely chopped

SAUCE

3 tablespoons butter

3 tablespoons all-purpose flour

2 ¼ cups milk

Salt and pepper

2 large egg yolks

❖   ❖   ❖   ❖   ❖

1. Preheat the oven to 400 degrees. Set the veal in a roasting pan and rub with the butter. Spread the carrots, onions, and bones around the meat. Season with salt and pepper. Transfer to the oven and roast for 30 minutes. Reduce the oven temperature to 350 degrees. Turn the meat, pour 1 ½ cups of boiling water around it, and roast for 1 hour, basting several times with the pan juices

2. Meanwhile, make the stuffing: In a medium saucepan, melt 2 tablespoons of the butter over low heat. Add the onions, cover, and cook until very soft, about 30 minutes. Transfer the onions to a bowl. Using an immersion blender, puree the onions.

3. In the same pan, melt the remaining 2 tablespoons of butter over low heat. Add the mushrooms and cook, stirring often, for 15 minutes. Add to the onions. Reserve one-quarter of the stuffing.

4. Make the sauce: In a small saucepan, melt the butter over medium heat. Whisk in the flour until it starts foaming. Whisk in 1 ½ cups of the milk. Season with salt and pepper. Bring to a boil, whisking. The sauce will be thick.

5. Transfer the meat to a cutting board, cover loosely with foil, and let stand for 10 minutes. Strain the pan juices into a warmed sauceboat. Stir 3 tablespoons of the sauce into the larger amount of stuffing. Slice the meat crosswise ½ inch thick without cutting all the way through. Spread some of this creamy stuffing inside each cut. Transfer the meat to an oven-proof platter.

6. Stir the reserved stuffing into the remaining sauce along with the remaining ¾ cup of milk and reheat. Remove the pan from the heat and beat in the egg yolks.

continued

7. Preheat the broiler. Spoon this sauce over the meat and transfer to the top shelf of the broiler to reheat. Serve the meat, passing the pan juices separately.

From Françoise:
• The veal roast can be cooked and stuffed up to 1 hour in advance. Cover it loosely with foil and keep warm in a low oven. Just before serving, reheat the roast under the broiler.

• Serve the veal Orloff with sautéed potatoes, broiled tomato halves, and celery hearts braised in the pan juices.

CREAMY VEAL STEW
- *Blanquette de veau* -

❖ EASY   ❖ MODERATE   ❖ 1 HOUR, 30 MINUTES   ❖ SERVES 4

2 pounds boneless veal shoulder, cut into
 1½-inch pieces
½ lemon
1 carrot, peeled
1 onion stuck with 1 whole clove
1 bouquet garni made with parsley, thyme, and
 bay leaf

Salt and pepper
1½ tablespoons butter
1½ tablespoons all-purpose flour
Chopped parsley leaves for sprinkling

❖ ❖ ❖ ❖ ❖

1. Rub and moisten the pieces of veal with the lemon half so they stay white. In a flameproof casserole of cold water, combine the veal, carrot, onion, and bouquet garni and season with salt and pepper. Cover and bring to a boil over medium-high heat, then reduce the heat to low and simmer, skimming occasionally, for 1 hour and 15 minutes.

2. When the stew has been simmering for 45 minutes, in a small saucepan, melt the butter over medium heat. Whisk in the flour until it starts foaming. Whisk in 1½ cups of the cooking liquid. Season with salt and pepper. Bring to a boil, whisking, then reduce the heat to low and cook for 10 minutes.

3. Using a slotted spoon, transfer the meat to a warmed serving dish. Spoon the sauce over it. Sprinkle with parsley and serve.

From Françoise:
• To make my sauce especially delicious, once it's cooked and off the heat, I whisk in 1 or 2 tablespoons of crème fraîche, 1 egg yolk, and a squeeze of lemon juice. The only problem with this enriched sauce is that you can't reheat it. (You would scramble the egg.) The only solution is to keep it warm in a hot, but not boiling, water bath.

• One of my young friends makes a tropical variation—she replaces half of the cooking liquid in the sauce with coconut milk.

- The boneless meat from the veal riblets makes a very tender blanquette.

- Serve this stew with boiled rice or potatoes cooked in the casserole for 30 minutes along with the veal.

BEEF RIB ROAST WITH SHALLOT BUTTER
- *Côte de boeuf à l'échalote* -

❖ VERY EASY   ❖ EXPENSIVE   ❖ 45 MINUTES, PLUS OPTIONAL OVERNIGHT CHILLING   ❖ SERVES 6

3-pound boneless beef rib roast, tied
Oil for brushing
Thyme leaves
1 bay leaf, crumbled

Cracked black peppercorns
Salt and pepper
7 tablespoons butter, softened
1 shallot, finely chopped

❖ ❖ ❖ ❖ ❖

1. In a shallow baking dish, brush the meat all over with oil and pat with the thyme, bay leaf, and cracked pepper. Cover and, if desired, refrigerate as long as overnight.

2. Preheat the oven to 425 degrees. Transfer the meat to a rack set in a roasting pan. Transfer to the oven and roast for about 30 minutes, turning the meat halfway through and basting several times with the pan juices.

3. Transfer the meat to a cutting board and remove the string. Season with salt and pepper.

Cover loosely with foil and let stand for 10 minutes.

4. Meanwhile, in a small saucepan, melt 1 tablespoon of the butter over medium-low heat. Add the shallot and cook until soft. Remove the pan from the heat and, using a fork, mash in the remaining 6 tablespoons of butter. Season with salt and pepper.

5. Carve the roast across the grain. Serve on warmed plates with the shallot butter.

CLASSIC BEEF RIB ROAST

- Côte de boeuf rôtie -

❖ VERY EASY ❖ EXPENSIVE ❖ 45 MINUTES ❖ SERVES 6

3 ½-pound boneless beef rib roast, tied
Oil for brushing

2 tablespoons butter, softened
Salt and pepper

❖ ❖ ❖ ❖ ❖

1. Preheat the oven to 425 degrees. In a roasting pan, brush the meat all over with oil.

2. Transfer to the oven and roast for about 30 minutes, turning the meat, brushing it with the butter halfway through and basting several times with the pan juices.

3. Transfer the meat to a cutting board and remove the string. Season with salt and pepper. Cover loosely with foil and let stand for 10 minutes. Carve the roast across the grain and serve.

From Françoise:

• The general rule for cooking a boneless beef rib roast is 9 to 10 minutes per pound.

• Serve the sliced roast on warmed plates.

• For a simple luxury, top each serving with a flavored butter such as *beurre maître d'hôtel* (softened butter mixed with chopped parsley, salt, pepper, and lemon juice) or *beurre d'échalote* (with finely chopped shallot).

BEEF RIB ROAST WITH CHABLIS SAUCE

- Côte de boeuf au chablis -

❖ EASY ❖ EXPENSIVE ❖ 45 MINUTES ❖ SERVES 6

3 ½-pound boneless beef rib roast, tied
Oil for brushing
Salt and pepper
7 tablespoons butter, softened

2 or 3 shallots, finely chopped
1 ½ cups Chardonnay wine, preferably Chablis
1 teaspoon all-purpose flour

1. Preheat the oven to 425 degrees. In a roasting pan, brush the meat all over with oil.

2. Transfer to the oven and roast for about 30 minutes, reducing the oven temperature to 400 degrees and turning the meat halfway through.

3. Transfer the meat to a cutting board and remove the string. Season with salt and pepper. Cover loosely with foil and let stand for 10 minutes.

4. Meanwhile, in a small saucepan, melt 1 tablespoon of the butter over medium-low heat. Add the shallots and cook until soft. Add the wine, season with salt and pepper, and simmer until reduced by half. Stir in any juices from the roasting pan.

5. In a cup, mash 1 teaspoon of the butter with the flour. Gradually whisk this paste into the simmering sauce. Remove the pan from the heat and gradually whisk in the remaining butter until it melts creamily. Pour into a warmed sauceboat.

6. Carve the roast across the grain and serve with the sauce.

From Françoise:

• You can roast the meat either on a rack in the roasting pan or directly in a roasting pan.

• Roast the meat in the center of the oven.

• It is very important to let the meat rest for 10 minutes after roasting. Transfer it to a cutting board and cover it loosely with foil to keep it warm. Or turn off the oven and leave the meat in it.

• You can keep the sauce warm in a hot, but not boiling, water bath. Do not reheat the sauce or it will separate.

RIB STEAKS WITH SHALLOT AND PARSLEY SAUCE
- *Entrecôtes Bercy* -

❖ EASY	❖ EXPENSIVE	❖ 15 MINUTES	❖ SERVES 4

2 boneless beef rib steaks, about ¾ pound each
Oil for brushing
Salt and pepper
6 tablespoons dry white wine

1 shallot, finely chopped
Chopped parsley
2 tablespoons butter, softened
1 teaspoon all-purpose flour

❖ ❖ ❖ ❖ ❖

1. Set a large skillet over medium-high heat. Brush the steaks on both sides with oil. Add the steaks to the skillet and cook until well browned on the bottom, 2 to 4 minutes. Turn the steaks, season with salt and pepper, and cook until well browned, 2 to 4 minutes.

Transfer to a cutting board and let stand for 5 minutes.

continued

2. Meanwhile, in the same skillet, reduce the heat to medium, add the wine, 1 teaspoon of water, the shallot, and parsley and season with salt and pepper. Simmer, scraping up any brown bits from the bottom, for 1 minute.

3. In a cup, mash the butter with the flour. Gradually whisk this paste into the simmering sauce until it thickens.

4. Cut each steak in half. Transfer to warmed plates, pour the sauce over the steaks, and serve.

From Françoise:
• A good steak is bright red and marbled with fat.

• You can also use strip steaks.

RIB STEAKS WITH WHITE WINE SAUCE
- *Entrecôtes marchand de vin* -

❖ EASY   ❖ EXPENSIVE   ❖ 15 MINUTES   ❖ SERVES 4

1 tablespoon oil
2 boneless beef rib steaks, about 1 pound each
Salt and pepper
7 tablespoons butter, softened

2 or 3 shallots, finely chopped
1½ cups dry white wine
1 teaspoon all-purpose flour

❖ ❖ ❖ ❖ ❖

1. In a large skillet, heat the oil over medium-high heat. Add the steaks to the skillet and brown them well, turning once, 2 to 4 minutes per side. Season with salt and pepper. Transfer to a cutting board and let stand for 5 minutes.

2. Meanwhile, in the same skillet, reduce the heat to medium-low and melt 1 tablespoon of the butter. Add the shallots and cook until soft. Add the wine, season with salt and pepper, and simmer, scraping up any brown bits from the bottom, until reduced by half.

3. In a cup, mash 1 teaspoon of the butter with the flour. Gradually whisk this paste into the simmering sauce until it thickens. Remove the pan from the heat and gradually whisk in the remaining butter until it melts creamily. Season with salt and pepper. Pour into a warmed sauceboat.

4. Cut each steak in half. Transfer to warmed plates and serve with the sauce.

STEAK TARTARE

- *Steak tartare* -

❖ VERY EASY   ❖ MODERATE   ❖ 10 MINUTES   ❖ SERVES 4

1 pound ground lean top beef round or sirloin

4 small onions, finely chopped (optional)

Chopped parsley leaves

3 tablespoons small capers

4 teaspoons Dijon mustard

Salt and pepper

4 large egg yolks

❖ ❖ ❖ ❖ ❖

1. In a bowl, lightly mix the ground meat with the onions, if using, the parsley, capers, and mustard and season with salt and pepper.

2. Shape the mixture into 4 patties. Transfer to cold plates. Make an indentation in each patty, add an egg yolk, and serve.

From Françoise:
• Please note that the finished dish contains raw meat and raw egg.

• Make sure the meat is freshly ground by your butcher and is of the best quality.

• Prepare this dish just before serving.

• You can make steak tartare in so many ways. Leave out any ingredients you don't like and add others, such as ketchup, Worcestershire sauce, cayenne pepper, finely chopped garlic, and fines herbes (parsley, chives, chervil, tarragon).

RIB STEAKS WITH RED WINE SAUCE AND POACHED MARROW

- *Entrecôtes bordelaise aux échalotes* -

❖ EASY   ❖ EXPENSIVE   ❖ 30 MINUTES   ❖ SERVES 4

BORDELAISE SAUCE

2 tablespoons butter

1 or 2 shallots, finely chopped

1 cup Cabernet or Merlot wine, preferably from Bordeaux

1 teaspoon tomato paste

Salt and pepper

1 teaspoon all-purpose flour

Salt

2 ounces beef bone marrow

2 boneless beef rib steaks, about ¾ pound each

Pepper

Chopped parsley leaves for sprinkling

continued

1. Make the Bordelaise sauce: In a small saucepan, melt 1 tablespoon of the butter over medium-low heat. Add the shallot and cook until soft. Add ¼ cup of the wine and simmer until it evaporates. Stir in the remaining ¾ cup of wine, the tomato paste, and ⅓ cup of water and season with salt and pepper. In a small cup, mash the remaining 1 tablespoon of butter with the flour. Gradually whisk this paste into the simmering sauce. Reduce the heat to low and cook for 4 to 5 minutes.

2. Bring a medium saucepan of salted water to a boil. Using a knife dipped in hot water, cut the marrow crosswise into thick slices. Transfer the marrow slices to a metal strainer. Dip them into the gently boiling water for 1 minute, then remove the pan from the heat. Let stand for 2 minutes, then drain the marrow and keep warm.

3. Set a large skillet over medium-high heat. Add the steaks to the skillet and brown them well, turning once, 2 to 4 minutes per side. Season with salt and pepper. Transfer to a cutting board and let stand for 5 minutes.

4. Meanwhile, add the sauce to the skillet and simmer, scraping up any brown bits from the bottom. Cut each steak in half and transfer to a warmed platter. Arrange the marrow on the steaks, pour the sauce on top, sprinkle with parsley, and serve.

From Françoise:

• A steak is medium rare when it's being seared on the second side and pearls of blood start to appear on the surface. The center is pink and warm.

• A steak is very rare—"bleu"—when the steak has been seared on both sides and the center remains cool and almost raw.

BEEF TENDERLOIN STEAKS WITH SAUTÉED POTATOES
- Chateaubriands aux pommes de terres -

❖ EASY	❖ EXPENSIVE	❖ 1 HOUR	❖ SERVES 4

1 ½ pounds potatoes, peeled and cut into
  ½-inch dice
5 tablespoons butter
Salt
2 center-cut beef tenderloins, tied,
  about 1 pound each

Pepper
Watercress or parsley sprigs for decorating
  (optional)

❖　❖　❖　❖　❖

1. Slowly bring the potatoes to a boil in a large saucepan of water, then drain. In a large skillet, melt 3 tablespoons of the butter over medium-low heat. Add the potatoes and cook, stirring occasionally, until golden brown on all sides, 20 to 30 minutes. Season with salt and cover.

2. Meanwhile, in another large skillet, melt the remaining 2 tablespoons of butter over medium-high heat. Add the steaks and cook until well browned on all sides and rare to medium rare, 4 to 8 minutes. Season with salt and pepper. Transfer the meat to a cutting board, remove the string, and let stand for 5 minutes.

3. Transfer the meat to a warmed platter and surround with the potatoes. Decorate with the watercress or parsley, if desired, and serve.

From Françoise:
• The "chateaubriand" is a thick piece of beef tenderloin, averaging 1 pound.

• Try to cut the potatoes in pieces of the same size so they cook evenly.

• Béarnaise sauce is the classic accompaniment to chateaubriand steak.

FRENCH HAMBURGERS
- *Steaks hachés* -

❖ VERY EASY   ❖ INEXPENSIVE   ❖ 15 MINUTES   ❖ SERVES 4

1 pound ground beef chuck
2 tablespoons butter

Salt and pepper
Chopped parsley for sprinkling

❖ ❖ ❖ ❖ ❖

1. Lightly shape the beef into 4 patties.

2. In a large skillet, melt the butter over medium-high heat. Add the burgers and brown them well, turning once, 3 to 4 minutes per side. Season with salt and pepper and transfer to a warmed platter.

3. Sprinkle with the parsley and serve.

From Françoise:
• Serving hamburgers with béarnaise sauce, usually reserved for expensive cuts, gives them a certain splendor. But since this is not a lofty dish, feel free to use a store-bought sauce.

• The cooking time for a hamburger is always a little longer than for a steak.

• French steaks hachés are not served on buns.

STEAK TARTARE BURGERS

- *Steaks hachés à la russe* -

❖ VERY EASY   ❖ INEXPENSIVE   ❖ 15 MINUTES   ❖ SERVES 4

1 pound ground beef chuck

1 tablespoon Dijon mustard

1 tablespoon chopped parsley leaves

1 tablespoon small capers

Salt and pepper

3 tablespoons butter

All-purpose flour for dusting

❖ ❖ ❖ ❖ ❖

1. In a bowl, lightly mix the beef with the mustard, parsley, and capers and season with salt and pepper. Shape into 4 patties.

2. In a large skillet, melt the butter over medium-high heat. Lightly dust the burgers with the flour, patting off the excess. Add to the skillet and brown them well, turning once, 3 to 4 minutes per side. Transfer to plates and serve.

From Françoise:

• Sear the burgers over fairly high heat so they get browned and crusty.

• You can play around with this recipe. Leave out the capers or mustard and add other ingredients, such as finely chopped garlic and chopped cornichons, if you prefer.

STEAKS WITH CREAMY GREEN PEPPERCORN SAUCE

- *Steaks au poivre vert* -

❖ EASY   ❖ EXPENSIVE   ❖ 15 MINUTES   ❖ SERVE 4

4 boneless beef sirloin, strip, or tenderloin steaks, about 7 ounces each

2 tablespoons crushed green peppercorns

2 tablespoons butter

1 tablespoon oil

2 tablespoons Cognac or rum

2 tablespoons crème fraîche

Salt and pepper

❖ ❖ ❖ ❖ ❖

1. Pat the steaks on both sides with the green peppercorns. In a large skillet, melt the butter in the oil over medium-high heat. Add the steaks and brown them well, turning once, 2 to 3 minutes per side. Transfer to a warmed platter.

2. Discard the fat in the skillet. Add the Cognac or rum and bring to a boil. Tilt the pan and carefully ignite. When the flames subside, add the crème fraîche, season with salt and pepper, and simmer, scraping up any brown bits stuck to the bottom, until slightly thickened. Pour over the steaks and serve.

From Françoise:

• Serve with potato chips or fried potatoes and grilled tomato halves.

• The flavor of green peppercorns is more subtle than that of black pepper, but it's still spicy!

BROILED HERB-CRUSTED STEAKS
- Steaks grillés aux herbes -

❖ EASY   ❖ EXPENSIVE   ❖ 15 MINUTES   ❖ SERVES 4

4 boneless beef steaks, 5 to 7 ounces each
Oil for brushing
Dried herbs, such as thyme, rosemary,
  or crumbled bay leaves

Salt and pepper
3 tablespoons butter

❖ ❖ ❖ ❖ ❖

1. Preheat the broiler. On a broiler pan, brush the steaks on both sides with oil and pat with the dried herbs. Broil the steaks, turning once, 2 to 3 minutes per side.

2. Transfer the steaks to a cutting board and let stand for 5 minutes. Transfer to a warmed platter. Season with salt and pepper, top with the butter, and serve.

From Françoise:
• It is important to broil the steaks at high heat or they won't sear properly.

• If you use a grill pan on top of the stove, set it over high heat for several minutes before adding the meat.

• Do not use a fork to turn the meat or the juices will run out. Use tongs instead.

• A piece of meat for the grill should weigh between 5 ounces and half a pound. The thinner the steak the quicker it cooks.

• The general rule for cooking steaks is 1 minute on each side for ½-inch-thick steaks; 2 to 3 minutes per side for 1-inch steaks; and 3 to 4 minutes for 1 ½-inch steaks.

STEAKS WITH CREAMY BLACK PEPPER SAUCE

- *Steaks au poivre* -

❖ EASY   ❖ EXPENSIVE   ❖ 15 MINUTES   ❖ SERVE 4

4 thick tenderloin or boneless beef sirloin steaks

1 teapoon cracked black peppercorns

3 tablespoons butter

Salt

3 tablespoons Cognac

❖ ❖ ❖ ❖ ❖

1. Pat the steaks on both sides with the peppercorns. In a large skillet, melt 1 tablespoon of the butter over medium-high heat. Add the steaks and brown them well, turning once, 3 to 4 minutes per side. Season with salt. Transfer to a warmed platter.

2. Discard the fat in the skillet. Add the Cognac and bring to a boil. Tilt the pan and carefully ignite. When the flames subside, season with salt and simmer, scraping up any bits stuck to the bottom, until slightly thickened. Remove the pan from the heat and gradually whisk in the remaining 2 tablespoons of butter until it melts creamily. Pour over the steaks and serve.

From Françoise:

• Serve with potato chips and watercress sprigs, sprinkled with balsamic vinegar.

• Pepper from the grinder is too fine for this recipe. Crack whole peppercorns in a mortar or spread them on a cutting board, cover with paper towels (so they don't fly all over the place), and crush using a rolling pin.

• Discard the fat used to cook the steaks. Add fresh butter to make the sauce.

• When the flames from the Cognac die down, I find a little bit of added crème fraîche is even better than butter. It's your choice.

PAN-SEARED STEAKS

- *Steaks à la poêle* -

❖ EASY   ❖ MODERATE   ❖ 10 MINUTES   ❖ SERVES 4

2 tablespoons butter
4 beef steaks

Salt and pepper

❖ ❖ ❖ ❖ ❖

1. In a large skillet, melt the butter over medium-high heat. Add the steaks and brown them well, turning once, 2 to 3 minutes per side. Season with salt and pepper. Transfer to a warmed platter and serve.

From Françoise:
• When you can get it, garnish the steaks with watercress sprigs. It's always appealing. Any remaining watercress can go to make a side salad.

PAN-SEARED STEAKS WITH ONIONS

- *Steaks à la lyonnaise* -

❖ EASY   ❖ MODERATE   ❖ 15 MINUTES   ❖ SERVES 4

3 tablespoons butter
2 or 3 onions, thinly sliced
Salt and pepper

4 beef steaks
6 tablespoons dry white wine

❖ ❖ ❖ ❖ ❖

1. In a large skillet, melt 2 tablespoons of the butter over medium heat. Add the onions and cook, stirring occasionally, until golden brown. Season with salt and pepper. Transfer to a bowl.

2. In the same skillet, heat the remaining 1 tablespoon of butter over medium-high heat. Add the steaks and brown them well, turning once, 2 to 3 minutes per side. Season with salt. Transfer to a warmed platter and top with the onions.

3. Add the wine to the skillet and boil, scraping up any brown bits on the bottom, until slightly thickened. Pour over the steaks and serve.

From Françoise:
• I recommend steaks from the tenderloin, strip steaks, rib steaks, or sirloin steaks. Or if you prefer steaks with long "fibers" that are juicy and tasty, look for skirt steak, flank steak (not too thick), or hanger steak.

BEEF TENDERLOIN STEAKS WITH FOIE GRAS AND TRUFFLES

- *Tournedos Rossini au foie gras* -

❖ INTERMEDIATE ❖ EXPENSIVE ❖ 1 HOUR ❖ SERVES 4

VEAL STOCK

2 tablespoons butter

1 veal bone, cracked

1 carrot, peeled

1 onion, chopped

1 teaspoon all-purpose flour

6 tablespoons dry white wine

½ teaspoon tomato paste

1 bouquet garni made with parsley, thyme,
  and bay leaf

Salt and pepper

4 slices of white sandwich bread

4 tablespoons (½ stick) butter

4 beef tenderloin steaks, tied, about 1½ inches
  thick

Salt and pepper

4 slices of foie gras terrine or foie gras mousse

4 black truffle slices

6 tablespoons port

❖ ❖ ❖ ❖ ❖

1. Make the veal stock: In a large saucepan, melt the butter over medium heat. Add the veal bone, carrot, onion, and flour and lightly brown. Add the wine, ¾ cup of water, the tomato paste, and bouquet garni and season with salt and pepper. Bring to a boil, stirring, then reduce the heat to low and cook for 30 minutes.

2. Meanwhile, using a saucer as a guide, cut rounds out of the bread slices slightly larger than the steaks. In a large skillet, melt 2 tablespoons of the butter over medium heat. Add the bread and cook until golden.

3. Wipe out the skillet. In it melt the remaining 2 tablespoons of butter over medium-high heat. Add the steaks and cook until well browned on all sides and rare to medium rare, 4 to 8 minutes. Transfer to a cutting board, remove the string, and season with salt and pepper. Set each steak on a toast and top with a slice of foie gras and truffle.

4. In the same skillet, add the port and boil, scraping up any brown bits on the bottom, until slightly thickened. Strain the veal stock into the skillet, bring to a boil, and taste for seasoning. Pour into a warmed sauceboat.

5. Transfer the steaks to a warmed platter or dishes and pass the sauce separately.

From Françoise:
• You can use 1 cup of store-bought veal stock instead of homemade.

BEEF TENDERLOIN STEAKS WITH PEA-STUFFED ARTICHOKE BOTTOMS

- *Tournedos clamart* -

❖ INTERMEDIATE   ❖ EXPENSIVE   ❖ 20 MINUTES   ❖ SERVES 4

1 cup canned petit pois peas

4 to 8 canned artichoke bottoms, depending on the size

3 tablespoons butter

4 beef tenderloin steaks, tied, about 1 ½ inches thick

Salt and pepper

6 tablespoons Madeira

6 tablespoons broth or water

MEAT & POULTRY

❖ ❖ ❖ ❖ ❖

1. In separate saucepans, reheat the peas and artichoke bottoms in their water.

2. In a large skillet, melt 2 tablespoons of the butter over medium-high heat. Add the steaks and cook until well browned on all sides and rare to medium rare, 4 to 8 minutes. Transfer to a cutting board, remove the string, and season with salt and pepper.

3. Drain the peas and artichoke bottoms. Swirl the remaining 1 tablespoon of butter into the peas. Spoon the peas into the artichoke bottoms.

4. In the same skillet, add the Madeira and broth or water and boil, scraping up any brown bits on the bottom, until reduced by half. Taste for seasoning. Pour into a warmed sauceboat.

5. Arrange the steaks in the center of a warmed platter and surround with the stuffed artichokes. Serve, passing the sauce separately.

From Françoise:

• A "tournedos" is a thick tenderloin steak that's often wrapped in a piece of barding fat and tied. You can remove the fat before serving.

• This is a good dinner-party dish for beginning cooks. It's expensive, but it's fast and impressive.

• Serve with potato chips and a green salad, and your menu is done.

ROASTED BEEF TENDERLOIN WITH CREAMY RED CURRANT SAUCE

- *Filet de boeuf grand veneur* -

❖ ADVANCED   ❖ EXPENSIVE   ❖ 1 HOUR, 15 MINUTES, PLUS 2 DAYS MARINATING   ❖ SERVES 4

2-pound beef tenderloin roast

4 tablespoons (½ stick) butter

1½ tablespoons all-purpose flour

2 cups beef broth

Salt and pepper

2 tablespoons crème fraîche

2 tablespoons red currant jelly

MARINADE

1½ cups red wine

6 tablespoons red wine vinegar

2 tablespoons oil

1 onion, chopped

2 carrots, peeled and chopped

2 shallots, chopped

2 garlic cloves, crushed

½ celery rib, chopped

1 bouquet garni made with parsley, thyme, and bay leaf

3 whole peppercorns

2 whole cloves

❖ ❖ ❖ ❖ ❖

1. In a gratin dish, combine the tenderloin with the marinade ingredients. Cover and refrigerate, turning the meat occasionally, for 2 days.

2. Scrape the marinade off the meat; transfer the meat to a roasting pan and pat dry. Strain the marinade, reserving the liquid. In a flameproof casserole, melt 2 tablespoons of the butter over medium heat. Add the vegetables from the marinade, sprinkle with the flour, and cook until lightly browned. Add the marinade and broth and bring to a boil, then reduce the heat to low and cook for 30 minutes. Taste for seasoning.

3. Meanwhile, preheat the oven to 425 degrees. Brush the meat all over with the remaining 2 tablespoons of butter. Transfer to the oven and roast, turning once, for 20 to 25 minutes for rare meat. Remove the string and season with salt and pepper. Transfer to a cutting board and cover loosely with foil.

4. Strain the broth into a saucepan. Bring to a simmer over medium heat and whisk in the crème fraîche. Cook until slightly thickened. Remove the pan from the heat and whisk in the red currant jelly. Taste for seasoning. Pour into a warmed sauceboat.

5. Transfer the meat to a warmed platter and serve, passing the sauce separately.

From Françoise:

• Serve with steamed potatoes, Pommes Dauphine (page 585), or even boiled noodles tossed with butter.

BEEF TENDERLOIN IN A GOLDEN PASTRY CRUST
- *Filet de boeuf en croûte* -

❖ ADVANCED ❖ EXPENSIVE ❖ 1 HOUR, 30 MINUTES ❖ SERVES 6

2 tablespoons butter, plus more for brushing
3-pound beef tenderloin roast
Salt and pepper
1 large egg yolk, lightly beaten with a little water
Madeira Sauce (page 640)

TWO-FORK DOUGH
1 ¾ cups all-purpose flour
1 cup (2 sticks) unsalted butter, softened
1 teaspoon salt
½ to ¾ cup water

❖ ❖ ❖ ❖ ❖

1. In a large skillet, melt the butter over medium-high heat. Add the meat and brown well on all sides for about 15 minutes. Season with salt and pepper. Transfer to a cutting board and let cool completely.

2. Make the two-fork dough: Spread the flour out on a clean work surface. Create a well in the center of the flour. With a knife, cut the butter in pieces and drop into the well. Dissolve the salt in the water and add to the well. With two forks, one in each hand, mix until the dough comes together. With your hand, press into a ball. Wrap with plastic wrap and refrigerate until firm, 15 to 20 minutes.

3. Preheat the oven to 425 degrees. On a lightly floured work surface, roll out the dough to a rectangle slightly less than ¼ inch thick. Set the meat on the dough. Bring the long sides of the dough up and over the meat, then brush the seam with the beaten egg yolk and press to seal. Trim off any excess dough from the short sides and brush with the egg wash. Fold the ends to enclose the meat and transfer the

bundle to a baking sheet lightly brushed with butter, seam side down. Brush with the beaten egg. If desired, cut out leaves or other decorations from the dough scraps and glue them on with beaten egg; brush the decorations with egg, too.

4. Bake for about 20 minutes. Cover loosely with foil if the pastry gets too dark. Transfer the meat to a cutting board and let rest for 10 minutes. Transfer to a warmed platter and serve, passing the Madeira sauce separately.

From Françoise:

• The beef tenderloin can be browned and the sauce and dough prepared in advance. Refrigerate until using. You will need 45 minutes to assemble and bake the tenderloin before serving.

• The secret to a beef tenderloin in pastry that's easy to wrap: The meat must be cooked and completely cooled first. If the meat is still warm, it will soften and moisten the dough, making it very difficult to work with.

CLASSIC ROAST BEEF
- Rôti de boeuf au four -

❖ EASY   ❖ MODERATE   ❖ 40 MINUTES   ❖ SERVES 4

2-pound beef roast, such as eye of round, tied
2 tablespoons butter, softened

Salt and pepper

❖ ❖ ❖ ❖ ❖

1. Preheat the oven to 425 degrees. In a roasting pan, brush the meat all over with the butter. Season with salt.

2. Transfer to the oven and roast for 25 to 30 minutes, turning the meat halfway through and basting several times with the pan juices.

3. Transfer the meat to a cutting board and remove the string. Season with salt and pepper. Cover loosely with foil and let stand for 10 minutes.

4. Carve the meat across the grain. Transfer to a warmed platter and serve, passing the pan juices separately.

From Françoise:
• The general rule for cooking a roast beef is 12 to 15 minutes per pound.

• Serve with any kind of potatoes—mashed, sautéed, fried, in Gratin Dauphinois (page 573), in croquettes.

• You can make the pan juices more flavorful by adding a quartered onion and a small sliced carrot to the roasting pan.

• Halfway through cooking, pour a little hot water into the roasting pan.

POT-ROASTED BEEF
- Rôti de boeuf à la cocotte -

❖ EASY   ❖ MODERATE   ❖ 50 MINUTES   ❖ SERVES 4

1 tablespoon butter
1 tablespoon oil

2-pound beef roast, such as eye of round, tied
Salt and pepper

1. In a flameproof casserole, melt the butter in the oil over medium-high heat. Add the beef roast and brown it well on all sides for 5 minutes. Partially cover and cook for 25 minutes.

2. Transfer the roast to a cutting board and remove the string. Season with salt and pepper. Cover loosely with foil and let stand for 10 minutes.

3. Add 1 or 2 tablespoons of water to the casserole and boil, scraping up any brown bits on the bottom, until slightly thickened. Taste for seasoning.

4. Carve the roast across the grain into thin slices and transfer to a warmed platter. Serve, passing the pan juices separately.

From Françoise:

• It's easier to brown the beef in a skillet than in a casserole. The meat colors better and you're less likely to burn yourself. Transfer the browned meat to a casserole and continue with the recipe.

BACON-WRAPPED MEATLOAF

- *Rôti haché au bacon* -

❖ EASY   ❖ INEXPENSIVE   ❖ 40 MINUTES   ❖ SERVES 4

1 ¼ pounds ground beef
½ cup dry bread crumbs
Salt and pepper

½ pound bacon slices
2 tablespoons butter, softened

❖ ❖ ❖ ❖ ❖

1. Preheat the oven to 450 degrees. In a bowl, mix the beef with the bread crumbs and season with salt and pepper. On a work surface, shape the mixture into a loaf.

2. On a large sheet of plastic wrap or wax paper, overlap the bacon slices to form a rectangle. Set the meatloaf on the bacon and wrap the plastic around it, pressing to help the bacon adhere. Peel off the plastic and reposition any slices of bacon. Using long pieces of kitchen string, tie the meatloaf at 1-inch intervals. Rub the butter all over the bacon and season with salt and pepper. Transfer to a baking sheet and bake on the top shelf of the oven for 20 minutes.

3. Transfer the meatloaf to a cutting board and remove the string. Cover loosely with foil and let stand for 10 minutes. Cut the meatloaf into thick slices, arrange on a heated platter, and serve.

From Françoise:

• The bread crumbs are essential for keeping the meatloaf moist.

• Using a serrated knife will make slicing the meatloaf much easier.

• Serve with fried or sautéed potatoes or with a good dish of pasta.

BEEF SIMMERED IN BROTH
- *Boeuf à la ficelle* -

❖ VERY EASY　　　❖ MODERATE　　　❖ 45 MINUTES　　　❖ SERVES 6

1 onion, studded with a whole clove
1 carrot, peeled and sliced crosswise
1 bouquet garni made with parsley, thyme,
　and bay leaf

Salt and pepper
2-pound boneless strip steak, tied
Sea salt, cornichons, Dijon and flavored
　mustards, and horseradish sauce for serving

❖　❖　❖　❖　❖

1. In a large saucepan of water, combine the onion with the carrot and bouquet garni and season with salt and pepper. Bring to a boil over medium-high heat, then reduce the heat to medium and simmer for 20 minutes.

2. Add the strip steak to the gently boiling broth, cover, and cook until rare, about 20 minutes. Transfer to a cutting board and remove the string. Cover loosely with foil and let stand for 10 minutes.

3. Transfer to a warmed serving dish and serve with the condiments in small bowls.

From Françoise:
• Buy a piece of meat of at least 2 pounds. Any leftovers can be used in myriad ways—to make shepherd's pie, a steak sandwich, or salad.

FRENCH BEEF TENDERLOIN HOT POT
- *Fondue bourguignonne* -

❖ EASY　　　❖ EXPENSIVE　　　❖ 30 MINUTES　　　❖ SERVES 4

2 cups oil
1 ½ pounds beef tenderloin, cut into cubes

Chopped cornichons, Dijon mustard, flavored
　mustards, horseradish sauce, capers, and
　ketchup for serving

❖　❖　❖　❖　❖

1. In a fondue pot or medium saucepan set on a hot plate or chafing dish in the center of the table, heat the oil until shimmering. Set out the condiments in small bowls. Let guests cook their own meat to the desired doneness and season to their liking.

From Françoise:

• The wider the array of condiments the better. You might also include store-bought sauces such as béarnaise sauce, tartar sauce, aioli, and harissa.

• Using long-handled forks, spear each piece of meat well so it doesn't fall off in the hot oil.

• Do not fill the pot or saucepan more than two-thirds full.

• It's very easy to get oil stains and burns, so warn your guests to be careful.

FRENCH MOUSSAKA
- *Moussaka* -

❖ INTERMEDIATE   ❖ MODERATE   ❖ 1 HOUR, 15 MINUTES   ❖ SERVES 4

1 tablespoon butter, plus more for brushing

2 onions, finely chopped

1 pound raw or cooked boneless lamb shoulder or leg, finely chopped

1 shallot, finely chopped

¼ cup chopped parsley leaves

¼ pound white mushrooms, finely sliced

2 tomatoes, peeled, seeded, and coarsely chopped

4 garlic cloves, crushed

Salt and pepper

2 pounds eggplants, sliced crosswise ½ inch thick

All-purpose flour for dusting

6 tablespoons oil

1 large egg, lightly beaten

½ cup shredded Gruyère cheese

❖　❖　❖　❖　❖

1. Preheat the oven to 400 degrees. Brush a gratin dish with butter.

2. In a flameproof casserole, melt the 1 tablespoon of butter over medium heat. Add the onions and cook until lightly browned. Add the lamb, shallot, and 3 tablespoons of the parsley and cook, stirring often, until the lamb is cooked through. Add the mushrooms, tomatoes, and garlic and season with salt and pepper. Cook, stirring occasionally, for 15 minutes.

3. Dust the eggplant slices lightly with flour, patting off the excess.

4. In a large skillet, heat the oil over medium heat until shimmering. Add the eggplant

slices without crowding and cook until nicely browned on both sides. Transfer to a paper towel–lined platter as they are done. Repeat with the remaining eggplant.

5. Remove the casserole from the heat. Beat in the egg. In the gratin dish, spread half the eggplant slices, then cover with half the lamb mixture and sprinkle with half the cheese. Repeat the layering.

6. Set the gratin dish in a roasting pan and fill with hot water to come halfway up the side of the dish. Transfer to the top shelf of the oven and bake until melted and golden, about

continued

209

40 minutes. Sprinkle with the remaining 1 tablespoon of parsley, and serve hot.

From Françoise:
• This is a great way to use up a meaty leftover leg of lamb.

• For a creamy gratinéed dish, you can make a béchamel or Mornay sauce to spread between the layers and on top.

FRENCH SHEPHERD'S PIE
- *Hachis parmentier* -

❖ EASY   ❖ INEXPENSIVE   ❖ 1 HOUR   ❖ SERVES 4

Salt

2 pounds potatoes, peeled

3 tablespoons butter, plus more for brushing

1 onion, chopped

1 garlic clove, finely chopped

2 cups chopped leftover beef

Pepper

1 ½ cups milk

½ cup shredded Gruyère cheese or dry
   bread crumbs

❖   ❖   ❖   ❖   ❖

1. In a large saucepan of boiling salted water, cook the potatoes for 25 to 30 minutes. Drain.

2. Meanwhile, in a skillet, melt 1 tablespoon of the butter over low heat. Add the onion and cook until soft, about 10 minutes. Add the garlic and cook for 1 minute. Stir in the meat, season with salt and pepper, and cook for 5 minutes.

3. Preheat the oven to 425 degrees. In a small saucepan, heat the milk until barely simmering. Mash the potatoes. Beat in 1 tablespoon of butter, then the hot milk. Season with salt and pepper.

4. Brush a gratin dish with butter. Spread half the mashed potatoes in the dish, then spread with the meat mixture and top with the remaining potatoes. Sprinkle with the

cheese or bread crumbs. Dot with the remaining 1 tablespoon of butter. Bake on the top shelf of the oven for 15 minutes and serve.

From Françoise:
• This shepherd's pie could be served as a starter if you have only a little leftover cooked meat. Try to keep roughly the same proportions.

• If serving it as an entrée, start the meal with a soup, offer a green salad as a side dish, and finish with a cheese or dessert.

• If you don't have enough leftover beef (or lamb), you can supplement what's on hand with a little cooked sausage meat.

• As an alternative, you might try replacing the beef with shredded duck confit—it's delicious.

GOLDEN GRATIN OF BEEF AND EGGPLANT SLICES WITH TOMATO SAUCE

- Hachis fin de boeuf aux aubergines -

❖ EASY   ❖ INEXPENSIVE   ❖ 45 MINUTES   ❖ SERVES 4

2 ½ cups finely chopped leftover beef

1 bunch of parsley, stems removed, leaves chopped

1 garlic clove, finely chopped

Salt and pepper

¼ cup oil

4 eggplants, sliced crosswise ½ inch thick

1 cup tomato sauce

¼ cup dry bread crumbs

½ cup shredded Gruyère cheese

2 tablespoons butter

❖ ❖ ❖ ❖ ❖

1. Preheat the oven to 425 degrees. In a bowl, combine the meat with the parsley and garlic. Season with salt and pepper.

2. In a large skillet, heat the oil over medium-high heat. Add the eggplant and cook, turning once, for 5 minutes per side.

3. Line a gratin dish with the eggplant slices. Spread the meat mixture on top, then add the tomato sauce. Sprinkle with the bread crumbs, then the cheese. Dot with the butter and bake on the top shelf of the oven until melted and golden, 15 to 25 minutes.

From Françoise:

• This is a great dish to make with any meat you have left over from a pot-au-feu.

• It can be assembled in advance, then baked just before serving.

MEAT & POULTRY

BEEF SIMMERED IN RED WINE WITH VEGETABLES

- *Boeuf bourguignon* -

❖ EASY ❖ MODERATE ❖ 2 HOURS, 20 MINUTES ❖ SERVES 4

2 tablespoons oil

2 pounds beef chuck, cut into 2-inch pieces

1 carrot, peeled and sliced crosswise

2 onions, thinly sliced

1 ½ tablespoons all-purpose flour

2 ½ cups red wine

Salt and pepper

1 garlic clove, crushed

1 bouquet garni made with parsley, thyme, and bay leaf

2 pounds potatoes, peeled, halved or quartered if large

Chopped parsley for sprinkling

❖ ❖ ❖ ❖ ❖

1. In a flameproof casserole, heat the oil over medium-high heat. Add the meat and cook until browned all over. Transfer the meat to a bowl. Stir in the carrot, onions, and flour and cook until lightly browned. Return the meat to the casserole, then add the red wine and bring to a boil, scraping up any brown bits on the bottom. Season with salt and pepper and add ¾ cup of water, the garlic, and bouquet garni. Reduce the heat to low, cover, and cook for 2 hours.

2. Meanwhile, steam the potatoes or cook them in boiling salted water for 25 to 30 minutes.

3. Using a slotted spoon, transfer the meat to a warmed serving dish. Strain the sauce over the meat. Sprinkle with the parsley and serve with the potatoes.

From Françoise:

• I like to let the pieces of meat marinate overnight in the wine with the carrot, onions, garlic, and bouquet garni before cooking them. The next day, I remove the pieces of meat and pat them dry, then proceed with the recipe.

• If your casserole is small, brown the meat in batches in a skillet.

BEER-BRAISED BEEF STEW WITH ONIONS
- Carbonade -

❖ EASY ❖ MODERATE ❖ 3 HOURS, 30 MINUTES ❖ SERVES 4

3 tablespoons butter

2 pounds beef chuck, cut into 2-inch pieces

5 onions, thinly sliced

1 tablespoon all-purpose flour

2 cups beer

1 tablespoon sugar

1 bouquet garni made with parsley, thyme,
  and bay leaf

Salt and pepper

❖ ❖ ❖ ❖ ❖

1. In a flameproof casserole, melt the butter over medium-high heat. Add the meat and cook until nicely browned all over. Remove the meat to a bowl. Add the onions to the pot and cook until lightly browned. Stir in the flour. Return the meat to the pot and add the beer, 2 cups of water, the sugar, and bouquet garni, and season with salt and pepper.

2. Cover and bring to a simmer, then reduce the heat to low and cook over low heat until the meat is very tender, 2 hours and 30 minutes to 3 hours. Remove the bouquet garni. Transfer the stew to a warmed serving dish, and serve.

From Françoise:
• Serve with boiled potatoes.

BRAISED BEEF WITH CARROTS
- Boeuf mode aux carottes -

❖ EASY ❖ MODERATE ❖ 2 HOURS, 25 MINUTES ❖ SERVES 4

2 tablespoons oil

2-pound beef chuck roast, tied

2 pounds carrots, peeled and sliced crosswise

1 onion, thinly sliced

1 calf's foot, cut in half

1 tablespoon tomato paste

1 ½ cups dry white wine

1 garlic clove, crushed

1 bouquet garni made with parsley, thyme,
  and bay leaf

Salt and pepper

continued

1. In a flameproof casserole, heat the oil over medium-high heat. Add the beef and cook until browned all over. Add 1 of the carrots, the onion, calf's foot, tomato paste, wine, 1 ½ cups of water, the garlic, and bouquet garni. Season with salt and pepper. Cover and bring to a boil, then reduce the heat to low and cook for 1 hour and 30 minutes.

2. Add the remaining carrots and cook for 45 minutes.

3. Transfer the beef and calf's foot to a cutting board. Remove the string. Slice the beef across the grain and cut the calf's foot into pieces; arrange on a warmed serving dish. Surround with the carrots, strain the sauce over the top, and serve.

From Françoise:

• Have your butcher cut the calf's foot in half.

• You might add some thinly sliced mushrooms to the casserole 15 minutes before the end of cooking.

BEEF STEW WITH PEARL ONIONS, MUSHROOMS, AND BACON
- Boeuf vigneronne -

❖ EASY   ❖ MODERATE   ❖ 3 HOURS   ❖ SERVES 6

3 tablespoons oil

3 pounds beef chuck, cut into 2-inch pieces

3 tablespoons butter

2 shallots, chopped

1 garlic clove, chopped

1 carrot, peeled and sliced crosswise

1 bouquet garni made with parsley, thyme, and bay leaf

Salt and pepper

2 tablespoons all-purpose flour

3 cups full-bodied red wine

½ pound thick-sliced pancetta or bacon, cut crosswise into ¼-inch-thick strips

12 pearl onions, peeled

½ pound white mushrooms, halved or quartered if large

❖ ❖ ❖ ❖ ❖

1. In a large skillet, heat the oil over medium-high heat. Add the meat and brown on all sides.

2. In a flameproof casserole, melt 1 tablespoon of the butter. Add the shallots, garlic, carrot, and bouquet garni and season with salt and pepper. Stir in the flour and cook until lightly browned. Add the meat and wine. Cover and bring to a boil, then reduce the heat to low and cook for 2 hours.

3. Meanwhile, in a large skillet, melt 1 tablespoon of the butter over medium heat. Add the

pancetta or bacon and pearl onions and cook until lightly browned. Add to the casserole and cook for 30 minutes.

4. In the same skillet, melt the remaining 1 tablespoon of butter over medium heat. Add the mushrooms, season with salt and pepper, and cook, stirring, until lightly browned. Add them to the stew just before serving.

5. Remove the bouquet garni. Transfer the stew to a warmed serving dish and serve.

From Françoise:
• Serve with penne or other pasta shapes moistened with pan juices from the stew.

BRAISED BEEF WITH VEGETABLES
- *Pot-au-feu* -

❖ EASY   ❖ MODERATE   ❖ 3 HOURS, 30 MINUTES   ❖ SERVES 6 TO 8

3 leeks, white and light green parts only, halved crosswise
3 carrots, peeled and sliced 2 inches thick
2 turnips, peeled and quartered
1 celery rib, sliced 2 inches thick
1 onion stuck with 3 whole cloves
1 garlic clove, crushed
1 bouquet garni made with parsley, thyme, and bay leaf

1 beef bone
Salt
1 to 1½ pounds short ribs
1 to 1½ pounds beef shin or chuck blade
1 beef marrow bone
6 or 8 toasts
Sea salt, cornichons, and Dijon mustard for serving

❖ ❖ ❖ ❖ ❖

1. In a large pot, bring 3 quarts of water to a boil with the leeks, carrots, turnips, celery, onion, garlic, bouquet garni, and beef bone. Season with salt.

2. Add the short ribs and beef shin or chuck blade to the simmering broth, reduce the heat to low, and cook, skimming occasionally, for 1 hour and 30 minutes to 2 hours. Add the marrow bone and cook for 1 hour.

3. Using a slotted spoon, transfer the meat, leeks, carrots, turnips, and celery to a warmed serving dish. Scoop out the marrow and add to the dish.

4. Strain the broth. Add the toasts to soup plates, ladle some of the broth over them, and serve. Serve the meats and vegetables after the broth, with the condiments (sea salt, cornichons, and mustard).

continued

From Françoise:

• Three things are necessary to make a good pot-au-feu: enough meat, half marbled with fat (short ribs) and half lean (shin or blade); an assortment of vegetables; and long, slow cooking.

• The meat will taste better if you add it to simmering broth. However, the broth will taste better if you add the meat to cold water.

• Plug both sides of the marrow bone with kosher salt to help keep the marrow in the bone.

• Instead of serving the broth with the toasts, you might cook 6 or 8 tablespoons of tapioca or vermicelli in the simmering broth.

BRAISED BEEF WITH TOMATO AND NEW POTATOES
- *Estouffat catalan* -

❖ EASY	❖ MODERATE	❖ 2 HOURS	❖ SERVES 4

2 tablespoons oil
2 pounds beef eye round roast, cut into thick
  slices
2 tablespoons butter
4 carrots, peeled and sliced crosswise
2 onions, thinly sliced

¾ cup dry white wine
2 tablespoons tomato paste
1 bouquet garni made with parsley, thyme,
  and bay leaf
Salt and pepper
1 ½ pounds new potatoes, peeled

❖ ❖ ❖ ❖ ❖

1. In a large skillet, heat the oil over medium-high heat. Add the beef and brown well on 2 sides. Using a slotted spoon, transfer the pieces of meat to a bowl as they are done.

2. In a flameproof casserole, melt the butter over medium heat. Add the carrots and onions and lightly brown. Stir in the wine, tomato paste, and bouquet garni and season with salt and pepper. Return the meat to the pot and set the potatoes on top. Cover, raise the heat, and bring to a boil, then reduce the heat to low and cook for 1 hour and 30 minutes. Transfer to a warmed serving dish and serve.

From Françoise:

• You can transfer the pot to a moderate 325-degree oven for the long, slow cooking. It's nice because the heat is more even than on the top of the stove, and there's less chance of the ingredients sticking to the pot.

• L'estouffat, also called "estouffade," is excellent reheated.

MARINATED BEEF STEW WITH COUNTRY HAM

- *Daube béarnaise au jambon cru de pays* -

❖ EASY   ❖ MODERATE   ❖ 4 TO 5 HOURS, PLUS OVERNIGHT MARINATING   ❖ SERVES 10

5 ½ pounds beef chuck, cut into 2 ½-inch pieces

Fresh pork rind for lining (optional)

All-purpose flour for dusting

1 thick slice dry-cured ham, cut into dice

1 bouquet garni made with parsley, thyme,
   and bay leaf

1 red chile

Salt and pepper

MARINADE

3 cups full-bodied red wine

2 tablespoons oil

Thyme sprigs

1 bay leaf

Peppercorns

2 onions, each stuck with a whole clove

2 garlic cloves, crushed

❖ ❖ ❖ ❖ ❖

1. In a large bowl, combine the meat with the marinade ingredients. Cover and refrigerate overnight.

2. Line a flameproof casserole with the pork rind, if using. Scrape the marinade off the meat. Dust the meat lightly with flour, patting off the excess.

3. Add the meat to the casserole with the ham. Add the marinade, bouquet garni, and red chile and season with salt and pepper. Cover and cook over very low heat for 4 to 5 hours.

From Françoise:

• It's the even and slow cooking of the daube that gives it its moistness and tenderness. If you're using a regular cast-iron casserole, it's best to transfer it to a 300-degree oven for the long cooking because the heat is more even than on the top of the stove, and there's less chance of the ingredients sticking to the pot.

• A daube is not only wonderful reheated, but it may be even better. So you can make it in advance and serve it for two meals or freeze part of it for another time.

• Steamed rice, boiled potatoes, and macaroni or penne pasta are the best accompaniments.

BEEF STEW WITH TOMATOES, MUSHROOMS, AND OLIVES

- *Estouffade à la provençale* -

❖ EASY ❖ MODERATE ❖ 3 HOURS, 15 MINUTES ❖ SERVES 4

2 tablespoons butter

5 ounces thick-sliced pancetta or bacon,
  cut crosswise into ¼-inch-thick strips

2 pounds beef chuck, cut into 2-inch pieces

3 onions, quartered

1 tablespoon all-purpose flour

1 teaspoon tomato paste

4 or 5 tomatoes, peeled, seeded, and chopped

2 cups red wine

2 cups beef broth or water

3 garlic cloves, crushed

1 bouquet garni made with parsley, thyme,
  and bay leaf

Salt and pepper

5 ounces white mushrooms, quartered
  lengthwise

½ cup black or green olives

❖ ❖ ❖ ❖ ❖

1. In a flameproof casserole, melt the butter over medium heat. Add the pancetta or bacon and lightly brown over medium heat. Using a slotted spoon, transfer to a bowl.

2. Increase the heat to medium-high, add the beef, and cook until nicely browned all over. Transfer the pieces as they are done to another bowl. Add the onions to the pot and lightly brown. Return the beef to the pot. Stir in the flour and cook until lightly browned. Add the tomato paste, tomatoes, wine, broth or water, garlic, and bouquet garni. Season with pepper and, lightly, with salt. Cover and bring to a boil, then reduce the heat to low and cook for 2 hours.

3. Add the mushrooms, pancetta or bacon, and olives and cook for 1 hour. Transfer the stew to a warmed serving dish and serve.

From Françoise:

• To remove some of the saltiness from the pancetta or bacon and the olives, cook them in boiling water for 5 minutes, then drain before using them.

• Serve with plain boiled pasta or potatoes, which go beautifully with this savory sauce.

• Both estouffade and daube taste better if you transfer them to a 300-degree oven halfway through cooking.

BEEF STEW WITH BACON, TOMATOES, AND BLACK OLIVES

- Estouffade de boeuf arlésienne -

❖ EASY   ❖ MODERATE   ❖ 3 HOURS, 15 MINUTES   ❖ SERVES 6

1 tablespoon oil

7 ounces thick-sliced pancetta or bacon, cut crosswise into ¼-inch-thick strips

3 pounds beef chuck, cut into 2-inch pieces

3 onions, quartered

2 tablespoons all-purpose flour

3 cups dry white wine

3 garlic cloves, crushed

1 bouquet garni made with parsley, thyme, and bay leaf

Salt and pepper

4 or 5 tomatoes, peeled, seeded, and chopped

¾ cup black olives

Chopped parsley leaves for sprinkling

❖ ❖ ❖ ❖ ❖

1. In a flameproof casserole, heat the oil over medium heat. Add the pancetta or bacon and lightly brown. Using a slotted spoon, transfer to a bowl.

2. Increase the heat to medium-high, add the beef, and brown on all sides. Transfer the pieces as they are done to another bowl. Add the onions to the pot and lightly brown. Return the beef to the pot. Stir in the flour and cook until lightly browned. Add the wine, ¾ cup of water, the garlic, and bouquet garni and season with pepper and, lightly, with salt. Cover and bring to a boil, then reduce the heat to low and cook for 2 hours.

3. Add the tomatoes, bacon, and olives and cook for 1 hour. Transfer the stew to a warmed serving dish, sprinkle with parsley, and serve.

From Françoise:

• Serve with plain boiled pasta or potatoes—they go beautifully with this savory sauce.

219

MARINATED BEEF STEW WITH TOMATOES, BLACK OLIVES, AND ORANGE

Daube provençale

❖ EASY   ❖ MODERATE   ❖ 3 HOURS, PLUS OVERNIGHT MARINATING   ❖ SERVES 6

3 pounds beef chuck, cut into 2-inch pieces

2 tablespoons butter

7 ounces thick-sliced pancetta or bacon,
  cut crosswise into ¼-inch-thick strips

7 ounces fresh pork rind (optional)

4 onions, quartered

1 long strip of orange zest

Salt and pepper

2 tomatoes, peeled, seeded, and chopped

¾ cup black olives

Chopped parsley leaves for sprinkling

MARINADE

3 cups dry white wine

3 garlic cloves, crushed

2 tablespoons oil

Thyme sprigs

1 bay leaf

Parsley sprigs

❖ ❖ ❖ ❖ ❖

1. In a large bowl, combine the beef with the marinade ingredients. Cover and refrigerate overnight.

2. In a flameproof casserole, melt the butter over medium heat. Add the pancetta or bacon and lightly brown. Using a slotted spoon, transfer to a bowl.

3. Scrape the marinade off the beef and pat dry. Increase the heat to medium-high, add the beef and, if using, pork rind to the casserole and brown on all sides. Transfer the pieces as they are done to another bowl. Add the onions to the pot and lightly brown. Return the meat to the pot with the marinade ingredients and orange zest and season with pepper and,

lightly, with salt. Cover and bring to a boil, then reduce the heat to low and cook for 2 hours.

4. Add the tomatoes, bacon, and olives and cook for 30 minutes. Transfer the stew to a warmed serving dish, removing the pork rind (if using), sprinkle with parsley, and serve.

From Françoise:

• Oil is indispensable in the marinade because it helps the marinade keep all its flavor. You might also add ¼ cup of Cognac to make it even more luscious.

TANGY SAUTÉED BEEF AND ONIONS

- *Miroton* -

2 tablespoons butter

3 or 4 onions, sliced

1 tablespoon all-purpose flour

3 cups chopped leftover beef

1 tablespoon tomato paste

1 cup beef broth

Salt and pepper

4 or 5 cornichons, sliced crosswise

1 teaspoon vinegar

Chopped parsley leaves for sprinkling

❖ ❖ ❖ ❖ ❖

1. In a large skillet, melt the butter over medium heat. Add the onions and lightly brown. Stir in the flour, beef, tomato paste, and broth and season with salt and pepper. Cook for 10 minutes, then cover and cook for 5 minutes.

2. Just before serving, stir in the cornichons and vinegar. Transfer to a warmed serving dish, sprinkle with parsley, and serve.

From Françoise:

• If you've made a pot-au-feu, you can use the broth from that. Otherwise, white wine or water will do.

MEAT & POULTRY

PAPRIKA-RUBBED BEEF TENDERLOIN SKEWERS

- *Brochettes de boeuf Zingara* -

1 ½ pounds beef tenderloin, cut into
  1 ½-inch pieces

Oil for brushing

2 teaspoons paprika

Thyme leaves for sprinkling

8 strips of lemon zest

8 bay leaves

Salt and pepper

Watercress sprigs for decorating

14 tablespoons (1 ¾ sticks) butter, melted

continued

1. In a gratin dish, brush the meat with oil and sprinkle with the paprika and thyme. Cover and refrigerate for 1 hour.

2. Heat a grill or the broiler. On each of 4 long metal skewers, thread 1 piece of meat, 1 strip of lemon zest, and 1 bay leaf, then repeat; finish the skewer with another piece of meat. Season with salt and pepper.

3. Grill or broil the skewers until charred on all sides, 4 to 5 minutes. Transfer to a warmed platter, decorate with the watercress, and serve, passing the melted butter in a sauceboat.

From Françoise:
• For more flavorful meat, brush the skewers with olive oil.

BEEF CROQUETTES
- Croquettes de boeuf -

❖ EASY   ❖ INEXPENSIVE   ❖ 30 MINUTES   ❖ SERVES 4

2 cups finely chopped leftover beef
1 onion, finely chopped
Finely chopped parsley
½ cup dry bread crumbs

1 large egg
Thyme leaves
Salt and pepper
2 tablespoons butter, plus more for brushing

❖ ❖ ❖ ❖ ❖

1. Preheat the oven to 400 degrees. In a bowl, combine the beef with the onion, parsley, bread crumbs, egg, and thyme. Season with salt and pepper. Shape the mixture into 4 croquettes.

2. Brush a gratin dish with butter. Add the croquettes and dot with the butter. Transfer to the oven and bake for 15 minutes.

From Françoise:
• A few variations: You might use finely chopped garlic or shallot instead of the onion. Snipped chives could stand in for the parsley. Marjoram or a little cumin could be substituted for the thyme.

• To make your own bread crumbs, grind day-old bread in a food processor or, if it's really stale, crush it with a rolling pin into fine crumbs.

• If you like, lightly brown the onion in a little butter before mixing it into the meat.

GRATIN OF MEAT-STUFFED CRÊPES
- Crêpes farcies à la viande -

❖ INTERMEDIATE   ❖ INEXPENSIVE   ❖ 1 HOUR, 30 MINUTES, PLUS 1 HOUR RESTING   ❖ SERVES 4

MEAT &
POULTRY

CRÊPES
½ cup all-purpose flour
¾ cup milk or water
1 large egg, lightly beaten
1 tablespoon butter, melted, plus more
  for brushing
¼ teaspoon salt

SAUCE
2 tablespoons butter
3 ounces thick-sliced pancetta or bacon,
  cut crosswise into ¼-inch-thick strips
1 shallot, finely chopped
1 garlic clove, finely chopped

3 tablespoons tomato paste
1 bouquet garni made with parsley, thyme,
  and bay leaf
Salt and pepper
1 teaspoon all-purpose flour

FILLING
4 to 5 tablespoons dry bread crumbs
6 tablespoons milk
1 cup finely chopped leftover beef
1 small shallot, finely chopped
Chopped parsley leaves
1 large egg yolk
Salt and pepper

❖   ❖   ❖   ❖   ❖

1. Make the crêpes: In a medium bowl, whisk the flour with the milk or water, egg, 1 tablespoon of the melted butter, and the salt. Cover and let stand for at least 1 hour.

2. Meanwhile, make the sauce: In a small saucepan, melt 1 tablespoon of the butter over medium heat. Add the pancetta or bacon and shallot and lightly brown. Add the garlic, tomato paste, 2 ¼ cups of water, and the bouquet garni and season with salt and pepper. Reduce the heat to low, cover, and cook for 20 minutes.

3. Make the filling: In a bowl, soak the bread crumbs in the milk, then squeeze dry. Mix in the beef, shallot, parsley, and egg yolk and season with salt and pepper.

4. Lightly brush a 7-inch skillet with melted butter and heat over medium heat. Whisk the batter and add about 2 tablespoons to the

skillet, swirling to coat the bottom. Cook until the edges begin to brown, about 30 seconds. Flip using a thin-bladed spatula and cook for 20 seconds. Slide onto a plate and repeat with the remaining batter, stacking the crêpes as they're cooked.

5. Preheat the oven to 350 degrees. Lightly brush the bottom of a gratin dish with butter. Spread about 1 tablespoon of filling over each crêpe and roll up. Arrange the crêpes in the gratin dish.

6. Remove the bouquet garni from the sauce. In a cup, mash the remaining 1 tablespoon of butter with the flour. Gradually whisk this paste into the simmering sauce. Spoon the sauce over the crêpes and bake until the filling is hot, 20 to 25 minutes. Serve right away.

continued

• The number of crêpes you'll get from these quantities varies—let's say something like 4 to 6, depending on the thickness of the crêpes and the size of your pan.

• Despite the long list of ingredients, this recipe is not very difficult to make, and it's a great dish for supper. What's more, it's economical.

WHITE BEAN STEW WITH SAUSAGE, LAMB, AND GOOSE CONFIT

- *Cassoulet* -

❖ INTERMEDIATE ❖ EXPENSIVE ❖ 4 HOURS, 30 MINUTES ❖ SERVES 6 TO 8

1 ½ pounds dried white beans

½-pound piece of bacon

½ pound fresh pork rind, chopped

2 carrots, peeled and sliced lengthwise

4 onions, 1 onion stuck with 2 whole cloves and 3 onions, chopped

3 garlic cloves, crushed

1 bouquet garni made with parsley, thyme, and bay leaf

Salt and pepper

3 tablespoons butter

1 pound lamb shoulder or neck

¾ pound boneless shoulder end of pork loin

1 pound French garlic sausage or kielbasa

2 shallots, chopped

2 or 3 tomatoes, peeled, seeded, and chopped

1 tablespoon tomato paste

3 pieces of goose or duck leg confit

Fresh bread crumbs for sprinkling

❖ ❖ ❖ ❖ ❖

1. In a large pot, generously cover the beans with water and bring to a boil. Cook for 15 minutes, then drain. Return the beans to the pot and add the bacon, pork rind, carrot, onion stuck with cloves, 1 garlic clove, the bouquet garni, and water to cover by 2 inches. Cover and bring to a boil, then reduce the heat to low and cook until tender, 1 hour and 30 minutes to 2 hours, seasoning with salt and pepper halfway through.

2. Meanwhile, in a flameproof casserole, melt 2 tablespoons of the butter over medium heat. Add the lamb and pork in batches and cook until nicely browned all over. Stir in the sausage, chopped onions, shallots, and 2 remaining garlic cloves. Add the tomatoes and tomato paste and season with salt and pepper. Add enough bean broth to barely cover the meats. Cover, bring to a boil, then reduce the heat to low and cook for 1 hour.

3. Preheat the oven to 200 degrees. Remove the meats to a cutting board and slice. Drain the beans, reserving the broth. Remove the bouquet garni, carrots, and onion from the beans and discard. In a large gratin dish, spread half the pork rind. Layer half the beans, meats, and confit on top, seasoning with pepper between the layers. Repeat, finishing with a layer of

bacon, pork rind, and sausage. Moisten with some of the reserved bean broth. Sprinkle with the bread crumbs and dot with the remaining 1 tablespoon of butter. Transfer to the oven and bake for 1 hour.

From Françoise:
• Instead of butter, it would be appropriate to use goose or duck fat to brown the meat in Step 2.

• If possible, blanch the pork rind before adding it to the casserole.

• Cassoulet is the subject of much debate with partisans for Castelnaudary, Toulouse, or other regions. Wherever it comes from, a well-prepared cassoulet is delicious. This is a basic recipe for the succulent pork, lamb, and bean stew, as one celebrated culinary dictionary describes it.

LAMB AND WHITE BEAN STEW
- *Haricot de mouton* -

❖ EASY   ❖ INEXPENSIVE   ❖ 2 HOURS, PLUS OVERNIGHT SOAKING   ❖ SERVES 4

½ pound dried white beans
3 tablespoons butter
2 ½ pounds lamb shoulder, breast, neck, or riblets, cut into 1 ½- to 2-inch pieces
2 onions, quartered
1 tablespoon all-purpose flour

1 garlic clove, crushed
1 bouquet garni made with parsley, thyme, and bay leaf
Salt and pepper
Chopped parsley leaves for sprinkling

❖ ❖ ❖ ❖ ❖

1. In a bowl, generously cover the beans with water and let soak overnight. Drain.

2. In a flameproof casserole, melt the butter over medium heat. Add the lamb and lightly brown on all sides. Transfer the pieces as they are done to another bowl. Add the onions to the pot and lightly brown. Return the lamb to the pot and stir in the flour, then 2 cups of water. Add the beans, garlic, and bouquet garni and season with salt and pepper. Cover and bring to a boil, then reduce the heat to low and cook for 1 hour and 30 minutes.

3. Transfer to a warmed serving dish, sprinkle with parsley, and serve.

From Françoise:
• While the lamb cooks, check it from time to time to see if the water is evaporating too quickly. Add a little if needed.

• Lamb breast, neck, and riblets are not as easy to find as lamb shoulder, but they are very tasty in this long-simmered dish, and a bargain.

BROILED LAMB CHOPS WITH PARSLEY BUTTER
- Côtelettes d'agneau grillées -

❖ VERY EASY   ❖ EXPENSIVE   ❖ 15 MINUTES   ❖ SERVES 4

8 lamb chops
Oil for brushing
2 tablespoons butter, softened

Chopped parsley leaves
Salt and pepper

❖ ❖ ❖ ❖ ❖

1. Heat the broiler. On a broiler pan, brush the chops on both sides with oil and broil, turning once, 2 to 3 minutes per side.

2. Meanwhile, mash the butter with the parsley and season with salt and pepper.

3. Transfer the chops to a warmed platter. Season with salt and pepper, top with the parsley butter, and serve.

From Françoise:
• Lamb, whether grilled, pan-seared, or roasted, is generally cooked medium-rare.

CLASSIC PAN-SEARED LAMB CHOPS
- Côtelettes d'agneau à la poéle -

❖ VERY EASY   ❖ EXPENSIVE   ❖ 15 MINUTES   ❖ SERVES 4

2 tablespoons butter
8 lamb chops

Salt and pepper

❖ ❖ ❖ ❖ ❖

1. In a large skillet, melt the butter over medium-high heat. Add the chops and cook, turning once, until golden brown, 3 to 4 minutes per side. Season with salt and pepper, transfer to a warmed platter, and serve.

From Françoise:
• Heat the dinner plates before serving the lamb. It's always nice to serve hot food on warmed plates, but especially so when serving lamb so the fat doesn't congeal quickly.

CLASSIC ROASTED LAMB SHOULDER
- Épaule d'agneau rôtie -

❖ VERY EASY   ❖ EXPENSIVE   ❖ 1 HOUR, 15 MINUTES   ❖ SERVES 4

3-pound lamb shoulder, tied
3 garlic cloves, halved lengthwise

Oil for brushing
Salt and pepper

❖   ❖   ❖   ❖   ❖

1. Preheat the oven to 400 degrees. Using a small, sharp knife, make 6 evenly spaced 1-inch incisions in the lamb. Push half a garlic clove into each incision. Brush the lamb with the oil and season with salt and pepper. Set the lamb in a roasting pan.

2. Transfer to the oven and roast for about 1 hour, turning the meat halfway through cooking and basting several times with the pan juices.

3. Transfer to a cutting board and remove the string. Cover loosely with foil and let stand for 10 minutes before carving.

From Françoise:

• Sprinkle thyme leaves on the lamb before roasting it. The herb only adds to the flavor.

• The general rule for roasting lamb is 20 to 25 minutes per pound.

• Halfway through cooking you can brush the meat with softened butter, but not too much because the pan juices are already a little fatty.

• Serve with green beans; shell beans, fresh or dried; Pommes Dauphine (page 585); or Gratin Dauphinois (page 573).

MEAT &
POULTRY

NUTMEG-BRAISED LAMB AND RICE PILAF
- Agneau au riz et aux épices -

❖ EASY   ❖ MODERATE   ❖ 1 HOUR, 10 MINUTES   ❖ SERVES 4

1 tablespoon butter
4 pounds lamb neck, cut into 1½-inch pieces
2 onions, quartered
1 garlic clove, crushed
1 bouquet garni made with parsley, thyme,
    and bay leaf

Freshly grated nutmeg
Salt and pepper
1½ cups rice

continued

1. In a flameproof casserole, melt the butter over medium-high heat. Add the lamb and brown well on all sides. Add the onions, water to barely cover, the garlic, and bouquet garni and season with nutmeg, salt, and pepper. Cover and bring to a boil, then reduce the heat to low and cook for 40 minutes.

2. Add the rice and, if needed, boiling water to barely cover the meat. Cover and cook over low heat for 20 minutes. Remove the bouquet garni and serve.

SPICY BRAISED LAMB AND VEGETABLES WITH COUSCOUS

- Couscous -

❖ ADVANCED	❖ EXPENSIVE	❖ 3 HOURS	❖ SERVES 8

2 pounds lamb neck or shoulder,
  cut into 2-inch pieces

4 onions, quartered lengthwise

Pinch of saffron threads

Salt

½ cup olive oil

3 tablespoons tomato paste

3 tablespoons harissa, plus more for serving

2 garlic cloves, crushed

2 carrots, peeled and halved lengthwise

2 turnips, peeled and halved lengthwise

3-pound chicken, cut into 8 serving pieces

4 small zucchini, cut into 2-inch lengths

2 tomatoes, coarsely chopped

1 to 2 teaspoons ras el hanout

1 teaspoon ground cumin

8 tablespoons butter, cut into ¼-inch dice

2 cups couscous

1 cup fresh or frozen petit pois peas

1 cup canned chickpeas, drained and rinsed

½ cup golden raisins

2 peeled roasted peppers

❖ ❖ ❖ ❖ ❖

1. In a flameproof casserole, combine 2 quarts of water with the lamb, onions, saffron, salt, olive oil, tomato paste, the 3 tablespoons of harissa, and the garlic. Cover and bring to a simmer over medium-high heat, then reduce the heat to low and cook for 30 minutes.

2. Add the carrots, turnips, and chicken to the lamb and cook for 1 hour. Add the zucchini, tomatoes, ras el hanout, and cumin, and cook for 30 minutes.

3. Meanwhile, in a large saucepan, melt 1 ½ tablespoons of the butter over medium heat. Add the couscous and cook, stirring, until lightly toasted, about 3 minutes. Stir in 2 cups of water, 1 cup of lamb cooking broth, and a large pinch of salt and bring to a boil. Cover, remove from the heat, and let stand until the liquid has been absorbed, about 10 minutes. Fluff with a fork.

4. In a medium saucepan, combine 2 cups of lamb broth with the peas, chickpeas, raisins,

roasted peppers, and harissa to taste; heat through.

5. Mound the couscous in a large warmed serving dish and dot with the remaining 6 ½ tablespoons of butter. Add the meat and vegetables to a warmed serving dish and moisten with some of the broth. Serve the couscous, meat, and vegetables, passing more harissa at the table.

From Françoise:
• You can replace the chicken with chicken giblets. Or add boiled beef to the meats.

• The vegetables can be expanded to include eggplant, artichoke bottoms, cabbage, and fresh shell beans.

• Traditionally, mint green tea is served with couscous. Or pour a light red wine.

CURRIED LAMB STEW

- Sauté de mouton au curry -

❖ EASY   ❖ MODERATE   ❖ 1 HOUR, 20 MINUTES   ❖ SERVES 4

2 tablespoons oil

2 pounds boneless lamb shoulder,
 cut into 1 ½-inch pieces

4 onions, thinly sliced

1 tablespoon all-purpose flour

2 to 3 teaspoons curry powder

1 tablespoon tomato paste

1 garlic clove, crushed

1 bouquet garni made with parsley, thyme,
 and bay leaf

Salt and pepper

❖   ❖   ❖   ❖   ❖

1. In a flameproof casserole, heat the oil over medium-high heat. Add the lamb and brown well on all sides. Transfer the pieces as they are done to a bowl. Add the onions to the pot and lightly brown. Return the lamb to the pot. Stir in the flour and cook until lightly browned. Add the curry powder, 3 cups of water, the tomato paste, garlic, and bouquet garni and season with salt and pepper. Cover and bring to a boil, then reduce the heat to low and cook for 1 hour. Remove the bouquet garni and serve.

From Françoise:
• For lamb braises and stews, choose less expensive cuts such as the neck, breast, riblets, and shoulder.

• Store-bought curry powders can vary in spiciness, so add it gingerly. You can always add more.

• Serve with steamed or boiled rice.

• To soften the pungency and add richness to the stew, stir 1 or 2 tablespoons of crème fraîche into the sauce.

BRAISED LAMB CHOPS WITH SLICED POTATOES AND ONIONS
- Côtelettes d'agneau Champvallon -

❖ EASY   ❖ MODERATE   ❖ 1 HOUR   ❖ SERVES 4

3 tablespoons butter

4 lamb chops

2 pounds potatoes, peeled and thinly sliced

2 large onions, thinly sliced

Salt and pepper

2 garlic cloves, finely chopped

1 bouquet garni made with parsley, thyme, and bay leaf

2 cups meat broth

❖   ❖   ❖   ❖   ❖

1. In a large skillet, melt the butter over medium-high heat. Add the chops and cook, turning once, until golden brown, 3 to 4 minutes per side. Transfer to a plate. Add the potatoes and onions to the skillet and lightly brown. Season with salt and pepper.

2. In a flameproof casserole, layer half the potatoes and onions. Cover with the lamb chops, garlic, and bouquet garni and spread the remaining potatoes and onions on top. Pour in the broth. Cover and bring to a boil over medium-high heat, then reduce the heat to low and cook for 30 to 40 minutes.

From Françoise:

• For a special dinner, choose rib or loin chops. But if, as a cost-saving measure, you buy shoulder, blade, or leg chops, I promise the result will be equally irresistible.

• If your skillet is too small to fit all the potatoes at once comfortably, brown them in batches.

• Try cooking the lamb chops in the oven at 350 degrees; they will cook more evenly than on top of the stove. The same is true for anything cooked in a casserole.

PARSLEY AND GARLIC–CRUSTED RACK OF LAMB
- Carré d'agneau persillade -

❖ EASY   ❖ EXPENSIVE   ❖ 20 MINUTES   ❖ SERVES 4

2 tablespoons butter

1 ½-pound rack of lamb, bones frenched (8 chops)

Salt and pepper

Finely chopped parsley leaves

1 garlic clove, finely chopped

Dry bread crumbs

1. Preheat the oven to 450 degrees. In a large skillet, melt 1 tablespoon of the butter over medium-high heat. Add the rack, fat side down, and cook until nicely browned, about 3 minutes. Turn and sear the meaty side of the rack, about 2 minutes longer.

2. Transfer the rack to a roasting pan, fat side up. Roast in the upper third of the oven for 15 minutes, turning the meat halfway through cooking and seasoning with salt and pepper.

3. Meanwhile, in a bowl, combine the parsley with the garlic and bread crumbs and season with salt and pepper. Using a wooden spoon, pat this mixture over the meat and dot with the remaining 1 tablespoon of butter. Return the rack to the oven for a few minutes. Transfer to a cutting board, cover loosely with foil, and let stand for 10 minutes before carving.

From Françoise:

• The rack of lamb can be prepared through Step 2 and set aside for 15 to 20 minutes. Pat on the parsley crust and return the lamb to the oven for 5 minutes to reheat it and crisp the topping. Before the lamb goes back in the oven, you can be baking a first course or side dish like a quiche Lorraine, cheese soufflé, or gratin.

• The secret to carving a rack of lamb: Using a large, sharp chef's knife, cut between the individual chops until you reach the bottom, then feel around with the tip of the knife for the joint between the bones and cut through it.

CLASSIC ROAST LEG OF LAMB
- *Gigot rôti* -

❖ EASY ❖ EXPENSIVE ❖ 1 HOUR ❖ SERVES 6

4-pound leg of lamb

4 or 5 garlic cloves, halved lengthwise

2 tablespoons butter, softened

Salt and pepper

❖ ❖ ❖ ❖ ❖

1. Preheat the oven to 450 degrees. Using a small, sharp knife, make 8 or 10 evenly spaced 1-inch incisions in the lamb. Push half a garlic clove into each incision. Brush the lamb with the butter and season with salt and pepper. Set the lamb in a roasting pan or on a rimmed baking sheet.

2. Transfer to the oven and roast for 35 to 40 minutes, basting several times with the pan juices. Transfer to a cutting board, cover loosely with foil, and let stand for 10 minutes. Carve the leg and serve with the pan juices.

From Françoise:

• The general rule for roasting leg of lamb is 10 to 15 minutes a pound, depending on the size; for instance, 30 minutes for a 2-pound leg and 35 to 40 minutes for a 3-pound leg; and 40 to 45 minutes for a 5-pound leg.

continued

- The traditional accompaniments to roasted leg of lamb are buttery haricots verts or green beans and flageolet beans.

- To get more for your money, buy at least a 3-pound leg of lamb.

- Lamb leftovers don't lend themselves easily to being reheated. One of the best things you can do is serve them cold with cornichons, mayonnaise, and a green salad.

ROAST LEG OF LAMB WITH STUFFED ARTICHOKES AND TOMATOES
- *Gigot Richelieu* -

❖ INTERMEDIATE   ❖ EXPENSIVE   ❖ 1 HOUR, 30 MINUTES   ❖ SERVES 8

2 pounds new potatoes, peeled

4 tablespoons (½ stick) butter, softened

Salt and pepper

4 ½-pound leg of lamb

2 garlic cloves, halved lengthwise

4 tomatoes, halved horizontally

8 cooked artichoke bottoms

STUFFING

2 tablespoons butter

2 shallots, finely chopped

¼ pound white mushrooms, chopped

6 tablespoons dry white wine

Salt and pepper

❖   ❖   ❖   ❖   ❖

1. In a large saucepan, cover the potatoes with water and bring to a boil; drain. Return the potatoes to the pan, add 2 tablespoons of the butter, and season with salt and pepper. Cook the potatoes in the butter until nicely browned, then partly cover and cook until tender, about 45 minutes.

2. Meanwhile, preheat the oven to 450 degrees. Using a small, sharp knife, make 4 evenly spaced 1-inch incisions in the lamb. Push half a garlic clove into each incision. Season the lamb with salt and pepper. Set in a roasting pan or on a rimmed baking sheet.

3. Transfer to the oven and roast for 45 to 55 minutes, basting several times with the

pan juices. Transfer to a cutting board, cover loosely with foil, and let stand for 10 minutes.

4. Meanwhile, make the stuffing: In a medium saucepan, melt the butter over medium heat. Add the shallots and mushrooms and cook until lightly browned. Add the wine and season with salt and pepper. Simmer until the juices evaporate.

5. In a large skillet, melt the remaining 2 tablespoons of butter. Add the tomatoes cut side down and lightly brown them, turning once, 5 minutes per side. Transfer to a work surface. In the same pan, reheat the artichoke bottoms.

6. Mound the stuffing on the tomatoes and artichoke bottoms. Partially carve the lamb and transfer to a very large platter. Surround with the potatoes, tomatoes, and artichokes and serve, passing the pan juices separately.

From Françoise:
• Use your largest platter to serve this dish. Or cover a large tray or baking sheet with foil and arrange the sliced lamb, lamb leg, and vegetables on it.

BRAISED LEG OF LAMB WITH VEGETABLES
- *Gigot à l'anglaise* -

❖ EASY   ❖ EXPENSIVE   ❖ 1 HOUR, 15 MINUTES   ❖ SERVES 6

½ pound carrots, peeled and sliced 2 inches thick

2 turnips, peeled and quartered

1 large onion stuck with 2 whole cloves

1 bouquet garni made with parsley, thyme, and bay leaf

Salt and pepper

4-pound leg of lamb

2 garlic cloves, halved lengthwise

❖ ❖ ❖ ❖ ❖

1. Fill a large pot halfway with water and bring to a boil over medium-high heat with the carrots, turnips, onion, and bouquet garni. Season with salt and pepper.

2. Using a small, sharp knife, make 4 evenly spaced 1-inch incisions in the lamb. Push half a garlic clove into each incision. Add the lamb to the simmering broth, cover, reduce the heat to low, and cook for 50 minutes to 1 hour.

3. Transfer the lamb to a cutting board and carve. Arrange the sliced lamb on a warmed serving dish and surround with the carrots and turnips. Ladle some of the broth over the top and serve.

From Françoise:
• Don't be put off by the lamb's grayish exterior. It's rosy and succulent on the inside.

• Serve with fried potatoes, mashed potatoes, or Gratin Dauphinois (page 573) and buttery green beans or dried white beans, flageolets, or, in season, fresh shell beans.

• For a sauce, try a very English mint sauce or a very French béarnaise sauce.

LAMB STEW WITH EGGPLANT
- Fricassée d'agneau aux aubergines -

❖ EASY   ❖ MODERATE   ❖ 2 HOURS   ❖ SERVES 4

1 pound small, firm eggplants, cut into chunks
Salt
1 ½ pounds boneless lamb shoulder,
  cut into 1 ½-inch pieces
All-purpose flour for dusting
¾ cup oil
2 onions, chopped
3 or 4 ripe tomatoes, chopped

1 tablespoon tomato paste
½ teaspoon ground turmeric
1 bouquet garni made with parsley, thyme,
  and bay leaf
1 or 2 pinches of cayenne pepper
Pepper
Juice of ½ lemon

❖ ❖ ❖ ❖ ❖

1. In a colander, sprinkle the eggplants with salt and let stand for 15 minutes. Pat dry with paper towels.

2. Meanwhile, lightly dust the lamb with the flour, patting off the excess. In a flameproof casserole, heat 2 tablespoons of the oil over medium-high heat. Add the lamb and brown well on all sides. Stir in the onions, then the tomatoes, tomato paste, turmeric, and bouquet garni. Season with the cayenne, salt, and pepper and cook, stirring, for 5 to 6 minutes.

3. In a large skillet, heat the remaining oil over medium-high heat. Add the eggplant and lightly brown on all sides. Transfer to the casserole with ¾ cup of water. Cover and bring to a boil, then reduce the heat to low and cook for 1 hour. Add the lemon juice and cook until the meat is tender and the eggplant has cooked almost to a puree, about 30 minutes.

4. Remove the bouquet garni. Transfer the stew to a warmed serving dish and serve.

SLOW-COOKED LAMB WITH POTATOES AND ONIONS
- Collier de mouton à l'étouffée -

❖ EASY   ❖ INEXPENSIVE   ❖ 2 HOURS, 15 MINUTES   ❖ SERVES 4

3 pounds lamb neck, cut into 2-inch pieces
1 bouquet garni made with parsley, thyme,
  and bay leaf
Salt and pepper

2 pounds russet potatoes, peeled and sliced
  crosswise
½ pound onions, thinly sliced
1 or 2 shallots, sliced

1. In a flameproof casserole, barely cover the lamb with water. Add the bouquet garni, season with salt and pepper, and bring to a boil over medium-high heat. Spread one-third of the potatoes over the top, then the onions, then the shallots, and finish with the remaining potatoes. Season with salt and pepper. Reduce the heat to low, cover, and cook for 2 hours, stirring occasionally.

2. Remove the bouquet garni. Transfer to a warmed serving dish and serve.

BRAISED LAMB MEATBALLS IN TOMATO SAUCE
- Boulettes de mouton -

❖ EASY ❖ MODERATE ❖ 1 HOUR ❖ SERVES 4

1 pound ground lamb shoulder
1 large onion, finely chopped or grated
1 large egg
Freshly grated nutmeg
Salt and pepper

All-purpose flour for dusting
2 tablespoons butter
1 cup meat broth
3 tablespoons tomato paste

❖ ❖ ❖ ❖ ❖

1. Preheat the oven to 350 degrees. In a bowl, mix the lamb with the onion and egg. Season with nutmeg, salt, and pepper. Shape the mixture into 8 meatballs. Lightly dust them with flour, patting off the excess.

2. In a large skillet, melt the butter over medium-high heat. Add the meatballs and brown well on all sides. Transfer them as they are done to a gratin dish.

3. In a saucepan, gradually whisk the meat broth into the tomato paste and bring to a boil. Pour the tomato sauce over the meatballs and bake for 45 minutes, basting often.

From Françoise:

• Serve with steamed or boiled rice.

• The meatballs should be lightly floured. They are browned first in the skillet, but the real cooking takes place with the tomato sauce in the oven.

• You could also cook the meatballs and tomato sauce in a covered casserole over low heat on top of the stove. What's important for getting tender, juicy meatballs is slow, even heat.

LAMB STEW WITH SPRING CARROTS, TURNIPS, AND PEAS

- *Navarin printanier* -

❖ EASY ❖ MODERATE ❖ 1 HOUR, 30 MINUTES ❖ SERVES 4

3 tablespoons butter

2 ½ pounds lamb neck or breast,
cut into 1 ½-inch pieces

4 onions, thinly sliced

1 tablespoon all-purpose flour

1 tablespoon tomato paste

1 bouquet garni made with parsley, thyme,
and bay leaf

Salt and pepper

1 pound young spring carrots, cut into 1 ½-inch
pieces

1 pound small young turnips, peeled and
quartered

2 cups shelled peas (about 2 pounds in the shell)

1 pound new potatoes, halved or quartered
if large

❖ ❖ ❖ ❖ ❖

1. In a flameproof casserole, melt the butter over medium heat. Add the lamb and lightly brown on all sides. Transfer to a bowl as the pieces are done. Add the onions to the casserole and lightly brown them. Stir in the flour and lightly brown it. Return the lamb to the pot and barely cover with water. Add the tomato paste and bouquet garni and season with salt and pepper. Cover and bring to a boil, then reduce the heat to low and cook for 45 minutes.

2. Add the carrots, turnips, peas, and potatoes and cook until tender, about 30 minutes. Remove the bouquet garni. Transfer the stew to a warmed serving dish and serve.

From Françoise:
• If the cooking liquid hasn't reduced sufficiently when the meat is tender, remove the meat and vegetables and simmer until slightly thickened.

CUMIN-MARINATED LAMB SKEWERS

- Brochettes d'Afrique du Nord -

❖ EASY ❖ MODERATE ❖ 40 MINUTES, PLUS 1 HOUR MARINATING ❖ SERVES 4

1 ½ pounds boneless lamb shoulder,
  cut into 1 ½-inch pieces
Thyme leaves, for sprinkling
1 teaspoon cumin seeds
Salt and pepper

2 onions, cut into 8 wedges
1 red bell pepper, cut into 8 pieces
4 bay leaves, halved
Oil for brushing

❖ ❖ ❖ ❖ ❖

1. In a gratin dish, sprinkle the lamb with the thyme and cumin. Season with salt and pepper. Cover and refrigerate for 1 hour.

2. Heat a grill or the broiler. On each of 4 long metal skewers, thread 1 piece of meat, 1 onion wedge, 1 piece of bell pepper, and 1 bay leaf half, then repeat; finish the skewer with another piece of lamb. Brush with the oil.

3. Grill or broil the skewers, until charred on all sides, about 10 minutes. Transfer to a warmed platter and serve.

From Françoise:

• Plain rice is the best accompaniment to these lamb skewers. But couscous would also be an appropriate side dish.

• For a less expensive dish, replace the shoulder of lamb with a more ordinary cut. The butcher can steer you to offcuts that would also be delicious in this recipe.

MEAT &
POULTRY

POT-ROASTED LAMB SHOULDER WITH ONIONS

- *Épaule de mouton à la cocotte* -

❖ EASY   ❖ EXPENSIVE   ❖ 1 HOUR, 15 MINUTES   ❖ SERVES 4

3-pound lamb shoulder, tied
2 garlic cloves, halved lengthwise
Oil for brushing

2 tablespoons butter
2 onions, quartered
Salt and pepper

❖ ❖ ❖ ❖ ❖

1. Using a small, sharp knife, make 4 evenly spaced 1-inch incisions in the lamb. Push half a garlic clove into each incision. Brush the lamb with oil.

2. In a flameproof casserole, melt the butter over medium-high heat. Add the lamb and brown on all sides. Remove the lamb to a plate. Add the onions to the pot and lightly brown. Return the lamb to the pot, reduce the heat to medium, and cook for 25 minutes. Turn the meat and season with salt and pepper. Reduce the heat to low, cover, and cook for 20 to 25 minutes.

3. Transfer the meat to a cutting board and remove the string. Cover loosely with foil and let stand for 10 minutes. Add 2 or 3 tablespoons of boiling water to the casserole and cook at high heat, scraping up any brown bits stuck to the bottom, for 5 minutes.

4. Carve the meat, transfer to a warmed platter, and serve, passing the pan juices separately in a warmed sauceboat.

From Françoise:
• Since I like my dishes well-flavored, I often add a bouquet garni and a diced carrot to the casserole.

• It's always a good idea to let a roast rest before carving it so the juices can spread throughout the meat.

POT-ROASTED LAMB SHOULDER
WITH WHITE BEANS AND TOMATO
- *Épaule de mouton bretonne* -

❖ EASY   ❖ EXPENSIVE   ❖ 2 HOURS, PLUS OVERNIGHT SOAKING   ❖ SERVES 4

½ pound dried white beans

1 bouquet garni made with parsley, thyme, and bay leaf

2 garlic cloves, crushed

Salt and pepper

3-pound lamb shoulder, tied

Oil for brushing

2 tablespoons butter

2 onions, quartered

3 tablespoons tomato paste

❖ ❖ ❖ ❖ ❖

MEAT & POULTRY

1. In a bowl, cover the beans generously with water and let soak overnight. Drain. The next day, in a flameproof casserole, cover the beans generously with water. Add the bouquet garni and 1 of the garlic cloves and season with pepper. Bring to a boil over medium-high heat, then reduce the heat to low and cook until tender, 1 hour and 30 minutes to 2 hours. Drain.

2. Meanwhile, brush the lamb with oil. In another flameproof casserole, melt the butter over medium-high heat. Add the lamb and brown on all sides. Remove the lamb to a plate. Add the onions to the pot and lightly brown. Return the lamb to the pot and add the remaining garlic clove and season with salt and pepper. Reduce the heat to low, cover, and cook for 1 hour and 30 minutes.

3. Transfer the lamb to a cutting board, remove the string, and cover loosely with foil. Stir the tomato paste and beans into the casserole and cook gently for 5 to 10 minutes. Carve the lamb and arrange on a platter. Surround with the beans and serve.

From Françoise:

• You can use canned white beans to make this recipe. Add them to the casserole with the tomato paste in Step 3.

• A little bit of chopped parsley brightens up the dish.

• The cooking time for the beans depends on how fresh they are. This year's beans take less time to cook than older beans. They are tender when you can easily crush them with a fork.

LAMB AND RICE WITH SWEET SPICES

- *Agneau au riz à l'orientale* -

❖ EASY ❖ MODERATE ❖ 1 HOUR, 10 MINUTES ❖ SERVES 4

2 tablespoons butter or oil

2 ½ pounds lamb neck, cut into 1 ½-inch pieces

2 onions, quartered

1 garlic clove, crushed

1 bouquet garni made with parsley, thyme,
 and bay leaf

Freshly grated nutmeg

1 or 2 pinches ground cinnamon

Salt and pepper

1 ½ cups rice, rinsed

❖ ❖ ❖ ❖ ❖

1. In a flameproof casserole, melt the butter or heat the oil over medium-high heat. Add the lamb and brown well on all sides. Add the onions, garlic, bouquet garni, and enough water to barely cover. Season with nutmeg, cinnamon, salt, and pepper. Cover and bring to a boil, then reduce the heat to low and cook for 40 minutes.

2. Add the rice and, if needed, boiling water to barely cover the meat. Cover and cook over low heat for 20 minutes. Remove the bouquet garni and serve.

From Françoise:

• This North African dish is also called *adjem-pilaf,* which means "pilgrim's pilaf."

• The nutmeg and cinnamon are not essential, but they do lend an exotic flavor to the dish. Still, don't overdo it.

GARLICKY PORK CHOPS WITH TOMATO

- *Côtes de porc à la tomate* -

❖ EASY ❖ INEXPENSIVE ❖ 30 MINUTES ❖ SERVES 4

2 tablespoons butter

4 pork chops

2 onions, quartered

3 tablespoons tomato paste

1 garlic clove, finely chopped

1 bouquet garni made with parsley, thyme,
 and bay leaf

Salt and pepper

1. In a large skillet, melt the butter over medium-high heat. Add the pork chops and cook until nicely browned on the bottom, 2 to 3 minutes. Turn them, add the onions, and cook until browned.

2. In a bowl, gradually whisk ¾ cup of water into the tomato paste. Pour into the skillet and add the garlic and bouquet garni. Season with salt and pepper, reduce the heat to low, cover, and cook for 20 minutes.

3. Transfer the chops to a warmed platter. Remove the bouquet garni. Simmer the sauce until it thickens slightly. Pour over the chops and serve.

From Françoise:
• This is a beginner's dish yet it's still unique.

• You have many choices of side dishes here: potatoes, spinach, endives, and Brussels sprouts for vegetables, and also pasta or rice.

• If you're pan-frying pork, choose quick-cooking cuts like chops (rib, loin, or blade), tenderloin, or the shoulder end of the loin.

CRUSTY PORK CHOPS WITH VINEGAR
- *Côtes de porc panées* -

❖ EASY   ❖ MODERATE   ❖ 30 MINUTES   ❖ SERVES 4

All-purpose flour for dredging
2 large eggs, lightly beaten
4 to 5 tablespoons dry bread crumbs
Salt and pepper

4 pork chops
3 tablespoons butter, plus more if needed
2 tablespoons vinegar

❖ ❖ ❖ ❖ ❖

1. In separate soup plates, spread the flour, eggs, and bread crumbs. Season the eggs with salt and pepper. Season the pork chops with salt and pepper, then dredge lightly in flour and dip in the eggs, letting any excess drip back into the plate. Dredge the chops in the bread crumbs, pressing lightly to help the crumbs adhere.

2. In a large skillet, melt the butter over medium heat. Add the chops and cook, turning once, until golden brown, 8 to 10 minutes per side. Transfer to a warmed platter. Add the vinegar to the skillet and boil, scraping up any brown bits on the bottom, for 1 or 2 minutes. Pour the vinegar pan sauce over the pork chops and serve at once.

From Françoise:
• You can skip the vinegar pan sauce if you like. In that case, serve the pork chops with lemon wedges to perk up the flavor.

CLASSIC PAN-SEARED PORK CHOPS
- Côtes de porc -

❖ VERY EASY   ❖ INEXPENSIVE   ❖ 20 MINUTES   ❖ SERVES 4

2 tablespoons butter
4 pork chops

Salt and pepper

❖ ❖ ❖ ❖ ❖

1. In a large skillet, melt the butter over medium-high heat. Add the pork chops and cook, turning once, until nicely browned. Reduce the heat to medium and cook for 7 to 8 minutes per side, covering the skillet when the chops are almost cooked. Season with salt and pepper. Transfer to a warmed platter and serve.

From Françoise:
• Pork can be a bit bland, so I like to add herbs or other seasonings. Sometimes I sprinkle thyme leaves over the meat when it goes into the pan. Or I add fresh or dried rosemary, marjoram, curry powder, or paprika—there's no lack of options.

PAN-SEARED PORK CHOPS WITH APPLES
- Côtes de porc à la flamande -

❖ VERY EASY   ❖ INEXPENSIVE   ❖ 30 MINUTES   ❖ SERVES 4

3 tablespoons butter
4 pork chops
Salt and pepper

4 Golden Delicious apples, peeled, quartered,
 and thinly sliced

❖ ❖ ❖ ❖ ❖

1. In a large skillet, melt 2 tablespoons of the butter over medium high-heat. Add the pork chops and cook, turning once, until nicely browned. Reduce the heat to medium and cook for 7 to 8 minutes per side. Season with salt and pepper. Transfer the chops to a warmed platter.

2. In the same skillet, melt the remaining 1 tablespoon of butter over medium-high heat.

Add the apples and cook, turning once, until nicely browned, 5 to 6 minutes. Arrange on the platter around the pork chops and serve.

From Françoise:
• Serve with potatoes, either boiled or mashed.

• The sautéed apples should not be seasoned—no salt, no sugar.

PORK CUTLETS WITH WHITE WINE
AND SHALLOT PAN SAUCE

- *Grillades de porc au vin blanc* -

❖ VERY EASY   ❖ INEXPENSIVE   ❖ 20 MINUTES   ❖ SERVES 4

2 tablespoons butter

4 thin pork cutlets

1 shallot, finely chopped

2 teaspoons all-purpose flour

1 ½ cups dry white wine

1 teaspoon tomato paste

Salt and pepper

Chopped parsley leaves for sprinkling

❖ ❖ ❖ ❖ ❖

MEAT &
POULTRY

1. In a large skillet, melt 1 tablespoon of the butter over medium-high heat. Add the pork cutlets and cook, turning once, until nicely browned. Transfer to a plate.

2. In the same skillet, melt the remaining 1 tablespoon of butter over medium heat. Add the shallot and cook until lightly browned. Stir in the flour and lightly brown. Stir in the wine and tomato paste and season with salt and pepper. Boil, scraping up any brown bits on the bottom, for about 2 minutes.

3. Return the cutlets to the pan, reduce the heat to low, and finish cooking in the pan sauce, about 5 minutes. Transfer to a warmed platter. Sprinkle with parsley and serve.

From Françoise:

• Don't brown the shallot in the skillet at the same time as the pork cutlets—the shallot will darken and turn bitter.

PAN-SEARED PORK CUTLETS WITH CREAMY TARRAGON SAUCE

- *Grillades de porc à l'estragon* -

❖ VERY EASY ❖ INEXPENSIVE ❖ 30 MINUTES ❖ SERVES 4

4 thin pork cutlets

2 tablespoons oil, plus more for brushing

Thyme leaves for sprinkling

1 bay leaf, crumbled

Salt and pepper

1 ½ cups dry white wine

3 tarragon sprigs, stems removed

1 teaspoon cornstarch

½ cup crème fraîche

❖ ❖ ❖ ❖ ❖

1. In a gratin dish, brush the pork cutlets on both sides with oil and sprinkle with the thyme and bay leaf. Cover and refrigerate for about 20 minutes.

2. In a large skillet, heat 1 tablespoon of the oil over medium-high heat. Add the pork cutlets and cook, turning once, until nicely browned. Reduce the heat to medium and cook for 5 to 6 minutes per side. Season with salt and pepper. Transfer to a plate.

3. Discard the fat in the skillet. Add the wine and boil, scraping up any brown bits on the bottom. Add the tarragon, season with salt and pepper, and simmer until reduced by half.

4. Meanwhile, in a cup, mix the cornstarch with the crème fraîche. Whisk this into the pan sauce and bring to a boil.

5. Return the cutlets to the skillet and reheat briefly in the pan sauce, turning once. Transfer the cutlets to a warmed platter. Pour the pan sauce over them and serve.

From Françoise:

• Pork cutlets and pork chops cooked at too high a heat are tough and stringy. Brown them over fairly high heat, then reduce the heat to finish cooking them more gently.

POT-ROASTED PORK RIB ROAST WITH ORANGE SAUCE

- *Carré de porc braisé à l'orange* -

❖ EASY   ❖ MODERATE   ❖ 1 HOUR, 30 MINUTES   ❖ SERVES 4

2 tablespoons butter

3-pound bone-in pork rib roast

1 onion, thinly sliced

1 carrot, peeled and thinly sliced crosswise

1 teaspoon tomato paste

¾ cup dry white wine

2 garlic cloves, crushed

1 bouquet garni made with parsley, thyme,
  and bay leaf

Salt and pepper

4 oranges

¼ cup orange liqueur

❖ ❖ ❖ ❖ ❖

1. In a flameproof casserole, melt the butter over medium-high heat. Add the pork and cook until nicely browned on all sides. Stir in the onion, carrot, tomato paste, wine, garlic, and bouquet garni and season with salt and pepper. Reduce the heat to low, cover, and cook for about 1 hour.

2. Meanwhile, using a vegetable peeler, remove the zest from 2 of the oranges in strips. Cut them into fine julienne strips. Squeeze the juice of these 2 oranges into a small saucepan. Bring another small saucepan of water to a boil. Add the julienned zest and boil for 3 minutes, then drain. Bring the orange juice to a boil, add the zest, and simmer for 4 to 5 minutes.

3. Transfer the pork to a cutting board and cover loosely with foil. Strain the pan juices,

then return to the casserole. Add the orange juice, zest, and orange liqueur and simmer, scraping up the brown bits on the bottom, for 5 minutes.

4. Using a sharp knife, peel the remaining 2 oranges, removing all the white pith. Thinly slice them crosswise, removing any seeds. Transfer the pork to a warmed platter. Arrange the orange slices around the meat, pour the sauce over the pork, and serve.

From Françoise:

• Just 2 or 3 minutes of boiling the orange zest in water helps to remove any bitterness, then simmering it briefly in the orange juice amplifies its natural flavor. Don't neglect these two important steps.

PORK SKEWERS WITH PINEAPPLE

- *Brochettes de porc grillées à l'ananas* -

❖ EASY   ❖ MODERATE   ❖ 1 HOUR   ❖ SERVES 4

4 thick slices of pineapple, cut into chunks

1 pork kidney, cut into chunks

1 pound boneless pork shoulder end of loin,
    cut into chunks

7 ounces thick-sliced bacon, cut crosswise
    into ¼-inch-thick strips

4 sweet Italian sausages, each cut crosswise
    into 4 pieces

4 bay leaves

Oil for brushing

Salt and pepper

Freshly grated nutmeg

A few pinches of paprika

❖ ❖ ❖ ❖ ❖

1. Heat a grill or grill pan. On each of 4 long metal skewers, thread assorted chunks of pineapple, kidney, pork loin, bacon, sausage, and bay leaf. Brush the skewers with oil.

2. Grill the skewers over medium-low heat until charred on all sides, about 20 minutes. Season with salt, pepper, nutmeg, and paprika. Transfer to a warmed platter and serve.

COLD ROAST PORK

- *Rôti de porc froid charcutière* -

❖ EASY   ❖ MODERATE   ❖ 1 HOUR, 10 MINUTES   ❖ SERVES 4

1 onion stuck with 1 whole clove

1 bouquet garni made with parsley, thyme,
    and bay leaf

Salt and pepper

2 tablespoons butter

2-pound pork tenderloin or boneless sirloin

Mayonnaise, béarnaise sauce, tartar sauce, Dijon
    and flavored mustards, cornichons, and other
    pickles for serving

❖ ❖ ❖ ❖ ❖

1. In a flameproof casserole, combine 6 cups of water with the onion and bouquet garni. Season with salt and pepper and bring to a boil.

2. Meanwhile, in a large skillet, melt the butter over medium-high heat. Add the pork and cook until nicely browned on all sides. Transfer the meat to the boiling water, reduce

the heat to low, cover, and cook for about 45 minutes.

3. Transfer the pork to a cutting board and pat dry with paper towels. Set the same skillet over medium-high heat. Add the pork and cook again until browned on all sides. Let cool slightly, then refrigerate until cold before serving with the condiments.

From Françoise:
• Serve the cold roast pork with highly seasoned store-bought condiments of every variety.

• Do not wash or wipe out the skillet between browning the pork the first and second times.

CLASSIC POT-ROASTED PORK
- *Rôti de porc bonne femme* -

❖ VERY EASY   ❖ INEXPENSIVE   ❖ 2 HOURS, 15 MINUTES   ❖ SERVES 4

3 tablespoons butter
3-pound pork tenderloin, boneless shoulder end of loin, or rib roast, tied
6 pearl onions, peeled
2 pounds potatoes, peeled and halved if large

1 bouquet garni made with parsley, thyme, and bay leaf
Salt and pepper
Chopped parsley leaves for serving

❖ ❖ ❖ ❖ ❖

1. In a flameproof casserole, melt the butter over medium-high heat. Add the pork roast and cook until nicely browned on all sides. Reduce the heat to low, cover, and cook for 1 hour and 15 minutes.

2. Add the onions, potatoes, and bouquet garni and season with salt and pepper. Cook over low heat for about 45 minutes, turning the potatoes halfway through cooking.

3. Transfer the meat to a cutting board and remove the string. Cover loosely with foil and let stand for 10 minutes. Remove the bouquet garni.

4. Carve the meat and transfer to a warmed platter. Arrange the potatoes and onions around the pork. Sprinkle with parsley and serve.

From Françoise:
• Roast pork tenderloin gets a little dry but slices nicely. Roast pork sirloin is good and less expensive. The most succulent cut is the shoulder end of the loin.

• Pork roast has a much better flavor if, 1 or 2 hours before cooking, you rub it with crushed garlic and let it marinate with dry white wine, thyme sprigs, bay leaf, rosemary, sage, salt, and pepper. For a special occasion, you could add a little Cognac to the marinade.

POT-ROASTED PORK WITH CHESTNUT PUREE

- *Rôti de porc aux marrons* -

❖ EASY   ❖ MODERATE   ❖ 2 HOURS   ❖ SERVES 4

**2-pound boneless pork shoulder end of loin
  or sirloin roast, tied
1 garlic clove, crushed
3 tablespoons butter**

**1 onion, quartered
Salt and pepper
1 pound canned unsweetened chestnut puree**

❖   ❖   ❖   ❖   ❖

1. Rub the pork roast all over with the garlic clove. In a flameproof casserole, melt 2 tablespoons of the butter over medium-high heat. Add the pork and nicely brown all over. Transfer the pork to a plate. Add the onion to the casserole and lightly brown. Return the pork to the casserole, stir in 2 tablespoons of water, and season with salt and pepper. Reduce the heat to low, cover, and cook for 1 hour and 15 minutes, turning the pork several times.

2. Transfer the pork to a cutting board, remove the string, and cover loosely with foil. Transfer the pan juices and onion to a bowl.

3. In the same casserole, heat the chestnut puree. Stir in the remaining 1 tablespoon of butter and some of the reserved pan juices and season with salt and pepper.

4. Carve the meat and transfer to a warmed platter. Pour some of the remaining pan juices over the meat and serve with the chestnut puree.

From Françoise:

• You could serve whole chestnuts, fresh or precooked, instead of the puree. To prepare chestnuts in the shell, boil them for 30 minutes, then peel and add to the pork in the casserole 20 minutes before the end of cooking. If you're serving canned chestnuts, drain and rinse them, then reheat for 5 minutes in the casserole with the pork.

MARINATED PORK ROAST WITH GOLDEN SLICED POTATOES

- *Rôti de porc boulangère* -

❖ EASY ❖ INEXPENSIVE ❖ 2 HOURS, 30 MINUTES, PLUS OVERNIGHT MARINATING ❖ SERVES 4

2-pound boneless pork roast

2 tablespoons butter, plus more for brushing

2 pounds potatoes, peeled and thinly sliced

3 onions, thinly sliced

Salt and pepper

1 thyme sprig

½ bay leaf

2 whole cloves

MARINADE

1 onion, sliced

4 whole cloves

1 tablespoon oil

Thyme sprigs

Bay leaf

¾ cup dry white wine

Pepper

❖ ❖ ❖ ❖ ❖

1. In a large bowl, combine the pork with the marinade ingredients. Cover and refrigerate overnight, turning the meat occasionally.

2. Generously brush the bottom of a flame-proof casserole with butter. In it layer half the potatoes and onions. Season lightly with salt. Brush the marinade off the pork and set it on top of the potatoes. Cover with the remaining potatoes and onions and season with salt and pepper. Add the thyme, bay leaf, and whole cloves. Strain the marinade into the casserole. Dot with the butter. Cover and cook over low heat for 2 hours.

From Françoise:

• You could also cook the pork in a 350-degree oven instead of on top of the stove.

• If the potatoes start to stick to the bottom of the casserole on your stove's lowest heat, set a heat diffuser on the burner. It's very effective against little cooking accidents—always a possibility with long-simmered dishes that you get tired of checking.

PORK AND GREENS MEATLOAF
- *Farci saintongeais* -

❖ EASY ❖ INEXPENSIVE ❖ 1 HOUR, 15 MINUTES ❖ SERVES 6

20 slices crustless white sandwich bread
   (about ½ pound)
1 ¼ cups milk
2 tablespoons butter, plus more for brushing
1 onion, finely chopped
½ pound ground pork
1 pound green cabbage, chopped

½ pound spinach, large stems removed, chopped
3 lettuce leaves, chopped
2 ounces sorrel, large stems removed, chopped
Mixed chopped parsley, chives, and chervil leaves
4 large eggs
Salt and pepper

❖ ❖ ❖ ❖ ❖

1. Preheat the oven to 400 degrees. In a food processor, grind the bread slices into crumbs. Soak these fresh bread crumbs in the milk, then squeeze dry.

2. In a skillet, melt the butter over medium heat. Add the onion and cook until lightly browned.

3. In a large bowl, combine the pork with the bread crumbs, cabbage, spinach, lettuce, sorrel, herbs, browned onion, and eggs. Season with salt and pepper and beat well.

4. Spread the mixture in a gratin dish and bake in the oven for 1 hour.

ROAST PORK WITH STUFFED APPLES
- *Rôti de porc suédoise* -

❖ EASY ❖ MODERATE ❖ 1 HOUR, 15 MINUTES, PLUS OVERNIGHT SOAKING ❖ SERVES 4

12 pitted prunes
1 ½-pound boneless sirloin or tenderloin roast
Salt and pepper

5 tablespoons butter
2 pounds apples

❖ ❖ ❖ ❖ ❖

1. In a bowl, soak the prunes in water to cover overnight.

2. Preheat the oven to 400 degrees. Make a deep lengthwise slit in the pork, leaving about

1 inch of meat attached. Open the roast and season with salt and pepper. Arrange a few prunes in a row along the slit. Close the roast and tie at 2-inch intervals with kitchen string. Season the pork all over with salt and pepper.

3. In a large skillet, melt 2 tablespoons of the butter over medium-high heat. Add the pork and cook until nicely browned on all sides. Transfer to a roasting pan and dot with 1 tablespoon of butter. Transfer to the oven and roast for 10 minutes. Pour ¾ cup of boiling water around the roast and roast for 15 minutes, basting the meat occasionally.

4. Meanwhile, peel the apples. Using a sharp knife, cut a thin slice from the top and bottom of each apple. Working from the stem end and using a corer or sharp knife, remove the interior core and seeds to within ½ inch of the bottom. Add 1 or 2 prunes to each apple and dot with the remaining 2 tablespoons of butter. Arrange the apples around the pork and roast for 25 to 30 minutes.

5. Transfer the pork to a cutting board and remove the string. Cover loosely with foil and let stand 10 minutes. Carve the pork and arrange on a warmed platter. Serve with the stuffed apples and pan juices.

From Françoise:
• If you're in a hurry, soak the prunes in hot water for 1 hour.

• Serve with boiled potatoes.

CLASSIC OVEN-ROASTED PORK

- Rôti de porc au four -

❖ VERY EASY   ❖ MODERATE   ❖ 1 HOUR, 30 MINUTES   ❖ SERVES 4

3 tablespoons butter

2-pound pork roast, tied

Salt and pepper

❖ ❖ ❖ ❖ ❖

1. Preheat the oven to 350 degrees. In a large skillet, melt 2 tablespoons of the butter over medium-high heat. Add the pork and cook until nicely browned on all sides.

2. Transfer the pork to a roasting pan. Season with salt and pepper and dot with the remaining 1 tablespoon of butter. Transfer to the oven and roast for 15 minutes. Pour ¾ cup of water around the meat and roast for 1 hour, basting several times with the pan juices.

3. Transfer the pork to a cutting board and remove the string. Cover loosely with foil and let stand for 10 minutes. Carve the pork and arrange on a warmed platter. Serve with the pan juices.

From Françoise:
• Some people like to make incisions in the pork and insert garlic halves before roasting the meat as they would do for a lamb roast. It's a good idea. As for me, I like to slip fragrant sprigs of thyme or rosemary under the string used to tie the roast.

• For roasting pork in the oven, choose the tenderloin, sirloin, shoulder end of loin, or rib roast.

• The roast will be better seared if you brown it in a skillet before transferring it to the oven.

MARINATED PORK ROAST WITH SAGE

- *Rôti de porc à la sauge* -

❖ EASY   ❖ MODERATE   ❖ 1 HOUR, 45 MINUTES, PLUS OVERNIGHT MARINATING   ❖ SERVES 4

2-pound boneless pork roast, tied
12 sage leaves
Salt and pepper
2 tablespoons butter

MARINADE
1 onion, sliced
4 whole cloves
1 tablespoon oil
Thyme sprigs
Bay leaf
¾ cup dry white wine
Pepper

❖ ❖ ❖ ❖ ❖

1. In a large bowl, combine the pork with the marinade ingredients. Cover and refrigerate overnight, turning the meat occasionally.

2. Preheat the oven to 350 degrees. Brush the marinade off the pork. Strain the marinade and reserve. Using a small, sharp knife, make 12 evenly spaced 1-inch incisions in the pork. Push a sage leaf into each incision. Set the pork in a roasting pan, season with salt and pepper, and dot with the butter.

3. Transfer the pork to the oven and roast for 1 hour and 30 minutes, turning the meat halfway through cooking and basting several times

with the reserved marinade. After an hour, loosely cover the pork with foil.

4. Transfer the pork to a cutting board and remove the string. Cover loosely with foil and let stand for 10 minutes. Carve the pork and arrange on a warmed platter. Serve with the pan juices.

From Françoise:
• Serve with boiled potatoes, potato gratin, pasta, or a green seasonal vegetable, boiled until tender and then sautéed in a skillet with butter.

CURED PORK SHOULDER WITH GREEN LENTILS

- *Petit salé aux lentilles* -

❖ EASY   ❖ MODERATE   ❖ 2 HOURS, PLUS 2 TO 3 HOURS SOAKING   ❖ SERVES 4

1½ pounds salt-cured pork shoulder

½ pound green lentils

1 carrot, peeled and halved lengthwise

1 onion stuck with 1 whole clove

1 garlic clove, crushed

1 bouquet garni made with parsley, thyme, and bay leaf

Salt and pepper

❖   ❖   ❖   ❖   ❖

1. In a large bowl of water, soak the pork for 2 to 3 hours, changing the water several times. Drain.

2. Bring a large saucepan of water to a boil over medium-high heat. Add the pork and cook for 5 minutes. Drain.

3. Fill the same saucepan with water and bring to a boil over medium-high heat. Add the lentils and boil until almost tender, about 20 minutes. Drain.

4. In the same saucepan, combine the pork with the lentils, carrot, onion, garlic, and bouquet garni. Barely cover with water. Cover and bring to a boil over medium-high heat, then reduce the heat to low and cook for 1 hour and 30 minutes. Season with salt and pepper halfway through cooking.

From Françoise:

• If the pork shoulder is partially cured, it doesn't need the long soaking. You can simply run cold water over it to remove any excess salt.

• Green lentils that are tender keep their shape but are easily crushed between the fingers. Beware of package cooking times, which are often too short, especially for older lentils. Also, people who have trouble digesting beans should cook them for at least an hour.

• You might add a sausage, smoked or not; bacon or pancetta; or the more economical pork rind.

• Serve with Dijon and flavored mustards.

PORK STEW WITH PAPRIKA
- Ragoût de porc au paprika -

❖ EASY   ❖ INEXPENSIVE   ❖ 1 HOUR, 30 MINUTES

3 tablespoons butter

2 ½ pounds boneless pork shoulder end of loin,
　cut into 1 ½-inch pieces

4 onions, chopped

Paprika

4 tomatoes, peeled, seeded, and chopped

1 tablespoon tomato paste

1 garlic clove, finely chopped

1 bouquet garni made with parsley, thyme,
　and bay leaf

Salt and pepper

1 ½ pounds potatoes, peeled and quartered

❖ ❖ ❖ ❖ ❖

1. In a flameproof casserole, melt the butter over medium-high heat. Add the pork and onions and lightly brown. Stir in the paprika, tomatoes, tomato paste, garlic, bouquet garni, and ½ cup of water. Season with salt and pepper. Reduce the heat to low, cover, and cook for 40 minutes.

2. Add the potatoes and cook for 30 minutes. Transfer the stew to a serving dish and serve.

From Françoise:
• The secret to a meltingly tender ragout: Cook the stew in a heavy cast-iron casserole in a 275-degree oven.

PORK MEATLOAF RING WITH TOMATO SAUCE
- Turban de porc haché -

❖ EASY   ❖ INEXPENSIVE   ❖ 1 HOUR, 20 MINUTES   ❖ SERVES 4

2 tablespoons butter, plus more for brushing

4 slices crustless white sandwich bread

1 large onion, chopped

1 ½ pounds ground pork

2 garlic cloves, finely chopped

1 large egg, lightly beaten

Salt and pepper

Store-bought tomato sauce, heated

❖ ❖ ❖ ❖ ❖

1. Preheat the oven to 350 degrees. Butter a 7-inch ring mold. In a food processor, grind the bread slices into crumbs.

2. In a skillet, melt the 2 tablespoons of butter over medium heat. Add the onion and cook until lightly browned.

3. In a bowl, mix the pork with the bread crumbs, onion, garlic, and egg and season with salt and pepper. Pack the meat mixture into the ring mold. Set it in a roasting pan and fill with water to come halfway up the sides of the mold. Transfer to the oven and bake for 1 hour.

4. Run a knife around the meatloaf. Invert a round platter over the mold. Holding the mold and platter together, quickly invert the meatloaf onto the platter. Spoon some of the tomato sauce over and around the meatloaf and serve, passing the remaining tomato sauce separately.

From Françoise:

• Serve with mashed potatoes, pasta, or a seasonal green vegetable.

STUFFED HEN BRAISED WITH VEGETABLES

- *Poule au pot* -

❖ INTERMEDIATE   ❖ EXPENSIVE   ❖ 4 HOURS   ❖ SERVES 6 TO 8

2 veal bones

1 veal shank

4 ½- to 5-pound braising hen, neck and giblets
   reserved

1 onion stuck with 2 whole cloves

1 celery rib

1 bouquet garni made with parsley, thyme,
   and bay leaf

Salt and pepper

3 carrots, peeled and sliced 2 inches thick

3 turnips, peeled and quartered

3 leeks, white and light green parts only,
   halved crosswise

6 or 8 toasts

STUFFING

1 cup dry bread crumbs

¾ cup milk

5 ounces dry-cured ham, such as *jambon de
   Bayonne*, prosciutto, or serrano ham,
   finely chopped

3 ounces ground veal

3 ounces sausage meat

1 ounce chicken liver pâté

Liver from the hen, chopped

5 garlic cloves, finely chopped

Finely chopped parsley leaves

Pinch of thyme leaves

1 large egg

Pinch of freshly grated nutmeg

Salt and pepper

❖ ❖ ❖ ❖ ❖

1. Fill a large pot halfway with water and bring to a boil. Add the veal bones and shank and boil for 5 minutes. Drain.

2. Rinse out the pot and fill with cold water. Return the veal bones and shank to the pot with the hen's neck and giblets, the onion, celery, and bouquet garni and season with salt and pepper. Bring to a boil, skimming often, then lower the heat and simmer uncovered.

continued

3. Meanwhile, make the stuffing: In a bowl, soak the bread crumbs in the milk, then squeeze dry. In a large bowl, mix the bread crumbs with the ham, veal, sausage meat, pâté, liver, garlic, parsley, thyme, and egg and season with nutmeg, salt, and pepper.

4. Pack the stuffing into the hen. Using kitchen string, tie the legs together and the wings together. Add the hen to the simmering broth, bring back to a simmer, then reduce the heat to low and cook until tender, 2 hours and 30 minutes to 3 hours, adding the carrots, turnips, and leeks after 1 hour.

5. Transfer the hen to a cutting board, remove the string, and carve into serving pieces. Arrange the hen pieces, stuffing, leeks, carrots, and turnips in a warmed serving dish.

6. Strain the broth, reserving the veal shank for another use. Add the toasts to soup plates, ladle some of the broth over them, and serve. Serve the hen, stuffing, and vegetables as a separate course after the broth.

From Françoise:
• The cooking time will be much shorter for a young chicken that's 3 or 3 ½ pounds.

• You won't be able to pack all the stuffing into a smaller bird, so wrap the extra in several layers of cheesecloth, tie with kitchen string, and simmer alongside the chicken.

• You may omit the chicken liver pâté if you like.

BRAISED HEN WITH CREAMY SAUCE AND MUSHROOMS
- Poule à l'ivoire -

❖ INTERMEDIATE   ❖ MODERATE   ❖ 3 HOURS   ❖ SERVES 4

2 onions
2 leeks, halved crosswise
2 carrots, halved crosswise
1 celery rib
3 ½-pound braising hen, legs and wings tied
½ lemon, plus 1 teaspoon lemon juice
½ pound white mushrooms, halved or quartered
  if large
1 tablespoon butter
Salt

SAUCE
3 tablespoons butter
3 tablespoons all-purpose flour
Salt and pepper
2 large egg yolks
2 tablespoons crème fraîche

❖ ❖ ❖ ❖ ❖

1. Bring a large pot of salted water to a boil over medium-high heat. Add the onions, leeks, carrots, and celery and boil for 15 minutes.

2. Rub the hen with a lemon half and its juice. Add the hen to the broth and cook at a gentle boil until tender, about 2 hours and 30 minutes.

3. Meanwhile, in a medium saucepan, barely cover the mushrooms with water and add the butter and 1 teaspoon of lemon juice. Season with salt. Bring to a boil over medium-high heat, then reduce the heat to low and simmer until tender, about 5 minutes. Drain.

4. Just before serving, make the sauce: In a small saucepan, melt the butter over medium heat. Whisk in the flour until it starts foaming. Whisk in 2 cups of the cooking broth. Season with salt and pepper. Bring to a boil, whisking, then reduce the heat to very low and cook for 10 minutes. In a small bowl, beat the egg yolks with the crème fraîche. Remove the pan from the heat and gradually whisk in the yolk mixture.

5. Transfer the hen to a cutting board, remove the string, and carve into serving pieces. Arrange on a warmed platter, spoon some of the sauce over the bird, and decorate with the mushrooms. Serve, passing the remaining sauce separately.

From Françoise:

• Rubbing the bird with lemon helps to keep the skin white (ivory), but it's not essential.

• Serve with rice cooked in some of the broth.

• If you use a young bird, it will be tender in 45 minutes to 1 hour.

BRAISED COUSCOUS-STUFFED HEN WITH SPICES

Poule farcie au couscous braisée à la cocotte

❖ INTERMEDIATE   ❖ INEXPENSIVE   ❖ 3 HOURS, 15 MINUTES   ❖ SERVES 6

STUFFING
¾ cup currants
Salt
⅔ cup couscous
¾ cup almonds, chopped
1 teaspoon ras el hanout (see note)
1 tablespoon butter

4 ½-pound braising hen
1 onion, finely chopped
Pinch of ground ginger
Pinch of saffron
¼ cup olive oil
Salt and pepper

❖ ❖ ❖ ❖ ❖

1. In a small bowl, cover the currants with hot water. In a small saucepan, bring ¾ cup of water to a boil and add salt. Stir in the couscous, cover, remove from the heat, and let stand for 5 minutes.

2. Drain the currants and stir into the couscous along with the almonds, ras el hanout,

and butter. Season with salt. Pack the couscous into the hen. Using kitchen string, tie the legs together and the wings together.

3. In a flameproof casserole, stir the onion with the ginger, saffron, and olive oil. Season with

continued

257

salt and pepper. Set the hen in the casserole and fill with boiling water to come halfway up the sides of the hen. Cover and bring to a boil over medium-high heat, then reduce the heat to low, partially cover, and cook until tender, 2 to 3 hours.

4. Transfer the hen to a cutting board, remove the string, and carve into serving pieces. Arrange the hen pieces and stuffing on a warmed platter.

5. Set the casserole over high heat and reduce the cooking liquid to 1 cup. Serve the hen and stuffing, passing the reduced cooking liquid separately.

From Françoise:

• Ras el hanout is a particular spice mix that originated in North Africa and is used often in the south of France. It is more aromatic than spicy and reminiscent of curry in some ways. The typical components are cardamom, nutmeg, cinnamon, cloves, turmeric, black pepper, chili pepper, ginger, and cumin. Look for it in specialty shops.

• Serve with more couscous or boiled rice or pasta.

• You can also make this recipe with a young bird, which will be tender in half the time.

SLOW-COOKED HEN WITH PANCETTA AND CARROTS
- *Poule en daube* -

❖ EASY   ❖ INEXPENSIVE   ❖ 3 HOURS, 15 MINUTES   ❖ SERVES 6 TO 8

½ pound thick-sliced pancetta, cut crosswise
  into ¼-inch-thick strips
1 calf's foot, split in half
1 bouquet garni made with parsley, thyme,
  and bay leaf
2 carrots, peeled and sliced crosswise
1 onion, thinly sliced

4 ½– to 5-pound braising hen, cut into serving
  pieces
Salt and pepper
¾ cup dry white wine
¼ cup Cognac

❖ ❖ ❖ ❖ ❖

1. In a flameproof casserole, spread the pancetta, calf's foot, bouquet garni, carrots, and onion. Set the hen pieces on top and season with salt and pepper. Pour in the wine, Cognac, and enough water to barely cover the hen. Cover and bring to a boil over medium-high heat, then reduce the heat to low and cook until the hen is tender, about 3 hours.

2. Transfer the hen pieces to a warmed serving dish. Strain the cooking liquid over and serve.

From Françoise:

• You could use bacon instead of pancetta for a slightly smoky flavor.

• Serve with steamed new potatoes.

• The hen is delicious served cold. Serve it with a green salad and cornichons.

BRAISED HEN WITH CURRY

- *Poule créole* -

❖ EASY   ❖ INEXPENSIVE   ❖ 3 HOURS   ❖ SERVES 6 TO 8

5 tablespoons butter

4 ½- to 5-pound braising hen, cut into
  serving pieces

2 onions, 1 quartered, 1 finely chopped

2 teaspoons curry powder

2 garlic cloves, crushed

1 bouquet garni made with parsley, thyme,
  and bay leaf

Salt and pepper

1 cup rice

½ pound white mushrooms, thinly sliced

❖ ❖ ❖ ❖ ❖

1. In a flameproof casserole, melt 3 tablespoons of the butter over medium-high heat. Add the hen and lightly brown all over. Remove to a bowl. Add the quartered onion to the casserole and cook, stirring, until lightly browned. Stir in 1 teaspoon of the curry powder, the garlic, and bouquet garni. Return the hen to the pot and season with salt and pepper. Barely cover the hen with water. Cover and bring to a boil, then reduce the heat to low and cook until tender, 2 to 3 hours.

2. Meanwhile, in a small saucepan, melt the remaining 2 tablespoons of butter over medium heat. Add the chopped onion and cook, stirring, until lightly browned. Stir in the rice and the remaining 1 teaspoon of curry powder, then 2 cups of the cooking liquid. Increase

the heat to medium-high, and bring to a boil, then cover and reduce the heat to low and cook for 17 to 20 minutes, adding the mushrooms halfway through cooking.

3. Spread the rice in a warmed serving dish. Arrange the hen pieces in the dish and serve.

From Françoise:

• Curry powder can be more or less spicy, so add a little to start and taste. You can always add more.

• Rinse the rice under cold running water and drain it well before cooking it.

• If there isn't enough cooking liquid to cook the rice, add water to make the 2 cups.

CLASSIC ROAST CHICKEN

- *Poulet rôti au four* -

❖ EASY   ❖ MODERATE   ❖ 1 HOUR, 30 MINUTES   ❖ SERVES 4

3 ½-pound chicken
Salt and pepper

2 tablespoons butter, softened

❖ ❖ ❖ ❖ ❖

1. Preheat the oven to 400 degrees. Season the cavity of the chicken with salt and pepper and add 1 tablespoon of the butter. Using kitchen string, tie the legs together and the wings together. Brush the remaining 1 tablespoon of butter all over the outside of the chicken.

2. Set the chicken on 1 leg in a roasting pan, transfer to the oven, and roast for about 1 hour, turning the chicken on the other leg after 20 minutes, then breast side up during the final 20 minutes.

3. Transfer the chicken to a cutting board, remove the string, and let stand for 10 minutes.

4. Meanwhile, add a few tablespoons of boiling water to the roasting pan and boil, scraping up any brown bits stuck to the bottom, for 1 minute. Pour into a warmed sauceboat. Carve the chicken, arrange on a warmed platter, and serve with the pan juices.

From Françoise:
• You can also add the chicken liver and a few herb sprigs, such as tarragon and thyme, to the cavity of the chicken, but not too much.

RICE-STUFFED ROAST CHICKEN

- *Poulet farci au riz* -

❖ EASY ❖ MODERATE ❖ 1 HOUR, 45 MINUTES ❖ SERVES 4

STUFFING

2 tablespoons butter

2 shallots, finely chopped

3 tablespoons rice

6 tablespoons chicken broth

¼ pound white mushrooms, chopped

3 ounces smoked ham, finely chopped

Liver and heart from the chicken, chopped

½ teaspoon paprika

Salt and pepper

¼ cup Cognac

1 large egg

3 ½-pound chicken, giblets reserved

2 tablespoons butter, softened, plus more
  for brushing

Salt and pepper

❖ ❖ ❖ ❖ ❖

1. Make the stuffing: In a small saucepan, melt
1 tablespoon of the butter over medium-low
heat. Add the shallots and cook until softened.
Stir in the rice. Add the chicken broth, increase
the heat, cover, and bring to a boil, then reduce
the heat to low and cook for 15 to 17 minutes.

2. Preheat the oven to 400 degrees. Brush a
roasting pan with butter.

3. Finish the stuffing: In another small saucepan, melt the remaining 1 tablespoon of butter
over medium heat. Add the mushrooms, ham,
and chicken liver and heart and season with
the paprika, salt, and pepper. Add the Cognac
and bring to a boil, then tilt the pan and carefully ignite. When the flames subside, reduce
the heat to low, cover, and cook for 5 minutes.
Remove the pan from the heat and mix in the
cooked rice and the egg.

4. Pack the stuffing into the chicken. Using
kitchen string, tie the legs together and the
wings together. Brush the 2 tablespoons of
butter all over the chicken. Set the chicken on
1 leg in the roasting pan and season with salt
and pepper. Transfer to the oven and roast for

about 1 hour, turning the chicken on the other
leg after 20 minutes, then breast side up during the final 20 minutes.

5. Transfer the chicken to a cutting board, remove the string, and let stand for 10 minutes.
Add a few tablespoons of boiling water to the
roasting pan and boil, scraping up any brown
bits stuck to the bottom, for 1 minute. Pour
into a warmed sauceboat. Carve the chicken,
arrange on a warmed platter with the stuffing,
and serve with the pan juices.

From Françoise:

• Neither the Cognac nor the paprika is essential; it's up to you.

• The smoked ham can be replaced by less
expensive bacon.

• It's always a good idea to let a roasted bird
rest for 10 minutes before serving. It will be
more succulent that way.

• Serve with rice, of course, but also English
peas, green beans, or haricots verts, spinach,
salsify, carrots, or braised celery.

SPIT-ROASTED CHICKEN

- *Poulet rôti à la broche* -

❖ EASY   ❖ MODERATE   ❖ 1 HOUR, 15 MINUTES   ❖ SERVES 4

3 ½-pound chicken, giblets reserved
2 tablespoons butter

Salt and pepper

❖   ❖   ❖   ❖   ❖

1. Stuff the chicken with the liver and butter. Season inside and out with salt and pepper. Using kitchen string, tie the legs together and the wings together. In a rotisserie oven, set a spit in the center of the oven. Pass the spit through the cavity of the bird and place in the oven. Place a pan at the bottom of the oven to catch the cooking juices. Spit-roast the bird until it is well browned, about 1 hour, basting often.

2. Transfer the bird to a cutting board and remove the string. Season again with salt and pepper and let stand for 10 minutes. Skim any collected juices from the cutting board and the oven pan. Carve the bird, transfer to a warmed platter with the liver, and serve, passing the juices in a warmed sauceboat.

From Françoise:

• You could also add herbs to the cavity to flavor the bird. Sprigs of tarragon and thyme are very good, as well as a little rosemary and bay leaf or even juniper berries.

• For most rotisseries, you don't need to baste during cooking.

• The liver cooked inside the chicken is delectable, but you could save it for another recipe.

• Serve with all kinds of vegetables, including unadorned watercress sprigs. You really have a choice here, because pretty much everything goes with rotisserie chicken. Two of the fastest choices are plain watercress and potato chips.

SAVORY MEAT-STUFFED ROAST CHICKEN

- *Poulet farci à la viande* -

❖ INTERMEDIATE ❖ INEXPENSIVE ❖ 1 HOUR, 30 MINUTES ❖ SERVES 4

STUFFING

2 tablespoons butter

2 onions, finely chopped

Gizzard from the chicken, finely chopped

¼ pound ground pork

¼ pound ground veal

Liver from the chicken, finely chopped

1 large egg

½ teaspoon thyme leaves

Freshly grated nutmeg

Salt and pepper

3 ½-pound chicken, giblets reserved

2 tablespoons butter, softened

Salt and pepper

❖ ❖ ❖ ❖ ❖

1. Preheat the oven to 400 degrees. Make the stuffing: In a medium skillet, melt the butter over low heat. Add the onions and chicken gizzard and cook for 10 minutes. Remove the skillet from the heat and mix in the ground pork and veal, chicken liver, egg, and thyme. Season with nutmeg, salt, and pepper.

2. Pack the stuffing into the chicken. Using kitchen string, tie the legs together and the wings together. Brush the butter all over the chicken and season with salt and pepper. Set the chicken on 1 leg in a roasting pan. Transfer to the oven and roast for about 1 hour, turning the chicken on the other leg after 20 minutes, then breast side up during the final 20 minutes.

3. Transfer the bird to a cutting board, remove the string, and let stand for 10 minutes. Spoon the stuffing into a bowl. Carve the bird, transfer to a warmed platter, and serve with the stuffing.

From Françoise:

• If you grind the meat yourself, buy a mixture of fatty (shoulder end of the loin) and lean (shoulder) cuts of pork so you get a stuffing that's neither too dry nor too fatty.

• You could add a little fresh bread crumbs, chopped fines herbes (parsley, chives, chervil, tarragon), or finely chopped mushrooms to the stuffing. It's entirely up to your imagination.

POT-ROASTED CHICKEN WITH GREEN OLIVES, TOMATOES, AND GOLDEN POTATOES

- *Poulet à la corse* -

❖ EASY   ❖ MODERATE   ❖ 1 HOUR, 30 MINUTES   ❖ SERVES 4

3 ½-pound chicken

Salt and pepper

5 tablespoons butter

¼ pound thick-sliced pancetta or bacon,
  cut crosswise into ¼-inch-thick strips

¼ cup Cognac

¾ cup pitted green olives

2 ounces white mushrooms, thinly sliced

4 tomatoes, peeled, seeded, and chopped

1 garlic clove, crushed

Salt and pepper

2 pounds new potatoes, peeled and diced

Mixed chopped parsley, chives, chervil, and
  tarragon leaves for sprinkling

❖ ❖ ❖ ❖ ❖

1. Season the cavity of the chicken with salt and pepper. Using kitchen string, tie the legs together and the wings together. In a flame-proof casserole, melt 2 tablespoons of the butter over medium heat. Add the pancetta or bacon and cook until lightly browned. Remove to a bowl. Add the chicken and lightly brown all over. Return the pancetta or bacon to the casserole. Add the Cognac and bring to a boil, then tilt the pot and carefully ignite.

2. In a small saucepan, cover the olives with cold water. Bring to a boil over medium-high heat and simmer for 1 to 2 minutes, then drain.

3. Add the olives, mushrooms, tomatoes, and garlic to the casserole. Season with pepper and, lightly, with salt. Cover and bring to a boil, then reduce the heat to low and cook for about 1 hour.

4. Meanwhile, in a large skillet, melt the remaining 3 tablespoons of butter over medium heat. Add the potatoes and cook until tender and nicely browned on all sides. Season with salt and pepper and cover toward the end of cooking.

5. Transfer the chicken to a cutting board and remove the string. Cover loosely with foil and let stand for 10 minutes. Set the chicken in a warmed serving dish and spoon the vegetables, including the potatoes, and pan juices around it. Sprinkle with the herbs and serve.

From Françoise:
• The point of briefly boiling the green olives in water is to remove some of the saltiness. If you skip this step, because you're in a hurry or you forget, take it into account when seasoning the dish.

• The Cognac and mushrooms are nice but not essential.

• To keep the potatoes from sticking to the skillet as they brown, boil them first for 5 minutes, then pat them dry scrupulously.

POT-ROASTED CHICKEN WITH SPRING VEGETABLES

- *Poulet aux légumes printaniers* -

❖ EASY ❖ MODERATE ❖ 2 HOURS ❖ SERVES 4

4 tablespoons (½ stick) butter, softened

1 pound green beans

10 small spring onions

2 cups shelled peas (about 2 pounds in the shell)

1 bunch tender, young carrots, trimmed

1 bouquet garni made with parsley, thyme, and bay leaf

3 ½-pound chicken, legs and wings tied

Salt and pepper

1 teaspoon all-purpose flour

❖ ❖ ❖ ❖ ❖

MEAT & POULTRY

1. Preheat the oven to 300 degrees. Brush a small flameproof casserole with the butter, reserving 1 teaspoon. Spread the green beans, onions, peas, carrots, and bouquet garni. Set the chicken on top and season with salt and pepper. Cover and set over low heat for 5 minutes, then transfer to the oven and roast for about 1 hour and 15 minutes.

2. Transfer the chicken to a cutting board and remove the string and bouquet garni. Cover loosely with foil. Bring the pan juices to a boil. In a cup, blend the flour with the reserved 1 teaspoon of butter. Whisk this paste into the simmering pan juices until slightly thickened. Transfer the chicken to a warmed platter and arrange the vegetables around it. Moisten with the pan juices and serve.

From Françoise:

• If you don't have an oven, you can cook this dish entirely on top of the stove, though the cooking will be more even in the oven.

• The vegetable proportions can be changed according to your taste and the seasons.

CITRUS-MARINATED CHICKEN

- *Poulet au citron vert et à l'orange* -

❖ EASY ❖ INEXPENSIVE ❖ 1 HOUR, PLUS OVERNIGHT MARINATING ❖ SERVES 4

MARINADE

Juice of ½ orange

Juice of ½ lime

1 shallot, thinly sliced

1 teaspoon oil

Few dashes of hot sauce

3 ½-pound chicken, split in half lengthwise and backbone removed

3 tablespoons butter, softened

Salt and pepper

continued

265

1. For the marinade: In a gratin dish, combine all the ingredients. Add the chicken and turn to coat. Then cover and refrigerate overnight, turning the chicken 2 or 3 times.

2. Preheat the oven to 475 degrees. Brush the marinade off the chicken, reserving the marinade, and set the chicken, skin side up, in a roasting pan. Pat the chicken dry. Brush the skin with the butter and season with salt and pepper. Transfer to the upper third of the oven and roast for 40 minutes, basting often with some of the reserved marinade.

3. Transfer the chicken to a cutting board and let stand for 10 minutes. Meanwhile, skim the fat off the cooking juices in the roasting pan. Add a little of the reserved marinade and water (3 tablespoons in all) to the pan and boil, scraping up any brown bits stuck to the bottom, for 1 minute. Pour into a warmed sauceboat. Cut the chicken into serving pieces, arrange on a warmed platter or plates, and serve with the pan juices.

From Françoise:
• Split the chicken in half lengthwise by cutting out the backbone with a large, sharp knife or poultry shears. Then open up the chicken and flatten it, pressing on the breastbone with the heel of your hand. It's fairly easy, but you can also have your butcher do it.

CRUSTY MUSTARD-GRILLED CHICKEN WITH SHALLOT SAUCE
- *Poulet à la diable* -

❖ INTERMEDIATE　　❖ INEXPENSIVE　　❖ 40 MINUTES　　❖ SERVES 4

3 ½-pound chicken, split in half lengthwise and
　backbone removed
8 slices of day-old crustless white sandwich bread
Dijon mustard for brushing
3 tablespoons butter

SAUCE
1 tablespoon butter
2 shallots, finely chopped
¼ cup dry white wine
¼ cup vinegar
¼ cup chicken broth
Salt and pepper

❖　❖　❖　❖　❖

1. Preheat the oven to 475 degrees. Set the chicken, skin side up, on a broiler pan. Transfer to the upper third of the oven and roast for 30 minutes.

2. Meanwhile, make the sauce: In a small saucepan, melt the butter over medium-low heat.

Add the shallots and cook until soft. Add the wine, vinegar, and chicken broth and season with salt and pepper. Reduce the heat to low and simmer for 10 minutes.

3. In a food processor, grind the bread slices into crumbs.

4. Remove the chicken from the oven. Heat the broiler to high. Brush the skin with the mustard. Pat the bread crumbs on the mustard and dot with the butter. Broil in the oven until the crumbs are crisp and browned.

5. Pour the sauce into a warmed sauceboat. Transfer the chicken to a warmed platter and serve with the sauce.

From Françoise:

• Garnish the platter with watercress sprigs.

• Serve with potato chips or sautéed potatoes and broiled tomatoes.

SPICED CHICKEN PILAF

- *Poulet à la martiniquaise* -

❖ INTERMEDIATE ❖ EXPENSIVE ❖ 1 HOUR ❖ SERVES 4

2 tablespoons butter

3 ½–pound chicken, cut into serving pieces

2 onions, thinly sliced

1 carrot, peeled and sliced crosswise

½ teaspoon curry powder

Pinch of saffron

1 garlic clove, crushed

1 bouquet garni made with parsley, thyme, and bay leaf

Salt and pepper

¾ cup rice

❖ ❖ ❖ ❖ ❖

1. In a flameproof casserole, melt the butter over medium-high heat. Add the chicken and lightly brown all over. Remove to a bowl. Add the onions and carrot to the casserole and cook, stirring, until lightly browned. Stir in the curry powder, saffron, garlic, and bouquet garni. Return the chicken to the pot and season with salt and pepper. Add 2 cups of water. Cover and bring to a boil, then reduce the heat to low and cook for 20 minutes.

2. Rinse the rice in cold running water and drain well. Add to the chicken and cook until tender, 17 to 20 minutes.

3. Remove the bouquet garni. Transfer the pilaf to a warmed serving dish and serve.

QUICK CHICKEN WITH MUSHROOMS AND SHALLOT
- *Poulet à la va-vite* -

❖ EASY ❖ INEXPENSIVE ❖ 45 MINUTES ❖ SERVES 4

3 tablespoons butter

3 ½-pound chicken, cut into serving pieces

1 shallot, chopped

1 tomato, chopped

1 bouquet garni made with parsley, thyme,
  and bay leaf

1 ½ cups dry white wine

Salt and pepper

½ pound white mushrooms, thinly sliced

Chopped parsley leaves for sprinkling

❖ ❖ ❖ ❖ ❖

1. In a large skillet, melt 2 tablespoons of the butter over medium-high heat. Add the chicken and lightly brown all over. Remove to a flameproof casserole and set over medium heat with the remaining 1 tablespoon of butter, the shallot, tomato, bouquet garni, and wine. Season with salt and pepper. Cover and bring to a boil, then reduce the heat to low and cook for about 30 minutes, adding the mushrooms halfway through cooking.

2. Remove the bouquet garni. Transfer the chicken and vegetables to a warmed serving dish. Sprinkle with parsley and serve.

CHICKEN WITH RED PEPPERS, CURRANTS, AND SPICES
- *Poulet à la grecque* -

❖ EASY ❖ MODERATE ❖ 1 HOUR, 30 MINUTES ❖ SERVES 4

3 ½-pound chicken, cut into serving pieces

Salt and pepper

Curry powder for dusting

4 tablespoons (½ stick) butter

3 shallots, finely chopped

4 onions, finely chopped

4 garlic cloves, finely chopped

3 tomatoes, peeled, seeded, and chopped

2 red bell peppers, chopped

1 cup currants

1 tablespoon sugar (optional)

Pinch of saffron

1 ½ cups dry white wine

1. Season the chicken with salt and pepper and dust lightly with curry powder, patting off the excess.

2. In a flameproof casserole, melt 2 tablespoons of the butter over medium-high heat. Add the chicken and lightly brown all over. Remove the chicken to a plate and pour off the fat in the casserole. Add the remaining 2 tablespoons of butter and melt. Stir in the shallots, onions, and garlic, reduce the heat to medium-low, and cook until softened. Stir in the tomatoes and bell peppers and cook gently for 15 minutes.

3. Stir in the currants, sugar, if using, and saffron and set the chicken pieces on top. Season

with salt and pepper and pour in the wine. Increase the heat to medium-high, cover, and bring to a boil, then reduce the heat to low and cook for 1 hour.

4. Transfer the chicken and vegetables to a warmed serving dish and serve.

From Françoise:

• The pieces of chicken need plenty of room for browning, so sauté them in batches.

• Plump the currants in boiling water, then drain before adding them to the casserole.

• Serve with boiled rice.

CHICKEN WITH MUSHROOMS AND TOMATOES
- *Poulet sauté minute* -

❖ EASY ❖ MODERATE ❖ 35 MINUTES ❖ SERVES 4

3 tablespoons butter	Juice of ½ lemon
3 ½–pound chicken, cut into serving pieces	1 thyme sprig
1 shallot, finely chopped	½ bay leaf
¼ cup Cognac (optional)	Salt and pepper
1 large tomato, peeled, seeded, and chopped	Chopped parsley leaves for sprinkling
¼ pound white mushrooms, thinly sliced	

❖ ❖ ❖ ❖ ❖

1. In a large skillet, melt 2 tablespoons of the butter over medium-high heat. Add the chicken pieces and lightly brown all over. Remove to a flameproof casserole as they are done and set over medium heat with the remaining 1 tablespoon of butter and the shallot. Add the Cognac, if using, and bring to a boil, then tilt the pan and carefully ignite. When the flames subside, add the tomato, mushrooms, lemon

juice, thyme, and bay leaf. Season with salt and pepper. Cover and bring to a boil, then reduce the heat to low and cook for about 25 minutes.

2. Remove the thyme and bay leaf. Transfer the chicken and vegetables to a warmed serving dish. Sprinkle with parsley and serve.

continued

• Sear only 3 or 4 pieces of the chicken at a time or they won't brown properly.

• Serve with mashed potatoes, sautéed cauliflower, pasta, or rice.

COGNAC-FLAMED CHICKEN WITH CREAMY TARRAGON SAUCE
- *Poulet flambé à l'estragon* -

❖ EASY   ❖ MODERATE   ❖ 1 HOUR   ❖ SERVES 4

2 tablespoons butter

1 tablespoon oil

3 ½–pound chicken, cut into serving pieces

¼ cup Cognac

3 shallots, finely chopped

6 tablespoons dry white wine

3 tarragon sprigs, leaves chopped, stems reserved

Salt and pepper

2 large egg yolks

3 tablespoons crème fraîche

❖   ❖   ❖   ❖   ❖

1. In a flameproof casserole, melt the butter in the oil over medium-high heat. Add the chicken pieces and lightly brown all over. Add the Cognac and bring to a boil, then tilt the pot and carefully ignite. When the flames subside, remove the chicken to a plate. Stir the shallots into the casserole and add the wine and 6 tablespoons of water. Return the chicken to the pot with the tarragon stems and season with salt and pepper. Cover and bring to a boil, then reduce the heat to low and cook for about 30 minutes.

2. Transfer the chicken to a warmed platter. Simmer the cooking juices until reduced and well flavored. Remove the tarragon stems. In a small bowl, whisk the egg yolks into the crème fraîche. Remove the casserole from the heat and whisk in the yolk mixture. Whisk in the tarragon leaves, pour over the chicken, and serve.

From Françoise:
• To flame the Cognac, bring it to a boil in the casserole and ignite it carefully with a long match.

• Do not let the shallots color at all when you add them to the casserole or they will turn bitter.

• If your sauce seems a little thin, whisk in a small amount of potato starch blended with a little cold water. Most important, do not let the sauce come to a boil once you have whisked in the egg-yolk-and-crème-fraîche mixture or it will separate.

CHICKEN WITH TOMATOES, MUSHROOMS, OLIVES, AND ALMONDS

- Poulet sauté tomates et olives -

❖ EASY　　　❖ INEXPENSIVE　　　❖ 1 HOUR, 15 MINUTES　　❖ SERVES 4

3 ½-pound chicken, cut into serving pieces

All-purpose flour for dusting

3 tablespoons olive oil

1 onion, chopped

1 ½ cups dry white wine

3 garlic cloves, crushed

2 red chiles

Salt and pepper

½ pound tomatoes, chopped

½ pound small white mushrooms

¾ cup pitted green olives

½ cup sliced almonds

❖　❖　❖　❖　❖

1. Dust the chicken pieces lightly with flour, patting off the excess. In a large skillet, heat the olive oil over medium-high heat. Add the chicken pieces and lightly brown all over. Remove to a plate. Add the onion to the skillet and cook, stirring, until lightly browned. Return the chicken to the skillet and add the wine, 1 ½ cups of water, the garlic, and chiles and season with salt and pepper. Cover and bring to a boil, then reduce the heat to low and cook for 30 to 35 minutes.

2. Add the tomatoes, mushrooms, olives, and almonds and cook for 25 minutes. Transfer the chicken and vegetables to a warmed serving dish and serve.

From Françoise:

• Serve with kidney beans, seasoned with butter and hot sauce.

• If your green olives are very salty or slightly bitter, add them to a small saucepan of cold water to cover and bring them just to a boil, then drain before adding them to the casserole.

271

CHICKEN WITH BACON AND THYME

- *Poulet sauté au thym* -

❖ EASY   ❖ MODERATE   ❖ 1 HOUR   ❖ SERVES 4

3 ½-pound chicken, cut into 8 serving pieces
4 thin bacon slices, halved crosswise
8 or 16 thyme sprigs, depending on size
3 tablespoons butter
1 tablespoon all-purpose flour
1 onion, chopped

2 tomatoes, peeled, seeded, and chopped
3 garlic cloves, crushed
1 cup dry white wine
Salt and pepper
20 pitted green olives

❖ ❖ ❖ ❖ ❖

1. Top each piece of chicken with a half bacon slice and 1 or 2 thyme sprigs and tie with kitchen string. In a flameproof casserole, melt the butter over medium-high heat. Add the chicken pieces and lightly brown on all sides. Stir in the flour. Add the onion, tomatoes, garlic, and wine and season with salt and pepper. Cover and bring to a boil, then reduce the heat to low and cook for about 40 minutes.

2. If the olives are very salty or bitter, add them to a small saucepan of cold water and bring just to a boil. Drain and add them to the chicken.

3. Remove the string from the chicken. Transfer the chicken and sauce to a warmed serving dish and serve.

From Françoise:
• Chicken broth can replace the wine in this dish.

• You have an array of side dishes to choose from to accompany this Provençal-inspired chicken—steamed or boiled rice, mashed or sautéed potatoes, English peas—but recipes from the south of France are especially appropriate, such as tomatoes provençale and ratatouille.

CHICKEN WITH A VELVETY PEPPER STEW

- *Poulet basquaise* -

❖ EASY   ❖ MODERATE   ❖ 1 HOUR, 15 MINUTES   ❖ SERVES 4

5 tablespoons oil
3 ½-pound chicken, cut into serving pieces
2 or 3 onions, chopped
2 pounds tomatoes, peeled, seeded, and chopped

½ pound red bell peppers, cut into 1-inch pieces
2 or 3 garlic cloves, crushed
Piment d'Espelette (see note)
Salt and pepper
1 ¼ cups rice

1. In a flameproof casserole, heat 3 tablespoons of the oil over medium-high heat. Add the chicken pieces and lightly brown on all sides. Add the onions, tomatoes, bell peppers, and garlic and season with piment d'Espelette, salt, and pepper. Cover and bring to a boil, then reduce the heat to low, partly cover, and cook for 45 to 50 minutes.

2. Meanwhile, in a medium saucepan, heat the remaining 2 tablespoons of oil over medium heat. Add the rice and cook, stirring, for 1 minute. Add 2 ½ cups of water and bring to a boil, then reduce the heat to low, cover, and cook for 17 to 20 minutes.

3. Spread the rice in a warmed serving dish. Set the chicken and vegetables on top and serve.

From Françoise:
• Piment d'Espelette is a hot red pepper grown in the southwest of France, Basque country. You could substitute red chili pepper.

• For a more elegant presentation, pack the cooked rice into buttered ramekins, then unmold on a platter around the chicken.

• If you have some leftover roast chicken on hand, make the velvety pepper stew in Step 1, then nestle the chicken, cut into pieces, in the stew and reheat.

CALVADOS-FLAMED CHICKEN WITH CREAMY SAUCE
- *Poulet sauté Vallée d'Auge* -

❖ EASY   ❖ MODERATE   ❖ 1 HOUR, 15 MINUTES   ❖ SERVES 4

3 tablespoons butter

1 tablespoon oil

3 ½-pound chicken, cut into serving pieces

Salt and pepper

¼ cup Calvados

2 large egg yolks

½ cup crème fraîche

❖   ❖   ❖   ❖   ❖

1. In a large skillet, melt 1 tablespoon of the butter in the oil over medium heat. Add the chicken and cook on all sides without browning. Remove the chicken to a plate. Discard the fat in the skillet. Melt the remaining 2 tablespoons of butter in the skillet. Return the chicken to the pan and season with salt and pepper. Increase the heat to medium-high, add the Calvados, and bring to a boil, then tilt the pan and carefully ignite. When the flames subside, reduce the heat, cover, and cook for about 1 hour.

2. Transfer the chicken to a warmed platter. In a small bowl, whisk the egg yolks with the crème fraîche. Remove the skillet from the heat. Whisk the yolk mixture into the pan juices until they thicken slightly. Pour this sauce over the chicken and serve.

From Françoise:
• If the pan juices are fatty, skim them before whisking in the yolk mixture.

• Serve with thickly sliced apples sautéed in butter without any seasoning at all.

RICH STUFFED CHICKEN

- Farce riche -

❖ EASY ❖ MODERATE ❖ 1 HOUR, 15 MINUTES ❖ SERVES 4

2 tablespoons butter

2 onions, chopped

3 ounces ground pork

3 ounces ground veal

Chicken liver and gizzard, finely chopped

1 large egg

Thyme leaves

1 bay leaf, crumbled

Freshly grated nutmeg

Salt and pepper

3 ½- to 4-pound chicken

Butter, for brushing

❖ ❖ ❖ ❖ ❖

1. In a large skillet, melt the butter over medium-low heat. Add the onions and cook until softened. Transfer to a bowl and mix with the pork, veal, chicken liver and gizzard, egg, thyme, and bay leaf. Season with nutmeg, salt, and pepper.

2. Pack the stuffing into the chicken and, using kitchen string, tie the legs together and the wings together before cooking.

3. Preheat the oven to 400 degrees. Put the chicken in a large, buttered pie plate. Roast for 50 minutes to 1 hour, turning and basting it with cooking juices from time to time.

CHICKEN WITH RYE BREAD AND BEEF MARROW STUFFING

- Farce à l'anglaise -

❖ EASY ❖ MODERATE ❖ 1 HOUR, 30 MINUTES ❖ SERVES 4

2 slices crustless rye bread, cut into chunks

3 tablespoons butter

2 onions, chopped

2 ounces beef marrow

2 chicken livers, chopped

Freshly grated nutmeg

Salt and pepper

3 ½- to 4-pound chicken

1. In a food processor, grind the rye bread into crumbs. In a large skillet, melt the butter over medium-low heat. Add the onions and cook, stirring occasionally, until lightly browned.

2. Meanwhile, bring a medium saucepan of salted water to a boil. Add the marrow, then remove the pan from the heat and let stand for 5 minutes. Drain the marrow and chop.

3. Remove the skillet from the heat. Stir in the bread crumbs, marrow, and chicken livers and season with nutmeg, salt, and pepper.

4. Pack the stuffing into the chicken and, using kitchen string, tie the legs together and the wings together before cooking.

5. Roast the chicken as in step 3 on page 274.

CHICKEN WITH PORK AND TARRAGON STUFFING
- *Farce à l'estragon* -

❖ EASY ❖ MODERATE ❖ 1 HOUR, 15 MINUTES ❖ SERVES 4

½ pound white mushrooms, finely chopped
¼ pound ground pork
3 ounces chicken livers, chopped
1 shallot, finely chopped

1 garlic clove, finely chopped
Several tarragon sprigs, leaves chopped
Salt and pepper
3 ½- to 4-pound chicken

❖ ❖ ❖ ❖ ❖

1. In a bowl, mix the mushrooms with the pork, chicken livers, shallot, garlic, and tarragon leaves and season with salt and pepper.

2. Pack the stuffing into the chicken and, using kitchen string, tie the legs together and the wings together before cooking.

3. Roast the chicken as in step 3 on page 274.

CHICKEN WITH CORN STUFFING

- Farce au maïs -

❖ EASY   ❖ MODERATE   ❖ 1 HOUR, 15 MINUTES   ❖ SERVES 4

2 tablespoons butter

2 ounces sausage meat

2 ounces chicken livers, chopped

10 pitted green olives, chopped

1 bell pepper, chopped

4 Boston lettuce leaves, finely sliced

Corn kernels from 2 ears of corn, cooked

Salt and pepper

1 large egg, lightly beaten

3 ½- to 4-pound chicken

❖ ❖ ❖ ❖ ❖

1. In a large skillet, melt the butter over medium heat. Add the sausage meat, chicken livers, olives, bell pepper, and lettuce and cook, breaking up the sausage with a wooden spoon, until the sausage is cooked through. Stir in the corn and season with salt and pepper. Remove the skillet from the heat and mix in the egg.

2. Pack the stuffing into the chicken and, using kitchen string, tie the legs together and the wings together before cooking.

3. Roast the chicken as in step 3 on page 274.

TURKEY WITH LIVER STUFFING

- Farce aux foies de volaille -

❖ EASY   ❖ MODERATE   ❖ 1 HOUR, 15 MINUTES   ❖ SERVES 6 TO 8

½ pound pancetta, finely chopped

2 onions, chopped

1 pound chicken livers, cut into ¼-inch dice

3 tablespoons butter, melted

4 cups bread crumbs, made from crustless
   white sandwich bread

Salt and pepper

8- to 10-pound turkey or goose

❖ ❖ ❖ ❖ ❖

1. In a large skillet, cook the pancetta over medium heat, stirring, until just beginning to brown. Add the onions and livers, reduce the heat to low, and cook for 10 minutes.

2. Transfer the chicken liver mixture to a bowl, mix with the melted butter and bread crumbs. Season with salt and pepper. Let cool completely before stuffing the bird.

3. Roast the chicken as in step 3 on page 274.

TURKEY WITH CHESTNUT STUFFING

- *Farce aux marrons* -

❖ EASY   ❖ MODERATE   ❖ 1 HOUR, 15 MINUTES   ❖ SERVES 6 TO 8

3 ounces ground veal

3 ounces ground pork

3 ounces pancetta, finely chopped

2 ½ ounces chicken livers, finely chopped

1 large egg

¾ cup fresh bread crumbs

1 or 2 shallots, finely chopped

¼ cup Cognac

3 ounces cooked, peeled chestnuts, crumbled

Salt and pepper

8- to 10-pound turkey or goose

❖ ❖ ❖ ❖ ❖

1. In a bowl, mix the ground veal with the pork, pancetta, chicken livers, egg, bread crumbs, shallots, Cognac, and chestnuts. Season with salt and pepper. Pack into the bird.

2. Roast the chicken as in step 3 on page 274.

MEAT & POULTRY

TURKEY WITH LIVER AND PORCINI MUSHROOM STUFFING

- *Farce périgourdine* -

❖ EASY   ❖ MODERATE   ❖ 1 HOUR, 15 MINUTES   ❖ SERVES 6 TO 8

4 small brioches, chopped

½ cup milk

2 tablespoons butter

½ pound turkey or chicken livers, chopped

2 shallots, chopped

5 ounces porcini or white mushrooms, stems chopped, caps cut into ¼-inch dice

Salt and pepper

8- to 10-pound turkey or goose

❖ ❖ ❖ ❖ ❖

1. In a bowl, soak the brioches in the milk, then squeeze dry.

2. In a large skillet, melt the butter over medium heat. Add the livers and shallots and sauté. Transfer to a bowl and mix with the brioches and mushrooms and season with salt and pepper. Pack into the bird.

3. Roast the chicken as in step 3 on page 274.

277

TURKEY WITH NUT STUFFING

- Farce aux noix -

❖ EASY ❖ MODERATE ❖ 1 HOUR, 15 MINUTES ❖ SERVES 6 TO 8

20 slices crustless white sandwich bread

3 tablespoons butter

2 onions, chopped

½ pound white mushrooms, finely chopped

2 ounces walnuts, coarsely chopped

1 ounce cashews, coarsely chopped

1 ounce Brazil nuts, coarsely chopped

1 tablespoon chopped parsley leaves

2 large eggs, lightly beaten

Salt and pepper

Chicken broth, if needed

8- to 10-pound turkey or goose

❖ ❖ ❖ ❖ ❖

1. In a food processor, grind the bread into crumbs.

2. In a large skillet, melt the butter over medium-low heat. Add the onions and cook until softened, about 5 minutes. Stir in the mushrooms and cook, stirring, for 5 minutes.

Transfer to a bowl and mix in the bread crumbs, all the nuts, the parsley, and eggs. Season with salt and pepper. If needed, mix in a little chicken broth so the stuffing holds together. Pack into the bird.

3. Roast the chicken as in step 3 on page 274.

CHICKEN CUTLETS WITH CREAMY TARRAGON SAUCE

- Escalopes à la normande -

❖ EASY ❖ MODERATE ❖ 25 MINUTES ❖ SERVES 4

2 tablespoons butter

4 chicken cutlets

6 tablespoons dry white wine

3 tarragon sprigs, leaves chopped,
  stems reserved

3 tablespoons crème fraîche

Salt and pepper

❖ ❖ ❖ ❖ ❖

1. In a large skillet, melt the butter over medium-high heat. Add the chicken cutlets, reduce the heat to medium, and cook, turning once, until lightly browned, 3 to 4 minutes per side. Add the wine and tarragon stems, cover, and bring to a boil, then reduce the heat to low and cook for 10 minutes.

2. Transfer the chicken to a warmed platter. Add 1 or 2 tablespoons of water to the skillet and boil, scraping up any brown bits stuck to the bottom, for 1 minute. Remove the tarragon stems. Stir in the crème fraîche and tarragon leaves and simmer for 1 minute. Pour over the chicken and serve.

From Françoise:

• Serve with peeled potatoes baked in the oven or quartered ones and sautéed in butter.

• This recipe can also be made with veal chops. It's the same for all the chicken cutlet recipes, though the veal chops take longer to cook since they are generally thicker.

CRISPY CHICKEN-STUFFED CRÊPES

- Crêpes farcies de blancs de poulet -

❖ INTERMEDIATE   ❖ INEXPENSIVE   ❖ 45 MINUTES, PLUS 1 HOUR RESTING   ❖ SERVES 4

CRÊPES

¾ cup all-purpose flour

1 cup water

1 large egg, lightly beaten

2 tablespoons butter, melted, plus more
 for brushing

¼ teaspoon salt

FILLING

2 ½ tablespoons butter

1 ½ tablespoons all-purpose flour

1 cup milk

Salt and pepper

½ cup shredded Gruyère cheese

1 to 2 cups leftover chopped chicken

1 tablespoon crème fraîche

❖ ❖ ❖ ❖ ❖

1. Make the crêpes: In a medium bowl, whisk the flour with the water, egg, 2 tablespoons of the melted butter, and the salt. Cover and let stand for at least 1 hour.

2. Meanwhile, make the filling: In a small saucepan, melt 1 ½ tablespoons of the butter over medium heat. Whisk in the flour until it starts foaming. Whisk in the milk. Season with salt and pepper. Bring to a boil, whisking. Remove the pan from the heat and whisk in 6 tablespoons of the cheese, the chicken, and the crème fraîche.

3. Lightly brush a 7- or 8-inch skillet with melted butter and heat over medium heat. Whisk the batter and add 2 to 3 tablespoons

to the skillet, swirling to coat the bottom. Cook until the edge begins to brown, about 30 seconds. Flip using a thin-bladed spatula and cook for 20 seconds. Slide onto a plate and repeat with the remaining batter, stacking the crêpes as they're cooked.

4. Preheat the oven to 425 degrees. Lightly brush the bottom of a gratin dish with butter. Spread about 1 tablespoon of filling over each crêpe and roll up or fold into quarters. Arrange the crêpes in the gratin dish. Sprinkle the remaining 2 tablespoons of cheese over the top and dot with the remaining 1 tablespoon of butter.

continued

5. Transfer to the top shelf of the oven and bake until melted and golden, about 10 minutes, and serve.

From Françoise:
• Crêpes are a really good vehicle for leftover chicken. In addition, since this dish can be prepared and assembled in advance and simply gratinéed in the oven just before serving, it should be on the make-ahead list of every busy cook.

CHICKEN POT PIE WITH GREEN OLIVES
- *Tourte de poulet aux olives* -

❖ ADVANCED   ❖ MODERATE   ❖ 2 HOURS   ❖ SERVES 4 TO 6

PÂTE BRISÉE

1 ¼ cups all-purpose flour

½ teaspoon salt

5 tablespoons butter, cut into pieces

3 tablespoons butter

3 ½-pound chicken, cut into serving pieces

7 ounces thick-sliced pancetta, cut crosswise
  into ¼-inch-thick strips

¼ pound small spring onions

1 tablespoon all-purpose flour

1 pound tomatoes, seeded and chopped

1 cup pitted green olives

1 bouquet garni made with parsley, thyme, and
  bay leaf

Pepper

❖ ❖ ❖ ❖ ❖

1. Make the pâte brisée: In a bowl, combine the flour with the salt and butter. Rub the butter into the flour between your palms. Sprinkle in ¼ cup of water and knead briefly until large crumbs form. Press into a disk. On a lightly floured surface, scrape the dough away from you with the heel of your hand in a long sliding motion, then press into a disk; repeat 3 times. Press into a disk, wrap, and refrigerate.

2. In a large skillet, melt the butter over medium heat. Add the chicken pieces and lightly brown all over. Remove to a plate. Add the pancetta and onions and cook, stirring, until just beginning to brown. Stir in the flour. Return the chicken to the skillet and add the

tomatoes, green olives, and bouquet garni and season with pepper. Cover and bring to a boil, then reduce the heat to low and cook for 30 minutes. The sauce should be well reduced; if needed, uncover and simmer until almost dry. Remove the chicken meat from the bones; discard the skin and bones. Cut the meat into large pieces and return to the skillet. Remove the bouquet garni.

3. Preheat the oven to 350 degrees. Spread the chicken mixture in a deep pie dish.

4. On a lightly floured work surface, roll the dough into a round ⅛ inch thick. Drape the dough on top of the pie dish. The dough round will be slightly larger than the dish. Brush the edge of the dough with water and pinch it around the rim to seal. Trim off any overhanging dough.

5. Brush the top with water. Poke a hole in the center of the pie and insert a foil "chimney" to allow steam to escape. Set on a baking sheet, transfer to the oven, and bake for 1 hour and 15 minutes. Serve warm.

From Françoise:
• Instead of making the dough, you can, of course, buy a rolled pie crust.

ROOSTER SIMMERED IN RED WINE
- Coq au vin -

❖ EASY   ❖ MODERATE   ❖ 2 HOURS, 30 MINUTES   ❖ SERVES 6

3 tablespoons butter

3 ounces fresh pork rind, chopped (optional)

4 ½-pound rooster, cut into serving pieces, liver pureed

1 onion, thinly sliced

2 shallots, thinly sliced

1 carrot, peeled and thinly sliced

3 garlic cloves, thinly sliced

2 tablespoons all-purpose flour

¼ cup Cognac or marc

3 cups red wine

1 tablespoon tomato paste

1 bouquet garni made with parsley, thyme, and bay leaf

Salt and pepper

¼ pound thick-sliced pancetta, cut crosswise into ¼-inch-thick strips

½ pound white mushrooms, thinly sliced

Freshly chopped parsley leaves for sprinkling

❖ ❖ ❖ ❖ ❖

1. In a flameproof casserole, melt the butter with the pork rind, if using, over medium-high heat. Add the rooster pieces and lightly brown all over. Remove to a plate. Add the onion, shallots, carrot, and garlic and cook, stirring, until just beginning to brown. Stir in the flour. Return the rooster to the skillet. Add the Cognac and bring to a boil, then tilt the pan and carefully ignite. When the flames subside, add the wine, ¾ cup of water, the tomato paste, and bouquet garni and season with salt and pepper. Cover and bring to a boil, then reduce the heat to low and cook until tender, 1 hour and 30 minutes to 2 hours.

2. Meanwhile, in a small saucepan, combine the pancetta with water to cover. Bring to a boil and simmer for a few seconds, then drain. Set over medium heat and cook, stirring, until just beginning to brown. Add the mushrooms, increase the heat to medium-high, and cook for 5 minutes. Transfer to a warmed serving dish.

3. Add the rooster pieces to the mushroom mixture. If the sauce is too thin, simmer it for a few minutes. Add the pureed liver and immediately remove the casserole from the heat.

continued

Strain the sauce over the bird. Sprinkle with parsley and serve.

From Françoise:
• You can also use a large braising hen instead of a rooster.

• Choose a good, full-bodied wine for simmering the rooster.

• Serve with steamed or boiled potatoes.

• If you can get fresh rooster's blood, mix it with a dash of vinegar and finely chopped onion. Add it to the sauce at the same time as the liver in Step 3.

MARINATED ROOSTER SIMMERED IN RED WINE
- Coq au chambertin -

❖ EASY   ❖ MODERATE   ❖ 2 HOURS, 30 MINUTES, PLUS 2 HOURS MARINATING   ❖ SERVES 6

MARINADE
3 cups Chambertin or other Pinot Noir wine
2 tablespoons oil
1 onion, thinly sliced
2 shallots, thinly sliced
1 carrot, thinly sliced
3 garlic cloves, thinly sliced
1 bouquet garni made with parsley, thyme, and bay leaf
1 whole clove
3 black peppercorns

4 ½-pound rooster, cut into serving pieces, liver pureed
3 tablespoons butter
3 ounces fresh pork rind, chopped (optional)
1 tablespoon all-purpose flour
¾ cup Cognac
1 tablespoon tomato paste
Salt and pepper
¼ pound thick-sliced pancetta, cut crosswise into ¼-inch-thick strips
½ pound white mushrooms, thinly sliced
Freshly chopped parsley leaves for sprinkling

❖ ❖ ❖ ❖ ❖

1. For the marinade: In a large bowl, combine all the ingredients. Add the rooster, cover, and refrigerate for 2 hours, turning the rooster occasionally. Remove the rooster, reserving the marinade. Pat dry the rooster pieces and vegetables.

2. In a flameproof casserole, melt the butter with the pork rind, if using, over medium-high heat. Add the rooster pieces and lightly brown all over. Remove to a plate. Add the vegetables from the marinade and cook, stirring, until just beginning to brown. Stir in the flour. Return the rooster to the skillet. Add the Cognac and bring to a boil, then tilt the pan and carefully ignite. When the flames subside, add the wine from the marinade, ¾ cup of water, the tomato paste, and the bouquet garni from the marinade and season with salt and pepper. Cover and bring to a boil, then reduce the heat to low and cook until tender, 1 hour and 30 minutes to 2 hours.

3. Meanwhile, in a small saucepan, cook the pancetta over medium-high heat, stirring, until just beginning to brown. Add the mushrooms and cook for 5 minutes. Transfer to a warmed serving dish.

4. Add the rooster pieces to the mushroom mixture. If the sauce is too thin, simmer it for a few minutes. Add the pureed liver and immediately remove the casserole from the heat. Strain the sauce over the bird. Sprinkle with parsley and serve.

From Françoise:

• Serve with potatoes or egg noodles.

• The secret to a velvety sauce: The pureed liver, added to the sauce just before serving, thickens it slightly. Do not let the sauce boil after adding the liver or it will separate.

• Chambertin, a burgundy wine of great reputation, is very strong and has a rich bouquet. However, a more modest wine, such as a Côtes du Rhône or a Beaujolais, may be used for this recipe.

ROOSTER SIMMERED IN WHITE WINE
- Coq au riesling -

❖ EASY   ❖ MODERATE   ❖ 2 HOURS, 30 MINUTES   ❖ SERVES 6

4 tablespoons (½ stick) butter

4 ½–pound rooster, cut into serving pieces

3 shallots, finely chopped

2 tablespoons all-purpose flour

1 bouquet garni made with parsley, thyme, and bay leaf

1 celery rib, sliced 2 inches thick

3 cups Riesling or other dry white wine

Salt and pepper

½ pound white mushrooms, halved or quartered if large and thinly sliced

1 tablespoon lemon juice

¾ cup crème fraîche

❖ ❖ ❖ ❖ ❖

1. In a flameproof casserole, melt 3 tablespoons of the butter over medium heat. Add the rooster pieces and cook all over without browning. Remove to a plate. Stir in the shallots and flour. Return the rooster to the skillet. Add the bouquet garni, celery, wine, and enough water to barely cover the rooster. Season with salt and pepper. Cover and bring to a boil, then reduce the heat to low and cook until tender, 1 hour and 30 minutes to 2 hours.

2. Meanwhile, in a small saucepan, combine the mushrooms with the lemon juice and remaining 1 tablespoon of butter and barely cover with water. Season with salt and pepper. Bring to a boil over medium-high heat, then reduce the heat to low and simmer for 5 minutes, then drain.

3. Add the rooster pieces to a warmed serving dish. Simmer the sauce until reduced by

continued

one-third, about 10 minutes. Strain the sauce into a saucepan. Add the mushrooms and crème fraîche and simmer for 1 minute. Pour the sauce over the bird and serve.

From Françoise:

• Riesling is a dry white wine from Alsace. You can, of course, replace it with another, less expensive dry white wine—so long as it's good quality.

• You can use a large braising hen instead of a rooster.

• Be careful not to let the shallots brown or they will become bitter.

• Serve with boiled rice or rice pilaf.

BRAISED DUCK WITH ORANGE SAUCE
- Canard braisé à l'orange -

❖ INTERMEDIATE	❖ EXPENSIVE	❖ 2 HOURS	❖ SERVES 4

4 tablespoons (½ stick) butter
3 ½- to 4 ½-pound duck, neck, wing tips, and gizzard reserved
1 onion, chopped
1 ½ cups dry white wine
1 carrot, thinly sliced
1 bouquet garni made with parsley, thyme, and bay leaf

Salt and pepper
2 oranges
1 ½ cups Curaçao or orange liqueur
1 tablespoon potato starch
2 tablespoons red currant jelly
Juice of ½ lemon

❖ ❖ ❖ ❖ ❖

1. In a medium saucepan, melt 2 tablespoons of the butter over medium-high heat. Add the duck neck, wing tips, gizzard, and onion and cook until lightly browned. Add the wine, ¾ cup of water, the carrot, and bouquet garni and season with salt and pepper. Bring to a boil, then reduce the heat to low and cook for 1 hour.

2. In a flameproof casserole, melt the remaining 2 tablespoons of butter over medium-high heat. Add the duck and cook until nicely browned all over. Season with salt and pepper. Strain the broth from Step 1 over the duck. (Discard the vegetables and duck parts from the broth.) Bring to a boil, then reduce the heat to low and cook for about 50 minutes.

3. Using a vegetable peeler, remove the zest from 1 orange in strips. Cut it into fine julienne. Add to a small saucepan of cold water and bring to a boil, then drain. In a bowl, combine the zest with ¾ cup of the Curaçao.

4. Using a sharp knife, peel the oranges, removing all the white pith. Thinly slice them crosswise, removing any seeds.

5. Transfer the duck to a cutting board, cover loosely with foil, and let stand for 10 minutes.

6. Meanwhile, skim the fat off the cooking liquid in the casserole. Simmer until slightly thickened. In a bowl, mix the potato starch

with the red currant jelly and the remaining ¾ cup of Curaçao; whisk this mixture into the simmering liquid. Add the lemon juice, orange slices, and zest in Curaçao and simmer, whisking, for 2 to 3 minutes.

7. Carve the duck and transfer to a warmed serving dish. Spoon the sauce and oranges over the duck and serve.

From Françoise:

• This recipe is more intimidating to read than to execute. The first step—making the broth—is neither difficult nor long, but it is important because the quality of your sauce depends on it.

• Make carving the duck easy: Using a heavy knife, simply cut it into quarters, removing the backbone. You don't need to cut the duck breasts off the bone and thinly slice them lengthwise into *aiguillettes* (long strips). That's typically reserved for really large duck breasts.

• Peeling a piece of citrus fruit "à vif" is using a very sharp knife to cut off the entire peel including the bitter white pith down to the juicy flesh.

• Briefly simmering citrus zest removes the bitter flavor.

DUCK WITH CREAMY TARRAGON PAN SAUCE AND APPLES

- *Canard normande à l'estragon* -

❖ EASY   ❖ EXPENSIVE   ❖ 1 HOUR, 15 MINUTES   ❖ SERVES 4

3 ½- to 4 ½-pound duck
Tarragon sprigs, leaves chopped, stems reserved
Salt and pepper
4 tablespoons (½ stick) butter
⅓ cup Calvados

4 apples, peeled, cored, and thickly sliced lengthwise
¾ cup dry white wine
¾ cup crème fraîche

❖   ❖   ❖   ❖   ❖

1. Stuff the duck with the tarragon stems. Season inside and out with salt and pepper. Using kitchen string, tie the legs together and the wings together.

2. In a flameproof casserole, melt 2 tablespoons of the butter over medium-high heat. Add the duck and cook until nicely browned all over. Discard the fat in the casserole. Add the Calvados and bring to a boil, then tilt the pot and carefully ignite. When the flames subside, reduce the heat to medium-low and cook the duck for 45 minutes to 1 hour, turning the bird 2 or 3 times. If the pot gets dry, add 2 or 3 tablespoons of water during cooking.

3. Transfer the duck to a cutting board and remove the string and tarragon stems. Cover loosely with foil and let stand for 10 minutes.

continued

4. Meanwhile, in a large skillet, melt the remaining 2 tablespoons of butter over medium heat. Add the apples and cook, turning once, until golden brown.

5. Skim any fat off the pan juices in the casserole. Add the wine and simmer, scraping up any brown bits stuck to the bottom, until reduced by half. Stir in the crème fraîche and tarragon leaves and bring to a boil. Pour into a warmed sauceboat.

6. Set the duck on a warmed platter, surround with the apples, and serve with the sauce.

From Françoise:
• If it looks like there aren't enough apples, add small, peeled new potatoes to the duck in the casserole halfway through cooking. They will be ready to serve at the same time.

BRAISED DUCK WITH SPRING TURNIPS
- Canard braisé aux navets -

❖ EASY   ❖ EXPENSIVE   ❖ 2 HOURS   ❖ SERVES 4

4 tablespoons (½ stick) butter
3 ½- to 4 ½-pound duck, neck, wing tips, and
  gizzard reserved
1 onion, chopped
¾ cup dry white wine
1 carrot, thinly sliced

1 bouquet garni made with parsley, thyme,
  and bay leaf
Salt and pepper
2 pounds small young turnips, quartered
5 ounces spring onions

❖ ❖ ❖ ❖ ❖

1. In a medium saucepan, melt 2 tablespoons of the butter over medium-high heat. Add the duck neck, wing tips, gizzard, and onion and cook until lightly browned. Add the wine, 1 ½ cups of water, the carrot, and bouquet garni and season with salt and pepper. Bring to a boil, then reduce the heat to low and cook for 1 hour.

2. In a flameproof casserole, melt the remaining 2 tablespoons of butter over medium-high heat. Add the duck and cook until nicely browned all over. Season with salt and pepper. Strain the broth from Step 1 over the duck. (Discard vegetables and duck parts from

broth.) Bring to a boil, then reduce the heat to low, cover, and cook for 10 minutes. Add the turnips and spring onions and cook for 40 to 50 minutes.

3. Transfer the duck to a cutting board and carve into serving pieces. Transfer to a warmed serving dish. Spoon the turnips and onions around the duck and serve.

From Françoise:
• If the duck renders a lot of fat when you brown it in Step 2, discard the fat before adding the broth.

- If you're not using tender spring turnips and onions, boil them for 5 minutes and drain well before adding them to the casserole.

- The broth can be prepared through Step 1 and refrigerated for up to 1 day.

POT-ROASTED DUCK WITH OLIVES
- Canard aux olives -

❖ EASY   ❖ EXPENSIVE   ❖ 1 HOUR, 10 MINUTES   ❖ SERVES 4

MEAT &
POULTRY

3 tablespoons butter
3 ½- to 4 ½-pound duck, legs and wings tied
1 teaspoon all-purpose flour
¾ cup dry white wine
¾ cup chicken broth

1 bouquet garni made with parsley, thyme,
 and bay leaf
Salt and pepper
1 cup pitted green olives

❖ ❖ ❖ ❖ ❖

1. In a flameproof casserole, melt the butter over medium-high heat. Add the duck and cook until nicely browned all over. Remove to a plate. Stir in the flour. Return the duck to the pot and add the wine, broth, and bouquet garni. Season with pepper and, lightly, with salt. Cover and bring to a boil, then reduce the heat to low and cook for about 1 hour.

2. Meanwhile, add the olives to a small saucepan of cold water and bring to a boil, then drain. Add to the duck.

3. Discard the bouquet garni. Remove the string from the duck. Transfer the duck and olives to a warmed serving dish and serve with the pan juices.

CLASSIC ROAST DUCK ON TOAST
- Caneton rôti sur canapé -

❖ EASY   ❖ EXPENSIVE   ❖ 1 HOUR, 15 MINUTES   ❖ SERVES 2

5 tablespoons butter, 2 tablespoons softened
3-pound duck, legs and wings tied
Salt and pepper
6 tablespoons dry white wine

1 large shallot, finely chopped
4 slices crustless white bread, toasted

continued

1. Preheat the oven to 400 degrees. In a flame-proof casserole, melt 2 tablespoons of the butter over medium-high heat. Add the duck and cook until nicely browned all over. Season with salt and pepper.

2. Transfer the casserole to the oven and roast the duck, uncovered, for 40 to 45 minutes, basting several times with the pan juices.

3. Transfer the duck to a cutting board and remove the string. Cover loosely with foil and let stand for 10 minutes.

4. Meanwhile, skim the fat off the pan juices in the casserole. Add the wine and boil, scraping up any brown bits stuck to the bottom, for 1 minute. Pour into a warmed sauceboat.

5. In a small saucepan, melt 1 tablespoon of the butter over medium-low heat. Add the shallot and cook until softened. Beat in the softened butter and season with salt and pepper. Spread the shallot butter on the toasts. Arrange on a warmed platter.

6. Carve the duck into quarters lengthwise, cutting out the backbone. Set each duck quarter on a toast and serve, passing the pan sauce separately.

POT-ROASTED DUCK WITH PEACHES
- *Caneton aux pêches* -

❖ EASY ❖ EXPENSIVE ❖ 1 HOUR, 15 MINUTES ❖ SERVES 4

3 tablespoons butter
1 tablespoon oil
3 ½- to 4 ½-pound duck, legs and wings tied
1 onion, cut into ¼-inch dice
1 carrot, peeled and cut into ¼-inch dice
1 teaspoon all-purpose flour
¾ cup dry white wine

¾ cup chicken broth
1 bouquet garni made with parsley, thyme, and bay leaf
Salt and pepper
1 tablespoon Cognac
4 peaches, peeled and halved

❖ ❖ ❖ ❖ ❖

1. In a flameproof casserole, melt 1 ½ tablespoons of the butter in the oil over medium-high heat. Add the duck and cook until nicely browned all over. Transfer to a plate and discard the fat in the pot.

2. In the same casserole, melt the remaining 1 ½ tablespoons of butter over medium-high heat. Add the onion and carrot and cook, stirring occasionally, until lightly browned. Stir in the flour and cook until lightly browned. Stir in the wine and broth, scraping up any brown bits stuck to the bottom, and bring to a boil. Return the duck to the casserole, add the bouquet garni, and season with salt and pepper. Reduce the heat to low, cover, and cook for about 50 minutes.

3. Transfer the duck to a cutting board and remove the string. Cover loosely with foil and let stand for 10 minutes.

4. Meanwhile, skim the fat off the pan juices in the casserole. Strain the pan juices and return to the casserole. Add the Cognac and set over medium heat. Add the peaches and cook, uncovered, until tender.

5. Transfer the duck to a warmed serving platter. Using a slotted spoon, arrange the peaches around the bird. Simmer the pan juices until slightly thickened and well flavored and serve with the duck.

From Françoise:
• If you have a yen for this dish out of peach season, you can make it with well-drained store-bought peaches in syrup.

ROAST TURKEY STUFFED WITH CHESTNUTS
- *Dindonneau farci aux marrons* -

❖ INTERMEDIATE   ❖ MODERATE   ❖ 3 HOURS   ❖ SERVES 8

3 ½ pounds chestnuts in the shell, scored

1 pound sausage meat

6 ½- to 7 ½-pound turkey, liver and heart chopped

Thyme leaves

Salt and pepper

3 tablespoons butter, softened

❖ ❖ ❖ ❖ ❖

1. Bring a large pot of water to a boil. Add the chestnuts and cook at a gentle boil for 30 minutes. Take 1 chestnut out of the water at a time and while still hot, hold it with a kitchen towel and peel with a paring knife. Crumble the chestnuts.

2. Preheat the oven to 425 degrees. In a bowl, combine the chestnuts with the sausage meat, turkey liver and heart, and thyme. Season with salt and pepper and beat until mixed. Pack the stuffing into the turkey. Using kitchen string, tie the legs together and the wings together. Brush the butter all over the bird. Season the outside with salt and pepper.

3. Set the turkey in a roasting pan and transfer to the oven. Roast until the turkey is well browned, about 45 minutes, then reduce the

oven temperature to 350 degrees. Continue roasting, basting the bird often, for 1 hour and 15 minutes.

4. Transfer the turkey to a cutting board and remove the string. Cover loosely with foil and let stand for 20 minutes. Spoon the stuffing into a bowl. Carve the turkey and arrange on a warmed platter. Serve with the stuffing.

From Françoise:
• If you're roasting a larger bird, cook it for longer at a lower temperature. Most important, baste it often—every 10 minutes.

• Instead of cooking and peeling raw chestnuts in the shell, you could use 2 pounds of peeled and cooked vacuum-packed chestnuts.

ROAST TURKEY WITH PORCINI STUFFING

- Dinde farcie aux cèpes -

❖ INTERMEDIATE ❖ EXPENSIVE ❖ 3 HOURS ❖ SERVES 10

4 slices of crustless white bread, chopped

6 tablespoons milk

½ pound jarred or canned whole porcini
  mushrooms, stems chopped, caps cut into
  ¼-inch dice

5 ounces ground veal

5 ounces ground pork

½ cup port

1 large egg

8 ½- to 9 ½-pound turkey, liver chopped

Salt and pepper

3 tablespoons butter, softened

❖ ❖ ❖ ❖ ❖

1. Preheat the oven to 350 degrees. In a large
bowl, mix the bread with the milk, porcini
mushrooms, veal, pork, 6 tablespoons of the
port, the egg, and turkey liver. Season with salt
and pepper. Pack the stuffing into the turkey.
Using kitchen string, tie the legs together and
the wings together. Brush the butter all over
the bird. Season the outside with salt and
pepper.

2. Set the turkey in a roasting pan, transfer to
the oven, and roast, basting the bird often, for
2 hours and 30 minutes.

3. Transfer the turkey to a cutting board and
remove the string. Cover loosely with foil and
let stand for 30 minutes.

4. Meanwhile, skim the fat off the pan juices
in the roasting pan. Add the remaining 2
tablespoons of port and boil, scraping up any
brown bits stuck to the bottom, until slightly
thickened and well flavored. Pour into a
warmed sauceboat.

5. Spoon the turkey stuffing into a bowl. Carve
the turkey and arrange on a warmed platter.
Serve with the stuffing and pan juices.

CLASSIC ROAST TURKEY

- Dindonneau rôti -

❖ EASY ❖ MODERATE ❖ 2 HOURS, 15 MINUTES ❖ SERVES 8

6 ½- to 7 ½-pound turkey, liver and heart chopped

Salt and pepper

Thyme leaves

4 tablespoons (½ stick) butter, softened

1. Preheat the oven to 425 degrees. Season the cavity of the turkey with salt and pepper and add the thyme and 2 tablespoons of the butter. Using kitchen string, tie the legs together and the wings together. Brush the remaining 2 tablespoons of butter all over the bird. Season the outside with salt and pepper.

2. Set the turkey in a roasting pan and transfer to the oven. Roast until the turkey is well browned, about 45 minutes, then reduce the oven temperature to 350 degrees. Continue roasting, basting the bird often, for 1 hour and 15 minutes.

3. Transfer the turkey to a cutting board and remove the string. Cover loosely with foil and let stand for 20 minutes.

4. Meanwhile, skim the fat off the pan juices in the roasting pan. Add 1 ¼ cups of boiling water and simmer, scraping up any brown bits stuck to the bottom, until slightly thickened and well flavored. Season to taste and pour into a warmed sauceboat.

5. Carve the turkey, arrange on a warmed platter, and serve with the pan juices.

From Françoise:
• Serve with potatoes in some form, like chips, croquettes, or mashed. Sautéed mushrooms, braised celery, English peas, and pureed chestnuts are also fine accompaniments.

BRAISED TURKEY WITH AROMATIC VEGETABLES
- *Dinde braisée* -

❖ EASY   ❖ INEXPENSIVE   ❖ 1 HOUR, 15 MINUTES   ❖ SERVES 4

2 tablespoons butter
1 ½ pounds turkey pieces
1 carrot, peeled and cut into ¼-inch dice
1 onion, cut into ¼-inch dice

¼ cup Cognac
1 bouquet garni made with parsley, thyme, and bay leaf
Salt and pepper

❖   ❖   ❖   ❖   ❖

1. In a flameproof casserole, melt the butter over medium-high heat. Add the turkey and cook until lightly browned on all sides. Remove the turkey to a plate. Add the carrot and onion and cook, stirring, until nicely browned. Add the Cognac and bring to a boil, then tilt the pot and carefully ignite. When the flames subside, add 1 ½ cups of water, the turkey, and the bouquet garni. Season with salt and pepper. Cover and bring to a boil, then reduce the heat to low and cook for about 1 hour.

2. Remove the bouquet garni. Transfer the turkey and vegetables to a warmed serving dish.

From Françoise:
• A hen, large chicken, or goose can also be prepared in the same way.

• Serve with sautéed or mashed potatoes, pasta, rice pilaf, or chestnuts.

ROAST HALF TURKEY WITH RICH MEAT STUFFING
- *Demi-dinde farcie* -

❖ EASY   ❖ MODERATE   ❖ 1 HOUR, 30 MINUTES   ❖ SERVES 4 OR 5

2 small brioches

Warm milk for moistening

4- to 5-pound half turkey, liver chopped

7 ounces ham, finely chopped

5 ounces ground veal

5 ounces ground pork

1 large egg

Salt and pepper

2 tablespoons butter

❖ ❖ ❖ ❖ ❖

1. Preheat the oven to 350 degrees. Tear the brioches into pieces and add to a large bowl; stir in enough milk just to moisten. Mix in the turkey liver, ham, veal, pork, and egg. Season with salt and pepper.

2. Pack the stuffing into the cavity of the turkey. Wrap with foil to hold the stuffing in place and set, foil side down, in a roasting pan. Dot the skin of the turkey with the butter. Transfer to the oven and roast for 45 minutes to 1 hour, turning the bird and removing the foil halfway through cooking to allow the stuffing to brown.

3. Transfer the turkey to a cutting board, cover loosely with foil, and let stand for 10 minutes.

4. Meanwhile, add ½ cup of boiling water to the pan juices in the roasting pan and simmer, scraping up any brown bits stuck to the bottom, until slightly thickened and well flavored. Taste for seasoning and pour into a warmed sauceboat.

5. Spoon the turkey stuffing into a bowl. Carve the turkey, arrange on a warmed platter, and serve with the stuffing and pan juices.

From Françoise:
• A whole turkey is split lengthwise in half, and the backbone removed, to make a half turkey.

CASSEROLE-ROASTED QUAILS WITH GRAPES
- *Cailles aux raisins* -

❖ EASY   ❖ MODERATE   ❖ 30 MINUTES   ❖ SERVES 4

8 tablespoons (1 stick) butter

8 quails, legs and wings tied, livers reserved

8 slices of crustless white sandwich bread

¼ cup Cognac

Salt and pepper

½ pound grapes, peeled if desired

1. In a flameproof casserole, melt 2 tablespoons of the butter over medium-high heat. Add the quails and cook until nicely browned all over. Reduce the heat to medium-low, cover, and cook for about 10 minutes.

2. Meanwhile, in a large skillet, melt 3 tablespoons of the butter. Working in batches, add the bread slices and cook until golden on both sides. Transfer to a work surface.

3. Wipe out the skillet. In it melt 2 tablespoons of the butter over medium-high heat. Add the quail livers and quickly sear on both sides. Add 2 tablespoons of the Cognac and bring to a boil, then tilt the skillet and carefully ignite. When the flames subside, remove the pan from the heat and mash the livers with a fork. Mash in the remaining 1 tablespoon of butter and season with salt and pepper. Spread the liver mixture over the toasts.

4. Transfer the quails to a cutting board and remove the string. Cover loosely with foil and let stand for 10 minutes.

5. Meanwhile, skim the fat off the pan juices in the casserole. Add the remaining 2 tablespoons of Cognac and bring to a boil, scraping up any brown bits stuck to the bottom, then tilt the pot and carefully ignite. When the flames subside, add the grapes, reduce the heat to low, cover, and cook for 2 minutes.

6. Arrange the liver toasts on a warmed platter. Set a quail on each and serve with the grapes.

From Françoise:
• You may tie a piece of barding fat around each quail if you like before browning them in Step 1. Remove the string and fat in Step 4.

• If your quails do not have their giblets, substitute 4 chicken livers in Step 3.

• Grapes are easy to peel with a small, sharp knife.

• Partridges can be prepared in the same way as these quails. Using 4 partridges, the proportions are the same, but the cooking time is a bit longer. Plan on 25 to 30 minutes of pot-roasting.

ROASTED QUAILS
- Cailles rôties -

❖ EASY	❖ MODERATE	❖ 40 MINUTES	❖ SERVES 4

2 tablespoons butter
8 quails, legs and wings tied

Salt and pepper
¼ to ½ cup Cognac

❖ ❖ ❖ ❖ ❖

1. Preheat the oven to 425 degrees. In a flameproof casserole, melt the butter over medium-high heat. Add the quails and cook until nicely browned all over. Season with salt and pepper.

2. Transfer the casserole to the oven and roast the birds, uncovered, for 20 to 25 minutes.

continued

3. Remove the string from the quails and set them on a warmed platter. Add the Cognac to the casserole and bring to a boil, scraping up any brown bits stuck to the bottom, then tilt the pot and carefully ignite. When the flames subside, pour over the quails and serve at once.

From Françoise:

• You might tie a piece of barding fat around each quail if you like before browning them in Step 1. Remove the string and fat in Step 3.

• The quails can also be cooked in the casserole on the stovetop with the pot partially covered. The cooking time will be about the same.

GUINEA HENS WITH CREAMY TARRAGON SAUCE
- *Pintade à l'estragon* -

❖ EASY   ❖ MODERATE   ❖ 45 MINUTES   ❖ SERVES 4

2 small guinea hens, about 2 pounds each
4 tarragon sprigs, stems reserved,
   leaves chopped
5 tablespoons plus 1 teaspoon butter
¾ cup dry white wine

1 bouquet garni made with parsley, thyme,
   and bay leaf
Salt and pepper
1 teaspoon all-purpose flour
1 tablespoon crème fraîche
4 slices of crustless white sandwich bread

❖ ❖ ❖ ❖ ❖

1. Preheat the oven to 350 degrees. Stuff the cavity of each guinea hen with 1 tarragon stem. Using kitchen string, tie the legs together and the wings together. In a flameproof casserole, melt 2 tablespoons of the butter over medium heat. Add the hens and cook until lightly browned all over. Add the wine, 6 tablespoons of water, the bouquet garni, and remaining 2 tarragon stems. Season with salt and pepper. Cover and bring to a boil, then transfer to the oven and cook for 30 to 35 minutes, turning the birds halfway through cooking.

2. Transfer the birds to a cutting board and remove the string. Cover loosely with foil and let stand for 10 minutes.

3. Meanwhile, strain the pan juices in the casserole and return to the pot. In a cup, blend the flour with 1 teaspoon of the butter. Whisk this paste into the simmering pan juices. Add the tarragon leaves and crème fraîche and simmer for 5 minutes. Pour into a warmed sauceboat.

4. In a large skillet, melt the remaining 3 tablespoons of butter. Add the bread slices and cook until golden on both sides. Transfer to a warmed platter.

5. Slice each guinea hen in half lengthwise, cutting out the backbone. Set each half on a toast and serve, passing the sauce separately.

From Françoise:
• Serve with buttered noodles.

POT-ROASTED GUINEA HENS WITH POTATOES, ONIONS, AND MUSHROOMS

- *Pintade grand-mère* -

❖ EASY   ❖ MODERATE   ❖ 1 HOUR, 15 MINUTES   ❖ SERVES 4

1 ½ pounds potatoes, peeled and cut into chunks
½ pound pearl onions, peeled
2 small guinea hens, about 2 pounds each
Salt and pepper

5 tablespoons butter
½ pound white mushrooms, quartered lengthwise
Chopped parsley leaves for sprinkling

❖ ❖ ❖ ❖ ❖

1. Bring a large pot of water to a boil over medium-high heat. Add the potatoes and onions and cook at a gentle boil for 5 minutes. Drain.

2. Season the cavity of each guinea hen with salt and pepper. Using kitchen string, tie the legs together and the wings together. In a flameproof casserole, melt 3 tablespoons of the butter over medium heat. Add the hens and cook until lightly browned all over. Remove to a platter. Add the potatoes and onions to the casserole and cook until lightly browned. Return the hens to the pot and season with salt and pepper. Cover and cook for 40 to 50 minutes.

3. In a skillet, melt the remaining 2 tablespoons of butter over medium-high heat. Add the mushrooms and season with salt and pepper. Cook, stirring occasionally, for 5 minutes. Add to the casserole and cook for 5 minutes. Sprinkle with parsley and serve.

From Françoise:

• You could prepare a chicken in the same way. One chicken would serve 4 people, or even 6 if it's larger than 3 ½ pounds. Cook it for 1 hour, because even though guinea hen can be eaten when the juices are still a little pink, chicken must be cooked until the juices run clear. At least that's my opinion!

ROASTED GUINEA HENS ON TOAST

- *Pintade rôtie sur canapé* -

❖ EASY   ❖ MODERATE   ❖ 45 MINUTES   ❖ SERVES 4

2 small guinea hens, about 2 pounds each,
  hearts, livers, and giblets reserved
Salt and pepper

4 tablespoons (½ stick) butter
4 slices of crustless white sandwich bread

continued

1. Preheat the oven to 400 degrees. Season the cavity of each guinea hen with salt and pepper. Using kitchen string, tie the legs together and the wings together. Set the hens in a roasting pan, transfer to the oven, and roast for about 35 minutes.

2. Transfer the birds to a cutting board and remove the string. Cover loosely with foil and let stand for 10 minutes.

3. Meanwhile, cut the hen livers and hearts into ¼-inch dice. In a large skillet, melt 1 tablespoon of the butter over medium-high heat. Add the livers, hearts, and giblets and sear. Drain them, then transfer to a bowl and mash with a fork. Season with salt and pepper.

4. Wipe out the skillet. In it melt the remaining 3 tablespoons of butter. Add the bread slices and cook until golden on both sides. Spread the giblet mixture over the toasts and transfer to a warmed platter.

5. Slice each guinea hen in half lengthwise, cutting out the backbone. Set each half on a toast and serve.

From Françoise:
• You might tie a piece of barding fat around each guinea hen if you like before roasting them in Step 1. Remove the string and fat in Step 2.

GUINEA HEN WITH MUSHROOMS

- *Pintade aux champignons et pain doré* -

❖ ADVANCED   ❖ EXPENSIVE   ❖ 1 HOUR, 45 MINUTES   ❖ SERVES 4

3 ½-pound guinea hen, neck and giblets reserved
5 tablespoons butter, 2 tablespoons softened
1 onion, chopped
1 carrot, chopped
1½ cups dry white wine
1 bouquet garni made with parsley, thyme,
   and bay leaf

Salt and pepper
¼ pound small white mushrooms
¼ lemon
2 slices of crustless white sandwich bread,
   cut into 4 triangles
2 ounces thick-sliced pancetta, cut crosswise
   into ¼-inch-thick strips

❖ ❖ ❖ ❖ ❖

1. Preheat the oven to 400 degrees. Set the guinea hen in a roasting pan and brush with the 2 tablespoons of softened butter. Transfer to the oven and roast until half-cooked, about 20 minutes. Transfer the hen to a cutting board and cut into serving pieces. Then cut and scrape the meat off the bones, keeping the meat in the largest possible pieces. Reserve the bones and pan juices.

2. In a saucepan, melt 2 tablespoons of the butter over medium-high heat. Add the reserved hen bones, neck, and giblets and cook until nicely browned. Add the wine, reserved pan

juices, 1 ½ cups of water, and the bouquet garni. Season with salt and pepper. Bring to a boil, then reduce the heat to low and cook, uncovered, for 1 hour.

3. In a flameproof casserole, strain the broth over the hen pieces, reserving the liver. Cover and bring to a boil over medium-high heat, then reduce the heat to low and cook for about 20 minutes.

4. Remove stems from the mushrooms (reserve for stock). Rub the mushroom caps with the lemon and its juice. In a saucepan, melt 1 tablespoon of butter, add the mushrooms, and cook, stirring occasionally, until tender, about 3 minutes.

5. In a large skillet, melt the remaining 2 tablespoons of butter over medium heat. Add the bread triangles and cook until golden on both sides. Transfer to a plate. In the same skillet, cook the pancetta until just beginning to brown. Finely chop the liver and add. Season

with salt and pepper and cook until browned on the outside and still pink on the inside. Mash with a fork.

6. Transfer the guinea hen to a warmed serving dish. Stir the mashed liver into the sauce remaining in the casserole and spoon over the bird. Surround with the mushrooms and toasts and serve.

From Françoise:
• Whole birds don't always come with their giblets, but you can usually buy them separately. If you forget, you can add a chicken bouillon cube in Step 2 to give the broth more flavor.

• A good guinea hen should have the same qualities as a chicken: a pliable breastbone, transparent skin, and not too much fat.

• Rubbing the mushroom caps with lemon keeps them white, but it's not critical.

BRAISED GOOSE WITH AROMATIC VEGETABLES
- *Oie en fricassée* -

❖ EASY	❖ MODERATE	❖ 2 HOURS	❖ SERVES 4

2 tablespoons butter

2 pounds goose pieces

½ pound carrots, peeled and cut into chunks

½ pound turnips, peeled and cut into chunks

1 onion, coarsely chopped

1 tablespoon all-purpose flour

1 garlic clove, crushed

1 bouquet garni made with parsley, thyme, and bay leaf

Salt and pepper

1 pound new potatoes, peeled and cut into chunks

continued

1. In a flameproof casserole, melt the butter over medium-high heat. Add the goose pieces and cook until lightly browned on all sides. Remove to a bowl. Add the carrots, turnips, and onion and cook, stirring occasionally, until lightly browned. Stir in the flour. Return the goose to the pot and add water to barely cover. Add the garlic and bouquet garni and season with salt and pepper. Cover and bring to a boil, then reduce the heat to low and cook for about 1 hour and 20 minutes.

2. Add the potatoes and cook for 30 minutes longer. Remove the bouquet garni and serve in a warmed serving dish.

From Françoise:

• Turkey can be prepared in the same way as goose; recipes that work for one would be good for the other.

• Add the potatoes toward the end of cooking so they don't fall apart.

• As a variation, you might add ¾ cup of dry white wine and ¾ cup of water to the casserole instead of just water. And a teaspoon of tomato paste will add depth of flavor.

ROAST GOOSE WITH STUFFED APPLES
- Oie rôtie aux pommes -

❖ EASY   ❖ EXPENSIVE   ❖ 3 HOURS   ❖ SERVES 6

2 pounds small apples
4 tablespoons (½ stick) butter, softened
1 tablespoon dry bread crumbs

Salt and pepper
6 ½– to 7 ½–pound goose
Thyme leaves for sprinkling

❖ ❖ ❖ ❖ ❖

1. Preheat the oven to 425 degrees. Peel the apples. Working from the stem end and using a melon baller, apple corer, or small, sharp knife, remove the interior core and seeds to within ½ inch of the bottom. In a cup, mash 3 tablespoons of the butter with the bread crumbs and season with salt and pepper. Spoon some of the butter mixture into each apple. Pack the apples into the goose. Using kitchen string, tie the legs together and the wings together.

2. Set the goose in a roasting pan and brush with the remaining 1 tablespoon of butter. Season with salt and pepper. Transfer to the oven and roast until browned all over, 15 to 20 minutes. Reduce the oven temperature to 350 degrees, sprinkle the goose with thyme, and add 2 or 3 tablespoons of boiling water to the pan. Roast the goose for about 2 hours longer, basting often during cooking.

3. Transfer the goose to a cutting board and remove the string. Cover loosely with foil and let stand for 10 minutes.

4. Meanwhile, skim the fat off the pan juices in the roasting pan. Add ¾ cup of water and simmer, scraping up any brown bits stuck to

the bottom, until slightly thickened and well flavored. Taste for seasoning and pour into a warmed sauceboat.

5. Transfer the apples to a warmed platter. Carve the goose and arrange on the platter. Serve, passing the pan juices separately.

ROAST GOOSE STUFFED WITH CHESTNUTS
- *Oie farcie aux marrons* -

❖ EASY   ❖ EXPENSIVE   ❖ 3 HOURS, 30 MINUTES   ❖ SERVES 8

3 ½ ounces ground veal

3 ½ ounces ground pork

3 ½ ounces pancetta, finely chopped

7 ½- to 8 ½-pound goose, liver finely chopped

2 shallots, finely chopped

5 ounces cooked, peeled chestnuts, crumbled

Salt and pepper

5 tablespoons butter

Watercress sprigs for decorating

❖   ❖   ❖   ❖   ❖

1. Preheat the oven to 425 degrees. In a bowl, mix the ground veal with the pork, pancetta, goose liver, shallots, and chestnuts. Season with salt and pepper. Pack the stuffing into the goose. Using kitchen string, tie the legs together and the wings together.

2. Set the goose in a roasting pan and brush the legs with the butter. Season with salt and pepper. Transfer to the oven and roast the goose for 30 minutes. Reduce the oven temperature to 400 degrees and add 2 or 3 tablespoons of boiling water to the pan. Roast the goose for about 2 hours and 30 minutes longer, basting often during cooking.

3. Transfer the goose to a cutting board and remove the string. Cover loosely with foil and let stand for 10 minutes.

4. Meanwhile, skim the fat off the pan juices in the roasting pan. Add ¾ cup of water and

simmer, scraping up any brown bits stuck to the bottom, until slightly thickened and well flavored. Season to taste and pour into a warmed sauceboat.

5. Spoon the stuffing into a bowl. Carve the goose and arrange on a warmed platter. Decorate with the watercress sprigs and serve with the stuffing, passing the pan juices separately.

From Françoise:
• If a roasting bird browns too quickly, cover it loosely with a sheet of foil.

• The secret to flavorful store-bought cooked chestnuts: Cook them gently in chicken broth—homemade or not—for 15 minutes. That's enough time for them to absorb the flavors of the broth. Add a little of the cooking liquid to the crumbled chestnuts.

ROAST GOOSE WITH SAUERKRAUT AND APPLES
- *Oie rôtie à la choucroute* -

❖ EASY   ❖ EXPENSIVE   ❖ 5 HOURS, 30 MINUTES, PLUS OVERNIGHT SOAKING   ❖ SERVES 8 TO 10

7 ½ pounds sauerkraut

10 ounces fresh pork rind

1-pound chunk of bacon

1 carrot, peeled

2 onions, stuck with 3 whole cloves total

30 juniper berries

1 bouquet garni made with parsley, thyme,
   and bay leaf

20 black peppercorns

Salt and pepper

6 tablespoons butter

3 cups dry white wine, preferably from Alsace

1 pound French garlic sausage or kielbasa

10 frankfurters

10 new potatoes, peeled

7 ½- to 8 ½-pound goose

8 to 10 small apples

❖ ❖ ❖ ❖ ❖

1. In a large bowl, cover the sauerkraut generously with water and let soak overnight, changing the water 2 or 3 times.

2. Drain the sauerkraut and squeeze out as much of the water as possible. Spread on a large, clean kitchen towel.

3. Add the pork rind to a large saucepan of water and bring to a boil. Simmer it for 2 to 3 minutes, then drain. In a flameproof casserole, spread the pork rind. Cover with half the sauerkraut, the bacon, carrot, onions, juniper berries, bouquet garni, peppercorns, and a little salt, then spread the remaining sauerkraut on top. Add 3 tablespoons of the butter and the wine. Cover and bring to a boil over medium-high heat, then reduce the heat to low and cook for 2 hours and 30 minutes. Add the sausage, frankfurters, and potatoes and cook for 30 minutes longer.

4. Preheat the oven to 450 degrees. Meanwhile, season the goose inside and out with salt and pepper. Tie the legs together and the wings together. Set the goose in a roasting pan, transfer to the oven, and roast until browned all over, 15 to 20 minutes. Reduce the oven temperature to 350 degrees and add 2 or 3 tablespoons of boiling water to the pan. Roast the goose for about 2 hours, basting often during cooking.

5. Peel the apples. Working from the stem end and using a melon baller, apple corer, or small, sharp knife, remove the interior core and seeds to within ½ inch of the bottom. In a cup, mash the remaining 3 tablespoons of butter and season with salt and pepper. Spoon some of the butter into each apple. Arrange the apples around the goose in the pan and roast for 30 minutes longer.

6. Transfer the goose to a cutting board and remove the string. Cover loosely with foil and let stand for 10 minutes.

7. Carve the goose and slice the sausage. Mound some of the sauerkraut on your largest platter. Arrange some of the goose, sausage slices, frankfurters, and potatoes on the sauerkraut and serve.

From Françoise:

• Preparing this dish is not complicated, but it is time-consuming and does require you to work through a series of simple steps. That said, it is one of the quintessential special-occasion dishes to serve at home in France. It looks very festive and makes a wonderful all-in-one dish to serve a crowd.

• You can use two platters or replenish your platter as needed.

• I serve the pan juices with the goose only if they are very well skimmed of fat.

STUFFED ROAST GOOSE WITH HOMEMADE APPLESAUCE
- Oie farcie de la Saint-Michel -

❖ EASY   ❖ EXPENSIVE   ❖ 3 HOURS, 45 MINUTES   ❖ SERVES 6 TO 8

1 pound large onions, unpeeled

Crustless bread

Milk

Sage sprigs, leaves chopped, or 2 tablespoons
   crumbled dried sage leaves

Freshly grated nutmeg

Salt and pepper

8- to 10-pound goose

3 tablespoons butter, softened

2 pounds apples, peeled and chopped

❖ ❖ ❖ ❖ ❖

1. Preheat the oven to 400 degrees. Set the onions on a baking sheet and roast in the oven for about 45 minutes. Remove the onions and increase the oven temperature to 425 degrees. Peel and coarsely chop the onions.

2. Weigh the onions and cut the same weight of bread into cubes. Add the bread to a bowl and soak in enough milk to cover. Pour off the milk and squeeze the bread dry. Mix in the onions and sage and season with nutmeg, salt, and pepper.

3. Pack the stuffing into the goose and, using kitchen string, tie the legs together and the wings together. Set the goose in a roasting pan and brush the legs with the butter. Season with

salt and pepper. Transfer to the oven and roast until browned all over, 15 to 20 minutes. Reduce the oven temperature to 350 degrees and add 2 to 3 tablespoons of boiling water to the pan. Roast the goose for about 2 hours and 30 minutes longer, basting often during cooking.

4. Meanwhile, add the apples to a flameproof casserole and season with salt and pepper. Cover and cook over low heat until the apples fall apart, about 30 minutes.

5. Transfer the goose to a cutting board and remove the string. Cover loosely with foil and let stand for 10 minutes.

continued

6. Meanwhile, skim the fat off the pan juices in the roasting pan. Add ¾ cup of water and simmer, scraping up any brown bits stuck to the bottom, until slightly thickened and well flavored. Season to taste and pour into a warmed sauceboat.

7. Spoon the stuffing into a bowl. Carve the goose and arrange on a warmed platter. Serve with the stuffing, passing the applesauce and pan juices separately.

From Françoise:
• Serve with steamed new potatoes or Pommes Dauphine (page 585).

• Do not try to save time by cooking the onions in a microwave oven. After a few minutes, your onions will turn into empty containers, with most of the onion gone.

POT-ROASTED SQUABS ON TOASTS
- *Pigeons cocotte bec à bec* -

❖ EASY   ❖ EXPENSIVE   ❖ 50 MINUTES   ❖ SERVES 4

2 squabs, about 1 pound each
Barding fat
6 tablespoons butter

Salt and pepper
4 slices of crustless white sandwich bread

❖ ❖ ❖ ❖ ❖

1. Preheat the oven to 400 degrees. Wrap each squab in a piece of barding fat and tie with kitchen string. In a flameproof casserole, melt 3 tablespoons of the butter over medium-high heat. Add the squabs and cook until nicely browned all over. Season with salt and pepper. Transfer the casserole to the oven and cook the squabs, uncovered, for about 35 minutes.

2. In a large skillet, melt the remaining 3 tablespoons of butter over medium heat. Add the bread slices and cook until golden on both sides. Transfer to a warmed platter.

3. Remove the barding fat and string from the squabs. Return them to the casserole and roast until nicely browned, about 5 minutes.

4. Transfer the squabs to a cutting board, cover loosely with foil, and let stand for 10 minutes.

5. Meanwhile, skim the fat off the pan juices in the casserole. Add 2 or 3 tablespoons of water and simmer, scraping up any brown bits stuck to the bottom, until slightly thickened and well flavored. Season to taste and pour into a warmed sauceboat.

6. Slice each squab in half lengthwise, cutting out the backbone. Set each half on a toast and serve, passing the pan juices separately.

From Françoise:
• Like all young birds, a squab has a flexible beak. The tail end piece is light colored, its skin is rosy, and the flesh is deep red.

• Don't expect to cut out the bitter green part of the liver because a young squab doesn't have it.

• You can also cook smaller squabs of about 10 ounces each in this manner. Reduce the cooking time to 15 or 20 minutes.

• If you prefer to cook small guinea hens this way, quarter them lengthwise first, cutting out the backbone.

• You can also add Cognac to the pan juices in the casserole instead of water. Carefully ignite them and when the flames subside, add some grapes and cook for a few minutes, uncovered, to heat through.

SQUABS WITH ENGLISH PEAS
- *Pigeons aux petits pois* -

❖ EASY   ❖ EXPENSIVE   ❖ 1 HOUR, 15 MINUTES   ❖ SERVES 4

2 tablespoons butter

3 ounces thick-sliced pancetta, cut crosswise into ¼-inch-thick strips

2 squabs, about 1 pound each

3 pounds peas in the pod, shelled, or 3 cups shelled peas

Salt and pepper

❖ ❖ ❖ ❖ ❖

1. In a flameproof casserole, melt the butter over medium heat. Add the pancetta and cook until just beginning to brown. Using a slotted spoon, transfer the pancetta to a bowl. Add the squabs to the casserole, increase the heat to medium-high, and cook until nicely browned all over. Return the pancetta to the pot with the peas and ¾ cup of water. Season with pepper and, lightly, with salt. Cover and bring to a boil, then reduce the heat to low and cook for about 45 minutes.

2. Spoon the peas into a warmed serving dish. Set the squabs on top and serve.

From Françoise:

• If you come across older squabs, you'll recognize them by their bluish skin and skinny necks and feet. Cook them longer, about 1 hour, with vegetables in a tightly closed casserole, as in this recipe, for example.

ROASTED SQUABS STUFFED WITH COUSCOUS, RAISINS, AND ALMONDS

- *Pigeons farcis aux raisins* -

❖ EASY ❖ EXPENSIVE ❖ 1 HOUR, PLUS 30 MINUTES SOAKING ❖ SERVES 4

⅔ cup raisins

Salt

⅔ cup couscous

½ cup almonds, chopped

Pepper

2 squabs, about 1 pound each, giblets reserved

Barding fat

2 tablespoons butter, softened

❖ ❖ ❖ ❖ ❖

1. Preheat the oven to 350 degrees. In a small bowl, soak the raisins in hot water for 30 minutes. In a small saucepan, bring ¾ cup of water to a boil and add salt. Stir in the couscous, cover, remove from the heat, and let stand for 5 minutes.

2. Drain the raisins and stir into the couscous along with the almonds. Season with salt and pepper. Pack the couscous into the squabs. Using kitchen string, tie the legs together and the wings together. Wrap each squab in a piece of barding fat and tie with kitchen string. Brush with the butter.

3. Set the squabs on 1 leg in a roasting pan. Transfer the pan to the oven and roast the squabs for 30 minutes, turning them on the other leg after 15 minutes. Remove the barding fat and string, season with salt and pepper, and roast until browned all over, about 10 minutes longer.

4. Transfer the squabs to a cutting board, cover loosely with foil, and let stand for 10 minutes.

5. Meanwhile, skim the fat off the juices in the pan. Add 2 or 3 tablespoons of water and simmer, scraping up any brown bits stuck to the bottom, until slightly thickened and well flavored. Season to taste and pour into a warmed sauceboat.

6. Spoon the stuffing into a bowl. Slice each squab in half lengthwise, cutting out the backbone. Transfer to a warmed platter and serve with the stuffing, passing the pan juices separately.

From Françoise:
• For a faster version, buy ready-made couscous and reheat it with a little butter in a steamer or in the microwave. Use a fork to remove any lumps. Or use the proportions of couscous and water given in the recipe and cook, covered, in the microwave for 2 minutes, stirring halfway through and letting it rest briefly before removing the cover.

RABBIT WITH RATATOUILLE
- *Lapin en ratatouille* -

RATATOUILLE

2 tablespoons butter

2 garlic cloves, crushed

1 onion, chopped

1 pound tomatoes, peeled, seed, and chopped

2 red bell peppers, diced

1 tablespoon tomato paste

1 red chile

1 bouquet garni made with parsley, thyme,
  and bay leaf

Salt and pepper

2 tablespoons oil

3 ½-pound rabbit, cut into serving pieces

3 tablespoons butter

1 onion, quartered

1 tablespoon all-purpose flour

1 ½ cups dry white wine

Salt and pepper

1 ½ cups rice, rinsed

Chopped parsley leaves for sprinkling

❖ ❖ ❖ ❖ ❖

1. Make the ratatouille: In a skillet, melt the butter over medium-high heat. Add the garlic, onion, tomatoes, bell peppers, tomato paste, red chile, and bouquet garni. Season with salt and pepper. Bring to a boil, then simmer, uncovered, until almost all the liquid has evaporated. Remove the chile and bouquet garni.

2. Meanwhile, in a flameproof casserole, heat the oil over medium-high heat. Add the rabbit pieces and cook until nicely browned on all sides. Remove the rabbit to a bowl. Discard the fat in the pot. Add the butter and onion to the pot and cook until lightly browned. Return the rabbit to the pot and stir in the flour. Add the wine and ratatouille and season with salt and pepper. Cover and bring to a boil, then reduce the heat to low and cook for 45 minutes.

3. Meanwhile, bring a large saucepan of water to a boil. Add the rice and cook until al dente,

about 10 minutes. Drain in a colander and rinse under cold running water, then drain again well. Stir the rice into the ratatouille and cook until tender, 5 to 7 minutes.

4. Transfer the rabbit and ratatouille to a warmed serving dish. Sprinkle with parsley and serve.

From Françoise:

• The rice absorbs all the delicious flavors of the sauce. Add it to the casserole just before serving or it will get soggy.

• You can also cook the rice until tender separately, either Creole style (in a lot of boiling water) or as a pilaf (sautéing it first in butter or oil, then cooking it, covered, over low heat with twice its volume of water or broth).

MEAT & POULTRY

RABBIT WITH ROQUEFORT SAUCE
- *Lapin au roquefort* -

❖ EASY   ❖ MODERATE   ❖ 1 HOUR, 15 MINUTES   ❖ SERVES 4

1 tablespoon oil

3 ½-pound rabbit, cut into serving pieces

1 onion, chopped

2 tablespoons butter

2 shallots, finely chopped

Salt and pepper

½ cup crumbled Roquefort cheese

2 or 3 tablespoons crème fraîche

❖ ❖ ❖ ❖ ❖

1. In a large skillet, heat the oil over medium-high heat. Add the rabbit pieces and cook until nicely browned on all sides. Remove the rabbit to a bowl. Add the onion and cook until lightly browned.

2. In a flameproof casserole, melt the butter over medium-low heat. Add the rabbit and onion, sprinkle the shallots on top, and season with pepper and, lightly, with salt. Stir to mix. Cover and cook for 30 minutes.

3. In a bowl, blend the cheese with the crème fraîche. Pour over the rabbit and cook for 20 to 30 minutes longer. If the sauce is too thin, uncover the pot during the last 15 minutes of cooking. Transfer to a warmed serving dish and serve.

From Françoise:

• Serve with buttered pasta.

• The secret to perfectly seasoned dishes made with Roquefort: Do not oversalt because the cheese is already quite salty. Don't stint on the pepper, however, which suits Roquefort very well.

RABBIT ASPIC TERRINE

- *Lapin en gelée* -

❖ EASY   ❖ MODERATE   ❖ 2 HOURS, 40 MINUTES, PLUS OVERNIGHT CHILLING   ❖ SERVES 4

1 calf's foot, split in half

3 tablespoons butter

3 ½-pound rabbit, cut into serving pieces

5 ounces thick-sliced pancetta, cut crosswise
   into ¼-inch-thick strips

3 shallots, finely chopped

3 garlic cloves, crushed

2 carrots, halved

2 whole cloves

1 bouquet garni made with parsley, thyme,
   and bay leaf

Salt and pepper

2 cups dry white wine

Boston lettuce leaves for decorating

Cornichons and Dijon mustard for serving

MEAT &
POULTRY

❖   ❖   ❖   ❖   ❖

1. Add the calf's foot to a large saucepan of cold water and bring to a boil. Simmer for 5 minutes, then drain.

2. In a flameproof casserole, melt the butter over medium-high heat. Add the rabbit pieces and cook until nicely browned on all sides. Remove to a bowl as they are done. Add the pancetta and cook until lightly browned. Return the rabbit to the pot with the shallots, garlic, carrots, cloves, and bouquet garni. Season with salt and pepper. Add the wine and enough water to come three-quarters of the way up the rabbit. Cover and bring to a boil, then reduce the heat to low and cook for 2 hours.

3. Transfer the rabbit to a cutting board and cut and scrape the meat off the bones. Add to

1 or 2 bowls. Strain the cooking liquid over the rabbit, cover, and refrigerate until the liquid sets, about 12 hours, or overnight.

4. Line a platter with the lettuce. Unmold the aspic on top and serve with the cornichons and mustard.

From Françoise:

• It's easy to remove the meat from the bones when the rabbit is cooked until very tender.

• Don't hesitate to pull the meat off the bones in large shreds, but don't chop it because it's nice to find large chunks of meat when you're eating.

MARINATED RABBIT WITH PRUNES
- *Lapin à la flamande* -

❖ EASY   ❖ MODERATE   ❖ 1 HOUR, PLUS OVERNIGHT MARINATING   ❖ SERVES 4

MARINADE

2 carrots, coarsely chopped

3 onions, coarsely chopped

1 celery rib, coarsely chopped

2 garlic cloves, coarsely chopped

1 shallot, coarsely chopped

2 whole cloves

Thyme sprigs

Bay leaves

1 cup vinegar

1 cup dry white wine

2 tablespoons oil

Salt and pepper

3 ½-pound rabbit, cut into serving pieces

2 tablespoons butter

1 pound pitted prunes, halved

1 tablespoon red currant or blueberry jelly

Salt and pepper

❖ ❖ ❖ ❖ ❖

1. For the marinade: In a large bowl, combine all the ingredients. Add the rabbit and turn to coat. Cover and refrigerate overnight, turning the rabbit 2 or 3 times.

2. Remove the rabbit and pat dry with paper towels. In a large saucepan, bring the marinade to a boil and simmer for 5 minutes.

3. Meanwhile, in a flameproof casserole, melt the butter over medium-high heat. Add the rabbit pieces and cook until nicely browned on all sides. Strain the marinade over the rabbit. Bring to a boil, then reduce the heat to low and simmer for 40 to 45 minutes, adding the prunes halfway through.

4. Using a slotted spoon, transfer the rabbit and prunes to a warmed serving dish. Whisk the jelly into the cooking liquid and simmer until slightly thickened and well flavored. Season with salt and pepper to taste and pour into a warmed sauceboat. Serve the rabbit, passing the sauce separately.

From Françoise:

• Serve with boiled new potatoes.

• The secret to an unctuous sauce: It needs to be sufficiently reduced by the end of cooking. If it's too thin, pour it into a saucepan and boil, uncovered, until it thickens slightly.

HERB-MARINATED RABBIT WITH HAM STUFFING

- *Lapin farci à la normande* -

❖ ADVANCED   ❖ MODERATE   ❖ 2 HOURS, 30 MINUTES, PLUS OVERNIGHT MARINATING   ❖ SERVES 4

MARINADE

Thyme leaves

Bay leaves, crumbled

Rosemary leaves, chopped

1 tablespoon oil

3 ½–pound rabbit

1 tablespoon butter

¼ pound white mushrooms, finely chopped

3 or 4 pearl onions, peeled

Fresh pork rind for lining (optional)

1 ½ cups dry white wine

⅓ cup Calvados, Cognac, or other eau-de-vie

Salt and pepper

STUFFING

½ pound ham, finely chopped

2 rabbit livers, finely chopped

½ cup fresh bread crumbs

½ cup snipped chives

1 large egg

⅓ cup Calvados, Cognac, or other eau-de-vie

½ teaspoon ground allspice

Salt and pepper

MEAT & POULTRY

❖ ❖ ❖ ❖ ❖

1. For the marinade: In a gratin dish, combine all the ingredients. Add the rabbit and rub all over with the herb mixture. Cover and refrigerate overnight, turning the rabbit 2 or 3 times.

2. For the stuffing: In a large bowl, mix the ham with the livers, bread crumbs, chives, egg, and Calvados or other eau-de-vie. Season with the allspice, salt, and pepper. Pack the stuffing into the rabbit's chest cavity. Fold the flaps over the stuffing and sew or skewer closed. Using kitchen string, tie the legs together.

3. Preheat the oven to 350 degrees. In a saucepan, melt the butter over low heat. Add the mushrooms and cook, stirring occasionally, for 10 minutes. Push the mushrooms to one side of the pan, add the onions, and lightly brown them.

4. Line a flameproof casserole with the pork rind, if using. Spread two-thirds of the mushrooms and all the onions on top. Add

the stuffed rabbit, and cover with the remaining mushrooms, the wine, Calvados, or other eau-de-vie. Season with salt and pepper. Bring to a boil over medium-high heat, then tilt the pot and carefully ignite. When the flames subside, cover and transfer to the oven, then cook for 1 hour and 30 minutes.

5. Transfer the rabbit to a cutting board. Spoon the stuffing into a bowl. Cut the rabbit into serving pieces and arrange on a platter. Serve with the stuffing and mushrooms and onions.

From Françoise:

• The secret to a successful stuffed rabbit: If possible, blanch the pork rind before adding it to the casserole. Add the pork rind to a large saucepan of water and bring to a boil, simmer for 2 to 3 minutes, then drain.

continued

- If you don't have a second rabbit liver (or any—rabbits aren't always sold with their giblets), you can replace it with chicken, lamb, or pork liver.

- If the cooking juices evaporate too quickly during cooking, add a little boiling water. But not too much because the more concentrated the sauce, the better it will taste.

SAUTÉED RABBIT WITH AROMATIC VEGETABLES
- *Lapin sauté* -

❖ EASY ❖ MODERATE ❖ 1 HOUR ❖ SERVES 4

3 tablespoons butter
2 ¾-pound rabbit, cut into serving pieces
15 pearl onions, peeled
2 shallots, finely chopped
2 garlic cloves, chopped

2 thyme sprigs
½ bay leaf
Salt and pepper
Chopped parsley leaves for sprinkling

❖ ❖ ❖ ❖ ❖

1. In a flameproof casserole, melt the butter over medium-high heat. Add the rabbit pieces and cook until nicely browned on all sides. Remove the rabbit to a bowl. Add the pearl onions and cook until lightly browned. Return the rabbit to the pot with the shallots, garlic, thyme, bay leaf, and 2 tablespoons of water. Season with salt and pepper. Cover and bring to a boil, then reduce the heat to low and cook for 45 minutes.

2. Remove the thyme and bay leaf. Transfer the rabbit and vegetables to a warmed serving dish, sprinkle with the parsley, and serve.

From Françoise:
- This recipe is good for a very young rabbit. The aromatic vegetables add flavor to the rabbit's mild taste.

- Add 20 minutes to the cooking time for a rabbit that's 3 pounds or more.

- Serve with steamed or boiled rice, potato chips or fries, or pasta.

ROAST RABBIT WITH MUSTARD

- *Lapin rôti à la moutarde* -

❖ EASY ❖ MODERATE ❖ 1 HOUR, 10 MINUTES ❖ SERVES 4

4-pound rabbit loin
Salt and pepper
2 tablespoons Dijon mustard

¼ pound caul fat
Chopped parsley leaves for sprinkling

❖ ❖ ❖ ❖ ❖

1. Preheat the oven to 350 degrees. Season the rabbit loin with salt and pepper. Brush with the mustard. Wrap in the caul fat and set in a roasting pan. Transfer to the oven and roast for 40 to 45 minutes.

2. Transfer the rabbit to a cutting board, cover loosely with foil, and let stand for 10 minutes.

3. Meanwhile, add ¼ cup of water to the roasting pan and bring to a boil, scraping up any brown bits stuck to the bottom, until slightly thickened and well flavored. Season with salt and pepper to taste.

4. Remove the caul fat from the rabbit and transfer to a warmed serving dish. Pour the pan juices over the rabbit, sprinkle with the parsley, and serve.

From Françoise:

• If you bought a very large rabbit to get the loin for this dish, use the rest of the rabbit (except the front legs) to make a stew.

• You can also roast a whole rabbit. It's less attractive but very good. Wrap the entire rabbit, brushed with the mustard, in the caul fat, which helps the mustard keep all of its flavor and discourages it from drying out.

• Caul fat can usually be special ordered from a butcher. Barding fat can also be used, but it makes the rabbit a little greasy.

• Rabbit is also good spit-roasted.

MEAT &
POULTRY

CREAMY RABBIT STEW

- *Lapin en blanquette* -

❖ EASY   ❖ MODERATE   ❖ 1 HOUR, 30 MINUTES   ❖ SERVES 4

3 ½-pound rabbit, cut into serving pieces

1 lemon, halved

2 carrots, finely chopped

2 leeks, white and light green parts only, finely chopped

1 celery rib, finely chopped

1 onion, stuck with a whole clove

1 garlic clove, crushed

1 bouquet garni made with parsley, thyme, and bay leaf

Salt and pepper

½ pound mushrooms, quartered lengthwise

POULETTE SAUCE

3 tablespoons butter

3 tablespoons all-purpose flour

Salt and pepper

1 large egg yolk

❖ ❖ ❖ ❖ ❖

1. Bring a flameproof casserole of water to a boil. Add the rabbit pieces and cook for 2 to 3 minutes. Drain in a colander under cold running water.

2. Wipe out the casserole. Rub the rabbit pieces with a lemon half and its juice. In the same casserole, combine the rabbit with the carrots, leeks, celery, onion, garlic, and bouquet garni, and barely cover with water. Season with salt and pepper. Bring to a boil over medium-high heat, then reduce the heat to low and cook for 45 minutes. Drain, discarding vegetables and bouquet garni. Return rabbit to the cooking liquid.

3. Meanwhile, in a small saucepan, combine the mushrooms with a little lemon juice and the rabbit cooking liquid to barely cover. Bring to a boil over medium-high heat, then reduce the heat to low and cook for 5 minutes. Drain, reserving the cooking liquid.

4. Make the poulette sauce: In a small sauce-pan, melt the butter over medium heat. Whisk

in the flour until it starts foaming. Whisk in 2 cups of the rabbit and mushroom cooking liquids and season with salt and pepper. Bring to a boil, whisking, then reduce the heat to very low and cook for 5 minutes. In a cup, blend the egg yolk with a little of the hot sauce. Remove the pan from the heat, then whisk this mixture into the sauce.

5. Transfer the rabbit and mushrooms to a warmed serving dish. Pour over the poulette sauce and serve.

From Françoise:

• To make a very flavorful stew, add all the vegetables specified. Don't be put off by the length of the list, though—if you don't have everything at hand, use what you have.

• Once the egg yolk is added to the sauce, do not allow it to boil.

• If you serve the rabbit with rice, cook it in the rabbit cooking liquid. Do not add any salt.

RABBIT STEW WITH SHALLOTS
- *Lapin aux échalotes* -

❖ EASY   ❖ MODERATE   ❖ 45 MINUTES   ❖ SERVES 4

¼ cup oil

3 ½–pound rabbit, cut into serving pieces

6 shallots, chopped

1 tablespoon all–purpose flour

¾ cup dry white wine

1 bouquet garni made with parsley, thyme,
  and bay leaf

Salt and pepper

Chopped parsley for sprinkling

❖ ❖ ❖ ❖ ❖

1. In a flameproof casserole, heat the oil over medium-high heat. Add the rabbit pieces and cook until nicely browned on all sides. Remove the pieces as they are done to a bowl. Stir in the shallots and the flour and cook until lightly browned. Return the rabbit to the pot. Add the wine and bouquet garni and season with salt and pepper. Cover and bring to a boil, then reduce the heat to low and cook for 25 minutes.

2. Add the parsley and cook for 5 minutes longer. Remove the bouquet garni. Transfer the rabbit, shallots, and sauce to a warmed serving dish and serve.

From Françoise:

• You can gain some time by browning half the rabbit pieces in a skillet and half in the casserole. Add the skillet rabbit to the casserole rabbit and proceed with the recipe. You can also bring the wine to a boil before adding it to the casserole.

• Make sure the casserole is large enough so the rabbit pieces can be braised in one layer.

• This dish can be made 1 hour in advance and reheated just before serving.

MEAT &
POULTRY

RABBIT STEW WITH PRUNES AND PANCETTA
- *Lapin aux pruneaux* -

❖ EASY   ❖ MODERATE   ❖ 2 HOURS, PLUS OVERNIGHT MARINATING AND SOAKING   ❖ SERVES 4

MARINADE

3 cups red wine

¼ cup Cognac

2 carrots, thinly sliced crosswise

2 large onions, thinly sliced crosswise

1 bouquet garni made with parsley, thyme,
   and bay leaf

Peppercorns

3 ½-pound rabbit, cut into serving pieces

½ pound pitted prunes, halved

2 tablespoons butter

3 ounces thick-sliced pancetta, cut crosswise
   into ¼-inch-thick strips

½ pound pearl onions

1 heaping tablespoon all-purpose flour

❖ ❖ ❖ ❖ ❖

1. For the marinade: In a large bowl, combine all the ingredients. Add the rabbit pieces, cover, and refrigerate overnight, turning the rabbit 2 or 3 times. In a bowl, generously cover the prunes with water and let soak overnight.

2. Remove the rabbit and pat dry with paper towels. In a flameproof casserole, melt the butter over medium-high heat. Add the pancetta and pearl onions and cook until lightly browned. Using a slotted spoon, transfer the pancetta and pearl onions to a bowl. Add the rabbit pieces to the casserole and cook until nicely browned on all sides. Stir in the flour and cook until lightly browned. Strain enough of the marinade over the rabbit to barely cover it. Cover and bring to a boil, then reduce the heat to low and simmer for 45 minutes.

3. Add the reserved pancetta, pearl onions, and prunes to the rabbit and cook for 45 minutes.

4. Transfer the rabbit mixture and sauce to a warmed serving dish and serve.

From Françoise:

• For this recipe you will need a large, mature rabbit since it simmers for a long time. If you have any leftovers, they are very good reheated.

• Hare can be prepared in the same way. If you can get the fresh blood from the hare, mix it with a dash of vinegar—which keeps the blood from coagulating—and add it to the sauce, off the heat, just before serving. Or you might be able to special order pork blood from a butcher.

• Serve with steamed or boiled new potatoes.

RABBIT STEW WITH PANCETTA AND MUSHROOMS
- *Lapin en gibelotte* -

❖ EASY ❖ MODERATE ❖ 1 HOUR, 15 MINUTES ❖ SERVES 4

2 tablespoons butter

3 ounces thick-sliced pancetta, cut crosswise
  into ¼-inch-thick strips

5 pearl onions, peeled

3 ½-pound rabbit, cut into serving pieces

1 tablespoon all-purpose flour

¾ cup dry white wine

2 garlic cloves, crushed

1 bouquet garni made with parsley, thyme,
  and bay leaf

Salt and pepper

¼ pound white mushrooms, halved

❖ ❖ ❖ ❖ ❖

1. In a flameproof casserole, melt the butter
over medium-high heat. Add the pancetta and
pearl onions and cook until lightly browned.
Using a slotted spoon, transfer the pancetta
and pearl onions to a bowl.

2. Add the rabbit pieces to the casserole and
cook until nicely browned on all sides. Stir
in the flour and cook until lightly browned.
Return the pancetta and pearl onions to the
pot. Add the wine, garlic, and bouquet garni
and season with salt and pepper. Cover and
bring to a boil, then reduce the heat to low and
simmer for 45 minutes.

3. Add the mushrooms to the rabbit and cook
for 15 minutes.

4. Remove the bouquet garni. Transfer the
rabbit and sauce to a warmed serving dish
and serve.

From Françoise:
• A rabbit should weigh at least 3 pounds to
be economical. If it weighs any less, it won't be
meaty enough. If it's much more, it's probably
more mature and may be drier.

• Serve with boiled or steamed new potatoes or
prepared in a gratin, or à la dauphinoise, à la
lyonnaise, à la bordelaise, and so on.

MEAT &
POULTRY

CHARCUTERIE & OTHER MEATS

PAN-SAUTÉED BRAINS WITH CAPERS, LEMON, AND CRISPY CROUTONS

- *Cervelle grenobloise* -

❖ INTERMEDIATE ❖ MODERATE ❖ 1 HOUR, 30 MINUTES ❖ SERVES 4

2 tablespoons vinegar

2 veal brains or 1 beef brain

Salt

1 bouquet garni made with parsley, thyme, and bay leaf

Pepper

All-purpose flour for dusting

5 tablespoons butter

3 tablespoons capers

Juice of ½ lemon

2 slices of day–old crustless white sandwich bread, cut into cubes

Chopped parsley leaves for sprinkling

❖ ❖ ❖ ❖ ❖

1. In a large bowl of cold water mixed with 1 tablespoon of the vinegar, soak the brains in the refrigerator for 15 minutes. Drain in a colander, then rinse under cold running water, using your fingers to pull away as much membrane and connective tissue as possible.

2. In a large saucepan of water, combine the salt, the remaining 1 tablespoon of vinegar, and the bouquet garni. Bring to a boil over medium-high heat, then reduce the heat to medium-low. Add the brains and cook, without boiling, for 15 to 20 minutes. Remove the pan from the heat and let cool completely.

3. Carefully drain the brains and pat dry with paper towels. Cut into slices about ½ inch thick. Season with salt and pepper and dust lightly with flour, patting off the excess.

4. In a large skillet, melt 2 tablespoons of the butter over medium heat. Add the brain slices and cook, turning once, until lightly browned, a few minutes on each side. Transfer to a warmed platter and sprinkle with the capers and lemon juice.

5. In the same skillet, melt the remaining 3 tablespoons of butter over medium heat. Add the bread cubes and cook until golden all over. Using a slotted spoon, transfer the croutons to the platter, sprinkle with parsley, and serve.

From Françoise:
• If you ask, the butcher might be willing to clean the brains for you.

• I don't recommend soaking the brains for longer than called for because they might fall apart.

• By waiting until the brains are completely cooled and firm in Step 2, you will get neat slices.

POACHED BRAINS WITH LEMON-PARSLEY BUTTER
- *Cervelle maître-d'hôtel* -

❖ INTERMEDIATE   ❖ MODERATE   ❖ 1 HOUR   ❖ SERVES 4

2 tablespoons vinegar

2 veal brains

Salt

1 bouquet garni made with parsley, thyme,
    and bay leaf

Juice of ½ lemon

2 tablespoons chopped parsley leaves

7 tablespoons butter

❖　❖　❖　❖　❖

1. In a large bowl of cold water mixed with
1 tablespoon of the vinegar, soak the brains
in the refrigerator for 15 minutes. Drain in a
colander, then rinse under cold running water,
using your fingers to pull away as much membrane and connective tissue as possible.

2. In a large saucepan of water, combine the
salt, the remaining 1 tablespoon of vinegar,
and the bouquet garni. Bring to a boil over
medium-high heat, then reduce the heat to medium-low. Add the brains and cook, without
boiling, for 15 to 20 minutes. Remove the pan
from the heat and let cool completely.

3. Carefully drain the brains and pat dry with
paper towels. Transfer to a warmed platter and
sprinkle with the lemon juice and parsley.

4. In a small saucepan, melt the butter over
medium heat. Pour it over the brains and serve
immediately.

From Françoise:

• If you're preparing lamb or pork brains, buy
2 per person. The poaching time will be about
5 minutes less.

• The cooking liquid for brains should not
come to a full boil but barely simmer. Brains
that are cooked at a rolling boil will fall apart
and lose their unique texture, which is firm
yet moist.

• Adding vinegar to the cooking liquid keeps
the brains from turning grayish.

CHARCUTERIE & OTHER MEATS

PAN-SEARED BRAIN WITH LEMON AND PARSLEY
- *Cervelle meunière* -

❖ INTERMEDIATE   ❖ MODERATE   ❖ 1 HOUR, 15 MINUTES   ❖ SERVES 4

2 tablespoons vinegar

1 beef brain

Salt

1 bouquet garni made with parsley, thyme,
   and bay leaf

2 whole cloves

1 garlic clove, crushed

Pepper

All-purpose flour for dusting

3 tablespoons butter

Juice of ½ lemon

Chopped parsley leaves for sprinkling

❖ ❖ ❖ ❖ ❖

1. In a large bowl of cold water mixed with 1 tablespoon of the vinegar, soak the brain in the refrigerator for 15 minutes. Drain in a colander, then rinse under cold running water, using your fingers to pull away as much membrane and connective tissue as possible.

2. In a large saucepan of water, combine the salt, the remaining 1 tablespoon of vinegar, the bouquet garni, cloves, and garlic. Bring to a boil over medium-high heat and cook for 5 minutes, then reduce the heat to medium-low. Add the brain and cook, without boiling, for 15 to 20 minutes. Remove the pan from the heat and let cool completely.

3. Carefully drain the brain and pat dry with paper towels. Cut into slices. Season with salt and pepper and dust lightly with flour, patting off the excess.

4. In a large skillet, melt the butter over medium heat. Add the brain slices and cook, turning once, until lightly browned, a few minutes on each side.

5. Transfer to a warmed platter and pour over the pan juices. Sprinkle with the lemon juice and parsley and serve.

From Françoise:
• Beef brains, which are firm, are perfect for this kind of recipe. Take advantage of them, as they are less expensive than veal brains.

BRAISED VEAL HEART WITH CARROTS

- *Coeur de veau braisé aux carottes* -

❖ INTERMEDIATE   ❖ INEXPENSIVE   ❖ 2 HOURS, 30 MINUTES   ❖ SERVES 4

3 tablespoons butter

2-pound veal heart, trimmed

2 pounds carrots, peeled and thinly sliced

2 onions, thinly sliced

1 garlic clove, crushed

1 bouquet garni made with parsley, thyme,
  and bay leaf

Salt and pepper

❖   ❖   ❖   ❖   ❖

1. In a flameproof casserole, melt the butter over medium heat. Add the veal heart and cook until browned all over. Add the carrots, onions, garlic, bouquet garni, and 1 ½ cups of water. Season with salt and pepper. Cover and bring to a boil, then reduce the heat to low and cook for about 2 hours.

2. Remove the bouquet garni. Transfer the veal heart to a cutting board and cut into slices about ½ inch thick. Spread the carrots and pan juices in a warmed serving dish. Arrange the heart slices on top and serve.

From Françoise:

• Have your butcher prepare the veal heart for cooking, in particular removing any tough inner membranes.

SLOW-COOKED VEAL HEARTS WITH PANCETTA, PEARL ONIONS, AND POTATOES

- *Coeurs de veau bonne femme* -

❖ INTERMEDIATE   ❖ MODERATE   ❖ 1 HOUR, 15 MINUTES   ❖ SERVES 4

3 tablespoons butter

2 veal hearts, trimmed

7 ounces thick-sliced pancetta, cut crosswise
  into ¼-inch-thick strips

7 ounces pearl onions, peeled

1 ½ pounds potatoes, peeled and diced

1 bouquet garni made with parsley, thyme,
  and bay leaf

Salt and pepper

Chopped parsley leaves for sprinkling

continued

1. In a flameproof casserole, melt the butter over medium heat. Add the veal hearts and cook until browned all over. Add 6 tablespoons of water, cover, and bring to a boil, then reduce the heat to low and cook for 20 minutes.

2. Add the pancetta, pearl onions, potatoes, bouquet garni, and 6 tablespoons of water to the casserole. Season with salt and pepper. Increase the heat to medium, cover, and bring to a boil, then reduce the heat to low and cook for about 35 minutes.

3. Remove the bouquet garni. Transfer to a warmed serving dish, sprinkle with parsley, and serve.

From Françoise:
• Beef heart, which is much larger than veal heart, is also less expensive. The cooking time, however, is longer—almost 2 hours of simmering.

BRAISED VEAL HEARTS WITH BREAD STUFFING
- Coeurs de veau farcis -

❖ INTERMEDIATE ❖ MODERATE ❖ 1 HOUR, 30 MINUTES ❖ SERVES 4

STUFFING
1 tablespoon butter
1 onion, finely chopped
2 ounces kidney fat, finely chopped
Finely chopped parsley leaves
¾ cup fresh bread crumbs
1 large egg
Salt and pepper

2 veal hearts, trimmed
Caul fat for wrapping
2 tablespoons butter
1 onion, chopped
1 teaspoon all-purpose flour
1 pound carrots, peeled and sliced crosswise
1 teaspoon tomato paste
1 bouquet garni made with parsley, thyme, and
    bay leaf
6 tablespoons dry white wine
Salt and pepper

❖ ❖ ❖ ❖ ❖

1. Make the stuffing: In a medium skillet, melt the butter over medium heat. Add the onion and cook until lightly browned. In a large bowl, mix the kidney fat with the parsley, bread crumbs, egg, and onion. Season with salt and pepper.

2. Cut the veal hearts almost in half lengthwise, leaving them attached on one side. Trim them so they can be stuffed, reserving the meat. Pack the stuffing into the hearts. Close and wrap each heart in a piece of caul fat.

3. In a flameproof casserole, melt the butter over medium heat. Add the veal hearts and cook until browned all over. Transfer to a plate. Add the onion to the pot and cook until lightly browned. Stir in the flour. Return the

hearts to the pot and add the meat trimmings, carrots, tomato paste, bouquet garni, wine, and 1 ½ cups of water. Season with salt and pepper. Cover and bring to a simmer, then reduce the heat to low and cook for about 1 hour. Transfer to a warmed serving dish and serve.

From Françoise:
• Caul fat is a fine, webbed membrane of pork or lamb fat. It can usually be special-ordered from a butcher.

PAN-SEARED LIVER WITH ANCHOVIES
- *Foie aux anchois* -

❖ EASY   ❖ INEXPENSIVE   ❖ 20 MINUTES   ❖ SERVES 4

2 salt-packed anchovies
2 tablespoons butter
2 tablespoons mixed chopped parsley, chives, chervil, and tarragon

4 slices of beef or lamb liver
All-purpose flour for dusting
Pepper
1 lemon, half juiced, half cut into 4 slices

❖ ❖ ❖ ❖ ❖

1. Using your fingers, remove the bones from the anchovies. Add the fillets to a sieve and rinse under warm water to remove some of the saltiness. In a bowl, mash the fillets with a fork.

2. In a large skillet, melt the butter over low heat. Add the mashed anchovies and herbs and cook for 3 to 4 minutes.

3. Dust the liver slices lightly with the flour, patting off the excess. Add them to the skillet, increase the heat to medium-low, and cook for 3 minutes on each side. Season with pepper and sprinkle the lemon juice over the top.

4. Arrange the liver on a warmed platter. Pour over the pan juices, top each slice of liver with a lemon slice, and serve.

From Françoise:
• The delicate flavor of veal liver would be overwhelmed by this pungent sauce. In France the *foie de génisse* is used to make this dish and the following foie en meurette; *génisse* is a female calf that is slightly older than the typical veal calf. In the United States beef or lamb liver would be the closest equivalent.

WINE-BRAISED LIVER

- *Foie en meurette* -

❖ EASY   ❖ INEXPENSIVE   ❖ 30 MINUTES   ❖ SERVES 4

4 thick slices of beef or lamb liver, diced
1 teaspoon all-purpose flour, plus more
  for dusting
3 tablespoons butter
1 onion, finely chopped

1½ cups red wine
1 thyme sprig
1 bay leaf
Salt and pepper
Chopped parsley leaves for serving

❖ ❖ ❖ ❖ ❖

1. Dust the liver lightly with the flour, patting off the excess. In a large skillet, melt 2 tablespoons of the butter over medium heat. Add the liver and cook, stirring, for 5 minutes. Using a slotted spoon, transfer the liver to a warmed serving dish.

2. Add the onion to the same skillet and cook until lightly browned. Add the wine, thyme, and bay leaf. Season with salt and pepper. Bring to a simmer and cook for 5 minutes.

3. In a cup, mash the remaining 1 tablespoon of butter with the 1 teaspoon of flour.

Gradually whisk this mixture into the skillet and let simmer for a few minutes, until slightly thickened. Pour the sauce over the liver, sprinkle with the parsley, and serve.

From Françoise:
• Serve with boiled or steamed rice or new potatoes.

• For a more elegant presentation, pack the rice into a buttered ring mold, then unmold onto a round platter and spoon the liver into the center.

PAN-SEARED LIVER WITH ONIONS

- *Foie aux oignons à la lyonnaise* -

❖ EASY   ❖ INEXPENSIVE   ❖ 15 MINUTES   ❖ SERVES 4

3 tablespoons butter
2 large onions, chopped
Salt and pepper
4 slices of beef, lamb, or veal liver

All-purpose flour for dusting
6 tablespoons vinegar
Chopped parsley leaves for sprinkling

1. In a large skillet, melt 2 tablespoons of the butter over medium-low heat. Add the onions and cook until softened. Season with salt and pepper. Reduce the heat to low, cover, and cook for 5 minutes. Transfer to a plate.

2. Dust the liver lightly with the flour, patting off the excess. In the same skillet, melt the remaining 1 tablespoon of butter over medium-low heat. Add the liver slices and cook for 3 to 4 minutes on each side. Season with salt and pepper. Increase the heat to high, return the onions to the pan with the vinegar, and simmer for a few seconds.

3. Transfer the liver slices to a warmed platter and sprinkle with the parsley. Surround with the onions and serve.

From Françoise:
• Dusting the liver slices with flour discourages the hot butter from sputtering the way it can when you add something moist.

PAN-SAUTÉED VEAL LIVER WITH BALSAMIC VINEGAR
- *Foie sauté* -

❖ EASY　　　❖ EXPENSIVE　　　❖ 15 MINUTES　　　❖ SERVES 4

4 slices of veal liver, about ¼ pound each
All-purpose flour for dusting
3 tablespoons butter

Salt and pepper
1 tablespoon balsamic vinegar

❖　❖　❖　❖　❖

1. Dust the liver slices lightly with the flour, patting off the excess. In a large skillet, melt 2 tablespoons of the butter over medium heat. Add the liver and cook for 2 to 3 minutes on each side. Season with salt and pepper and transfer to a warmed platter.

2. In the same skillet, add the balsamic vinegar and the remaining 1 tablespoon of butter. Increase the heat to high and bring to a boil, shaking the pan. Pour over the liver and serve.

From Françoise:
• Add a little chopped parsley just before serving.

• Chicken livers can be prepared in the same way. Serve them on a bed of mesclun, arugula, or other greens.

CHARCUTERIE & OTHER MEATS

CREAMY LIVER RAMEKINS WITH TOMATO COMPOTE

- *Mousselines de foie* -

❖ INTERMEDIATE ❖ INEXPENSIVE ❖ 50 MINUTES ❖ SERVES 4

BÉCHAMEL SAUCE
1 tablespoon butter
1 tablespoon all-purpose flour
¾ cup milk
Salt and pepper

½ pound pork liver or chicken livers,
 finely chopped

1 onion, finely chopped
Finely chopped parsley leaves, plus sprigs
 for decorating
1 large egg
2 tablespoons crème fraîche
Salt and pepper
1 tablespoon butter, plus more for brushing
2 tomatoes, peeled, seeded, and chopped

❖ ❖ ❖ ❖ ❖

1. Make the béchamel: In a small saucepan, melt the butter over medium heat. Whisk in the flour until it starts foaming. Whisk in the milk. Season with salt and pepper. Bring to a boil, whisking, until thickened.

2. Preheat the oven to 400 degrees. In a bowl, mix the liver with the onion, chopped parsley, egg, crème fraîche, and béchamel sauce. Season with salt and pepper. Brush 4 ramekins with butter. Fill the ramekins with the liver mixture to come ¼ inch below the rim. Set the ramekins in a roasting pan and fill the pan with hot water to come halfway up the sides of the ramekins. Transfer to the oven and bake for 30 minutes.

3. Meanwhile, in a small saucepan, melt the remaining 1 tablespoon of butter. Add the tomatoes, season with salt and pepper, and cook until reduced slightly.

4. Run a knife around the ramekins. Invert a dish over the top of each. Holding the dish and ramekin together, quickly invert the ramekin onto the dish. Decorate with the tomato compote and parsley sprigs and serve.

From Françoise:
• Instead of decorating the ramekins with tomato compote, you could garnish them with 4 white mushroom caps or thinly sliced white mushrooms simmered in a little water. Add dollop of crème fraîche.

STUFFED TOMATOES WITH CHICKEN LIVERS

- *Foies de volaille aux tomates* -

❖ EASY   ❖ INEXPENSIVE   ❖ 50 MINUTES   ❖ SERVES 4

4 tomatoes, halved crosswise and seeded

Salt

2 tablespoons oil

¼ cup dry bread crumbs

3 garlic cloves, finely chopped

Chopped parsley leaves

3 tablespoons butter

4 chicken livers, halved

Pepper

2 tablespoons vinegar

❖ ❖ ❖ ❖ ❖

1. Preheat the oven to 425 degrees. Sprinkle the tomatoes with salt and set, cut side down, on a plate to drain. Pat dry with paper towels. In a large skillet, heat the oil over medium-high heat. Add the tomatoes, cut side down, and cook, turning once, for 4 minutes.

2. In a bowl, combine the bread crumbs with the garlic and parsley. Set the tomatoes, cut side up, in a roasting pan. Mound with the bread stuffing and dot with 1 tablespoon of the butter. Transfer to the upper third of the oven and bake until browned, about 15 minutes.

3. Meanwhile, melt 1 tablespoon of the remaining butter over medium-high heat. Add the chicken livers, season with salt and pepper, and cook until browned on the outside and still rosy in the center. Transfer them to a plate.

4. Add the vinegar to the same skillet and simmer, scraping up any brown bits stuck to the bottom. Add the remaining 1 tablespoon of butter along with the chicken livers and reheat. Transfer the stuffed tomatoes to a warmed platter, top with the chicken livers and pan juices, and serve.

From Françoise:

• There's very little waste with chicken livers. Using a small, sharp knife, just remove the sinewy bit between the two lobes and trim off any green part.

CHARCUTERIE & OTHER MEATS

BRAISED CALF'S HEAD WITH VINAIGRETTE
- Tête de veau vinaigrette -

❖ INTERMEDIATE   ❖ INEXPENSIVE   ❖ 2 HOURS, 30 MINUTES   ❖ SERVES 4

1 boned, rolled calf's head

Salt

2 tablespoons vinegar

1 carrot, halved lengthwise

1 bouquet garni made with parsley, thyme,
  and bay leaf

12 black peppercorns

VINAIGRETTE

3 tablespoons vinegar

1 tablespoon Dijon mustard

½ cup plus 1 tablespoon oil

Salt and pepper

Chopped chervil or parsley leaves

❖ ❖ ❖ ❖ ❖

1. Add the calf's head to a large pot of cold salted water. Bring to a boil over medium-high heat, then reduce the heat and simmer for 10 minutes. Drain in a colander and rinse under cold running water, then drain again.

2. In the same pot, combine the salt, vinegar, carrot, bouquet garni, and peppercorns and cover with cold water. Bring to a boil over medium-high heat, then reduce the heat to medium, add the calf's head, and cook at a gentle boil for 2 hours.

3. Meanwhile, in a bowl, whisk the vinegar with the mustard. Blend in the oil and season with salt and pepper. Whisk in the chervil or parsley.

4. Drain the calf's head well, transfer to a cutting board, and pat dry with paper towels. Cut into slices and arrange on a serving dish. Pour over the vinaigrette and serve.

From Françoise:

• A calf's head can be special-ordered from a butcher. Have the butcher prepare it for cooking.

• Cook the calf's head soon after buying it because offal does not keep as well as other meat.

• Calf's head can also be served cold, but it's harder to digest.

• Serve it with a pungent sauce, such as tartar sauce or simply with Dijon mustard.

• Rinse the fresh calf's head under cold running water to remove impurities. Scrub it with a brush if needed.

• You can prepare beef or lamb tongue in the same way. Buy 5 or 6 lamb tongues to make 4 servings.

BEEF TONGUE WITH MADEIRA SAUCE

- *Langue de boeuf sauce madère* -

❖ INTERMEDIATE ❖ MODERATE ❖ 3 HOURS ❖ SERVES 10

Salt

1 beef tongue, trimmed

2 carrots

2 leeks

1 small turnip

1 onion

3 garlic cloves, crushed

1 bouquet garni made with parsley, thyme,
  and bay leaf

1 whole clove

Pepper

Madeira Sauce (page 640)

❖ ❖ ❖ ❖ ❖

1. Bring a large pot of salted water to a boil
over medium-high heat. Add the tongue and
cook for 5 minutes, then drain. Return the
tongue to the pot and add the carrots, leeks,
turnip, onion, garlic, bouquet garni, and clove.
Season with salt and pepper. Cover with cold
water, bring to a simmer over medium heat,
and cook for 2 hours and 30 minutes.

2. Drain the tongue. Trim it and peel. Cut into
thin slices on the diagonal. Arrange the slices
on a warmed platter and pour over some of the
Madeira sauce. Serve, passing the remaining
sauce separately.

From Françoise:

• Serve with Pommes Duchesse (page 587).
Pipe the potatoes around a platter and arrange
the slices of tongue in the center.

• To peel the tongue, use a small, sharp knife
to make an incision in the skin down the
length of the tongue without cutting into the
meat. Pull off the skin.

• Use the tongue cooking liquid to make the
Madeira sauce.

CHARCUTERIE & OTHER MEATS

VEAL TONGUE IN A PIQUANT SAUCE
- Langue de veau sauce piquante -

❖ INTERMEDIATE   ❖ MODERATE   ❖ 2 HOURS, 30 MINUTES   ❖ SERVES 4

Salt
1 veal tongue, trimmed
1 carrot, sliced crosswise
1 leek, halved crosswise
1 turnip, quartered
1 onion, quartered
2 garlic cloves, crushed
1 bouquet garni made with parsley, thyme,
    and bay leaf
1 whole clove
Salt and pepper

PIQUANT SAUCE
3 ½ tablespoons butter
1 ½ tablespoons all-purpose flour
1 tablespoon tomato paste
1 tomato, peeled, seeded, and chopped
1 shallot, finely chopped
6 tablespoons dry white wine
6 tablespoons vinegar
Pepper
3 cornichons, sliced crosswise
Chopped parsley leaves

❖ ❖ ❖ ❖ ❖

1. Bring a large pot of salted water to a boil over medium-high heat. Add the tongue and cook for 10 minutes. Drain in a colander and rinse under cold running water. Return the tongue to the pot and add the carrot, leek, turnip, onion, garlic, bouquet garni, and clove. Season with salt and pepper. Cover generously with cold water, bring to a simmer over medium heat, and cook for 45 minutes.

2. Ladle 2 cups of the cooking liquid through a sieve into a measuring cup. Cook the tongue about 30 minutes longer.

3. Make the piquant sauce: In a medium saucepan, melt 1 ½ tablespoons of the butter over medium heat. Whisk in the flour until it starts foaming and turns a blond color. Whisk in the reserved 2 cups of cooking liquid, the tomato paste, and tomato and bring to a boil, whisking, until thickened. Reduce the heat to very low, partially cover, and cook for about 25 minutes.

4. In a small skillet, melt 1 tablespoon of the remaining butter over medium heat. Add the shallot and cook until softened. Add the wine, vinegar, and pepper. Bring to a simmer, then cook until reduced by half. Add to the sauce and cook for 10 minutes, then strain. Remove the pan from the heat and whisk in the cornichons, parsley, and remaining 1 tablespoon of butter.

5. Drain the tongue. Trim and peel it. Cut into thin slices on the diagonal. Arrange the slices on a warmed platter and pour over some of the sauce. Serve, passing the remaining sauce separately.

From Françoise:
• Serve with boiled new potatoes or mashed potatoes.

• Veal tongue reheated in its sauce is just as good or even better.

TOMATO-BRAISED VEAL TONGUE
- *Langue de veau braisée à la tomate* -

✧ INTERMEDIATE　　　✧ MODERATE　　　✧ 2 HOURS　　　✧ SERVES 4

1 veal tongue
4 tablespoons (½ stick) butter
10 pearl onions, peeled
1 tablespoon all-purpose flour
3 tablespoons tomato paste

1 bouquet garni made with parsley, thyme,
　and bay leaf
1 garlic clove, crushed
Salt and pepper

✧　✧　✧　✧　✧

1. Carefully scrub the tongue under cold running water. Add to a large saucepan and cover generously with cold water. Bring to a boil over medium-high heat, then reduce the heat to medium and simmer for 10 minutes. Drain in a colander, rinse under cold running water, and drain again. Using a small, sharp knife, scrape off the skin. Wipe it well to remove any trimmings.

2. In a flameproof casserole, melt 2 tablespoons of the butter over medium heat. Add the tongue and cook until browned all over. Remove it to a plate and discard the fat.

3. In the same casserole, melt the remaining 2 tablespoons of butter over medium heat. Add the pearl onions and cook until lightly browned. Stir in the flour. Add the tomato paste, 2 ¼ cups of water, the tongue, bouquet garni, and garlic clove. Season with salt and pepper. Cover and bring to a boil, then reduce the heat to low and cook for about 1 hour and 30 minutes.

4. Remove the bouquet garni. Transfer the tongue and sauce to a warmed serving dish and serve.

From Françoise:
• Peeling the tongue requires a little time and patience, but the result is worth the effort. Start by scraping the tongue with a small, sharp knife. Slide the point of the knife under the skin and pull on the loosened skin. It's not too difficult with a little perseverance.

• I often add 20 pitted green olives to this dish 15 minutes before the end of cooking. Season lightly with salt if you're going to add olives.

CHARCUTERIE
& OTHER MEATS

BRAISED SWEETBREADS WITH CREAMY CHABLIS SAUCE

- *Ris de veau au chablis* -

❖ INTERMEDIATE   ❖ EXPENSIVE   ❖ 50 MINUTES, PLUS 1 HOUR WEIGHTING   ❖ SERVES 4

1 ½ pounds veal sweetbreads

Salt

1 small canned truffle, cut into slivers,
   juice reserved (optional)

2 tablespoons butter

1 small carrot, peeled and cut into ¼-inch dice

1 onion, cut into ¼-inch dice

1 tablespoon all-purpose flour

1 ½ cups Chablis or other unoaked Chardonnay
   wine

1 bouquet garni made with parsley, thyme,
   and bay leaf

Pepper

½ cup crème fraîche

❖ ❖ ❖ ❖ ❖

1. Add the sweetbreads to a large saucepan of salted water and heat slowly until barely simmering. Cook, without boiling, for 5 minutes. Drain in a colander and rinse under cold running water, then drain again. Use your fingers to pull away as much membrane and connective tissue as possible. Pat dry with paper towels. Transfer the sweetbreads to a gratin dish, set another dish on top, and weigh down with cans of food for 1 hour.

2. If using the truffle, make small evenly spaced incisions in the sweetbreads with a small, sharp knife. Push a truffle sliver into each incision.

3. In a flameproof casserole, melt the butter over medium-low heat. Add the carrot and onion and cook until softened. Stir in the flour. Add the Chablis or other wine, the truffle juice, if using, sweetbreads, and bouquet garni. Season with salt and pepper. Cover and bring to a simmer, then reduce the heat to low and cook for about 20 minutes.

4. Transfer the sweetbreads to a warmed serving dish. Strain the cooking liquid and return it to the casserole. Add the crème fraîche and simmer until slightly thickened. Pour over the sweetbreads and serve.

From Françoise:
• The most important thing in variety meats is freshness. Buy them from a top butcher.

CLASSIC BRAISED VEAL SWEETBREADS

- *Ris de veau braisées* -

❖ INTERMEDIATE ❖ EXPENSIVE ❖ 1 HOUR, PLUS 1 HOUR WEIGHTING ❖ SERVES 4

1 ½ pounds veal sweetbreads
Salt
3 ½ tablespoons butter
1 small carrot, peeled and cut into ¼-inch dice
2 onions, cut into ¼-inch dice

1 tablespoon all-purpose flour, plus more
 for dusting
1 teaspoon tomato paste
Pepper

❖   ❖   ❖   ❖   ❖

1. Add the sweetbreads to a large saucepan of salted water and heat slowly until barely simmering. Cook, without boiling, for 5 minutes. Drain in a colander and rinse under cold running water, then drain again. Use your fingers to pull away as much membrane and connective tissue as possible. Pat dry with paper towels. Transfer the sweetbreads to a gratin dish, set another dish on top, and weigh down with cans of food for 1 hour.

2. In a flameproof casserole, melt 1 ½ tablespoons of the butter over medium heat. Add the carrot and onions and cook until lightly browned. Stir in the flour. Add the tomato paste and 2 cups of water. Season with salt and pepper. Bring to a boil, then reduce the heat and cook, uncovered, for about 30 minutes.

3. Season the sweetbreads with salt and pepper. Dust lightly with flour, patting off the excess. In a large skillet, melt the remaining 2 tablespoons of the butter over medium-high heat. Add the sweetbreads and cook until lightly browned all over. Transfer the sweetbreads to the casserole. Reduce the heat to low, cover, and cook for 20 to 25 minutes.

4. Transfer the sweetbreads to a warmed serving dish. Strain the cooking liquid over the sweetbreads and serve.

From Françoise:
• If the sauce seems thin, whisk in a little potato starch mixed with a little cold water and simmer until slightly thickened.

• Braised English peas are the traditional accompaniment to this dish.

CHARCUTERIE & OTHER MEATS

BRAISED VEAL SWEETBREADS IN TOASTED BRIOCHE
- *Ris de veau en brioche* -

❖ INTERMEDIATE   ❖ EXPENSIVE   ❖ 1 HOUR, PLUS 1 HOUR WEIGHTING   ❖ SERVES 4

1 pound veal sweetbreads

Salt

3 tablespoons butter, 1 tablespoon softened

1 onion, chopped

1 carrot, peeled and chopped

1 tablespoon all-purpose flour

1 tablespoon tomato paste

1 ½ cups dry white wine

¾ cup Madeira

1 bouquet garni made with parsley, thyme, and bay leaf

Pepper

¼ pound small white mushrooms, quartered lengthwise

¼ pound cooked beef tongue, cut into ¼-inch dice

1 ham slice, cut into ¼-inch dice

1 tablespoon canned black truffle peelings, juice reserved

1 large or 4 small brioches

❖ ❖ ❖ ❖ ❖

1. Add the sweetbreads to a large saucepan of salted water and heat slowly until barely simmering. Cook, without boiling, for 5 minutes. Drain in a colander and rinse under cold running water, then drain again. Use your fingers to pull away as much membrane and connective tissue as possible. Reserve the trimmings. Pat dry with paper towels. Transfer the sweetbreads to a gratin dish, set another dish on top, and weigh down with cans of food for 1 hour.

2. In a flameproof casserole, melt 1 tablespoon of the butter over medium-high heat. Add the sweetbreads and cook until lightly browned all over. Transfer to a plate. Add the onion, carrot, reserved sweetbreads trimmings, and the flour to the casserole, stirring. Add the tomato paste, wine, 6 tablespoons of the Madeira, and the bouquet garni. Season with salt and pepper. Return the sweetbreads to the pot, cover, reduce the heat to low, and cook for 15 minutes.

3. Preheat the oven to 400 degrees. Remove the sweetbreads to a cutting board and dice them. In a large saucepan, melt 1 tablespoon of the remaining butter over medium-high heat. Add the mushrooms and cook. Add the tongue, ham, the truffle with its juice, the sweetbreads, and remaining 6 tablespoons of Madeira. Strain the sweetbreads cooking liquid into the pan and season with pepper. Reduce the heat to low, cover, and cook for 10 minutes.

4. Cut a "hat" out of each brioche, then carefully cut out much of the bread, leaving a sturdy shell. Brush the insides with the remaining 1 tablespoon of softened butter. Set the brioches on a baking sheet and toast lightly in the oven. Spoon the filling into the brioches, top with their "hats," and serve.

From Françoise:

• This recipe can be prepared through Step 3 several hours in advance or even refrigerated overnight. Reheat gently and toast the brioches just before serving.

BRAISED VEAL SWEETBREADS WITH MADEIRA SAUCE

- *Ris de veau sauce madère* -

❖ INTERMEDIATE ❖ EXPENSIVE ❖ 1 HOUR, 15 MINUTES ❖ SERVES 4

1 ½ pounds veal sweetbreads

Salt

4 ½ tablespoons butter

1 carrot, peeled and cut into ¼-inch dice

2 onions, cut into ¼-inch dice

1 tablespoon all-purpose flour, plus more for dusting

1 teaspoon tomato paste

2 cups beef broth

Pepper

¼ pound small white mushrooms, thinly sliced

4 to 5 tablespoons Madeira

❖ ❖ ❖ ❖ ❖

1. Add the sweetbreads to a large saucepan of salted water and heat slowly until barely simmering. Cook, without boiling, for 5 minutes. Drain in a colander and rinse under cold running water, then drain again. Use your fingers to pull away as much membrane and connective tissue as possible. Pat dry with paper towels. Transfer the sweetbreads to a gratin dish, set another dish on top, and weigh down with cans of food for 1 hour.

2. In a flameproof casserole, melt 1 ½ tablespoons of the butter over medium heat. Add the carrot and onions and cook until lightly browned. Stir in the flour. Add the tomato paste and beef broth. Season lightly with salt and pepper. Bring to a boil, then reduce the heat to low and cook, uncovered, for about 30 minutes.

3. Meanwhile, in a small saucepan, combine the mushrooms with 1 tablespoon of the butter and barely cover with water. Season with salt and pepper. Bring to a boil and simmer for 5 minutes. Strain the cooking liquid into the casserole and reserve the mushrooms.

4. Season the sweetbreads with salt and pepper. Dust lightly with flour, patting off the excess. In a large skillet, melt the remaining 2 tablespoons of the butter over medium-high heat.

Add the sweetbreads and cook until lightly browned all over. Transfer the sweetbreads to the casserole. Reduce the heat to low, cover, and cook for 20 to 25 minutes.

5. Transfer the sweetbreads to a warmed serving dish. Strain the cooking liquid into a saucepan and add the Madeira and reserved mushrooms. Simmer for 1 minute. Pour over the sweetbreads and serve.

From Françoise:

• I have made veal sweetbreads without pressing them. They aren't quite as neat looking, but they taste just as good, and it saves an hour of prep time.

• Typically sweetbreads are sold ready to cook, but it's a good idea to ask. If they are not cleaned, add them to a bowl of cold vinegar water and refrigerate for 12 hours or overnight, changing the water 2 or 3 times.

• If the sauce looks thin, whisk in ⅓ teaspoon of potato starch mixed with a tiny amount of cold water.

• Artichokes Clamart (page 501) are very good with this dish.

CHARCUTERIE & OTHER MEATS

CREAMY SWEETBREADS, MARROW, AND BRAINS IN CRISP PUFF PASTRY

- *Vol-au-vent financière* -

❖ ADVANCED ❖ EXPENSIVE ❖ 45 MINUTES, PLUS 1 HOUR WEIGHTING ❖ SERVES 6 TO 8

1½ pounds veal sweetbreads

Salt

1 tablespoon vinegar

5 ounces veal marrow, cleaned

1 beef brain, cleaned

2 tablespoons butter

1 onion, chopped

1 carrot, peeled and chopped

1 tablespoon all-purpose flour

1 tablespoon tomato paste

1½ cups dry white wine

¾ cup Madeira

1 bouquet garni made with parsley, thyme,
  and bay leaf

Pepper

¼ pound white mushrooms, quartered lengthwise

1 small canned black truffle, finely chopped,
  juice reserved

¼ pound thinly sliced cooked chicken breast

12 pitted green olives

9-inch baked puff pastry shell or 8 small baked
  puff pastry shells

❖ ❖ ❖ ❖ ❖

1. Add the sweetbreads to a large saucepan of salted water and heat slowly until barely simmering. Cook, without boiling, for 5 minutes. Drain in a colander and rinse under cold running water, then drain again. Use your fingers to pull away as much membrane and connective tissue as possible. Reserve the trimmings. Pat dry with paper towels. Transfer the sweetbreads to a gratin dish, set another dish on top, and weigh down with cans of food for 1 hour.

2. Meanwhile, bring a large saucepan of salted water to a boil with the vinegar over medium-high heat. Add the marrow and brain and reduce the heat to low. Remove the pan from the heat when the water is barely simmering. Let cool.

3. In a flameproof casserole, melt 1 tablespoon of the butter over medium heat. Add the

sweetbreads and cook until lightly browned all over. Transfer to a plate. Add the onion, carrot, reserved sweetbreads trimmings, and the flour to the casserole, stirring. Add the tomato paste, wine, 6 tablespoons of the Madeira, and the bouquet garni. Season with salt and pepper. Return the sweetbreads to the pot, reduce the heat to low, cover, and cook for 15 minutes.

4. Preheat the oven to 300 degrees. Remove the sweetbreads to a cutting board and dice them. Drain the marrow and brain and dice them. In a large saucepan, melt the remaining 1 tablespoon of butter over medium-high heat. Add the mushrooms and cook. Add the truffle with its juice, the sweetbreads, marrow, brain, chicken, olives, and the remaining 6 tablespoons of Madeira. Strain the sweetbreads cooking liquid into the pan and season with pepper. Reduce the heat to low, cover, and cook for 10 minutes.

5. Set the puff pastry shell(s) on a baking sheet and warm in the oven. Spoon the filling into the pastry shell(s) and serve.

From Françoise:

• The secret to tasty canned truffles: Add them to whatever dish you're making along with their liquid, which has absorbed much of the truffle flavor.

WINE-BRAISED TRIPE WITH PANCETTA AND TOMATO
- *Tripes à la niçoise* -

❖ EASY ❖ INEXPENSIVE ❖ 2 HOURS, 30 MINUTES ❖ SERVES 4

1 ¼ pounds blanched tripe, cut into pieces
Salt
2 tablespoons butter
3 ounces thick-sliced pancetta, cut crosswise
   into ¼-inch-thick strips
1 tablespoon all-purpose flour
3 tablespoons tomato paste

1 ½ cups dry white wine
1 onion stuck with 2 whole cloves
1 garlic clove, crushed
1 bouquet garni made with parsley, thyme,
   and bay leaf
Pepper
¼ cup Cognac

❖ ❖ ❖ ❖ ❖

1. Add the tripe to a pot of boiling, salted water and cook for 10 minutes, then drain.

2. In a flameproof casserole, melt the butter over medium-high heat. Add the pancetta and cook until lightly browned. Stir in the flour. Stir in the tomato paste and wine and bring to a simmer.

3. Add the tripe, onion, garlic, and bouquet garni. Season with salt and pepper. Cover and bring to a boil, then reduce the heat to low and cook for about 2 hours.

4. Remove the bouquet garni. Stir in the Cognac. Transfer the tripe and sauce to a warmed serving dish and serve.

From Françoise:

• This dish is so good reheated I recommend doubling the recipe so you can make a second meal of it. It can be refrigerated for at least 2 days.

• Tripe can sometimes be found blanched and cooked. If you have a source for it, you need to simmer the cooked tripe for only 30 minutes in Step 3. But in that case you also need to simmer the cooking liquid for 30 minutes beforehand.

• You can stir a few green olives into this dish just before serving. Add them first to a pan of cold water and bring to a boil, then drain to remove some of the saltiness.

CHARCUTERIE & OTHER MEATS

TRIPE WITH ONIONS
- Gras-double à la lyonnaise -

❖ EASY   ❖ INEXPENSIVE   ❖ 25 MINUTES   ❖ SERVES 4

2 tablespoons butter

2 onions, chopped

2 pounds cooked tripe, cut into large pieces

Salt and pepper

2 tablespoons vinegar

Chopped parsley leaves for sprinkling

❖ ❖ ❖ ❖ ❖

1. In a large skillet, melt the butter over medium heat. Add the onions and cook until lightly browned. Add the tripe, season with salt and pepper, and cook, stirring often, for 15 minutes.

2. Transfer the tripe and onions to a warmed serving dish. In the same skillet, add the vinegar and bring to a simmer, scraping up any brown bits stuck to the bottom. Pour over the tripe, sprinkle with the parsley, and serve very hot.

From Françoise:

• If you are using uncooked tripe, simmer it in a court bouillon (seasoned broth of water cooked with sliced carrot, sliced onion, bouquet garni, peppercorns, salt, and white wine) until tender, about 1 hour and 30 minutes.

SAUTÉED TRIPE WITH PARSLEY AND GARLIC
- Gras-double en persillade -

❖ VERY EASY   ❖ INEXPENSIVE   ❖ 20 MINUTES   ❖ SERVES 4

3 tablespoons butter

2 pounds cooked tripe, cut into thin strips

Salt and pepper

Leaves from ½ bunch of parsley, chopped

2 garlic cloves, finely chopped

❖ ❖ ❖ ❖ ❖

1. In a large saucepan, melt the butter over medium-high heat. Add the tripe, season with salt and pepper, and cook for about 10 minutes. Transfer to a warmed serving dish, sprinkle with the parsley and garlic, and serve.

From Françoise:

• Different kinds of tripe can be prepared in the same way. They aren't expensive and go well with the most modest vegetable—the potato—in all its forms: sautéed, fried, boiled, mashed. Tripe and potatoes together make a copious main dish.

PRESSURE-COOKER TRIPE WITH PANCETTA AND TOMATO

Gras-double à la provençale

❖ EASY   ❖ INEXPENSIVE   ❖ 2 HOURS   ❖ SERVES 4 TO 6

2 to 3 pounds uncooked tripe, cut into 2-inch pieces

Salt

3 tablespoons butter

3 ounces thick-sliced pancetta, cut crosswise
   into ¼-inch-thick strips

1 tablespoon all-purpose flour

2 tablespoons tomato paste

1½ cups dry white wine

1 onion stuck with 2 whole cloves

1 garlic clove, crushed

1 bouquet garni made with parsley, thyme,
   and bay leaf

Pepper

2 tablespoons Cognac

❖   ❖   ❖   ❖   ❖

1. Add the tripe to a pot of boiling, salted water and cook for 10 minutes, then drain.

2. In a pressure cooker, melt the butter. Add the pancetta and cook until lightly browned. Stir in the flour. Stir in the tomato paste and wine and bring to a simmer.

3. Add the tripe, onion, garlic, and bouquet garni. Season with salt and pepper. Add the Cognac and bring to a boil, then tilt the pot and carefully ignite. When the flames subside, lock the lid in place and bring to high pressure. Reduce the heat to maintain high pressure and cook for 1 hour and 30 minutes.

4. Remove the bouquet garni. Transfer the tripe and sauce to a warmed serving dish and serve.

From Françoise:

• This recipe can be prepared entirely in advance and reheated in the oven, on top of the stove, or, much more quickly, in the microwave in individual portions of 1 cup.

CHARCUTERIE & OTHER MEATS

GOLDEN GRATINÉED TRIPE WITH TOMATO SAUCE
- Gras-double au gratin -

❖ EASY ❖ INEXPENSIVE ❖ 1 HOUR, 15 MINUTES ❖ SERVES 4

TOMATO SAUCE
2 tablespoons butter
1 small carrot, peeled and finely chopped
1 onion, finely chopped
1 tablespoon all-purpose flour
2 tablespoons tomato paste
1 tomato, chopped
1 teaspoon sugar

1 bouquet garni made with parsley, thyme, and bay leaf
6 tablespoons dry white wine
Salt and pepper

2 pounds cooked tripe, cut into thin strips
¾ cup shredded Gruyère cheese

❖ ❖ ❖ ❖ ❖

1. Make the tomato sauce: In a saucepan, melt the butter over medium-high heat. Add the carrot and onion and cook until lightly browned. Stir in the flour. Add the tomato paste, tomato, sugar, bouquet garni, wine, and 2 cups of water. Season with salt and pepper. Reduce the heat to low, partially cover, and cook heat for about 30 minutes.

2. Meanwhile, preheat the oven to 425 degrees. Spread the tripe in a gratin dish. Cover with half the cheese, then the tomato sauce, and finish with the remaining cheese. Transfer to the top shelf of the oven and bake until the tripe is hot and the cheese is melted and golden, about 30 minutes.

From Françoise:
• Serve with boiled new potatoes.

• Using store-bought tomato sauce will save you a good half hour of prep time.

CRUSTY GRATIN OF PIG'S FEET
- Pieds de porc panés au four -

❖ EASY ❖ INEXPENSIVE ❖ 25 MINUTES ❖ SERVES 4

Oil for brushing
4 breaded pig's feet

Dijon mustard for serving

1. Preheat the oven to 400 degrees. Brush a gratin dish with oil. Arrange the pig's feet in the dish and bake for 15 to 20 minutes. Serve with Dijon mustard.

From Françoise:
• I serve this very humble dish to guests who appreciate pig's feet. To give it a more epicurean feel, I set out cornichons, flavored mustards, and prepared Béarnaise Sauce (page 138), which I heat up. Believe me, even store-bought condiments make a difference.

• When you buy a breaded pig's foot, what you typically get, in fact, is half a foot. Ask for either whole feet or halves, according to your appetite.

BRAISED CALF'S FEET WITH OLIVES
- *Pieds de veau aux olives* -

❖ INTERMEDIATE　　❖ INEXPENSIVE　　❖ 2 HOURS　　❖ SERVES 4

4 calf's feet, split lengthwise

2 cups dry white wine

1 onion stuck with 2 cloves

1 carrot, halved lengthwise

1 bouquet garni made with parsley, thyme, and bay leaf

Salt and pepper

2 tablespoons butter

2 tablespoons all-purpose flour

1 tablespoon tomato paste

¾ cup dry white wine

1 cup pitted green olives

1 large egg yolk

❖　❖　❖　❖　❖

1. Bring a large saucepan of water to a boil. Add the calf's feet and cook for 5 minutes. Drain them in a colander under cold running water and drain again.

2. Return the calf's feet to the saucepan and add 6 cups of water, 1 ¼ cups of the wine, the onion, carrot, and bouquet garni. Season with salt and pepper. Bring to a boil over medium-high heat, then reduce the heat to medium and cook at a gentle boil, uncovered, for 45 minutes.

3. Using tongs, transfer the calf's feet to a cutting board. Remove the bones. Strain the cooking liquid and reserve.

4. Wipe out the saucepan. In it melt the butter over medium heat. Whisk in the flour until it starts foaming. Whisk in the tomato paste, remaining ¾ cup of wine, and reserved cooking liquid. Season with salt and pepper. Bring to a boil, whisking, until it thickens slightly. Add the calf's feet and olives, reduce the heat to low, cover, and cook for 45 minutes.

5. In a cup, blend the egg yolk with a little of the hot sauce. Remove the pan from the heat, then gradually whisk this mixture into the sauce. Transfer the calf's feet and sauce to a warmed serving dish and serve.

From Françoise:
• Serve with boiled new potatoes or rice.

SLOW-COOKED CALF'S FEET IN CREAMY SAUCE

- *Pieds de veau à la poulette* -

❖ INTERMEDIATE ❖ INEXPENSIVE ❖ 2 HOURS ❖ SERVES 4

4 calf's feet, split lengthwise

2 cups dry white wine

1 onion stuck with 2 cloves

1 carrot, halved lengthwise

1 bouquet garni made with parsley, thyme,
   and bay leaf

Salt and pepper

POULETTE SAUCE

2 tablespoons butter

2 tablespoons all-purpose flour

Salt and pepper

1 large egg yolk

❖ ❖ ❖ ❖ ❖

1. Bring a large saucepan of water to a boil. Add the calf's feet and cook for 5 minutes. Drain them in a colander under cold running water and drain again.

2. Return the calf's feet to the saucepan and add 4 cups of water, the wine, onion, carrot, and bouquet garni. Season with salt and pepper. Bring to a boil over medium-high heat, then reduce the heat to medium and cook at a gentle boil, uncovered, for 45 minutes.

3. Using tongs, transfer the calf's feet to a cutting board. Remove the bones. Strain the cooking liquid and reserve.

4. Make the poulette sauce: Wipe out the saucepan. In it melt the butter over medium heat. Whisk in the flour until it starts foaming. Whisk in the reserved cooking liquid and season with salt and pepper. Bring to a boil,

whisking, until it thickens slightly. Add the calf's feet, reduce the heat to low, cover, and cook for 45 minutes.

5. In a cup, blend the egg yolk with a little of the hot sauce. Remove the pan from the heat, then gradually whisk this mixture into the sauce. Transfer the calf's feet and sauce to a warmed serving dish and serve.

From Françoise:

• If you sprinkle the dish with a little chopped parsley or chervil just before serving, it will be even better.

• Adding a few sautéed mushrooms and lemon juice to the sauce is also a good idea.

• Serve with steamed new potatoes—and that's all!

GRILLED KIDNEY, SAUSAGE, AND BACON SKEWERS

- *Rognons grillés en brochettes* -

❖ INTERMEDIATE ❖ EXPENSIVE ❖ 40 MINUTES ❖ SERVES 4

8 lamb or sheep kidneys

4 large white mushrooms, quartered lengthwise

3-ounce piece of bacon, cut into 8 cubes

4 small sweet Italian sausages

Oil for brushing

❖ ❖ ❖ ❖ ❖

1. Preheat a grill or broiler. If there is any membrane surrounding the kidneys, peel it off. Cut the kidneys in half horizontally. Remove the connective tissue and fat.

2. On each of 4 long metal skewers, thread assorted chunks of kidney, mushroom, and bacon. Finish with a sausage. Brush the skewers with oil.

3. Grill or broil the skewers until charred on all sides, 10 to 15 minutes. Transfer to a warmed platter and serve.

From Françoise:

• Have your butcher prepare the kidneys for cooking, removing the membrane, connective tissue, and fat.

• Lamb and sheep kidneys are perfect for skewers because they're small.

• If using pork kidneys, cut them into 4 or 6 pieces each. Two are enough for 4 servings.

• Serve with plain rice and grilled tomatoes.

CHARCUTERIE & OTHER MEATS

PAN-SAUTÉED VEAL KIDNEYS AND SAUSAGE WITH MUSTARD PAN SAUCE

- *Rognons sautés à la moutarde* -

❖ INTERMEDIATE ❖ EXPENSIVE ❖ 15 MINUTES ❖ SERVES 4

3 tablespoons butter

4 sweet Italian sausages

4 large white mushroom caps

Salt and pepper

2 veal kidneys, halved horizontally or cut into
  1 ½-inch pieces

¾ cup dry white wine

1 tablespoon Dijon mustard

continued

1. In a large skillet, melt 1 tablespoon of the butter over medium-high heat. Add the sausages and mushroom caps and cook until lightly browned all over. Season with salt and pepper and transfer to a warmed serving dish.

2. In the same skillet, melt the remaining 2 tablespoons of butter over medium-high heat. Add the kidneys and cook for about 5 minutes. Season with salt. Using tongs or a slotted spoon, transfer them to the serving dish. Discard the pan juices.

3. Add the wine to the skillet and simmer, scraping up any brown bits stuck to the bottom, until slightly thickened. Remove the pan from the heat and stir in the mustard. Pour over the kidneys and serve with the sausages and mushroom caps.

From Françoise:
• The secret to mustard that doesn't separate when heated: Whisk it or, using a wooden spoon, stir it vigorously into the hot sauce or mixture off the heat. If it must be reheated, use only the gentle warmth of a water bath.

VEAL KIDNEYS WITH CREAMY MUSHROOMS
- *Rognons aux champignons* -

❖ INTERMEDIATE   ❖ EXPENSIVE   ❖ 15 MINUTES   ❖ SERVES 4

3 tablespoons butter
½ pound white mushrooms, diced
1 tablespoon fresh lemon juice
Salt and pepper

2 veal kidneys, diced
¼ cup port, Madeira, or vermouth
2 tablespoons crème fraîche

❖ ❖ ❖ ❖ ❖

1. In a large skillet, melt 1 tablespoon of the butter over medium-high heat. Add the mushrooms and lemon juice and season with salt and pepper. Cook for 5 minutes. Using a slotted spoon, transfer them to a bowl. Pour off the cooking liquid.

2. In the same skillet, melt the remaining 2 tablespoons of butter over medium-high heat. Add the kidneys and cook for about 5 minutes. Using a slotted spoon, transfer them to the bowl. Discard the pan juices.

3. Add the port, Madeira, or vermouth to the skillet. Add the mushrooms, then the kidneys, season with salt and pepper, and reheat for a few seconds over medium-high heat. Stir in the crème fraîche, scraping up any brown bits stuck to the bottom. Transfer to a warmed serving dish and serve at once.

From Françoise:
• If you let kidneys boil for more than a few seconds, they'll get tough.

• Pork kidneys can be prepared in the same way as veal kidneys.

• Have your butcher prepare the kidneys for cooking, removing the membrane, connective tissue, and fat.

COGNAC-FLAMED VEAL KIDNEYS

- *Rognons flambés au cognac* -

❖ INTERMEDIATE　　❖ EXPENSIVE　　　　❖ 20 MINUTES　　　❖ SERVES 4

2 veal kidneys or 4 pork kidneys
2 tablespoons butter
Salt and pepper

¼ cup Cognac
¼ cup crème fraîche

❖　❖　❖　❖　❖

1. If there is any membrane surrounding the kidneys, peel it off. Cut the kidneys in half horizontally. Remove the connective tissue and fat. Cut the kidneys into 1 ½-inch pieces.

2. In a large skillet, melt the butter over medium-high heat. Add the kidneys and cook for about 5 minutes. Season with salt and pepper.

3. Add the Cognac to the skillet and simmer, scraping up any brown bits stuck to the bottom. Tilt the pan and carefully ignite. When the flames subside, using a slotted spoon, transfer the kidneys to a warmed serving dish. Stir the crème fraîche into the skillet and simmer for a few seconds. Pour over the kidneys and serve.

From Françoise:
• Veal kidneys are expensive, but pork kidneys are more affordable. They can be special-ordered from a butcher.

• Serve with boiled new potatoes, lightly sprinkled with chopped parsley.

• Transfer the flamed kidneys to a rack set over a dish to drain while preparing the pan sauce. Discard any liquid that accumulates. Don't add it to the sauce; it's not very tasty.

CHARCUTERIE & OTHER MEATS

PAN-SEARED PORK KIDNEYS WITH PARSLEY BUTTER

- *Rognons de porc maître d'hôtel* -

❖ INTERMEDIATE　　❖ MODERATE　　　　❖ 15 MINUTES　　　❖ SERVES 4

4 tablespoons (½ stick) butter, 2 tablespoons
　softened
1 small bunch parsley, chopped

4 pork kidneys
Salt and pepper

continued

1. In a bowl, mash the 2 tablespoons of softened butter with the parsley.

2. If there is any membrane surrounding the kidneys, peel it off. Cut the kidneys almost but not entirely in half horizontally. Remove the connective tissue and fat.

3. In a large skillet, melt the remaining 2 tablespoons of butter over medium-high heat. Add the kidneys and cook, turning once, for 2 to 3 minutes per side. Season with salt and pepper.

4. Using tongs, transfer the kidneys to a warmed platter. Dot with the parsley butter and serve.

From Françoise:

• Marinate the kidneys for 2 to 3 hours before cooking them. Drizzle with oil and set 1 thyme sprig and ½ bay leaf on top. You can use this oil to cook them instead of butter.

• It's important to discard the kidney pan juices; they're not very tasty.

• Serve with buttered artichoke bottoms and potato chips, warmed in the oven. Set the kidneys in the center of a platter and arrange the artichokes and chips at either end. And, if you have any watercress sprigs, that green note will make your dish look very appealing.

BOILED OXTAIL WITH VEGETABLES AND BUTTERY CROUTONS
- *Queues de boeuf en marmite* -

❖ INTERMEDIATE   ❖ MODERATE   ❖ 3 HOURS   ❖ SERVES 4

2-pound oxtail, thickly sliced crosswise
Salt
3 leeks, white and light green parts only,
   cut into 2-inch pieces
2 carrots, peeled and cut into 2-inch pieces
1 turnip, peeled and quartered lengthwise
1 celery rib, cut into 2-inch pieces

1 onion stuck with 4 cloves
1 garlic clove, crushed
1 bouquet garni made with parsley, thyme,
   and bay leaf
12 slices of baguette
2 tablespoons butter, softened

❖ ❖ ❖ ❖ ❖

1. In a flameproof casserole, cover the oxtail generously with cold water. Bring to a boil over medium-high heat, then drain. Add 2 quarts of water and salt and bring to a simmer over medium heat. Add the leeks, carrots, turnip, celery, onion, garlic, and bouquet garni, reduce the heat to low, and cook for about 2 hours and 30 minutes.

2. Meanwhile, preheat the oven to 350 degrees. Brush the baguette slices with the butter and spread on a baking sheet. Toast in the oven until lightly browned.

3. Discard the bouquet garni. Serve the broth, oxtail, and vegetables, passing the croutons separately.

From Françoise:

• Bringing the oxtail to a boil and then draining it eliminates a lot of the foam later on.

• To make a more flavorful broth, add 1 teaspoon of potato starch mixed with ¼ cup of cherry brandy to the simmering liquid just before serving.

• Serve with boiled new potatoes and an assortment of condiments, such as sea salt, cornichons, and flavored mustards.

JUICY BAKED BOUDIN BLANC SAUSAGES
- *Boudins blancs au four* -

❖ VERY EASY   ❖ EXPENSIVE   ❖ 25 MINUTES   ❖ SERVES 4

4 boudin blanc sausages (about 1 pound total)

❖ ❖ ❖ ❖ ❖

1. Preheat the oven to 425 degrees. Tear off 4 sheets of parchment or foil and wrap each sausage, twisting the ends to seal.

2. Set the sausages on an oven rack and bake for about 20 minutes, turning once halfway through cooking. Transfer to a work surface and remove the parchment or foil. Arrange on a warmed platter and serve.

From Françoise:
• Boudin blanc is a smooth, white, veal-and-pork sausage similar to bockwurst. It's traditionally served as a first course in France on Christmas or for New Year's dinner and absolutely delicious when it's well made but disappointing otherwise. If you don't have a good source for sausages, serve something else.

• The parchment or foil wrapper helps keep the sausages from bursting during cooking, which they can easily do. As an added precaution, prick them with a needle or a thin metal cake tester before cooking—not a fork, which would make larger holes.

• You can also arrange the wrapped sausages on a baking sheet, then transfer them to the oven for cooking.

CHARCUTERIE & OTHER MEATS

JUICY BAKED BLOOD SAUSAGES

- *Boudins noirs au four* -

❖ VERY EASY   ❖ INEXPENSIVE   ❖ 25 MINUTES   ❖ SERVES 4

4 blood sausages (about 1 pound total)   **Dijon mustard for serving**

❖ ❖ ❖ ❖ ❖

1. Preheat the oven to 425 degrees. Tear off 4 sheets of parchment or foil and wrap each sausage, twisting the ends to seal.

2. Set the sausages on an oven rack and bake for about 20 minutes, turning once halfway through cooking. Transfer to a work surface and remove the parchment or foil. Arrange on a warmed platter and serve with the mustard.

From Françoise:
• Serve with a green salad and sautéed potatoes or apples, mashed potatoes, or applesauce. Pour a simple wine, like Beaujolais, to accompany this rustic dish.

• You can cook blood sausage without wrapping it, but it's more likely to burst in the oven.

JUICY PAN-SEARED BLOOD SAUSAGES

- *Boudins noirs sautés* -

❖ VERY EASY   ❖ INEXPENSIVE   ❖ 12 MINUTES   ❖ SERVES 4

1 tablespoon oil   **4 blood sausages (about 1 pound total)**

❖ ❖ ❖ ❖ ❖

1. In a large skillet, heat the oil over medium-high heat. Add the sausages and sear on all sides. Reduce the heat to medium and cook for 7 to 8 minutes. Arrange on a warmed platter and serve.

From Françoise:
• Prick the sausages with a needle or a thin metal cake tester before cooking to discourage them from bursting.

• Serve with sautéed potatoes or apples, mashed potatoes, chestnut puree, or applesauce.

• To make this into a really fast meal, consider serving it with potato chips or cooked, vacuum-packed chestnuts reheated with a little butter.

PAN-SAUTÉED ANDOUILLETTE SAUSAGES
- *Andouillettes à la poéle* -

❖ VERY EASY   ❖ INEXPENSIVE   ❖ 15 MINUTES   ❖ SERVES 4

1 tablespoon oil

4 andouillette sausages (about 1 pound total)

Dijon mustard for serving

❖ ❖ ❖ ❖ ❖

1. In a large skillet, heat the oil over medium-high heat. Add the sausages and cook until lightly browned all over. Reduce the heat to low and cook for 10 to 12 minutes. Arrange on a warmed platter or plates and serve with the mustard.

From Françoise:
• Andouillettes are coarse chitterling (tripe) sausages.

• Serve with fried or mashed potatoes. And don't forget to pass the mustard at the table.

• Prick the sausages with a needle or a thin metal cake tester before cooking to discourage them from bursting.

CHARCUTERIE & OTHER MEATS

BRAISED ANDOUILLETTE SAUSAGES
WITH SLICED POTATOES

- Andouillettes braisées aux pommes de terre -

❖ EASY   ❖ INEXPENSIVE   ❖ 1 HOUR   ❖ SERVES 4

3 tablespoons butter, plus more for brushing

1 ½ pounds potatoes, peeled and thinly sliced

Salt and pepper

4 andouillette sausages (about 1 pound total)

Dijon mustard for brushing

1 ½ cups dry white wine

❖ ❖ ❖ ❖ ❖

1. Preheat the oven to 350 degrees. Brush a gratin dish with butter. Spread the potato slices in the dish and season with salt and pepper. Dot with 2 tablespoons of the butter.

2. In a large skillet, melt the remaining 1 tablespoon of butter over medium-high heat. Add the sausages and cook until lightly browned all over. Arrange them in the gratin dish, brush generously with mustard, and pour the wine around them. Transfer to the oven and bake for about 45 minutes. Serve in the gratin dish.

From Françoise:

• Use a food processor or mandoline slicer to cut thin, even potato slices.

• If the dish looks like it's beginning to dry out, cover it loosely with a sheet of foil three-quarters of the way through cooking.

WINE-BRAISED ANDOUILLETTE SAUSAGES
- *Andouillettes braisées au vin blanc* -

❖ EASY   ❖ INEXPENSIVE   ❖ 1 HOUR   ❖ SERVES 4

**4 tablespoons (½ stick) butter, softened,
plus more for brushing**
4 andouillette sausages (about 1 pound total)

2 ¼ cups dry white wine
Dijon mustard for serving

❖ ❖ ❖ ❖ ❖

1. Preheat the oven to 350 degrees. Brush a gratin dish with butter. Arrange the sausages in the dish and brush with the 4 tablespoons of softened butter. Pour in the wine. Transfer to the oven and bake until the wine is completely absorbed, about 45 minutes. Serve in the gratin dish, passing the mustard separately.

From Françoise:
• Serve with a green salad and mashed potatoes.

• If the wine looks like it's evaporating too quickly, cover the dish loosely with a sheet of foil.

CHARCUTERIE & OTHER MEATS

PAN-SAUTÉED PORK SAUSAGES
- *Saucisses à la poêle* -

❖ VERY EASY   ❖ INEXPENSIVE   ❖ 15 MINUTES   ❖ SERVES 4

2 tablespoons butter

4 pork sausages (about 1 pound total)

❖ ❖ ❖ ❖ ❖

1. In a large skillet, melt the butter over medium-high heat. Add the sausages and cook until lightly browned all over. Reduce the heat to low and cook for 10 to 12 minutes. Arrange on a warmed platter or plates and serve.

From Françoise:
• All uncooked ground pork sausages, such as Toulouse sausage, Italian sausage, *crépinettes*

(wrapped in caul fat), and chipolatas, can be prepared in this way. The cooking time will vary slightly depending on the size of the sausage.

• Serve with starchy side dishes for absorbing the delicious fat, such as potatoes, rice, split peas, lentils, and cabbage.

SAUSAGE-STUFFED CRÊPES WITH CREAMY TOMATO SAUCE

- Crêpes aux saucisses -

❖ INTERMEDIATE   ❖ INEXPENSIVE   ❖ 1 HOUR   ❖ SERVES 4

CRÊPES

¾ cup all-purpose flour

1 cup water or milk

1 large egg, lightly beaten

2 tablespoons butter, melted, plus more
  for brushing

¼ teaspoon salt

SAUCE

2 tablespoons butter

1 shallot, finely chopped

1 garlic clove, finely chopped

2 tablespoons all-purpose flour

1 tablespoon tomato paste

1 bouquet garni made with parsley, thyme,
  and bay leaf

Salt and pepper

1 tablespoon butter

4 sweet Italian sausages

❖ ❖ ❖ ❖ ❖

1. Make the crêpes: In a medium bowl, whisk the flour with the water or milk, egg, 2 tablespoons of the melted butter, and the salt. Cover and let stand at least 1 hour.

2. Meanwhile, make the sauce: In a small saucepan, melt the butter over medium-low heat. Add the shallot and garlic and cook until softened. Whisk in the flour until it starts foaming. Whisk in the tomato paste, then 2 cups of cold water and the bouquet garni. Season with salt and pepper. Bring to a boil, whisking, until slightly thickened. Reduce the heat to very low and cook, uncovered, for 15 minutes.

3. In a large skillet, melt the butter for the sausages over medium heat. Add the sausages and cook until lightly browned all over, about 15 minutes.

4. Lightly brush a 7- or 8-inch skillet with melted butter and heat over medium heat.

Whisk the batter and add 2 to 3 tablespoons to the skillet, swirling to coat the bottom. Cook until the edge begins to brown, about 30 seconds. Flip using a thin-bladed spatula and cook for 20 seconds. Slide onto a plate and repeat with the remaining batter, stacking the crêpes as they're cooked.

5. Remove the bouquet garni from the sauce. Roll each sausage in a crêpe and arrange on a warmed serving dish. Spoon the sauce over the top and serve.

From Françoise:

• This recipe makes about 8 crêpes, so you'll have extras for another recipe.

• If you serve sausage-stuffed crêpes as a main dish, I think you're doing the right thing. In that case, you'll want 2 crêpes and 2 sausages per person—you'll have enough batter with this recipe, since it makes enough for 8 crêpes.

POACHED FRANKFURTERS
- *Saucisses pochées* -

❖ VERY EASY   ❖ INEXPENSIVE   ❖ 15 MINUTES   ❖ SERVES 4

8 frankfurters

❖ ❖ ❖ ❖ ❖

1. Bring a large saucepan of water to a boil over medium-high heat. Add the frankfurters and cook at a gentle boil for 10 minutes. Drain. Arrange on a warmed platter or plates and serve.

From Françoise:
• Serve with—besides sauerkraut—mashed potatoes, braised green cabbage, dried beans, pasta, or rice.

SLOW-COOKED SAUSAGES WITH BUTTERY CABBAGE
- *Chipolatas au chou* -

❖ EASY   ❖ INEXPENSIVE   ❖ 1 HOUR   ❖ SERVES 4

2-pound green cabbage, core and outer leaves removed, thinly sliced
Salt
5 tablespoons butter
1 onion, thinly sliced

1 carrot, peeled and thinly sliced crosswise
1 garlic clove, crushed
Pepper
8 small sweet Italian sausages
2 tablespoons vinegar

❖ ❖ ❖ ❖ ❖

1. Bring a large pot of salted water to a boil. Add the cabbage and cook for 10 minutes. Drain in a colander, pressing on the cabbage to remove as much water as possible.

2. In a flameproof casserole, melt 3 tablespoons of the butter over medium heat. Add the onion and carrot and cook until lightly browned. Add the cabbage and garlic and season with salt and pepper. Reduce the heat to low, cover, and cook for 40 minutes.

3. Meanwhile, in a large skillet, melt the remaining 2 tablespoons of butter over medium-low heat. Add the sausages and cook until lightly browned all over, about 5 minutes.

4. Spread the cabbage in a warmed serving dish. Arrange the sausages on top.

continued

CHARCUTERIE & OTHER MEATS

5. In the same skillet, bring the vinegar to a simmer, scraping up any brown bits stuck to the bottom. Pour over the sausages and serve.

From Françoise:

• Look for a green cabbage that's tightly packed.

• This simple country recipe makes a quickly prepared meal-in-one dish.

• For a slightly sweet and more intensely flavored dish, stir balsamic vinegar into the pan juices.

BRAISED CURED PORK AND SAUSAGES WITH SAUERKRAUT

- *Choucroute* -

❖ EASY ❖ EXPENSIVE ❖ 4 HOURS, 30 MINUTES, PLUS OVERNIGHT SOAKING ❖ SERVES 6

4 ½ pounds raw sauerkraut

10 ounces fresh pork rind

1-pound chunk of bacon

1 calf's foot, split in half

1 smoked pork shoulder

1 carrot, peeled

2 onions, stuck with 3 whole cloves total

20 juniper berries

1 bouquet garni made with parsley, thyme, and bay leaf

10 black peppercorns

7 tablespoons butter

2 cups dry white wine, preferably from Alsace

Salt and pepper

1 pound new potatoes, peeled

1 pound French garlic sausage or kielbasa

10 frankfurters

Dijon mustard for serving

❖ ❖ ❖ ❖ ❖

1. In a large bowl, cover the sauerkraut generously with water and let soak overnight, changing the water 2 or 3 times.

2. Drain the sauerkraut and squeeze out as much of the water as possible. Spread on a large, clean kitchen towel.

3. Add the pork rind, bacon, calf's foot, and pork shoulder to a large pot of water and bring to a boil over medium-high heat. Reduce the heat and simmer for 5 minutes, then drain.

4. In a flameproof casserole, spread out the pork rind. Cover with half the sauerkraut, the carrot, onions, juniper berries, bouquet garni, and peppercorns. Add the bacon, calf's foot, pork shoulder, and butter. Spread the remaining sauerkraut on top. Add the wine and enough water to barely cover the sauerkraut.

Season with salt and pepper. Cover and bring to a boil over medium-high heat, then reduce the heat to low and cook for about 3 hours and 30 minutes, removing the bacon after 1 hour and the pork shoulder after 1 hour and 30 minutes.

5. Bring a large saucepan of salted water to a boil. Add the potatoes and cook for 15 minutes. Using a slotted spoon, transfer the potatoes to the sauerkraut for 15 minutes to finish cooking. Return the bacon and pork shoulder to the pot to reheat.

6. Add the sausage and frankfurters to the same boiling water and cook through.

7. Slice the pork shoulder, sausage, and bacon. Spread the sauerkraut on a large warmed platter and arrange the sliced meats and frankfurters on top. Serve hot, passing the potatoes and mustard separately.

From Françoise:
• When you're preparing choucroute, make a large batch because it's a long process. I've given you the proportions for at least 6 servings. This is a dish that reheats well or can be served at room temperature with sliced hard-boiled eggs and beets, as in Germany.

• If your sauerkraut is fresh, you don't need to soak it. It will have more flavor that way.

• If you don't want to pick through the spices and aromatic vegetables when you're eating the choucroute, you can wrap them in cheesecloth before adding them to the pot and remove them before serving.

• To make a quick version of choucroute, reheat prepared sauerkraut with a little dry white wine, poached sausages, sliced ham, and slices of parboiled bacon.

CHARCUTERIE & OTHER MEATS

WINE-BRAISED SAUSAGE WITH WARM POTATO SALAD

- *Saucisson chaud et pommes à l'huile* -

❖ EASY   ❖ MODERATE   ❖ 1 HOUR, 15 MINUTES   ❖ SERVES 4

½ pound new potatoes, unpeeled

¾ cup dry white wine

1 French garlic sausage or kielbasa
  (about 1 pound)

1 tablespoon vinegar

3 tablespoons oil

1 small onion, finely chopped

1 shallot, finely chopped

Salt and pepper

Chopped parsley leaves for sprinkling

❖ ❖ ❖ ❖ ❖

1. Add the potatoes to a large saucepan of salted water. Bring to a boil over medium-high heat and cook until tender, about 30 minutes.

2. Meanwhile, in another large saucepan, bring the wine and 4 cups of water to a boil over medium-high heat. Add the sausage, reduce the heat to medium, and cook at a gentle boil for 15 to 25 minutes. Drain, reserving 6 table-spoons of the cooking liquid. Slice the sausage.

3. In a salad bowl, whisk the vinegar with the oil, onion, and shallot. Season with salt and pepper.

4. Drain and peel the potatoes. Slice them into the vinaigrette. Add the sausage slices and reserved cooking liquid and toss to coat. Sprinkle with the parsley and serve hot.

From Françoise:

• The sausage can be cooked in water without the wine.

• You might add a little warmed white wine to the salad bowl instead of the sausage cooking liquid. It's very good!

BOILED SMOKED PORK AND SAUSAGES
WITH VEGETABLES

- *Potée alsacienne* -

❖ EASY   ❖ EXPENSIVE   ❖ 2 HOURS, 40 MINUTES   ❖ SERVES 6 TO 8

1 green cabbage, quartered and cored

1 pound smoked ham shank or smoked pork
  knuckle or shoulder

½ pound carrots, peeled and cut into
  2-inch pieces

½ pound turnips, peeled and quartered

½ pound leeks, white and light green parts only,
  cut into 2-inch pieces

2 garlic cloves, crushed

1 bouquet garni made with parsley, thyme,
  and bay leaf

1 ½ pounds new potatoes, peeled

1 pound French garlic sausage or kielbasa

4 small pork sausages

Dijon mustard for serving

❖ ❖ ❖ ❖ ❖

1. Bring a large pot of water to a boil. Add the cabbage and cook for 10 minutes, then drain.

2. Bring another large pot of water to a boil. Add the cabbage, ham or pork, carrots, turnips, leeks, garlic, and bouquet garni and simmer for 2 hours.

3. Add the potatoes and garlic sausage and cook for 30 minutes. In a medium skillet, cook the small pork sausages over medium-high heat until nicely browned all over.

4. Remove the bouquet garni. Transfer the ham or pork and garlic sausage to a cutting board and slice. Transfer all the meats and vegetables to a warmed serving dish. Moisten with some of the broth and serve, passing the mustard separately.

From Françoise:

• Follow the directions on the meat wrapper or consult your butcher about the length of presoaking time needed for salt-cured or smoked pork.

CHARCUTERIE & OTHER MEATS

357

BOILED CURED PORK AND SAUSAGES
WITH VEGETABLES

- *Potée limousine* -

❖ EASY   ❖ EXPENSIVE   ❖ 3 HOURS   ❖ SERVES 6 TO 8

1 green cabbage, quartered and cored

1 pound salt-cured pork knuckle or belly

7-ounce piece of bacon

½ pound carrots, peeled and cut into
  2-inch pieces

½ pound turnips, peeled and quartered

½ pound leeks, white and light green parts only,
  cut into 2-inch pieces

2 garlic cloves, crushed

1 bouquet garni made with parsley, thyme,
  and bay leaf

1 ½ pounds new potatoes, peeled

4 small pork sausages

Dijon mustard for serving

❖ ❖ ❖ ❖ ❖

1. Bring a large pot of water to a boil. Add the cabbage and cook for 10 minutes, then drain.

2. Bring another large pot of water to a boil. Add the cabbage, pork, bacon, carrots, turnips, leeks, garlic, and bouquet garni and simmer for 2 hours.

3. Add the potatoes and cook until tender, about 30 minutes. In a medium skillet, cook the small pork sausages over medium-high heat until nicely browned all over.

4. Remove the bouquet garni. Transfer the pork and bacon to a cutting board and slice. Transfer all the meats and vegetables to a warmed serving dish. Moisten with some of the broth and serve, passing the mustard separately.

From Françoise:

• Follow the directions on the meat wrapper or consult your butcher about the length of presoaking time needed for salt-cured or smoked pork.

BOILED CURED PORK AND SAUSAGES WITH DRIED BEANS AND VEGETABLES

- *Potée lorraine* -

❖ EASY ❖ EXPENSIVE ❖ 2 HOURS, 30 MINUTES ❖ SERVES 6 TO 8

1 pound smoked pork shoulder

4 carrots, peeled and cut into 2-inch pieces

2 turnips, peeled and quartered

4 leeks, white and light green parts only,
   cut into 2-inch pieces

2 onions, 1 thinly sliced, 1 stuck with 3 whole cloves

1 garlic clove, crushed

1 celery rib, cut into 2-inch pieces

1 bouquet garni made with parsley, thyme,
   and bay leaf

1 green cabbage, quartered and cored

½ pound dried white beans

7-ounce piece of bacon

6 or 8 new potatoes, peeled

1 pound French garlic sausage or kielbasa

Salt and pepper

Dijon mustard for serving

❖ ❖ ❖ ❖ ❖

1. In a large pot, combine the pork with the carrots, turnips, leeks, onions, garlic, celery, and bouquet garni. Cover generously with water and bring to a boil over medium-high heat, then reduce the heat and cook at a gentle boil for 1 hour.

2. Meanwhile, bring another large pot of water to a boil. Add the cabbage and cook for 10 minutes, then remove. Add the dried beans to the boiling water and cook for 15 minutes; drain. Add the cabbage, dried beans, and bacon to the pot of pork and vegetables and cook for 1 hour.

3. Add the potatoes and sausage and cook until tender, about 30 minutes. Season with salt and pepper if needed.

4. Remove the bouquet garni and onion stuck with cloves. Transfer the pork, sausage, and bacon to a cutting board and slice. Transfer all the meats and vegetables to a warmed serving dish. Moisten with some of the broth and serve, passing the mustard separately.

From Françoise:

• Follow the directions on the meat wrapper or consult your butcher about the length of presoaking time needed for salt-cured or smoked pork.

BAKED HAM STEAKS WITH CREAMY SPINACH

- *Jambon à la florentine* -

❖ EASY ❖ MODERATE ❖ 40 MINUTES ❖ SERVES 4

4 ham steaks, about ½ pound each,
  cut ¼ inch thick
¼ cup port
3 ½ pounds spinach, tough stems removed

2 tablespoons butter
2 or 3 tablespoons crème fraîche
Salt and pepper

❖ ❖ ❖ ❖ ❖

1. Preheat the oven to 150 degrees. Spread the ham slices in a gratin dish. Add the port, cover with foil, and bake for 20 to 25 minutes.

2. Meanwhile, bring a large pot of water to a boil. Add the spinach and cook for 5 minutes. Drain in a colander and press on the spinach to remove as much water as possible. Coarsely chop the spinach.

3. In a flameproof casserole, melt the butter over medium-high heat. Add the spinach and cook for 2 to 3 minutes, stirring, to dry it out a bit. Add the crème fraîche and season with salt and pepper. Reduce the heat to low, cover, and cook for 10 minutes.

4. Spread the spinach on a large warmed serving dish. Arrange the ham slices on top, pour in the cooking juices, and serve.

From Françoise:
• It takes some effort to clean, blanch, drain, and cook all the spinach, but this dish is easily made by a beginner. Or you could try a little less baby spinach, which usually doesn't need to be stemmed or cleaned, though it is more expensive.

• Instead of port, you can use another sweet or fortified wine, such as Madeira, muscat, or vermouth.

• Don't bake the ham at too high a temperature or it will toughen. Cover it with foil to keep it moist.

• You can also gently heat the ham slices in a skillet.

• Try to squeeze as much water as possible out of the spinach.

BRAISED HAM WITH MADEIRA-MUSHROOM SAUCE

- Jambon braisé au madère -

❖ ADVANCED   ❖ EXPENSIVE   ❖ 1 HOUR   ❖ SERVES 8 TO 10

3 tablespoons butter

2 pounds veal bones, cracked

2 onions, finely chopped

2 carrots, peeled and finely chopped

2 shallots, finely chopped

10 ounces mushrooms, one-third finely chopped,
  two-thirds thinly sliced

1 tablespoon all-purpose flour

1 tablespoon tomato paste

1 garlic clove, crushed

1 bouquet garni made with parsley, thyme,
  and bay leaf

1 ½ cups Madeira

1 ½ cups dry white wine

Salt and pepper

7 ½- to 8-pound bone-in baked ham, skin
  removed and fat trimmed to ¼ inch

❖ ❖ ❖ ❖ ❖

1. In a large flameproof casserole, melt the butter over medium heat. Add the veal bones, onions, carrots, shallots, and finely chopped mushrooms and cook until lightly browned. Stir in the flour. Add the tomato paste, garlic, bouquet garni, Madeira, and wine. Season with pepper and, lightly, with salt. Bring to a simmer, then add the ham, reduce the heat to low, cover, and cook for 30 minutes, turning the ham halfway through.

2. Transfer the ham to a cutting board and cover loosely with foil. Bring the sauce to a simmer and cook until slightly thickened and well flavored. Strain into a saucepan.

3. Add the sliced mushrooms to the sauce and cook over low heat while carving the ham. Arrange the ham slices on a warmed platter and pass the sauce separately.

From Françoise:

• Serve with buttery or creamy spinach. Or, for a more elevated accompaniment, spread the cooked spinach in baked tartlet shells.

HAM BAKED IN A GOLDEN PASTRY CRUST

- *Jambon en croûte* -

❖ ADVANCED   ❖ EXPENSIVE   ❖ 1 HOUR, 30 MINUTES   ❖ SERVES 8 TO 10

PÂTE BRISÉE

3 cups all-purpose flour

1 teaspoon salt

14 tablespoons (1 ¾ sticks) unsalted butter,
  cut into pieces

Butter for brushing

7 ½- to 8-pound boneless cooked ham

1 large egg, lightly beaten with a little water

Madeira Sauce (page 640)

❖ ❖ ❖ ❖ ❖

1. Make the pâte brisée: In a bowl, combine the flour with the salt and butter. Rub the butter into the flour between your palms. Sprinkle over 1 cup of water and knead briefly until large crumbs form. Press into a disk. On a lightly floured surface, scrape the dough away from you with the heel of your hand in a long sliding motion, then press into a disk; repeat 3 times. Wrap and refrigerate until firm, 15 to 20 minutes.

2. Preheat the oven to 400 degrees. Lightly brush a baking sheet with butter. On a lightly floured surface, roll two-thirds of the dough to a round ⅛ inch thick. Wrap the dough around the rolling pin and transfer it to the baking sheet. Set the ham on the round, narrow side up. Bring the dough up around the ham, patting it into place. Roll out the rest of the dough ⅛ inch thick and cut it into a round to fit over the top of the ham. Brush the edge of the bottom dough with beaten egg and press the top round in place. Pinch the edges together to seal them. Brush with beaten egg. If desired, cut out leaves or other decorations from the dough scraps and glue them on with beaten egg; brush the decorations with egg, too.

3. Bake for about 1 hour. Cover loosely with foil and reduce the oven temperature to 350 degrees if the pastry gets too dark. Transfer the ham to a cutting board and let rest for 10 minutes. Transfer to a warmed platter and serve, passing the Madeira sauce separately.

From Françoise:

• Serve with braised spinach or peas.

• You can buy a sliced ham that has been reshaped.

• Using a serrated knife makes slicing much easier.

WINE-BRAISED HAM STEAKS WITH BUTTERY SPLIT PEA PUREE

- *Jambon Saint-Germain* -

❖ EASY   ❖ MODERATE   ❖ 1 HOUR, 30 MINUTES   ❖ SERVES 4

1 cup green split peas (about ½ pound)

1 carrot, halved crosswise

1 onion stuck with 1 clove

A few Boston lettuce leaves

1 bouquet garni made with parsley, thyme,
  and bay leaf

Salt and pepper

4 ham steaks, about ½ pound each,
  cut ¼ inch thick

1 cup dry white wine

3 tablespoons butter

3 tablespoons crème fraîche

SAUCE

1 tablespoon butter

1 tablespoon all-purpose flour

1 teaspoon tomato paste

1 cup broth or water

Salt and pepper

❖ ❖ ❖ ❖ ❖

1. Add the split peas to a large saucepan with water just to cover and bring to a boil over medium-high heat. Cook for 15 minutes, then drain. Cover the split peas generously with water and add the carrot, onion, lettuce, and bouquet garni. Season with salt and pepper. Cover and bring to a simmer over medium heat, then reduce the heat to low and cook until very tender, about 1 hour.

2. Meanwhile, preheat the oven to 150 degrees. Spread the ham steaks in a gratin dish. Add the wine, cover with foil, and bake for 20 to 25 minutes. Drain, reserving the cooking liquid.

3. Make the sauce: In a small saucepan, melt the butter over medium heat. Whisk in the flour until it starts foaming. Whisk in the tomato paste, then the broth or water. Season with salt and pepper. Bring to a boil, whisking, then reduce the heat to very low and cook for 10 minutes.

4. Drain the split peas. Remove the bouquet garni. Using a potato masher or an infusion blender, mash the peas. Beat in the butter, crème fraîche, and ham cooking liquid.

5. Spread the split peas on a warmed serving dish. Arrange the ham steaks on top, pour over the sauce, and serve.

From Françoise:

• Many people cook split peas in water, period— no onion, bouquet garni, lettuce, or carrot. The result? It's not terrific. So follow my recipe. It's so much better, and at very little cost.

• For a more refined dinner, replace the white wine with Madeira or port.

• Reheated ham should not boil, or it will get tough.

• You could also add a bouillon cube with 1 cup of water in Step 3 instead of using prepared broth or plain water.

PORT-BRAISED HAM STEAKS WITH CREAMY MUSHROOM SAUCE

- Jambon braisé au porto -

❖ EASY ❖ MODERATE ❖ 35 MINUTES ❖ SERVES 4

---

4 ham steaks, about ½ pound each,
  cut ¼ inch thick
¼ cup port
¼ pound white mushrooms, thinly sliced

Juice of ½ lemon
2 tablespoons crème fraîche
Salt and pepper
1 large egg yolk

❖ ❖ ❖ ❖ ❖

1. Preheat the oven to 150 degrees. Spread the ham slices in a gratin dish. Add the port, cover, and heat for 20 to 25 minutes.

2. Meanwhile, in a medium saucepan, barely cover the mushrooms with water and add the lemon juice. Bring to a boil over medium-high heat, then drain. Add the crème fraîche, season with salt and pepper, and simmer for 1 minute. Remove the pan from the heat and whisk in the egg yolk and the port from the ham.

3. Arrange the ham slices on a warmed platter. Pour the mushroom sauce over the top and serve.

From Françoise:

• You can also prepare this ham with Madeira, sherry, or another fortified wine. Their sweetness mellows the ham's saltiness.

• If you don't have a lid that fits your gratin dish exactly, simply wrap a sheet of foil or parchment paper around it.

JELLIED FRESH HAM TERRINE

- *Rouelle de jambon en gelée* -

❖ ADVANCED   ❖ INEXPENSIVE   ❖ 2 HOURS, 30 MINUTES, PLUS OVERNIGHT CHILLING   ❖ SERVES 4

2 tablespoons butter

1 tablespoon oil

3 ½- to 4 ½-pound bone-in fresh ham

7 ounces fresh pork rind, cut into pieces

1 pound veal bones, cracked

2 carrots, sliced crosswise

4 large onions, thinly sliced

1 small celery rib

2 or 3 garlic cloves, crushed

1 bouquet garni made with parsley, thyme, and bay leaf

2 whole cloves

Salt and pepper

¾ cup dry white wine

❖ ❖ ❖ ❖ ❖

1. In a large skillet, melt the butter in the oil over medium-high heat. Add the ham and cook until lightly browned all over.

2. Add the pork rind and veal bones to a large saucepan of water and bring to a boil. Simmer for 5 minutes, then drain in a colander under cold running water.

3. In a flameproof casserole, spread out the pork rind, veal bones, carrots, and onions. Set the ham on top. Tuck the celery, garlic, bouquet garni, and cloves around it. Season with salt and pepper and add the wine. Bring to a boil over medium-high heat, then add 1 ½ cups water. Cover and bring back to a boil, then reduce the heat to low and cook for about 2 hours.

4. Transfer the ham to a cutting board. Carve the ham into pieces. Spread in a deep dish and strain the cooking liquid on top. Refrigerate overnight until the liquid sets.

From Françoise:

• Serve with a green salad and cornichons.

• On chilly days, try this hot with pasta, dried beans, lentils—or a good split pea puree, which no one makes anymore!

• The cut of fresh ham you want comes from the meatiest part of the leg.

CHARCUTERIE & OTHER MEATS

WILD GAME

HARE AND PANCETTA TERRINE
- Terrine de lièvre -

❖ ADVANCED   ❖ EXPENSIVE   ❖ 3 HOURS, PLUS MARINATING AND CHILLING   ❖ SERVES 10 TO 12

MARINADE

3 cups white or red wine

6 tablespoons vinegar

3 tablespoons oil

1 onion, thinly sliced

1 small carrot, thinly sliced crosswise

2 shallots, thinly sliced

1 celery rib, thinly sliced

1 garlic clove, crushed

1 whole clove

1 parsley sprig

1 thyme sprig

¼ bay leaf

3 black peppercorns

5 ½-pound hare, kidney and liver reserved

2 ½ pounds pancetta, cut into chunks

¾ pound pork fat, cut into chunks

3 large eggs

2 tablespoons potato starch

Salt and pepper

½ pound sliced barding fat or bacon

1 bay leaf

❖ ❖ ❖ ❖ ❖

1. Make the marinade: In a large bowl, combine all the ingredients.

2. Cut and scrape the hare meat off the bones. Cut the loin meat into ½-inch strips and reserve. Cut the remaining meat, the kidneys, and liver into large pieces. Add all the hare meat to the marinade with the pancetta and pork fat. Cover and refrigerate for 1 to 2 days.

3. Using a slotted spoon, transfer the hare meat, pancetta, and pork fat to a bowl and pat dry with paper towels. Strain and pour the marinade into a large saucepan. Simmer over medium heat until reduced to 1 cup, 30 to 40 minutes.

4. Preheat the oven to 350 degrees. Reserve the hare strips. Coarsely grind the remaining meats and fat. Using a wooden spoon, mix in the eggs, potato starch, and a few tablespoons of the reduced marinade; the mixture should not be too loose. Season with salt and pepper.

Cook a piece of the ground meat in a skillet and taste. Add salt and pepper to the remaining meat if necessary.

5. Line a terrine with the barding fat or bacon, reserving some for the top. Spread one-half of the ground meat in the terrine, then lay in the reserved hare strips lengthwise. Cover with the remaining ground meat and the bay leaf. Lay the remaining barding fat or bacon on top and cover with the lid.

6. Set the terrine in a roasting pan and fill the pan with hot water to come halfway up the terrine. Bake for about 1 hour and 30 minutes. Remove the lid and bake for 15 minutes.

7. Let cool for 30 minutes. Press the terrine with a weight until completely cooled. Refrigerate for at least 2 days before serving.

From Françoise:

• You can substitute rabbit for the hare.

PHEASANT, VEAL, AND PORK TERRINE
- Terrine de faisan -

❖ ADVANCED ❖ EXPENSIVE ❖ 3 HOURS, PLUS MARINATING AND CHILLING ❖ SERVES 10 TO 12

MARINADE

1 cup red or white wine

¾ cup Madeira (optional)

1 tablespoon oil

1 onion, thinly sliced

1 small carrot, thinly sliced crosswise

1 garlic clove, crushed

1 bouquet garni made with parsley, thyme,
   and bay leaf

3 black peppercorns

2 ½– to 3 ½–pound pheasant

½ pound boneless veal shoulder, cut into chunks

½ pound boneless pork shoulder, cut into chunks

3 ½ ounces pork fat

1 tablespoon canned black truffle peelings,
   juice reserved

Salt and pepper

½ pound sliced barding fat or bacon

15 shelled pistachios, skin removed

❖ ❖ ❖ ❖ ❖

1. Make the marinade: In a large bowl, combine all the ingredients.

2. Cut and scrape the pheasant meat off the bones. Cut some of the breast meat into ½-inch strips and reserve. Cut the remaining meat into large pieces. Add all the pheasant meat with the veal and pork to the marinade. Cover and refrigerate for 1 to 2 days.

3. Preheat the oven to 350 degrees. Drain the meat, reserving the marinade liquid. Reserve the pheasant strips. Coarsely grind the remaining meats and pork fat. Using a wooden spoon, mix in a little of the marinade and truffle juice; the mixture should be a little loose. Season with salt and pepper. Cook a piece of the ground meat in a skillet and taste. Add salt and pepper to the remaining meat if necessary.

4. Line a terrine with the barding fat or bacon, reserving some for the top. Spread one-half of the ground meat in the terrine, then lay in the reserved pheasant strips lengthwise and spread the pistachios and truffles over the top. Cover with the remaining ground meat. Lay the remaining barding fat or bacon on top and cover with the lid.

5. Set the terrine in a roasting pan and fill the pan with hot water to come halfway up the terrine. Bake for about 1 hour and 30 minutes. Remove the lid and bake for 15 minutes.

6. Let cool for 30 minutes. Press the terrine with a weight until completely cooled. Refrigerate for at least 2 days before serving.

WILD GAME

CLASSIC ROASTED PHEASANT WITH LIVER TOASTS
- Faisan rôti -

❖ EASY   ❖ EXPENSIVE   ❖ 1 HOUR, 25 MINUTES   ❖ SERVES 4

4 tablespoons (½ stick) butter, plus more
  for brushing
3 ½-pound pheasant, liver reserved
Salt and pepper

Sliced barding fat
8 slices of crustless white sandwich bread,
  each cut into 2 triangles

❖ ❖ ❖ ❖ ❖

1. Preheat the oven to 400 degrees. Brush a roasting pan lightly with butter. Season the cavity of the pheasant with salt and pepper. Using kitchen string, tie the barding fat around the pheasant. Tie the legs together and the wings together. Set the bird in the roasting pan, transfer to the oven, and roast for about 1 hour.

2. Transfer the bird to a cutting board and remove the barding fat and string. Cover loosely with foil and let stand for 10 minutes.

3. Meanwhile, coarsely chop the pheasant liver. In a large skillet, melt 1 tablespoon of the butter over medium-high heat. Add the liver and sear. Drain, then transfer to a bowl and mash with a fork. Season with salt and pepper.

4. Wipe out the skillet. In it melt the remaining 3 tablespoons of butter over medium heat. Add the bread triangles in batches and cook until golden on both sides. Spread the liver mixture over the toasts.

5. Add 2 tablespoons of boiling water to the juices in the roasting pan and simmer, scraping up any brown bits stuck to the bottom. Taste for seasoning and pour into a warmed sauceboat.

6. Transfer the pheasant to a warmed platter. Surround with the liver toasts and serve, passing the pan juices separately.

From Françoise:
• You can wrap the pheasant in sliced pancetta instead of barding fat.

• If your pheasant is no longer young—the breastbone isn't pliable—you're better off pot-roasting it than oven-roasting it, for instance, following the recipe for Pot-Roasted Partridges with Buttery Cabbage and Sausage on page 381.

POT-ROASTED PHEASANT WITH WALNUT AND CURRANT STUFFING

- *Faisan farci aux noix* -

❖ ADVANCED   ❖ EXPENSIVE   ❖ 1 HOUR, 30 MINUTES, PLUS 2 HOURS MARINATING   ❖ SERVES 4

STUFFING

⅓ cup currants

½ cup Cognac

½ cup dry coarse bread crumbs

6 tablespoons milk

2 cups walnut halves

Pheasant liver and heart, chopped

1 large egg

Salt and pepper

3 ½-pound pheasant

Salt and pepper

Sliced barding fat or pancetta

5 tablespoons butter

1 carrot, peeled and chopped

1 onion, chopped

1 bouquet garni made with parsley, thyme,
    and bay leaf

4 slices of crustless white sandwich bread,
    each cut into 2 triangles

❖ ❖ ❖ ❖ ❖

1. Make the stuffing: In a small bowl, soak the currants in the Cognac for at least 2 hours. Drain, reserving the Cognac. In another small bowl, soak the bread crumbs in the milk, then squeeze dry. Reserve 12 of the walnut halves and coarsely chop the rest. In a medium bowl, mix the bread crumbs with the currants, chopped walnuts, liver, heart, and egg. Season well with salt and pepper.

2. Preheat the oven to 350 degrees. Pack the stuffing into the pheasant. Season the outside with salt and pepper. Using kitchen string, tie the barding fat or pancetta around the bird. Tie the legs together and the wings together.

3. In a flameproof casserole, melt 3 tablespoons of the butter over medium heat. Add the pheasant and cook until nicely browned all over. Add the carrot, onion, and bouquet garni. Transfer the pot to the oven and roast, uncovered, for 10 minutes, then cover and cook for about 1 hour.

4. Meanwhile, in a large skillet, melt the remaining 2 tablespoons of butter over medium heat. Add the bread triangles in batches and cook until golden on both sides.

5. Transfer the bird to a cutting board and remove the barding fat and string. Cover loosely with foil and let stand for 10 minutes. Spoon the stuffing into a bowl.

6. Meanwhile, add the reserved Cognac to the juices in the roasting pan and simmer, scraping up any brown bits stuck to the bottom. Tilt the pan and carefully ignite. When the flames subside, taste for seasoning.

7. Transfer the pheasant to a warmed platter. Decorate with the reserved walnut halves and the toasts. Strain the pan juices over the bird and serve with the stuffing.

continued

WILD GAME

From Françoise:

• Coarsely chop the walnut haves using a large chef's knife. They become too finely chopped when ground in a food processor.

• If you like, you can spread a little of the stuffing or some store-bought liver pâté on the toasts and top with a walnut half.

• Serve with sautéed potatoes, fries, or chips and unsweetened applesauce.

SLOW-COOKED PHEASANT WITH RED WINE SAUCE
- Salmis de faisan -

❖ ADVANCED　　　　❖ EXPENSIVE　　　　❖ 1 HOUR, 45 MINUTES　　　　❖ SERVES 4

7 tablespoons butter

3 ½-pound pheasant, head, wingtips, neck, and giblets reserved

1 tablespoon all-purpose flour

¾ cup dry white wine

1 onion, cut into ¼-inch dice

1 carrot, peeled and cut into ¼-inch dice

1 tablespoon tomato paste

¾ cup Cognac

1 bouquet garni made with parsley, thyme, and bay leaf

4 black peppercorns

Salt and pepper

5 ounces white mushrooms, quartered lengthwise

8 slices of crustless white sandwich bread, each cut into 2 triangles

1 tablespoon canned black truffle peelings, juice reserved

❖　❖　❖　❖　❖

1. In a medium saucepan, melt 1 tablespoon of the butter over medium-high heat. Add the pheasant head, wingtips, neck, and giblets and cook until well browned. Stir in the flour. Add 6 tablespoons of the wine and ¾ cup of water. Cover and bring to a boil, then reduce the heat to low and cook for 30 minutes. Strain the broth.

2. Cut the pheasant into 4 serving pieces, removing the back. In a flameproof casserole, melt 2 tablespoons of the remaining butter over medium heat. Add the pheasant pieces and cook until nicely browned all over. Add the onion, carrot, and tomato paste. Add the Cognac and bring to a simmer, then tilt the pot and carefully ignite. When the flames subside, add the remaining 6 tablespoons of wine, the broth, bouquet garni, and peppercorns. Season with salt. Cover and bring to a boil, then reduce the heat to low and cook for 1 hour.

3. Meanwhile, in a medium skillet, melt 1 tablespoon of the remaining butter over medium-high heat. Add the mushrooms,

season with salt and pepper, and cook, stirring occasionally, until tender.

4. In a large skillet, melt the remaining 3 tablespoons of butter over medium heat. Add the bread triangles in batches and cook until golden on both sides.

5. Using tongs, transfer the pheasant pieces to a warmed serving dish. Add the mushrooms and truffle peelings and juice to the casserole

and cook until slightly thickened. Remove the bouquet garni. Pour the sauce over the pheasant, add the toasts to the dish, and serve.

From Françoise:

• This recipe can be prepared through Step 3 several hours in advance. Just before serving, reheat the pheasant gently in the sauce along with the mushrooms and truffles. Fry the bread triangles at the same time.

MARINATED HARE STEW WITH MUSHROOMS
- *Civet de lièvre* -

❖ ADVANCED   ❖ EXPENSIVE   ❖ 3 HOURS, PLUS 1 TO 2 DAYS MARINATING   ❖ SERVES 6

MARINADE

3 cups red wine

3 tablespoons oil

3 tablespoons vinegar

1 carrot, thinly sliced crosswise

2 shallots, thinly sliced

1 onion, thinly sliced

1 garlic clove, crushed

1 bouquet garni made with parsley, thyme, and bay leaf

1 sage sprig

1 tarragon sprig

6 black peppercorns

2 whole cloves

1 hare, cut into serving pieces, blood and liver reserved

½ pound thick-sliced pancetta, cut crosswise into ¼-inch-thick strips

7 tablespoons butter

1 tablespoon all-purpose flour

1 tablespoon tomato paste

¼ cup Cognac or other eau-de-vie

Salt and pepper

6 slices of baguette

1 ounce pork fat, chopped

12 pearl onions, peeled

1 pound small white mushrooms

❖   ❖   ❖   ❖   ❖

1. Make the marinade: In a large bowl, combine all the ingredients. Add the hare pieces and liver, cover, and refrigerate for 1 to 2 days, turning the hare occasionally. Drain the hare, liver, and vegetables, reserving the marinade. Pat the hare pieces, liver, and vegetables dry with paper towels.

2. Add the pancetta to a small saucepan of cold water and bring to a boil, then drain.

3. In a flameproof casserole, melt 2 tablespoons of the butter. Add the blanched pancetta and

continued

373

cook until lightly browned. Remove to a bowl. Add the hare pieces to the pot and cook until nicely browned all over. Remove to the bowl. Add the vegetables from the marinade and cook, stirring, until lightly browned. Stir in the flour, then the tomato paste. Return the hare and pancetta to the pot. Add the Cognac or other eau-de-vie and bring to a boil, then tilt the pot and carefully ignite. When the flames subside, add the herbs and spices and enough wine from the marinade to cover the hare. Season with salt and pepper. Cover and bring to a boil, then reduce the heat to low and cook until tender, about 2 hours.

4. Meanwhile, in a large skillet, melt 3 tablespoons of the remaining butter over medium heat. Add the baguette slices and cook until golden on both sides. Transfer to a plate. Add the pork fat to the skillet, reduce the heat to low, and cook until melted. Coarsely chop the hare liver, add to the skillet, increase the heat to medium-high, and cook until nicely browned on the outside and still rosy inside. Mash the liver with the fat in the skillet. Spread the liver mixture over the baguette toasts.

5. Using tongs, transfer the hare pieces to a warmed serving dish. Strain the cooking liquid into a medium saucepan, reserving the pancetta. Add the pearl onions and reserved pancetta to the pan and simmer until the sauce is slightly thickened and well flavored, about 15 minutes.

6. Meanwhile, in a large saucepan, melt the remaining 2 tablespoons of butter over medium-high heat. Add the mushrooms and cook, stirring occasionally, until tender. Add them to the hare.

7. Just before serving, remove the sauce from the heat. Using a wooden spoon, stir in the blood. Pour the sauce over the hare and serve with the liver toasts.

From Françoise:
• Bacon can be substituted for the pancetta.

• Instead of the pork fat, you can use pancetta or bacon and cook it until the fat melts.

• If you can get the fresh blood from the hare, mix it with a dash of vinegar—which keeps the blood from coagulating—and refrigerate until using. Or you might be able to special order pork blood from a butcher.

PAN-SEARED VENISON CHOPS WITH JUNIPER BERRY SAUCE

- Côtelettes de chevreuil au genièvre -

❖ EASY   ❖ EXPENSIVE   ❖ 1 HOUR, 30 MINUTES   ❖ SERVES 4

3 tablespoons butter

8 venison chops, bones reserved

1 small onion, chopped

1 small carrot, peeled and chopped

1 garlic clove, crushed

10 juniper berries, crushed

1 teaspoon tomato paste

1 tablespoon all-purpose flour

5 tablespoons sloe gin

6 tablespoons vinegar

1 ½ cups red wine

1 bouquet garni made with parsley, thyme, and bay leaf

4 black peppercorns

Salt

½ tablespoon oil

❖   ❖   ❖   ❖   ❖

1. In a medium saucepan, melt 1 tablespoon of the butter over medium heat. Add the venison bones, onion, carrot, and garlic and cook until nicely browned. Add the juniper berries and tomato paste. Stir in the flour. Add ¼ cup of the sloe gin and bring to a simmer. Tilt the pan and carefully ignite. When the flames subside, add the vinegar, wine, bouquet garni, and peppercorns. Season with salt. Cover and bring to a boil, then reduce the heat to low and cook for 1 hour. Strain the broth.

2. In a large skillet, melt 1 tablespoon of the remaining butter in the oil over high heat. Add the venison chops and cook until nicely browned on both sides, about 2 minutes per side for rare meat. Transfer the chops to a warmed platter.

3. Add the remaining 1 tablespoon of sloe gin and the broth to the skillet. Bring to a simmer, scraping up any brown bits stuck to the bottom, and cook for 1 minute. Remove the skillet from the heat and whisk in the remaining tablespoon of butter until it melts creamily. Pour the sauce over the venison and serve.

From Françoise:

• Since preparing the sauce takes a fairly long time, I recommend doing it several hours in advance. The quality won't suffer.

• If the broth cooks down too quickly, add a little water, though what you want is a reduced and unctuous sauce for serving.

• Scrape the bottom of the skillet well with a wooden spoon to get all the delicious flavor from the browned cooking juices.

• Venison chops don't need marinating. But if you really want to marinate them, you can add them to one of the game marinades and refrigerate for a few hours.

WILD GAME

ROAST VENISON WITH BUTTERY APPLES

- *Rôti de chevreuil aux pommes* -

❖ INTERMEDIATE   ❖ EXPENSIVE   ❖ 1 HOUR, 45 MINUTES, PLUS 2 DAYS MARINATING   ❖ SERVES 4

MARINADE

2 tablespoons oil

2 onions, thinly sliced

2 carrots, thinly sliced

2 shallots, thinly sliced

3 cups white or red wine

½ cup vinegar

1 celery rib, thinly sliced

2 garlic cloves, crushed

1 bouquet garni made with parsley, thyme,
   and bay leaf

2 whole cloves

3 black peppercorns

1 rosemary sprig

2-pound boneless venison roast, tied

3 tablespoons butter, plus more for brushing

Salt

2 pounds apples

❖ ❖ ❖ ❖ ❖

1. Make the marinade: In a medium sauce-pan, heat the oil over medium heat. Add the onions, carrots, and shallots and cook until lightly browned. Add the wine, vinegar, celery, garlic, bouquet garni, cloves, peppercorns, and rosemary. Bring to a boil over medium-high heat, then reduce the heat to low and sim-mer, uncovered, for 30 to 40 minutes. Let cool completely.

2. In a large bowl, pour the marinade over the venison. Cover and refrigerate for 2 days, turn-ing the meat occasionally.

3. Preheat the oven to 425 degrees. Drain the venison and pat dry with paper towels. Reserve the vegetables, herbs, and spices. Brush a roasting pan lightly with butter. Spread out the reserved vegetables, herbs, and spices in the pan and set the meat on top. Season with salt.

4. Peel the apples. Working from the stem end and using a melon baller, apple corer, or small, sharp knife, remove the interior core

and seeds to within ½ inch of the bottom. Add the 3 tablespoons of butter to the insides and arrange the apples around the meat.

5. Transfer the pan to the oven and roast the meat for 30 to 40 minutes. Transfer the meat to a cutting board and remove the string. Cover loosely with foil and let stand for 10 minutes. Arrange the apples on a warmed platter.

6. Meanwhile, add ¼ cup of water to the roast-ing pan. Bring to a simmer, scraping up any brown bits stuck to the bottom, and cook until slightly thickened and well flavored. Season to taste. Strain into a warm sauceboat.

7. Set the meat on the platter and serve, pass-ing the pan juices separately.

From Françoise:

• The venison roast can be from the tenderloin, leg, or rib.

- The general rule for roasting venison is 15 to 20 minutes per pound. The cooking time can be shorter or longer, depending on the firmness of the meat.

- With all game, and with venison in particular, serve chestnut puree, unsweetened applesauce, cranberry or blueberry jelly, but also steamed or boiled new potatoes.

ROAST VENISON LEG WITH CREAMY RED CURRANT SAUCE
- Gigue de chevreuil grand veneur -

❖ INTERMEDIATE ❖ EXPENSIVE ❖ 3 HOURS, PLUS 2 DAYS MARINATING ❖ SERVES 8

WILD GAME

4 ½-pound bone-in leg of venison, boned and tied, trimmings and bones reserved

2 tablespoons oil

MARINADE

2 cups dry white wine

¼ cup oil

1 onion, thinly sliced

1 carrot, thinly sliced

2 shallots, thinly sliced

1 garlic clove, crushed

1 bouquet garni made with parsley, thyme, and bay leaf

Black peppercorns

GRAND VENEUR SAUCE

2 ½ ounces pork fat, chopped

1 veal bone, cracked

1 onion, chopped

1 carrot, peeled and chopped

3 tablespoons all-purpose flour

1 garlic clove, crushed

Salt

2 black peppercorns, crushed

2 tablespoons crème fraîche

1 tablespoon red currant jelly

❖ ❖ ❖ ❖ ❖

1. Make the marinade: In a large bowl, combine the boned leg of venison and trimmings with the marinade ingredients. Cover and refrigerate for 2 days, turning the meat occasionally. Remove the venison and trimmings and pat dry. Reserve the marinade.

2. Make the grand veneur sauce: In a large saucepan, melt the pork fat over low heat. Add the venison trimmings and bones, veal bone, onion, and carrot, increase the heat to medium, and cook until nicely browned. Stir in the flour and cook until browned. Add the garlic and reserved marinade, including the bouquet garni. Season with salt. Bring to a boil, then reduce the heat to low and cook, uncovered, for 1 hour and 30 minutes. Add the peppercorns and cook for 30 minutes longer.

3. Preheat the oven to 450 degrees. Heat a roasting pan in the oven. Meanwhile, in a large skillet, heat the oil over high heat. Add the

continued

venison and cook until nicely browned all over. Transfer the meat to the hot roasting pan and cook for 40 to 50 minutes, depending on the desired doneness.

4. Transfer the meat to a cutting board and remove the string. Cover loosely with foil and let stand for 10 minutes.

5. Strain the grand veneur sauce into a saucepan. Bring to a simmer and whisk in the crème fraîche. Cook until slightly thickened. Remove the pan from the heat and whisk in the red currant jelly. Taste for seasoning; it should be peppery. Pour into a warmed sauceboat.

6. Carve the venison and arrange on a warmed platter. Serve with the grand veneur sauce.

From Françoise:
• Serve with Pommes Dauphine (page 585) and baked tartlet shells or toasts spread with jelly. You can also pass red currant, cranberry, or blueberry jelly separately.

MARINATED BOAR STEW
- Sauté de marcassin -

❖ INTERMEDIATE   ❖ EXPENSIVE   ❖ 1 HOUR, 30 MINUTES, PLUS 2 TO 3 DAYS MARINATING   ❖ SERVES 4

2 pounds boneless shoulder of young boar,
   cut into 1½-inch pieces
3 tablespoons oil
1 tablespoon all-purpose flour
1 teaspoon tomato paste
3 tomatoes, peeled, seeded, and chopped
Salt and pepper
2 cups beef broth

MARINADE
2 cups dry white wine
6 tablespoons oil
1 onion, thinly sliced
1 carrot, peeled and thinly sliced
2 shallots, thinly sliced
1 garlic clove, crushed
1 bouquet garni made with parsley, thyme,
   and bay leaf
5 black peppercorns

❖   ❖   ❖   ❖   ❖

1. Make the marinade: In a large bowl, combine the pieces of meat with the marinade ingredients. Cover and refrigerate for 2 to 3 days, turning the meat occasionally. Drain the meat and vegetables and pat dry. Reserve the remaining marinade.

2. In a flameproof casserole, heat the oil over high heat. Add the meat and cook until nicely browned on all sides. Remove to a bowl. Add the marinade vegetables, sprinkle with the flour, and cook, stirring often, until lightly browned. Return the meat to the pot and add the tomato paste, tomatoes, and remaining marinade. Season with salt and pepper. Bring to a boil and cook, uncovered, for 10 minutes. Add the broth, cover, and bring to a boil, then reduce the heat to low and cook for about 1 hour and 15 minutes.

3. Remove the bouquet garni. Transfer the stew to a warmed serving dish and serve.

From Françoise:
• Serve with sliced country bread fried in butter until golden, boiled new potatoes, and unsweetened applesauce.

• The secret to flavorful frozen young boar: Add the meat to the marinade ingredients without defrosting it first. It has plenty of time to defrost in the refrigerator while absorbing all the aromatic flavors.

ROASTED YOUNG BOAR WITH CREAMY RED CURRANT SAUCE
- *Marcassin rôti sauce grand veneur* -

❖ ADVANCED   ❖ EXPENSIVE   ❖ 1 HOUR, 30 MINUTES, PLUS 2 DAYS MARINATING   ❖ SERVES 6 TO 8

3 ½-pound boneless young boar roast, tied, trimmings reserved
2 tablespoons butter, softened
Salt and pepper

MARINADE
1 cup red wine
6 tablespoons vinegar
6 tablespoons oil
2 onions, thinly sliced
2 carrots, peeled and thinly sliced
1 celery rib, thinly sliced

1 garlic clove, crushed
1 bouquet garni made with parsley, thyme, and bay leaf
5 black peppercorns

SAUCE
3 ½ ounces pork fat, chopped
3 tablespoons all-purpose flour
Salt and pepper
¼ cup crème fraîche
1 teaspoon Dijon mustard
1 teaspoon red currant jelly

❖ ❖ ❖ ❖ ❖

1. Make the marinade: In a large bowl, combine the meat and trimmings with the marinade ingredients. Cover and refrigerate for 2 days, turning the meat occasionally. Remove the meat, trimmings, and vegetables and pat dry. Reserve the marinade.

2. Make the sauce: In a large saucepan, melt the pork fat over low heat. Add the meat trimmings and marinade vegetables, increase the heat to medium, and cook until nicely

browned. Stir in the flour and cook until lightly browned. Add 1 ½ cups of the reserved marinade with the bouquet garni and 3 cups of water. Season with salt and pepper. Bring to a boil, then reduce the heat to low and cook, uncovered, for 1 hour.

3. Meanwhile, preheat the oven to 425 degrees. Set the meat in a roasting pan and brush with

continued

the butter. Season with salt and pepper. Transfer to the oven and roast for 30 to 35 minutes.

4. Transfer the meat to a cutting board and remove the string. Cover loosely with foil and let stand for 10 minutes.

5. Add ¾ cup of the reserved marinade to the roasting pan and simmer, scraping up any brown bits stuck to the bottom, for 2 to 3 minutes. Strain in the sauce. Bring to a simmer and whisk in the crème fraîche. Cook until slightly thickened. Remove the pan from the heat and whisk in the mustard and red currant jelly. Taste for seasoning. Pour into a warmed sauceboat.

6. Carve the meat and arrange on a warmed platter. Serve with the sauce.

From Françoise:

• The boar roast can be from the leg, shoulder end of the loin, or center rib.

• Serve with a chestnut puree, enriched with butter and crème fraîche.

• Since this dish takes a long time to prepare, it's best to make it for at least 8 people. If you're serving just 2 or 3 people, buy 5-ounce boar tenderloin steaks instead of the roast. Reduce the marinade quantities by one-third and marinate the steaks for only 3 or 4 hours. Cut the ingredients for the sauce in half.

• If you don't use the red currant jelly in the sauce, what you have is a poivrade sauce, which is also delicious.

• Cranberry or blueberry jelly can replace the red currant jelly.

DOUBLE-CRUSTED PIE WITH YOUNG BOAR AND PRUNES
- Tourte au marcassin à la mode d'Agen -

❖ ADVANCED   ❖ MODERATE   ❖ 1 HOUR, 45 MINUTES, PLUS 1 DAY MARINATING   ❖ SERVES 6

MARINADE

3 tablespoons oil

1 small carrot, chopped

1 onion, chopped

1 or 2 shallots, chopped

1 small celery rib, chopped

1 garlic clove, crushed

3 cups red wine

6 tablespoons vinegar

1 bouquet garni made with parsley, thyme, and bay leaf

3 black peppercorns

1 whole clove

1¼ pounds boneless shoulder of young boar, cut into chunks

1 pound boneless pork top loin (shoulder end of the loin), cut into chunks

1 pound pitted prunes

Salt and pepper

1 large egg, lightly beaten

PÂTE BRISÉE

1½ cups all-purpose flour

¾ teaspoon salt

7 tablespoons unsalted butter, cut into pieces

1. Make the marinade: In a saucepan, heat the oil over medium heat. Add the carrot, onion, and shallots and cook until lightly browned. Add the remaining marinade ingredients, bring to a boil, then reduce the heat to low and cook, uncovered, for 30 minutes. Let cool completely. In a large bowl, combine the boar, pork, and prunes with the cooled marinade. Cover and refrigerate for 1 day.

2. Make the pâte brisée: In a bowl, combine the flour with the salt and butter. Rub the butter into the flour between your palms. Sprinkle over 5 or 6 tablespoons of water and knead briefly until large crumbs form. Press into a disk. On a lightly floured surface, scrape the dough away from you with the heel of your hand in a long sliding motion, then press into a disk; repeat 3 times. Divide into 2 disks, wrap, and refrigerate until firm, 15 to 20 minutes.

3. Scrape the marinade off the meats and prunes. Discard the marinade. Coarsely chop the meat. Season with salt and pepper.

4. Preheat the oven to 400 degrees. On a lightly floured work surface, roll 1 disk into a round. Wrap the dough around the rolling pin and fit it into an 8-inch springform pan.

5. Roll the second disk into a round. Spread half the meat in the shell. Arrange the prunes on top and cover with the remaining meat. Brush the edges of the rounds with water. Press the second round on top, pinching the edges together to seal. Poke a hole in the center of the pie and insert a foil "chimney" to allow steam to escape. Brush the top with the beaten egg. Set on a baking sheet, transfer to the oven, and bake for about 45 minutes.

From Françoise:

• To soften dried-out prunes quickly, add them to a bowl, cover with water, tea, or wine, and cook in the microwave oven on high for about 1 minute. Let the prunes cool in the liquid. Be careful not to overcook the prunes or they'll toughen.

POT-ROASTED PARTRIDGES WITH BUTTERY CABBAGE AND SAUSAGE

- *Perdrix en chartreuse* -

❖ INTERMEDIATE   ❖ EXPENSIVE   ❖ 2 HOURS, 30 MINUTES   ❖ SERVES 4

2-pound Savoy cabbage, cut into 8 wedges and cored

3 tablespoons butter, plus more for brushing

10 ounces thick-sliced pancetta, cut crosswise into ¼-inch-thick strips

2 partridges, about 1 pound each, legs and wings tied

2 carrots, peeled and sliced crosswise

1 onion, thinly sliced

½ pound sweet Italian sausage, sliced crosswise

Salt and pepper

continued

1. Bring a large pot of water to a boil. Add the cabbage and boil for 10 minutes. Drain.

2. In a flameproof casserole, melt the butter over low heat. Add the pancetta and cook until just beginning to brown. Push to the side of the pot. Add the partridges, increase the heat to medium-high, and cook until nicely browned all over. Add the cabbage, carrots, onion, and sausage. Reduce the heat to low, cover, and cook for 1 hour and 30 minutes to 2 hours.

3. Transfer the partridges to a cutting board and remove the string. Cover loosely with foil and let stand for 10 minutes.

4. Meanwhile, brush a soufflé or other deep baking dish with butter. Line the bottom and sides with the sliced carrots and sausage tightly packed together. Pack the cabbage inside.

5. Invert a round platter over the soufflé dish. Holding the dish and platter together, quickly invert the cabbage mold onto the platter. Set the partridges on the cabbage and serve.

From Françoise:
• Pheasant can be prepared in the same way using the same proportions.

VINE LEAF–ROASTED YOUNG PARTRIDGES
Perdreaux rôtis à la feuille de vigne

❖ EASY ❖ EXPENSIVE ❖ 40 MINUTES ❖ SERVES 4

4 small young partridges, livers reserved
6 tablespoons butter, 2 tablespoons softened
Salt and pepper
4 fresh grapevine leaves

Sliced barding fat
Pinch of thyme leaves
4 slices of crustless white sandwich bread

❖ ❖ ❖ ❖ ❖

1. Preheat the oven to 350 degrees. Brush the partridges with the 2 tablespoons of softened butter. Season with salt and pepper. Press 1 vine leaf on the breast of each partridge, then wrap in the barding fat. Using kitchen string, tie the vine leaves and barding fat in place. Tie the legs together and the wings together. Set the birds in a roasting pan, transfer to the oven, and roast for 15 minutes, basting with the pan juices.

2. Take the partridges out of the oven. Remove the barding fat and vine leaves, reserving the leaves. Return the partridges to the oven and roast until browned all over, about 5 minutes.

3. Transfer the partridges to a cutting board and remove the string. Cover loosely with foil and let stand for 10 minutes.

4. Meanwhile, coarsely chop the partridge livers. In a large skillet, melt 1 tablespoon of the

butter over medium-high heat. Add the livers, season with salt, pepper, and the thyme, and sear. Drain, then transfer to a bowl and mash with a fork.

5. Wipe out the skillet. In it melt the remaining 3 tablespoons of butter over medium heat. Add the bread slices in batches and cook until golden on both sides. Spread the liver mixture over the toasts. Arrange on a warmed platter.

6. Set each partridge on a liver toast, top with a vine leaf, and serve.

From Françoise:
• Brined vine leaves, also called grape leaves, can be substituted for fresh leaves. Pat them dry with paper towels before using.

• Instead of using barding fat, you can wrap the partridges in sliced pancetta or bacon, which you'll probably want to eat!

• If you cook 2 larger partridges to serve 4 people, roast them for at least 25 minutes. But if the birds are much larger, they're probably not young anymore. You're better off braising them in a casserole.

• Serve with potato chips or sautéed potatoes and watercress sprigs. Or you might peel some large grapes and sauté them in butter with a sprinkling of sugar as an accompaniment. (Unpeeled grapes are okay, too.) Moisten them with a little Cognac or other eau-de-vie just before serving.

• Young partridges can be prepared in the same ways as squabs.

SEAFOOD

FISH FILLETS STEAMED ON A PLATE
WITH LEMON AND BUTTER

- *Filets de poisson à la vapeur* -

❖ EASY   ❖ MODERATE   ❖ 15 MINUTES   ❖ SERVES 4

1 ½ pounds thin, skinless fish fillets
Juice of 1 lemon

Salt and pepper
2 tablespoons butter, cut into ¼-inch dice

❖ ❖ ❖ ❖ ❖

1. Bring a large saucepan of water to a boil.

2. Lay the fish fillets, skinned side down, on a plate larger than the saucepan. Drizzle with lemon juice, season with salt and pepper, and dot with the butter. Cover with a second plate and set on the saucepan. Steam for 10 to 12 minutes, depending on the thickness of the fillets. Transfer to a platter or plates and serve.

From Françoise:
• This is a dish for serious fish lovers. Use only super-fresh, pristine fish.

• For a guest on a diet, you can prepare this fish without the butter. It's delicious just sprinkled with chopped herbs.

SAUTÉED FISH FILLETS WITH CURRY CRUMBS

- *Poisson pané au curry* -

❖ EASY   ❖ MODERATE   ❖ 15 MINUTES   ❖ SERVES 4

All-purpose flour for dredging
2 large eggs, lightly beaten
1 cup dry bread crumbs
Salt and pepper

1 ½ pounds skinless fish fillets
2 teaspoons curry powder
3 tablespoons butter
1 tablespoon oil

❖ ❖ ❖ ❖ ❖

1. In separate soup plates, spread the flour, eggs, and bread crumbs. Season the eggs with salt and pepper. Season the fish fillets with salt and pepper and dust lightly with the curry powder, patting off the excess. Then dredge them lightly in flour and dip in the eggs, letting the excess drip back into the plate. Dredge the fish in the bread crumbs, pressing lightly to help the crumbs adhere.

2. In a large skillet, melt the butter in the oil over medium heat. Add the fish and cook, turning once, until golden brown, 4 to 5 minutes per side. Transfer to a warmed platter and serve.

From Françoise:
• Curry powder is a blend of various ground spices, and the recipe varies according to the brand, though it usually contains ginger, coriander, saffron, chile powder, cumin, and cloves.

• If the fish fillets look a little dry on the plate, drizzle them with lemon juice.

CRISPY FISH FILLETS WITH LEMON
- *Poisson pané à l'anglaise* -

❖ EASY ❖ MODERATE ❖ 15 MINUTES ❖ SERVES 4

All-purpose flour for dredging
2 large eggs, lightly beaten
1 cup dry bread crumbs
Salt and pepper
1½ pounds thin skinless fish fillets or four 5- or 6-ounce skinless fish fillets

3 tablespoons butter
1 tablespoon oil
Chopped parsley leaves for sprinkling
1 lemon, cut into 4 wedges

❖ ❖ ❖ ❖ ❖

SEAFOOD

1. In separate soup plates, spread the flour, eggs, and bread crumbs. Season the eggs with salt and pepper. Season the fish fillets with salt and pepper, then dredge them lightly in flour and dip in the eggs, letting the excess drip back into the plate. Dredge the fish in the bread crumbs, pressing lightly to help the crumbs adhere.

2. In a large skillet, melt the butter in the oil over medium heat. Add the fish and cook, turning once, until golden brown, 4 to 5 minutes per side, depending on the thickness. Transfer to a warmed platter and sprinkle with parsley. Serve with the lemon wedges.

From Françoise:
• This great classic can be made with many different kinds of fish, whole or filleted. The weight of the fillets can vary from one variety of fish to another.

• Start out with a good amount of butter and oil. The fish needs to bathe comfortably in the fat to cook without sticking.

• Do not pierce the fish with a fork while it cooks. Instead, shake the pan sharply to keep the fish from sticking.

• You could baste the fish with more melted butter just before serving, but that might be a bit much.

continued

• Make your own bread crumbs by grinding stale bread in the food processor, or crushing it on a cutting board. Cover it with a kitchen towel so the crumbs don't go everywhere.

• To dress up this dish, pass Béarnaise Sauce, homemade (page 632) or store-bought, at the table. Warm it up while the fish cooks. A further refinement: Surround the fish with warm artichoke bottoms filled with the sauce.

PAN-SEARED FISH FILLETS WITH BUTTER AND LEMON
- *Poisson meunière* -

❖ EASY   ❖ MODERATE   ❖ 10 MINUTES   ❖ SERVES 4

1 ½ pounds skinless fish fillets
Salt and pepper
All-purpose flour for dusting

3 tablespoons butter
Juice of 1 lemon
Chopped parsley leaves for sprinkling

❖ ❖ ❖ ❖ ❖

1. Season the fish fillets with salt and pepper and dust lightly with flour, patting off the excess.

2. In a large skillet, melt the butter over medium heat. Add the fish and cook, turning once, until lightly browned, 3 to 4 minutes per side.

3. Transfer the fish to a warmed platter. Pour the pan juices on top and drizzle with lemon juice. Sprinkle with parsley and serve.

From Françoise:
• You can also cook whole, small (one-serving) flat fish this way. If they are any larger, cut them crosswise into steaks first.

• Remember to lightly dust the fish with flour before cooking, patting off the excess. The flour absorbs any moisture and makes the fish brown beautifully in the hot butter.

• The cooking time, of course, depends on the thickness of the fillets.

• If you don't have any lemons in the house, warm a few drops of vinegar in the skillet after the fish has come out, then pour the pan juices over the fish.

ROLLED POACHED FISH FILLETS IN A CREAMY SAUCE WITH TARRAGON

- *Paupiettes de filets de poisson à la crème* -

❖ EASY ❖ MODERATE ❖ 25 MINUTES ❖ SERVES 4

1 ½ pounds thin, skinless fish fillets

Salt and pepper

1 tarragon sprig, stem removed

Splash of vinegar

1 bouquet garni made with parsley, thyme,
  and bay leaf

1 ½ tablespoons butter

1 ½ tablespoons all-purpose flour

1 cup court-bouillon (page 393)

Crème fraîche or 1 large egg yolk

❖ ❖ ❖ ❖ ❖

1. Season the fish fillets with salt and pepper. Sprinkle the skinned side of the fillets with the tarragon leaves. Carefully roll up, jelly-roll style. Spear with toothpicks or tie with kitchen string.

2. Transfer them to a skillet that fits them snugly. Barely cover them with water and add the vinegar. Tuck in the bouquet garni. Set over low heat and cook until it reaches a bare simmer. Remove the pan from the heat.

3. Meanwhile, in a small saucepan, melt the butter over medium heat. Whisk in the flour until it starts foaming. Whisk in the court-bouillon. Season with salt and pepper. Bring to a boil, whisking, then reduce the heat to very low and cook for 10 minutes. Whisk in the crème fraîche or remove the pan from the heat and whisk in the egg yolk.

4. Drain the fish and remove the toothpicks or string. Transfer to a warmed serving dish, pour the sauce over the top, and serve.

From Françoise:
• Serve with plain rice or steamed new potatoes.

SEAFOOD

OVEN-POACHED FISH FILLETS WITH MUSHROOMS AND CREAMY SAUCE

- *Filets de poisson bonne femme* -

✧ EASY　　　✧ MODERATE　　　✧ 30 MINUTES　　　✧ SERVES 4

1 tablespoon butter, softened, plus more
  for brushing
½ pound white mushrooms, thinly sliced
2 shallots, finely chopped

1 ½ pounds skinless fish fillets
6 tablespoons dry white wine
Salt and pepper
1 teaspoon all-purpose flour

✧　✧　✧　✧　✧

1. Preheat the oven to 400 degrees. Brush a roasting pan with butter. Spread the mushrooms and shallots in the dish and cover with the fish fillets. Add the wine and ¾ cup of water and season with salt and pepper. Cover with foil, transfer to the oven, and poach for 10 to 20 minutes, depending on the thickness of the fish.

2. In a cup, mash the 1 tablespoon of butter with the flour. Using a slotted fish slice, transfer the fish to a warmed serving dish. Set the roasting pan over medium heat. Gradually whisk in the paste and simmer for 1 to 2 minutes. Pour over the fish and serve.

From Françoise:

• You can replace the white wine with the juice of half a lemon. Make up the difference in cooking liquid by adding more water.

• If you're preparing this for company, add a few cooked, shelled shrimp and mussels or cockles and a little crème fraîche to the roasting pan after the fish comes out.

• Serve with plain rice.

FROMAGE BLANC–BAKED FISH FILLETS WITH BASIL

- *Filets de poisson au fromage blanc et au basilic* -

❖ EASY ❖ MODERATE ❖ 35 MINUTES ❖ SERVES 4

2 tablespoons butter, cut into ¼-inch dice,
 plus more for brushing
6 tablespoons fromage blanc
6 tablespoons crème fraîche
Shredded basil leaves

1½ pounds thin, skinless fish fillets
Salt and pepper
Juice of ½ lemon
1 tablespoon dry bread crumbs

❖ ❖ ❖ ❖ ❖

1. Preheat the oven to 350 degrees. Generously butter a gratin dish. In a bowl, blend the fromage blanc with the crème fraîche and basil.

2. Spread the fish fillets on a platter. Season with salt and pepper. Drizzle with the lemon juice. Brush all over with the fromage blanc mixture. Fold the fillets in thirds.

3. Arrange them in the gratin dish, ends down. Sprinkle with the bread crumbs and dot with

the 2 tablespoons of butter. Transfer the fish to the oven and bake for about 25 minutes.

From Françoise:
• You can use frozen fish fillets to make this recipe without defrosting them. You won't be able to fold them, but otherwise proceed with the recipe, baking the fish a little longer.

SEAFOOD

CRISPY FISH AND MASHED POTATO PIE

- *Gratin de filets de poisson façon parmentier* -

❖ EASY ❖ MODERATE ❖ 1 HOUR ❖ SERVES 4

1 tablespoon vinegar
2 onions, halved and stuck with 2 whole cloves total
1 shallot, thinly sliced
1 bouquet garni made with parsley, thyme,
 and bay leaf
Salt
Black peppercorns
1½ pounds skinless fish fillets

2 pounds potatoes, peeled
1½ cups milk
3 tablespoons butter, plus more for brushing
Salt and pepper
4 hard–boiled eggs, sliced crosswise
½ cup shredded Gruyère cheese
Dry bread crumbs for sprinkling

continued

1. In a large sauté pan, make the court-bouillon: Combine 2 quarts of water with the vinegar, onions, shallot, bouquet garni, salt, and peppercorns. Bring to a boil over medium-high heat, then reduce the heat to low and simmer for 15 minutes. Let cool slightly.

2. Add the fish fillets to the court-bouillon. Set over medium heat, and when it comes to a simmer, adjust the heat so the fish cooks at a bare simmer for 10 to 15 minutes. Drain and break up the fish into large flakes.

3. Meanwhile, in a large saucepan of boiling salted water, cook the potatoes for 25 to 30 minutes. Drain.

4. Preheat the oven to 425 degrees. In a small saucepan, heat the milk over medium-low heat until barely simmering. Mash the potatoes. Beat in 2 tablespoons of the butter, then the hot milk. Season with salt and pepper.

5. Brush a gratin dish with butter. Spread half the mashed potatoes in the dish. Layer the fish, egg slices, and remaining mashed potatoes on top. Sprinkle with the cheese and bread crumbs. Dot with the remaining 1 tablespoon of butter. Transfer to the top shelf of the oven and bake until melted and golden, 10 to 15 minutes, and serve.

FLAKY ROLLED FISH PASTRY
- *Biscuit roulé au poisson* -

❖ INTERMEDIATE   ❖ MODERATE   ❖ 50 MINUTES   ❖ SERVES 6 TO 8

DOUGH
1 ¼ cups all–purpose flour
½ teaspoon salt
1 teaspoon baking powder
5 tablespoons unsalted butter, cut into pieces
1 large egg, lightly beaten
Milk for brushing

FILLING
2 tablespoons butter
1 onion, finely chopped
10 ounces cooked, flaked fish
Fresh lemon juice
Salt and pepper

❖ ❖ ❖ ❖ ❖

1. Make the dough: In a bowl, whisk the flour with the salt and baking powder. Add the butter and rub it into the flour between your palms. Add the egg and knead briefly until large crumbs form. Press into a disk. On a lightly floured surface, scrape the dough away from you with the heel of your hand in a long sliding motion, then press into a disk; repeat 3 times. Wrap and refrigerate until firm, 15 to 20 minutes.

2. Make the filling: In a large skillet, melt the butter over medium-low heat. Add the onion and cook until softened. Stir in the fish. Season with lemon juice, salt, and pepper.

3. Preheat the oven to 425 degrees. On a lightly floured work surface, roll the dough into a 10-by-12-inch rectangle about ⅛ inch thick. Spread the filling over the dough, leaving a

1-inch border. Roll up into a log, tucking in the ends as you go. Brush the log with milk. Pinch the seam to seal. Brush the log again with milk. Carefully transfer to a baking sheet.

4. Bake in the oven for 20 to 25 minutes. Set on a warmed platter and serve hot.

From Françoise:
• Use a large serrated knife to cut the log into neat slices.

• You can also serve tomato sauce with this fish pastry.

• If needed, reheat the pastry in the oven.

POACHED WHOLE FISH IN COURT-BOUILLON
- *Poisson au court-bouillon* -

❖ EASY   ❖ MODERATE   ❖ 30 MINUTES   ❖ SERVES 4

COURT-BOUILLON
1 tablespoon vinegar
2 onions, halved and stuck with 2 whole cloves total
1 shallot, thinly sliced
1 bouquet garni made with parsley, thyme, and bay leaf

Salt
Black peppercorns

2 ½-pound whole fish, cleaned, with head

❖ ❖ ❖ ❖ ❖

1. In a large sauté pan, make the court-boullion: Combine 2 quarts of water with the vinegar, onions, shallot, bouquet garni, salt, and peppercorns. Bring to a boil over medium-high heat, then reduce the heat to low and simmer for 15 minutes. Let cool slightly.

2. Rinse the fish and add it to the court-bouillon. Set over medium heat, and when it comes to a simmer, adjust the heat so the fish cooks at a bare simmer for 10 to 15 minutes, depending on the size.

3. Drain the fish and serve it warm, or let it cool completely in the court-bouillon and serve at room temperature.

From Françoise:
• Hake, porgy, cod, skate, pike, and salt cod can all be poached in a court-bouillon. You can also prepare fish steaks the same way, poaching them for only 5 minutes.

• The court-bouillon should simmer for at least 15 minutes to be flavorful.

• Never let fish cook at a rolling boil; it will toughen or break up.

• A whole fish easily falls apart during cooking. To keep it together, you might swaddle it in plenty of cheesecloth and tie the ends before

continued

SEAFOOD

adding it to the court-bouillon. Gently lift the fish out of the pan by the 2 cheesecloth ends and snip off the wrapper before serving.

• Serve warm poached fish with caper, curry, or tomato sauce. Serve cold poached fish with a simple vinaigrette, or mayonnaise or tartar sauce. (See the Sauces chapter, page 623.)

GOLDEN GRATINÉED FISH IN SCALLOP SHELLS
- Coquilles de poisson gratinées -

❖ INTERMEDIATE ❖ MODERATE ❖ 40 MINUTES ❖ SERVES 4

1 tablespoon vinegar

2 onions, halved and stuck with 2 whole cloves total

1 shallot, thinly sliced

1 bouquet garni made with parsley, thyme, and bay leaf

Salt

Black peppercorns

1-pound whole fish, cleaned, with head

2 tablespoons butter, cut into ¼-inch dice

MORNAY SAUCE

3 tablespoons butter

3 tablespoons all-purpose flour

2 cups milk

Salt and pepper

½ cup shredded Gruyère cheese

About 12 large scallop shells

❖ ❖ ❖ ❖ ❖

1. In a large sauté pan, make the court-bouillon: Combine 2 quarts of water with the vinegar, onions, shallot, bouquet garni, salt, and peppercorns. Bring to a boil over medium-high heat, then reduce the heat to low and simmer for 15 minutes. Let cool slightly.

2. Rinse the fish and add it to the court-bouillon. Set over medium heat, and when it comes to a simmer, adjust the heat so the fish cooks at a bare simmer for 10 minutes. Let it cool completely in the court-bouillon.

3. Meanwhile, make the Mornay sauce: In a small saucepan, melt the butter over medium heat. Whisk in the flour until it starts foaming. Whisk in the milk. Season with salt and pepper. Bring to a boil, whisking, then reduce the heat to very low and cook for 5 minutes.

Remove the pan from the heat and whisk in ¼ cup of the cheese.

4. Preheat the oven to 425 degrees. Drain the fish. Flake the fish, discarding the skin and bones. Fold the fish into the Mornay sauce. Spread the fish mixture in the scallop shells. Sprinkle the remaining cheese over the tops and dot with the butter.

5. Transfer the scallop shells to a baking sheet. Slide it onto the top shelf of the oven and bake until the tops are melted and golden, about 10 minutes; serve.

From Françoise:

• The Mornay sauce should be a little thicker than usual.

- If you don't especially like Mornay sauce, you can make this dish with Béchamel Sauce (page 634). Omit the Gruyère cheese and sprinkle dry bread crumbs over the top to get a golden crust.

- Almost all kinds of fish, even the most inexpensive ones, are suitable for this recipe.

- For the sauce—Mornay or Béchamel—you can replace the milk with the court-bouillon you used to poach the fish. If you do, don't salt it first.

CRISPY FRIED WHITEBAIT
- *Friture de petits poissons* -

❖ EASY   ❖ MODERATE   ❖ 20 MINUTES   ❖ SERVES 4

All-purpose flour for dredging
1 ½ to 2 pounds whole whitebait, cleaned,
  with heads
Salt

4 cups oil for frying
Parsley sprigs
1 lemon, cut into wedges

❖ ❖ ❖ ❖ ❖

1. Spread the flour in a large bowl. Rinse the fish and pat dry. Season the fish with salt, then toss them in the flour. Transfer the fish to a large sieve and tap to remove the excess flour.

2. In a large skillet, heat the oil to 375 degrees. Gently drop the fish into the oil without crowding and fry until golden, 1 to 3 minutes. Using a slotted spoon, transfer the fish to paper towels to drain as they are done. Transfer to a platter and keep warm in a low oven while frying the remaining fish. Serve very hot with the parsley and lemon wedges.

From Françoise:
- The smaller the fish, the hotter the oil must be when you add the fish, and the shorter the cooking time.

- Serve with Mayonnaise (page 624), mixed with a bit of chopped fines herbes.

- For a fun presentation, serve the fish in paper cones.

SEAFOOD

GOLDEN PAN-SAUTÉED HERRING WITH LEMON
- Harengs frais meunière -

❖ EASY   ❖ MODERATE   ❖ 15 MINUTES   ❖ SERVES 4

4 medium whole fresh herring, cleaned,
  with heads, roe reserved
Salt and pepper
All-purpose flour for dusting

2 tablespoons butter
1 tablespoon oil
1 lemon, cut into wedges

❖ ❖ ❖ ❖ ❖

1. Rinse the fish and pat dry. Season with salt and pepper and dust lightly with flour, patting off the excess.

2. In a large skillet, melt the butter in the oil over medium heat. Add the fish and cook, turning once, until lightly browned, 6 to 7 minutes per side.

3. Transfer the fish to a warmed platter and serve with the lemon wedges.

From Françoise:
• If herring doesn't entirely agree with you, try serving it with a pungent mustard sauce.

• Herring roe is delicious sautéed in butter. Try cooking it for 10 minutes over medium heat.

OVEN-BRAISED FRESH HERRING
WITH POTATOES AND ONIONS
- Harengs frais boulangère -

❖ EASY   ❖ MODERATE   ❖ 1 HOUR   ❖ SERVES 4

3 tablespoons butter, plus more for brushing
1½ pounds potatoes, peeled and thinly sliced
3 onions, thinly sliced
4 medium whole fresh herring, cleaned,
  with heads

Salt and pepper
1 shallot, finely chopped
Chopped parsley leaves

1. Preheat the oven to 350 degrees. Generously butter a gratin dish or roasting pan large enough to hold both the fish and potatoes. Spread the potatoes and onions in the dish. Rinse the fish and pat dry. Arrange the fish on top, add 6 tablespoons of water, and season with salt and pepper. Dot with the 3 tablespoons of butter. Transfer the dish to the oven and bake for about 45 minutes.

2. Sprinkle the fish with the shallot and parsley and serve.

From Françoise:

• The only problem with this dish is the herring bones. Otherwise, it's an excellent all-in-one recipe for lunch or dinner. The cooking takes a little time, but the fish doesn't require any attention once it's in the oven.

• If your fish is very fresh, you can hold it for a day or two in the refrigerator; any longer isn't a good idea. Have the fishmonger clean it for you or do it yourself as soon as you get it home so it keeps better. Wrap it in foil to contain the smell and store it in the coldest part of your refrigerator. Do not under any circumstances keep the fish in water; it will degrade quickly.

SMOKED HERRING WITH EGG, MUSTARD, AND SHALLOT SAUCE

- Harengs sauce Lucas -

❖ EASY   ❖ MODERATE   ❖ 20 MINUTES   ❖ SERVES 4

4 hard-boiled eggs, whites and yolks separated
1 shallot, coarsely chopped
Chopped parsley leaves
1 tablespoon Dijon mustard

5 tablespoons oil
¼ cup vinegar
1 pound smoked herring fillets, cut into pieces

❖ ❖ ❖ ❖ ❖

1. In a food processor, finely chop the egg yolks with the shallot, parsley, and mustard. Blend in the oil a few drops at a time to begin, then in a steady stream. Mix in the vinegar.

2. Finely chop or shred the egg whites. Spread the herring on a platter. Spoon the sauce over the top. Decorate with the egg whites and serve.

From Françoise:

• Vacuum-packed smoked herring needs only to be wiped off before using.

• If you don't have a food processor, you can mash the egg yolks, shallot, parsley, and mustard with a fork, then blend in the oil and vinegar using a whisk or electric beater to emulsify the sauce.

MARINATED SMOKED HERRING IN OIL

- *Harengs saurs à l'huile* -

❖ EASY   ❖ MODERATE   ❖ 15 MINUTES, PLUS 24 HOURS MARINATING   ❖ SERVES 4

1 pound smoked herring fillets

1 onion, thinly sliced

½ carrot, peeled and thinly sliced

Thyme sprigs

Bay leaves

1 garlic clove, crushed

Whole cloves to taste

1 small dried chile (optional)

1 ½ cups oil

❖ ❖ ❖ ❖ ❖

1. Rinse the herring under cold running water and pat dry with paper towels.

2. Layer them in a bowl with the onion, carrot, thyme, bay leaves, garlic, cloves, and chile, if using. Pour the oil over the top, cover, and refrigerate for at least 24 hours.

From Françoise:

• Vacuum-packed smoked herring isn't especially salty, so it is typically ready to serve. If that isn't the case, soak the fish in water or milk for an hour, turning it several times.

• This herring can be refrigerated for several days.

PAN-SEARED FRESH SARDINES WITH PARSLEY

- *Sardines fraîches poêlées et persillés* -

❖ EASY   ❖ MODERATE   ❖ 20 MINUTES   ❖ SERVES 4

1 ½ pounds fresh whole sardines, cleaned,
  with heads (about 24)

All-purpose flour for dusting

4 to 6 tablespoons butter

Salt and pepper

Chopped parsley leaves

1 lemon, cut into wedges (optional)

❖ ❖ ❖ ❖ ❖

1. Rinse the fish and pat dry. Dust lightly with flour, patting off the excess.

2. In a large skillet, melt 2 tablespoons of the butter over medium heat. Add the fish in batches and cook, turning once, until lightly browned, 2 to 3 minutes per side. Add more butter with each batch.

3. Transfer the fish as they are done to a warmed platter and season with salt and pepper. Sprinkle with parsley and serve with the lemon wedges, if using.

From Françoise:
• Sardines don't need to have their scales scraped off. They will come off when you wipe them with paper towels.

• To remove the fishy odor from a skillet, rub it with salt or boil a little vinegar in it. Better yet, designate one skillet for cooking fish.

• If your sardines have come right out of the water and are still firm, sauté them without dusting them with flour first.

CRISPY FRESH SARDINES WITH LEMON, GARLIC, AND PARSLEY

- Sardines fraîches gratinées -

❖ EASY   ❖ MODERATE   ❖ 30 MINUTES   ❖ SERVES 4

2 dozen small whole sardines
4 tablespoons (½ stick) butter, plus more
   for brushing
Salt and pepper

2 tablespoons dry bread crumbs
Juice of ½ lemon
1 small garlic clove, finely chopped
Chopped parsley leaves for sprinkling

❖ ❖ ❖ ❖ ❖

1. Preheat the oven to 400 degrees. Remove the sardine heads; the insides will come out at the same time. Rinse the fish and pat dry.

2. Brush a gratin dish with butter. Arrange the sardines in the dish and season with salt and pepper. Sprinkle with the bread crumbs and dot with the 4 tablespoons butter.

3. Transfer the fish to the oven and bake for 15 minutes. Drizzle the fish with the lemon juice, garlic, and parsley, and serve.

From Françoise:
• In some coastal regions of France, sardines fished straight from the sea are sprinkled with coarse salt. If yours are salted, you won't need to season them in Step 2.

SEAFOOD

GRILLED FRESH SARDINES
- *Sardines fraîches grillées* -

❖ EASY   ❖ MODERATE   ❖ 15 MINUTES   ❖ SERVES 4

**2 dozen small whole sardines, cleaned,
with heads**

**2 tablespoons oil
1 lemon, cut into wedges**

❖ ❖ ❖ ❖ ❖

1. Preheat a grill pan over high heat. Rinse the fish and pat dry. Lightly brush the fish with oil.

2. Grill the fish, turning once, until charred, 1 to 2 minutes per side. Transfer to a warmed platter and serve with the lemon wedges.

From Françoise:
• Sardines really need to be superfresh. You can check for freshness in several ways: no fishy smell. The skin is shiny and the scales aren't loose. The eyes aren't sunken and they're clear and bright. The fish is rigid and the flesh is firm and elastic. The gills are red and shiny, which you can tell by lifting them.

SARDINES IN OIL WITH HARD-BOILED EGGS
- *Sardines à l'huile* -

❖ VERY EASY   ❖ INEXPENSIVE   ❖ 15 MINUTES   ❖ SERVES 4

**8 oil-packed whole sardines
1 or 2 hard-boiled eggs, sliced crosswise or
yolks and whites chopped separately
Chopped parsley leaves for sprinkling**

**1 lemon, cut into wedges (optional)
Vinegar mixed with finely chopped shallots for
serving (optional)**

❖ ❖ ❖ ❖ ❖

1. Arrange the sardines on a platter. Decorate with the sliced or chopped yolks and whites and sprinkle with the parsley to get patches of vivid color. Serve, passing the lemon wedges and shallot vinegar, if using, separately.

From Françoise:
• Sardines packed in oil are easy to use—all you have to do is open a can—but that doesn't mean people will like them. So make a little effort and *your* sardines in oil will help establish your reputation as a cook.

- Vintage canned sardines are highly prized for their flavor. The French, Portuguese, and Spanish keep them for several years before opening them.

- The lemon or vinegar helps cut the strong flavor of these oily fish.

MONKFISH AND PANCETTA SKEWERS
- *Brochettes de lotte au lard* -

❖ EASY ❖ MODERATE ❖ 30 MINUTES, PLUS 2 HOURS MARINATING ❖ SERVES 4

MARINADE
6 tablespoons oil
Juice of ½ lemon
1 fennel rib, thinly sliced (optional)
1 thyme sprig
1 bay leaf
Salt and pepper

1 pound monkfish fillets, cut into cubes
¼ pound pancetta, cut into cubes
7 ounces white mushrooms, thickly sliced
Oil for brushing
Salt and pepper
1 lemon, cut into wedges

❖ ❖ ❖ ❖ ❖

1. Make the marinade: In a large bowl, combine all the ingredients. Add the monkfish, cover, and refrigerate for 2 hours, turning the fish occasionally. If using wood skewers, soak them in water.

2. Preheat the oven to 425 degrees. Brush the marinade off the monkfish. On metal or wood skewers, thread pieces of monkfish, pancetta, and mushroom.

3. Transfer the skewers to a large baking sheet, brush with oil, and season with salt and pepper. Bake on the top shelf of the oven, turning once, for 5 to 6 minutes on each side.

4. Transfer the skewers to a warmed platter and serve with the lemon wedges.

From Françoise:
- Don't attempt this dish with just any fish; most fall apart when skewered. You need a firm-fleshed fish like monkfish. If you can't find monkfish, porgy is more fragile, but it's still worth a try.

- You can also broil the skewers or cook them on a grill.

- I like to vary my skewers by adding different ingredients, like cherry tomatoes, pieces of bell pepper, and bay leaves.

SEAFOOD

MONKFISH AND CHORIZO SKEWERS

- Brochettes de lotte au chorizo -

❖ EASY   ❖ MODERATE   ❖ 25 MINUTES, PLUS 1 HOUR MARINATING   ❖ SERVES 4

1 ½ pounds monkfish fillets, cut into cubes

3 tablespoons olive oil

Juice of 1 lemon

Salt and pepper

3 tablespoons butter

7 ounces chorizo, sliced into pieces

Bay leaves

3 ½ ounces Canadian bacon, cut into thick strips

❖ ❖ ❖ ❖ ❖

1. In a large bowl, combine the monkfish with the olive oil and half the lemon juice. Season with salt and pepper. Cover and refrigerate for 1 hour, turning occasionally. If using wood skewers, soak them in water.

2. Meanwhile, in a small saucepan, melt the butter. Add the remaining lemon juice and season with salt and pepper. Transfer to a sauceboat.

3. Preheat the grill or broiler. Drain the monkfish, reserving the marinade. On metal or wood skewers, thread pieces of monkfish, chorizo, bay leaves, and Canadian bacon.

4. Transfer the skewers to a large baking sheet and brush with the reserved marinade. Grill or broil the skewers, turning once, for about 5 minutes on each side, basting often with the marinade.

5. Transfer the skewers to a warmed platter and serve with the lemon-butter sauce.

From Françoise:
• Serve with plain rice.

WINE-BRAISED MONKFISH WITH TOMATOES, CARROTS, AND MUSHROOMS

- *Lotte braisée aux légumes* -

❖ EASY   ❖ MODERATE   ❖ 1 HOUR, 15 MINUTES   ❖ SERVES 4

Four 6-ounce monkfish fillets

All-purpose flour for dusting

3 tablespoons butter

1 pound carrots, peeled and sliced crosswise

½ pound onions, thinly sliced

5 ounces tomatoes, peeled, seeded, and chopped

¾ cup dry white wine

1 garlic clove, crushed

1 bouquet garni made with parsley, thyme, and
  bay leaf

Salt and pepper

½ pound white mushrooms, quartered lengthwise

❖ ❖ ❖ ❖ ❖

1. Dust the fish lightly with flour, patting off the excess. In a flameproof casserole, melt the butter over medium-high heat. Add the fish and cook, turning once, until lightly browned, about 2 minutes per side. Remove the fish to a plate. Add the carrots and onions and cook, stirring occasionally, until lightly browned. Add the tomatoes, fish, wine, garlic, and bouquet garni. Season with salt and pepper. Cover and bring to a simmer, then reduce the heat to low and cook for 50 minutes.

2. Add the mushrooms to the casserole and cook for 10 minutes.

3. Remove the bouquet garni. Transfer the fish, vegetables, and sauce to a warmed serving dish and serve.

From Françoise:

• The white wine adds flavor but it's not indispensable. You can leave it out if you like.

• If you sauté the mushrooms in a little butter before adding them to the casserole, they will be even tastier.

• Serve with new potatoes cooked in their skins.

SEAFOOD

MONKFISH WITH JULIENNE VEGETABLES AND CREAMY SAUCE

- *Lotte sauce Suchet* -

❖ EASY   ❖ MODERATE   ❖ 45 MINUTES   ❖ SERVES 4

2 tablespoons butter

½ carrot, peeled and cut into julienne strips

1 leek, white part only, cut into julienne strips

1 small celery rib, cut into julienne strips

Four 6-ounce monkfish fillets

¾ cup dry white wine

Salt and pepper

SAUCE

2 tablespoons butter

2 tablespoons all-purpose flour

½ cup crème fraîche

Salt and pepper

❖   ❖   ❖   ❖   ❖

1. In a flameproof casserole, melt the butter over medium-low heat. Add the carrot, leek, and celery and cook until softened, about 5 minutes. Add the fish, wine, and ¾ cup of water. Season with salt and pepper. Cover and bring to a simmer, then reduce the heat to low and cook for 10 minutes.

2. Using a slotted spoon, transfer the fish to a warmed serving dish. Strain the cooking liquid into a glass measuring cup and add the vegetables to the serving dish.

3. Make the sauce: In a small saucepan, melt the butter over medium heat. Whisk in the flour until it starts foaming. Whisk in 1 ½ cups of the cooking liquid. Bring to a boil, whisking, then reduce the heat to very low and cook for 2 minutes. Whisk in the crème fraîche and season with salt and pepper. Pour the sauce over the fish and serve.

From Françoise:

• You can enrich the sauce even more with an egg yolk. Whisk it into the crème fraîche, then remove the sauce from the heat and whisk in this egg yolk mixture.

MONKFISH WITH AROMATIC TOMATO SAUCE

- *Lotte à l'américaine* -

❖ INTERMEDIATE ❖ EXPENSIVE ❖ 45 MINUTES ❖ SERVES 4

Four 6-ounce monkfish fillets
Salt and pepper
2 tablespoons plus 1 teaspoon all-purpose flour
5 tablespoons butter
1 shallot, finely chopped

¼ cup Cognac
1½ cups dry white wine
½ pound tomatoes, chopped
Cayenne pepper

❖ ❖ ❖ ❖ ❖

1. Season the fish with salt and pepper. Dust it lightly with 2 tablespoons of the flour, patting off the excess. In a flameproof casserole, melt 3 tablespoons of the butter over medium-high heat. Add the fish and cook, turning once, until lightly browned, about 2 minutes per side.

2. Add the shallot and Cognac to the casserole and bring to a boil, then tilt the pot and carefully ignite. When the flames subside, add the wine, ¾ cup of water, and the tomatoes. Season with cayenne. Cover and bring to a simmer, then reduce the heat to low and cook for 30 minutes.

3. Using a slotted fish slice, transfer the fish to a warmed serving dish.

4. In a cup, mash the remaining 2 tablespoons of butter with the 1 teaspoon of flour. Gradually whisk this paste into the simmering sauce and cook for 1 minute. Pour the sauce over the fish and serve.

From Françoise:
• The tomatoes can be peeled and seeded or not, however you like it.

• When I can't find good fresh tomatoes, I use 2 tablespoons of tomato paste instead. Or I add a little tomato paste to the tomatoes to boost the flavor.

• You might also whisk a little crème fraîche into the sauce just before serving.

• The perfect accompaniment to this dish is plain rice. That is to say, rice cooked in plenty of boiling, salted water for 15 to 17 minutes.

SEAFOOD

OVEN-BAKED COD WITH TOMATOES AND ONIONS
- Cabillaud bressane -

❖ EASY   ❖ INEXPENSIVE   ❖ 40 MINUTES   ❖ SERVES 4

2 tablespoons butter, cut into ¼-inch dice,
  plus more for brushing
3 tomatoes, peeled and sliced
2 large onions, thinly sliced

Four 6-ounce cod fillets
Salt and pepper
1 cup chicken broth
2 tablespoons dry bread crumbs

❖ ❖ ❖ ❖ ❖

1. Preheat the oven to 350 degrees. Brush a gratin dish with butter. Spread the tomatoes and onions in the dish. Set the fish on top and season with salt and pepper. Add the broth, sprinkle with the bread crumbs, and dot with the 2 tablespoons of butter.

2. Transfer to the oven and bake for about 30 minutes, basting the fish occasionally with the juices.

From Françoise:
• This is a great dish for fledgling cooks. There's nothing tricky about it. It's also inexpensive yet refined. If you want to make the dish a little more special, mash ½ tablespoon of butter with the same amount of flour and whisk this paste into the simmering sauce for a few minutes before serving. It will make your sauce very creamy.

• If you are using older onions that are pretty strong, boil the slices in water for 5 minutes before spreading them in the dish to remove any bitterness.

• Serve with plain rice or boiled new potatoes.

PAN-ROASTED COD WITH POTATOES AND ONIONS
- Cabillaud pageottière -

❖ EASY   ❖ INEXPENSIVE   ❖ 45 MINUTES   ❖ SERVES 4

1½ pounds small new potatoes, peeled
  and quartered
¼ pound small onions, quartered
4 tablespoons (½ stick) butter
Four 6-ounce cod fillets

1 bouquet garni made with parsley, thyme,
  and bay leaf
Juice of ½ lemon
Salt and pepper
Chopped parsley leaves for serving

1. Preheat the oven to 400 degrees. In a flame-proof gratin dish, combine the potatoes, onions, and 3 tablespoons of the butter. Transfer to the oven and bake for 10 minutes. Reduce the oven temperature to 350 degrees.

2. Push the potatoes and onions to the sides and add the fish, bouquet garni, and lemon juice. Season with salt and pepper and dot with the remaining 1 tablespoon of butter. Return to the oven and bake for 30 minutes.

3. Remove the bouquet garni. Sprinkle with parsley and serve.

From Françoise:
• If you use frozen cod, let it defrost completely before cooking.

BAKED COD WITH CURRIED TOMATOES
- *Cabillaud à l'indienne* -

❖ EASY　　　　❖ MODERATE　　　　❖ 45 MINUTES　　　　❖ SERVES 4

2 tablespoons butter, cut into ¼-inch dice, plus more for brushing
3 tomatoes, peeled and halved
2 large onions, thinly sliced
1 garlic clove, crushed

Chopped parsley leaves
1 to 2 teaspoons curry powder
Four 6-ounce cod fillets
Salt and pepper
6 tablespoons dry white wine

❖　❖　❖　❖　❖

1. Preheat the oven to 350 degrees. Brush a gratin dish with butter. Spread the tomatoes, onions, garlic, and parsley in the dish. Stir in the curry powder. Add the fish and season with salt and pepper. Add the wine and dot with the 2 tablespoons of butter.

2. Transfer to the oven and bake for about 30 minutes, basting the fish occasionally with the pan juices.

From Françoise:
• Cod is a fairly mild fish and benefits from some spicing up.

• Curry powder can be more or less fiery, depending on how much chile it has. Add it sparingly, then taste and adjust the seasoning.

• Serve with plain rice cooked in plenty of boiling, salted water for 15 to 17 minutes.

SEAFOOD

ROASTED COD WITH PARSLEY AND SHALLOT
- *Cabillaud au four à la flamande* -

❖ EASY   ❖ MODERATE   ❖ 30 MINUTES   ❖ SERVES 4

3 tablespoons butter, cut into ¼-inch dice,
   plus more for brushing
Chopped parsley leaves for sprinkling
1 shallot, finely chopped
Four 6-ounce cod fillets

6 tablespoons dry white wine
Juice of ½ lemon
Freshly grated nutmeg
Salt and pepper
2 tablespoons dry bread crumbs

❖ ❖ ❖ ❖ ❖

1. Preheat the oven to 425 degrees. Brush a roasting pan with butter. Sprinkle the parsley and shallot in the pan and set the fish on top. Pour in the wine and lemon juice. Season with nutmeg, salt, and pepper. Dot with 2 tablespoons of the butter.

2. Transfer to the oven and bake for about 15 minutes, basting the fish occasionally with the pan juices.

3. Using a slotted fish slice, transfer the fish to warmed plates. Stir in the bread crumbs, more parsley, and the remaining 1 tablespoon of butter into the roasting pan. Spoon over the fish and serve.

From Françoise:
• Use dry white wine for cooking fish because sweet white wine turns the sauce a grayish color.

POACHED PIKE IN COURT-BOUILLON
- *Brochet au court-bouillon* -

❖ EASY   ❖ MODERATE   ❖ 30 MINUTES   ❖ SERVES 4

1 tablespoon vinegar
2 onions, halved and stuck with 2 whole cloves total
1 shallot, thinly sliced
1 bouquet garni made with parsley, thyme,
   and bay leaf

Salt
Black peppercorns
2 ½-pound whole pike, cleaned, with head

1. In a large sauté pan, make the court-bouillon: Combine 2 quarts of water with the vinegar, onions, shallot, bouquet garni, salt, and peppercorns. Bring to a boil over medium-high heat, then reduce the heat to low and simmer for 15 minutes. Let cool slightly.

2. Rinse the fish and add it to the court-bouillon. Set over medium heat, and when it comes to a simmer, adjust the heat so the fish cooks at a bare simmer for about 10 minutes, depending on the size.

3. Drain the fish and serve it warm, or let it cool completely in the court-bouillon and serve at room temperature.

From Françoise:

• Pike is often served warm with beurre blanc, a delicate butter sauce that's quite tricky to make. I recommend pairing the fish simply with melted butter.

• Cold poached pike needs mayonnaise prepared with lots of pungent Dijon mustard or a tartar sauce flavored with fresh herbs (see recipe, page 626).

• A whole fish easily falls apart during cooking. To keep it together, you might swaddle it in plenty of cheesecloth and tie the ends before adding it to the court-bouillon. Gently lift the fish out of the pan by the 2 cheesecloth ends and snip off the wrapper before serving.

BROILED MACKEREL WITH FINES HERBES AND CRÈME FRAÎCHE

- *Maquereaux grillés à la crème fraîche* -

4 small whole mackerel, cleaned, with heads
2 tablespoons oil
½ cup crème fraîche

Salt and pepper
Mixed chopped parsley, chervil, chives, and
  tarragon leaves for sprinkling

❖ ❖ ❖ ❖ ❖

1. Rinse the fish and pat dry. Make 3 shallow crosswise slashes on both sides of each fish. Brush with the oil. Transfer the fish to a broiler pan.

2. Preheat the broiler. Broil the fish on the top shelf of the oven, turning once, for 3 to 4 minutes per side.

3. Meanwhile, in a small saucepan, warm the crème fraîche.

4. Transfer the fish to a warmed platter. Season with salt and pepper. Brush the fish with the crème fraîche, sprinkle with the herbs, and serve.

From Françoise:

• You can also grill the fish on the barbecue. A fat bouquet of thyme, rosemary, or dried fennel tucked in the coals underneath gives the fish a fragrant perfume.

• Sometimes I add a teaspoon of Dijon mustard to the crème fraîche.

SEAFOOD

MACKEREL MARINATED IN WHITE WINE

- *Maquereaux marinés au vin blanc* -

❖ EASY   ❖ MODERATE   ❖ 45 MINUTES, PLUS 2 TO 3 HOURS MARINATING   ❖ SERVES 4

2 cups dry white wine

½ pound carrots, peeled and thinly sliced

2 onions, thinly sliced

1 garlic clove, crushed

1 bouquet garni made with parsley, thyme, and bay leaf

1 teaspoon coriander seeds

Salt

6 to 8 black peppercorns

4 to 8 small whole mackerel, cleaned, with heads

❖ ❖ ❖ ❖ ❖

1. In a large sauté pan, combine the wine with 1 cup of water, the carrots, onions, garlic, bouquet garni, coriander seeds, salt, and peppercorns. Bring to a boil over medium-high heat, then reduce the heat to low and simmer for 15 minutes. Let cool slightly.

2. Rinse the fish and pat dry. Transfer them to a flameproof gratin dish. Pour the court-bouillon over the fish along with the aromatics. Bring to a simmer slowly over medium-low heat, then reduce the heat to low and cook at a bare simmer for 12 to 15 minutes.

3. Remove the bouquet garni. Let the fish cool slightly in the court-bouillon, then refrigerate for 2 to 3 hours. Serve cold.

From Françoise:

• Coriander is often sold as seeds, which is what you need for this recipe. It looks like peppercorns but isn't peppery at all.

• I prepare small fresh herring in exactly the same way. Watch out for the bones!

OVEN-BRAISED MACKEREL WITH CURRY SAUCE

- *Maquereaux à l'indienne sauce curry* -

❖ EASY   ❖ MODERATE   ❖ 1 HOUR   ❖ SERVES 4

4 medium whole mackerel, cleaned, with heads
¾ cup dry white wine
Salt and pepper
2 tablespoons butter
1 onion, chopped
1 teaspoon curry powder
1 cup long-grain rice

CURRY SAUCE
3 tablespoons butter
3 tablespoons all-purpose flour
1 to 2 teaspoons curry powder

❖   ❖   ❖   ❖   ❖

1. Preheat the oven to 350 degrees. Rinse the fish and pat dry. Arrange the fish in a gratin dish and add the wine and ¾ cup of water. Season with salt and pepper. Transfer to the oven and bake for 15 to 20 minutes.

2. Meanwhile, in a medium saucepan, melt the butter over medium-low heat. Add the onion and curry powder and cook until softened. Stir in the rice. Add 2 cups of water and season with salt and pepper. Increase the heat to medium-high, bring to a boil, then reduce the heat to low, cover, and cook until the rice is tender and the water is absorbed, 17 to 20 minutes.

3. Fluff the rice and spread it on a warmed serving dish. Drain the fish well, reserving the broth, and set them on the rice.

4. Make the curry sauce: In a saucepan, melt the butter over medium heat. Whisk in the flour and curry powder until they start foaming. Whisk in 2 cups of the broth. Bring to a boil, whisking, then reduce the heat to very low and cook for about 10 minutes.

5. Pour the sauce over the fish and serve.

From Françoise:
• Small mackerel are much better than the large, fatty ones.

• If you're nervous about making the curry sauce because it's hard to know how to dose the curry powder, start off with the smaller amount and add more to taste.

SEAFOOD

MARINATED TUNA IN CAPER-TOMATO SAUCE

- *Thon à la provençale* -

MARINADE

6 tablespoons oil

Thyme

Bay leaf

Rosemary

Juice of 1 lemon

8 black peppercorns

Six 6-ounce tuna fillets

6 oil-packed anchovy fillets, halved

2 onions, finely chopped

3 garlic cloves, finely chopped

1 ½ pounds tomatoes, peeled, seeded, and
  chopped

1 cup dry white wine

Salt and pepper

1 tablespoon capers, drained

Chopped parsley leaves

1 tablespoon butter

❖ ❖ ❖ ❖ ❖

1. Make the marinade: In a gratin dish, combine all the ingredients.

2. Using a small, sharp knife, make 2 evenly spaced 1-inch incisions in each tuna fillet. Push half an anchovy fillet into each incision. Add the tuna to the marinade and turn to coat. Cover and refrigerate overnight, turning the fish occasionally.

3. Brush the marinade off the tuna. In a flame-proof casserole, cook the tuna over medium-high heat until lightly browned on both sides. Add the onions, garlic, tomatoes, wine, and 6 tablespoons of water. Season with salt and pepper. Cover and bring to a simmer, then reduce the heat to low and cook for 20 minutes.

4. Using a slotted fish slice, transfer the tuna to a warmed serving dish. If needed, simmer the sauce until slightly thickened. Remove the pot from the heat and stir in the capers, parsley, and butter until the butter melts creamily.

5. Pour the sauce over the tuna and serve.

From Françoise:
• This dish can also be served cold, as a first course.

BRAISED TUNA WITH ONIONS, TOMATOES, AND CORNICHONS

Thon bonne femme

❖ EASY   ❖ MODERATE   ❖ 40 MINUTES   ❖ SERVES 4

3 tablespoons butter

1 tablespoon oil

Four 6-ounce tuna fillets

5 onions, thinly sliced

1 tablespoon all-purpose flour

4 tomatoes, chopped

1 ½ cups dry white wine

1 bouquet garni made with parsley, thyme, and bay leaf

Salt and pepper

4 cornichons, sliced crosswise

Chopped parsley for sprinkling

❖ ❖ ❖ ❖ ❖

1. In a flameproof casserole, melt the butter in the oil over medium-high heat. Add the tuna and cook until lightly browned on both sides. Remove the fish to a plate.

2. Add the onions to the casserole, reduce the heat to medium-low, and cook until softened. Stir in the flour. Add the tomatoes, wine, 1 ½ cups of water, and the bouquet garni. Season with salt and pepper. Cover and bring to a sim-

mer, then reduce the heat to low and cook for 25 minutes.

3. Transfer the tuna and sauce to a warmed serving dish. Sprinkle with the cornichons and parsley and serve.

From Françoise:
• Serve with boiled new potatoes.

TUNA WITH VELVETY TOMATO AND PEPPER STEW

- Thon frais braisé aux tomates et aux poivrons -

❖ EASY   ❖ MODERATE   ❖ 1 HOUR, 30 MINUTES   ❖ SERVES 4

2 tablespoons oil

Four 6-ounce tuna fillets

1 onion, thinly sliced

1 carrot, peeled and thinly sliced

1 bell pepper, thinly sliced

1 tomato, sliced

1 garlic clove, crushed

1 bouquet garni made with parsley, thyme,
  and bay leaf

6 tablespoons dry white wine or water

Salt and pepper

VEGETABLE STEW

2 tablespoons oil

½ pound onions, chopped

½ pound tomatoes, chopped

½ pound bell peppers, thinly sliced

1 garlic clove, crushed

1 bouquet garni made with parsley, thyme,
  and bay leaf

Salt and pepper

❖ ❖ ❖ ❖ ❖

1. In a flameproof casserole, heat the oil over medium-high heat. Add the tuna and cook until lightly browned on both sides. Add the onion, carrot, bell pepper, tomato, garlic, bouquet garni, and wine or water. Season with salt and pepper. Cover and bring to a simmer, then reduce the heat to low and cook for 30 to 40 minutes.

2. Make the vegetable stew: In a large skillet, heat the oil over medium heat. Stir in all the ingredients and season with salt and pepper. Cook, uncovered, for 30 minutes.

3. Using a slotted fish slice, transfer the tuna to a warmed serving dish. Pour the tuna cooking liquid through a sieve, pressing on the vegetables, into the vegetable stew. Remove the bouquet garni. Pour the vegetable stew over the tuna and serve.

From Françoise:

• If you like spicy food, add a small chile to the vegetable stew.

• Serve this dish hot, with boiled rice, or cold with rice salad.

GOLDEN GRATINÉED SALT COD WITH GRUYÈRE

- *Morue sauce Mornay au gratin* -

❖ EASY   ❖ MODERATE   ❖ 1 HOUR, PLUS 12 HOURS SOAKING   ❖ SERVES 4

1 to 1¼ pounds skinless salt cod fillet
Salt
1½ pounds potatoes, unpeeled
2 tablespoons butter, cut into ¼-inch dice

COURT-BOUILLON
1 onion, halved and stuck with 3 whole cloves total
1 bouquet garni made with parsley, thyme,
  and bay leaf

1 garlic clove, crushed
A little salt

MORNAY SAUCE
3 tablespoons butter
3 tablespoons all-purpose flour
2 cups milk
Salt and pepper
¾ cup shredded Gruyère cheese

❖ ❖ ❖ ❖ ❖

1. In a bowl, soak the salt cod in plenty of cold water at room temperature for 12 hours, changing the water at least 3 times.

2. In a large saucepan of boiling salted water, cook the potatoes for 25 to 30 minutes. Drain, peel, and slice crosswise.

3. Meanwhile, make the court-bouillon: In a large sauté pan, combine 2 quarts of water with the onion, bouquet garni, garlic, and salt. Drain the salt cod and add it to the court-bouillon. Bring it to a simmer, then remove the pan from the heat. Drain the cod well. Flake the fish, removing any bones.

4. Preheat the oven to 425 degrees. Make the Mornay sauce: In a small saucepan, melt the butter over medium heat. Whisk in the flour

until it starts foaming. Whisk in the milk. Season with salt and pepper. Bring to a boil, whisking, then reduce the heat to very low and cook for 5 minutes. Remove the pan from the heat and whisk in ¼ cup of the cheese.

5. In a gratin dish, layer half the Mornay sauce, the potatoes, the cod, and the remaining Mornay sauce. Sprinkle with the remaining ½ cup of cheese and dot with the 2 tablespoons of butter. Bake on the top shelf of the oven until melted and golden, about 10 minutes, and serve.

From Françoise:
• Adding 2 or 3 pinches of curry powder to the Mornay sauce at the same time as the flour gives the dish a nice flavor.

SEAFOOD

PAN-SEARED SALT COD WITH DIJON MUSTARD

- *Morue à la moutarde* -

❖ EASY   ❖ MODERATE   ❖ 30 MINUTES, PLUS 12 HOURS SOAKING   ❖ SERVES 4

1 to 1 ¼ pounds skinless salt cod fillet
A little salt

2 tablespoons butter
1 or 2 tablespoons Dijon mustard

❖ ❖ ❖ ❖ ❖

1. In a bowl, soak the salt cod in plenty of cold water at room temperature for 12 hours, changing the water at least 3 times.

2. In a large sauté pan, combine 2 quarts of water with the salt. Drain the salt cod and add it to the pan. Set over medium heat, and when it comes to a simmer, adjust the heat so the fish cooks at a bare simmer for 15 minutes. Drain the fish well and pat dry.

3. In a large skillet, melt the butter over medium-high heat. Add the fish and cook until lightly browned on both sides. Remove the pan from the heat and stir in the mustard. Transfer the fish and sauce to a warmed platter and serve.

From Françoise:

• This recipe comes from my mother. It's especially good for beginning cooks. The only thing to watch for is not to return the pan to the heat once the mustard has been stirred in, or it will separate.

• It's remarkably good with plain boiled potatoes. You might sprinkle them with a mixture of chopped herbs, such as parsley, chives, tarragon, and chervil.

• If you have any leftovers of salt cold poached in a court-bouillon, you can proceed directly to Step 3.

GOLDEN GRATINÉED SALT COD WITH POTATOES
- *Morue au gratin* -

❖ EASY   ❖ MODERATE   ❖ 1 HOUR, PLUS 12 HOURS SOAKING   ❖ SERVES 4

1 pound skinless salt cod fillet

Salt

1 pound potatoes, unpeeled

1 bouquet garni made with parsley, thyme,
  and bay leaf

½ cup shredded Gruyère cheese

2 tablespoons butter, cut into ¼-inch dice

BÉCHAMEL SAUCE

3 tablespoons butter

3 tablespoons all-purpose flour

2 cups milk

Salt and pepper

❖ ❖ ❖ ❖ ❖

1. In a bowl, soak the salt cod in plenty of cold water at room temperature for 12 hours, changing the water at least 3 times.

2. In a large saucepan of boiling salted water, cook the potatoes for 25 to 30 minutes. Drain, peel, and slice crosswise.

3. Drain the salt cod. In a large sauté pan, combine 2 quarts of water with the fish, bouquet garni, and a little salt. Bring it to a simmer over medium-high heat, then remove the pan from the heat. Let the fish cool slightly in the court-bouillon, then drain well. Flake the fish, removing any bones.

4. Preheat the oven to 425 degrees. Make the béchamel sauce: In a small saucepan, melt the butter over medium heat. Whisk in the flour until it starts foaming. Whisk in the milk. Season with salt and pepper. Bring to a boil, whisking, then reduce the heat to very low and cook for 5 minutes.

5. In a gratin dish, layer half the béchamel sauce, the potatoes, the cod, and the remaining béchamel sauce. Sprinkle with the cheese and dot with the butter. Bake on the top shelf of the oven until melted and golden, about 10 minutes, and serve.

From Françoise:
• I learned the secret to perfect salt cod in Portugal: Soak it for so long that you need to add a little salt when you cook it.

• My first choice is the long-soak method—at least 12 hours—but you can soak salt cod more quickly in warm water for 6 hours, changing the water at least 3 times.

SEAFOOD

SALT COD PAELLA

- *Paella de morue* -

❖ INTERMEDIATE ❖ MODERATE ❖ 1 HOUR, 30 MINUTES, PLUS 12 HOURS SOAKING ❖ SERVES 4

1 pound skinless salt cod fillet

1 pound mussels, scrubbed and debearded

1 shallot, finely chopped

1 tablespoon butter

7 ounces thick-sliced pancetta, cut crosswise
    into ¼-inch-thick strips

5 ounces chorizo, sliced crosswise

2 onions, chopped

3 red bell peppers, thinly sliced

3 tomatoes, peeled, seeded, and diced

½ bay leaf

3 garlic cloves, crushed

Salt and pepper

2 tablespoons oil

Chopped parsley leaves

Thyme leaves

Pinch of saffron threads

1 cup rice

❖ ❖ ❖ ❖ ❖

1. In a bowl, soak the salt cod in plenty of cold water at room temperature for 12 hours, changing the water at least 3 times.

2. Add the mussels, shallot, and ¾ cup of water to a pot. Cover and cook over high heat, stirring once or twice, just until the mussels open, 3 to 5 minutes. Using a slotted spoon, transfer the mussels to a bowl. Pour the broth through a fine strainer lined with a moistened paper towel.

3. In a flameproof casserole, melt the butter over medium heat. Add the pancetta and cook until just beginning to brown. Add the chorizo, onions, bell peppers, tomatoes, bay leaf, and garlic. Season with salt and pepper. Reduce the heat to low, cover, and cook for 20 minutes.

4. Drain the salt cod and pat dry. In a large skillet, heat the oil over medium-high heat. Add the fish, parsley, and thyme and cook until lightly browned on both sides. Break up the fish into large pieces, removing any bones.

5. Stir the fish, mussels in the shell, saffron, and rice into the casserole. Add the mussel broth and enough water to barely cover the rice. Reduce the heat to low and cook, uncovered, until the rice is tender and the water is absorbed, 25 to 30 minutes. Taste and adjust the seasoning, if needed, before serving.

From Françoise:

• Chorizo is often spicy, but since paella is traditionally a highly seasoned dish, you might also add 1 or 2 pinches of cayenne pepper or a small dried chile to taste.

• You can use roasted red peppers in a jar instead of fresh bell peppers.

• In Step 5, add a little boiling water to the pot if the liquid evaporates before the rice is tender.

• If your pancetta is especially salty, cook it in boiling water for 2 minutes, then drain, before adding it in Step 3.

RUSTIC SALT COD WITH ONIONS, TOMATOES, AND CORNICHONS
- *Morue à la portugaise* -

❖ EASY ❖ MODERATE ❖ 1 HOUR, PLUS 12 HOURS SOAKING ❖ SERVES 4

1 ¼ pounds skinless salt cod fillet

3 tablespoons butter

5 ounces onion, chopped

2 garlic cloves, chopped

½ pound tomatoes, peeled, seeded, and chopped

Salt and pepper

1 bouquet garni made with parsley, thyme,
  and bay leaf

3 or 4 cornichons, sliced crosswise

❖ ❖ ❖ ❖ ❖

1. In a bowl, soak the salt cod in plenty of cold water at room temperature for 12 hours, changing the water at least 3 times.

2. Preheat the oven to 350 degrees. In a medium saucepan, melt 2 tablespoons of the butter over medium heat. Add the onion, garlic, and tomatoes and cook for 5 to 10 minutes.

3. Scrape the tomato mixture into a gratin dish. Season with salt and pepper and tuck in the bouquet garni. Drain the salt cod and pat dry. Cut into large cubes. Add the cod to the dish and dot with the remaining 1 tablespoon of butter.

4. Transfer the dish to the oven and bake for 30 to 40 minutes, turning the fish halfway through cooking so it absorbs the sauce and stays moist. Sprinkle with the cornichons and serve.

From Françoise:
• One or two tablespoons of tomato paste can replace the fresh tomatoes here, or even boost their flavor. It's often a good idea to amplify the taste of fresh tomatoes with a little tomato paste, especially when they're not in season.

• You can substitute fresh cod for the salt cod in this recipe, without soaking it first of course.

SEAFOOD

COLD POACHED HAKE WITH VEGETABLE SALAD
- Colin froid parisienne -

❖ EASY   ❖ MODERATE   ❖ 1 HOUR, 30 MINUTES   ❖ SERVES 4

COURT-BOUILLON

1 tablespoon vinegar

2 onions, halved and stuck with 2 whole cloves
  total

1 shallot, thinly sliced

1 bouquet garni made with parsley, thyme,
  and bay leaf

Salt

Black peppercorns

2 ½-pound whole hake, cleaned, with head

1 cup asparagus tips

¾ cup mayonnaise

1 cup frozen or canned mixed diced vegetables

1 small can oil-packed anchovy fillets, drained

1 lemon, thinly sliced

❖   ❖   ❖   ❖   ❖

1. In a large sauté pan, make the court-bouillon: Combine 2 quarts of water with the vinegar, onions, shallot, bouquet garni, salt, and peppercorns. Bring to a boil over medium-high heat, then reduce the heat to low and simmer for 15 minutes. Let cool slightly.

2. Rinse the fish and add it to the court-bouillon. Set over medium heat, and when it comes to a simmer, adjust the heat so the fish cooks at a bare simmer for about 10 minutes, depending on the size. Let it cool completely in the court-bouillon.

3. Meanwhile, bring a medium saucepan of water to a boil. Add the asparagus tips and cook until barely tender, about 3 minutes. Using a slotted spoon, transfer the asparagus to a colander and rinse under cold running water, then drain well and pat dry with paper towels. In a bowl, fold them into ¼ cup of the mayonnaise.

4. Add the frozen vegetables to the boiling water and cook until tender. Drain in a colander and rinse under cold running water, then drain well. Pat the mixed vegetables dry with paper towels. In a bowl, fold them into ¼ cup of the mayonnaise.

5. Drain the fish well and pat dry. Remove the skin by scraping it gently. Transfer the fish to a long platter. Mound some of the asparagus salad at one end of the fish and some of the mixed vegetable salad at the other. Decorate the fish with rosettes of the remaining mayonnaise. Arrange the anchovies in a crosshatch pattern on top, and decorate with the lemon slices. Serve, passing the remaining asparagus and chopped vegetable salads separately.

From Françoise:

• I prefer fresh hake, but if you use a large frozen fish, always let it defrost completely in the refrigerator before cooking.

• If you don't have a fish poaching rack, which is very practical for cooking a whole fish but one more piece of equipment to have around, you can swaddle your fish in plenty of cheesecloth and tie the ends before adding it to the court-bouillon. Gently lift the fish out of the pan by the 2 cheesecloth ends and snip off the wrapper before serving.

• If you have the time, make your own mix of diced vegetables using fresh corn kernels, lima beans, peas, carrots, green beans, and turnips.

PAN-SEARED HAKE WITH TOMATOES AND SHALLOTS
- *Colin basquaise* -

❖ EASY   ❖ MODERATE   ❖ 30 MINUTES   ❖ SERVES 4

Four 6-ounce hake fillets
All-purpose flour for dusting
3 tablespoons butter
1 tablespoon oil

1 onion, chopped
2 shallots, chopped
1 pound tomatoes, peeled, halved, and seeded
Salt and pepper

❖ ❖ ❖ ❖ ❖

1. Dust the fish lightly with flour, patting off
the excess. In a large sauté pan, melt the butter
in the oil over medium heat. Add the fish and
cook, turning once, until lightly browned,
about 2 minutes per side.

2. Add the onion, shallots, and tomatoes
and season with salt and pepper. Reduce the
heat to low, partially cover, and cook for 15
minutes. Transfer the fish and tomatoes to a
warmed serving dish and serve.

From Françoise:
• I often add a coarsely chopped red bell pepper to this dish along with the tomatoes.

• Just before serving, I like to enrich the
tomatoes slightly with 1 tablespoon of crème
fraîche.

SEAFOOD

PAN-SEARED HAKE WITH BUTTER AND LEMON
- *Colin meunière* -

❖ EASY   ❖ MODERATE   ❖ 20 MINUTES   ❖ SERVES 4

Four 6-ounce skinless hake fillets
Salt and pepper
All-purpose flour for dusting

3 tablespoons butter
Chopped parsley leaves for sprinkling
1 lemon, cut into wedges

❖ ❖ ❖ ❖ ❖

1. Season the fish fillets with salt and pepper
and dust lightly with flour, patting off the
excess.

2. In a large skillet, melt the butter over
medium heat. Add the fish and cook, turning

continued

once, until lightly browned, 5 to 7 minutes per side.

3. Transfer the fish to a warmed platter. Pour the pan juices on top. Sprinkle with the parsley and serve with the lemon wedges.

From Françoise:

• When you buy hake fillets, make sure the flesh is pearly white and firm. It shouldn't be sticky or have a fishy smell.

SOUFFLÉED HAKE WITH SHRIMP SAUCE
- *Colin sauce crevette* -

❖ INTERMEDIATE   ❖ MODERATE   ❖ 1 HOUR, 30 MINUTES   ❖ SERVES 4

Butter for brushing

1 cup dry bread crumbs

¾ cup milk

1 pound cooked hake fillet, flaked

4 large eggs, separated

Salt and pepper

SHRIMP SAUCE

3 tablespoons butter

3 tablespoons all-purpose flour

1 teaspoon tomato paste

Milk

Salt and pepper

Cayenne pepper

Paprika

8 large cooked, shelled shrimp, halved
    horizontally

❖   ❖   ❖   ❖   ❖

1. Preheat the oven to 350 degrees. Generously brush a ring mold with butter.

2. In a large bowl, soak the bread crumbs in the milk. Squeeze them dry and pour off the excess milk. Add the fish and egg yolks and season with salt and pepper. Mash with a fork.

3. Beat the egg whites with a pinch of salt until stiff. Mix one-quarter of the egg whites into the fish mixture, then fold this lightened mixture into the remaining whites.

4. Scrape the fish mixture into the ring mold, filling it three-quarters full. Transfer to a

roasting pan and fill it with hot water to come halfway up the sides of the mold. Transfer the pan to the oven and bake the soufflé until risen and browned, about 45 minutes.

5. Meanwhile, make the shrimp sauce: In a medium saucepan, melt the butter over medium heat. Whisk in the flour until it starts foaming. Whisk in the tomato paste, fish broth (from poaching the fish), and enough milk to make 2 cups. Season with salt, pepper, cayenne, and paprika. Bring to a boil, whisking, then reduce the heat to very low and cook for 10 minutes. Remove the pan from the heat and stir in the shrimp.

6. Remove the ring mold from the water bath. Run a knife around the soufflé. Invert a round platter over the mold. Holding the mold and platter together, quickly invert the soufflé onto the platter. Spoon some of the sauce over and around the soufflé and serve, passing the remaining shrimp sauce separately.

From Françoise:
• See Poached Whole Fish in Court-Bouillon (page 393) for how to cook the hake.

• Fold the beaten egg whites into the fish mixture using a rubber spatula or a wooden spoon so the whites don't deflate.

• If you don't have a ring mold, you can use a soufflé dish.

• You can also make this recipe using steamed fresh fish or canned tuna or salmon.

FRIED FLOUNDER
- Carrelets frits -

❖ INTERMEDIATE ❖ MODERATE ❖ 30 MINUTES ❖ SERVES 4

All-purpose flour for dredging
4 small (one-person) whole flounders, cleaned,
  with heads

Salt and pepper
Oil for frying
1 lemon, cut into wedges

❖ ❖ ❖ ❖ ❖

1. Spread the flour in a large dish. Rinse the fish and pat dry. Season the fish with salt and pepper, then dredge them in the flour, patting off the excess.

2. In a large skillet, heat the oil to 375 degrees. Gently drop the fish 1 or 2 at a time into the oil and fry them, turning once, until golden, 2 to 3 minutes per side. Using a slotted fish slice, carefully transfer the fish to paper towels to drain as they are done. Transfer to a platter and keep warm in a low oven while frying the remaining fish. Serve very hot with the lemon wedges.

From Françoise:
• Carrelet is an orange-spotted flounder or fluke from the English Channel. It's also known as plie in France and plaice in England.

SEAFOOD

PAN-SEARED FLOUNDER WITH BUTTER AND LEMON
- *Carrelet meunière* -

❖ EASY   ❖ MODERATE   ❖ 30 MINUTES   ❖ SERVES 4

4 small (one-person) whole flounders, cleaned, with heads
Salt and pepper

All-purpose flour for dusting
6 tablespoons butter
1 lemon, cut into wedges

❖ ❖ ❖ ❖ ❖

1. Rinse the fish and pat dry. Season the fish with salt and pepper and dust lightly with flour, patting off the excess.

2. In a large skillet, melt 3 tablespoons of the butter over medium heat. Add the fish in 2 batches and cook, turning once, until lightly browned, 6 to 7 minutes per side.

3. Transfer the fish to a warmed platter and cook the remaining fish in the remaining 3 tablespoons of butter. Transfer to the platter and serve with the lemon wedges.

From Françoise:
• If you buy larger flounders, have your fishmonger cut them crosswise into steaks. But don't purchase too large a fish that won't fit in your skillet.

STUFFED PAN-ROASTED PORGY WITH LEMON
- *Dorade au citron* -

❖ EASY   ❖ MODERATE   ❖ 40 MINUTES   ❖ SERVES 4

2-pound whole porgy, cleaned, with head
3 shallots, finely chopped
Chopped parsley leaves from 1 large bunch
1 garlic clove, finely chopped

1 lemon, cut into thin half moons
Thyme leaves for sprinkling
Salt and pepper
1 tablespoon butter, cut into ¼-inch dice

❖ ❖ ❖ ❖ ❖

1. Preheat the oven to 400 degrees. Rinse the fish and pat dry. In a bowl, mix the shallots with the parsley and garlic. Pack the fish with this stuffing and secure with toothpicks. Make

3 deep crosswise slashes on 1 side of the fish and insert the lemon slices in the incisions. Sprinkle with thyme leaves and season with salt and pepper.

2. Set the fish in a roasting pan and dot with the butter. Bake in the oven for about 30 minutes. Remove the toothpicks, transfer the fish to a platter, and serve.

From Françoise:
• Here's another recipe for beginners, yet it's refined and original. I've had a lot of success with it.

• You can replace the 3 shallots with 1 onion.

• Instead of using parsley in the stuffing, you can add chives, chervil, tarragon, cilantro, or whatever you like.

LEMON-MARINATED PORGY WITH SAFFRON TOMATO SAUCE
- *Dorade au safran* -

❖ EASY ❖ MODERATE ❖ 40 MINUTES, PLUS 2 HOURS MARINATING ❖ SERVES 4

2 ½- to 3-pound whole porgy, cleaned, with head
Juice of 1 lemon
Salt and pepper
3 tablespoons butter

2 onions, chopped
4 tomatoes, peeled, seeded, and chopped
Pinch of saffron threads

❖ ❖ ❖ ❖ ❖

SEAFOOD

1. Rinse the fish and pat dry. In a gratin dish, combine the fish with the lemon juice and season with salt and pepper. Cover and refrigerate for 2 hours, turning occasionally.

2. In a flameproof casserole, melt the butter over medium heat. Add the onions and cook until softened. Add the tomatoes and saffron and season with salt and pepper. Reduce the heat to low, cover, and cook for 15 minutes.

3. Transfer the fish to the casserole. Cover and cook over low heat for about 20 minutes.

From Françoise:
• Serve with plain rice or pasta.

PAN-ROASTED PORGY WITH
BREAD AND MUSHROOM STUFFING
- *Dorade farcie* -

❖ EASY   ❖ MODERATE   ❖ 1 HOUR, 15 MINUTES   ❖ SERVES 4

2 ½- to 3-pound whole porgy, cleaned, with head

¾ cup dry white wine

2 tablespoons butter, cut into ¼-inch dice

STUFFING

6 tablespoons milk

½ cup dry bread crumbs

1 tablespoon butter

½ pound white mushrooms, thinly sliced

1 shallot, finely chopped

1 large egg yolk

Chopped parsley leaves

Salt and pepper

❖ ❖ ❖ ❖ ❖

1. Preheat the oven to 400 degrees. Rinse the fish and pat dry.

2. Make the stuffing: In a small saucepan, warm the milk. Add the bread crumbs and let soak, then squeeze dry, discarding the excess milk.

3. In a skillet, melt the 1 tablespoon of butter over medium heat. Add the mushrooms and shallot and cook, stirring occasionally, until tender. In a bowl, mix the mushrooms and shallot with the bread crumbs, egg yolk, and parsley. Season with salt and pepper. Pack the stuffing into the fish and secure with toothpicks.

4. Set the fish in a gratin dish, pour in the wine, and dot with the 2 tablespoons of butter. Transfer the dish to the oven and bake for 40 to 50 minutes. Remove the toothpicks and serve in the gratin dish.

From Françoise:

• You can also cover the stuffing with a piece of barding fat and tie it with kitchen string. Or even easier, use a piece of foil or parchment paper.

• The white wine adds flavor to the fish but it's not essential. If you use water, it will be just as good, but then add the juice of ½ lemon.

BAKED PORGY ON A BED OF MUSHROOMS AND SHALLOTS

- *Dorade aux champignons* -

❖ EASY ❖ MODERATE ❖ 45 MINUTES ❖ SERVES 4

2 tablespoons butter, cut into ¼-inch dice,
  plus more for brushing
¼ pound white mushrooms, thinly sliced
3 shallots, finely chopped

2 ½-pound whole porgy, cleaned, with head
Salt and pepper
Chopped parsley for sprinkling
3 thyme sprigs

❖ ❖ ❖ ❖ ❖

1. Preheat the oven to 400 degrees. Brush a gratin dish with butter. Spread the mushrooms and shallots in the dish. Rinse the fish and pat dry. Set the fish on top and pour in ¾ cup of water. Season with salt and pepper. Sprinkle with parsley and top with the thyme sprigs. Dot with the 2 tablespoons of butter.

2. Transfer the dish to the oven and bake for about 30 minutes, basting often with the pan juices. Serve in the gratin dish.

From Françoise:

• I often recommend serving fish in its cooking dish because it's tricky to transfer a large fish to another dish. Gratin dishes are perfectly presentable, even very attractive.

• Just before serving, you can squeeze lemon juice over the fish if you like. Or pass lemon wedges at the table.

SEAFOOD

GRATIN OF WHITING WITH ZUCCHINI AND TOMATOES

- *Tian de merlan aux courgettes* -

❖ EASY ❖ MODERATE ❖ 1 HOUR ❖ SERVES 4

1 garlic clove
1 ½ pounds whiting fillets
Salt and pepper
4 small zucchini, sliced crosswise ½ inch thick
All-purpose flour for dusting
¼ cup oil

3 tablespoons butter, cut into ¼-inch dice
1 pound tomatoes, quartered
Dry bread crumbs for sprinkling

continued

1. Preheat the oven to 425 degrees. Rub a gratin dish with the garlic clove. Spread the whiting fillets in the dish and season with salt and pepper.

2. Lightly dust the zucchini slices with flour, patting off the excess. In a large skillet, heat the oil over medium-high heat. Add the zucchini in batches and cook until lightly browned on both sides. Using a slotted spoon, transfer the zucchini to the gratin dish as they are done.

3. Discard most of the oil in the skillet. Melt 1 tablespoon of butter in the remaining oil over medium-high heat. Add the tomatoes and cook, then spread over the zucchini in the dish.

4. Sprinkle the top with bread crumbs and dot with the remaining 2 tablespoons of butter. Transfer the dish to the oven and bake for 20 to 30 minutes. Serve in the gratin dish.

FRIED WHITING PATTIES WITH POTATOES AND PARSLEY
- *Croquettes de merlan à la tunisienne* -

❖ EASY ❖ MODERATE ❖ 1 HOUR ❖ SERVES 4

½ pound potatoes, unpeeled
6 tablespoons butter
1 onion, finely chopped
1 pound skinless whiting fillets

Chopped parsley leaves from 1 bunch
2 large eggs, lightly beaten
Salt and pepper
All-purpose flour for dredging

❖ ❖ ❖ ❖ ❖

1. In a large saucepan of boiling salted water, cook the potatoes for 25 to 30 minutes.

2. Meanwhile, in a large skillet, melt 2 table-spoons of the butter over medium-low heat. Add the onion and cook until softened. In a food processor, grind the fish fillets with the parsley.

3. Drain and peel the potatoes. In a large bowl, mash the potatoes. Beat in the eggs, onion, and fish mixture. Season with 1 teaspoon of salt and with pepper. Shape into balls the size of a small egg, then flatten into patties. Spread the flour in a soup plate. Dredge the patties in the flour, patting off the excess.

4. Wipe out the skillet. In it melt 2 tablespoons of the butter over medium heat. Add half the patties and cook, turning once, until golden brown, about 5 minutes per side. Transfer to paper towels to drain as they are done, then arrange on a warmed platter. Repeat with the remaining patties and butter. Serve hot.

From Françoise:
• If you lightly beat the eggs first, they will blend more easily into the mixture.

• Cook the patties in batches so they don't stick together in the skillet, adding more fresh butter with the second batch. Keep them warm while you fry the rest. Pass lemon wedges at the table.

PAN-SEARED WHITING WITH GARLIC, PARSLEY, AND CORNICHONS

- *Merlans à la biarrotte* -

❖ EASY　　　❖ MODERATE　　　❖ 30 MINUTES　　　❖ SERVES 4

4 whole whiting, cleaned, without heads

Salt and pepper

1 teaspoon all-purpose flour, plus more
　for dusting

2 tablespoons butter

1 tablespoon oil

3 garlic cloves, finely chopped

Chopped parsley leaves

3 cornichons, sliced crosswise

1 large egg yolk

3 tablespoons vinegar

❖　❖　❖　❖　❖

1. Rinse the fish and pat dry. Cut them cross-wise into thick steaks. Season with salt and pepper and dust lightly with flour, patting off the excess.

2. In a large skillet, melt 1 tablespoon of the butter in the oil over medium heat. Add the fish steaks and cook until lightly browned on both sides. Transfer to a warmed serving dish.

3. In the same skillet, melt the 1 remaining tablespoon of butter over medium heat. Add the garlic, parsley, and 1 teaspoon of flour and cook until foaming. Whisk in ½ cup of water

and the cornichons and season with salt and pepper. Bring to a boil, whisking. In a cup, blend the egg yolk with the vinegar. Remove the pan from the heat and whisk in the egg yolk mixture until the sauce thickens slightly.

4. Pour the sauce over the fish and serve at once.

From Françoise:

• The egg yolk should thicken the sauce lightly off the heat. If it doesn't, return it to low heat briefly, whisking continuously. Do not let the sauce boil.

SEAFOOD

PAN-ROASTED WHITING WITH SHALLOTS AND RED WINE

- Merlans marchande de vin -

❖ EASY　　　　❖ MODERATE　　　　❖ 25 MINUTES　　　　❖ SERVES 4

4 whole whiting, cleaned, with heads
All-purpose flour for dusting
Salt and pepper
1 ½ cups red wine

2 shallots, chopped
2 tablespoons dry bread crumbs
2 tablespoons butter, cut into ¼-inch dice

❖　❖　❖　❖　❖

1. Rinse the fish and pat dry. Dust lightly with the flour, patting off the excess. Arrange the fish in a gratin dish. Season with salt and pepper. Pour in the wine and sprinkle the shallots around the fish. Sprinkle the top with the bread crumbs and dot with the butter.

2. Transfer the dish to the oven and bake for 15 to 20 minutes. Serve in the dish.

From Françoise:
• The red wine turns purplish when you cook it. If you don't like the color, whisk in a little bit of tomato paste to make it redder.

LOOKS-LIKE-OPERA-GLASSES DEEP-FRIED WHITING

- Merlans frits en lorgnettes -

❖ ADVANCED　　　　❖ MODERATE　　　　❖ 35 MINUTES　　　　❖ SERVES 4

4 whole whiting, cleaned, with heads
All-purpose flour for dredging
2 large eggs, lightly beaten
Dry bread crumbs for dredging

Salt and pepper
4 cups oil for frying
Chopped parsley leaves
1 lemon, cut into wedges

❖　❖　❖　❖　❖

1. Rinse the fish and pat dry. Using a sharp flexible knife, cut along the backbone of each fish from just behind the head to the tail. Slip the knife between the bones and the flesh on each side to release the fillets. The 2 fillets should still be attached to the head. Snip the backbone at both ends with scissors and pull it out along with the attached fine bones.

2. In separate soup plates, spread the flour, eggs, and bread crumbs. Season the eggs with salt and pepper. Season the fish fillets (still attached to the head) with salt and pepper, then dredge lightly in flour and dip in the eggs, letting the excess drip back into the plate. Dredge the fillets in the bread crumbs, pressing lightly to help the crumbs adhere. Roll up each fish fillet and secure it with a toothpick.

3. In a large skillet, heat the oil to 375 degrees. Gently drop the fish into the oil without crowding and fry until golden. Using a slotted spoon, transfer the fish to paper towels to drain as they are done. Remove the toothpicks. Transfer to a platter and keep warm in a low oven while frying the remaining fish. Serve very hot with parsley and the lemon wedges.

GOLDEN PAN-SAUTÉED WHITING WITH LEMON
- *Merlans meunière* -

❖ EASY ❖ MODERATE ❖ 25 MINUTES ❖ SERVES 4

4 whole whiting, cleaned, with heads
Salt and pepper
All-purpose flour for dusting
3 tablespoons butter

1 tablespoon oil
Chopped parsley leaves for sprinkling
1 lemon, cut into wedges

❖ ❖ ❖ ❖ ❖

1. Rinse the fish and pat dry. Season with salt and pepper and dust lightly with flour, patting off the excess.

2. In a large skillet, melt the butter in the oil over medium heat. Add the fish and cook, turning once, until lightly browned, 5 to 7 minutes per side.

3. Transfer the fish to a warmed platter, sprinkle with parsley, and serve with the lemon wedges.

From Françoise:
• Whiting is a fish that's delicate and easy to digest. Look for very fresh ones; they're shiny and firm.

POACHED SOLE WITH CREAMY MUSHROOM SAUCE
- Filets de sole Célestine -

❖ INTERMEDIATE   ❖ EXPENSIVE   ❖ 1 HOUR   ❖ SERVES 4

4 whole soles, cleaned and filleted,
  heads and bones reserved
½ pound white mushrooms
1 tablespoon butter
1 lemon

FISH STOCK
¾ cup dry white wine
1 onion, thinly sliced
1 small carrot, thinly sliced

1 bouquet garni made with parsley, thyme,
  and bay leaf
Salt
Black peppercorns

SAUCE
3 tablespoons butter
3 tablespoons all-purpose flour
2 tablespoons crème fraîche
Salt and pepper

❖ ❖ ❖ ❖ ❖

1. Make the fish stock: In a large saucepan, combine the reserved fish heads and bones with the wine, 2 ¼ cups of water, the onion, carrot, bouquet garni, salt, and peppercorns. Bring to a simmer, then cook at a bare simmer for 30 minutes.

2. Meanwhile, reserve 8 of the nicest mushroom caps. Chop all the remaining mushrooms. In a medium saucepan, melt the butter over medium heat. Add the chopped mushrooms, mushroom caps, and 1 tablespoon of water. Squeeze in a little lemon juice. Cook for 5 minutes. Drain and reserve the mushroom broth.

3. Fold the sole fillets in half. Arrange them in a large skillet. Pour the fish stock through a fine strainer lined with a paper towel over them. Bring slowly to a simmer over medium-low heat, then reduce the heat to low and cook at a bare simmer for 4 minutes. Using a slotted spoon, transfer the fillets to a warmed serving dish.

4. Make the sauce: In a medium saucepan, melt the butter. Whisk in the flour and cook until foaming. Whisk in the reserved mushroom broth and enough fish stock to make 2 cups. Season with salt and pepper. Bring to a boil, whisking, then reduce the heat to very low and cook for 10 minutes. Whisk in the crème fraîche and chopped mushrooms.

5. Pour the sauce over the sole, decorate with the mushroom caps, and serve at once.

From Françoise:
• Have your fishmonger fillet the soles, but ask to keep the carcasses.

• To save on cleanup, use the same saucepan to cook the mushrooms and the sauce.

POACHED SOLE WITH MUSSELS IN VELVETY SAUCE

- *Filets de sole Marguery* -

❖ INTERMEDIATE   ❖ EXPENSIVE   ❖ 1 HOUR   ❖ SERVES 4

1 pound mussels, scrubbed and debearded

1½ pounds skinless sole fillets

¾ cup dry white wine

1 bouquet garni made with parsley, thyme,
   and bay leaf

Salt and pepper

8 large cooked, shelled shrimp, tail on

SAUCE

1½ tablespoons butter

1½ tablespoons all-purpose flour

Salt and pepper

❖ ❖ ❖ ❖ ❖

1. Add the mussels to a large pot. Cover and cook over high heat, stirring once or twice, just until they open, 3 to 5 minutes. Remove the pot from the heat. Remove the meat from the shells and reserve. Discard the shells and any unopened mussels. Pour the broth through a fine strainer lined with a moistened paper towel.

2. In a large saucepan, combine the sole fillets with the wine, 1 cup of water, the reserved mussel broth, and bouquet garni. Season with salt and pepper. Bring to a simmer slowly over medium-low heat, then remove from the heat. Using a slotted fish slice, transfer the fillets to a warmed serving dish. Surround with the mussels and shrimp.

3. Make the sauce: In a small saucepan, melt the butter over medium heat. Whisk in the flour and cook until foaming. Whisk in 1 cup of the fish broth. Season with salt and pepper. Bring to a boil, whisking, then reduce the heat to very low and cook for 10 minutes.

4. Pour the sauce over the sole and serve at once.

From Françoise:

• Use dry white wine in this recipe. Sweet white wine tends to turn gray when cooked.

• Before pouring the sauce over the fish, taste it for seasoning and adjust if needed.

SEAFOOD

PAN-SEARED SOLE WITH BUTTER AND LEMON
- *Sole meunière* -

❖ EASY   ❖ EXPENSIVE   ❖ 25 MINUTES   ❖ SERVES 4

4 small (one-person) whole soles, cleaned,
  with heads
Salt and pepper
All-purpose flour for dusting

4 tablespoons (½ stick) butter
Chopped parsley for sprinkling
1 lemon, cut into wedges

❖ ❖ ❖ ❖ ❖

1. Rinse the fish and pat dry. Season the fish with salt and pepper and dust lightly with flour, patting off the excess.

2. In a large skillet, melt 2 tablespoons of the butter over medium-high heat. Add 2 of the fish and cook, turning once, until lightly browned, 3 to 4 minutes per side.

3. Transfer the fish to a warmed platter and cook the remaining 2 fish in the remaining 2 tablespoons of butter. Transfer to the platter and pour the pan juices over the fish. Sprinkle with parsley and serve, passing the lemon wedges separately.

From Françoise:

• To make a good sole meunière, you must dust the fish lightly with flour. (A "meunière" is a miller's wife.) Without this protective coating, the moist fish would stick to the skillet.

• Don't cook the sole over too high a heat or it might adhere to the pan. Don't try to turn them with a fork; they may break apart.

• To serve 4, you could also buy 2 larger soles and cook them 5 minutes per side.

• Sole fillets can be prepared in exactly the same way.

STUFFED SOLE FILLETS WITH CREAMY SAUCE
- *Filets de sole farcis, sauce crème* -

❖ ADVANCED   ❖ EXPENSIVE   ❖ 45 MINUTES   ❖ SERVES 4

1 ¾ pounds skinless sole fillets
2 tablespoons crème fraîche
1 small egg white
Salt and pepper

½ pound white mushrooms, thinly sliced
¾ cup dry white wine
1 teaspoon butter
1 teaspoon all-purpose flour

1. Preheat the oven to 350 degrees. In a food processor, grind 1 fish fillet with 1 tablespoon of the crème fraîche, the egg white, salt, and pepper.

2. On a work surface, spread the skinned side of the remaining fillets with the stuffing. Roll up the fillets and tie with kitchen string.

3. In a roasting pan, spread the mushrooms. Set the fish on top. Pour in the wine and press a sheet of foil or parchment paper on top. Transfer to the oven and poach for 15 to 20 minutes.

4. Using a slotted spoon, transfer the fish and mushrooms to a warmed serving dish. Remove the string. In a cup, mash the butter with the flour. Gradually whisk this paste into the pan juices and simmer for a few seconds until slightly thickened. Whisk in the remaining 1 tablespoon of crème fraîche.

5. Pour the sauce over the fish and serve.

From Françoise:
• Serve with steamed new potatoes or plain rice.

PAN-SEARED LEMON SOLE WITH BUTTER AND LEMON
- *Sole meunière* -

❖ EASY   ❖ MODERATE   ❖ 30 MINUTES   ❖ SERVES 4

4 small (one-person) whole lemon soles, cleaned, with heads
Salt and pepper

All-purpose flour for dusting
4 tablespoons (½ stick) butter
1 lemon, cut into wedges

❖ ❖ ❖ ❖ ❖

1. Rinse the fish and pat dry. Season the fish with salt and pepper and dust lightly with flour, patting off the excess.

2. In a large skillet, melt 2 tablespoons of the butter over medium heat. Add 2 of the fish and cook, turning once, until lightly browned, 5 to 7 minutes per side.

3. Transfer the fish to a warmed platter and cook the remaining 2 fish in the remaining 2 tablespoons of butter. Transfer to the platter and pour the pan juices over the fish. Serve, passing the lemon wedges separately.

From Françoise:
• Lemon sole has a more delicate texture than Dover sole, but you can use lemon sole to make any of the sole recipes.

• In order to brown properly, the sole should have plenty of room in the skillet, so cook them in 2 or 3 batches, depending on the size of the fish.

GOLDEN GRATINÉED SKATE WINGS

- *Raie à la vénitienne* -

❖ EASY   ❖ MODERATE   ❖ 30 MINUTES   ❖ SERVES 4

4 pieces skinned skate wing, not filleted
  (about 2 ½ pounds in all)
Salt and pepper
All-purpose flour for dusting
2 tablespoons butter
1 ½ cups milk

1 garlic clove, crushed
1 thyme sprig
½ bay leaf
1 whole clove
⅓ cup shredded Gruyère cheese

❖   ❖   ❖   ❖   ❖

1. Preheat the oven to 400 degrees. Season the fish with salt and pepper and dust lightly with flour, patting off the excess.

2. In a large skillet, melt the butter over medium heat. Add the fish in batches and cook, turning once, until very lightly browned.

3. Transfer the fish pieces as they are done to a gratin dish. Add the milk, garlic, thyme, bay leaf, and clove. Transfer the dish to the oven and bake for 10 to 15 minutes. Remove from the oven and discard the aromatics.

4. Increase the oven temperature to 450 degrees. Sprinkle the cheese over the fish, slide it on the top shelf of the oven, and bake for a few minutes until melted and lightly browned. Serve in the gratin dish.

From Françoise:
• This recipe is remarkably good with all parts of the skate wing. But if you can find skate cheeks, they are especially delicious.

• Finishing the baking on the top shelf makes the cheese brown more quickly because that's the hottest spot in the oven.

SKATE WITH CAPERS, LEMON, AND CRISPY CROUTONS
- *Raie grenobloise* -

❖ EASY   ❖ MODERATE   ❖ 30 MINUTES   ❖ SERVES 4

4 pieces skate wing, not filleted
 (about 2 ½ pounds in all)
6 tablespoons vinegar
Salt
1 lemon

8 tablespoons (1 stick) butter,
 cut into tablespoons
3 slices of crustless bread, cut into ¼-inch dice
2 tablespoons capers, drained
Chopped parsley for sprinkling

❖ ❖ ❖ ❖ ❖

1. In a large sauté pan, combine the skate with water to cover and 5 tablespoons of the vinegar. Season with salt. Bring to a simmer over medium heat, skimming, then reduce the heat to low and cook at a bare simmer for 15 minutes. Using a slotted fish slice, transfer the skate to a platter lined with paper towels. Remove the skin, if any. Transfer to a warmed serving dish and sprinkle with the remaining 1 tablespoon of vinegar.

2. Using a sharp knife, peel the lemon, removing all the white pith. Cut in between the membranes to release the sections. Cut the sections into ¼-inch dice.

3. In a large skillet, melt the butter over medium heat. Add the bread and cook until golden brown all over. Add the capers and lemon dice and heat through. Pour over the fish, sprinkle with parsley, and serve.

From Françoise:
• Don't worry if your skate has a faint ammonia smell; it's not bad. Skate is the only fish that benefits from brief aging. In fact, its firm and elastic flesh is more tender after a few days.

SEAFOOD

POACHED SKATE WITH BROWN BUTTER SAUCE

- *Raie au court-bouillon beurre noisette* -

❖ EASY   ❖ MODERATE   ❖ 30 MINUTES   ❖ SERVES 4

4 pieces skate wing, not filleted
  (about 2 ½ pounds in all)
6 tablespoons vinegar
Salt

8 tablespoons (1 stick) butter,
  cut into tablespoons
Chopped parsley for sprinkling

❖ ❖ ❖ ❖ ❖

1. In a large sauté pan, combine the skate with water to cover and 5 tablespoons of the vinegar. Season with salt. Bring to a simmer, skimming, then cook at a bare simmer for 15 minutes. Using a slotted fish slice, transfer the skate to a platter lined with paper towels. Remove the skin, if any. Transfer to a warmed serving dish and sprinkle with the remaining 1 tablespoon of vinegar.

2. In a small saucepan, melt the butter over low heat and cook until lightly browned. Pour over the fish, sprinkle with parsley, and serve.

WINE-POACHED JOHN DORY WITH HERBS

- *Saint-pierre au four* -

❖ EASY   ❖ EXPENSIVE   ❖ 40 MINUTES   ❖ SERVES 4

2 tablespoons butter, cut into ¼-inch pieces,
  plus more for brushing
2 ½- to 3-pound whole John Dory, cleaned,
  with head

2 tarragon sprigs or fennel fronds
Salt and pepper
¾ cup dry white wine or water

❖ ❖ ❖ ❖ ❖

1. Preheat the oven to 400 degrees. Brush a gratin dish with butter. Rinse the fish and pat dry. Set in the dish. Stuff with the herbs and 1 tablespoon of the butter. Season with salt and pepper. Pour in the wine or water and dot with the remaining 1 tablespoon of butter.

2. Transfer to the oven and bake for 30 minutes, basting occasionally with the pan juices.

From Françoise:

• John Dory is a prized mild, flat, white ocean fish. It has a large head, so if yours won't fit in your skillet, have the fishermonger cut off the head.

• This fish has a black skin on the inside. Peel it off if it hasn't already been removed. If you have any trouble, rub it with salt and it will detach easily.

JOHN DORY STUFFED WITH PARSLEY BREAD CRUMBS
- *Saint-pierre farci à l'anglaise* -

❖ EASY   ❖ EXPENSIVE   ❖ 50 MINUTES   ❖ SERVES 4

5 tablespoons butter, plus more for brushing

1 large egg

2 tablespoons chopped parsley leaves

Salt and pepper

Freshly grated nutmeg

1 lemon

1 cup dry bread crumbs

2 ½– to 3–pound whole John Dory, cleaned, with head

1 carrot, peeled and thinly sliced

1 onion, thinly sliced

❖ ❖ ❖ ❖ ❖

1. Preheat the oven to 400 degrees. In a small saucepan, barely melt 3 tablespoons of the butter. In a large bowl, beat the egg with the parsley and season with salt, pepper, and nutmeg. Squeeze in a little lemon juice. Beat in the bread crumbs and the softly melted butter. Rinse the fish and pat dry. Pack the stuffing into the fish. Secure with the toothpicks.

2. Brush a gratin dish with butter. Spread the carrot and onion in the dish. Set the fish on top. Pour in ¾ cup of water and dot with the remaining 2 tablespoons of butter.

3. Transfer the fish to the oven and bake for 30 minutes, basting occasionally with the pan juices. Just before serving, drizzle with more lemon juice. Remove the toothpicks and serve.

From Françoise:

• John Dory is an exquisite fish and my favorite. It's expensive, though, especially when you take into account the large head, so there's even less meat.

• The fillets of John Dory can be cooked à la meunière (see page 434). It's simple and delicious.

• You can use dry white wine instead of water here. It will give the dish more flavor.

SEAFOOD

BROILED RED MULLET WITH HERBS
- *Rouget grillés aux herbes* -

❖ EASY   ❖ EXPENSIVE   ❖ 10 MINUTES, PLUS 30 MINUTES MARINATING   ❖ SERVES 4

¾ cup oil

Juice of ½ lemon

½ teaspoon dried rosemary leaves

½ teaspoon dried thyme leaves

Parsley sprigs, plus chopped parsley leaves
  for serving

Fennel fronds

Salt and pepper

4 whole red mullets, cleaned, with heads
  (6 to 7 ounces each)

❖ ❖ ❖ ❖ ❖

1. In a gratin dish, combine the oil with the lemon juice, rosemary, thyme, parsley sprigs, and fennel. Season with salt and pepper. Rinse the fish and pat dry. Make 3 shallow cross-wise slashes on both sides of each fish. Add to the marinade and turn to coat. Cover and refrigerate for 30 minutes, turning the fish occasionally.

2. Preheat the broiler. Brush the marinade off the fish and transfer them to a broiler pan. Broil the fish on the top shelf of the oven, turning once, for 3 to 4 minutes per side. Brush the fish occasionally with the marinade.

3. Transfer the fish to a warmed platter. Sprinkle with the chopped parsley and serve.

From Françoise:
• If your red mullets are freshly fished, you don't have to remove the insides. Some people like this part, especially the liver.

• You can make your own dried herbs by removing the leaves when they're fresh and storing them in jars.

ROSEMARY-MARINATED MULLET WITH SAFFRON

- Rougets marinés et cuits au four -

❖ EASY   ❖ EXPENSIVE   ❖ 45 MINUTES   ❖ SERVES 4

2 tablespoons butter, cut into ¼-inch dice,
  plus more for brushing
2 tablespoons olive oil
Chopped rosemary leaves
1 onion, thinly sliced
1 lemon, thinly sliced

1 garlic clove, thinly sliced
Salt and pepper
2 large whole red mullets, cleaned, with heads
Pinch of saffron threads or finely chopped ginger
6 tablespoons dry white wine

1. Brush a gratin dish with butter. In it combine the olive oil with the rosemary, onion, lemon slices, and garlic. Season with salt and pepper. Rinse the fish and pat dry. Add to the marinade and turn to coat. Cover and refrigerate for a few minutes, turning the fish occasionally.

2. Preheat the oven to 425 degrees. Sprinkle the fish with the saffron or ginger and dot with the butter. Pour in the wine. Transfer the dish to the oven and bake for 25 minutes. Serve in the dish.

SEAFOOD

PAN-SEARED RED MULLET WITH MUSHROOMS IN PARCHMENT

- Rougets en papillotes -

❖ EASY   ❖ EXPENSIVE   ❖ 40 MINUTES   ❖ SERVES 4

4 tablespoons (½ stick) butter
½ pound white mushrooms, finely chopped
1 shallot, finely chopped
Salt and pepper
6 tablespoons milk
All-purpose flour for dredging

4 whole red mullets, cleaned, with heads
  (6 to 7 ounces each)
1 tablespoon oil, plus more for brushing

continued

1. Preheat the oven to 425 degrees.

2. In a large skillet, melt 2 tablespoons of the butter over medium-low heat. Add the mushrooms and shallot, season with salt and pepper, and cook, stirring, until tender and all the liquid is evaporated.

3. In 2 separate soup bowls, add the milk and flour. Season the milk with salt and pepper. Rinse the fish and pat dry. Dip the fish in the milk, letting it drip back into the plate, then dredge lightly in flour, patting off the excess.

4. In a large skillet, melt the remaining 2 tablespoons of butter in the oil over medium heat. Add the fish and cook, turning once, until lightly browned, about 5 minutes per side.

5. Tear off 4 very large sheets of parchment paper or foil and fold them in half. Open each one up and brush with oil. On one half pile a quarter of the mushrooms alongside the folded edge. Set a fish on top. Fold the other half of the sheet over the fish and pleat it all around to seal, if using parchment; if using foil, fold in the edges. Transfer the papillotes to 2 baking sheets and bake for about 5 minutes.

6. Serve the fish in the papillotes and let guests open them at the table.

From Françoise:
• You can replace the sautéed mushrooms with anchovy butter, made by mashing softened butter with anchovy fillets. But then don't add any salt.

• Rouget is considered one of the most exquisite fish. It has deep rosy skin and varies in size from about 6 inches to 1 foot. It has very few bones, apart from the backbone, which is easily removed. The flesh is firm and lends itself to many different kinds of preparations. The tiniest rougets de roche are sometimes grilled without removing their entrails when they're superfresh, like woodcocks, which is why they are sometimes called *bécasses de mer* (woodcocks of the sea).

BAKED RED GURNARD WITH AROMATIC VEGETABLES
- *Grondins au four* -

❖ EASY   ❖ MODERATE   ❖ 40 MINUTES   ❖ SERVES 4

2 tablespoons butter, cut into ¼-inch dice, plus more for brushing
1 carrot, peeled and thinly sliced
1 onion, thinly sliced
1 shallot, thinly sliced

4 whole red gurnard or red mullets, cleaned, with heads (6 to 7 ounces each)
Salt and pepper
6 tablespoons dry white wine

❖   ❖   ❖   ❖   ❖

1. Preheat the oven to 400 degrees. Brush a gratin dish with butter. Spread the carrot, onion, and shallot in the dish. Rinse the fish and pat dry. Make 3 deep crosswise slashes on both

sides of each fish. Set in the dish and season with salt and pepper. Pour in the wine and 6 tablespoons of water and dot with the butter.

2. Transfer the fish to the oven and bake for about 30 minutes. Serve in the dish.

From Françoise:
• Grondin (red gurnard) is a large, common rockfish with a sharp dorsal fin, less prized than rouget. Red mullet is a good substitute.

• The fillets of the red gurnard are fairly thick; make the cuts deep so the fish cooks all the way through.

• If your kitchen has a fishy smell after cooking seafood, you can remove it by burning a lump of sugar, a piece of orange peel, or even apple peel.

WINE-BRAISED POLLACK WITH CARROTS, TOMATOES, AND MUSHROOMS
- *Lieu braisé* -

❖ EASY   ❖ MODERATE   ❖ 45 MINUTES   ❖ SERVES 4

2 tablespoons butter
1 carrot, peeled and cut into ½-inch dice
1 onion, cut into ½-inch dice
1 ½ pounds pollack fillets
1 garlic clove, crushed

1 shallot, chopped
2 tomatoes, peeled, seeded, and chopped
¾ cup dry white wine
Salt and pepper
¼ pound mushrooms, cut into ½ inch dice

❖ ❖ ❖ ❖ ❖

1. In a flameproof casserole, melt the butter over medium heat. Add the carrot and onion and cook until lightly browned. Add the fish, garlic, shallot, tomatoes, wine, and 6 table-spoons of water. Season with salt and pepper. Cover and bring to a simmer, then reduce the heat to low and cook for 20 minutes

2. Add the mushrooms and cook for 10 min-utes. Transfer the fish and sauce to a warmed serving dish and serve.

From Françoise:
• Pollack is a fish in the cod family.

• Your sauce will be more luscious if you stir in a little crème fraîche, off the heat, just before serving.

• You can leave out the wine and use water and a splash of vinegar or lemon juice instead.

• If the sauce looks thin, simmer it, uncovered, once the fish has come out, for 5 to 10 min-utes, until it thickens slightly.

SEAFOOD

PAN-SEARED POLLACK WITH BUTTER AND LEMON
- *Lieu meunière* -

❖ EASY   ❖ MODERATE   ❖ 25 MINUTES   ❖ SERVES 4

Four 6-ounce skinless pollack fillets
Salt and pepper
All-purpose flour for dusting

2 tablespoons butter
Chopped parsley leaves for sprinkling
1 lemon, cut into wedges

❖ ❖ ❖ ❖ ❖

1. Season the fish fillets with salt and pepper and dust lightly with flour, patting off the excess.

2. In a large skillet, melt the butter over medium heat. Add the fish and cook, turning once, until lightly browned, 5 to 7 minutes per side, depending on the thickness.

3. Transfer the fish to a warmed platter. Pour the pan juices on top. Sprinkle with the parsley and serve with the lemon wedges.

From Françoise:
• Pollack is a fairly fragile fish, so make sure the butter is not too hot when you add the fillets and cook them over medium heat.

• Pollack is similar to hake but less expensive and also not as flavorful, so season it well with salt, pepper, lemon, and parsley.

BROILED TURBOT
Turbot grillé

❖ VERY EASY   ❖ EXPENSIVE   ❖ 30 MINUTES   ❖ SERVES 4

Four 6-ounce skinless turbot fillets
Salt and pepper

2 tablespoons oil

❖ ❖ ❖ ❖ ❖

1. Preheat the broiler. Season the fish with salt and pepper and brush with the oil. Transfer the fillets to a broiler pan. Broil the fish on the top shelf of the oven, turning once, for 7 to 10 minutes per side, then serve.

OVEN-POACHED TURBOT WITH CREAMY TOMATO SAUCE

- Turbot duglére -

❖ EASY ❖ EXPENSIVE ❖ 45 MINUTES ❖ SERVES 4

2 tablespoons butter

1 onion, finely chopped

1 shallot, finely chopped

2 tomatoes, peeled, seeded, and finely chopped

Four 6-ounce skinless turbot fillets

¾ cup dry white wine

Salt and pepper

1 teaspoon all-purpose flour

Chopped parsley leaves for sprinkling

❖ ❖ ❖ ❖ ❖

1. Preheat the oven to 400 degrees. In a medium saucepan, melt 1 tablespoon of the butter over medium-low heat. Add the onion and shallot and cook until softened. Add the tomatoes and cook for 5 minutes.

2. Scrape the tomato mixture into a roasting pan. Set the fish on top and pour in the wine and ¾ cup of water. Season with salt and pepper.

3. Transfer to the oven and cook for 20 to 30 minutes. Using a slotted fish slice, transfer the fillets to a warmed serving dish. In a cup, mash the remaining 1 tablespoon of butter with the flour. Set the roasting pan over medium heat and gradually whisk in the paste. Let simmer until slightly thickened, about 2 minutes, then pour over the fish. Sprinkle with parsley and serve.

From Françoise:

• I like to save half a tomato and finely chop it, then add it the sauce just before serving. It adds a hit of fresh flavor to the dish. What's more, it's pretty.

• You can whisk 2 or 3 tablespoons of crème fraîche into the sauce just before serving.

SEAFOOD

POACHED HADDOCK WITH MELTED BUTTER
- *Haddock poché* -

❖ VERY EASY ❖ MODERATE ❖ 25 MINUTES ❖ SERVES 4

1 pound skinless smoked haddock fillet
2 cups milk

7 tablespoons butter

❖ ❖ ❖ ❖ ❖

1. Wash the haddock in several changes of cold water. In a sauté pan, combine the haddock with the milk and 2 cups of water. Bring to a simmer slowly over medium-low heat, then reduce the heat to low and cook at a bare simmer for about 15 minutes.

2. Meanwhile, in a small saucepan, melt the butter.

3. Using a slotted fish slice, transfer the fish to a warmed platter. Pour the butter over the top, and serve.

From Françoise:

• Don't salt the haddock. It's already salted; in fact, sometimes it's too salty and you need to soak it in cold water for an hour or two.

• I like to add the juice of half a lemon to the melted butter. It's exquisite.

• You can sprinkle the fish with chopped parsley leaves just before serving.

BROILED HADDOCK WITH LEMON AND PARSLEY
- *Haddock grillé* -

❖ EASY ❖ MODERATE ❖ 20 MINUTES, PLUS 2 HOURS MARINATING ❖ SERVES 4

1 pound skinless smoked haddock fillet,
  cut into 4 pieces
¾ cup oil

1 lemon
Chopped parsley leaves for sprinkling

❖ ❖ ❖ ❖ ❖

1. In a gratin dish, combine the haddock with the oil and turn to coat. Cover and refrigerate for 2 hours.

2. Preheat the broiler. Scrape the oil off the fish. Transfer the fillets to a broiler pan. Broil the fish on the top shelf of the oven, turning once, for 8 to 10 minutes per side.

3. Transfer the fish to a warmed platter. Drizzle with lemon juice, sprinkle with the parsley, and serve.

From Françoise:
• Haddock is small fresh cod that has been salted and smoked, so it keeps longer than fresh fish. Its color is vibrant yellow.

• You can also grill the haddock on a barbecue or in a grill pan on top of the stove. Preheat the grill or grill pan until hot before adding the well-oiled fish.

• You could serve this haddock with sauerkraut.

HERB-STUFFED GRAY MULLET WITH AROMATIC VEGETABLES

- *Mulet farci aux aromates* -

❖ EASY   ❖ MODERATE   ❖ 1 HOUR, 15 MINUTES   ❖ SERVES 4

STUFFING
6 tablespoons milk
½ cup dry bread crumbs
Mixed chopped parsley, chives, chervil, thyme, and tarragon leaves
Salt and pepper

2 ½- to 3-pound whole gray mullet, cleaned, with head

2 tablespoons butter, cut into ¼-inch dice, plus more for brushing
1 carrot, peeled and thinly sliced
1 onion, thinly sliced
1 shallot, thinly sliced
1 garlic clove, thinly sliced
1 bouquet garni made with parsley, thyme, and bay leaf
¾ cup dry white wine

❖ ❖ ❖ ❖ ❖

1. Preheat the oven to 400 degrees. Make the stuffing: In a small saucepan, warm the milk. Add the bread crumbs and let soak, then squeeze dry, discarding the excess milk. In a bowl, mix the bread crumbs with the herbs. Season well with salt and pepper.

2. Rinse the fish and pat dry. Pack the stuffing into the fish and secure with toothpicks.

3. Brush a gratin dish with butter and spread the carrot, onion, shallot, garlic, and bouquet garni in the bottom. Set the fish on top. Pour in the wine and dot with the 2 tablespoons of butter. Transfer the dish to the oven and bake for about 45 minutes. Remove the toothpicks and serve in the gratin dish.

From Françoise:
• What to do if you have too much stuffing? Shape it into balls, dust lightly with flour, and surround the fish with them. They make an inexpensive and attractive garnish.

• Gray mullet sometimes has a slightly muddy taste. As a precaution, rinse the inside with a little vinegar.

POACHED CONGER EEL IN AROMATIC BROTH

- *Congre au court-bouillon* -

❖ EASY ❖ MODERATE ❖ 45 MINUTES ❖ SERVES 4

1 tablespoon vinegar

2 onions, halved and stuck with 2 whole cloves total

1 shallot, thinly sliced

1 bouquet garni made with parsley, thyme, and bay leaf

Salt

Black peppercorns

2 ½–pound whole conger eel, cleaned, with head

❖ ❖ ❖ ❖ ❖

1. In a large sauté pan, combine 2 quarts of water with the vinegar, onions, shallot, bouquet garni, salt, and peppercorns. Bring to a boil over medium-high heat, then reduce the heat and simmer for at least 15 minutes. Let cool slightly.

2. Rinse the fish and add it to the court-bouillon. Set over medium heat, and when it comes to a simmer, adjust the heat so the fish cooks at a bare simmer for 10 to 15 minutes, depending on the size.

3. Drain the fish and serve it warm, or let it cool completely in the court-bouillon and serve at room temperature.

From Françoise:

• Conger eel is a large ocean fish resembling a freshwater eel. It has a lot of flavor—and even more bones. You should serve only a center-cut piece. The rest of the fish can be added to flavor fish soups or stews, but don't eat it.

• I recommend serving it cold, in scallop shells, which allows you to remove all the small bones before serving.

• To make this recipe more quickly, prepare a concentrated court-bouillon, using only 1 quart of water. After 15 minutes of simmering, add 1 quart of cold water, and you won't need to let it cool much before adding the fish.

• Conger eel is usually served hot with caper sauce, béchamel sauce, or sauce bâtarde (see the Sauces chapter, page 623).

WHITE WINE–BRAISED CONGER EEL WITH PEARL ONIONS AND CREAMY SAUCE

- *Congre braisé au vin blanc* -

❖ EASY   ❖ MODERATE   ❖ 1 HOUR   ❖ SERVES 4

¼ pound pearl onions, peeled

2-pound center-cut piece of conger eel

1 teaspoon all-purpose flour, plus more for dusting

3 tablespoons butter

1 cup dry white wine

1 garlic clove, crushed

1 bouquet garni made with parsley, thyme, and bay leaf

Salt and pepper

❖ ❖ ❖ ❖ ❖

1. Bring a medium saucepan of water to a boil. Add the pearl onions and cook for 2 minutes; drain.

2. Rinse the fish and pat dry. Dust lightly with flour. In a flameproof casserole, melt 2 tablespoons of the butter over medium heat. Add the fish and cook until lightly browned all over. Transfer to a plate. Add the pearl onions and cook until lightly browned. Return the fish to the pot and add the wine, garlic, and bouquet garni. Season with salt and pepper. Cover and bring to a simmer, then reduce the heat to low and cook for 40 minutes.

3. Using a slotted spoon, transfer the fish and onions to a warmed serving dish. Remove the bouquet garni. In a cup, mash the remaining 1 tablespoon of butter with the 1 teaspoon of flour. Gradually whisk in this paste and simmer for 2 minutes. Pour over the fish and serve.

From Françoise:

• Conger eel is relatively inexpensive, but very boney, especially in the tail end, which is why I recommend using a center-cut piece in this recipe.

• Give this sauce a little color by adding 1 or 2 tablespoons of snipped chives just before serving.

SEAFOOD

PROVENÇAL FISH STEW WITH SAFFRON
- *Bouillabaisse* -

❖ INTERMEDIATE ❖ EXPENSIVE ❖ 1 HOUR ❖ SERVES 6 TO 8

¼ cup olive oil

3 onions, chopped

4 to 4 ½ pounds mixed whole white fish, cleaned
and cut into steaks if large, heads reserved

3 tomatoes, chopped

1 fennel bulb, chopped

1 bay leaf

1 summer savory or thyme sprig

1 strip of orange zest

Pinch of saffron threads

Salt and pepper

24 slices of baguette, toasted

ROUILLE

A small handful of fresh bread crumbs

1 ½ cups milk

3 or 4 garlic cloves

1 or 2 small red chiles or cayenne pepper to taste

Salt

¾ cup olive oil

❖ ❖ ❖ ❖ ❖

1. In a large flameproof casserole, heat the olive oil over medium-low heat. Add the onions and cook, stirring occasionally, until softened, about 5 minutes. Add the fish steaks and heads, shaking the pot to coat the fish in the oil. Add the tomatoes, fennel, bay leaf, summer savory or thyme, orange zest, and saffron. Season with salt and pepper. Generously cover with boiling water and cook at a rolling boil, uncovered, for 15 to 20 minutes.

2. Meanwhile, make the rouille: In a bowl, soak the bread crumbs in the milk, then squeeze out as much milk as possible, discarding the milk. Using a mortar or small food processor, grind the garlic and chiles, if using, to a paste. Add the bread crumbs, salt, and cayenne pepper, if using, and puree. Blend in the olive oil a few drops at a time to begin, then in a steady stream.

3. Remove the fish heads. Transfer the fish to a warmed serving dish. Set the baguette toasts in soup bowls. Ladle the broth over the toasts

and serve with the fish, passing the rouille at the table.

From Françoise:

• I like to add a splash of pastis. It replaces the fennel and lends a typically Provençal accent.

• You can also use stale bread or rub the toasts with garlic.

• Saffron is so expensive and rare a spice that it's sold in tiny quantities. But it's extremely pungent, too. Even a pinch adds a tremendous amount of flavor to a dish.

• Bouillabaisse is not a dish to make ahead. Serve it quickly.

• There are many different recipes for bouillabaisse. Some add potatoes. Others omit the fish heads—*rascasse* (gurnard or scorpion fish, in the rockfish family) excepted—and make a fish head broth separately to add to the stew.

BRAISED DOGFISH WITH ONIONS

- *Roussette braisée à la cocotte* -

❖ EASY   ❖ MODERATE   ❖ 45 MINUTES   ❖ SERVES 4

1-pound dogfish, cleaned, without head
Salt and pepper
All-purpose flour for dusting

3 tablespoons butter
¼ pound onions, quartered
¾ cup dry white wine

❖ ❖ ❖ ❖ ❖

1. Rinse the fish and pat dry. Slice crosswise into thick steaks. Season with salt and pepper, then dust lightly with flour, patting off the excess.

2. In a flameproof casserole, melt the butter over medium heat. Add the pieces of fish and cook until lightly browned all over. Add the onions and wine and season with salt and pepper. Cover and bring to a simmer, then reduce the heat to low and cook for 30 minutes.

3. Transfer the fish and onions to a warmed serving dish and serve.

From Françoise:

• Dogfish, from the Atlantic, is also called *salmonette* because of its pinkish skin.

• The white wine is not critical, but it does make a better sauce. You can add a little lemon juice to the pot instead.

• For a variation, prepare dogfish "à l'américaine": When the fish is browned, add 1 peeled, seeded, and chopped tomato to the pot along with a pinch of cayenne pepper, then proceed with the recipe.

• To make a Cognac-flamed sauce, whisk a paste of 1 tablespoon of softened butter mixed with 1 teaspoon of flour into the pan juices and simmer for 2 minutes. Return the fish to the pot, add ¼ cup of Cognac, bring to a simmer, then carefully ignite.

SEAFOOD

DOGFISH WITH SAFFRON TOMATO SAUCE ON TOASTS
- *Roussette marseillaise* -

❖ EASY   ❖ MODERATE   ❖ 30 MINUTES   ❖ SERVES 4

3 tablespoons butter

4 onions, finely chopped

2 garlic cloves, chopped

1 pound tomatoes, peeled, seeded, and chopped

¼ cup dry white wine or water

Pinch of saffron threads

Salt and pepper

1-pound dogfish, cleaned, without head

4 slices of country bread or crustless white
sandwich bread, toasted

❖ ❖ ❖ ❖ ❖

1. In a flameproof casserole, melt the butter over medium-high heat. Add the onions and cook until lightly browned. Add the garlic, tomatoes, wine or water, and saffron. Season with salt and pepper. Cook for 5 minutes.

2. Rinse the fish and pat dry. Slice crosswise into 4 thick steaks. Add to the casserole, reduce the heat to low, cover, and cook for 30 minutes.

3. Arrange the toasts on a warmed platter. Set a piece of fish on top of each toast with some sauce. Serve, passing the remaining sauce separately.

CRISPY DOGFISH WITH LEMON
- *Roussette panée* -

❖ EASY   ❖ MODERATE   ❖ 15 MINUTES   ❖ SERVES 4

All-purpose flour for dredging

2 large eggs, lightly beaten

1 cup dry bread crumbs

Salt and pepper

1-pound dogfish, cleaned, without head

4 cups oil for frying

1 lemon, cut into 4 wedges

❖ ❖ ❖ ❖ ❖

1. In separate soup plates, spread the flour, eggs, and bread crumbs. Season the eggs with salt and pepper.

2. Rinse the fish and pat dry. Cut crosswise into thin steaks. Season with salt and pepper, then dredge them lightly in flour and dip in the eggs, letting the excess drip back into the

plate. Dredge the fish in the bread crumbs, pressing lightly to help the crumbs adhere.

3. In a large skillet, heat the oil to 375 degrees. Gently drop the fish into the oil without crowding and fry until golden, 1 to 3 minutes.

Using a slotted spoon, transfer the fish to paper towels to drain as they are done. Transfer to a platter and keep warm in a low oven while frying the remaining fish. Serve very hot with the lemon wedges.

BROILED SALMON WITH LEMONY-PARSLEY BUTTER
- *Saumon frais grillé* -

❖ EASY   ❖ MODERATE   ❖ 25 MINUTES   ❖ SERVES 4

MAÎTRE D'HÔTEL BUTTER
7 tablespoons butter, softened
1 tablespoon chopped parsley
½ tablespoon fresh lemon juice
Salt and pepper

Four 6-ounce salmon fillets
Salt and pepper
2 tablespoons oil

❖   ❖   ❖   ❖   ❖

1. Make the maître d'hôtel butter: In a bowl, beat the softened butter with the parsley and lemon juice. Season with salt and pepper.

2. Preheat the broiler. Season the salmon fillets with salt and pepper. Brush with the oil. Transfer to a broiler pan. Broil on the top rack of the oven, turning once, for 5 to 8 minutes per side, depending on the thickness of the fillets.

3. Transfer the salmon fillets to a warmed platter and serve with the flavored butter.

From Françoise:

• If you use a grill pan or barbecue, heat it until very hot. Add the salmon fillets and grill, rotating the fish once until seared with crosshatch grill marks, then turn the fillets and repeat on the second side.

• You can also serve the salmon with melted butter, seasoned with lemon juice, or with Béarnaise Sauce (page 632).

• Open the kitchen windows when you're grilling or broiling inside. Burn a lump of sugar, or a piece of orange peel or apple peel, to remove the inevitable fishy smell.

SEAFOOD

COLD POACHED SALMON IN ASPIC

- Saumon froid en Bellevue -

❖ ADVANCED ❖ MODERATE ❖ 2 HOURS, PLUS OVERNIGHT CHILLING ❖ SERVES 8 TO 10

COURT-BOUILLON

3 cups dry white wine

2 onions, thinly sliced

2 carrots, thinly sliced

1 bouquet garni made with parsley, thyme, and bay leaf

Salt

Black peppercorns

5 ½– to 6-pound whole salmon, cleaned, with head

GARNISH

1 envelope (1 tablespoon) unflavored powdered gelatin

10 small tomatoes

Salt

Tarragon sprigs, stems removed

1 ½ cups canned mixed diced vegetables, drained and patted dry

10 hard-boiled eggs, halved

MAYONNAISE

2 large egg yolks

Salt and pepper

2 teaspoons Dijon mustard

2 cups oil

1 to 2 tablespoons vinegar

❖ ❖ ❖ ❖ ❖

1. Make the court-bouillon: In a fish poacher, combine 1 quart of water with the wine, onions, carrots, bouquet garni, salt, and peppercorns. Bring to a boil over medium-high heat, then reduce the heat to medium and simmer for 30 minutes. Remove the poacher from the heat and add 1 quart of cold water to cool it quickly.

2. Rinse the salmon and add it to the court-bouillon, topping it off with more cold water, if needed to cover the fish. Set over medium heat, and when it comes to a simmer, adjust the heat so the fish cooks at a bare simmer for 10 minutes. Let it cool completely in the court-bouillon, then cover and refrigerate overnight.

3. In a small saucepan, sprinkle the gelatin over ½ cup of water. Let stand until spongy, about 3 minutes. Set the saucepan over medium heat until the water is warm and the gelatin melts, about 1 minute. Let cool—but it should still be liquid.

4. Cut a thin slice off the top of each tomato. Using a spoon, hollow out the insides, leaving a sturdy shell. Sprinkle with salt and turn upside down on a plate to drain.

5. Remove the salmon from the court-bouillon and pat dry. Set on a cake rack over a large dish. Carefully remove the skin on top. Brush the pink flesh with the liquid aspic. Dip tarragon leaves in the aspic then use to decorate the fish. Brush a second time with the aspic to make the tarragon stick and make a shiny coating. Carefully transfer the salmon to a large platter or a tray lined with a white napkin. Refrigerate overnight until set.

6. Meanwhile, make the mayonnaise: Using a mortar or small food processor, blend the egg yolks with the salt, pepper, and mustard. Blend in the oil a few drops at a time to begin, then in a steady stream. Mix in the vinegar and 2 tablespoons of the liquid aspic.

7. In a bowl, fold the diced vegetables with 1 cup of the mayonnaise. Spoon the vegetables into the tomatoes, mounding slightly.

8. To serve, surround the salmon with the stuffed tomatoes, alternating with the hard-boiled eggs. Serve, passing the remaining mayonnaise separately.

From Françoise:

• In Step 1, you can even add ice cubes to chill the court-bouillon quickly.

• If there is any aspic left, let it set completely, then coarsely crush it with a fork and use to decorate the platter.

• Please note that the finished dish contains raw egg.

SALMON TARTARE

- *Tartare de saumon* -

❖ EASY   ❖ MODERATE   ❖ 35 MINUTES   ❖ SERVES 4

1 shallot, finely chopped
½ lemon
1 pound skinless center-cut salmon fillet
Salt and pepper

2 tablespoons olive oil
Mixed chopped herbs such as parsley, chives, chervil, mint, and tarragon

❖ ❖ ❖ ❖ ❖

1. In a bowl, sprinkle the shallot with a teaspoon of the lemon juice.

2. Rinse the salmon fillet and pat dry. Run your fingers over the flesh and pull out any bones with tweezers. Cut into ¼-inch dice. Transfer to a bowl, season with salt, and refrigerate for at least 10 minutes and as long as 30 minutes.

3. Season with pepper and fold in the shallot and remaining lemon juice, olive oil, and herbs. Mound the tartare in chilled glasses and serve.

From Françoise:

• Instead of serving the tartare in glasses, you can pile it on salad plates lined with lettuce leaves—mâche, for instance.

• I like to vary the seasonings, as I do for beef tartare, adding diced zucchini, mango (it's very good), tomatoes, lemon sections, grated ginger.

• For a slightly iodine flavor, you might fold raw diced oysters into the salmon. Serve the tartare in the oyster shells.

• If you prefer a creamy texture, stir a little mayonnaise into the tartare.

• Serve with chilled glasses of vodka or aquavit.

SEAFOOD

PAN-SEARED SALMON FILLETS WITH BUTTER AND LEMON

- *Saumon frais meunière* -

❖ EASY   ❖ MODERATE   ❖ 20 MINUTES   ❖ SERVES 4

Four 6-ounce skinless salmon fillets
Salt and pepper
All-purpose flour for dusting

3 tablespoons butter
Parsley sprigs
1 lemon, cut into wedges

❖ ❖ ❖ ❖ ❖

1. Season the salmon fillets with salt and pepper and dust lightly with flour, patting off the excess.

2. In a large skillet, melt the butter over medium heat. Add the salmon and cook, turning once, until lightly browned, 5 to 7 minutes per side, depending on the thickness of the fillets.

3. Transfer the salmon to a warmed platter. Decorate with the parsley and lemon wedges and serve.

From Françoise:
• To dress up this dish, set the sautéed salmon fillets on a bed of watercress sprigs and surround with grilled tomato halves, lemon wedges, and potato chips.

• You could also serve the salmon with steamed small new potatoes, sprinkled with chopped parsley, and with a sauceboat of melted butter.

• Frozen salmon can be prepared in the same way; defrost it first in the refrigerator.

EEL STEW WITH RED WINE

- *Matelote d'anguilles* -

❖ INTERMEDIATE   ❖ MODERATE   ❖ 1 HOUR, 10 MINUTES   ❖ SERVES 4

3 cups red wine

1 carrot, peeled and thinly sliced

¼ pound yellow onions, thinly sliced

1 bouquet garni made with parsley, thyme,
   and bay leaf

Salt

Black peppercorns

1 ½ pounds eels, cleaned and skinned

¼ pound pearl onions, peeled

6 tablespoons butter

¼ pound thick-sliced pancetta, cut crosswise
   into ¼-inch-thick strips

½ pound white mushrooms, cut into ¼-inch dice

1 tablespoon all-purpose flour

4 slices of country bread or crustless white
   sandwich bread

❖   ❖   ❖   ❖   ❖

1. In a large sauté pan, make the court-bouillon: Combine the wine with the carrot, yellow onions, bouquet garni, salt, and peppercorns. Bring to a boil over medium-high heat, then reduce the heat to medium and simmer for 15 minutes. Let cool slightly.

2. Rinse the eels and add them to the court-bouillon. Set over medium heat, and when it comes to a simmer, adjust the heat so the eels cook at a bare simmer for 10 minutes. Remove the pan from the heat, leaving the eels in the court-bouillon.

3. In a small saucepan, barely cover the pearl onions with court-bouillon. Partially cover and cook over low heat until completely dry.

4. In a medium skillet, melt 1 tablespoon of the butter over medium heat. Add the pancetta and cook until just beginning to brown. Add the mushrooms and cook for 5 minutes.

5. Remove the eels from the court-bouillon. Strain the court-bouillon into a flameproof casserole and bring to a simmer. Discard the aromatics. In a cup, mash 2 tablespoons of the remaining butter with the flour. Gradually whisk this paste into the simmering court-bouillon. Add the eels, pearl onions, pancetta, and mushrooms, reduce the heat to low, cover, and cook for 10 minutes.

6. Meanwhile, in a large skillet, melt the remaining 3 tablespoons of butter over medium heat. Add the bread and cook until golden on both sides.

7. Transfer the toasts to a warmed serving dish, spoon the eel stew on top, and serve.

From Françoise:

• Serve with steamed or boiled new potatoes, sprinkled with chopped parsley.

• Since this stew is cooked with red wine, pour a red wine to accompany it.

SEAFOOD

PAN-SEARED TROUT WITH BUTTERY ALMONDS

- Truites aux amandes -

❖ EASY   ❖ MODERATE   ❖ 30 MINUTES   ❖ SERVES 4

¾ cup milk

All-purpose flour for dredging

Salt and pepper

4 whole trout, cleaned, with heads

4 tablespoons (½ stick) butter

½ cup sliced almonds

1 lemon, thinly sliced (optional)

❖ ❖ ❖ ❖ ❖

1. In 2 separate soup bowls, add the milk and flour. Season the milk with salt and pepper. Rinse the fish and pat dry. Dip the fish in the milk, letting it drip back into the bowl, then dredge lightly in flour, patting off the excess.

2. In a large skillet, melt 2 tablespoons of the butter over medium heat. Add the fish and cook, turning once, until lightly browned, 7 to 8 minutes per side.

3. In a small saucepan, melt the remaining 2 tablespoons of butter with the almonds and cook until lightly browned.

4. Transfer the trout to a serving platter and decorate with the lemon slices, if using. Pour the almonds and butter over the fish and serve.

From Françoise:

• Watch the cooking of the fish and the almonds closely, as they can easily burn and trout is delicate.

• If you like, decorate the lemon by cutting thin grooves in the peel before slicing it into rounds.

• You may need to sauté the trout two at a time with 1 tablespoon of butter per batch if your skillet is too small. The fish should fit comfortably so they brown nicely.

WINE-BRAISED TROUT WITH CREAM AND CHIVES

- *Truites à la crème et à la ciboulette* -

❖ EASY   ❖ MODERATE   ❖ 20 MINUTES   ❖ SERVES 4

Butter for brushing

1 shallot, finely chopped

4 whole trout, cleaned, with heads

1 ½ cups dry white wine

1 tablespoon snipped chives

Juice of ½ lemon

Salt and pepper

¼ cup crème fraîche

❖ ❖ ❖ ❖ ❖

1. Preheat the oven to 425 degrees. Brush a roasting pan with butter. Scatter the shallot in the bottom. Set the trout in the pan and add the wine, chives, and lemon juice. Season with salt and pepper. Transfer to the oven and poach for 10 minutes.

2. Using a slotted fish slice, transfer the trout to a warmed serving dish. Add the crème fraîche to the pan juices and bring to a simmer for a few seconds until the sauce thickens slightly. Pour over the trout and serve.

From Françoise:
• Serve with steamed new potatoes, sprinkled with chopped parsley.

• If you use an attractive gratin dish (porcelain, for instance) instead of a roasting pan, you can serve the trout in it. You'll need to pour the pan juices into a saucepan to reduce with the crème fraîche, then pour them over the fish in the gratin dish. Wipe the rim of the dish before serving.

• Ask your fishmonger to empty your trout by the gills instead of cutting through the belly so the fish won't break during cooking and will look nicer. Or do it yourself.

SEAFOOD

TROUT SIMMERED IN AROMATIC BROTH

- *Truites au bleu* -

❖ EASY ❖ MODERATE ❖ 30 MINUTES ❖ SERVES 4

COURT-BOUILLON
¾ cup vinegar
1 onion, thinly sliced
1 carrot, peeled and thinly sliced
1 bouquet garni made with parsley, thyme,
   and bay leaf

Salt
Black peppercorns

4 whole live trout
Vinegar

❖ ❖ ❖ ❖ ❖

1. Make the court-bouillon: In a large sauté pan, combine 2 quarts of water with the vinegar, onion, carrot, bouquet garni, salt, and peppercorns. Bring to a boil over medium-high heat, then reduce the heat to medium and simmer for 15 minutes.

2. Working quickly, clean the trout through the gills. Rinse them and sprinkle with plenty of vinegar. Add them to the simmering court-bouillon. When it returns to a bare simmer, remove the pan from the heat.

3. Spread the onion and carrot from the court-bouillon in the bottom of a warmed serving dish. Set the trout on top and pour in a little court-bouillon. Serve at once.

From Françoise:
• Serve with a sauceboat of melted butter and steamed potatoes, sprinkled with parsley.

• Truites au bleu can also be served cold. Let the trout cool completely in the court-bouillon.

• The secret to the blue color: Add the trout to the vinegary court-bouillon just after they're killed. Don't be surprised if the trout curl up and the flesh breaks a little when added to the simmering court-bouillon. It really can't be avoided.

COCKLES WITH SHALLOTS AND CRISPY CRUMBS
- *Coques à la nantaise* -

❖ EASY ❖ MODERATE ❖ 20 MINUTES, PLUS 30 MINUTES SOAKING ❖ SERVES 4

2 pounds cockles
Salt
3 tablespoons butter
2 shallots, finely chopped

6 tablespoons muscadet or other dry white wine
½ cup fresh or dry bread crumbs
Chopped parsley leaves for sprinkling

❖ ❖ ❖ ❖ ❖

1. Add the cockles to a large bowl of heavily salted water and let soak for 30 minutes; drain.

2. Preheat the oven to 425 degrees. Transfer the cockles to a large pot. Cover and cook over high heat, stirring once or twice, just until they open, 3 to 5 minutes. Remove the pot from the heat. Remove the meat from the shells and reserve. Discard the shells and any unopened cockles. Pour the broth through a fine strainer lined with a moistened paper towel.

3. Rinse out the pot. In it melt 1 tablespoon of the butter over medium-low heat. Add the shallots and wine and cook until softened. Add the cockles, ¼ cup of the bread crumbs, and enough of the cockle broth to moisten them. Cover and simmer for 1 minute.

4. Spread the cockle mixture in scallop shells or individual gratin dishes. Sprinkle the remaining ¼ cup of bread crumbs and the parsley on top and dot with the remaining 2 tablespoons of butter. Set on a baking sheet, transfer to the oven, and bake for a few minutes until nicely browned.

From Françoise:
• To make this a more substantial dish, serve it with plain rice or boiled new potatoes.

• Soaking the cockles in salted water for at least 30 minutes makes them disgorge any sand and grit, which falls to the bottom of the bowl.

• You can replace the 2 shallots with 1 onion.

• To make your own fresh bread crumbs quickly, grind crustless bread in a food processor. Crumbled toast can also be used.

• Mussels and small clams can be prepared this way, too.

SEAFOOD

COCKLES AND MACARONI WITH
CREAMY TOMATO SAUCE
- *Coques aux coquillettes* -

❖ EASY   ❖ MODERATE   ❖ 45 MINUTES, PLUS 30 MINUTES SOAKING   ❖ SERVES 4

3 pounds cockles

Salt

½ pound macaroni

¼ cup shredded Gruyère cheese

SAUCE

2 tablespoons butter

2 tablespoons all-purpose flour

8-ounce can tomato sauce

Salt and pepper

Cayenne pepper

❖　❖　❖　❖　❖

1. Add the cockles to a large bowl of heavily salted water and let soak for 30 minutes; drain.

2. Transfer the cockles to a large pot. Cover and cook over high heat, stirring once or twice, just until they open, 3 to 5 minutes. Remove the pot from the heat. Remove the meat from the shells and reserve. Discard the shells and any unopened cockles. Pour the broth through a fine strainer lined with a moistened paper towel into a glass measuring cup.

3. Bring a large saucepan of salted water to a boil. Add the macaroni and cook, stirring occasionally, until al dente; drain.

4. Meanwhile, make the sauce: In a small saucepan, melt the butter over medium heat. Whisk in the flour until it starts foaming. Whisk in the cockle broth with enough water to make 2 cups, then the tomato sauce. Season with salt, pepper, and cayenne. Bring to a boil, whisking, until thickened. Add the cockles, reduce the heat to low, and cook for 2 to 3 minutes.

5. Transfer the macaroni to a serving bowl. Add the cockle sauce and toss to coat. Sprinkle with the cheese and serve.

From Françoise:

• This is also a good recipe to make with fresh tagliatelle noodles. And you can substitute mussels for the cockles.

MOLDED RICE PILAF WITH COCKLES
AND CREAMY SAUCE

- Pilaf de coques -

❖ EASY   ❖ MODERATE   ❖ 1 HOUR, PLUS 30 MINUTES SOAKING   ❖ SERVES 4

---

2 pounds cockles

Salt

4 tablespoons (½ stick) butter, plus more
  for brushing

1 onion, finely chopped

¼ pound white mushrooms, cut into ¼-inch dice

1 ¼ cups long-grain rice

1 bouquet garni made with parsley, thyme,
  and bay leaf

SAUCE

1 ½ tablespoons butter

1 ½ tablespoons all-purpose flour

Pepper

1 large egg yolk

❖ ❖ ❖ ❖ ❖

1. Add the cockles to a large bowl of heavily salted water and let soak for 30 minutes; drain.

2. Meanwhile, in a medium saucepan, melt 3 tablespoons of the butter over medium-low heat. Add the onion and mushrooms and cook until softened. Stir in the rice. Add 2 ½ cups of water and the bouquet garni. Bring to a boil, then reduce the heat to low, cover, and cook until the rice is tender and the water is absorbed, 17 to 20 minutes.

3. Transfer the cockles to a large pot. Cover and cook over high heat, stirring once or twice, just until they open, 3 to 5 minutes. Remove the pot from the heat. Remove the meat from the shells and reserve. Discard the shells and any unopened cockles. Pour the broth through a fine strainer lined with a moistened paper towel into a glass measuring cup.

4. Remove the bouquet garni. In a large bowl, combine the rice with the cockles. Brush a soufflé or other deep baking dish with butter.

Pack the cockles and rice into the dish and keep warm.

5. Make the sauce: In a small saucepan, melt the butter over medium heat. Whisk in the flour until it starts foaming. Whisk in the cockle broth with enough water to make 1 cup. Season with pepper. Bring to a boil, whisking, then reduce the heat to very low and cook for 10 minutes. Remove the pan from the heat and whisk in the egg yolk.

6. Invert a round platter over the soufflé dish. Holding the dish and platter together, quickly invert the rice pilaf onto the platter. Pour the sauce around the pilaf and serve.

From Françoise:

• Small clams or mussels can also be used in this recipe.

• The usual proportion of water to rice when making pilaf is 2 to 1. The cooking time can vary somewhat depending on the origin of the rice.

SEAFOOD

GOLDEN GRATINÉED SHELLFISH WITH
SHALLOT AND PARSLEY BUTTER

- Coquillages farcis 1 -

❖ EASY   ❖ MODERATE   ❖ 40 MINUTES   ❖ SERVES 4

¾ cup (1 ½ sticks) butter, softened
1 shallot, finely chopped
Chopped parsley leaves
Salt and pepper

6 dozen mussels, cockles, or small clams,
  scrubbed and bearded
1 ½ cups fresh bread crumbs

❖   ❖   ❖   ❖   ❖

1. In a bowl, beat the softened butter with the shallot and parsley. Season with salt and pepper.

2. Using a small, sharp knife, carefully open the shellfish. Detach the meat from the shells, keeping the meat in its shell, and transfer to individual gratin dishes. Dot with the shallot and parsley butter. Set on a baking sheet.

3. Just before serving, preheat the broiler. Sprinkle the bread crumbs over the tops.

Transfer the baking sheet to the top rack of the oven and broil until the shellfish is nicely browned, 3 to 5 minutes. Serve at once.

From Françoise:
• This dish can be prepared through Step 2 and refrigerated for several hours. Broil the shellfish just before serving.

• The secret to perfect gratinéed shellfish: Broil them very quickly at high heat. Cooked slowly, they become rubbery.

GOLDEN GRATINÉED SHELLFISH WITH
GARLICKY CURRY BUTTER

- Coquillages farcis 2 -

❖ EASY   ❖ MODERATE   ❖ 40 MINUTES   ❖ SERVES 4

7 tablespoons butter, softened
2 garlic cloves, finely chopped
1 teaspoon curry powder

Salt and pepper
6 dozen mussels, cockles, or small clams,
  scrubbed and debearded

1. In a bowl, beat the softened butter with the garlic. Season with the curry, salt, and pepper.

2. Using a small, sharp knife, carefully open the shellfish. Detach the meat from the shells, keeping the meat in its shell, and transfer to individual gratin dishes. Dot with the curry butter. Set on a baking sheet.

3. Just before serving, preheat the broiler. Transfer the baking sheet to the top rack of the oven and broil until the shellfish is nicely browned, 3 to 5 minutes. Serve at once.

PERIWINKLES COOKED IN AROMATIC BROTH

- Bigorneaux au court-bouillon -

❖ EASY ❖ INEXPENSIVE ❖ 15 MINUTES ❖ SERVES 4

1 pound periwinkles

1 bouquet garni made with parsley, thyme,
  and bay leaf

1 garlic clove, crushed

1 shallot, chopped

1 whole clove

1 small dried red chile

¾ cup dry white wine

1 teaspoon salt

Cracked black pepper

❖ ❖ ❖ ❖ ❖

1. Wash the periwinkles in several changes of cold water.

2. In a large saucepan, combine the periwinkles with the bouquet garni, garlic, shallot, clove, chile, wine, salt, and cracked pepper. Add enough water to barely cover. Bring to a boil over medium heat, then reduce the heat to low and cook at a gentle boil for 10 minutes. Let the periwinkles cool slightly or completely in the broth before serving.

From Françoise:
• Periwinkles make a fun, hands-on hors d'oeuvre or first course.

• Stick several large pins into a cork and set them out on the table when you serve the periwinkles. They are the best tools for picking out the meat inside the shell.

• Select large and lively periwinkles. Pay attention to how they smell when you wash them; one bad periwinkle could spoil the whole bunch.

SEAFOOD

BOILED PERIWINKLES

- *Bigorneaux au naturel* -

❖ EASY   ❖ INEXPENSIVE   ❖ 15 MINUTES   ❖ SERVES 4

1 pound periwinkles

1 bouquet garni made with parsley, thyme,
   and bay leaf

1 garlic clove, crushed

1 shallot, chopped

1 whole clove

1 teaspoon salt

Cracked black pepper

❖ ❖ ❖ ❖ ❖

1. Wash the periwinkles in several changes of
cold water.

2. In a large saucepan, combine the periwinkles
with the bouquet garni, garlic, shallot, clove,

salt, and pepper. Add enough water to barely
cover. Bring to a boil over medium heat, then
reduce the heat to low and cook at a gentle boil
for 10 minutes. Let the periwinkles cool slightly
or completely in the broth before serving.

SIMPLE PAN-SEARED SEA SCALLOPS

- *Coquilles Saint-Jacques simplement poêlées* -

❖ EASY   ❖ EXPENSIVE   ❖ 15 MINUTES   ❖ SERVES 4

2 tablespoons butter

12 sea scallops

Salt and pepper

1 tablespoon chopped parsley leaves

1 lemon, cut into 4 wedges

❖ ❖ ❖ ❖ ❖

1. In a large skillet, melt the butter over
medium-high heat. When it foams, add the
scallops and cook, turning once, until nicely
browned, 3 to 4 minutes, depending on the
size. Season with salt and pepper.

2. Transfer the scallops to a warmed platter,
sprinkle with the parsley, and serve with the
lemon wedges.

From Françoise:
• Serve the scallops as is, at their unadorned best,
or on a mesclun salad, drizzled with extra-virgin
olive oil and balsamic or raspberry vinegar.

• You might also sear them in olive oil, adding
minced garlic just before serving.

• If the scallops are really very large, cut them
in half horizontally.

466

POACHED SEA SCALLOPS IN A CREAMY SAUCE

- *Coquilles Saint-Jacques à la crème* -

❖ INTERMEDIATE   ❖ EXPENSIVE   ❖ 30 MINUTES   ❖ SERVES 4

16 sea scallops

1 bouquet garni made with parsley, thyme,
   and bay leaf

2 shallots, chopped

1 onion stuck with 2 whole cloves

Salt and pepper

1 ½ cups dry white wine

SAUCE

2 tablespoons butter

1 ½ tablespoons all–purpose flour

2 large egg yolks

2 tablespoons crème fraîche

❖ ❖ ❖ ❖ ❖

1. In a large saucepan, combine the scallops with the bouquet garni, shallots, and onion. Season with salt and pepper. Add the wine and 1 ½ cups of water. Bring slowly to a simmer over medium-low heat, then reduce the heat to low and cook at a bare simmer for 3 to 4 minutes. Using a slotted spoon, remove the scallops to a bowl. Pour the broth through a fine strainer into a glass measuring cup.

2. Make the sauce: In a small saucepan, melt the butter over medium heat. Whisk in the flour until it starts foaming. Whisk in 1 cup of the reserved scallop broth. Bring to a boil, whisking, then reduce the heat to low and cook for 2 to 3 minutes. The sauce should be thin.

3. In a small bowl, whisk the egg yolks with the crème fraîche. Whisk in a little of the hot sauce. Remove the pan from the heat and whisk in this mixture until slightly thickened.

4. Spoon some of the sauce into a warmed serving dish. Arrange the scallops in the dish, cover with the remaining sauce, and serve.

From Françoise:

• If you like, serve the scallops with boiled or steamed rice.

• The secret to firm and juicy poached scallops: They should not boil, but cook in barely simmering water for 3 to 5 minutes, depending on the thickness. Cooking them for too long or at a rolling boil toughens them.

SEAFOOD

GRATIN OF SEA SCALLOPS AND MUSHROOMS IN CREAMY SAUCE

- Coquilles Saint-Jacques au gratin -

❖ INTERMEDIATE   ❖ EXPENSIVE   ❖ 35 MINUTES   ❖ SERVES 4

¾ cup dry white wine

2 shallots, chopped

2 tablespoons butter

1 bouquet garni made with parsley, thyme, and bay leaf

Salt and pepper

¼ pound white mushrooms, cut into ¼-inch dice

Juice of ½ lemon

8 sea scallops

SAUCE

2 tablespoons butter

1½ tablespoons all-purpose flour

1 large egg yolk

❖ ❖ ❖ ❖ ❖

1. In a large saucepan, combine the wine, shallots, 1 tablespoon of the butter, and the bouquet garni. Season with salt and pepper. Bring to a boil over medium heat and simmer for 3 minutes. Add the mushrooms and lemon juice, reduce the heat to low, and cook for 10 minutes.

2. Add the scallops and cook at a bare simmer for 2 minutes. Using a slotted spoon, remove the scallops and mushrooms to a bowl. Pour the broth through a fine strainer into a glass measuring cup.

3. Preheat the oven to 425 degrees. Make the sauce: In a small saucepan, melt the butter over medium heat. Whisk in the flour until it starts foaming. Whisk in the scallop broth with

enough water to make 1 cup. Bring to a boil, whisking, then reduce the heat to very low and cook for 5 minutes. Remove the pan from the heat and whisk in the egg yolk until slightly thickened.

4. Slice the scallops horizontally. Spread the scallops and mushrooms in scallop shells or individual gratin dishes. Spoon the sauce over the tops and dot with the remaining 1 tablespoon of butter. Set on a baking sheet and bake on the top shelf of the oven for a few minutes until lightly browned. Serve at once.

From Françoise:

• You can sprinkle dry bread crumbs over the scallops before browning them in the oven.

CRUSTY GRATIN OF SEA SCALLOPS AND MUSHROOMS IN CREAMY SAUCE

- *Coquilles Saint-Jacques sauce Mornay* -

❖ INTERMEDIATE   ❖ EXPENSIVE   ❖ 1 HOUR   ❖ SERVES 4

¾ cup dry white wine

1 onion, sliced

1 whole clove

1 bouquet garni made with parsley, thyme, and bay leaf

Salt and pepper

8 sea scallops

½ pound white mushrooms, thinly sliced

2 ½ tablespoons butter

Juice of ½ lemon

Dry bread crumbs for sprinkling

MORNAY SAUCE

2 tablespoons butter

1 ½ tablespoons all-purpose flour

Salt and pepper

1 tablespoon crème fraîche

1 large egg yolk

❖ ❖ ❖ ❖ ❖

1. In a large saucepan, combine the wine, ¾ cup of water, the onion, clove, and bouquet garni. Season with salt and pepper. Bring to a boil over medium heat and simmer for 3 minutes.

2. Add the scallops, reduce the heat to low, and cook at a bare simmer for 2 minutes. Using a slotted spoon, remove the scallops to a bowl. Pour the broth through a fine strainer into a glass measuring cup.

3. In a medium saucepan, combine the mushrooms with ½ tablespoon of the butter, the lemon juice, and a little water. Season with salt and pepper. Cook over medium heat for 5 minutes. Add the mushroom broth to the measuring cup.

4. Preheat the oven to 425 degrees. Make the Mornay sauce: In a small saucepan, melt the butter over medium heat. Whisk in the flour until it starts foaming. Whisk in the scallop and mushroom broths with enough water, if needed, to make 1 cup. Season with salt and pepper. Bring to a boil, whisking, and cook over very low heat for 5 minutes. In a small bowl, whisk the crème fraîche with the egg yolk. Remove the pan from the heat and whisk in the egg yolk mixture until slightly thickened.

5. Spoon some of the Mornay sauce into 4 scallop shells or individual gratin dishes. Top with the scallops and mushrooms and cover with the remaining sauce. Sprinkle bread crumbs over the top and dot with the remaining 2 tablespoons of butter. Set on a baking sheet and bake on the top shelf of the oven for a few minutes until lightly browned. Serve at once.

From Françoise:

• If the scallops are very thick, cut them in half or even thirds horizontally and reduce the poaching time.

SEAFOOD

PAN-SEARED SEA SCALLOPS WITH SHALLOT, GARLIC, AND PARSLEY BUTTER

- Coquilles Saint-Jacques à la provençale -

❖ EASY   ❖ EXPENSIVE   ❖ 30 MINUTES   ❖ SERVES 4

3 tablespoons butter

12 sea scallops

Salt and pepper

4 shallots, finely chopped

2 garlic cloves, finely chopped

Chopped parsley leaves for sprinkling

❖ ❖ ❖ ❖ ❖

1. In a large skillet, melt the butter over high heat. When it foams, add the scallops, season with salt and pepper, and cook, turning once, until nicely browned, about 2 minutes. Add the shallots and garlic, reduce the heat to low, cover, and cook for 2 minutes.

2. Transfer the scallops with the buttery pan juices to a warmed platter, sprinkle with parsley, and serve very hot.

SCALLOPS WITH MUSHROOMS AND HERB CRUMBS

- Coquilles Saint-Jacques nantaise -

❖ EASY   ❖ EXPENSIVE   ❖ 45 MINUTES   ❖ SERVES 4

2 tablespoons butter

1 shallot or garlic clove, chopped

¼ pound white mushrooms, chopped

Salt and pepper

1 ¼ cups muscadet or other dry white wine

8 sea scallops, cut into ¼-inch dice

About 1 cup day-old bread crumbs

Mixed chopped parsley, chervil, and chives

❖ ❖ ❖ ❖ ❖

1. In a large skillet, melt 2 tablespoons of the butter over low heat. Add the shallot or garlic and mushrooms and cook until tender. Season with salt and pepper. Add the wine and cook for 20 minutes.

2. Add the scallops and cook at a bare simmer for 5 minutes. Add just enough bread crumbs to absorb the pan juices; the mixture should not be thick. Stir in the herbs.

3. Preheat the broiler. Spread the scallop mixture in 4 scallop shells or individual gratin dishes. Set on a baking sheet and broil on the top shelf of the oven for a few minutes until nicely browned. Serve at once.

BOILED CRAB
- Crabe au naturel -

❖ EASY   ❖ MODERATE   ❖ 30 MINUTES   ❖ SERVES 4

Salt
1 bouquet garni made with parsley, thyme,
   and bay leaf

Pepper
1 large Dungeness crab (2 ½ to 3 ½ pounds) or
   2 medium crabs

❖ ❖ ❖ ❖ ❖

1. Bring a large pot of salted water to a boil with the bouquet garni and pepper. Add the crab and cook for 20 to 30 minutes, depending on the size.

2. Drain in a colander, then rinse under cold running water and drain well again.

From Françoise:

• Crustaceans should be purchased while still alive. They should be energetic and heavy for their size. If you buy them precooked, smell them to make sure they are fresh. Crab can be a bargain at certain times; take advantage of it.

• Using a large, heavy knife, cut the crab into 4 serving pieces. Pass nutcrackers and nut picks at the table and let your guests extract the flavorful flesh using their fingers. Set out finger bowls for cleaning up—any simple bowls will do.

SEAFOOD

CRAB SOUFFLÉ
- Soufflé de crabe -

❖ ADVANCED　　　　❖ EXPENSIVE　　　　❖ 1 HOUR　　　　❖ SERVES 4

2 tablespoons butter, plus more for brushing

2 tablespoons all-purpose flour

3 ½ ounces lump crabmeat, shredded,
  juice reserved

About 1 cup milk

Salt and pepper

3 large eggs

❖　❖　❖　❖　❖

1. Preheat the oven to 350 degrees. Generously brush a soufflé dish with butter.

2. In a medium saucepan, melt the 2 tablespoons of butter over medium heat. Whisk in the flour until it starts foaming. Whisk in the crab juice with enough milk to make 1 cup. Season with salt and pepper. Bring to a boil, whisking, then reduce the heat to very low and cook for 5 minutes. Remove the pan from the heat.

3. Break the eggs, adding the whites to a large bowl and the yolks to the saucepan. Mix in the yolks with the crabmeat. Beat the egg whites with a pinch of salt until stiff. Mix one-quarter of the egg whites into the crab mixture, then fold this lightened mixture into the remaining whites.

4. Scrape the crab mixture into the soufflé dish, filling it three-quarters full. Transfer to the oven and bake until risen and browned, 25 to 30 minutes. Serve immediately.

From Françoise:

• This soufflé can be very economical if you're starting with about 3 ½ ounces of leftover fish that was poached in court-bouillon (seasoned broth). If by any chance you've kept the court-bouillon, cook it for about 15 minutes until well flavored and reduced to about 1 cup. Use this broth to make your soufflé base in Step 2 instead of milk. Season lightly with salt and pepper.

• If you like, add a little Worcestershire sauce to the soufflé base before folding in the egg whites.

• If you want your soufflé to rise more evenly, run a table knife around the edge of the dish, making a groove, before baking.

CRISPY CRAB SPRING ROLLS

- *Pâté imperial au crabe* -

❖ INTERMEDIATE ❖ MODERATE ❖ 1 HOUR ❖ MAKES 12

2 tablespoons butter

3 onions, chopped

5 ounces ground pork

5 ounces white mushrooms, chopped

1 can (6.5 ounces) crab, drained

2 ounces bean threads (cellophane noodles),
  soaked in hot water for 30 minutes, drained,
  and cut into 2-inch pieces

2 large eggs, lightly beaten

½ teaspoon Asian fish sauce, plus more
  for serving

Salt and pepper

12 dried rice–paper rounds

Oil for frying

❖ ❖ ❖ ❖ ❖

In a large skillet, melt the butter over medium-low heat. Add the onions and cook until softened. Add the pork and cook, stirring and breaking it up with a wooden spoon, for 10 minutes. Add the mushrooms, crab, and bean threads and stir to mix. Stir in the eggs until lightly set. Remove from the heat and season with the ½ teaspoon of fish sauce, salt, and pepper.

5. Fill a large bowl with warm water. Dip 1 rice-paper round into the water and turn to moisten completely. Lay the round on a damp kitchen cloth. Set 1 tablespoon of the filling on the bottom third of the round. Using your fingers, shape the filling into a small cylinder. Lift the bottom edge over the filling, then fold in both sides. Roll into a small cylinder. Transfer seam side down to a platter. Continue to make the rolls with the remaining filling and rounds.

6. Pour about 1 ½ inches of oil into a large skillet and heat to 375 degrees. Add the rolls without crowding and fry until evenly golden all over, about 4 minutes. Using a slotted spoon, remove the rolls and drain on paper towels. Serve the spring rolls immediately, passing the fish sauce separately.

From Françoise:
• Serve with a green salad.

• To make mini spring rolls for a buffet or cocktail party, cut each round into quarters before stuffing it. Fry them and stick each spring roll with a toothpick.

• Rice-paper rounds, Asian fish sauce, and bean threads can be found in Asian markets and they are becoming easier to find in most supermarkets.

SEAFOOD

SAFFRON RICE PILAF WITH CRAB

- *Pilaf de crabe* -

❖ EASY   ❖ EXPENSIVE   ❖ 30 MINUTES   ❖ SERVES 4

3 tablespoons butter

1 onion, finely chopped

1 ¼ cups long-grain rice

6 ounces lump crabmeat, chopped, juice reserved

Salt and pepper

Pinch of saffron threads

❖ ❖ ❖ ❖ ❖

1. In a medium saucepan, melt 2 tablespoons of the butter over medium-low heat. Add the onion and cook until softened. Stir in the rice. Add the crab juice with enough water to make 2 ½ cups. Season lightly with salt and pepper. Add the saffron and crabmeat. Increase the heat to medium-high, bring to a boil, then reduce the heat to low, cover, and cook until the rice is tender and the water is absorbed, 17 to 20 minutes.

2. Add the remaining 1 tablespoon of butter, fluff the rice with a fork, and serve.

From Françoise:

• It's a project to cook a live crab and pick out the meat. I suggest it only when your guests do most of the work themselves, as in Boiled Crab (page 471). But if you have the patience, you can certainly prepare this rice pilaf with fresh crab.

• Saffron is so expensive and rare that it's sold in tiny quantities. But it's extremely pungent, too—even a pinch adds a tremendous amount of flavor to a dish.

BROILED, STUFFED DUNGENESS CRABS
- *Tourteau "Matoutou"* -

◆ EASY ◆ MODERATE ◆ 2 HOURS, 30 MINUTES ◆ SERVES 4

COURT-BOUILLON

Salt

¾ cup vinegar

1 bouquet garni made with parsley, thyme,
 and bay leaf

10 black peppercorns

1 carrot, peeled and thinly sliced

1 onion, thinly sliced

3 whole cloves

4 Dungeness crabs (about 1 pound each) or
 1 pound lump crabmeat

1 cup fresh bread crumbs

6 tablespoons dry white wine

3 tablespoons butter

3 scallions, finely chopped

1 garlic clove, fnely chopped

1 small dried chile

5 ounces ground pork

Salt and pepper

Dry bread crumbs for sprinkling

◆ ◆ ◆ ◆ ◆

1. Make the court-bouillon: Bring a large pot of salted water to a boil over medium-high heat with the vinegar, bouquet garni, peppercorns, carrot, onion, and cloves. Reduce the heat to medium and simmer for 10 minutes. Add the crabs and cook for about 10 minutes. Let them cool slightly in the broth. Pull the top shell off each crab, rinse, and reserve for stuffing. Crack the legs, claws, and bodies and extract all the meat.

2. In a bowl, soak the fresh bread crumbs in the wine and squeeze dry. In a skillet, melt 2 tablespoons of the butter over medium heat. Add the scallions, garlic, chile, and pork and sauté, breaking up the meat, until cooked through. Remove the skillet from the heat and mix in the crabmeat and squeezed bread crumbs. Season with salt and pepper.

3. Preheat the broiler. Lightly pack the stuffing into the reserved crab shells or individual gratin dishes. Set on a baking sheet. Sprinkle with dry bread crumbs and dot with the remaining 1 tablespoon of butter. Transfer to the top shelf of the oven and broil for a few minutes until nicely browned on top.

SEAFOOD

LANGOUSTINES IN CREAM SAUCE

- *Langoustines à la crème* -

❖ EASY   ❖ EXPENSIVE   ❖ 30 MINUTES   ❖ SERVES 4

Oil for brushing

2 ½ pounds langoustines

¼ cup Cognac

½ cup crème fraîche

Salt and pepper

Cayenne pepper

Juice of ½ lemon

❖ ❖ ❖ ❖ ❖

1. Brush a large skillet with oil and heat over very high heat. Add the langoustines and sear until deep pink. Add the Cognac and bring to a simmer, then tilt the pan and carefully ignite. When the flames subside, stir in the crème fraîche and season with salt, pepper, and cayenne. Reduce the heat to medium-low and simmer for 10 minutes.

2. Using a slotted spoon, transfer the langoustines to a bowl. Remove the heads. Arrange the tails on a warmed platter.

3. Bring the sauce to a simmer and cook until slightly thickened. Add the lemon juice. Strain the sauce over the langoustines and serve.

From Françoise:

• You can substitute jumbo or colossal shrimp in the shell for the langoustines. If you can find shrimp with their heads still on, that's even better.

• Steamed or boiled rice is the perfect accompaniment.

• Think about setting out 1 nutcracker per person when serving crustaceans. And finger bowls—especially when saucy langoustines are on the menu.

GRATIN OF LANGOUSTINES WITH CREAMY SHELLFISH SAUCE

- *Gratin de langoustines* -

❖ EASY   ❖ EXPENSIVE   ❖ 1 HOUR   ❖ SERVES 4 TO 6

2 tablespoons oil

4 pounds langoustines

1 small carrot, peeled and chopped

1 shallot, chopped

1 garlic clove, chopped

3 tablespoons Cognac

2 cups dry white wine

1 tablespoon tomato paste

1 bouquet garni made with parsley, thyme, and bay leaf

Salt and pepper

Cayenne pepper

1 large egg yolk

½ cup crème fraîche

❖ ❖ ❖ ❖ ❖

1. In a flameproof casserole, heat the oil over very high heat. Add the langoustines and sear until deep pink. Stir in the carrot, shallot, and garlic. Add the Cognac and bring to a boil, then tilt the pot and carefully ignite. When the flames subside, add the wine, tomato paste, bouquet garni, and 3 cups of water. Season with salt, pepper, and cayenne. Cover and bring to a boil, then reduce the heat to low and cook for 3 to 4 minutes.

2. Using a slotted spoon, transfer the langoustines to a bowl. Remove the heads and shells. Add the tails to a gratin dish. In a food processor, pulse the heads and shells until coarsely chopped. Strain the broth back into the casserole. Add the chopped heads and shells. Simmer over medium-high heat, uncovered, for 20 minutes. Pour through a fine strainer lined with a moistened paper towel into a saucepan.

3. Preheat the broiler. In a small bowl, whisk the egg yolk with the crème fraîche. Off the heat, whisk the egg yolk mixture into the reduced langoustine broth. Whisk over low heat briefly until the sauce thickens slightly; do not allow to boil. Pour over the langoustines. Transfer to the top shelf of the oven and broil for a few minutes until lightly browned.

From Françoise:

• If, after simmering the langoustine broth for 20 minutes, you think your sauce will still be too thin even when you add the egg yolk mixture, thicken it slightly first. In a cup, blend 1 tablespoon of softened butter with 1 tablespoon of flour. Gradually whisk this mixture into the simmering broth until it reaches the desired consistency. Then proceed to Step 3.

SEAFOOD

CURRIED LANGOUSTINE TARTLETS
- *Langoustines au curry en barquettes* -

❖ EASY　　　　❖ EXPENSIVE　　　　❖ 20 MINUTES　　　　❖ SERVES 4

5 ounces shelled langoustine tails
Salt and pepper
4 baked tartlet shells

CURRY SAUCE
1 tablespoon butter
1 tablespoon all-purpose flour
1 teaspoon curry powder
1 teaspoon crème fraîche
Salt and pepper

❖　❖　❖　❖　❖

1. In a medium saucepan, combine the langoustines with ¾ cup of water. Season with salt and pepper and bring to a boil. Drain the langoustines, reserving the broth. Cut the langoustines into ¼-inch dice.

2. Make the curry sauce: In a small saucepan, melt the butter over medium heat. Whisk in the flour until it starts foaming. Whisk in the reserved broth and curry powder. Bring to a boil, whisking. Whisk in the crème fraîche, reduce the heat to very low, and cook for 5 minutes. Taste for seasoning.

3. Preheat the broiler. Stir the langoustines into the sauce. Spoon the sauce into the tartlet shells and set on a baking sheet. Transfer to the top shelf of the oven and broil for a few minutes until lightly browned. Arrange on a warmed platter or plates and serve.

From Françoise:
• You can easily substitute shrimp for the langoustines in this recipe.

LANGOUSTINES IN AROMATIC SHELLFISH SAUCE

- *Langoustines à l'américaine* -

❖ INTERMEDIATE ❖ EXPENSIVE ❖ 20 MINUTES ❖ SERVES 4

2 tablespoons oil

2 ½ pounds langoustines

1 shallot, finely chopped

1 garlic clove, finely chopped

¼ cup Cognac

1 ½ cups dry white wine

2 tablespoons tomato paste

Salt and pepper

Cayenne pepper

1 tablespoon butter, softened

1 teaspoon all-purpose flour

❖ ❖ ❖ ❖ ❖

1. In a flameproof casserole, heat the oil over very high heat. Add the langoustines and sear until deep pink. Stir in the shallot and garlic. Add the Cognac and bring to a boil, then tilt the pot and carefully ignite. When the flames subside, add the wine, ¾ cup of water, and the tomato paste. Season with salt, pepper, and cayenne. Cover and bring to a boil, then reduce the heat to low and cook for about 10 minutes.

2. Using a slotted spoon, transfer the langoustines to a warmed serving dish. Simmer the broth until slightly thickened. In a cup, mash the butter with the flour. Gradually whisk this paste into the simmering broth.

3. Pour the sauce over the langoustines and serve.

From Françoise:

• Frozen shell-on langoustine tails work very well in this recipe. You'll need about 2 pounds of them. The shells are very important in making a flavorful sauce. Defrost the langoustines before using.

SEAFOOD

LANGOUSTINES FRITTERS

- Beignets de langoustines -

❖ INTERMEDIATE   ❖ EXPENSIVE   ❖ 30 MINUTES, PLUS 1 HOUR RESTING   ❖ SERVES 4

FRITTER BATTER
1 cup all-purpose flour
½ teaspoon salt
1 large whole egg, plus 2 large egg whites
1 tablespoon oil
½ to ⅔ cup beer or water

2 pounds langoustines
Salt and pepper
4 cups oil for frying

❖ ❖ ❖ ❖ ❖

1. Make the fritter batter: In a large bowl, whisk the flour with the salt, whole egg, and oil. Gradually whisk in the ½ cup beer or water. The mixture should be thicker than crêpe batter. Cover and let stand for 1 hour. Just before using the batter, beat the egg whites with a pinch of salt until stiff and fold into the batter.

2. Remove the langoustine heads and shells. Season the tails with salt and pepper.

3. In a large skillet, heat the oil to 375 degrees. Using a fork, dip the langoustines one at a time in the batter. Gently drop them into the oil without crowding. Fry the langoustines, turning them once, until puffed and golden, 1 to 3 minutes total. Using a slotted spoon, transfer the fritters to paper towels to drain. Keep warm in a low oven while frying the remaining langoustines. Season with salt and serve very hot.

From Françoise:
• For even more delectable fritters, marinate the langoustine tails for 2 hours in ½ cup of oil with the juice of 1 lemon, 1 finely chopped onion, thyme leaves, a bay leaf, and tarragon sprigs.

• Serve with Béarnaise Sauce (page 632).

• To make a lighter, Asian-style batter, use a mixture of half flour and half rice flour or potato starch.

• To remove the shells from langoustines, use an old pair of scissors to carefully snip the underside of the tail from top to bottom, then pull out the meat in 1 piece.

MOLDED RICE PILAF WITH LANGOUSTINES AND PEAS

- *Langoustines au riz et aux petits pois* -

❖ INTERMEDIATE   ❖ MODERATE   ❖ 45 MINUTES   ❖ SERVES 4

1 pound shelled langoustine tails

Salt and pepper

2 tablespoons butter, plus more for brushing

1 onion, finely chopped

3 ½ ounces dry-cured ham, cut into ¼-inch dice

¼ cup shelled peas

1 red bell pepper, half cut into ¼-inch dice,
  half cut into thin strips

1 cup long-grain rice

1 bouquet garni made with parsley, thyme,
  and bay leaf

❖ ❖ ❖ ❖ ❖

1. In a medium saucepan, barely cover the langoustines with water. Season with salt and pepper. Bring to a boil over medium-high heat, then reduce the heat and simmer for 3 to 4 minutes. Drain the broth into a glass measuring cup. Slice the langoustines crosswise, reserving a few whole tails for decorating.

2. In a medium saucepan, melt the butter over medium-low heat. Add the onion, ham, peas, and diced bell pepper and cook until softened. Stir in the rice. Add the langoustine broth with enough water, if necessary, to make 2 cups. Add the bouquet garni, raise the heat to medium-high, and bring to a boil, then reduce the heat to low, cover, and cook until the rice is tender and the water is absorbed, 17 to 20 minutes.

3. Remove the bouquet garni. In a large bowl, combine the rice with the sliced langoustines. Brush a soufflé or other deep baking dish with butter. Pack the langoustine pilaf into the dish and keep warm.

4. Invert a round platter over the soufflé dish. Holding the dish and platter together, quickly invert the pilaf onto the platter. Decorate with the reserved langoustine tails and red pepper strips and serve.

From Françoise:

• If you would like to serve a sauce with this pilaf, follow the directions for the one in Molded Rice Pilaf with Cockles and Creamy Sauce on page 463. Cook the rice in plain water in Step 2 above and use the reserved langoustine broth to make your sauce instead.

SEAFOOD

CREAMY SEAFOOD SALAD

- *Cocktail de fruits de mer* -

❖ VERY EASY　　❖ EXPENSIVE　　❖ 15 MINUTES　　❖ SERVES 4

⅓ cup mayonnaise

2 tablespoons ketchup

1 teaspoon Cognac

Pinch of cayenne pepper

1 small spring onion or scallion, finely chopped

3 ½ ounces lump crabmeat, shredded

3 ½ ounces cooked, shelled shrimp,
　cut into ¼-inch dice

2 hard-boiled eggs, chopped

Boston lettuce leaves for decorating

2 tomatoes, quartered lengthwise

❖　❖　❖　❖　❖

1. In a bowl, combine the mayonnaise with the ketchup, Cognac, cayenne, onion, crabmeat, shrimp, and eggs.

2. Line a platter, plates, or bowls with the lettuce. Mound the salad on top, decorate with the tomatoes, and serve.

From Françoise:

• I usually make this salad into a substantial and attractive starter, serving it on the same plate with mounds of crudités—dressed with vinaigrette, or not—like cucumber, tomato,

carrot, radish, celery, and celery root, depending on the season. My guests always love it, and it lets you serve a few more people with a little less seafood.

• You can also prepare this salad with langoustine or lobster meat, alone or in combination with other seafood.

• For a different presentation, slice the lettuce crosswise into thin ribbons, then pile it into glasses or bowls and top with the seafood salad.

SHRIMP SALAD IN A GLASS

- *Cocktail de crevettes* -

❖ EASY　　❖ MODERATE　　❖ 20 MINUTES　　❖ SERVES 4

½ pound cooked, shelled shrimp

1 teaspoon Cognac

¾ cup mayonnaise

1 tablespoon crème fraîche

Chopped chives or tarragon leaves

2 pinches of cayenne pepper

2 Boston lettuce leaves, sliced crosswise into
　thin strips

1. In a bowl, toss the shrimp with the Cognac and let marinate for 15 minutes.

2. Meanwhile, in another bowl, blend the mayonnaise with the crème fraîche, herbs, and cayenne. Reserve ¼ cup of the herb mayonnaise. Reserve 4 of the shrimp and fold the rest into the larger amount of mayonnaise.

3. In each glass, layer the lettuce strips and shrimp salad, finishing with more lettuce. Top with 1 tablespoon of the reserved mayonnaise and hook 1 shrimp on the rim. Chill until serving.

From Françoise:

• This recipe can be prepared through Step 2 and refrigerated for several hours, which is convenient, plus it tastes even better.

• Of course, if you make your own mayonnaise (page 624), this salad is more delicious.

SHRIMP SALAD TARTLETS
- *Tartelettes aux crevettes* -

❖ INTERMEDIATE   ❖ MODERATE   ❖ 45 MINUTES   ❖ SERVES 8

PÂTE BRISÉE
1 ¼ cups all-purpose flour
½ teaspoon salt
5 tablespoons unsalted butter, cut into pieces

7 ounces cooked, shelled small shrimp
Lemon Mayonnaise (page 624)
8 small Boston lettuce leaves
Chopped parsley leaves for sprinkling

❖ ❖ ❖ ❖ ❖

1. Make the pâte brisée: In a bowl, combine the flour with the salt and butter. Rub the butter into the flour between your palms. Sprinkle over ¼ cup of water and knead briefly until large crumbs form. Press into a disk. On a lightly floured surface, scrape the dough away from you with the heel of your hand in a long sliding motion, then press into a disk; repeat 3 times.

2. On a lightly floured work surface, roll the dough into a round about ⅛ inch thick. Wrap the dough around the rolling pin and unroll it over 8 tartlet pans packed together. Roll the pin over the pans and trim off any excess dough. Fit the dough into the pans and use the scraps to patch any cracks. Prick holes all over the bottom of the tartlet shells with a fork. Wrap and refrigerate until firm, 15 to 20 minutes.

3. Preheat the oven to 400 degrees. Cut rounds of foil slightly larger than the tartlet pans and roll up the edge. Fit them inside the tartlet shells. Bake until the crust is lightly browned and cooked through, 15 to 20 minutes. Transfer to a rack to cool completely, then unmold.

4. In a bowl, fold the shrimp into the mayonnaise. Line each tartlet shell with a lettuce leaf.

continued

SEAFOOD

Spread the shrimp salad on top, sprinkle with parsley, and serve.

From Françoise:
• This is a spectacular dish, and it's quick to assemble. Once your baked tartlet shells are cooled, all you need to do is add the shrimp salad. The tartlet shells can, of course, be baked in advance.

• You can use good, store-bought pie crust or puff pastry and mayonnaise. I recommend always having some extra on hand, along with cooked, shelled shrimp.

• The little foil shells help the dough keep its shape during baking. Don't forget to remove them for a few minutes to let the crust brown slightly.

BOILED SHRIMP

- *Crevettes au naturel* -

❖ EASY   ❖ MODERATE   ❖ 10 MINUTES   ❖ SERVES 4

Salt
1 bouquet garni made with parsley, thyme, and bay leaf

Pepper
1 pound shell-on shrimp

❖ ❖ ❖ ❖ ❖

1. Bring a large saucepan of heavily salted water to a boil with the bouquet garni and pepper. Add the shrimp, reduce the heat to low, and cook at a bare simmer for just 3 minutes.

2. Drain and serve cold or, preferably, warm.

From Françoise:
• If you're at the seaside, cook the shrimp in seawater. Naturally, it won't need salting.

• You can also simply sauté the shrimp over high heat in a large skillet filmed with oil for 3 minutes.

• Let your guests peel the shrimp themselves at the table.

• If your shrimp are sweet and tiny, you might like serving them on buttered toast, sprinkled with sea salt.

CRAYFISH IN AROMATIC BROTH

- *Écrevisses à la nage* -

❖ EASY ❖ EXPENSIVE ❖ 45 MINUTES ❖ SERVES 4

1 tablespoon butter

1 carrot, peeled and thinly sliced

1 onion, thinly sliced

3 cups dry white wine

1 bouquet garni made with parsley, thyme,
  and bay leaf

Salt

5 black peppercorns

Pinch of cayenne

24 crayfish

❖ ❖ ❖ ❖ ❖

1. In a large saucepan, melt the butter over medium-low heat. Add the carrot and onion and cook until softened. Add the wine, 3 cups of water, and the bouquet garni. Season with salt, the peppercorns, and cayenne. Increase the heat to medium-high, cover, and bring to a boil, then reduce the heat and cook at a gentle boil for 30 minutes.

2. Wash the crayfish in several changes of cold water.

3. Add the crayfish to the court-bouillon and cook for 10 minutes. Serve them hot or cold in the cooking liquid.

From Françoise:

• "À la nage" means served in its cooking broth.

• Because this is such a minimalist recipe—there's not much more to it than the pure flavor of the crayfish—you really need to start with the freshest, liveliest specimens. If they're not available, hold off on making this dish.

SEAFOOD

LOBSTER IN AROMATIC SHELLFISH SAUCE

- *Homard à l'américaine* -

❖ ADVANCED ❖ EXPENSIVE ❖ 45 MINUTES, PLUS 1 HOUR FREEZING ❖ SERVES 4

3 ½-pound lobster

Salt and pepper

5 tablespoons oil

1 carrot, peeled and finely chopped

1 shallot, finely chopped

¼ cup Cognac

3 or 4 tomatoes (about 10 ounces total),
  peeled, seeded, and chopped

1 ¼ cups dry white wine

1 tablespoon tomato paste

1 bouquet garni made with parsley, thyme,
  and bay leaf

Cayenne pepper

1 tablespoon butter, softened

1 tablespoon all-purpose flour

Mixed chopped parsley, chive, chervil, and
  tarragon leaves for sprinkling

❖ ❖ ❖ ❖ ❖

1. To cut up a live lobster, first freeze it for 1 hour to anesthetize it.

2. Place the lobster on a cutting board. Using a large chef's knife, cut off the claws and knuckles. Cut off the head and cut it in half lengthwise. Discard the sand sac from the head and reserve the tomalley (greenish-gray liver) and coral (eggs). Cut the tail crosswise into 5 or 6 pieces. Crack the claws and knuckles gently so they remain intact, leaving the meat in the shell. Season with salt and pepper.

3. In a large skillet, heat ¼ cup of the oil over high heat. Add the tail, claws, and knuckles and sear until the shells turn red. Remove the lobster to a bowl.

4. In a flameproof casserole, heat the remaining 1 tablespoon of oil over medium-high heat. Add the carrot and shallot and cook until lightly browned. Add the lobster and Cognac and bring to a boil, then tilt the pot and carefully ignite. When the flames subside, add the tomatoes, wine, 1 ¼ cups of water, the tomato

paste, and bouquet garni. Season with salt, pepper, and cayenne. Bring to a simmer, then cook for about 10 minutes.

5. Using a slotted spoon, transfer the lobster to a warmed serving dish. Strain the lobster broth into a saucepan. Simmer the broth until slightly thickened and well flavored. In a cup, mash the butter with the flour. Gradually whisk this paste into the simmering broth and cook for 3 minutes. Remove the pan from the heat and whisk in the tomalley and coral.

6. Pour the sauce over the lobster, sprinkle with herbs, and serve.

From Françoise:

• You can enrich the sauce with crème fraîche; add it with the tomalley and coral in Step 5.

• Serve with boiled or steamed rice.

• To flame the Cognac, bring it to a boil, then tilt the pot and light it with a long match.

ROASTED LOBSTER

- *Homard grillé* -

❖ EASY   ❖ EXPENSIVE   ❖ 45 MINUTES, PLUS 1 HOUR FREEZING   ❖ SERVES 4

3 ½–pound lobster

3 tablespoons butter, softened

Salt

Thyme leaves for sprinkling

2 bay leaves, halved

1 or 2 pinches of cayenne pepper

❖ ❖ ❖ ❖ ❖

1. To cut up a live lobster, first freeze it for 1 hour to anesthetize it.

2. Preheat the oven to 425 degrees. Place the lobster on a cutting board. Turn it on its back and split it down the middle from head to tail fan, being careful not to cut through to the back of the lobster shell. Remove the intestines. Gently pry the halves of the lobster apart.

3. Set the lobster on its back on a rimmed baking sheet or the bottom of a broiler pan. Brush the lobster tail meat with the butter. Season with salt, thyme, the bay leaves, and cayenne. Roast on the top shelf of the oven for 15 to 20 minutes, basting with the pan juices.

From Françoise:

• For a variation, once the lobster is cooked, set the baking sheet or broiler pan on the stove and whisk in 3 or 4 tablespoons of crème fraîche and 2 or 3 pinches of saffron threads just until the sauce comes to a simmer. Then pour it into a warmed sauceboat and serve it with the lobster. It's delicious.

• Crustaceans don't do well in the refrigerator for very long. Try to chill them for no longer than a day.

SEAFOOD

BOILED LOBSTER

- Homard au naturel -

❖ EASY   ❖ EXPENSIVE   ❖ 40 MINUTES, PLUS 1 HOUR FREEZING   ❖ SERVES 4

3 ½-pound lobster
Salt

1 bouquet garni made with parsley, thyme,
    and bay leaf
Pepper

❖ ❖ ❖ ❖ ❖

1. To cut up a live lobster, first freeze it for 1 hour to anesthetize it.

2. Bring a large pot of salted water to a boil with the bouquet garni and pepper. Using kitchen string, tie the lobster to a cutting board so it stays flat during cooking. Add the lobster to the court-bouillon and cook for about 10 minutes. Remove the lobster. Pierce the head and hold the lobster upside down to drain.

3. Remove the string. Using a large chef's knife, split the lobster in half down the middle from head to tail fan. Discard the intestines.

4. Just before serving, cut the lobster tail meat in half crosswise. Replace in the shell. Transfer to a platter and serve.

From Françoise:
• Serve with mayonnaise or tartar sauce.

• Set out nutcrackers and nut picks so every morsel can be extracted.

• Without getting fancy, it's a good idea to provide finger bowls. Your guests will need them when they are done taking the lobster apart. Small porcelain, glass, or ceramic bowls will do it. Fill them with warm water and add a slice of lemon or rose petals.

• Tying the lobster flat to a cutting board before cooking makes slicing it in half easier later on. If that seems complicated, though, add the lobster to the seasoned water without this step. The lobster will curl up a little, that's all.

COLD SPINY LOBSTER'S APOTHEOSIS
- *Langouste en Bellevue* -

❖ ADVANCED   ❖ EXPENSIVE   ❖ 1 HOUR, PLUS 1 HOUR FREEZING   ❖ SERVES 8 TO 10

5 ½–pound spiny lobster

Salt

1 bouquet garni made with parsley, thyme,
  and bay leaf

Pepper

1 envelope (1 tablespoon) unflavored powdered
  gelatin

1 ½ cups mayonnaise, preferably homemade
  (page 624)

1 lemon, thickly sliced

10 small tomatoes, halved

½ cup canned mixed diced vegetables, drained
  and mixed with mayonnaise

5 hard–boiled eggs, halved

Chopped chervil or tarragon leaves for sprinkling

Tender inner Boston lettuce leaves for decorating

❖ ❖ ❖ ❖ ❖

1. To cut up a live lobster, first freeze it for 1 hour to anesthetize it.

2. Bring a large pot of salted water to a boil with the bouquet garni and pepper. Using kitchen string, tie the lobster to a cutting board so it stays flat during cooking. Add the lobster to the court-bouillon and cook for 25 to 30 minutes. Drain.

3. Remove the string. Using a large chef's knife, cut off the head. Carefully snip the underside of the tail from top to bottom, then pull out the meat in 1 piece. Slice the tail meat crosswise into ½-inch-thick medallions. Spread on a cake rack.

4. In a small saucepan, sprinkle the gelatin over ¼ cup of water. Let stand until spongy, about

3 minutes. Set the saucepan over medium heat until the water is warm and the gelatin melts, about 1 minute. Let cool—but it should still be liquid—then stir into the mayonnaise.

5. Brush the lobster medallions with the mayonnaise and refrigerate until set.

6. To serve, reassemble the lobster on a platter with the head slightly raised. Thread a few lemon slices and tomato halves on a decorative skewer and plant it between the lobster's eyes. Starting at the head, slightly overlap the lobster medallions in a row down the tail. Fill the remaining tomatoes with a little of the diced vegetables in mayonnaise. Decorate the platter with the stuffed tomatoes, eggs, herbs, and lettuce leaves.

SEAFOOD

LOBSTER SALAD IN THE SHELL
- *Homard à la parisienne* -

❖ ADVANCED   ❖ EXPENSIVE   ❖ 1 HOUR, PLUS 1 HOUR FREEZING   ❖ SERVES 4

3 ½-pound lobster

Salt

1 bouquet garni made with parsley, thyme,
   and bay leaf

Pepper

2 cups canned mixed diced vegetables, drained
   and patted dry

Boston lettuce leaves for decorating

2 hard-boiled eggs, halved lengthwise

2 small tomatoes, halved

Parsley sprigs

MAYONNAISE

1 large egg yolk

Salt and pepper

1 teaspoon Dijon mustard

1 cup oil

1 or 2 teaspoons vinegar

❖ ❖ ❖ ❖ ❖

1. To cut up a live lobster, first freeze it for 1 hour to anesthetize it.

2. Bring a large pot of salted water to a boil with the bouquet garni and pepper. Add the lobster to the court-bouillon and cook for about 10 minutes. Remove the lobster. Pierce the head and hold the lobster upside down to drain.

3. Using a large chef's knife, split the lobster in half down the middle from head to tail fan. Discard the intestines. Remove the lobster tail meat from the shell and slice it crosswise ½ inch thick. Rinse the lobster shell and pat dry.

4. Meanwhile, make the mayonnaise: Using a mortar or small food processor, blend the egg yolk with the salt, pepper, and mustard. Blend in the oil a few drops at a time to begin, then in a steady stream. Mix in the vinegar.

5. In a bowl, fold the diced vegetables into ½ cup of the mayonnaise. Spread the vegetable salad in the lobster halves.

6. Line a platter with the lettuce. Transfer the lobster halves to the platter. Just before serving, arrange the tail slices on the vegetable salad. Surround the lobster with the eggs, tomatoes, and parsley. Decorate with rosettes of mayonnaise and serve, passing the remaining mayonnaise separately.

From Françoise:

• It takes some time and effort to prepare this lobster salad, but it is spectacular and can be made in advance.

• Be careful not to overcook the lobster so the meat doesn't become rubbery.

• Set out nutcrackers and nut picks so every morsel can be extracted.

• To save time, buy frozen lobster. It works very well in this recipe.

• Please note that the finished dish contains raw egg.

ROASTED MUSSELS WITH SHALLOT, GARLIC, AND PARSLEY BUTTER

- *Moules farcies* -

❖ EASY   ❖ INEXPENSIVE   ❖ 50 MINUTES   ❖ SERVES 4

---

7 tablespoons butter, softened

3 small shallots, finely chopped

1 or 2 garlic cloves, finely chopped

Chopped parsley leaves

Salt and pepper

3 to 4 pounds large mussels, scrubbed
   and debearded

❖ ❖ ❖ ❖ ❖

1. Preheat the oven to 425 degrees. In a bowl, beat 6 tablespoons of the butter with the shallots, garlic, and parsley. Season with salt and pepper.

2. Add the mussels and remaining 1 tablespoon of butter to a pot, cover, and cook over high heat, stirring once or twice, just until they open, 3 to 5 minutes. Remove the pot from the heat.

3. Reserve the mussel broth for another use. Detach the meat from the shells. Replace 2 or 3 mussels in a shell, discarding the extra shells and any unopened mussels. Transfer the mussels to individual gratin dishes or a large one. Dot with the flavored butter. Set on a baking sheet.

4. Transfer the baking sheet to the top rack of the oven and bake until the mussels are sizzling and lightly browned, 3 to 5 minutes. Serve at once.

From Françoise:

• I like to roast my stuffed mussels in individual gratin dishes. That makes serving easy and you don't lose any of the delectable sauce.

• For a crispy variation, sprinkle stale bread crumbs over the mussels before roasting them.

• If you can find large mussels, buy a dozen per person.

• Small, tender clams can also be prepared this way.

• These stuffed mussels can be prepared through Step 3 and refrigerated for several hours. Roast them in the oven just before serving.

SEAFOOD

MUSSELS WITH SHALLOT AND HERB VINAIGRETTE

- *Moules vinaigrette* -

❖ EASY   ❖ INEXPENSIVE   ❖ 15 MINUTES   ❖ SERVES 4

2 tablespoons vinegar

6 to 8 tablespoons oil

Salt and pepper

2 pounds mussels, scrubbed and debearded

1 shallot, finely chopped

Mixed chopped parsley, chive, chervil, and
  tarragon leaves for sprinkling

❖ ❖ ❖ ❖ ❖

1. In a salad bowl, whisk the vinegar with the
oil and season with salt and pepper.

2. Add the mussels to a pot, cover, and cook
over high heat, stirring once or twice, just until
they open, 3 to 5 minutes. Remove the pot
from the heat. Remove the mussel meat from
the shells and reserve. Discard the shells and
any unopened mussels. Reserve the mussel
broth for another use.

3. Add the mussels to the vinaigrette and toss
to coat. Sprinkle with the shallot and herbs
and serve.

From Françoise:

• You can make this recipe with cockles, too.
But you'll need to soak them in salted water
for at least 30 minutes first to make them
disgorge any sand and grit.

• Instead of vinaigrette, I sometimes like to
fold mussels or cockles into mayonnaise. It's
just as simple and it's richer and more refined.
Still, since mayonnaise is stiffer, I thin it with
a little of the mussel broth, vinegar, or even
water so it coats the shellfish more easily.
Don't leave out the herbs.

MUSSELS IN BUTTERY BROTH

- Moules marinière -

❖ EASY ❖ INEXPENSIVE ❖ 45 MINUTES ❖ SERVES 4

4 pounds mussels, scrubbed and debearded

2 shallots, finely chopped

¾ cup dry white wine

2 tablespoons butter, softened

1 teaspoon all-purpose flour

Pepper

Chopped parsley leaves for sprinkling

❖ ❖ ❖ ❖ ❖

1. Add the mussels, shallots, and wine to a pot. Cover and cook over high heat, stirring once or twice, just until they open, 3 to 5 minutes. Using a slotted spoon, transfer the mussels to a warmed serving dish.

2. Pour the broth through a fine strainer lined with a moistened paper towel. In a cup, mash the butter with the flour. Return the broth to the pot and bring to a simmer. Gradually whisk in the paste and cook until the broth thickens slightly. Season with pepper.

3. Pour the broth over the mussels. Sprinkle with the parsley and serve.

From Françoise:

• To keep the mussels warm while preparing the sauce, cover the serving dish and set it over a pan of barely simmering water.

• You can replace the butter with the same amount of crème fraîche.

SEAFOOD

MUSSELS WITH CREAMY CURRIED SAUCE
- *Moules à la charentaise* -

❖ EASY   ❖ INEXPENSIVE   ❖ 40 MINUTES   ❖ SERVES 4

3 to 4 pounds mussels, scrubbed and debearded

3 tablespoons butter

1 shallot or garlic clove, finely chopped

¾ cup dry white wine

Pepper

¼ cup Cognac

1 teaspoon all-purpose flour

½ teaspoon curry powder

1 large egg yolk

1 or 2 teaspoons crème fraîche

Juice of ½ lemon

Chopped parsley leaves for sprinkling

❖   ❖   ❖   ❖   ❖

1. In a large pot, combine the mussels with 2 tablespoons of the butter, the shallot or garlic, and wine. Season with pepper. Set over high heat, and when the mussels begin to open, add the Cognac. Bring to a simmer, then tilt the pot and carefully ignite. When the flames subside, cover the pot and cook, stirring once or twice, just until the mussels open, 3 to 5 minutes. Using a slotted spoon, transfer the mussels to a warmed serving dish. Pour the broth through a fine strainer lined with a moistened paper towel into a glass measuring cup.

2. In a saucepan, melt the remaining 1 tablespoon of butter over medium heat. Whisk in the flour and curry powder until it starts foaming. Whisk in 1 cup of the broth. Bring to a boil, whisking, then cook over very low heat for about 10 minutes. In a small bowl, whisk the egg yolk with the crème fraîche and lemon juice. Remove the pan from the heat and whisk in the egg yolk mixture. Whisk in the parsley.

3. Pour the sauce over the mussels and serve.

From Françoise:

• Here's a fantastic recipe; I wouldn't put it in the special occasion category because you use your fingers to eat it, but it does deserve a place there.

• Serve this dish to mussel lovers and pour a muscadet or Gros Plant wine to go with it. Your guests will be happy to discover it.

• I don't add any salt or pepper to the sauce because the broth is already plenty salty.

MUSSELS ON THE HALF SHELL WITH LEMONY SAUCE

- *Mouclade* -

❖ EASY   ❖ INEXPENSIVE   ❖ 30 MINUTES   ❖ SERVES 4

4 pounds mussels, scrubbed and debearded

2 tablespoons butter

2 tablespoons all-purpose flour

1 garlic clove, finely chopped

Pepper

1 large egg yolk

Juice of ½ lemon

Chopped parsley leaves for sprinkling

❖ ❖ ❖ ❖ ❖

1. Add the mussels to a pot, cover, and cook over high heat, stirring once or twice, just until they open, 3 to 5 minutes. Using a slotted spoon, transfer the mussels to a bowl and remove 1 shell from each. Arrange the mussels on the half shell in a warmed serving dish. Pour the broth through a fine strainer lined with a moistened paper towel into a glass measuring cup.

2. In a saucepan, melt the butter over medium heat. Whisk in the flour until it starts foaming. Whisk in the garlic and broth with enough water to make 2 cups. Bring to a boil, whisking, then reduce the heat to very low and cook for about 10 minutes. Season with pepper. Remove the pan from the heat and whisk in the egg yolk and lemon juice.

3. Pour the sauce over the mussels, sprinkle with parsley, and serve.

From Françoise:
• The mussel broth is generally salty enough not to require more seasoning. In fact, I don't recommend it.

SEAFOOD

SQUID SIMMERED IN GARLICKY TOMATO SAUCE

- *Encornets niçoise à la tomate* -

❖ EASY ❖ INEXPENSIVE ❖ 50 MINUTES ❖ SERVES 4

2 pounds squid

3 tablespoons butter

1 small onion or shallot, chopped

1 garlic clove, chopped

3 tablespoons tomato paste

1 thyme sprig

¼ bay leaf

2 whole cloves

Salt and pepper

❖ ❖ ❖ ❖ ❖

1. Using kitchen scissors, cut open the squid from top to bottom. Pull the head with the tentacles from inside. Remove the "pen." Cut off the tentacles right in front of the eyes and squeeze out the "beak." Peel off the skin. Slice the tentacles into ½-inch pieces. Rinse in cold running water.

2. In a flameproof casserole, melt the butter over medium-low heat. Add the onion or shallot and garlic and cook until softened. Add the squid, tomato paste, 1 ½ cups of water, the thyme, bay leaf, and cloves. Season with salt and pepper. Increase the heat to medium-high, cover, and bring to a boil, then reduce the heat to low and cook for about 30 minutes, removing the lid halfway through to let the sauce reduce. Transfer to a warmed serving dish and serve.

From Françoise:

• Serve with boiled new potatoes or plain rice for sopping up the delicious sauce.

• If you have any leftovers, they're just as good reheated or served as a first course at room temperature.

• Frozen squid, whole or cut into rings, is excellent.

BRAISED SQUID STUFFED WITH HAM AND OLIVES

- *Encornets farcis à la cocotte* -

❖ INTERMEDIATE ❖ INEXPENSIVE ❖ 2 HOURS, 15 MINUTES ❖ SERVES 8

8 squid

STUFFING

2 tablespoons butter

1 onion, finely chopped

1 slice of dry-cured ham, finely chopped

2 carrots, peeled and finely chopped

2 tomatoes, peeled, seeded, and chopped

Chopped parsley leaves

Salt and pepper

2 large egg yolks

10 pitted black olives, finely chopped

SAUCE

2 tablespoons butter

1 onion, thinly sliced

1 carrot, peeled and thinly sliced

1 tomato, peeled, seeded, and chopped

Salt and pepper

1 tablespoon vinegar

¾ cup dry white wine

Chopped parsley leaves

❖ ❖ ❖ ❖ ❖

1. Pull the head with the tentacles from inside the squid. Remove the "pen." Cut off the tentacles right in front of the eyes and squeeze out the "beak." Peel off the skin. Chop the tentacles. Rinse in cold running water.

2. Make the stuffing: In a saucepan, melt the butter over medium-low heat. Add the onion, cover, and cook until softened. Add the ham, carrots, tomatoes, parsley, and tentacles. Season with salt and pepper. Reduce the heat to low, cover, and cook for 5 minutes. Remove the pan from the heat and mix in the egg yolks. Return the pan to medium-high heat and cook, stirring constantly, for a few seconds to dry out the mixture without letting it stick. Remove the pan from the heat and mix in the olives.

3. Make the sauce: In a flameproof casserole, melt the butter over medium heat. Add the onion, carrot, and tomato and season with salt and pepper. Reduce the heat to low and cook for 10 minutes.

4. Pack the stuffing into the squid and close with toothpicks. Add the stuffed squid to the casserole. Add the vinegar, wine, and parsley. Cover and cook over low heat for 1 hour and 30 minutes.

5. Remove the toothpicks. Transfer to a serving dish and serve hot.

From Françoise:

• Serve with boiled or steamed rice or rice pilaf.

• This dish is also good served cold as a starter.

SEAFOOD

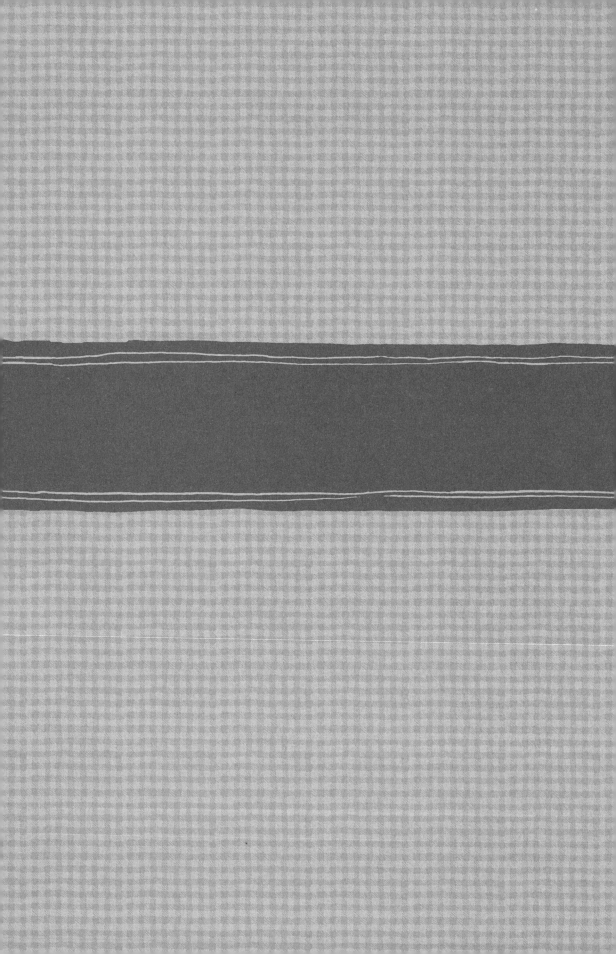

VEGETABLES

BOILED ARTICHOKES
- *Artichauts au naturel* -

❖ EASY   ❖ INEXPENSIVE   ❖ 50 MINUTES   ❖ SERVES 4

Salt   4 large artichokes
Vinegar

❖ ❖ ❖ ❖ ❖

1. Bring a large pot of salted water to a boil. Meanwhile, fill a large bowl with cold water and add the vinegar. Break off the artichoke stems. Pull off any tough, stringy outer leaves. Soak the artichokes in the vinegar water, leaves pointing down, for 5 minutes. Rinse the artichokes under cold running water, spreading the leaves apart, to dislodge any dirt.

2. Add the artichokes to the boiling water, cover, reduce the heat to medium, and simmer until you can easily remove a leaf, 30 to 45 minutes. Drain in a colander, leaves pointing down.

From Françoise:
• The artichokes need to be completely submerged in boiling water. Since they tend to bob on top of the water, weight them down with a cake rack or heatproof dish that fits inside your pot.

• The proportions for acidulated water are 1 tablespoon of vinegar or lemon juice to 1 quart of water.

WINE-BRAISED BABY ARTICHOKES
- *Artichauts à la barigoule* -

❖ EASY   ❖ MODERATE   ❖ 1 HOUR, 30 MINUTES   ❖ SERVES 4

8 very young chokeless artichokes
2 tablespoons oil
3 ½ ounces thick-sliced pancetta, cut crosswise into ¼–inch-thick strips
1 carrot, peeled and thinly sliced

2 large onions, thinly sliced
Salt and pepper
2 tomatoes, peeled, seeded, and chopped
¾ cup dry white wine
Chopped parsley leaves for sprinkling

1. Using kitchen scissors, snip off any tough leaves at the base of the artichokes. Snip off the tips of the remaining leaves. Peel and trim the stems, if any.

2. In a large saucepan, heat the oil over medium heat. Stir in the pancetta, carrot, and onions. Add the artichokes, leaves pointing up and packing them close together. Season with pepper and, lightly, with salt. Add the tomatoes and bring to a simmer. Add the wine and ¾ cup of water, cover, reduce the heat to low, and cook for about 1 hour and 15 minutes.

3. Transfer the artichokes to a serving dish with the broth, sprinkle with parsley, and serve warm. Or let the artichokes cool completely in the broth and serve at room temperature.

From Françoise:
• If you can't find these special chokeless artichokes, use regular baby artichokes: Snap off all of the dark green outer leaves. Using a sharp knife, slice off the top half of the leaves and peel and trim the stems. Halve the artichokes lengthwise and scoop out the hairy chokes. Proceed to Step 2.

BUTTERY PEA-STUFFED ARTICHOKE BOTTOMS
- Artichauts Clamart (fonds d') -

❖ EASY   ❖ INEXPENSIVE   ❖ 15 MINUTES   ❖ SERVES 4

1 cup canned petit pois peas
3 tablespoons butter
4 to 8 canned artichoke bottoms,
   depending on the size, drained

Salt and pepper
Chopped chervil or parsley leaves
   for sprinkling

❖   ❖   ❖   ❖   ❖

1. In a small saucepan, reheat the peas in their water.

2. In a large skillet, melt 1 ½ tablespoons of the butter over medium heat. Add the artichoke bottoms, season with salt and pepper, and warm them through.

3. Drain the peas, season with salt and pepper, and swirl in the remaining 1 ½ tablespoons of butter. Spoon the peas into the artichoke bottoms.

4. Transfer the artichoke bottoms to a warmed platter, sprinkle with herbs, and serve.

From Françoise:
• Try these stuffed artichokes as a side dish for a dinner party. They are extremely easy to make. You might serve them to dress up roasted meat or poultry, or even a simple steak.

• Of course you can make this recipe using fresh peas and artichokes. Preparing artichoke bottoms yourself is a project, but if you would like to try it, follow the directions in Artichoke Bottoms Stuffed with Mixed Vegetables (page 57).

VEGETABLES

EGGPLANT LOAF WITH TOMATO SAUCE

- *Pain d'aubergines à la tomate* -

❖ EASY   ❖ INEXPENSIVE   ❖ 1 HOUR, 30 MINUTES   ❖ SERVES 4

Salt

Vinegar

2 pounds eggplants, peeled and quartered

3 large eggs

Pepper

Butter for brushing

TOMATO SAUCE

1 ½ pounds tomatoes, chopped

2 onions, chopped

1 garlic clove, chopped

1 bouquet garni made with parsley, thyme,
  and bay leaf

Salt and pepper

2 tablespoons butter

1 teaspoon all-purpose flour

❖　❖　❖　❖　❖

1. Preheat the oven to 400 degrees. Bring a large saucepan of salted water to a boil with the vinegar. Add the eggplant and cook for 10 minutes. Drain. In a food processor, puree the eggplant. Add the eggs and blend until smooth. Season with salt and pepper.

2. Brush a soufflé dish or other deep baking dish with butter. Scrape in the eggplant puree. Set the dish in a roasting pan and add hot water to come halfway up the sides of the dish. Transfer to the oven and bake for about 45 minutes.

3. Meanwhile, make the tomato sauce: In a medium saucepan, combine the tomatoes, onions, garlic, and bouquet garni. Season with salt and pepper. Place over medium-low heat and cook, uncovered, for 45 minutes. Remove the bouquet garni. Puree the sauce using a food mill. Return the sauce to the pan and bring to a simmer. In a cup, mash the butter with the flour. Gradually whisk this paste into the sauce and cook until it thickens slightly.

4. Remove the baking dish from the roasting pan. Invert a round platter over the dish. Holding the dish and platter together, quickly invert the eggplant onto the platter. Pour the sauce over and around the eggplant and serve.

From Françoise:

• The secret to peeled or cut eggplants that don't darken: Add them immediately to boiling water with vinegar. The acidity prevents them for oxidizing, hence turning brown. This step isn't necessary if you're frying or sautéing eggplant.

• The proportions for acidulated water are 1 tablespoon of vinegar or lemon juice to 1 quart of water.

EGGPLANT SOUFFLÉ

- Zéphyr d'aubergines -

❖ EASY   ❖ INEXPENSIVE   ❖ 45 MINUTES   ❖ SERVES 4

3 tablespoons butter, plus more for brushing
Salt
Vinegar
1 pound eggplants, peeled and cut into chunks
1 ½ tablespoons all-purpose flour

¾ cup milk
Pepper
2 large eggs, separated
¾ cup shredded Gruyère cheese

❖ ❖ ❖ ❖ ❖

1. Preheat the oven to 400 degrees. Generously brush a soufflé dish with butter.

2. Bring a large saucepan of salted water to a boil with the vinegar. Add the eggplants and cook for 2 minutes. Drain well and finely chop.

3. In a large saucepan, melt 2 tablespoons of the butter over medium-high heat. Add the eggplants and cook, stirring often, until lightly browned. Stir in the flour. Gradually add the milk, stirring, until the mixture thickens. Season with salt and pepper. Remove the pan from the heat and mix in the egg yolks and cheese.

4. In a large bowl, beat the egg whites with a pinch of salt until stiff. Beat one-quarter of the egg whites into the eggplant mixture, then fold this lightened mixture into the remaining whites.

5. Scrape the eggplant mixture into the soufflé dish, filling it three-quarters full. Transfer to the oven and bake until risen and browned, about 25 minutes. Serve immediately.

From Françoise:
• Instead of using 1 large soufflé dish, try using individual ramekins for baking the eggplant mixture.

• The proportions for acidulated water are 1 tablespoon of vinegar or lemon juice to 1 quart of water.

VEGETABLES

SAUTÉED EGGPLANT WITH GARLIC AND PARSLEY

- *Aubergines sautées persillade* -

❖ EASY   ❖ INEXPENSIVE   ❖ 30 MINUTES, PLUS 30 MINUTES DRAINING   ❖ SERVES 4

4 large eggplants, sliced crosswise ½ inch thick
Salt
All-purpose flour for dusting
6 tablespoons oil

1 tablespoon butter
1 tablespoon chopped parsley leaves
2 garlic cloves, finely chopped

❖ ❖ ❖ ❖ ❖

1. In a colander, sprinkle the eggplant slices with salt and let them drain for 30 minutes.

2. Wipe the eggplant slices with paper towels. Dust lightly with flour, patting off the excess.

3. In a large skillet, heat the oil over medium-high heat until shimmering. Add the eggplant slices without crowding and cook until nicely browned about 5 minutes per side. Transfer to a warmed platter as they are done. Repeat with the remaining eggplant.

4. In a small saucepan, melt the butter over low heat. Add the parsley and garlic and cook until fragrant, about 1 minute. Pour over the eggplant and serve.

From Françoise:
• Don't peel the eggplants. They're very good with the skin.

• If possible, drain the sautéed eggplant slices on paper towels or on a cake rack. They will be less greasy that way.

FRIED EGGPLANT

- *Aubergines frites* -

❖ EASY   ❖ INEXPENSIVE   ❖ 20 MINUTES   ❖ SERVES 4

1 ¼ to 1 ½ pounds eggplants,
  sliced crosswise ¼ inch thick
All-purpose flour for dusting

4 cups oil for frying
Salt and pepper

❖ ❖ ❖ ❖ ❖

1. Wipe the eggplant slices with paper towels. Dust lightly with flour, patting off the excess.

2. In a large skillet, heat the oil to 375 degrees. Gently drop the eggplant slices into the oil

without crowding. Fry the eggplant slices, turning them once, until golden, 2 to 3 minutes total. Using a slotted spoon, transfer them to paper towels to drain. Keep warm in a low oven while frying the remaining slices. Season with salt and pepper and serve very hot.

GOLDEN BAKED EGGPLANT AND TOMATOES WITH GRUYÈRE

- *Aubergines et tomates au four* -

❖ EASY   ❖ INEXPENSIVE   ❖ 1 HOUR   ❖ SERVES 4

4 eggplants, halved lengthwise

Salt

6 tablespoons oil

Pepper

4 tomatoes, halved horizontally

2 garlic cloves, finely chopped

Chopped parsley leaves for sprinkling

½ cup shredded Gruyère cheese

1 tablespoon dry bread crumbs

❖ ❖ ❖ ❖ ❖

1. Sprinkle the eggplant halves with salt and let them drain for 30 minutes.

2. Preheat the oven to 350 degrees. Wipe the eggplant halves with paper towels. In a large skillet, heat the oil over medium-high heat until shimmering. Add the eggplant halves without crowding and cook, turning once, until nicely browned, about 5 minutes per side. Drain them. Transfer to a gratin dish and season with salt and pepper.

3. In the same skillet over medium heat, add the tomato halves cut side down. Cook, turning once, until lightly browned, about 2 minutes per side.

4. Set the tomato halves on the eggplants. Sprinkle with the garlic, parsley, cheese, and bread crumbs. Transfer to the top shelf of the oven and bake until nicely browned, 15 to 20 minutes.

From Françoise:

• This is a good summer dish or something to make when you're away on vacation in a sunny place. If you slip a slice of ham between the eggplant and the tomatoes, you have a main dish.

• Add the tomato halves to the skillet cut side down, so they are less likely to fall apart when you turn them over to brown the second side.

VEGETABLES

GRATINÉED ASPARAGUS WITH PARMESAN CHEESE
- *Asperges au parmesan gratinées* -

❖ EASY   ❖ MODERATE   ❖ 30 MINUTES   ❖ SERVES 4

Salt
2 pounds thick asparagus

½ cup grated Parmesan cheese
2 tablespoons butter, melted

❖ ❖ ❖ ❖ ❖

1. Preheat the oven to 400 degrees. Bring a large pot of salted water to a boil. Peel the asparagus stems. Rinse the asparagus under cold running water. Add to the boiling water and cook until tender, 12 to 15 minutes. Drain. Pat dry with paper towels and transfer to a gratin dish.

2. Sprinkle the tips and half the stems with the cheese. Pour the melted butter over the asparagus. Transfer to the top shelf of the oven and bake for 4 to 5 minutes until melted and nicely browned.

From Françoise:
• When peeling asparagus spears, lay each one flat on a work surface so it doesn't break.

• The secret to perfectly tender asparagus: Peel the stems like a potato; don't just scrub them. Using a vegetable peeler, start at the base and stop just below the tip.

• You don't need to use a knife to trim the bottoms because asparagus naturally breaks where it stops being tender.

BUTTERY GLAZED CARROTS
- *Carottes Vichy* -

❖ EASY   ❖ INEXPENSIVE   ❖ 1 HOUR   ❖ SERVES 4

2 pounds carrots, peeled and sliced crosswise
3 tablespoons butter
1 teaspoon sugar

Salt
Chopped parsley leaves

❖ ❖ ❖ ❖ ❖

1. In a large saucepan, combine the carrots with the butter, sugar, salt, and 2 cups of water. Cover and cook over low heat until the carrots are tender and the water evaporates, 30 to 45 minutes.

2. Transfer the carrots to a warmed serving dish. Sprinkle with parsley and serve.

From Françoise:

• If your carrots have been in the refrigerator for a while, cook them in boiling water first for 10 minutes, then drain.

• It goes without saying that Carrots Vichy should be prepared with Vichy water (a sparkling mineral water from springs near the city of Vichy), but that's rarely what happens at my house. Carrots Vichy are excellent even if you make them with tap water.

CARROT SOUFFLÉ
- *Carottes en soufflé* -

❖ INTERMEDIATE   ❖ INEXPENSIVE   ❖ 1 HOUR, 15 MINUTES   ❖ SERVES 4

3 tablespoons butter, plus more for brushing

Salt

1 pound carrots, peeled and thinly sliced

2 onions, thinly sliced

3 tablespoons all-purpose flour

1 ½ cups milk

Pinch of sugar

Pepper

2 large eggs, separated

❖ ❖ ❖ ❖ ❖

1. Preheat the oven to 400 degrees. Generously brush a soufflé dish with butter.

2. In a large saucepan, bring 2 cups of salted water to a boil. Add the carrots and onions and cook until tender, about 15 minutes. Drain. Puree the vegetables using a food mill or food processor.

3. In a medium saucepan, melt the 3 tablespoons of butter over medium heat. Whisk in the flour until it starts foaming. Whisk in the milk. Season with the sugar, salt, and pepper. Bring to a boil, whisking, then reduce the heat to very low and cook until thickened. Remove the pan from the heat and beat in the carrot puree and egg yolks.

4. In a large bowl, beat the egg whites with a pinch of salt until stiff. Beat one-quarter of the egg whites into the carrot mixture, then fold this lightened mixture into the remaining whites.

5. Scrape the carrot mixture into the soufflé dish, filling it three-quarters full. Transfer to the oven and bake until risen and browned, about 35 minutes. Serve immediately.

VEGETABLES

SLOW-COOKED CARROTS WITH PEARL ONIONS
- *Carottes braisées aux oignons* -

❖ EASY   ❖ INEXPENSIVE   ❖ 1 HOUR, 20 MINUTES   ❖ SERVES 4

3 tablespoons butter

2 pounds carrots, peeled and sliced crosswise

½ pound pearl onions, peeled

1 or 2 garlic cloves, crushed

1 bouquet garni made with parsley, thyme, and bay leaf

Salt and pepper

Chopped parsley leaves for sprinkling

❖ ❖ ❖ ❖ ❖

1. In a round flameproof casserole, melt the butter over medium-low heat. Add the carrots and pearl onions and cook, stirring, until slightly softened. Add the garlic and bouquet garni and season with salt and pepper. Set a soup plate on top of the casserole and fill it with cold water. Reduce the heat to very low and cook for about 1 hour, refilling the plate with cold water as needed.

2. Remove the bouquet garni. Transfer the carrots to a warmed serving dish. Sprinkle with parsley and serve.

From Françoise:

• Add a tablespoon of water to the casserole if the heat is too high and the carrots begin to stick.

• Just before serving, you can add 1 or 2 tablespoons of crème fraîche to the carrots. Or vary it with a sprinkling of chervil, cilantro, or even cumin.

DICED CARROTS AND POTATOES WITH CREAMY SAUCE
- *Carottes à la pompadour* -

❖ EASY   ❖ INEXPENSIVE   ❖ 30 MINUTES   ❖ SERVES 4

Salt

1 pound carrots, peeled and cut into ½-inch dice

1 pound potatoes, peeled and cut into ½-inch dice

BÉCHAMEL SAUCE

3 tablespoons butter

3 tablespoons all-purpose flour

2 cups milk

Salt and pepper

1. Bring 2 large saucepans of salted water to a boil. Add the carrots to one pan and the potatoes to the other and cook until tender, about 15 minutes.

2. Meanwhile, make the béchamel sauce: In a small saucepan, melt the butter over medium heat. Whisk in the flour until it starts foaming.

Whisk in the milk. Season with salt and pepper. Bring to a boil, whisking, then reduce the heat to very low and cook for 5 minutes.

3. Drain the vegetables and pat dry with paper towels. Spread in a gratin dish, cover with the béchamel sauce, and serve.

TOMATOES STUFFED WITH SHRIMP SALAD
- *Tomates farcies aux crevettes* -

❖ INTERMEDIATE   ❖ INEXPENSIVE   ❖ 40 MINUTES   ❖ SERVES 4

4 medium tomatoes
Salt
¼ pound small, cooked, shelled shrimp
Parsley sprigs

MAYONNAISE
1 large egg yolk
1 teaspoon Dijon mustard
¾ cup oil
1 tablespoon vinegar
Salt and pepper

❖ ❖ ❖ ❖ ❖

1. Cut a thin slice off the top of each tomato. Using a spoon, hollow out the insides, leaving a sturdy shell. Sprinkle with salt and turn upside down on a plate to drain.

2. Meanwhile, make the mayonnaise: In a small bowl, whisk the egg yolk with the mustard. Blend in the oil a few drops at a time to begin, then in a steady stream. Beat in the vinegar and season with salt and pepper.

3. In a bowl, fold ½ cup of the mayonnaise into the shrimp. Stuff the tomatoes with the shrimp salad, mounding it slightly. Decorate with mayonnaise rosettes and parsley sprigs. Transfer to a platter and serve.

From Françoise:
• Please note that the finished dish contains raw egg.

• You can use store-bought mayonnaise to make the shrimp salad instead.

• If you can find mayonnaise in a tube, it makes the decorating so much easier.

VEGETABLES

TOMATOES STUFFED WITH
CREAMY CUCUMBER SALAD

- Tomates farcies au concombre -

❖ EASY   ❖ INEXPENSIVE   ❖ 25 MINUTES, PLUS 2 HOURS DRAINING   ❖ SERVES 4

1 cucumber (about 1 pound), peeled

Salt

4 medium tomatoes (about 1 pound total)

1 tablespoon crème fraîche

1 teaspoon mayonnaise

Pepper

❖ ❖ ❖ ❖ ❖

1. Cut the cucumber in half lengthwise. Using a teaspoon, scoop out the seeds. Thinly slice the cucumber crosswise. In a colander, sprinkle the cucumber slices with salt and let drain for 2 hours.

2. Meanwhile, cut a thin slice off the top of each tomato. Using a spoon, hollow out the insides, leaving a sturdy shell. Sprinkle with salt and turn upside down on a plate to drain.

3. Squeeze out as much water as possible from the cucumber slices and pat dry with paper towels. In a bowl, combine the cucumbers with the crème fraîche, mayonnaise, and pepper and toss to coat. Stuff the tomatoes with the cucumber salad, mounding it slightly. Serve very cold.

From Françoise:

• Stir a little chopped parsley, chervil, chives, or mint into the cucumber salad.

TOMATOES STUFFED WITH MUSTARDY AVOCADOS

- Tomates farcies d'avocat -

❖ EASY   ❖ INEXPENSIVE   ❖ 10 MINUTES   ❖ SERVES 4

4 medium tomatoes

Salt

½ cup mayonnaise

Dijon mustard to taste

1 avocado, peeled, pitted, and cut into ¼-inch dice or mashed

Juice of ½ lemon

1. Cut a thin slice off the top of each tomato. Using a spoon, hollow out the insides, leaving a sturdy shell. Sprinkle with salt and turn upside down on a plate to drain.

2. In a bowl, blend the mayonnaise with the mustard. Fold in the avocado and lemon juice.

Stuff the tomatoes with the avocado salad, mounding it slightly, and serve.

From Françoise:
• Use ripe but firm avocados to make this recipe.

TOMATOES STUFFED WITH HERBED TUNA-AND-EGG SALAD
- *Tomates farcies au thon* -

❖ EASY   ❖ INEXPENSIVE   ❖ 15 MINUTES   ❖ SERVES 4

4 medium tomatoes
Salt
3 ½ ounces oil-packed tuna, flaked
2 hard-boiled eggs, chopped

1 teaspoon vinegar
Mixed chopped parsley, chervil, chives, and
    tarragon leaves
Pepper

❖ ❖ ❖ ❖ ❖

1. Cut a thin slice off the top of each tomato. Using a spoon, hollow out the insides, leaving a sturdy shell. Sprinkle with salt and turn upside down on a plate to drain.

2. In a bowl, combine the tuna, eggs, vinegar, and herbs. Season with salt and pepper and toss to mix. Stuff the tomatoes with the tuna salad, mounding it slightly, and serve.

From Françoise:
• To make a creamier filling, stir in 1 or 2 tablespoons of mayonnaise.

• For a pungent kick, add chopped capers.

VEGETABLES

ROASTED TOMATOES STUFFED WITH SEMOLINA AND HAM

- *Tomates à la semoule* -

❖ EASY ❖ INEXPENSIVE ❖ 40 MINUTES ❖ SERVES 4

2 tablespoons butter, cut into ¼-inch dice,
  plus more for brushing
4 large or 8 medium tomatoes
Salt
1 cup chicken broth
¼ cup semolina

Pepper
1 slice ham, finely chopped
⅓ cup shredded Gruyère cheese
1 large egg yolk
2 pinches of freshly grated nutmeg

❖ ❖ ❖ ❖ ❖

1. Preheat the oven to 400 degrees. Brush a gratin dish with butter.

2. Cut a thin slice off the top of each tomato. Using a spoon, hollow out the insides, leaving a sturdy shell. Sprinkle with salt and turn upside down on a plate to drain.

3. In a medium saucepan, bring the broth to a simmer over medium heat. Gradually add the semolina. Season with pepper and, lightly, with salt. Reduce the heat to low and cook, stirring occasionally, until thickened, about 10 minutes. Remove the pan from the heat and stir in the ham, cheese, egg yolk, and nutmeg.

4. Stuff the tomatoes with the semolina mixture, mounding it slightly. Set them in the gratin dish and dot with the 2 tablespoons of butter. Transfer them to the top shelf of the oven and bake for 12 to 15 minutes. Serve hot.

CRISPY MEAT-STUFFED TOMATOES

- *Tomates farcies à la viande* -

❖ EASY ❖ INEXPENSIVE ❖ 1 HOUR ❖ SERVES 4

2 tablespoons butter, cut into ¼-inch dice,
  plus more for brushing
4 large tomatoes
Salt
6 tablespoons milk
1 cup dry bread crumbs

2 cups chopped leftover meat
1 large egg
1 tablespoon chopped parsley leaves
1 onion, finely chopped
1 garlic clove, finely chopped
Pepper

1. Preheat the oven to 350 degrees. Brush a gratin dish with butter.

2. Cut a thin slice off the top of each tomato and reserve. Using a spoon, hollow out the insides, leaving a sturdy shell. Reserve the insides. Sprinkle the shells with salt and turn upside down on a plate to drain.

3. In a small saucepan, warm the milk. Remove from the heat, add ½ cup of the bread crumbs, and let soak, then squeeze dry, discarding the excess milk.

4. In a bowl, mix the soaked bread crumbs with the chopped meat, egg, parsley, onion, and garlic. Season with salt and pepper. Add a little of the reserved tomatoes, if needed, to make a moist mixture that holds together.

5. Stuff the tomatoes with the meat mixture, mounding it slightly. Set them in the gratin dish. Sprinkle with the remaining ½ cup of dry bread crumbs and dot with the 2 tablespoons of butter. Transfer them to the top shelf of the oven and bake for 30 minutes. Set the tomato lids on top and bake for 10 minutes more. Serve hot.

From Françoise:

• The salted tomatoes will drain better if you set them upside down on a cake rack over a plate.

• Pack the stuffed tomatoes close together in the gratin dish to discourage them from bursting.

• If you don't have any leftovers from a roast, you can make this stuffing with sausage meat. Cook it in a skillet, crumbling the meat with a wooden spoon, until cooked through.

ROASTED TOMATOES STUFFED WITH GREEN PEPPER RICE PILAF
- *Tomates parasol* -

❖ EASY   ❖ INEXPENSIVE   ❖ 50 MINUTES   ❖ SERVES 4

4 medium tomatoes

Salt

2 tablespoons butter, cut into ¼-inch dice, plus more for brushing

1 onion, finely chopped

1 cup long-grain rice

1 green bell pepper, cut into ¼-inch dice

Pepper

❖ ❖ ❖ ❖ ❖

1. Cut a thin slice off the top of each tomato and reserve. Using a spoon, hollow out the insides, leaving a sturdy shell. Sprinkle with salt and turn upside down on a plate to drain.

2. Meanwhile, in a medium saucepan, melt the 2 tablespoons of butter over medium-low

continued

heat. Add the onion and rice and cook for 2 minutes. Add 2 cups of water and the bell pepper and season with salt and pepper. Increase the heat to medium, bring to a boil, then cover, reduce the heat to low, and cook until the rice is tender and the water is absorbed, 17 to 20 minutes. Fluff the rice.

3. Meanwhile, preheat the oven to 350 degrees. Brush a gratin dish with butter.

4. Stuff the tomatoes with the rice pilaf, mounding it slightly. Set them in the gratin dish. Set the tomato lids on top. Transfer to the top shelf of the oven and bake for 20 to 25 minutes. Serve warm or at room temperature.

From Françoise:
• The rice must be completely tender before stuffing the tomatoes because it will not continue to cook in the oven.

• This is a good way to use up rice leftovers. If you don't have quite enough to fill the tomatoes, mix in some diced ham, black olives, and more bell pepper.

ROASTED TOMATOES WITH GRUYÈRE AND SHALLOT CRUMBS
- *Tomates au fromage* -

❖ EASY   ❖ INEXPENSIVE   ❖ 35 MINUTES   ❖ SERVES 4

2 tablespoons butter, cut into ¼-inch dice, plus more for brushing
½ cup shredded Gruyère cheese
3 shallots, finely chopped
Chopped parsley leaves

2 tablespoons dry bread crumbs
Salt and pepper
4 medium tomatoes, halved horizontally and seeded

❖ ❖ ❖ ❖ ❖

1. Preheat the oven to 350 degrees. Brush a gratin dish with butter.

2. In a bowl, toss the cheese with the shallots, parsley, and bread crumbs. Season with salt and pepper.

3. Arrange the tomatoes (cut side up) in the gratin dish, packing them close together. Sprinkle the cheese crumbs over the top and dot with the 2 tablespoons of butter. Transfer them to the top shelf of the oven and bake for 20 to 25 minutes. Serve hot.

From Françoise:
• Roasting the tomatoes on the top shelf of the oven allows them to brown nicely as they cook.

• These tomatoes are often served alongside pan-seared veal cutlets or chops. On a platter, surround the meat with the tomatoes and some potato chips, warmed in the oven.

ROASTED TOMATOES
- *Tomates grillées* -

❖ VERY EASY   ❖ INEXPENSIVE   ❖ 15 MINUTES   ❖ SERVES 4

2 tablespoons butter, cut into ¼-inch dice,
  plus more for brushing

8 small tomatoes, cored
Salt and pepper

❖ ❖ ❖ ❖ ❖

1. Preheat the oven to 400 degrees. Brush a gratin dish with butter.

2. Arrange the tomatoes in the dish and pierce the tops with the point of a knife. Dot with the 2 tablespoons of butter and season with salt and pepper. Transfer to the top shelf of the oven and bake for 10 to 12 minutes.

From Françoise:

• Select firm, unblemished tomatoes.

• If you peel the tomatoes before roasting them, they are less likely to burst.

• I like to serve these tomatoes with all kinds of roasts, or pan-seared or grilled meats, as well as with Crusty Mustard-Grilled Chicken with Shallot Sauce (page 266).

CREAMY PAN-SEARED TOMATO HALVES WITH ONIONS
- *Tomates à la crème* -

❖ EASY   ❖ INEXPENSIVE   ❖ 20 MINUTES   ❖ SERVES 4

2 tablespoons butter
6 medium tomatoes, halved horizontally
  and seeded

2 or 3 onions, finely chopped
Salt and pepper
1 or 2 tablespoons crème fraîche

❖ ❖ ❖ ❖ ❖

1. In a large skillet, melt the butter over low heat. When it foams, add the tomatoes cut side down, packing them close together. Sprinkle the onions on top and season with salt and pepper. Cover and cook for 15 minutes, turning the tomatoes halfway through.

2. Stir in the crème fraîche and simmer for 4 to 5 minutes. Transfer to a warmed serving dish and serve.

From Françoise:

• Serve with white meats, poultry, or rabbit.

GOLDEN GARLICKY TOMATOES

- *Tomates provençales* -

❖ EASY   ❖ INEXPENSIVE   ❖ 15 MINUTES   ❖ SERVES 4 TO 6

6 firm tomatoes, halved horizontally
Salt
4 garlic cloves, finely chopped
Chopped parsley leaves from 1 small bunch

2 to 3 tablespoons dry bread crumbs
5 tablespoons butter
Pepper

❖ ❖ ❖ ❖ ❖

1. Sprinkle the tomatoes with salt and turn cut side down on a plate to drain.

2. In a small bowl, toss the garlic with the parsley and bread crumbs.

3. In a large skillet, melt 2 tablespoons of the butter over medium-high heat. When it foams, add the tomatoes cut side down. Cover and cook, turning once, about 2 minutes per side. Season with salt and pepper.

4. Pack the tomatoes close together in the skillet. Sprinkle the tops with the garlic crumbs and dot with the remaining 3 tablespoons of butter. Cover and cook over medium heat for 10 minutes. Transfer to a warmed platter and serve.

From Françoise:

• If your skillet is too small to fit all the tomatoes, use two, adding half the ingredients to each.

• These tomatoes are especially good with sautéed veal chops or cutlets.

SAUTÉED SALSIFY

- *Salsifis sautés* -

❖ INTERMEDIATE   ❖ MODERATE   ❖ 1 HOUR   ❖ SERVES 4

Vinegar

2 pounds salsify

Salt

1 tablespoon all-purpose flour

3 tablespoons butter

Pepper

Chopped parsley leaves for sprinkling

❖ ❖ ❖ ❖ ❖

1. Fill a medium bowl with water and add the vinegar. Peel the salsify and trim the ends. Transfer the salsify to the water as you peel it. Slice the salsify crosswise 2 inches thick. Return the salsify to the water to keep it white.

2. Meanwhile, in a large saucepan, bring 6 cups of salted water to a boil. In a cup, blend the flour with ¼ cup cold water to make a slurry, then add to the boiling water. Drain the salsify. Add to the pan and cook until tender, 30 to 40 minutes. Drain.

3. In a large skillet, melt the butter over medium heat. Add the salsify and cook until nicely browned, about 10 minutes. Season with salt and pepper. Transfer to a warmed serving dish, sprinkle with parsley, and serve.

From Françoise:

• Start by soaking the salsify in a bowl of cold water to loosen the dirt and make it easier to peel.

• You can simplify the recipe by omitting the flour slurry, but the salsify won't be as white when it's cooked.

• The proportions for acidulated water are 1 tablespoon of vinegar or lemon juice to 1 quart of water.

VEGETABLES

SALSIFY FRITTERS

- Beignets de salsifis -

❖ ADVANCED ❖ MODERATE ❖ 1 HOUR, 20 MINUTES, PLUS 1 HOUR STANDING ❖ SERVES 4

FRITTER BATTER

1 cup all-purpose flour

Salt

1 large whole egg, plus 2 large egg whites

1 tablespoon oil

½ to ⅔ cup beer or water

Vinegar

1 ½ pounds salsify

Salt

1 tablespoon all-purpose flour

4 cups oil for frying

Pepper

❖ ❖ ❖ ❖ ❖

1. Make the fritter batter: In a large bowl, whisk the flour with ½ teaspoon of salt, the whole egg, and oil. Gradually whisk in the ½ cup of beer or water. The mixture should be thicker than crêpe batter; use more liquid if needed. Cover and let stand for 1 hour. Just before using, beat the egg whites with a pinch of salt until stiff and fold into the batter.

2. Meanwhile, fill a medium bowl with water and add the vinegar. Peel the salsify and trim the ends. Transfer the salsify to the water as you peel it. Slice the salsify crosswise 2 inches thick. Return the salsify to the water to keep it white.

3. In a large saucepan, bring 6 cups of salted water to a boil. In a cup, blend the flour with ¼ cup cold water to make a slurry, then add to the boiling water. Drain the salsify. Add to the pan and cook until tender, 30 to 40 minutes. Drain well.

4. In a large skillet, heat the oil to 375 degrees. Using a fork, dip the salsify one at a time in the batter. Gently drop them into the oil without crowding. Fry the salsify, turning them once, until puffed and golden, 1 to 3 minutes total. Using a slotted spoon, transfer the fritters to paper towels to drain. Keep warm in a low oven while frying the remaining salsify. Season with salt and pepper and serve very hot.

From Françoise:

• With the extra egg yolks from the batter, you can enrich a soup or a sauce (but use them quickly). Whisk 1 yolk with a little of the hot broth, sauce, or crème fraîche, then, off the heat, whisk this mixture into the soup or sauce.

• The proportions for acidulated water are 1 tablespoon of vinegar or lemon juice to 1 quart of water.

SAUTÉED SWISS CHARD STEMS

- *Bettes sautées* -

❖ EASY ❖ INEXPENSIVE ❖ 1 HOUR ❖ SERVES 4

Salt

2 pounds broad-stemmed Swiss chard

2 tablespoons butter

Pepper

❖ ❖ ❖ ❖ ❖

1. Bring a large saucepan of salted water to a boil.

2. Meanwhile, cut the green leaves off the Swiss chard stems and reserve for another use. Remove any tough strings from the stems and cut crosswise into pieces 1½ inches thick.

3. Add the stems to the boiling water and cook until tender, about 45 minutes. Drain well.

4. In a large saucepan, melt the butter over medium heat. Add the stems and cook until

nicely browned, about 10 minutes. Season with salt and pepper. Transfer to a warmed serving dish and serve.

From Françoise:

• Slice very broad stems in half lengthwise before boiling.

• If you're serving the Swiss chard with sautéed steaks or cutlets, add the boiled stems to the skillet after the meat comes out along with 1 or 2 tablespoons of boiling water and cook over high heat for a few minutes.

VEGETABLES

GOLDEN GRATINÉED SWISS CHARD STEMS

- *Bettes gratinées au fromage* -

❖ EASY   ❖ INEXPENSIVE   ❖ 1 HOUR, 15 MINUTES   ❖ SERVES 4

Salt
2 pounds broad-stemmed Swiss chard

2 tablespoons butter, cut into ¼-inch dice,
   plus more for brushing
1 cup shredded Gruyère cheese

❖ ❖ ❖ ❖ ❖

1. Bring a large saucepan of salted water to a boil.

2. Meanwhile, cut the green leaves off the Swiss chard stems and reserve for another use. Remove any tough strings from the stems and cut crosswise into pieces 1½ inches thick.

3. Add the stems to the boiling water and cook until tender, about 45 minutes. Drain well.

4. Meanwhile, preheat the oven to 425 degrees. Brush a gratin dish with butter.

5. Spread half the stems in the dish, then layer half the cheese and half the butter on top. Continue layering with the remaining stems, cheese, and butter.

6. Transfer the dish to the top shelf of the oven and bake until nicely browned, 10 to 15 minutes. Serve at once.

From Françoise:
• If the stems are very broad, slice them in half lengthwise before boiling.

• You can cook the Swiss chard leaves in plenty of boiling water, like spinach, then drain and simmer with butter or leftover pan juices. Chard leaves cook down a lot, so you need quite a bit to make 4 servings. Or you could always stir them into mashed potatoes. If you have only a little leftover pan juice, extend it with a little chicken broth. Don't add salt, since the broth is already seasoned.

BROCCOLI IN CREAMY ROQUEFORT SAUCE

- *Brocolis au roquefort* -

❖ EASY   ❖ INEXPENSIVE   ❖ 30 MINUTES   ❖ SERVES 4

Salt

2 broccoli bunches, cut into florets,
   stems peeled and cut into 1-inch pieces

½ cup crème fraîche

½ cup crumbled Roquefort cheese
   (about 2 ounces)

2 tablespoons milk

Pepper

❖   ❖   ❖   ❖   ❖

1. Bring a large saucepan of salted water to a boil. Add the broccoli and cook until tender, about 15 minutes. Drain well.

2. Meanwhile, in a medium saucepan, combine the crème fraîche with the cheese and milk. Cook over medium heat, swirling the pan until the cheese melts.

3. Spread the broccoli in a warmed serving dish. Pour the cheese sauce over the top and serve.

From Françoise:

• Some cooks throw out the broccoli stems, but this is an unnecessary waste. It's unfortunate because the stems are really very good, especially with this tasty sauce.

• Broccoli can be cooked until crisp-tender. In fact, the less it cooks the more it keeps its bright green color. It will also be greener and more vitamin-rich when drained immediately after cooking.

VEGETABLES

CELERY ROOT AND POTATO PUREE

- *Purée de céleri-rave et pommes de terre* -

❖ EASY   ❖ INEXPENSIVE   ❖ 50 MINUTES   ❖ SERVES 4

Salt

1 celery root, thickly peeled and quartered

3 or 4 potatoes, peeled

3 tablespoons butter

½ cup shredded Gruyère cheese

Pepper

❖   ❖   ❖   ❖   ❖

1. Bring a large saucepan of salted water to a boil. Add the celery root and potatoes, cover, and cook until tender, 20 to 30 minutes

2. Drain well, reserving 1 cup of the cooking water. Puree the vegetables using a food mill.

continued

Using a wooden spoon, gradually mix in the butter and enough of the reserved cooking liquid to make a light puree. Stir in the cheese and season with salt and pepper. Transfer to a warmed serving dish and serve.

From Françoise:

• I often mix a good amount of crème fraîche and a little hot milk into the pureed vegetables. This way you can leave out the Gruyère cheese, which not everybody likes.

• This puree is the classic partner to game dishes.

GOLDEN GRATIN OF CELERY ROOT WITH GRUYÈRE
- *Céleri-rave gratiné au fromage* -

❖ EASY   ❖ INEXPENSIVE   ❖ 50 MINUTES   ❖ SERVES 4

2 tablespoons butter, cut into ¼-inch dice, plus more for brushing
Salt

1 celery root, thickly peeled, quartered, and sliced ½ inch thick
1 ¼ cups shredded Gruyère cheese

❖ ❖ ❖ ❖ ❖

1. Preheat the oven to 425 degrees. Brush a gratin dish with butter.

2. Bring a large saucepan of salted water to a boil. Add the celery root and cook until tender, 20 to 30 minutes. Drain well.

3. Spread half the celery root slices in the gratin dish and layer half the cheese and half the 2 tablespoons of butter on top. Continue layering with the remaining celery root, cheese, and butter.

4. Transfer the dish to the top shelf of the oven and bake until nicely browned, 10 to 15 minutes. Serve at once.

From Françoise:

• Knock on the celery root (like a door) before buying it; it should feel "full." Or lift it; it should feel heavy for its size.

• Serve this gratin as a first course or as a side dish with white meat (veal cutlets, chicken, roast pork).

DICED CELERY ROOT SIMMERED WITH TOMATO, MUSHROOM, AND HAM SAUCE

- *Céleri-rave à l'italienne* -

❖ EASY   ❖ INEXPENSIVE   ❖ 1 HOUR   ❖ SERVES 4

SAUCE

2 tablespoons butter

¼ pound white mushrooms, chopped

1 onion, chopped

1 shallot, chopped

1 thin slice ham, finely chopped

2 tablespoons tomato paste

Salt and pepper

1 tablespoon all-purpose flour

1½- to 2-pound celery root, thickly peeled and
   cut into 1-inch cubes

1 tablespoon butter

Salt and pepper

Chopped parsley for sprinkling

❖ ❖ ❖ ❖ ❖

1. Make the sauce: In a large saucepan, melt 1 tablespoon of the butter over medium heat. Add the mushrooms, onion, and shallot and cook until lightly browned. Add the ham, ¾ cup of water, and the tomato paste and season with salt and pepper. Partly cover and bring to a simmer, then reduce the heat to low and cook until reduced by half, about 30 minutes.

2. Meanwhile, bring a large saucepan of water to a boil. Add the celery root and cook for 10 minutes. Drain well.

3. In a flameproof casserole, melt the 1 tablespoon of butter over medium-high heat. Add the celery root and cook until lightly browned. Season with salt and pepper.

4. Pour the sauce into the casserole. In a cup, mash the remaining 1 tablespoon of butter with the flour. Gradually whisk this paste into the sauce. Cover and cook over low heat for 10 minutes. Spoon into a warmed serving dish, sprinkle with parsley, and serve.

From Françoise:

• The sauce will have more finesse if you add a little dry white wine; reduce the water proportionately.

• This is a good recipe to make for anyone who doesn't yet know how good celery root is.

• If you don't add any ham, you can stir in 6 tablespoons of beef broth to make the sauce more flavorful.

VEGETABLES

TENDER CELERY RIBS WITH ANCHOVY DIPPING SAUCE
- Céleri en anchoïade -

❖ EASY   ❖ INEXPENSIVE   ❖ 15 MINUTES   ❖ SERVES 4

1 tender celery heart, ribs separated
12 oil- or salt-cured anchovy fillets
6 tablespoons olive oil

Splash of vinegar
Pepper

❖ ❖ ❖ ❖ ❖

1. Arrange the celery ribs in a glass or in a dish.

2. In a mortar or food processor, puree the anchovies. Gradually blend in the oil and vinegar. Season with pepper.

3. Scrape the anchovy sauce into a small bowl and serve with the celery for dipping.

From Françoise:
• If you're using salt-cured anchovies, soak them first for a few minutes in water to remove the salt. Pat dry with paper towels, then proceed with the recipe.

• Serve an assortment of raw vegetables with the anchovy sauce—cauliflower and broccoli florets; carrot, bell pepper, and cucumber sticks; and mushrooms.

TOMATO-BRAISED CELERY
- Céleri-branche braisé -

❖ EASY   ❖ INEXPENSIVE   ❖ 1 HOUR, 45 MINUTES   ❖ SERVES 4

SAUCE
2 tablespoons butter
1 carrot, peeled and cut into ¼-inch dice
1 onion, cut into ¼-inch dice
2 teaspoons all-purpose flour
1 teaspoon tomato paste
3 cups chicken broth

Salt
2 bunches of celery (about 2 pounds)
Pepper

1. Make the sauce: In a flameproof casserole, melt the butter over medium heat. Add the carrot and onion and cook until lightly browned. Stir in the flour, then the tomato paste. Pour in the broth, then bring to a simmer, reduce the heat to medium-low, and cook, uncovered, until reduced by half, about 45 minutes.

2. Meanwhile, bring a large saucepan of salted water to a boil. Separate the celery ribs and remove any tough strings. Cut the ribs in half crosswise. Add to the boiling water and cook for 10 minutes. Drain well.

3. Slice the celery ribs in half lengthwise. Add to the sauce and season with salt and pepper. Cover and cook for 45 minutes. Transfer to a warmed serving dish and serve.

From Françoise:

• I recommend serving this recipe with roasted veal or roast beef.

• Scattering Parmesan cheese shavings over the top would be lovely.

CORN CROQUETTES
- *Croquettes de maïs* -

❖ INTERMEDIATE   ❖ INEXPENSIVE   ❖ 30 MINUTES, PLUS 2 HOURS CHILLING   ❖ SERVES 4

3 ears of corn, shucked
5 tablespoons dry bread crumbs
7 tablespoons butter

THICK BÉCHAMEL SAUCE
2 tablespoons butter
2 tablespoons all-purpose flour
1 cup milk
Salt and pepper

❖ ❖ ❖ ❖ ❖

1. Bring a large saucepan of water to a boil. Add the corn and boil over medium-high heat until just tender, about 4 minutes; drain. When cool enough to handle, cut the corn kernels from the cobs; you will need 2 cups.

2. Make the thick béchamel sauce: In a small saucepan, melt the butter over medium heat. Whisk in the flour until it starts foaming. Whisk in the milk. Season with salt and pepper. Bring to a boil, whisking, until thickened.

3. Remove the sauce from the heat and mix in the corn. Spread in a shallow pan, cover, and refrigerate until cold and firm, about 2 hours.

4. Spread the bread crumbs in a soup plate. Turn the corn mixture out onto a work surface and roll into a cylinder about 1 inch in diameter. Cut it into 2 ½- to 3-inch pieces and dredge in the bread crumbs, pressing lightly to help the crumbs adhere.

5. In a large skillet, melt the butter over medium heat. When it foams, add the croquettes without crowding and fry until golden brown all over, 1 to 2 minutes per side. Transfer the croquettes to a warmed platter. Serve as soon as possible.

continued

VEGETABLES

From Françoise:

• You can also use canned corn, drained, or frozen corn kernels to make these croquettes. If you're using frozen corn, boil it for 2 minutes, then drain.

• This recipe can be prepared through Step 2 and refrigerated for up to 2 days.

• With these proportions you should get about 10 croquettes.

• The béchamel sauce needs to be thick enough so that the croquettes hold their shape.

• Serve corn croquettes with roasted meat or poultry.

VEGETABLE STEW WITH SOFTLY SCRAMBLED EGGS
- *Piperade* -

❖ EASY   ❖ INEXPENSIVE   ❖ 1 HOUR, 20 MINUTES   ❖ SERVES 4

6 tablespoons olive oil
1 ½ pounds tomatoes, peeled, seeded, and quartered
2 bell peppers, thinly sliced

1 garlic clove, crushed
Salt and pepper
4 or 6 large eggs, lightly beaten

❖ ❖ ❖ ❖ ❖

1. In a large skillet, heat the oil over low heat. Add the tomatoes, bell peppers, and garlic clove. Season with salt and pepper. Cover and cook for about 1 hour, removing the lid halfway through to let the liquid reduce.

2. Remove the garlic clove. Increase the heat to medium-high, add the eggs to the skillet, and cook, stirring constantly, until the eggs are softly scrambled, 2 to 3 minutes. Transfer to a warmed serving dish and serve

From Françoise:
• To make peeling tomatoes easy, cut a shallow cross in the bottom of each one, then add to boiling water until the skin begins to curl, about 1 minute; drain.

• It's completely normal for piperade to look a little lumpy.

• I add a pinch of the mildly hot ground chile *piment d'Espelette* to the stew for guests who like their food a little spicy.

• Try serving piperade in baked tartlet shells made with pie dough, or with phyllo dough. Brush sheets of phyllo with melted butter, stack them, and press them into tartlet pans, then trim the excess dough before baking.

CRISPY MEAT-STUFFED ZUCCHINI

- *Courgettes farcies à la viande* -

❖ EASY　　　　❖ INEXPENSIVE　　　　❖ 1 HOUR, 15 MINUTES　　　　❖ SERVES 4

4 large zucchini

6 tablespoons milk

½ cup dry bread crumbs

3 tablespoons butter

1 onion, finely chopped

2 cups chopped leftover meat

1 large egg

Chopped parsley leaves and chives

Salt and pepper

❖　❖　❖　❖　❖

1. Slice the zucchini in half lengthwise. Using a spoon, hollow out the insides, leaving a sturdy shell.

2. In a small saucepan, warm the milk. Add the bread crumbs and let soak, then squeeze dry, discarding the excess milk.

3. In a large skillet, melt 1 tablespoon of the butter over medium-low heat. Add the onion and cook until softened. Remove the pan from the heat and mix in the soaked bread crumbs, chopped meat, egg, and herbs. Season with salt and pepper.

4. Stuff the zucchini with the meat mixture, mounding it slightly. In a flameproof casserole, melt the remaining 2 tablespoons of butter over medium-high heat. Add the stuffed zucchini, cover, and cook for a few minutes, until lightly browned, then reduce the heat to low and cook for 40 to 45 minutes. Transfer the zucchini to a serving dish and serve.

From Françoise:

• When you hollow out the zucchini, you lose mostly seeds, so it's not wasteful.

VEGETABLES

ZUCCHINI WITH RICE AND TOMATOES

- *Courgettes à la marseillaise* -

❖ EASY　　　　❖ INEXPENSIVE　　　　❖ 1 HOUR, 15 MINUTES　　　　❖ SERVES 4

3 tablespoons olive oil

2 tomatoes, peeled, seeded, and coarsely chopped

1 onion, finely chopped

1 garlic clove, finely chopped

4 zucchini, cut into ½-inch dice

Salt and pepper

⅓ cup long-grain rice

continued

1. In a flameproof casserole, heat the oil over medium heat. Add the tomatoes, onion, and garlic and cook for 5 minutes. Add the zucchini and season with salt and pepper. Cover, reduce the heat to low, and cook for 30 minutes.

2. Rinse the rice in a colander under cold running water and drain. Stir into the zucchini mixture, cover, and cook over low heat until the rice is tender, about 25 minutes.

From Françoise:

• Peeling and seeding the tomatoes is not essential.

• Do not peel the zucchini, but do scrub them well to remove any grit.

• Zucchini usually release enough water to cook the rice without additional liquid, but if the rice looks dry before it's completely tender, add a little boiling water to the pot.

GRATINÉED ZUCCHINI WITH ONIONS
- *Courgettes à la lyonnaise* -

❖ EASY ❖ INEXPENSIVE ❖ 30 MINUTES ❖ SERVES 4

3 tablespoons oil
4 zucchini, thickly sliced crosswise
Salt and pepper

1 tablespoon butter
1 large onion, thinly sliced
⅓ cup shredded Gruyère cheese

❖ ❖ ❖ ❖ ❖

1. In a large skillet, heat the oil over medium-high heat. Add the zucchini slices without crowding and cook until lightly browned on both sides. Season with salt and pepper, cover, reduce the heat to low, and cook for 20 minutes.

2. Meanwhile, in a medium saucepan, melt the butter over low heat. Add the onions, cover, and cook for 15 minutes.

3. Preheat the broiler. In a gratin dish, layer the zucchini, onions, and cheese. Transfer to the top shelf of the oven and broil until the cheese is melted and nicely browned, 3 to 5 minutes.

ZUCCHINI AND TOMATOES WITH GARLIC AND PARSLEY CRUMBS

- *Courgettes gratinées au four* -

❖ EASY   ❖ INEXPENSIVE   ❖ 1 HOUR, PLUS 15 MINUTES DRAINING   ❖ SERVES 4

4 small zucchini, sliced crosswise

Salt

2 to 3 tablespoons olive oil

Pepper

2 garlic cloves, finely chopped

1 tablespoon chopped parsley leaves

2 tablespoons dry bread crumbs

4 tomatoes, halved horizontally

❖ ❖ ❖ ❖ ❖

1. In a colander, toss the zucchini with salt and let drain for 15 minutes. Pat dry with paper towels.

2. Preheat the oven to 350 degrees.

3. In a large skillet, heat the oil over medium-high heat. Add the zucchini slices without crowding and cook until lightly browned on both sides. Transfer the zucchini to a gratin dish and season with salt and pepper.

4. In a bowl, toss the garlic with the parsley and bread crumbs. Arrange the tomato halves on top of the zucchini. Sprinkle the top with the garlic and parsley crumbs. Transfer to the oven and bake on the top shelf for 30 minutes.

From Françoise:

• You can omit the bread crumbs, but that would be a shame. It's easy to make bread crumbs at home—grind stale bread or toast in a food processor—and it doesn't cost very much.

VEGETABLES

EASY RATATOUILLE

- *Ratatouille niçoise* -

❖ EASY   ❖ INEXPENSIVE   ❖ 2 HOURS   ❖ SERVES 4

3 to 4 tablespoons olive oil

3 large onions, thinly sliced

4 eggplants, cut into 1-inch chunks

4 zucchini, halved lengthwise and cut into
   1-inch chunks

1 pound tomatoes, coarsely chopped

2 bell peppers, cut into thin strips

2 garlic cloves, crushed

1 bouquet garni made with parsley, thyme,
   and bay leaf

Salt and pepper

continued

1. In a flameproof casserole, heat the olive oil over medium-low heat. Add the onions and cook until softened. Add the eggplants, zucchini, tomatoes, bell peppers, garlic, and bouquet garni. Season with salt and pepper.

2. Cover and bring to a simmer, then reduce the heat to low and cook until the vegetables are very tender, 1 hour to 1 hour and 30 minutes, removing the lid halfway through to reduce the cooking juices if needed.

3. Remove the bouquet garni and serve.

From Françoise:

• Stir the ratatouille during cooking or cook over very low heat because it tends to stick to the pot, especially the eggplant.

• I like to serve ratatouille very cold, as an hors-d'oeuvre.

LAMB-STUFFED ZUCCHINI WITH TOMATO SAUCE
- Courgettes à la tomate -

❖ EASY ❖ INEXPENSIVE ❖ 2 HOURS ❖ SERVES 4

3 tablespoons long-grain rice
1 ½ pounds large zucchini
½ pound ground lamb
3 small onions, finely chopped
Salt and pepper
¼ cup oil
2 bell peppers, cut into ¼-inch dice

1 to 2 teaspoons curry powder
¾ cup dry white wine
1 pound tomatoes, peeled, seeded, and
  coarsely chopped
½ pound white mushrooms, chopped
1 garlic clove, finely chopped

❖ ❖ ❖ ❖ ❖

1. Bring a small saucepan of water to a boil. Add the rice and cook for 5 minutes. Drain.

2. Trim the zucchini ends. Cut the zucchini crosswise into 2 ½-inch pieces. Using a spoon, hollow out the insides, leaving a sturdy shell.

3. In a bowl, mix the rice with the lamb and onions and season with salt and pepper. Stuff this mixture into the zucchini pieces. In a flameproof casserole, heat 3 tablespoons of the oil over medium-high heat. Add the stuffed zucchini and cook until lightly browned, turning gently. Add the bell peppers, curry powder, wine, and 2 cups of water and season with salt

and pepper. Reduce the heat to low, cover, and cook for 1 hour.

4. In a large saucepan, heat the remaining 1 tablespoon of oil over medium-high heat. Add the tomatoes, mushrooms, and garlic and cook for 5 minutes. Add to the casserole, cover, and cook for 20 to 30 minutes. Serve hot or let cool and serve at room temperature.

From Françoise:

• The stuffing can also be made with leftover cooked lamb and fresh bread crumbs. Beat in 1 or 2 large eggs to bind the mixture.

GRATINÉED FENNEL WITH GRUYÈRE

- Fenouil gratiné -

❖ EASY ❖ INEXPENSIVE ❖ 45 MINUTES ❖ SERVES 4

Salt

4 fennel bulbs

2 tablespoons butter, cut into ¼-inch dice,
   plus more for brushing

Pepper

½ cup shredded Gruyère cheese

❖ ❖ ❖ ❖ ❖

1. Bring a large saucepan of salted water to a boil. Trim the fennel and remove any strings or tough outer ribs. Cut the fennel in half lengthwise. Add to the boiling water and cook until tender, about 30 minutes. Drain well, pressing out any water.

2. Preheat the broiler. Brush a gratin dish with butter. Arrange the fennel halves in the dish. Season with salt and pepper. Sprinkle with the cheese and dot with the 2 tablespoons of

butter. Transfer to the top shelf of the oven and broil until the cheese is melted and nicely browned, 3 to 5 minutes.

From Françoise:

• Instead of broiling the fennel, you can brown it in a 425-degree oven for 10 to 15 minutes.

• This fennel is especially good with veal or all white meat.

VEGETABLES

FENNEL BRAISED WITH PANCETTA AND AROMATIC VEGETABLES

- Fenouil braisé -

❖ EASY ❖ INEXPENSIVE ❖ 1 HOUR, 30 MINUTES ❖ SERVES 4

Salt

4 fennel bulbs

3 tablespoons butter

¼ pound thickly sliced pancetta, cut crosswise
   into ¼-inch-thick strips

1 carrot, peeled and cut into ¼-inch dice

1 onion, cut into ¼-inch dice

1 bouquet garni made with parsley, thyme,
   and bay leaf

1 cup broth or water

Pepper

continued

1. Bring a large saucepan of salted water to a boil. Trim the fennel and remove any strings or tough outer ribs. Cut the fennel in half lengthwise. Add to the boiling water and cook for 10 minutes. Drain well, pressing out any water.

2. In a flameproof casserole, melt the butter over low heat. Add the pancetta and cook until lightly browned. Add the fennel, carrot, onion, bouquet garni, and broth or water. Season with salt and pepper. Cover and cook for 1 hour.

From Françoise:
• Braised fennel is delicious with roasted veal or veal cutlets or chicken.

CREAMY GRATINÉED SPINACH WITH GRUYÈRE
- *Épinards gratinés à la romaine* -

❖ EASY   ❖ INEXPENSIVE   ❖ 50 MINUTES   ❖ SERVES 6

3 pounds spinach, tough stems removed
1 tablespoon butter
1 slice pancetta, cut crosswise into
   ¼-inch-thick strips
1 garlic clove, crushed

Salt and pepper
2 large eggs
¼ cup milk
½ cup shredded Gruyère cheese, plus ½ cup
   shaved Gruyère

❖ ❖ ❖ ❖ ❖

1. Bring a large pot of water to a boil. Add the spinach and cook for 5 minutes. Drain and squeeze out as much water as possible. Coarsely chop.

2. In a flameproof casserole, melt the butter over low heat. Add the pancetta and cook until just beginning to brown. Add the spinach and garlic and season with salt and pepper. Cover and cook for 15 minutes.

3. Preheat the oven to 425 degrees. Spread the spinach mixture in a gratin dish. In a bowl, whisk the eggs with the milk and shredded cheese. Pour this over the spinach. Arrange the shaved cheese in a decorative pattern on top. Transfer to the top shelf of the oven and bake until the cheese is melted and nicely browned, 10 to 15 minutes.

From Françoise:
• If you like, you can use half shredded Gruyère and half grated Parmesan. Be careful that the Parmesan is not too strong or rancid. That happens sometimes; taste it first.

• Frozen spinach can also be prepared this way.

CREAMED SPINACH

- Épinards à la crème -

❖ EASY   ❖ INEXPENSIVE   ❖ 30 MINUTES   ❖ SERVES 8

4 pounds spinach, large stems removed
2 tablespoons butter

½ cup crème fraîche
Salt and pepper

❖ ❖ ❖ ❖ ❖

1. Bring a large pot of water to a boil. Add the spinach and cook for 5 minutes. Drain and squeeze out as much water as possible.

2. In a flameproof casserole, melt the butter over medium-high heat. Add the spinach and cook for 2 to 3 minutes to dry it out. Stir in ⅓ cup of the crème fraîche and season with salt and pepper. Reduce the heat to low, cover, and cook for 10 minutes.

3. Just before serving, stir in the remaining crème fraîche. Transfer to a warmed serving dish and serve.

From Françoise:

• To give the spinach more flavor, I add a pinch of freshly grated nutmeg, but that's all!

• Spinach can never be washed too well. The nooks and crannies hide the grit that crunches between your teeth.

• Dry out the spinach well before adding the crème fraîche or it will be watery.

• This is a wonderful side dish with white meats and their delicious pan juices, as well as with eggs.

VEGETABLES

SLOW-COOKED SPINACH WITH GARLIC

- Épinards braisés -

❖ EASY   ❖ INEXPENSIVE   ❖ 45 MINUTES   ❖ SERVES 8

4 pounds spinach, tough stems removed
3 tablespoons butter

1 garlic clove, chopped
Salt and pepper

❖ ❖ ❖ ❖ ❖

1. Bring a large pot of water to a boil. Add the spinach and cook for 5 minutes. Drain and squeeze out as much water as possible. Coarsely chop.

2. In a flameproof casserole, melt the butter over low heat. Add the spinach and garlic and

continued

season with salt and pepper. Cover and cook for 20 to 30 minutes. Transfer to a warmed serving dish and serve.

From Françoise:

• If you have any meat jus around, add it to the spinach, as it loves sauce.

GOLDEN CREAMY ENDIVES
- *Endives au gratin* -

❖ EASY   ❖ INEXPENSIVE   ❖ 1 HOUR, 30 MINUTES   ❖ SERVES 4

3 tablespoons butter
1 onion, thinly sliced
2 pounds endives, cored
½ lemon
Salt and pepper

MORNAY SAUCE
3 tablespoons butter
3 tablespoons all-purpose flour
2 cups milk
Salt and pepper
Freshly grated nutmeg
½ cup shredded Gruyère cheese

❖ ❖ ❖ ❖ ❖

1. In a flameproof casserole, melt 2 tablespoons of the butter over low heat. Stir in the onion, then add the endives and sprinkle with lemon juice. Season with salt and pepper. Cover and cook for 1 hour, turning the endives occasionally.

2. Preheat the oven to 425 degrees. Make the Mornay sauce: In a medium saucepan, melt the butter over medium heat. Whisk in the flour until it starts foaming. Whisk in the milk. Season with salt, pepper, and nutmeg. Bring to a boil, whisking, then reduce the heat to very low and cook for 5 minutes. Remove the pan from the heat and stir in the cheese.

3. Arrange the onions and endives in a gratin dish. Spoon the Mornay sauce over the top and dot with the remaining 1 tablespoon of butter. Transfer to the top shelf of the oven and bake until nicely browned, 10 to 15 minutes.

From Françoise:

• At my house, I often turn these endives into a main dish by wrapping each one in a thin slice of ham before arranging them in the gratin dish. Even people who don't especially like endives enjoy them this way.

• To remove any bitterness from the endives, cook them first in boiling water for 30 minutes, then transfer them to the gratin dish. Drain them very well and pat dry before adding the Mornay sauce or the dish will be watery.

• The lemon juice keeps the endives from turning brown during cooking.

BUTTERY ENDIVES WITH PANCETTA

- Endives à l'ardennaise -

❖ EASY ❖ INEXPENSIVE ❖ 1 HOUR ❖ SERVES 4

2 tablespoons butter
2 pounds endives, cored
Salt and pepper

¼ pound thickly sliced pancetta, cut crosswise
   into ¼-inch-thick strips
3 ½ ounces dry-cured ham, chopped

❖ ❖ ❖ ❖ ❖

1. In a flameproof casserole, melt the butter over medium heat. Add the endives and cook until lightly browned all over. Sprinkle with 2 tablespoons of water. Season with salt and pepper. Reduce the heat to very low, cover, and cook for 30 minutes.

2. Add the pancetta and ham and cook for 20 minutes. Transfer to a warmed serving dish.

From Françoise:
• You might add a sprinkling of lemon juice to the endives in Step 1.

• Baked ham can replace the dry-cured ham.

• Don't confuse endives with curly endives, sometimes called curly chicory or frisée.

VEGETABLES

BUTTERY ENDIVES WITH ONION

- Endives braisées -

❖ EASY ❖ INEXPENSIVE ❖ 1 HOUR, 15 MINUTES ❖ SERVES 4

3 tablespoons butter
2 pounds endives, cored
1 onion, thinly sliced

½ lemon
Salt and pepper

❖ ❖ ❖ ❖ ❖

1. In a flameproof casserole, melt the butter over medium heat. Add the endives and cook until lightly browned all over. Add the onion and sprinkle with lemon juice. Season with salt and pepper. Reduce the heat to low, cover, and cook for 1 hour, turning the endives occasionally.

2. Transfer to a warmed serving dish and serve.

From Françoise:
• To cook the endives more quickly, slice them in half lengthwise. It may not look as nice, but it's twice as fast.

BUTTERY GREEN BEANS

- Haricots verts à l'anglaise -

❖ EASY   ❖ INEXPENSIVE   ❖ 30 MINUTES   ❖ SERVES 4

2 pounds green beans, ends removed
Salt

2 tablespoons butter
Chopped parsley leaves

❖ ❖ ❖ ❖ ❖

1. Bring a large saucepan of water to a boil. Add the green beans and salt and cook until tender, 10 to 20 minutes. Drain well.

2. Transfer to a warmed serving dish. Top with the butter, sprinkle with the parsley, and serve.

From Françoise:
• To keep the color in the green beans bright, do not cover them when they're cooking.

• The beans taste better when they're al dente. Watch the cooking carefully.

• You can also make this recipe with green runner beans.

• Green beans are a very good accompaniment to roasted and sautéed meats.

BUTTERY SAUTÉED GREEN BEANS

- Haricots verts sautées -

❖ EASY   ❖ INEXPENSIVE   ❖ 30 MINUTES   ❖ SERVES 4

2 pounds green beans, ends removed
Salt
3 tablespoons butter

Pepper
Chopped parsley leaves

❖ ❖ ❖ ❖ ❖

1. Bring a large saucepan of water to a boil. Add the green beans and salt and cook until tender, 10 to 20 minutes. Drain well.

2. In a large skillet, melt the butter over medium-high heat. Add the beans and cook until well coated with the butter. Season with

pepper and sprinkle with parsley. Transfer to a warmed serving dish and serve.

From Françoise:
• You might add 1 finely diced garlic clove to the skillet when you sauté the green beans.

WHITE BEANS WITH PORK SAUSAGE AND BACON
- Haricots à la parisienne -

❖ EASY ❖ MODERATE ❖ 15 MINUTES ❖ SERVES 4

2 tablespoons butter

8 small pork sausages

1 bacon slice, cut crosswise into ¼-inch-thick strips

15-ounce can white beans, drained and rinsed

Salt and pepper

Chopped parsley leaves

❖ ❖ ❖ ❖ ❖

1. In a large skillet, melt the butter over medium-low heat. Add the sausages and bacon and cook until nicely browned. Stir in the beans, season with salt and pepper, and cook until heated through.

2. Transfer to a warmed serving dish. Sprinkle with the parsley and serve.

WHITE BEANS WITH CRUMBLED BLOOD SAUSAGE
- Haricots à l'ardéchoise -

❖ EASY ❖ MODERATE ❖ 2 HOURS, 30 MINUTES ❖ SERVES 4

¾ pound dried white beans

2 garlic cloves, crushed

Salt

2 tablespoons butter

2 onions, chopped

¾ cup dry white wine

1 tablespoon vinegar

7 ounces blood sausage, casing removed, crumbled

Pepper

Chopped parsley leaves

❖ ❖ ❖ ❖ ❖

1. In a large saucepan, generously cover the beans with water and bring to a boil. Cook for 15 minutes, then drain. Return the beans to the pan and add the garlic and boiling water to cover by 2 inches. Bring to a boil, then reduce the heat to low and cook, uncovered, until tender, 1 hour and 30 minutes to 2 hours, seasoning with salt halfway through.

2. Meanwhile, in another large saucepan, melt 1 tablespoon of the butter over medium heat. Add the onions and cook until lightly browned. Add ¾ cup of the bean broth, the wine, vinegar, and blood sausage. Season with

continued

537

salt and pepper. Cover and bring to a simmer, then reduce the heat to low and cook for 20 minutes.

3. Drain the beans and fold into the blood sausage mixture. Stir in the remaining 1 tablespoon of butter and the parsley. Transfer to a warmed serving dish and serve.

CREAMY WHITE BEAN PUREE
- *Mousse de haricots blancs* -

❖ EASY ❖ INEXPENSIVE ❖ 10 MINUTES ❖ SERVES 4

1 ½ cups milk
1 tablespoon cornstarch
Salt and pepper

A few pinches of allspice or freshly grated nutmeg
2 cups cooked white beans
2 tablespoons crème fraîche

❖ ❖ ❖ ❖ ❖

1. In a large saucepan over medium heat, heat the milk with the cornstarch and season with salt, pepper, and allspice or nutmeg. Add the white beans and heat through.

2. Puree the beans with the crème fraîche, using a blender or food processor. Transfer to a warmed serving dish and serve.

From Françoise:

• Stirring in a little walnut oil just before serving would give the puree a rich and nutty flavor.

• If using canned beans, drain and rinse them first.

• You can cook dried beans to make this dish a day ahead. Remember that they need to be parboiled first, then cooked for 1 hour and 30 minutes to 2 hours. Follow the directions in Buttery White Beans (page 539).

BUTTERY WHITE BEANS

- Haricots blancs au naturel -

❖ EASY   ❖ INEXPENSIVE   ❖ 2 HOURS, 30 MINUTES   ❖ SERVES 4

½ pound dried white beans
1 carrot, sliced lengthwise
1 onion stuck with 2 whole cloves
1 bouquet garni made with parsley, thyme,
   and bay leaf

Salt and pepper
2 tablespoons butter
Chopped parsley leaves for sprinkling

❖ ❖ ❖ ❖ ❖

1. In a large saucepan, generously cover the beans with water and bring to a boil. Cook for 15 minutes, then drain. Return the beans to the pan and add the carrot, onion, bouquet garni, and water to cover by 2 inches. Cover and bring to a boil, then reduce the heat to low and cook until tender, 1 hour and 30 minutes to 2 hours, seasoning with salt and pepper halfway through.

2. Drain the beans. Remove the bouquet garni, carrot, and onion. Transfer the beans to a warmed serving dish. Add the butter, sprinkle with parsley, and serve.

From Françoise:
• You can also make this recipe with flageolets, the pale green dried beans about the size of a fingernail.

FRESH SHELL BEANS WITH CRISP BUTTERY CRUMBS

- Haricots blancs gratinés -

❖ EASY   ❖ INEXPENSIVE   ❖ 1 HOUR, 30 MINUTES   ❖ SERVES 4

2 pounds fresh shell beans, pods removed
1 carrot, sliced lengthwise
1 onion stuck with 1 whole clove
1 bouquet garni made with parsley, thyme,
   and bay leaf
Salt and pepper

3 tablespoons butter, cut into ¼-inch dice,
   plus more for brushing
3 tablespoons dry bread crumbs

continued

1. In a large saucepan, generously cover the beans with water and bring to a boil. Cook for 5 minutes, then drain. Return the beans to the pan and add the carrot, onion, bouquet garni, and water to cover by 2 inches. Cover and bring to a boil, then reduce the heat to low and cook until tender, about 50 minutes, seasoning with salt and pepper halfway through.

2. Preheat the oven to 425 degrees. Brush a gratin dish with butter. Drain the beans, reserving 3 tablespoons of broth. Remove the bouquet garni, carrot, and onion. Spread the beans in the gratin dish and stir in 2 tablespoons of the butter and the reserved bean broth. Sprinkle with the bread crumbs and dot with the remaining 1 tablespoon of butter. Transfer to the top shelf of the oven and bake until nicely browned, 10 to 15 minutes.

From Françoise:
• You can add 1 or 2 tablespoons of crème fraîche or meat jus to your beans.

• Shell beans are a classic accompaniment to lamb—chops, shoulder, or special-occasion leg.

WHITE BEANS WITH LAMB AND BUTTERY CRUMBS
- *Gratin de haricots berrichonne* -

❖ EASY   ❖ INEXPENSIVE   ❖ 30 MINUTES   ❖ SERVES 4

2 tablespoons butter, cut into ¼-inch dice, plus more for brushing
15-ounce can white beans, drained and rinsed
½ cup dry bread crumbs
½ cup shredded Gruyère cheese

STUFFING
½ cup fresh bread crumbs
6 tablespoons milk
1 garlic clove, crushed
Parsley leaves
2 cups chopped leftover lamb
1 large egg
Salt and pepper

❖ ❖ ❖ ❖ ❖

1. Preheat the oven to 425 degrees. Brush a gratin dish with butter.

2. Make the stuffing: In a medium bowl, soak the bread crumbs in the milk, then squeeze dry, discarding the excess milk. Transfer to a food processor and finely chop with the garlic, parsley, lamb, and egg. Season well with salt and pepper.

3. In the gratin dish, layer half the beans and stuffing, then repeat. Sprinkle the dry bread crumbs and cheese on top and dot with the 2 tablespoons of butter.

4. Transfer to the top shelf of the oven and bake until the cheese is melted and nicely browned, 10 to 15 minutes. Serve.

From Françoise:
• Obviously, this dish can be prepared with dried beans cooked at home. Follow the directions in Buttery White Beans (page 539). It does take more time, but it's also more delicious.

BUTTERY FRESH SHELL BEANS WITH PARSLEY

- Haricots blancs frais persillés -

❖ EASY   ❖ INEXPENSIVE   ❖ 1 HOUR   ❖ SERVES 4

2 pounds fresh shell beans, pods removed

1 carrot, sliced lengthwise

1 onion stuck with 1 whole clove

1 bouquet garni made with parsley, thyme,
  and bay leaf

Salt and pepper

3 tablespoons butter

Chopped parsley leaves for sprinkling

❖ ❖ ❖ ❖ ❖

1. In a large saucepan, generously cover the
beans with water and bring to a boil. Cook for
5 minutes, then drain. Return the beans to the
pan and add the carrot, onion, bouquet garni,
and water to cover by 2 inches. Cover and bring
to a boil, then reduce the heat to low and cook
until tender, about 50 minutes, seasoning with
salt and pepper halfway through.

2. Drain the beans. Remove the bouquet garni,
carrot, and onion. Swirl in the butter. Transfer
to a warmed serving dish, sprinkle with parsley,
and serve.

PROVENÇAL WHITE BEANS

- Haricots blancs à la provençale -

❖ EASY   ❖ INEXPENSIVE   ❖ 2 HOURS, 30 MINUTES   ❖ SERVES 4

½ pound dried white beans

3 tablespoons butter

4 onions, 1 of which stuck with 2 whole cloves

1 garlic clove, crushed

1 shallot

3 tomatoes, peeled, seeded, and chopped

1 tablespoon tomato paste

Salt and pepper

Chopped parsley leaves for sprinkling

continued

541

1. In a large saucepan, generously cover the beans with water and bring to a boil. Cook for 15 minutes, then drain.

2. In a flameproof casserole, melt the butter over medium heat. Add the onions and cook until lightly browned all over. Add the garlic, shallot, and 1 cup of boiling water. Cover and bring to a boil, then reduce the heat to low and cook until tender, 1 hour and 30 minutes to 2 hours, adding boiling water as needed.

3. Halfway through, add the tomatoes and tomato paste and season with salt and pepper.

4. Remove the onions, shallot, and garlic. Transfer the beans to a warmed serving dish. Sprinkle with parsley and serve.

From Françoise:
• Don't add the tomatoes and tomato paste until halfway through cooking or the acidity will make the beans take much longer to cook.

FRESH SHELL BEANS WITH TOMATO SAUCE
- Haricots blancs à la bretonne -

❖ EASY ❖ INEXPENSIVE ❖ 1 HOUR, 30 MINUTES ❖ SERVES 4

2 pounds fresh shell beans, pods removed
1 carrot, thinly sliced crosswise
1 onion stuck with 2 whole cloves
1 garlic clove, chopped
1 shallot, chopped
1 bouquet garni made with parsley, thyme, and bay leaf
Salt and pepper

2 tablespoons butter
Chopped parsley leaves for sprinkling

TOMATO SAUCE
1 tablespoon butter
3 onions, finely chopped
4 tomatoes, peeled, seeded, and chopped
Salt and pepper

❖ ❖ ❖ ❖ ❖

1. In a large saucepan, generously cover the beans with water and bring to a boil. Cook for 5 minutes, then drain. Return the beans to the pan and add the carrot, onion, garlic, shallot, bouquet garni, and water to cover by 2 inches. Cover and bring to a boil, then reduce the heat to low and cook until tender, about 50 minutes, seasoning with salt and pepper halfway through.

2. Meanwhile, make the tomato sauce: In a medium saucepan, melt the butter over medium heat. Add the onions and cook until lightly browned. Add the tomatoes and season with salt and pepper. Cook, uncovered, for 20 minutes.

3. Drain the beans. Remove the bouquet garni and onion. Stir in the tomato sauce and 2 tablespoons of butter. Transfer to a warmed serving dish, sprinkle with parsley, and serve.

CREAMY WHITE BEANS

- *Mojettes à la crème* -

❖ EASY   ❖ INEXPENSIVE   ❖ 2 HOURS, 30 MINUTES   ❖ SERVES 4

¾ pound dried white beans

1 carrot, sliced lengthwise

1 onion stuck with 2 whole cloves

1 garlic clove, crushed

1 bouquet garni made with parsley, thyme,
   and bay leaf

Salt and pepper

2 tablespoons butter

2 tablespoons crème fraîche

Chopped parsley leaves for sprinkling

❖ ❖ ❖ ❖ ❖

1. In a large saucepan, generously cover the beans with water and bring to a boil. Cook for 15 minutes, then drain. Return the beans to the pan and add the carrot, onion, garlic, bouquet garni, and boiling water to cover by 2 inches. Cover and bring to a boil, then reduce the heat to low and cook until tender, 1 hour and 30 minutes to 2 hours, seasoning with salt and pepper halfway through.

2. Drain the beans. Remove the bouquet garni, carrot, garlic, and onion. Swirl in the butter and crème fraîche. Transfer the beans to a warmed serving dish. Sprinkle with parsley and serve.

From Françoise:

• When you can find fresh shell beans at the end of summer and in the early fall, try this dish, shortening the cooking time to about 50 minutes.

VEGETABLES

LENTILS SIMMERED WITH AROMATICS

- *Lentilles au naturel* -

❖ EASY   ❖ INEXPENSIVE   ❖ 45 MINUTES   ❖ SERVES 4 TO 6

¾ pound lentils

1 carrot, sliced crosswise into 4 lengths

1 onion stuck with 2 whole cloves

1 garlic clove, unpeeled

1 small dried red chile (optional)

1 bouquet garni made with parsley, thyme,
   bay leaf, and celery

Salt and pepper

continued

1. In a large saucepan, generously cover the lentils with water and bring to a boil. Cook for 5 minutes, then drain. Return the lentils to the pan and add the carrot, onion, garlic, chile, if using, bouquet garni, and boiling water to cover by 2 inches. Bring to a boil, then reduce the heat to medium-low and cook, uncovered, until tender, 20 to 30 minutes, seasoning with salt and pepper halfway through.

2. Drain the lentils if needed. Remove the carrot, onion, garlic, chile, and bouquet garni. Transfer to a warmed serving dish and serve.

From Françoise:

• There are so many things you can do with lentils once they're cooked; for instance, sauté them with chopped onions in butter, or serve them at room temperature in a salad with a mustardy vinaigrette and chopped scallions or shallots.

• The secret to lentils that are tender and keep their shape: Check on them after 20 minutes of cooking. Cooking time can vary depending on where they come from and how old they are.

LENTILS AND BACON WITH MUSTARD SAUCE
- *Lentilles à la dijonnaise* -

❖ EASY   ❖ INEXPENSIVE   ❖ 1 HOUR, 25 MINUTES   ❖ SERVES 4

½ pound lentils

1 carrot, sliced crosswise into 4 lengths

1 onion stuck with 1 whole clove

1 bouquet garni made with parsley, thyme, and bay leaf

Salt and pepper

1 tablespoon butter

4 slices bacon or smoked ham, cut crosswise into ¼-inch-thick strips

1 onion, finely chopped

1 tablespoon all-purpose flour

Dijon mustard to taste

Chopped parsley leaves for sprinkling

❖ ❖ ❖ ❖ ❖

1. In a large saucepan, combine the lentils with the carrot, onion, bouquet garni, and water to cover by 2 inches. Bring to a boil, then reduce the heat and cook at a gentle boil, uncovered, until tender, about 1 hour, seasoning with salt and pepper halfway through.

2. Meanwhile, in a medium saucepan, melt the butter over medium heat. Add the bacon or ham and cook until lightly browned. Remove to a dish. Add the onion and cook until lightly browned. Whisk in the flour until foaming. Whisk in 1 cup of the lentil broth until boiling. Season with pepper. Return the bacon or ham to the pan, reduce the heat to very low, and cook for 5 minutes. Remove the pan from the heat and stir in the mustard.

3. Drain the lentils if needed. Remove the carrot, onion, and bouquet garni. Stir in the sauce. Transfer to a warmed serving dish, sprinkle with parsley, and serve.

FAVA BEANS WITH SUMMER SAVORY BUTTER

- *Fèves à la sarriette* -

❖ INTERMEDIATE   ❖ MODERATE   ❖ 20 MINUTES   ❖ SERVES 4

2 pounds fresh fava beans, shelled
Salt
1 bouquet garni made with parsley, thyme,
   and bay leaf

1 small bunch summer savory or chervil
2 tablespoons butter, softened
Pepper

❖ ❖ ❖ ❖ ❖

1. Bring a medium saucepan of water to a boil. Add the fava beans and cook until barely tender, about 2 minutes. Drain and let cool slightly, then peel the beans.

2. Refill the saucepan with water and bring to a boil. Add the beans, salt, bouquet garni, and 1 herb sprig and cook until tender, 5 to 10 minutes.

3. Meanwhile, chop some of the herb leaves. In a cup, mash the herbs with the butter. Drain the beans. Remove the herb sprig. Swirl in the herb butter and season with salt and pepper. Transfer to a warmed serving dish and serve.

From Françoise:
• Fresh fava beans can be eaten raw, with a sprinkling of fine sea salt.

• You can also prepare this dish with dried fava beans, which of course will need parboiling and then longer cooking.

• To make a creamy version of this dish, swirl in 3 tablespoons of crème fraîche and chopped fines herbes (parsley, chives, chervil, tarragon) in Step 3 instead of the herb butter. Simmer for 1 minute and serve. It's lovely.

VEGETABLES

BUTTERY FAVA BEANS WITH BABY ARTICHOKES
- *Panaché de fèves et d'artichauts* -

❖ INTERMEDIATE   ❖ MODERATE   ❖ 1 HOUR, 30 MINUTES   ❖ SERVES 4

1 pound fresh fava beans, shelled

8 very young chokeless artichokes

3 tablespoons butter, softened

2 onions, finely chopped

Salt and pepper

Freshly grated nutmeg

❖ ❖ ❖ ❖ ❖

1. Bring a medium saucepan of water to a boil. Add the fava beans and cook until barely tender, about 2 minutes. Drain and let cool slightly, then peel the beans.

2. Using kitchen scissors, snip off any tough leaves at the base of the artichokes. Snip off the tips of the remaining leaves. Peel and trim the stems. Quarter the artichokes lengthwise.

3. In a large saucepan, melt 2 tablespoons of the butter over medium-low heat. Add the onions and cook until softened. Add the beans and artichokes and enough water to come half-way up the vegetables. Season with salt, pepper, and nutmeg. Cover and bring to a simmer, then reduce the heat to low, and cook until tender and the liquid evaporates, about 1 hour.

4. Swirl in the remaining 1 tablespoon of butter. Transfer the vegetables to a warmed serving dish and serve.

From Françoise:

• If you can't find these special chokeless artichokes, use regular baby artichokes: Snap off all of the dark green outer leaves. Using a sharp knife, slice off the top half of the leaves, and peel and trim the stem. Scrape out the hairy choke.

• The secret to tender fava beans: Remove the skin. It does require extra work, but the result is worth the effort.

LITTLE SAUSAGE-STUFFED CABBAGES
- *Choux farcis* -

❖ INTERMEDIATE   ❖ INEXPENSIVE   ❖ 1 HOUR, 15 MINUTES   ❖ SERVES 4

1 large green cabbage

1 pound sausage meat

1 tablespoon chopped parsley leaves

2 tablespoons butter

1 onion, cut into ¼-inch dice

1 carrot, peeled and cut into ¼-inch dice

1 celery rib, cut into ¼-inch dice

½ cup broth

Salt and pepper

❖ ❖ ❖ ❖ ❖

1. Bring a large pot of water to a boil. Carefully separate the cabbage leaves and add them to the pot. Cook for 2 minutes, then drain.

2. In a bowl, mix the sausage meat with the parsley. Stack the blanched cabbage leaves in 5 or 6 piles, putting the largest leaves on the bottom. Divide the sausage mixture among the piles. Wrap the cabbage leaves around the sausage and, using kitchen string, tie each one into a ball to look like a little cabbage.

3. In a flameproof casserole, melt the butter over medium heat. Add the onion, carrot, and celery and cook until lightly browned. Add the little cabbages and cook until lightly browned all over. Turn them nice side up, add the broth, and season with salt and pepper. Cover and bring to a simmer, then reduce the heat to low and cook for about 45 minutes.

4. Remove the strings. Transfer the cabbages to a warmed serving dish and serve.

From Françoise:
• These stuffed cabbages are also delicious at room temperature.

• You can stuff a whole large cabbage, too, but it's more difficult to reassemble. Cook it for a good half-hour longer.

• Chopped leftover beef, pork, or veal can be substituted for the sausage meat.

• To vary the dish, replace the parsley with cilantro, and add a little chopped ginger to the aromatics in the casserole.

VEGETABLES

SLOW-COOKED RED CABBAGE WITH VINEGAR AND APPLES

- Chou rouge à la flamande -

❖ EASY ❖ INEXPENSIVE ❖ 1 HOUR, 45 MINUTES ❖ SERVES 4

2 tablespoons butter

2-pound red cabbage, cored and sliced
  into thin strips

Salt and pepper

2 tablespoons vinegar

4 Golden Delicious apples, peeled, cored, and
  quartered lengthwise

1 teaspoon sugar

❖ ❖ ❖ ❖ ❖

1. In a flameproof casserole, melt the butter over medium-low heat. Add the cabbage, season with salt and pepper, and sprinkle with the vinegar. Reduce the heat to very low, cover, and cook for 1 hour. Add the apples and sugar and cook until tender, about 30 minutes.

2. Transfer to a warmed serving dish and serve.

From Françoise:
• Try adding a special vinegar, like balsamic, instead of the usual red wine vinegar.

• Cook the cabbage over very low heat or it might stick and burn. A heat diffuser is useful for this. Or line the bottom of the casserole with blanched pork skin.

• Serve with pork chops, pork roast, or pan-sautéed sausages.

• You can leave out the apples if you prefer.

RED WINE–BRAISED RED CABBAGE WITH BACON

- Chou rouge au vin rouge -

❖ EASY ❖ INEXPENSIVE ❖ 1 HOUR, 50 MINUTES ❖ SERVES 4

2 tablespoons butter

3 ½ ounces thick-sliced bacon, cut crosswise
  into ¼-inch-thick strips

2 onions, chopped

2-pound red cabbage, cored and sliced
  into thin strips

¾ cup red wine

Salt and pepper

1. In a flameproof casserole, melt the butter over medium-low heat. Add the bacon and onions and cook until lightly browned. Stir in the cabbage and red wine and season with salt and pepper. Reduce the heat to very low and cook until tender, about 1 hour and 30 minutes. Transfer to a warmed serving dish and serve.

From Françoise:

• This dish is perfectly suited to a pressure cooker. Add only ½ cup of red wine, as there's practically no evaporation with this method of cooking.

• Here's how to cut a cabbage into thin strips easily: Remove the large outer leaves and, using a large chef's knife, cut out the thick ribs. Stack the leaves and roll them up, then slice them crosswise into thin strips. Cut the cabbage heart into quarters before slicing. This method is simple, but it does take at least 15 minutes.

GOLDEN CREAMY CAULIFLOWER
- *Chou-fleur au gratin* -

❖ EASY   ❖ INEXPENSIVE   ❖ 40 MINUTES   ❖ SERVES 4

Salt
2-pound head of cauliflower, cut into florets
1 tablespoon butter, cut into ¼-inch pieces,
   plus more for brushing

MORNAY SAUCE
3 tablespoons butter
3 tablespoons all-purpose flour
2 cups milk
Salt and pepper
½ cup shredded Gruyère cheese

❖ ❖ ❖ ❖ ❖

1. Bring a large saucepan of salted water to a boil. Add the cauliflower and cook until tender, 15 to 20 minutes.

2. Meanwhile, make the Mornay sauce: In a medium saucepan, melt the butter over medium heat. Whisk in the flour until it starts foaming. Whisk in the milk. Season with salt and pepper. Bring to a boil, whisking, then reduce the heat to very low and cook for 10 minutes. Remove the pan from the heat and stir in ¼ cup of the cheese.

3. Preheat the broiler. Brush a broiler-safe gratin dish with butter. Drain the cauliflower well and spread in the gratin dish. Spoon the Mornay sauce over the top and dot with the remaining ¼ cup of cheese and 1 tablespoon of butter. Transfer to the top shelf of the oven and broil until the cheese is melted and nicely browned, 3 to 5 minutes.

From Françoise:

• You can also brown the dish on the top shelf of a 425-degree oven for 10 to 15 minutes. This is good to know for when you make the dish ahead and leave the browning until just before serving. Finishing the cooking in the oven will reheat the dish through.

VEGETABLES

continued

- Another alterative: Simply spoon the Mornay sauce over the well-drained cauliflower and serve.

- For a more substantial dish, surround the cauliflower in the gratin dish with boiled new potatoes and hard-boiled egg halves, then cover with the Mornay sauce.

BOILED CAULIFLOWER
- Chou-fleur au naturel -

❖ VERY EASY ❖ INEXPENSIVE ❖ 25 MINUTES ❖ SERVES 4

Salt

2-pound head of cauliflower, cut into florets

❖ ❖ ❖ ❖ ❖

1. Bring a large saucepan of salted water to a boil. Add the cauliflower and cook until tender, 15 to 20 minutes. Drain well.

2. Transfer to a warmed serving dish and serve.

From Françoise:
- If you're serving cauliflower at room temperature, sprinkle it with lemon juice instead of red wine vinegar so it looks better.

- Drain the cauliflower as soon as it's tender; don't let it sit in the water.

- There are so many ways to serve boiled cauliflower: Hot, with melted butter or warmed crème fraîche and chopped parsley; with béchamel or Mornay sauce; sautéed in butter over high heat. Cold, in a salad. Or pack the florets stem side up in a bowl, then invert on a platter.

CAULIFLOWER SOUFFLÉ
- Chou-fleur en gâteau -

❖ INTERMEDIATE ❖ INEXPENSIVE ❖ 1 HOUR, 20 MINUTES ❖ SERVES 4

Salt

2-pound head of cauliflower, cut into florets

3 large eggs, separated

½ cup shredded Gruyère cheese

THICK BÉCHAMEL SAUCE

4 tablespoons (½ stick) butter

¼ cup all-purpose flour

2 cups milk

Salt and pepper

1. Bring a large saucepan of salted water to a boil. Add the cauliflower and cook until very tender, 15 to 20 minutes.

2. Meanwhile, make the thick béchamel sauce: In a large saucepan, melt the butter over medium heat. Whisk in the flour until it starts foaming. Whisk in the milk. Season with salt and pepper. Bring to a boil, whisking, then reduce the heat to very low and cook for 10 minutes.

3. Preheat the oven to 350 degrees. Brush a soufflé dish with butter.

4. Drain the cauliflower well. Puree the cauliflower using a food mill or a food processor. Remove the béchamel sauce from the heat.

Beat in the cauliflower puree, the egg yolks, and cheese.

5. Beat the egg whites with a pinch of salt until stiff. Mix one-quarter of the egg whites into the cauliflower mixture, then fold this lightened mixture into the remaining whites.

6. Scrape the cauliflower mixture into the soufflé dish, filling it three-quarters full. Transfer to the oven and bake until risen and browned, about 40 minutes. Serve immediately.

From Françoise:
• I like to grate the equivalent of 2 pinches of nutmeg—no more—into the béchamel sauce for a delicate flavor.

LEEKS VINAIGRETTE
- *Poireaux à l'huile* -

❖ EASY ❖ INEXPENSIVE ❖ 40 MINUTES ❖ SERVES 4

Salt
2 pounds leeks, white and light green parts only

VINAIGRETTE
2 tablespoons vinegar
6 tablespoons oil
Salt and pepper

❖ ❖ ❖ ❖ ❖

1. Bring a large pot of salted water to a boil. Using kitchen string, tie the leeks in bundles. Add the leeks to the boiling water and cook until tender, 25 to 30 minutes.

2. Meanwhile, make the vinaigrette: In a small bowl, whisk the vinegar with the oil and season with salt and pepper.

3. Drain the leeks well. Remove the strings and pat dry. Arrange the leeks on a platter, drizzle with the vinaigrette, and serve warm or at room temperature.

continued

- If your leeks are sandy, slice them length-wise almost in half or in quarters (do not cut through the root end) and swish them in a large bowl of water to remove the grit.

- I like to thicken my vinaigrette a little with a teaspoon of Dijon mustard or mayonnaise.

- If serving the leeks at room temperature, drain them in a colander and rinse under cold running water, then drain well.

LEEKS WITH CREAMY SAUCE
- Poireaux sauce blanche -

❖ EASY ❖ INEXPENSIVE ❖ 1 HOUR ❖ SERVES 4

Salt
2 pounds leeks, white and light green parts only

SAUCE
3 tablespoons butter
3 tablespoons all-purpose flour
1 cup milk
Salt and pepper

❖ ❖ ❖ ❖ ❖

1. Bring a large pot of salted water to a boil. Using kitchen string, tie the leeks in bundles. Add the leeks to the boiling water and cook until tender, 25 to 30 minutes. Reserve 1 cup of the leek broth.

2. Meanwhile, make the sauce: In a large sauce-pan, melt the butter over medium heat. Whisk in the flour until it starts foaming. Whisk in the milk and the reserved leek broth. Season with salt and pepper. Bring to a boil, whisking, then reduce the heat to very low and cook for 10 minutes.

3. Drain the leeks well. Remove the strings and pat dry. Arrange the leeks in a warmed serving dish. Spoon the sauce over the top and serve.

From Françoise:
- Drain the leeks very well and pat them dry or the sauce will be watery.

GARLICKY SAUTÉED BRUSSELS SPROUTS
- Choux de Bruxelles sautés -

❖ EASY   ❖ INEXPENSIVE   ❖ 40 MINUTES   ❖ SERVES 4

2 pounds Brussels sprouts
Salt
3 tablespoons butter

1 garlic clove, finely chopped
Pepper
Chopped parsley leaves for sprinkling

❖ ❖ ❖ ❖ ❖

1. Bring a large saucepan of water to a boil. Add the Brussels sprouts, and when the water returns to a boil, drain them in a colander under cold running water.

2. Fill the same saucepan with salted water and bring to a boil. Add the Brussels sprouts and boil until tender, about 15 minutes. Drain again in a colander under cold running water then drain again well.

3. In a large skillet, melt the butter over medium heat. Add the Brussels sprouts and garlic and season with salt and pepper. Cook until lightly browned. Transfer to a warmed serving dish, sprinkle with parsley, and serve.

From Françoise:
• Serve as a side dish with pork or ham.

• You can also sauté some bacon or pancetta cut crosswise into ¼-inch-thick strips in the skillet until just beginning to brown before adding the Brussels sprouts.

VEGETABLES

SLOW-COOKED BRUSSELS SPROUTS WITH PANCETTA
- Choux de Bruxelles braisés -

❖ EASY   ❖ INEXPENSIVE   ❖ 50 MINUTES   ❖ SERVES 4

2 pounds Brussels sprouts
2 tablespoons butter
3 ½ ounces thick-sliced pancetta, cut crosswise into ¼-inch-thick strips

Salt and pepper
Chopped parsley leaves for sprinkling

continued

1. Bring a large saucepan of water to a boil. Add the Brussels sprouts, and when the water returns to a boil, drain them in a colander under cold running water, then drain again well.

2. In a flameproof casserole, melt the butter over low heat. Add the pancetta and cook until just beginning to brown. Add the Brussels sprouts and season with salt and pepper. Cover and cook until very tender, about 30 minutes. Transfer to a warmed serving dish, sprinkle with parsley, and serve.

From Françoise:
• Do not reduce the cooking time for the Brussels sprouts in Step 2. If anything, you might increase it for the most delicious flavor.

BUTTERY PEAS WITH PEARL ONIONS AND LETTUCE
- *Petits pois à la française* -

❖ EASY　　　❖ INEXPENSIVE　　　❖ 30 MINUTES　　　❖ SERVES 4

3 tablespoons butter
2 cups shelled peas (about 2 pounds in the shell)
6 pearl onions, peeled
1 head Boston lettuce, leaves separated
　and sliced into thin strips

Parsley sprigs
Chervil sprigs
1 teaspoon sugar
Salt and pepper

❖　❖　❖　❖　❖

1. In a large saucepan, melt 2 tablespoons of the butter over low heat. Add the peas, pearl onions, lettuce, parsley and chervil sprigs, sugar, and 1 tablespoon of water. Season with salt and pepper. Cover with a soup plate and fill the plate with cold water. Cook for 20 minutes, refilling the plate with cold water as needed.

2. Remove the herb sprigs and swirl in the remaining 1 tablespoon of butter. Transfer to a warmed serving dish and serve.

From Françoise:
• You can replace the chervil with mint if you like, or mix these herbs.

• This recipe is especially appropriate for tender spring peas.

• If the peas begin to stick to the bottom of the pan, add 2 or 3 tablespoons of boiling water.

• Throughout the cooking, the moisture from the peas evaporates and then condenses when it hits the cold soup plate, basting the peas. That's why I say to replenish the cold water often.

CHUNKY SPLIT PEA PUREE

- *Pois cassés en "purée st-germain"* -

❖ EASY   ❖ INEXPENSIVE   ❖ 1 HOUR, 30 MINUTES   ❖ SERVES 4

1 pound green split peas
2 tablespoons butter
3 ½ ounces sliced pancetta, finely chopped
1 small carrot, peeled and thinly sliced
1 onion, thinly sliced

2 or 3 Boston lettuce leaves, rolled and sliced
   crosswise into thin strips
1 bouquet garni made with parsley, thyme, and
   bay leaf
Salt and pepper

❖   ❖   ❖   ❖   ❖

1. In a large saucepan, generously cover the split peas with water and bring to a boil. Cook for 15 minutes. Drain in a colander under cold running water, then drain again well.

2. In a flameproof casserole, melt 1 tablespoon of the butter over medium heat. Add the pancetta and cook until lightly browned. Add the carrot, onion, split peas, lettuce, bouquet garni, and water to barely cover. Cover and bring to a simmer, then reduce the heat to low and cook until tender, about 1 hour, seasoning with salt halfway through. Add a little boiling water if the peas are dry.

3. Carefully drain the split peas. Remove the bouquet garni. Puree the peas using a food mill or food processor. Return the puree to the casserole and season with pepper. Stir the remaining 1 tablespoon of butter into this fairly thick puree. Transfer to a warmed serving dish and serve.

From Françoise:

• I often add 1 or 2 pinches of freshly grated nutmeg and 2 heaping tablespoons of crème fraîche to my split pea puree. Then I omit the pancetta.

• Be careful, because split pea puree tends to stick to the casserole. Set it in a water bath to keep the puree warm or use a nonstick pot.

VEGETABLES

BUTTERY GLAZED PEARL ONIONS
- *Oignons glacés* -

❖ EASY   ❖ MODERATE   ❖ 30 MINUTES   ❖ SERVES 4

¾ pound pearl onions

2 tablespoons butter

1 tablespoon sugar

Salt

❖ ❖ ❖ ❖ ❖

1. Bring a large saucepan of water to a boil. Add the pearl onions and cook for 3 minutes. Drain and peel.

2. In the same saucepan, melt the butter with the sugar over medium-low heat. Add the pearl onions and cook, stirring occasionally, until nicely browned and tender, about 20 minutes. Partly cover the pan halfway through cooking.

3. Season with salt. Transfer to a warmed serving dish and serve.

From Françoise:

• Parboiling pearl onions makes them much easier to peel.

• The secret to pearl onions that brown without burning: Add 1 or 2 teaspoons of cold water to the saucepan and cover. The cooking will proceed without incident.

STUFFED TURNIPS BRAISED IN CIDER
- *Navets farcis au cidre* -

❖ EASY   ❖ INEXPENSIVE   ❖ 1 HOUR, 15 MINUTES   ❖ SERVES 4

4 large round turnips

Butter for brushing

½ cup cider

¼ cup broth

Salt and pepper

STUFFING

½ pound sausage meat

1 large egg

Thyme leaves

1 bay leaf, crumbled

Mixed chopped parsley, chives, and chervil leaves

1 shallot, finely chopped

Salt and pepper

2 pinches of allspice

1. Preheat the oven to 400 degrees. Cut a thin slice off the top of each turnip. Using a melon baller, hollow out the insides, leaving a sturdy shell. Cut a thin slice off the bottoms so they can stand upright.

2. Make the stuffing: In a bowl, mix the sausage meat with the egg, thyme, bay leaf, parsley, chives, chervil, and shallot. Season with salt, pepper, and the allspice. Pack the stuffing into the turnips, mounding it slightly.

3. Brush a flameproof casserole with butter. Add the stuffed turnips. Pour in the cider and broth and season with salt and pepper. Transfer to the oven and cook until tender, about 45 minutes.

From Françoise:
• If you have 3 or 4 tablespoons of meat pan juices in the fridge, they're much better than the broth. These stuffed turnips are delicious with roasted veal, pork, or duck, and the juices from any of these meats would be perfect for braising the turnips.

BUTTERY GLAZED TURNIPS
- *Navets glacés* -

❖ EASY   ❖ INEXPENSIVE   ❖ 1 HOUR   ❖ SERVES 4

2 pounds small round turnips, peeled and
   cut into 1-inch cubes
4 tablespoons (½ stick) butter

Salt and pepper
Pinch of sugar

❖ ❖ ❖ ❖ ❖

1. Bring a large saucepan of water to a boil. Add the turnips and cook for 5 minutes. Drain them in a colander under cold running water and drain again.

2. In the same saucepan, melt 3 tablespoons of the butter over low heat. Add the turnips and 2 cups of water and season with salt and pepper. Cover and cook until the turnips are tender and the water evaporates, about 30 minutes. Add the remaining 1 tablespoon of butter and the sugar and stir for a few minutes over medium heat, uncovered, until the turnips are glazed and lightly browned. Transfer to a warmed serving dish and serve.

From Françoise:
• The skin on turnips is thick, so don't hesitate to peel them using a paring knife.

• If the pan looks too watery in Step 2 after 20 minutes, remove the lid and cook uncovered to evaporate the liquid.

VEGETABLES

SLOW-COOKED TURNIPS WITH SHALLOTS AND GARLIC
- *Navets braisés* -

❖ EASY   ❖ INEXPENSIVE   ❖ 1 HOUR, 10 MINUTES   ❖ SERVES 4

2 pounds small round turnips, peeled and
  cut into 1-inch pieces
2 tablespoons butter
1½ tablespoons all-purpose flour
1 teaspoon tomato paste
1 shallot, finely chopped

1 garlic clove, crushed
3 cups broth or water
1 bouquet garni made with parsley, thyme,
  and bay leaf
Salt and pepper

❖ ❖ ❖ ❖ ❖

1. Bring a large saucepan of water to a boil.
Add the turnips and cook for 5 minutes. Drain
them in a colander under cold running water,
then drain again well.

2. In the same saucepan, melt the butter over
medium heat. Add the turnips and cook, stirring, to coat. Stir in the flour. Add the tomato
paste, shallot, garlic, broth or water, and bouquet garni. Season with salt and pepper. Cover
and bring to a simmer, then reduce the heat
to low and cook until the turnips are tender,
about 45 minutes.

3. Remove the bouquet garni. Transfer to a
warmed serving dish and serve.

From Françoise:
• If you don't have any homemade broth in the
refrigerator, you don't need to make any especially for this dish. Use a good store-bought
broth and use less salt in Step 2. Prepared
broths usually are already seasoned.

• Choose turnips that are firm and
unblemished.

GARLICKY PAN-SEARED CHANTERELLES
- *Girolles sautées à l'ail* -

❖ EASY   ❖ EXPENSIVE   ❖ 40 MINUTES   ❖ SERVES 4

¼ cup oil
2 pounds chanterelle mushrooms
1 garlic clove, finely chopped

Salt and pepper
Chopped parsley leaves for sprinkling

1. In a large skillet, heat 3 tablespoons of the oil over medium heat. Add the mushrooms and cook until they release their liquid, about 5 minutes. Drain in a sieve, pressing on the mushrooms to remove as much water as possible.

2. In the same skillet, heat the remaining 1 tablespoon of oil over medium-high heat. Add the mushrooms and garlic and season with salt and pepper. Cook, stirring, for 5 minutes, then reduce the heat to low, cover, and cook for 15 minutes. Transfer to a warmed serving dish, sprinkle with parsley, and serve.

From Françoise:

• Try replacing the garlic with 1 finely chopped shallot.

• You can also fry some potatoes in another skillet and, just before serving, mix them with the chanterelles. That way you can make the flavor of these exquisite—and expensive—mushrooms go further.

CREAMY CHANTERELLE MUSHROOMS

- Girolles à la crème -

❖ EASY　　　❖ EXPENSIVE　　　❖ 35 MINUTES　　　❖ SERVES 4

1 tablespoon oil
3 pounds chanterelle mushrooms
3 tablespoons butter

Salt and pepper
⅓ cup crème fraîche

❖　❖　❖　❖　❖

1. In a large skillet, heat the oil over medium heat. Add the mushrooms and cook until they release their liquid, about 5 minutes. Drain in a sieve, pressing on the mushrooms to remove as much water as possible.

2. In the same skillet, melt the butter over low heat. Add the mushrooms and season with salt and pepper. Cover and cook for 15 minutes. Add the crème fraîche and bring to a simmer. Transfer to a warmed serving dish and serve.

From Françoise:

• It is essential to cook chanterelles twice. The first time they release their liquid, which is better off discarded.

• Serve as a side dish with a chicken, roasted veal, or sautéed veal cutlets.

• I like to add a sprinkling of chopped parsley or chervil just before taking the chanterelles to the table.

VEGETABLES

CREAMY MOREL MUSHROOMS

- *Morilles à la crème* -

❖ EASY   ❖ EXPENSIVE   ❖ 30 MINUTES   ❖ SERVES 4

3 tablespoons butter

3 pounds fresh morel mushrooms,
   halved or quartered lengthwise if large

Juice of ½ lemon

Salt

¾ cup crème fraîche

Pepper

❖ ❖ ❖ ❖ ❖

1. In a large skillet, melt 1 tablespoon of the butter over medium heat. Add the morels, squeeze in the lemon juice, and season with salt. Cook until the mushrooms release their liquid, about 10 minutes. Drain in a sieve over a small saucepan.

2. In the same skillet, heat the remaining 2 tablespoons of butter over medium-high heat. Add the mushrooms and cook, stirring, for 5 minutes. Add the crème fraîche and season with salt and pepper, then reduce the heat to low and cook for 10 minutes.

3. Meanwhile, simmer the reserved morel liquid until reduced by half; stir into the mushrooms. Transfer the morels to a warmed serving dish and serve.

From Françoise:

• Swish the morels quickly in a large bowl of water to dislodge any dirt hidden in the crevices and drain well.

• You can also make this dish with dried morels, which are expensive but very good. Buy 2 ounces to serve 4 people. You'll need to soak them first, then proceed to Step 2: Cover the mushrooms with warm water and let soak for 1 hour. Swish them around in the soaking water and let stand until all the grit falls to the bottom. Carefully remove the mushrooms, leaving the grit behind. Strain the morel soaking liquid and reduce it in Step 3. It has a lot of flavor.

• These creamy mushrooms are delicious with chicken, squab, or any kind of white meat.

PAN-SAUTÉED PORCINI MUSHROOMS WITH SHALLOTS AND PARSLEY
- Cèpes à la bordelaise -

❖ EASY ❖ EXPENSIVE ❖ 20 MINUTES ❖ SERVES 4

¼ cup oil

1 ½ pounds fresh porcini mushrooms, thinly sliced

2 shallots, finely chopped

1 tablespoon dry bread crumbs

Salt and pepper

½ lemon

Chopped parsley leaves

❖ ❖ ❖ ❖ ❖

1. In a large skillet, heat the oil over medium-high heat. Add the mushrooms and cook for 3 to 5 minutes, until browned. Add the shallots and bread crumbs and season with salt and pepper. Reduce the heat to medium and cook for 5 minutes.

2. Squeeze in a little lemon juice. Transfer the mushrooms to a warmed serving dish, sprinkle with parsley, and serve.

From Françoise:

• I like to fry some potatoes in another skillet and, just before serving, mix them with the porcini. That way you can make the flavor of these exquisite—and expensive—mushrooms go further.

• If you are using fresh porcini mushrooms to garnish a roast, then 1 or 1 ¼ pounds of them will suffice.

• In southwest France, finely chopped garlic often replaces the shallot.

VEGETABLES

CREAMY STUFFED MUSHROOMS
- Mousse de champignons en chapeaux -

❖ EASY ❖ INEXPENSIVE ❖ 20 MINUTES ❖ SERVES 4

1 ½ pounds large white mushrooms, stems and caps separated

2 cups milk

Salt and pepper

Freshly grated nutmeg

1 tablespoon fresh lemon juice

1 tablespoon cornstarch or potato starch

2 tablespoons crème fraîche (optional)

continued

1. In a medium saucepan, combine the mushrooms with the milk and season with salt, pepper, and nutmeg. Cook at a bare simmer, uncovered, for 10 minutes.

2. Drain the mushrooms, reserving the milk for another use. Reserve 8 of the nicest mushroom caps and keep warm.

3. In a food processor, puree the remaining mushrooms with the lemon juice, cornstarch or potato starch, and crème fraîche, if using.

4. Spoon the stuffing into the reserved mushroom caps, mounding it slightly. Transfer to a warmed platter and serve hot.

From Françoise:
• Serve as a first course or as a side dish with fish or meat.

• You can also puree all the mushrooms in Step 2 and use this delicate blend as a stuffing for artichoke bottoms, crêpes, an omelet, or veal or chicken cutlets.

PAN-SEARED MUSHROOMS WITH FINES HERBES
- Champignons sautés aux fines herbes -

❖ EASY   ❖ INEXPENSIVE   ❖ 15 MINUTES   ❖ SERVES 4

3 tablespoons butter
1 ½ pounds white mushrooms, thinly sliced
Salt and pepper

Juice of ½ lemon
Mixed chopped parsley, chives, chervil, and tarragon for sprinkling

❖ ❖ ❖ ❖ ❖

1. In a large skillet, melt the butter over medium-high heat. Add the mushrooms and season with salt, pepper, and lemon juice. Cook for 5 to 6 minutes.

2. Transfer to a warmed serving dish, sprinkle with the herbs, and serve.

From Françoise:
• I like to add a little chopped garlic—or even a lot—to the skillet when sautéing the mushrooms.

VELVETY CHESTNUT PUREE

- *Purée de marrons* -

❖ EASY   ❖ MODERATE   ❖ 1 HOUR   ❖ SERVES 4

2 pounds chestnuts in the shell, scored
3 cups milk

Salt
3 tablespoons butter, cut into ¼-inch dice

❖   ❖   ❖   ❖   ❖

1. Bring a large pot of water to a boil. Add the chestnuts and cook at a gentle boil for 10 minutes. Take 1 chestnut out of the water at a time and while still hot, hold it with a kitchen towel and peel off the shell and skin with a paring knife.

2. In a large saucepan, combine the chestnuts with the milk and season with salt. Cover and cook over low heat until soft, 30 to 40 minutes.

3. Drain the chestnuts, reserving the milk. Puree the chestnuts using a food mill or food processor, blending in the butter and a little of the reserved milk until smooth. Transfer to a warmed serving dish and serve.

From Françoise:
• Removing the chestnuts from the water one at a time makes them easier to peel.

• Instead of cooking the chestnuts in milk, you can cook them in beef or chicken stock flavored with some chopped celery. In this case, add a little sugar to sweeten it slightly.

SLOW-COOKED CHESTNUTS

- *Marrons braisés* -

❖ EASY   ❖ MODERATE   ❖ 1 HOUR, 15 MINUTES   ❖ SERVES 4

1 ½ to 2 pounds chestnuts in the shell, scored
3 tablespoons butter

1 cup beef broth
Salt and pepper

continued

1. Bring a large pot of water to a boil. Add the chestnuts and cook at a gentle boil for 10 minutes. Take one chestnut out of the water at a time and while still hot, hold it with a kitchen towel and peel off the shell and skin with a paring knife.

2. In a large saucepan, melt the butter over very low heat. Stir in the chestnuts. Add the broth and season with salt and pepper. Cover and cook for 45 minutes.

3. There should be just a little broth left in the pan. Transfer to a warmed serving dish and serve.

From Françoise:
• Instead of cooking and peeling raw chestnuts in the shell, you could use peeled and cooked vacuum-packed chestnuts. Add less broth and cook them for less time in Step 2.

• Avoid stirring the fragile chestnuts while they cook so they don't break apart.

• If it looks like there's too much broth toward the end of cooking, uncover the pan and let the broth reduce slightly.

• You can serve these braised chestnuts with any kind of roasted poultry.

WILTED DANDELION SALAD WITH BACON
- *Pissenlits au lard* -

❖ EASY   ❖ MODERATE   ❖ 25 MINUTES   ❖ SERVES 4

½ pound dandelion greens
1 shallot or garlic clove, finely chopped
Salt and pepper
1 teaspoon oil

5 ounces thick-sliced bacon, cut crosswise into
   ¼-inch-thick strips
2 tablespoons vinegar

❖ ❖ ❖ ❖ ❖

1. In a salad bowl, combine the dandelion greens and shallot or garlic. Season with pepper, and, lightly, with salt.

2. In a large skillet, heat the oil over medium heat. Add the bacon and cook, stirring occasionally, until nicely browned. Pour over the greens.

3. Quickly swirl the vinegar in the skillet and bring to a simmer, then pour over the greens. Toss to coat and serve immediately.

From Françoise:
• This salad must be eaten warm.

• Adding boiled new potatoes and hard-boiled eggs would turn this into a main dish.

• You might also toss garlic-rubbed baguette toasts in the salad, which would replace the shallots or garlic.

CREAMY WATERCRESS PUREE

- *Mousse de cresson* -

❖ EASY   ❖ MODERATE   ❖ 15 MINUTES   ❖ SERVES 4

Salt
4 bunches of watercress, stems removed
1 lemon wedge, peel and white pith removed,
  chopped

1 tablespoon cornstarch or potato starch
2 tablespoons crème fraîche
Pepper

❖   ❖   ❖   ❖   ❖

1. Bring a large saucepan of salted water to a boil. Reserve 20 of the nicest watercress leaves and add the remaining leaves to the boiling water. Cook for 2 minutes, then drain. Dry well using a salad spinner.

2. In a food processor, puree the still-warm watercress with the reserved raw leaves, the lemon flesh, cornstarch or potato starch, and crème fraîche. Season with pepper. Scrape into a bowl and serve.

From Françoise:
• Serve this puree with white meats, fish fillets, or even poached or hard-boiled eggs.

• Here's a fast way of preparing the watercress before washing it: Slice off the stems just below the leaves without undoing the bunches.

• You can use the watercress stems to make soup.

VEGETABLES

GOLDEN PUMPKIN GRATIN

- *Potiron au gratin* -

❖ EASY   ❖ INEXPENSIVE   ❖ 1 HOUR, 15 MINUTES   ❖ SERVES 4

2 pounds pumpkin, peeled, seeded, and
  cut into chunks
3 large potatoes, peeled and cut into chunks
1 onion, cut into chunks
Salt

3 tablespoons butter, cut into ¼-inch dice
¾ cup shredded Gruyère cheese
2 tablespoons dry bread crumbs

continued

1. In a large saucepan, combine the pumpkin, potatoes, and onion with 1 cup of water. Season with salt. Cover and bring to a boil, then reduce the heat to low and cook for 30 minutes.

2. Preheat the oven to 425 degrees. Drain the vegetables and mash them in a bowl with 2 tablespoons of the butter and ½ cup of the cheese. Spread in a gratin dish and sprinkle with the remaining ¼ cup of cheese and the bread crumbs. Dot with the remaining 1 tablespoon of butter.

3. Transfer to the top shelf of the oven and bake until the cheese is melted and nicely browned, 10 to 15 minutes.

From Françoise:
• The bread crumbs are not crucial, but they do make an appetizing, golden crust. Grinding a couple of dry toasts in the food processor will do the trick.

COOKED SALAD GREENS WITH CREAMY SAUCE
- Salade cuite -

❖ EASY   ❖ INEXPENSIVE   ❖ 1 HOUR, 15 MINUTES   ❖ SERVES 6

Salt
3 ½ pounds salad greens
1 or 2 garlic cloves, crushed

THICK BÉCHAMEL SAUCE
4 tablespoons (½ stick) butter
¼ cup all-purpose flour
2 ¼ cups milk
Salt and pepper
Pinch of freshly grated nutmeg

❖ ❖ ❖ ❖ ❖

1. Bring a large pot of salted water to a boil. Add the greens and garlic and cook for about 45 minutes. Drain and squeeze out as much water as possible. Coarsely chop.

2. Meanwhile, make the thick béchamel sauce: In a large saucepan, melt the butter over medium heat. Whisk in the flour until it starts foaming. Whisk in the milk. Season with salt, pepper, and nutmeg. Bring to a boil, whisking, then reduce the heat to very low and cook for 5 minutes.

3. Stir the greens into the béchamel sauce and cook for 5 minutes. Transfer to a warmed serving dish and serve.

From Françoise:
• All salad greens are good cooked: Boston lettuce, romaine, escarole, frisée. You can also use endive. This is a dish to make when greens are in season.

• I heartily recommend spreading the mixture of greens and béchamel sauce in a gratin dish and broiling it in the oven for a few minutes.

• To make the dish more substantial, add a few boiled new potatoes.

BELL PEPPERS STUFFED WITH RICE

- *Poivrons farcis au riz* -

❖ EASY   ❖ INEXPENSIVE   ❖ 1 HOUR, 30 MINUTES   ❖ SERVES 4

2 tablespoons oil

2 onions, 1 finely chopped, 1 thinly sliced

1 cup long–grain rice

Salt and pepper

1 thyme sprig

½ bay leaf

4 bell peppers

2 tomatoes, peeled, seeded, and chopped

2 garlic cloves, crushed

❖ ❖ ❖ ❖ ❖

1. In a medium saucepan, melt 1 tablespoon of the oil over medium-low heat. Add the chopped onion and the rice and cook for 2 minutes. Add 2 cups of water and season with salt and pepper. Add the thyme and bay leaf. Bring to a boil, then reduce the heat to low, cover, and cook until the rice is tender and the water is absorbed, 17 to 20 minutes. Remove the herbs and fluff the rice.

2. Cut a thin slice off the top of each bell pepper. Using a spoon, hollow out the insides, leaving a sturdy shell. Stuff each pepper with the rice, filling it three-quarters full. Replace the tops.

3. In a flameproof casserole, heat the remaining 1 tablespoon of oil over medium heat. Add the sliced onion and cook until softened. Add the tomatoes and garlic and season with salt and pepper. Pack the stuffed peppers close together in the casserole. Cover and cook for 30 minutes, basting the peppers with the juices from time to time. Transfer to a platter and serve warm or at room temperature.

From Françoise:

• You can also stuff the peppers with a mixture of half rice, half chopped leftover meat.

VEGETABLES

BUTTERY SPRING VEGETABLES

- *Jardinière de légumes* -

❖ EASY ❖ INEXPENSIVE ❖ 45 MINUTES ❖ SERVES 4

3 tablespoons butter

1 cup shelled peas (about 1 pound in the shell)

1 bunch of tender young carrots, tops removed

3 or 4 tender young round turnips

¼ pound haricots verts, ends removed

Several Boston lettuce leaves, sliced into thin strips

Parsley or chervil sprigs

Salt and pepper

½ pound small new potatoes, about 1 ½ inches in diameter, large ones halved

❖ ❖ ❖ ❖ ❖

1. In a large saucepan, melt 2 tablespoons of the butter over low heat. Stir in the peas, carrots, turnips, haricots verts, and lettuce to coat with the butter. Add 2 tablespoons of water and the parsley or chervil and season with salt and pepper. Cover with a soup plate and fill the plate with cold water. Cook for 10 minutes.

2. Add the potatoes and cook for 15 to 20 minutes, refilling the plate with cold water as needed. Remove the herb sprigs and swirl in the remaining 1 tablespoon of butter. Transfer to a warmed serving dish and serve.

From Françoise:

• I often stir chopped parsley leaves and a tablespoon of crème fraîche into my jardinière before taking it to the table. Believe me, my guests are no worse off for it.

• This dish is intended for the tender young spring harvest. The quantities of each vegetable can vary, as can the timing in this method of cooking very slowly in a tightly covered pan with almost no liquid. It depends on the age of the ingredients and your taste.

• Here's an alternative, as different vegetables do have varying cooking times: Boil them one at a time, then fish them off as they're done. Or use separate saucepans. You might also wrap each kind of vegetable in cheesecloth and cook them together in a large pot of boiling water, removing the carrots, peas, and so forth as they are tender. Toss with salt, pepper, butter, and herbs just before serving.

SLOW-COOKED VEGETABLE MEDLEY

- *Compote de légumes* -

❖ EASY   ❖ INEXPENSIVE   ❖ 1 HOUR, 15 MINUTES   ❖ SERVES 4 TO 6

3 tablespoons butter

1 onion, finely chopped

3 garlic cloves, finely chopped

2 leeks, white and light green parts only,
    thinly sliced

3 tomatoes, peeled, seeded, and chopped

1 tablespoon tomato paste

1 potato, peeled and cut into ¾-inch pieces

2 carrots, peeled and sliced crosswise
    ¾ inch thick

2 round turnips, peeled and cut into
    ¾-inch pieces

1 cup shelled peas (about 1 pound in the shell)

¼ pound green beans, ends removed

1 eggplant, cut into ¾-inch pieces

1 broccoli crown, cut into florets

2 zucchini, sliced crosswise into ¾-inch lengths

1 bouquet garni made with parsley, thyme,
    and bay leaf

Salt and pepper

❖ ❖ ❖ ❖ ❖

1. In a flameproof casserole, melt the butter over medium-low heat. Add the onion and garlic and cook until softened. Stir in the leeks, tomatoes, and tomato paste. Add the potato, carrots, turnips, peas, green beans, eggplant, broccoli, zucchini, bouquet garni, and 2 cups of water. Season with salt and pepper. Cover and bring to a simmer, then reduce the heat to low and cook for 50 to 60 minutes.

2. Transfer the vegetables to a warmed serving dish and serve.

From Françoise:

• If needed, add 1 or 2 tablespoons of water during the cooking, but the vegetables should steam in very little water, even fry slightly.

• You can use frozen peas and green beans, which will save you some prep time.

• If your casserole is a nice one, you can serve the vegetables directly from the pot.

VEGETABLES

BUTTERY SAUTÉED CHINESE ARTICHOKES
- *Crosnes sautés* -

❖ EASY   ❖ EXPENSIVE   ❖ 40 MINUTES   ❖ SERVES 4

Kosher salt
1 ½ pounds Chinese artichokes
2 tablespoons butter

Pepper
Mixed chopped parsley and chervil leaves
  for sprinkling

❖ ❖ ❖ ❖ ❖

1. Bring a large saucepan of salted water to a boil.

2. Meanwhile, in a colander, remove the skin of the Chinese artichokes by rubbing it with kosher salt. Rinse in cold running water. Add to the boiling water and cook until tender, 15 to 20 minutes. Drain well.

3. In a large skillet, melt the butter over medium-high heat. Add the Chinese artichokes and cook until lightly browned. Season with salt and pepper and sprinkle with the herbs. Transfer to a warmed serving dish and serve.

From Françoise:

• Crosnes, also known as Chinese or Japanese artichokes, are small, unusual caterpillar-shaped tubers with a mild flavor similar to artichokes.

• To save time, you could simply toss the Chinese artichokes with the salt, pepper, butter, and herbs just before serving.

POTATO PANCAKES

- *Petites crêpes de pommes de terre* -

❖ EASY   ❖ INEXPENSIVE   ❖ 40 MINUTES   ❖ SERVES 4

1 ¼ pounds baking potatoes

2 large eggs, beaten

1 tablespoon all-purpose flour

Salt and pepper

Oil for frying

❖   ❖   ❖   ❖   ❖

1. Peel the potatoes and coarsely shred them in a food processor or on a box grater. Rinse them in a colander under cold running water. Drain well, transfer to a large, clean kitchen towel, and squeeze dry.

2. In a large bowl, toss the potatoes with the eggs and flour and season with salt and pepper.

3. In a large skillet, heat a little oil over medium-high heat until shimmering. Drop 1 tablespoon of the potato mixture into the skillet and flatten with the back of a spoon. Make about 3 more pancakes and cook until golden on the bottom, 3 to 5 minutes. Flip the pancakes and cook until golden. Transfer to paper towels to drain. Repeat with the remaining potato mixture, adding oil as needed. Arrange on a warmed platter and serve hot.

From Françoise:

• Keep the potato pancakes warm in a low oven or in between 2 plates set on top of a pan of simmering water.

• Try mixing the potatoes with finely chopped garlic and herbs or with shredded Gruyère cheese and 1 or 2 pinches of freshly grated nutmeg before frying.

VEGETABLES

GOLDEN POTATO CAKE WITH FINES HERBES

- *Galette de pommes de terre aux fines herbes* -

❖ EASY   ❖ INEXPENSIVE   ❖ 45 MINUTES   ❖ SERVES 4

1 pound baking potatoes

Oil for frying

2 large eggs, beaten

1 or 2 garlic cloves, finely chopped

2 tablespoons chopped parsley leaves

Salt and pepper

Butter for brushing

continued

1. Peel the potatoes and finely shred them in a food processor or on a box grater. Rinse them in a colander under cold running water. Drain well, transfer to a large, clean kitchen towel, and squeeze dry.

2. Preheat the oven to 400 degrees. In a large skillet, heat a little oil over medium-high heat until shimmering. Add the potatoes in 2 or 3 batches and cook them, stirring, until partly tender, about 5 minutes. Transfer to a large bowl as they are done. Add more oil with each batch.

3. In a large bowl, mix together the eggs, garlic, parsley, and salt and pepper to taste.

4. Brush a pie plate or gratin dish with butter. Pack the potato mixture in the bottom. Transfer to the oven and bake until cooked through and nicely browned, about 15 minutes. Run a knife around the potatoes. Invert a platter over the dish. Holding the dish and platter together, quickly invert the potatoes onto the platter. Serve hot.

WARM POTATO SALAD WITH VINAIGRETTE
- *Pommes de terre à l'huile* -

❖ EASY   ❖ INEXPENSIVE   ❖ 40 MINUTES   ❖ SERVES 4

Salt
1 ½ pounds new potatoes, unpeeled
4 to 5 tablespoons dry white wine
Mixed chopped parsley, chervil, chives, and tarragon

VINAIGRETTE
1 ½ tablespoons vinegar
5 tablespoons oil
Salt and pepper

❖   ❖   ❖   ❖   ❖

1. Bring a large pot of water to a boil. Add the potatoes and cook until tender, 25 to 30 minutes.

2. Meanwhile, make the vinaigrette: In a small bowl, whisk the vinegar with the oil and season with salt and pepper.

3. Drain the potatoes well and pat dry. Peel the potatoes and slice them into a salad bowl. Sprinkle with the wine, then the vinaigrette. Toss with the herbs and serve warm or at room temperature.

From Françoise:
• Prepared with new potatoes, this salad is a delicacy.

• If you can find chervil, use lots of it in this recipe.

• This salad is best warm. If possible, make it just before serving.

• The white wine makes the potatoes moist and flavorful.

CREAMY GOLDEN POTATO GRATIN

- Gratin dauphinois -

❖ EASY   ❖ INEXPENSIVE   ❖ 1 HOUR, 20 MINUTES   ❖ SERVES 4

1 garlic clove

2 tablespoons butter, cut into ¼-inch dice,
   plus more for brushing

1½ cups milk

2 pounds potatoes, peeled and thinly sliced

½ cup shredded Gruyère cheese

1 large egg

Salt and pepper

❖ ❖ ❖ ❖ ❖

1. Preheat the oven to 400 degrees. Rub a gratin dish with the garlic clove and brush with butter. In a small saucepan, bring the milk to a bare simmer; remove from the heat.

2. Spread the potatoes in the gratin dish, sprinkle with ¼ cup of the cheese, and pour in 1 cup of the hot milk. Transfer to the oven and bake for 50 minutes, gently stirring the potatoes 2 or 3 times.

3. Reduce the oven temperature to 350 degrees. In a small bowl, lightly beat the egg with salt and pepper and the remaining ½ cup of milk. Pour this mixture over the potatoes. Sprinkle the remaining ¼ cup of cheese over the top and dot with the 2 tablespoons of butter. Return to the oven and bake until the cheese is melted and golden, 10 to 15 minutes.

From Françoise:

• Stirring the potatoes during baking helps them cook more evenly.

• Sometimes when you're baking a potato gratin, the sauce separates. But if you follow my method and add the beaten egg at a lower temperature almost at the last minute, you won't have this problem. The sauce will look like slightly thickened cream.

• You can also use cream instead of milk, in which case it will be entirely absorbed by the potatoes.

• If you don't like garlic, don't rub the gratin dish with it. It's not crucial. You might add a pinch of freshly grated nutmeg instead.

• This gratin is a nice accompaniment to white meats.

VEGETABLES

BUTTERY PARSLEY POTATOES
- *Pommes de terre persillées* -

❖ EASY   ❖ INEXPENSIVE   ❖ 40 MINUTES   ❖ SERVES 4

Salt

2 pounds new potatoes, peeled and
   quartered if large

3 tablespoons butter, melted

1 small bunch parsley, leaves chopped

❖ ❖ ❖ ❖ ❖

1. Bring a large pot of salted water to a boil. Add the potatoes and cook until tender, 20 to 25 minutes. Drain well.

2. In a large saucepan, dry out the potatoes over low heat for 5 minutes. Transfer them to a warmed serving dish. Pour the melted butter over them, sprinkle with the parsley, and serve.

From Françoise:
• These potatoes would be just as good with chopped chives or chervil.

• Add a little butter to the saucepan if you're afraid the potatoes will stick when you're drying them out.

CREAMY MASHED POTATOES
- *Purée de pommes de terre* -

❖ EASY   ❖ INEXPENSIVE   ❖ 50 MINUTES   ❖ SERVES 4

Salt

2 pounds baking potatoes, peeled

1½ to 2 cups milk

3 tablespoons butter, plus more for brushing

Salt and pepper

❖ ❖ ❖ ❖ ❖

1. Bring a large pot of salted water to a boil. Add the potatoes and cook until tender, 25 to 30 minutes. Drain.

2. In a small saucepan, heat the milk to a bare simmer. Mash or rice the potatoes or work them through a food mill. Beat in the butter, then, gradually, the hot milk. Season with salt and pepper.

3. Transfer to a warmed serving dish and serve as soon as possible.

From Françoise:

• The best mashed potatoes are tricky to make. They should be prepared at the last minute, and they require a fair amount of pot-washing, but what a sheer delight!

• New potatoes are not suitable because they can get gluey when mashed. Don't use an electric beater, either, which also tends to make the mixture elastic instead of fluffy.

• To get the lightest potatoes, work them through a ricer or a food mill.

• Really good mashed potatoes cannot be made in advance because they don't reheat well. You can keep them warm, however, by placing their bowl in a pan of hot water.

• Use more or less milk depending on whether you like your mashed potatoes thick or creamier.

CRISPY POTATO CROQUETTES
- Croquettes de pommes de terre -

❖ INTERMEDIATE ❖ INEXPENSIVE ❖ 1 HOUR, PLUS 2 HOURS CHILLING ❖ SERVES 4

Salt
1 ½ pounds baking potatoes, unpeeled
2 large eggs, separated
½ cup all-purpose flour

Pepper
½ cup dry bread crumbs
7 tablespoons butter

❖ ❖ ❖ ❖ ❖

1. Bring a large pot of salted water to a boil. Add the potatoes and cook until tender, about 30 minutes. Drain.

2. Peel the potatoes and return to the pot. Mash or rice them or work them through a food mill. Do not add any liquid. Off the heat, beat in the egg yolks and 1 tablespoon of the flour and season with salt and pepper.

3. Spread the potato mixture in a shallow pan, cover, and refrigerate until cold and firm, about 2 hours.

4. In separate soup plates, spread the remaining flour, the egg whites, lightly beaten, and bread crumbs. Turn the potato mixture out onto a work surface and roll into a cylinder

about 1 inch in diameter. Cut it into 2- to 2 ½-inch pieces and dredge in the flour, patting off the excess. Then dip in the egg whites, letting the excess drip back into the plate. Dredge in the bread crumbs, pressing lightly to help the crumbs adhere.

5. In a large skillet, melt the butter over medium heat. When it foams, add the croquettes without crowding and fry until golden brown all over, 1 to 2 minutes per side. Transfer the croquettes to a warmed platter. Serve as soon as possible.

From Françoise:
• Do not add any liquid to the mashed potatoes because a mixture that is too soft tends to fall apart when fried.

VEGETABLES

- Fry the croquettes in batches so it's easier to turn them without breaking them.

- Add plenty of butter or oil to the skillet, or the croquettes may stick to the bottom.

- To make garlicky potato croquettes, add finely chopped garlic and parsley or chives to the mashed potatoes, then proceed with the recipe.

- Older potatoes are better for making croquettes than new potatoes, which don't hold together as well.

FRIED POTATOES WITH PEARL ONIONS AND PANCETTA

- Pommes de terre à l'alsacienne -

❖ EASY   ❖ INEXPENSIVE   ❖ 1 HOUR   ❖ SERVES 4

2 pounds potatoes, peeled and halved or
   quartered if large
3 tablespoons butter
1 tablespoon oil
5 ounces pearl onions, peeled

¼ pound thick-sliced pancetta, cut crosswise
   into ¼-inch-thick strips
Salt and pepper
Mixed chopped parsley, chervil, chives,
   and tarragon

❖ ❖ ❖ ❖ ❖

1. Bring a large pot of water to a boil. Add the potatoes and cook just until the water comes back to a boil. Drain and pat dry.

2. In a large skillet, melt the butter in the oil over medium-high heat. Add the potatoes and pearl onions and cook, uncovered, until nicely browned, about 15 minutes.

3. Stir in the pancetta, partly cover, and cook for 15 to 25 minutes until the vegetables are tender and nicely browned. Season with salt and pepper. Transfer to a warmed serving dish, sprinkle with the herbs, and serve.

From Françoise:
- Do not cover the skillet while the potatoes are browning in Step 2, instead shake the pan often. Cover the skillet only partway when finishing the cooking in Step 3.

GOLDEN POTATOES AND ONIONS

- *Pommes de terre à la lyonnaise* -

❖ EASY ❖ INEXPENSIVE ❖ 1 HOUR ❖ SERVES 4

5 tablespoons butter
2 pounds potatoes, peeled and sliced

Salt and pepper
½ pound onions, thinly sliced

❖ ❖ ❖ ❖ ❖

1. Preheat the oven to 350 degrees. In a large skillet, melt 3 tablespoons of the butter over medium-high heat. Add the potatoes and cook until nicely browned. Season with salt and pepper. Transfer to a gratin dish.

2. In the same skillet, melt the remaining 2 tablespoons of butter over medium-high heat, add the onions, and cook until nicely browned. Season with salt and pepper. Spread the onions over the potatoes.

3. Transfer the gratin to the oven and bake until tender, 30 to 40 minutes.

From Françoise:

• If you cover the gratin dish with a sheet of buttered foil, the potatoes will be moister.

• You can also cook this dish entirely on top of the stove if your skillet is very big—large enough to hold all the potatoes easily. Cover the skillet when the potatoes and onions are golden.

• Serve with veal and pork roasts.

VEGETABLES

SLOW-COOKED POTATOES WITH TOMATOES AND BELL PEPPERS

- *Pommes de terre à l'espagnole* -

❖ EASY ❖ INEXPENSIVE ❖ 1 HOUR ❖ SERVES 4

3 tablespoons butter
2 pounds new potatoes, peeled and cut
  into chunks
3 or 4 onions, coarsely chopped
2 bell peppers, cut into 1 ½–inch pieces
1 pound tomatoes, peeled, seeded, and chopped

1 bouquet garni made with parsley, thyme,
  and bay leaf
1 garlic clove, crushed
Salt and pepper

continued

1. In a flameproof casserole, melt the butter over medium heat. Add the potatoes, onions, bell peppers, tomatoes, bouquet garni, garlic, and ¾ cup of water. Season with salt and pepper. Cover and bring to a simmer, then reduce the heat to low and cook for about 45 minutes.

From Françoise:
• It isn't essential to peel the tomatoes, but it is better. Score the bottoms and drop them in boiling water until the skin begins to curl, about 1 minute.

• Adding 1 tablespoon of vinegar to the pot before adding the water will make the potatoes more flavorful.

• This is a good, light vegetable dish for summer.

• It's an especially good partner for white meats.

GRATIN OF POTATOES AND ONIONS
- *Pommes de terre à la boulangère* -

❖ EASY ❖ INEXPENSIVE ❖ 1 HOUR, 10 MINUTES ❖ SERVES 4

5 tablespoons butter, cut into ¼-inch dice, plus more for brushing
4 or 5 onions, thinly sliced
Salt and pepper

2 pounds potatoes, peeled and thinly sliced
1 bouquet garni made with parsley, thyme, and bay leaf
1½ cups broth

❖ ❖ ❖ ❖ ❖

1. Preheat the oven to 400 degrees. Brush a gratin dish with butter.

2. In a large skillet, melt 2 tablespoons of the butter over medium-high heat. Add the onions and cook until nicely browned. Season with salt and pepper.

3. Spread half the potatoes in the gratin dish. Cover with the onions. Dot with 1 ½ tablespoons of the butter and add the bouquet garni. Top with the remaining potatoes and pour in the broth. Dot with the remaining 1 ½ tablespoons of butter and season with salt and pepper.

4. Transfer to the oven and bake until tender, about 45 minutes. Remove the bouquet garni and serve.

From Françoise:
• You might add a tablespoon of water in Step 2 if the onions start sticking.

• If the gratin dries out too quickly, reduce the oven temperature and cover the gratin dish with foil.

GRATIN OF SAUTÉED POTATOES AND ONIONS

- *Pommes marmiton* -

❖ EASY ❖ INEXPENSIVE ❖ 1 HOUR, 30 MINUTES ❖ SERVES 4

3 tablespoons butter, plus more for brushing

2 tablespoons oil

2 pounds potatoes, peeled and thinly sliced

1 ½ pounds sweet onions, thinly sliced

Salt and pepper

1 ½ cups broth

❖ ❖ ❖ ❖ ❖

1. Preheat the oven to 350 degrees. Brush a gratin dish with butter.

2. In a large skillet, melt the 3 tablespoons of butter in the oil over medium-high heat. Add the potatoes and onions in batches and cook until nicely browned.

3. Spread the potatoes and onions in the gratin dish. Pour in the broth. Season with pepper and, lightly, with salt. Transfer to the oven and bake until tender, 45 minutes to 1 hour. Serve hot.

From Françoise:

• If the top browns too quickly, cover it with foil.

• You can boil whole yellow onions in water for a few minutes before slicing them to soften the flavor.

FRIED POTATOES WITH SHALLOTS AND PARSLEY

- *Pommes de terre à la bordelaise* -

❖ EASY ❖ INEXPENSIVE ❖ 1 HOUR ❖ SERVES 4

2 pounds new potatoes, peeled and cut into ½-inch dice

3 tablespoons butter

Salt and pepper

4 shallots, finely chopped

Chopped parsley leaves for sprinkling

continued

1. In a large saucepan, cover the potatoes with water and bring to a boil. Drain well.

2. In a large skillet, melt the butter over medium heat. Add the potatoes and cook, stirring often, until tender and nicely browned, 20 to 30 minutes.

3. Season with salt and pepper. Add the shallots and parsley and cook, stirring, for a few moments. Serve immediately.

From Françoise:

• I can't emphasize enough to use a very large skillet for browning potatoes. They will cook much more evenly. If you don't have a very large one, well, use two and add half the ingredients to each, but that's more complicated.

• This brief boiling the potatoes in water, before the actual cooking, helps keep the potatoes from sticking in the skillet.

• Garlic could replace the shallots.

SLOW-COOKED POTATOES WITH BACON
- *Pommes de terre au lard* -

❖ EASY   ❖ INEXPENSIVE   ❖ 1 HOUR   ❖ SERVES 4

2 tablespoons butter
5 ounces thick-sliced bacon, cut crosswise
   into ¼-inch-thick strips
7 ounces onions, coarsely chopped

1 tablespoon all-purpose flour
2 cups water or broth
Salt and pepper
2 pounds potatoes, peeled and quartered

❖ ❖ ❖ ❖ ❖

1. In a flameproof casserole, melt the butter over medium heat. Add the bacon and cook until just beginning to brown. Add the onions and cook until nicely browned. Stir in the flour. Add the water or broth and season with salt and pepper. Bring to a simmer, stirring.

2. Add the potatoes, reduce the heat to low, cover, and cook until tender, 30 to 40 minutes. Transfer to a warmed serving dish and serve.

From Françoise:

• The potatoes will have more flavor if you use broth. You may not need to season the onions in Step 1, depending on the broth.

WINE-BRAISED POTATOES
- *Pommes de terre en matelote* -

❖ EASY　　　　❖ INEXPENSIVE　　　　❖ 1 HOUR, 10 MINUTES　　　　❖ SERVES 4

3 tablespoons butter

2 onions, thinly sliced

1 tablespoon all-purpose flour

¾ cup red wine

2 pounds potatoes, peeled and thinly sliced

1 bouquet garni made with parsley, thyme, and bay leaf

Salt and pepper

Chopped parsley leaves for sprinkling

❖　❖　❖　❖　❖

1. Preheat the oven to 350 degrees. In a flame-proof casserole, melt the butter over medium-high heat. Add the onions and cook until lightly browned. Stir in the flour. Add the wine and ¾ cup of water and stir to mix. Add the potatoes and bouquet garni. Season with salt and pepper. Cover and bring to a boil.

2. Transfer to the oven and cook until the potatoes are tender, 50 to 60 minutes. Remove the bouquet garni. Transfer the potatoes to a warmed serving dish. Sprinkle with parsley and serve.

From Françoise:

• The potatoes can be braised on top of the stove, but the cooking won't be as even and you'll need to stir them occasionally at the risk of breaking the potato slices. You could, however, cook them more easily, more evenly, and, obviously, more quickly in a pressure cooker. That would take only 15 or 20 minutes.

VEGETABLES

WARM POTATOES WITH CREAMY SAUCE
- *Pommes de terre à la béchamel* -

❖ EASY　　　　❖ INEXPENSIVE　　　　❖ 45 MINUTES　　　　❖ SERVES 4

Salt

2 pounds potatoes, unpeeled

BÉCHAMEL SAUCE

3 tablespoons butter

3 tablespoons all-purpose flour

2 cups milk

Salt and pepper

continued

1. Bring a large pot of salted water to a boil. Add the potatoes and cook until tender, 25 to 30 minutes. Drain.

2. Meanwhile, make the béchamel sauce: In a large saucepan, melt the butter over medium heat. Whisk in the flour until it starts foaming. Whisk in the milk. Season with salt and pepper. Bring to a boil, whisking, then reduce the heat to very low and cook for 10 minutes.

3. Peel the potatoes and slice them. Transfer to a warmed serving dish. Spoon the hot béchamel sauce over them and serve.

From Françoise:
• To vary the dish, you can stir different flavorings into the béchamel sauce just before serving; for instance, 1 tablespoon of capers, chopped or not; chopped parsley, chervil, or tarragon leaves; 1 tablespoon freshly grated horseradish or prepared horseradish; chopped mushrooms sautéed in butter; or shredded Gruyère cheese.

WARM POTATOES AND HARD-BOILED EGGS WITH CREAMY SAUCE

- *Pommes de terre à la percheronne* -

❖ EASY   ❖ INEXPENSIVE   ❖ 45 MINUTES   ❖ SERVES 4

Salt
2 pounds potatoes, unpeeled
6 hard-boiled eggs, quartered lengthwise

BÉCHAMEL SAUCE
3 tablespoons butter
3 tablespoons all-purpose flour
2 cups milk
Salt and pepper

❖ ❖ ❖ ❖ ❖

1. Bring a large pot of salted water to a boil. Add the potatoes and cook until tender, 25 to 30 minutes. Drain.

2. Meanwhile, make the béchamel sauce: In a large saucepan, melt the butter over medium heat. Whisk in the flour until it starts foaming. Whisk in the milk. Season with salt and pepper. Bring to a boil, whisking, then reduce the heat to very low and cook for 10 minutes.

3. Peel the potatoes and quarter them lengthwise. Layer them with the eggs in a warmed serving dish. Spoon the hot béchamel sauce over them and serve.

From Françoise:
• You can always enrich a béchamel sauce with a little crème fraîche.

MASHED POTATO CAKE WITH GRUYÈRE
- *Gâteau de pommes de terre* -

❖ EASY   ❖ INEXPENSIVE   ❖ 1 HOUR, 15 MINUTES   ❖ SERVES 4

Salt

2 pounds potatoes, peeled

3 tablespoons butter, cut into ¼-inch dice,
   plus more for brushing

¾ cup milk

2 large eggs, separated

Salt and pepper

½ cup shredded Gruyère cheese

❖   ❖   ❖   ❖   ❖

1. Bring a large pot of salted water to a boil. Add the potatoes and cook until tender, 25 to 30 minutes. Drain.

2. Preheat the oven to 400 degrees. Brush a gratin dish with butter.

3. In a small saucepan, heat the milk to a bare simmer. Mash or rice the potatoes or work them through a food mill. Beat in 2 tablespoons of the butter, then, gradually, the hot milk. Beat in the egg yolks. Season with salt and pepper.

4. In a large bowl, beat the egg whites with a pinch of salt until they hold stiff peaks. Stir one-quarter of the beaten whites into the potatoes, then gently fold this lightened mixture into the remaining whites.

5. Spread the potatoes in the gratin dish. Sprinkle with the cheese and dot with the remaining 1 tablespoon of butter. Transfer to the oven and bake until nicely browned, 25 to 30 minutes. Serve immediately.

From Françoise:

• To make this into a meal-in-one dish, finely chop 2 or 3 slices of baked ham and stir them into the mashed potatoes in Step 3. Or add flaked leftover fish.

• This potato cake should be fairly solid. It's not a soufflé. Don't expect it to rise dramatically, even if your egg whites are well beaten.

VEGETABLES

GOLDEN SAUTÉED POTATOES

- *Pommes sautées* -

❖ EASY ❖ INEXPENSIVE ❖ 50 MINUTES ❖ SERVES 4

Salt
**2 pounds large new potatoes, peeled and
  cut into even pieces**

3 tablespoons butter
Pepper

❖ ❖ ❖ ❖ ❖

1. Bring a large pot of salted water to a boil with the potatoes. When the water comes to a boil, drain the potatoes and pat dry.

2. In a large skillet, melt the butter over medium heat. Add the potatoes and cook, stirring often, until tender and nicely browned all over, about 30 minutes. Season with salt and pepper. Transfer to a warmed serving dish and serve.

From Françoise:
• It is easier and quicker to make sautéed potatoes if you parboil them first. The result is slightly different than if you cooked them directly in butter or oil, but it's also very good so long as you brown the potatoes well.

SAUTÉED NEW POTATOES WITH THYME

- *Pommes sautées au thym* -

❖ EASY ❖ INEXPENSIVE ❖ 45 MINUTES ❖ SERVES 4

Salt
1 ½ pounds small new potatoes, unpeeled
3 tablespoons butter

Fresh or dried thyme leaves
Pepper

❖ ❖ ❖ ❖ ❖

1. Bring a large pot of salted water to a boil. Add the potatoes and cook until tender, 25 to 30 minutes. Drain the potatoes.

2. In a large skillet, melt the butter over medium-high heat. Add the potatoes and cook until nicely browned all over. Season with thyme, salt, and pepper. Cover and cook until fragrant, 2 to 3 minutes. Transfer to a warmed serving dish and serve.

SAUTÉED POTATOES WITH CRISP CRUMBS
- *Pommes sablées* -

❖ EASY   ❖ INEXPENSIVE   ❖ 45 MINUTES   ❖ SERVES 4

Salt

1 ½ pounds potatoes, unpeeled

3 tablespoons butter

1 tablespoon dry bread crumbs

Pepper

❖ ❖ ❖ ❖ ❖

1. Bring a large pot of salted water to a boil. Add the potatoes and cook until tender, 25 to 30 minutes. Drain, peel, and dice or slice the potatoes.

2. In a large skillet, melt the butter over medium-high heat. Add the potatoes and cook, stirring often, until nicely browned, about 10 minutes.

3. Sprinkle with the bread crumbs and season with salt and pepper. Reduce the heat to medium and cook, stirring, for 2 to 3 minutes. Transfer to a warmed serving dish and serve.

CRISPY, CREAMY POTATO PUFFS
- *Pommes dauphine* -

❖ ADVANCED   ❖ INEXPENSIVE   ❖ 1 HOUR, 20 MINUTES   ❖ SERVES 6

Salt

1 pound baking potatoes, unpeeled

Pepper

4 cups oil for frying

CHOUX PASTRY

5 tablespoons butter, diced

½ teaspoon salt

⅔ cup all-purpose flour

3 large eggs

❖ ❖ ❖ ❖ ❖

1. Bring a large pot of salted water to a boil. Add the potatoes and cook until tender, 25 to 30 minutes. Drain.

2. Meanwhile, make the choux pastry: In a saucepan, bring ⅔ cup of water, the butter, and salt to a boil. When the butter melts, remove the pan from the heat, add all the flour at once, and beat well using a wooden spoon. Return the pan to low heat and beat until the dough is smooth and pulls away from the pan to form a ball. Off the heat, add

continued

585

the eggs, one at a time, beating well after each addition.

3. Peel the potatoes. Mash or rice the potatoes or work them through a food mill. Season with salt and pepper. Do not add any liquid. Beat them into the choux pastry and let cool.

4. In a large skillet, heat the oil to 375 degrees. Shape the potato mixture into balls about the size of a walnut. Gently drop them into the oil without crowding and fry, turning them once, until puffed and golden, 1 to 3 minutes total. Using a slotted spoon, transfer the puffs to paper towels to drain. Keep warm in a low oven while frying the remaining mixture. Season with salt and pepper and serve very hot.

From Françoise:
• Select baking potatoes like russets or Idahos to make this recipe.

• Follow the proportions and method closely in this recipe or you may be disappointed.

• Do not add any liquid to the mashed potatoes in Step 3, even if they look dry. They are supposed to.

• To shape the puffs, use a small spoon and scoop up a little of the potato mixture. Using a finger dipped in cold water—have a glass of water right next to you—gently push the ball off the spoon into the hot oil. To avoid burning yourself, drop in each ball as close to the oil as possible so it doesn't splash.

• The oil should not be too hot. If it is, the puffs will brown before they have had a chance to puff and cook through.

• Add the balls in small batches; they should have plenty of room for frying.

STUFFED BAKED POTATOES WITH GRUYÈRE
- *Pommes de terre farcies Arlie* -

❖ EASY   ❖ INEXPENSIVE   ❖ 1 HOUR, 30 MINUTES   ❖ SERVES 4

1 pound kosher salt
4 large, evenly shaped, smooth baking potatoes

STUFFING
4 tablespoons (½ stick) butter, cut into
  ¼-inch dice

2 tablespoons crème fraîche
1 tablespoon chopped chervil or chives
2 pinches of freshly grated nutmeg
Salt and pepper
½ cup shredded Gruyère cheese

❖ ❖ ❖ ❖ ❖

1. Preheat the oven to 425 degrees. Spread the salt in a small rimmed baking sheet. Set the potatoes on top, transfer to the oven, and bake until tender, 50 to 60 minutes. Let cool slightly. Leave the oven on.

2. Cut a thin slice off the top of each potato. Using a spoon, hollow out the insides, leaving a sturdy shell.

3. In a bowl, mash or rice the potatoes or work them through a food mill. Beat in 3 tablespoons of the butter, the crème fraîche, and chervil or chives. Season with nutmeg, salt, and pepper.

4. Pack the stuffing into the potatoes. Sprinkle with the cheese and dot with the remaining 1 tablespoon of butter. Return the potatoes to the oven and bake on the top shelf until the cheese is melted and nicely browned, 10 to 15 minutes.

From Françoise:
• You can bake the potatoes on the baking sheet without salt; the salt just keeps them from wobbling.

• There are so many ways to vary stuffed baked potatoes.

• Stuffed with mushrooms: Sauté sliced mushrooms in butter and mix them and 3 tablespoons of crème fraîche into the mashed potatoes. Serve without returning the potatoes to the oven.

• Gratinéed: Beat 2 eggs, 1 tablespoon of butter, chopped ham or chicken leftovers, 2 pinches of nutmeg, and shredded Gruyère cheese into the mashed potatoes. Broil for 3 to 5 minutes.

• Souffléed: Beat 2 egg yolks and 1 tablespoon shredded Gruyère cheese into the mashed potatoes. Season with salt and pepper. Fold in 2 egg whites, beaten until stiff. Return to a 400-degree oven and bake until puffed, about 10 minutes.

RICH MASHED POTATO GARNISH
- *Pommes duchesse* -

❖ INTERMEDIATE   ❖ INEXPENSIVE   ❖ 1 HOUR   ❖ SERVES 4

Salt
1 pound baking potatoes, unpeeled
Pepper

3 large egg yolks
1 large egg white, lightly beaten

❖ ❖ ❖ ❖ ❖

1. Bring a large pot of salted water to a boil. Add the potatoes and cook until tender, 25 to 30 minutes. Drain.

2. Preheat the oven to 400 degrees. Peel the potatoes. Mash or rice the potatoes or work them through a food mill. Season with salt and pepper. Do not add any liquid. Beat in the egg yolks.

3. Using a piping bag fitted with a large tip, pipe the potatoes around a heatproof platter or on a baking sheet. Brush with the egg white.

Transfer to the oven and bake until golden, 5 to 10 minutes.

From Françoise:
• You can either pipe the potatoes around the (heatproof) platter where you will set your roast or pipe them on a baking sheet and then transfer them to your serving dish.

• Do not add any liquid (aside from the egg yolks) to the mashed potatoes because they need to be dry to hold their shape for piping.

CRISPY STUFFED POTATO CROQUETTES
- Cassolettes duchesse -

❖ ADVANCED   ❖ INEXPENSIVE   ❖ 3 HOURS   ❖ SERVES 4

FILLING

¼ pound split peas or dried white beans

1 carrot, sliced lengthwise

1 onion stuck with 2 whole cloves

1 bouquet garni made with parsley, thyme,
  and bay leaf

Salt and pepper

1 tablespoon butter

2 or 3 tablespoons crème fraîche

Salt

1 pound baking potatoes, unpeeled

Pepper

3 large egg yolks

½ cup all-purpose flour

2 whole large eggs, lightly beaten

Dry bread crumbs

Oil for frying

❖ ❖ ❖ ❖ ❖

1. Make the filling: In a large saucepan, generously cover the peas or beans with water and bring to a boil. Cook for 15 minutes, then drain. Return the peas or beans to the pan and add the carrot, onion, bouquet garni, and water to cover by 2 inches. Cover and bring to a boil, then reduce the heat to low and cook until tender, 1 hour and 30 minutes to 2 hours, seasoning with salt and pepper halfway through.

2. Drain the peas or beans. Remove the bouquet garni, carrot, and onion. Work the peas or beans through a food mill into a bowl. Beat in the butter and crème fraîche.

3. Meanwhile, bring a large pot of salted water to a boil. Add the potatoes and cook until tender, 25 to 30 minutes. Drain.

4. Peel the potatoes. Mash or rice the potatoes or work them through a food mill. Season with salt and pepper. Do not add any liquid. Beat in the egg yolks. Spread the potato mixture in a shallow pan, cover, and refrigerate until cold and firm.

5. In separate soup plates, spread the flour, whole eggs, and bread crumbs. Season the eggs with salt and pepper. Turn the potatoes out onto a work surface and roll into a cylinder. Cut it into 8 croquettes and dredge in the flour, patting off the excess. Then dip in the eggs, letting the excess drip back into the plate. Dredge in the bread crumbs, pressing lightly to help the crumbs adhere. Transfer to a platter and refrigerate until firm, about 1 hour.

6. In a large skillet, heat the oil to 375 degrees. Gently drop the croquettes into the oil without crowding and fry, turning them once, until golden, 1 to 3 minutes total. Using a slotted spoon, transfer the croquettes to paper towels to drain. Keep warm in a low oven while frying the remaining croquettes.

7. Cut a thin slice off the top of each croquette. Using a small spoon, carefully hollow out the insides, leaving a sturdy shell.

8. Using a piping bag fitted with a plain tip or a small spoon, fill the croquettes with the stuffing. Serve hot.

From Françoise:

• Reserve a little of the pea or bean cooking broth in case it's needed to soften the stuffing. The stuffing should be thick but not so stiff that it can't be piped. If necessary, beat in some of the hot cooking broth.

• You could also use canned beans, drained and rinsed, to make the stuffing. Puree them and beat in the butter and crème fraîche as directed in Step 2.

• Keep the filling warm in a bowl set in a pan of hot water until ready to use.

• These croquettes are traditionally used as a garnish, arranged around a platter of roasted meat.

FOIL-BAKED POTATOES WITH CREAMY TOPPINGS
- *Pommes de terre en robe d'argent* -

❖ EASY ❖ INEXPENSIVE ❖ 1 HOUR, 15 MINUTES ❖ SERVES 4

---

4 large potatoes, unpeeled
Salt and pepper

CREAMY CHIVE AND HORSERADISH SAUCE
½ cup crème fraîche
1 teaspoon grated horseradish
2 teaspoons chopped chives

CREAMY GRUYÈRE AND ONION SAUCE
½ cup shredded Gruyère cheese
2 tablespoons butter, melted
¼ cup crème fraîche
1 or 2 small onions, finely chopped
Salt and pepper

❖ ❖ ❖ ❖ ❖

1. Preheat the oven to 400 degrees. Set each potato on a fairly large sheet of foil. Season with salt and pepper and wrap in the foil, twisting both ends. Set on a baking sheet and transfer to the oven. Bake until tender, about 1 hour.

2. Meanwhile, make the sauces: In 2 separate bowls, stir the ingredients for each sauce together.

3. Cut each potato in half lengthwise through the foil. Serve the potatoes in the foil and pass the sauces separately.

From Françoise:
• I also like to give the potatoes a garlicky flavor. I slice them in half lengthwise before baking them, add halved garlic cloves, then close them, then wrap in the foil. Excellent! I wouldn't use the horseradish, though, which doesn't go well with garlic.

VEGETABLES

CLASSIC POTATOES BOILED IN THEIR SKINS
- *Pommes de terre en robe des champs* -

❖ EASY   ❖ INEXPENSIVE   ❖ 35 MINUTES   ❖ SERVES 4

Salt
2 pounds potatoes, unpeeled

Butter or crème fraîche

❖ ❖ ❖ ❖ ❖

1. Bring a large pot of salted water to a boil. Add the potatoes and cook until tender, 25 to 30 minutes. Drain.

2. Serve the potatoes in their skins with butter or crème fraîche.

From Françoise:
• Don't forget to salt the water well or the potatoes will be bland.

HOMEMADE FRENCH FRIES
- *Pommes de terre frites* -

❖ INTERMEDIATE   ❖ INEXPENSIVE   ❖ 30 MINUTES   ❖ SERVES 4

2 quarts oil for deep-frying
2 pounds russet or Idaho potatoes,
** peeled and cut into ⅜-inch-thick fries**

Salt

❖ ❖ ❖ ❖ ❖

1. In a large pot, heat the oil to 325 degrees. Pat the potatoes thoroughly dry. Working in batches, fry the potatoes, stirring several times, until softened but not browned, 3 to 4 minutes. Using a slotted spoon, transfer to a paper towel-lined platter to drain and cool.

2. Heat the oil to 375 degrees. Fry the potatoes a second time until golden, 4 to 6 minutes.

Transfer to a paper towel-lined platter to drain. Sprinkle with salt and serve piping hot.

From Françoise:
• I fry my potatoes once before serving. Then I fry them a second time once everyone is at the table, so I can serve them very hot.

• Two quarts of oil is enough to cook 1 to 1 ½ pounds of potatoes at a time.

- The potatoes should be completely submerged in the hot oil to cook properly. If you add too many at once, the temperature of the oil will drop and the potatoes will cook too slowly and stick together, soaking up too much oil when you want them to be crisp and light.

- Please note that cut potatoes that aren't perfectly dry—that haven't been carefully wiped—can make the oil boil over. The moisture expands when it hits the hot oil and makes it froth up.

STEAMED POTATOES
- *Pommes de terre vapeur* -

❖ EASY   ❖ INEXPENSIVE   ❖ 1 HOUR   ❖ SERVES 4

**2 pounds new potatoes, peeled and
  cut in half if large**

Salt

❖   ❖   ❖   ❖   ❖

1. In a large saucepan fitted with a steamer basket, bring 1 inch of water to a boil over medium heat. Add the potatoes, cover, and steam until tender, 40 to 50 minutes.

2. Transfer the potatoes to a warmed serving dish, season with salt, and serve piping hot.

From Françoise:
- Serve steamed potatoes as an accompaniment to all kinds of meat in sauce and poached fish.

- The quality of the potatoes is important because there's nothing to hide anything less than perfect.

- Steamed potatoes are usually served sprinkled with chopped parsley.

- You may need to add boiling water to the saucepan when cooking for more than 30 minutes.

- Steamed potatoes will need seasoning. Salting the water does not flavor the potatoes.

- If you don't have a stacked metal steamer, you can steam the potatoes using a metal colander or steamer basket set in a pot or saucepan. Watch the level of water carefully so it doesn't all evaporate.

VEGETABLES

PASTA & RICE

HOMEMADE RAVIOLI
- *Ravioli frais* -

❖ INTERMEDIATE ❖ INEXPENSIVE ❖ 3 HOURS, PLUS 1 HOUR RESTING ❖ SERVES 4

1 ½ cups all-purpose flour, plus more for dusting

3 large whole eggs

1 teaspoon salt

Filling (pages 596–597)

1 large egg yolk, lightly beaten

Butter for brushing

Salt

Shredded Gruyère cheese for sprinkling

❖ ❖ ❖ ❖ ❖

1. Mound the flour on a work surface. Make a well in the middle of the flour and add the whole eggs, the 1 teaspoon of salt, and 1 tablespoon of cold water. Using a fork, beat together the eggs and water and gradually incorporate the flour. Knead the dough until very smooth and elastic. Cover and let rest for about 1 hour.

2. On a lightly floured work surface, roll the dough to as thin a sheet as possible. Cut it into two 5-inch-wide strips. Drop 1-teaspoon mounds of filling in two rows, about 2 inches apart, down the length of the dough. Brush a little beaten egg yolk on the dough around each mound of filling. Drape the second sheet of dough over the filling. Firmly press around each mound of filling, pressing out any air that may be trapped inside.

3. Using a pastry wheel or knife and a ruler, cut the ravioli into 2-inch squares. Firmly press around the edges to seal them. Transfer the finished ravioli to a baking sheet dusted with flour.

4. Preheat the oven to 425 degrees. Brush a gratin dish with butter. Bring a large pot of salted water to a boil. Add the ravioli and cook until they float and are tender, 3 to 5 minutes. Drain carefully. Spread the ravioli in the gratin dish, sprinkle with cheese, and bake on the top shelf of the oven until the cheese is melted and nicely browned, 10 to 15 minutes.

From Françoise:

• Alternatively, you can serve the ravioli with a Tomato Sauce (pages 642–645) or Mornay Sauce (page 635).

HOMEMADE CANNELLONI
- *Cannelloni frais* -

❖ INTERMEDIATE   ❖ INEXPENSIVE   ❖ 3 HOURS, PLUS 1 HOUR RESTING   ❖ SERVES 4

1½ cups all-purpose flour, plus more for dusting
3 large whole eggs
1 teaspoon salt
Butter for brushing

Salt
Filling (pages 596–597)
Shredded Gruyère cheese for sprinkling

❖ ❖ ❖ ❖ ❖

1. Mound the flour on a work surface. Make a well in the middle of the flour and add the whole eggs, the 1 teaspoon of salt, and 1 tablespoon of cold water. Using a fork, beat together the eggs and water and gradually incorporate the flour. Knead the dough until very smooth and elastic. Cover and let rest for about 1 hour.

2. On a lightly floured work surface, roll the dough to as thin a sheet as possible. Using a pastry wheel or knife and a ruler, cut the dough into rectangles about 2 ½ by 3 inches.

3. Preheat the oven to 425 degrees. Brush a gratin dish with butter. Bring a large pot of salted water to a boil. Add the pasta rectangles and cook until al dente. Drain carefully.

4. Spread the rectangles side by side on a clean kitchen towel. Put a heaping tablespoon of filling on each pasta rectangle and roll it up. Spread the cannelloni in the gratin dish, sprinkle with cheese, and bake on the top shelf of the oven until the cheese is melted and nicely browned, 10 to 15 minutes.

From Françoise:

• You can also spoon Tomato Sauce (pages 642–645) or Mornay Sauce (page 635) over the top and brown it, or not, in the oven.

• To stuff dried cannelloni, spoon or pipe the filling into the uncooked tubes. Arrange them in a buttered gratin dish without crowding because they swell when cooked. Generously cover them with a thin, hot tomato sauce. Cover with foil and bake in a 350-degree oven for 15 minutes. Remove the foil, sprinkle with shredded Gruyère cheese, and dot with butter, then bake for 10 minutes.

PASTA
& RICE

MEAT FILLING
- Farce à la viande -

❖ EASY ❖ MODERATE ❖ 10 MINUTES ❖ SERVES 4

1 cup finely chopped leftover meat
1 slice baked ham, finely chopped
1 shallot, finely chopped
Finely chopped parsley leaves

1 large egg
3 tablespoons shredded Gruyère cheese
Salt and pepper

❖ ❖ ❖ ❖ ❖

1. In a bowl, mix the leftover meat with the ham, shallot, parsley, egg, and cheese. Season with salt and pepper.

From Françoise:
• This recipe makes enough filling for one recipe of Homemade Ravioli (page 588) or Homemade Cannelloni (page 589).

CRAB FILLING
- Farce au crabe -

❖ EASY ❖ EXPENSIVE ❖ 20 MINUTES ❖ SERVES 4

3 tablespoons butter
2 tablespoons all-purpose flour
3 ½ ounces lump crabmeat, shredded, juice reserved

About 1 cup milk
Salt and pepper
¼ pound white mushrooms, finely chopped
Fresh lemon juice

❖ ❖ ❖ ❖ ❖

1. In a medium saucepan, melt 2 tablespoons of the butter over medium heat. Whisk in the flour until it starts foaming. Whisk in the crab juice with enough milk to make 1 cup. Season with salt and pepper. Bring to a boil, whisking.

2. In a medium skillet, melt the remaining 1 tablespoon of butter over medium-high heat. Add the mushrooms and squeeze in some lemon juice. Cook until tender and any liquid is evaporated.

3. Stir the mushrooms and crabmeat into the sauce and simmer briefly to blend the flavors.

From Françoise:
• This recipe makes enough filling for one recipe of Homemade Ravioli (page 588) or Homemade Cannelloni (page 589).

SPINACH FILLING

- Farce aux épinards -

❖ EASY   ❖ INEXPENSIVE   ❖ 10 MINUTES   ❖ SERVES 4

1 ½ cups finely chopped leftover beef

1 cooked lamb's brain, finely chopped

1 large egg

5 ounces finely chopped cooked spinach

3 tablespoons shredded Gruyère cheese

Salt and pepper

Freshly grated nutmeg

❖   ❖   ❖   ❖   ❖

1. In a bowl, mix the leftover beef with the brain, egg, spinach, and cheese. Season with salt, pepper, and nutmeg.

From Françoise:

• This recipe makes enough filling for one recipe of Homemade Ravioli (page 588) or Homemade Cannelloni (page 589).

BAKED GNOCCHI WITH GRUYÈRE

- Gnocchi à la romaine -

❖ EASY   ❖ INEXPENSIVE   ❖ 45 MINUTES   ❖ SERVES 4

2 cups milk

Salt

2 pinches of freshly grated nutmeg

3 tablespoons butter, plus more for brushing

¾ cup semolina flour

1 large egg yolk

¾ cup shredded Gruyère cheese

White pepper

❖   ❖   ❖   ❖   ❖

1. In a small saucepan, combine the milk, salt, and nutmeg with 2 tablespoons of the butter and bring to a boil over high heat. As soon as the water boils, add the semolina all at once and beat the dough with a wooden spoon until it thickens. Reduce the heat to low and cook for 10 minutes.

2. Remove the pan from the heat and beat the egg yolk into the dough, then ½ cup of the

cheese and the pepper until the dough is very smooth. Spread out the dough ½ inch thick in a cold pan and smooth the top. Let cool completely.

3. Preheat the oven to 375 degrees. Brush a baking sheet with butter. Stamp rounds out of the dough using a glass. Arrange the gnocchi

PASTA & RICE

continued

on the baking sheet. Sprinkle with the remaining ¼ cup of cheese and dot with the remaining 1 tablespoon of butter.

4. Transfer to the oven and bake until browned, about 10 minutes. Transfer to a warmed platter and serve.

PASTA WITH BUTTERY MUSHROOMS
- Pâtes sautées aux champignons -

❖ EASY   ❖ INEXPENSIVE   ❖ 20 MINUTES   ❖ SERVES 4

Salt
½ pound short or long pasta
2 tablespoons butter

5 ounces white mushrooms, thinly sliced
Pepper

❖ ❖ ❖ ❖ ❖

1. Bring a large saucepan of salted water to a boil. Add the pasta and cook, stirring occasionally, until al dente.

2. Meanwhile, in a large skillet, melt the butter over medium-high heat. Add the mushrooms and cook for 5 minutes. Season with salt and pepper.

3. Drain the pasta, reserving 1 cup of the pasta water. Add the pasta to the mushrooms with a little of the reserved water and cook for 2 to 3 minutes, until the liquid thickens slightly. Transfer to a warmed serving dish and serve.

PASTA WITH ROSEMARY BUTTER
- Pâtes au romarin -

❖ EASY   ❖ INEXPENSIVE   ❖ 20 MINUTES   ❖ SERVES 4

Salt
½ pound short or long pasta
2 tablespoons butter

1 rosemary sprig, leaves chopped
Pepper

1. Bring a large saucepan of salted water to a boil. Add the pasta and cook, stirring occasionally, until al dente. Drain, reserving 1 cup of the pasta water.

2. In the same saucepan, melt the butter over medium heat. Add the chopped rosemary leaves and cook until fragrant, about 1 minute.

3. Add the pasta to the rosemary butter with a little of the reserved water. Season with salt and pepper. Cook for 2 to 3 minutes, until the liquid thickens slightly. Transfer to a warmed serving dish and serve.

PASTA WITH ANCHOVY SAUCE

- *Pâtes aux anchois* -

❖ EASY   ❖ INEXPENSIVE   ❖ 20 MINUTES   ❖ SERVES 4

Salt
½ pound short or long pasta
2 tablespoons butter
10 anchovy fillets, chopped

1 tablespoon tomato paste
Pepper
Shredded Gruyère cheese

❖ ❖ ❖ ❖ ❖

1. Bring a large saucepan of salted water to a boil. Add the pasta and cook, stirring occasionally, until al dente. Drain, reserving 1 cup of the pasta water.

2. In the same saucepan, melt the butter over medium-low heat. Add the anchovies and cook until melted, about 1 minute. Stir in the tomato paste and season with pepper.

3. Add the pasta to the anchovies with a little of the reserved water. Cook for 2 to 3 minutes, until the liquid thickens slightly. Transfer to a warmed serving dish, sprinkle with cheese, and serve.

From Françoise:

• You can use either oil- or salt-cured anchovies in this recipe. If salt-cured, soak them in water briefly to remove the salt.

PASTA & RICE

PASTA WITH CREAMY ROQUEFORT SAUCE

- *Pâtes au roquefort* -

❖ EASY   ❖ MODERATE   ❖ 15 MINUTES   ❖ SERVES 4

Salt

½ pound fettuccine, tagliatelle, or linguine

1 cup crumbled Roquefort cheese
  (about 3 ½ ounces)

3 or 4 tablespoons crème fraîche

Pepper

2 garlic cloves, crushed

❖   ❖   ❖   ❖   ❖

1. Bring a large saucepan of salted water to a boil. Add the pasta and cook, stirring occasionally, until al dente.

2. Meanwhile, in a bowl, combine the cheese with the crème fraîche. Season with pepper.

3. Drain the pasta and return it to the pan. Add the cheese sauce and cook over low heat until the sauce is warmed through, 1 to 2 minutes. Rub a warmed serving dish with the garlic cloves. Add the pasta and serve.

PASTA WITH PESTO

- *Pâtes au basilic* -

❖ EASY   ❖ INEXPENSIVE   ❖ 25 MINUTES   ❖ SERVES 4

Salt

½ pound short or long pasta

1 bulb green garlic, root and green parts
  trimmed, outer layer removed, or 1 mature
  garlic clove

Pepper

10 to 15 large basil leaves

3 tablespoons olive oil

❖   ❖   ❖   ❖   ❖

1. Bring a large saucepan of salted water to a boil. Add the pasta and cook, stirring occasionally, until al dente.

2. Meanwhile, in a mortar or mini food processor, puree the garlic. Season with salt and pepper. Gradually add the basil leaves, working the

ingredients into a paste. Gradually blend in the olive oil as for a mayonnaise.

3. Drain the pasta and return it to the pan. Add the pesto and toss to coat. Transfer to a warmed serving dish and serve at once.

From Françoise:

• You can also make pasta with a creamy basil sauce. Warm 3 tablespoons of crème fraîche and blend with finely chopped garlic, salt, and pepper. Pour over the pasta and toss with shredded basil at the last minute.

• If you'd like less of a garlicky presence, rub the serving dish with the garlic clove instead of adding it to the sauce.

SPAGHETTI WITH ANCHOVY-TOMATO SAUCE
- *Spaghetti à la provençale* -

❖ EASY　　　　❖ INEXPENSIVE　　　　❖ 30 MINUTES　　　　❖ SERVES 4

Salt

½ pound spaghetti

3 tablespoons butter

2 pounds tomatoes, chopped

2 garlic cloves, crushed

1 onion, finely chopped

1 bouquet garni made with parsley, thyme, and bay leaf

Pepper

10 oil-cured anchovy fillets, chopped

❖　❖　❖　❖　❖

1. Bring a large saucepan of salted water to a boil. Add the pasta and cook, stirring occasionally, until al dente.

2. Meanwhile, in a medium saucepan, melt the butter over medium-high heat. Add the tomatoes and cook, stirring to coat with the butter. Stir in the garlic, onion, and bouquet garni. Season with salt and pepper. Reduce the heat to medium-low, cover, and cook for 15 minutes. Remove the bouquet garni. Puree the sauce in a food mill or food processor. Stir in the anchovies.

3. Drain the pasta and transfer to a warmed serving dish. Spoon the sauce over the top and serve.

From Françoise:

• You can in fact reheat pasta. First cook it until barely al dente, then drain it in a colander. Just before serving, add the pasta to a pot of boiling water and cook it for 2 minutes, then drain again. Add the sauce and serve at once.

PASTA & RICE

SPAGHETTI WITH CHUNKY TOMATO SAUCE
- *Spaghetti à la napolitaine* -

❖ EASY   ❖ INEXPENSIVE   ❖ 40 MINUTES   ❖ SERVES 4

2 tablespoons butter

1 ½ pounds tomatoes, chopped

2 garlic cloves, finely chopped

1 bouquet garni made with parsley, thyme,
   and bay leaf

Salt and pepper

½ pound spaghetti

½ cup shredded Gruyère cheese

❖   ❖   ❖   ❖   ❖

1. In a large saucepan, melt the butter over medium-low heat. Add the tomatoes, garlic, and bouquet garni. Season with salt and pepper. Cook, uncovered, for about 30 minutes. Remove the bouquet garni.

2. Meanwhile, bring a large saucepan of salted water to a boil. Add the pasta and cook, stirring occasionally, until al dente. Drain.

3. Add the pasta to the sauce with the cheese and toss to coat. Transfer to a warmed serving dish and serve.

From Françoise:

• Canned tomatoes can replace the fresh tomatoes in this dish.

• Keep an eye on the tomatoes as they cook. If the pan begins to dry out, cover it.

CORSICAN SPAGHETTI WITH MEAT SAUCE
- *Pastasciutta corse* -

❖ EASY   ❖ INEXPENSIVE   ❖ 45 MINUTES   ❖ SERVES 4

5 tablespoons butter

2 onions, finely chopped

¾ cup chopped leftover meat

1 pound tomatoes, peeled, seeded, and chopped

1 garlic clove, crushed

1 small red chile

Salt

½ pound spaghetti

¾ cup pitted green olives, sliced

½ cup shredded Gruyère cheese

1. In a large skillet, melt 2 tablespoons of the butter over medium heat. Add the onions and cook until nicely browned. Add the meat, tomatoes, garlic, and chile and season with salt. Bring to a simmer and cook, uncovered, for 30 minutes. Remove the chile.

2. Meanwhile, bring a large saucepan of salted water to a boil. Add the spaghetti and cook, stirring occasionally, until al dente. Drain and return to the pot.

3. Add the sauce, the remaining 3 tablespoons of butter, and the olives and toss to coat. Transfer to a warmed serving dish and serve, passing the cheese at the table.

From Françoise:

• To remove some of the saltiness from the olives, cook them in boiling water for 5 minutes, then drain before adding them.

• Chiles can be more or less spicy, so take care when using them.

• Any kind of leftover meat would work in this dish.

• To peel tomatoes easily, score the bottoms and drop them in boiling water until the skin begins to curl, about 1 minute.

PASTA WITH SIMPLE TOMATO SAUCE
- *Pâtes sautées à l'italienne* -

❖ EASY   ❖ INEXPENSIVE   ❖ 30 MINUTES   ❖ SERVES 4

Salt
½ pound short or long pasta
2 tablespoons butter or olive oil

4 tomatoes, sliced
2 garlic cloves, finely chopped
Pepper

❖   ❖   ❖   ❖   ❖

1. Bring a large saucepan of salted water to a boil. Add the pasta and cook, stirring occasionally, until al dente.

2. Meanwhile, in a large skillet, melt the butter over medium heat. Add the tomatoes and cook until browned, about 5 minutes.

3. Drain the pasta, reserving 1 cup of the water. Add the pasta and garlic to the tomatoes with a little of the reserved water. Season with salt and pepper. Cook for 2 to 3 minutes, until the liquid thickens slightly. Transfer to a warmed serving dish and serve.

From Françoise:

• This pasta is great because it finishes cooking in the sauce, absorbing all the flavor.

• If you like, garnish the dish with finely chopped basil.

• Other quick ideas: You can sauté all kinds of sliced vegetables (zucchini, eggplant, bell peppers) and even shrimp, shellfish, or diced squid, at the last minute in olive oil. Then add the pasta and a little water and cook for a few minutes to blend the flavors.

PASTA
& RICE

PASTA WITH SMOKED HAM AND TOMATO SAUCE
- *Pâtes calabraise* -

❖ EASY ❖ INEXPENSIVE ❖ 25 MINUTES ❖ SERVES 4

Salt

½ pound short or long pasta

2 tablespoons butter

1 onion, finely chopped

3 ½ ounces smoked ham or bacon,
   cut into ¼-inch dice

1 pound tomatoes, peeled, seeded, and chopped

1 garlic clove, crushed

1 bouquet garni made with parsley, thyme,
   and bay leaf

Pepper

½ cup shredded Gruyère or grated
   Parmesan cheese

❖ ❖ ❖ ❖ ❖

1. Bring a large saucepan of salted water to a boil. Add the pasta and cook, stirring occasionally, until al dente.

2. Meanwhile, in another large saucepan, melt the butter over medium heat. Add the onion and ham or bacon and cook until lightly browned. Add the tomatoes, garlic, and bouquet garni. Season with salt and pepper. Cook, uncovered, stirring occasionally, for 15 to 20 minutes. Remove the garlic and bouquet garni.

3. Drain the pasta, add to the sauce, and toss to coat. Transfer to a warmed serving dish, sprinkle with the cheese, and serve.

From Françoise:

• You can also sprinkle the pasta with a blend of Gruyère and Parmesan. The Parmesan adds pungency to the mix, while the Gruyère makes it creamy.

CRUNCHY EGG NOODLES WITH GRUYÈRE
- *Nouilles à l'alsacienne* -

❖ EASY ❖ INEXPENSIVE ❖ 20 MINUTES ❖ SERVES 4

Salt

½ pound wide egg noodles or short pasta

3 tablespoons butter

Pepper

½ cup shredded Gruyère cheese

1. Bring a large saucepan of salted water to a boil. Add three-quarters of the pasta and cook, stirring occasionally, until al dente. Drain. Return the pasta to the pan and, off the heat, swirl in 2 tablespoons of the butter. Season with salt and pepper.

2. In a medium skillet, melt the remaining 1 tablespoon of butter over medium heat. Add the remaining raw pasta and cook, stirring, until nicely browned. Transfer the boiled pasta to a warmed serving dish, top with the fried noodles, sprinkle with the cheese, and serve.

FETTUCCINE WITH MUSSELS AND SHRIMP
- Pâtes aux fruits de mer -

❖ INTERMEDIATE ❖ INEXPENSIVE ❖ 40 MINUTES ❖ SERVES 4

8 pounds mussels, scrubbed and debearded
1 shallot, finely chopped
1 bouquet garni made with parsley, thyme,
   and bay leaf
Salt
½ pound fettuccine, tagliatelle, or linguine
¼ pound small peeled shrimp

SAUCE
2 tablespoons butter
2 tablespoons all-purpose flour
3 tablespoons tomato paste
Salt and pepper

❖ ❖ ❖ ❖ ❖

1. Add the mussels to a pot with the shallot and bouquet garni. Cover and cook over high heat, stirring once or twice, just until they open, 3 to 5 minutes. Remove the pot from the heat. Remove the mussel meat from the shells and reserve. Discard the shells and any unopened mussels. Pour the broth through a fine strainer lined with a moistened paper towel into a glass measuring cup.

2. Bring a large saucepan of salted water to a boil. Add the pasta and cook, stirring occasionally, until al dente.

3. Meanwhile, make the sauce: In a small saucepan, melt the butter over medium heat. Whisk

in the flour until it starts foaming. Whisk in the reserved mussel broth with enough water to make 2 cups, then add the tomato paste. Season with salt and pepper. Bring to a boil, whisking, until thickened. Add the shrimp, reduce the heat to low, and cook for 1 to 2 minutes.

4. Drain the pasta and transfer it with the mussels to a warmed serving dish. Add the sauce and toss to coat. Serve at once.

From Françoise:
• You can also make this dish with cockles. Add them to a large bowl of heavily salted water and let soak for 30 minutes, then drain and proceed with the recipe.

PASTA & RICE

GOLDEN PASTA GRATIN WITH GRUYÈRE
- *Pâtes au gratin* -

❖ EASY ❖ INEXPENSIVE ❖ 30 MINUTES ❖ SERVES 4

Salt
½ pound macaroni, penne, or other short pasta
3 tablespoons butter, cut into ¼-inch dice

½ cup shredded Gruyère cheese
Pepper

❖ ❖ ❖ ❖ ❖

1. Preheat the oven to 425 degrees. Bring a large saucepan of salted water to a boil. Add the pasta and cook, stirring occasionally, until al dente. Drain.

2. Spread the pasta in a gratin dish. Stir in 2 tablespoons of the butter and ¼ cup of the cheese. Season with salt and pepper. Sprinkle with the remaining ¼ cup of cheese and dot with the remaining 1 tablespoon of butter.

3. Transfer to the top shelf of the oven and bake until the cheese is melted and golden, 10 to 15 minutes.

GOLDEN PASTA GRATIN WITH TOMATOES
- *Gratin aux tomates* -

❖ EASY ❖ INEXPENSIVE ❖ 30 MINUTES ❖ SERVES 4

Salt
½ pound macaroni, penne, or other short pasta
1 tablespoon oil
3 tomatoes, peeled, seeded, and chopped

Pepper
½ cup shredded Gruyère cheese
2 tablespoons butter, cut into ¼-inch dice

❖ ❖ ❖ ❖ ❖

1. Preheat the oven to 425 degrees. Bring a large saucepan of salted water to a boil. Add the pasta and cook, stirring occasionally, until al dente. Drain.

2. In a large skillet, heat the oil over medium-high heat until shimmering. Add the tomatoes and cook 2 to 3 minutes, stirring to coat. Stir in the pasta, tossing to coat with the tomatoes. Season with salt and pepper.

3. Spread the pasta in a gratin dish. Sprinkle with the cheese and dot with the butter. Transfer to the top shelf of the oven and bake until the cheese is melted and golden, 8 to 10 minutes.

LAYERED PASTA GRATIN WITH MEAT AND GRUYÈRE
- *Pâtes bonne femme* -

❖ EASY   ❖ INEXPENSIVE   ❖ 35 MINUTES   ❖ SERVES 4

Salt

½ pound short or long pasta

4 tablespoons (½ stick) butter

1 onion, chopped

1 ½ cups beef broth

1 ½ cups chopped leftover meat

1 cup shredded Gruyère cheese

❖ ❖ ❖ ❖ ❖

1. Bring a large saucepan of salted water to a boil. Add the pasta and cook, stirring occasionally, until al dente.

2. Meanwhile, preheat the oven to 425 degrees. In a medium saucepan, melt 1 tablespoon of the butter over medium heat. Add the onion and cook until lightly browned. Add the broth, reduce the heat to medium-low, and cook, uncovered, for 10 minutes.

3. In a large skillet, melt 2 tablespoons of the remaining butter over medium-high heat. Add the meat and cook until heated through.

4. Drain the pasta and return to the pan. Add the onion sauce, reduce the heat to medium-low, and cook for 5 minutes.

5. In a gratin dish, spread half the pasta, half the meat, and half the cheese. Repeat the layering, finishing with the cheese. Dot with the remaining 1 tablespoon of butter. Transfer to the top shelf of the oven and bake until the cheese is melted and nicely browned, 10 to 15 minutes.

From Françoise:
• This recipe is an excellent way of using up leftover beef, veal, or pork, but it's also worth cooking meat deliberately if needed. Simply sauté chopped raw meat in Step 3 until cooked through.

PASTA & RICE

BAKED EGG NOODLES WITH
CHICKEN LIVERS AND GRUYÈRE

- *Nouilles aux foies de volaille* -

✧ EASY ✧ INEXPENSIVE ✧ 30 MINUTES ✧ SERVES 4

Salt
½ pound wide egg noodles
3 tablespoons butter
2 chicken livers, chopped

1 onion, thinly sliced
Pepper
2 tablespoons crème fraîche
¾ cup shredded Gruyère cheese

✧ ✧ ✧ ✧ ✧

1. Bring a large saucepan of salted water to a boil. Add the pasta and cook, stirring occasionally, until al dente. Drain.

2. Meanwhile, in a medium saucepan, melt 1 tablespoon of the butter over medium-high heat. Add the chicken livers and onion and cook until nicely browned. Season with salt and pepper.

3. Heat the broiler. Toss the pasta with the chicken liver mixture, 1 tablespoon of the remaining butter, the crème fraiche, and ½ cup of the cheese. Spread the pasta in a gratin dish, sprinkle with the remaining ¼ cup of cheese, and dot with the remaining 1 tablespoon of butter.

4. Transfer to the top shelf of the oven and broil until the cheese is melted and browned, 3 to 5 minutes.

BAKED PASTA WITH EGGPLANTS, TOMATOES,
AND MUSHROOMS

- *Macaroni à la languedocienne* -

✧ EASY ✧ INEXPENSIVE ✧ 45 MINUTES ✧ SERVES 4

3 small eggplants, sliced crosswise ¼ inch thick
Salt
½ pound macaroni or penne
8 tablespoons (1 stick) butter, plus more
  for brushing
All-purpose flour for dusting

4 or 5 tomatoes, peeled, seeded, and chopped
1 garlic clove, finely chopped
Pepper
½ pound white mushrooms, cut into ¼-inch dice
½ cup shredded Gruyère cheese

1. In a colander, sprinkle the eggplant slices with salt and let them drain for about 30 minutes.

2. Meanwhile, bring a large saucepan of salted water to a boil. Add the pasta and cook, stirring occasionally, until al dente. Drain.

3. Preheat the oven to 425 degrees. Butter a gratin dish.

4. Wipe the eggplant slices with paper towels. Dust lightly with flour, patting off the excess.

5. In a large skillet, melt 6 tablespoons of the butter over medium-high heat. Add the eggplant slices without crowding and cook until nicely browned on both sides. Transfer to a platter as they are done. Repeat with the remaining eggplant. Return the eggplant to the skillet and add the tomatoes and garlic. Season with salt and pepper. Reduce the heat to medium-low, cover, and cook for 10 minutes. Add the mushrooms and cook for 10 minutes.

6. Spread the pasta in the gratin dish. Spoon the vegetables over the top. Sprinkle with the cheese and dot with the remaining 2 tablespoons of butter. Transfer to the top shelf of the oven and bake until the cheese is melted and nicely browned, 10 to 15 minutes.

FRENCH LASAGNA WITH CREAMY MEAT SAUCE
- *Lasagnes farcies au four* -

❖ INTERMEDIATE   ❖ MODERATE   ❖ 1 HOUR   ❖ SERVES 6

MEAT SAUCE
2 tablespoons butter
2 ounces thick-sliced pancetta,
 cut crosswise into ¼-inch-thick strips
½ pound ground beef
1 carrot, peeled and finely chopped
1 onion, finely chopped
1 celery rib, finely chopped
Chopped parsley leaves
¼ pound white mushrooms, finely chopped
1 teaspoon tomato paste
1 cup broth
Salt and pepper

BÉCHAMEL SAUCE
5 tablespoons butter
5 tablespoons all-purpose flour
3 cups milk
Salt and pepper
Freshly grated nutmeg

Salt
½ pound lasagna noodles
½ cup grated Parmesan or shredded
 Gruyère cheese

❖   ❖   ❖   ❖   ❖

1. Make the meat sauce: In a large saucepan, melt the butter over medium heat. Add the pancetta and cook until just beginning to brown. Add the beef and cook, breaking up the meat, until it is cooked through. Push the meat to one side. Add the carrot, onion,

PASTA
& RICE

continued

609

celery, and parsley and cook until softened. Add the mushrooms, tomato paste, and broth and season with pepper and, lightly, with salt. Reduce the heat to medium-low and cook for 20 minutes.

2. Preheat the oven to 350 degrees. Make the béchamel sauce: In a medium saucepan, melt the butter. Whisk in the flour until it starts foaming. Whisk in the milk. Season with salt, pepper, and nutmeg. Bring to a boil, whisking, then reduce the heat to very low and cook for 5 minutes.

3. Bring a large pot of salted water to a boil. Add the lasagna noodles and cook until al dente. Drain carefully. Spread the noodles side by side on a clean kitchen towel.

4. Spread a little of the meat sauce in the bottom of a 9-x-13-inch baking dish or other shallow baking dish. Arrange one-third of the lasagna noodles in a layer in the dish. Spread one-third of the meat sauce on top, then one-third of the béchamel sauce. Sprinkle with one-third of the cheese. Repeat the layering two more times, finishing with the cheese.

5. Transfer the dish to the oven and bake until the cheese is melted and golden, 25 to 30 minutes.

From Françoise:
• This dish can be prepared through Step 4, covered, and refrigerated overnight. Just before serving, bake it in the oven.

• You can use Homemade Cannelloni (page 589) to make this lasagna.

BAKED PASTA WITH HAM AND GRUYÈRE
- Charlotte de pâtes -

❖ INTERMEDIATE ❖ INEXPENSIVE ❖ 30 MINUTES ❖ SERVES 4

3 tablespoons butter, plus more for brushing
4 cups milk
Salt and pepper
½ pound short pasta

2 large eggs
2 ounces baked ham, finely chopped
½ cup shredded Gruyère cheese
Freshly grated nutmeg

❖ ❖ ❖ ❖ ❖

1. Preheat the oven to 350 degrees. Brush a soufflé dish or other deep baking dish with butter.

2. In a large saucepan, bring the milk to a simmer over medium heat. Season with salt and pepper. Add the pasta and cook, stirring occasionally, until al dente. Remove the pan from the heat. Do not drain.

3. In a small saucepan, melt 2 tablespoons of the butter over medium heat. In a bowl, beat the eggs lightly. Beat in the melted butter, the ham, and cheese and season with salt, pepper, and nutmeg. Stir into the pasta. Scrape the pasta mixture into the soufflé dish. Transfer to the oven and bake for 10 to 15 minutes.

4. Invert a round platter over the soufflé dish. Holding the dish and platter together, quickly invert the pasta onto the platter. Serve.

From Françoise:
• If you like, serve with tomato sauce.

• Do not drain the pasta even if it is floating in the milk. Any excess liquid will be absorbed during baking.

• To add an Italian note, stir a little grated Parmesan cheese into the mix.

BAKED PASTA WITH TOMATO SAUCE
- *Pâtes en timbale* -

❖ INTERMEDIATE ❖ INEXPENSIVE ❖ 1 HOUR ❖ SERVES 4

---

2 tablespoons butter, plus more for brushing
Salt
½ pound short pasta
¼ pound white mushrooms, thinly sliced
Pepper
1 slice of baked ham, finely chopped
½ cup shredded Gruyère cheese

TOMATO SAUCE
2 tablespoons butter
2 tablespoons all-purpose flour
1 tablespoon tomato paste
1 tomato, chopped
Salt and pepper

❖ ❖ ❖ ❖ ❖

1. Preheat the oven to 425 degrees. Brush a soufflé dish or other deep baking dish with butter.

2. Make the tomato sauce: In a medium saucepan, melt the butter over medium heat. Whisk in the flour until it starts foaming. Whisk in the tomato paste, tomato, and 2 cups of water. Season with salt and pepper. Bring to a boil, whisking, then reduce the heat to very low and cook for 20 minutes. Puree the sauce using a food mill or food processor.

3. Meanwhile, bring a large saucepan of salted water to a boil. Add the pasta and cook, stirring occasionally, until al dente.

4. In a medium skillet, melt 1 tablespoon of the butter over medium heat. Add the

mushrooms and cook until the juices evaporate and the mushrooms are tender. Season with salt and pepper.

5. Drain the pasta and return to the pan. Off the heat, stir in the mushrooms, ham, and tomato sauce. Scrape the pasta mixture into the soufflé dish. Sprinkle with the cheese and dot with the remaining 1 tablespoon of butter. Transfer to the upper third of the oven and bake for 10 to 15 minutes. Serve hot.

From Françoise:
• The ingredients in this recipe are flexible. You can use pasta or ham leftovers, a different cheese, wild mushrooms. It's all good.

• Do not cover the saucepan when the pasta is cooking; it will boil over.

PASTA & RICE

EGGS BAKED IN PASTA NESTS
- *Nïds de macaroni* -

❖ EASY	❖ INEXPENSIVE	❖ 50 MINUTES	❖ SERVES 4

Salt
2 ounces short-straight tube pasta
Butter for brushing
1 slice baked ham, finely chopped

4 large eggs
Pepper
Shredded Gruyère cheese

❖ ❖ ❖ ❖ ❖

1. Bring a large saucepan of salted water to a boil. Add the pasta and cook, stirring occasionally, until barely al dente. Drain.

2. Preheat the oven to 425 degrees. Generously brush 4 ramekins with butter. Arrange the pasta in a spiral in the bottom of each ramekin, packing it tightly. Line the sides of each ramekin with more pasta, packing it close together. Sprinkle one-quarter of the ham into each ramekin. Break an egg into each. Season with salt and pepper.

3. Set the ramekins in a roasting pan and fill it with boiling water to come halfway up the sides of the ramekins. Transfer to the oven and bake until the egg whites are set and the yolks are still soft, about 12 minutes.

4. Remove the ramekins from the water bath. Invert a round plate over each ramekin. Holding the dish and ramekin together, quickly invert the pasta nest onto the plate. Serve hot, passing the cheese separately.

From Françoise:
• Instead of cheese, you could serve this dish with tomato sauce. Also, try spooning a little crème fraîche and crumbled Roquefort cheese in the ramekin before adding the egg; omit the Gruyère cheese or tomato sauce.

SOFTLY SCRAMBLED EGGS WITH PASTA
- *Brouillade de macaroni* -

❖ EASY	❖ INEXPENSIVE	❖ 25 MINUTES	❖ SERVES 4

Salt
½ pound macaroni or other short pasta
2 tablespoons butter

4 or 6 large eggs
2 slices baked ham, finely chopped
½ cup shredded Gruyère cheese

1. Bring a large saucepan of salted water to a boil. Add the pasta and cook, stirring occasionally, until al dente. Drain.

2. In a large skillet, melt 1 tablespoon of the butter. In a bowl, beat the eggs to mix, then beat in the melted butter, the ham, and cheese.

3. In the same skillet, melt the remaining 1 tablespoon of butter over medium heat. Add the pasta and toss to coat with the butter. Pour in the egg mixture and cook, stirring continuously with a wooden spoon until they thicken creamily.

4. Spoon the eggs into a warmed serving dish and serve immediately.

RICE WITH GRUYÈRE

- *Risotto* -

❖ EASY   ❖ INEXPENSIVE   ❖ 25 MINUTES   ❖ SERVES 4

2 tablespoons butter
1 onion, finely chopped
1 ¼ cups rice
2 ½ cups water or broth

1 bouquet garni made with parsley, thyme, and bay leaf
Salt and pepper
½ cup shredded Gruyère cheese or grated Parmesan cheese

❖ ❖ ❖ ❖ ❖

1. In a medium saucepan, melt the butter over medium-low heat. Add the onion and cook until softened. Stir in the rice. Add the water or broth and the bouquet garni. Season with salt and pepper. Bring to a boil, then reduce the heat to low, cover, and cook until the rice is tender and the water is absorbed, 17 to 20 minutes.

2. Remove the bouquet garni. Add the cheese and fluff the rice. Transfer to a warmed serving dish and serve.

From Françoise:
• This is a good recipe for using up leftovers. If you have any peas in the refrigerator, for instance, add them to the rice with the cheese.

• Serve with eggs, braised meat, or pan-seared sausages.

PASTA & RICE

SAFFRON RICE WITH MUSHROOMS AND PARMESAN

- *Risotto à la milanaise* -

❖ EASY   ❖ INEXPENSIVE   ❖ 25 MINUTES   ❖ SERVES 4

3 tablespoons butter

1 onion, finely chopped

2 ounces mushrooms, finely chopped

1 ¼ cups rice

2 ½ cups water or broth

1 tablespoon tomato paste

Pinch of saffron threads

Salt and pepper

½ cup grated Parmesan cheese or shredded
   Gruyère cheese

❖　❖　❖　❖　❖

1. In a medium saucepan, melt 2 tablespoons of the butter over medium-low heat. Add the onion and mushrooms and cook until softened. Stir in the rice. Add the water or broth, tomato paste, and saffron. Season with salt and pepper. Bring to a boil, then reduce the heat to low, cover, and cook until the rice is tender and the water is absorbed, 17 to 20 minutes.

2. Add 6 tablespoons of the cheese and the remaining 1 tablespoon of butter. Fluff the rice and transfer to a warmed serving dish. Sprinkle the remaining 2 tablespoons of cheese over the top and serve.

RING MOLD OF RICE WITH CREAMY SEAFOOD SAUCE

- *Risotto de fruits de mer* -

❖ INTERMEDIATE   ❖ MODERATE   ❖ 45 MINUTES   ❖ SERVES 4

2 pounds mussels, scrubbed and debearded

Salt and pepper

2 tablespoons butter, plus more for brushing

1 onion, finely chopped

1 ¼ cups rice

2 ½ cups chicken broth

¼ pound lump crabmeat, picked over

SAUCE

1 ½ tablespoons butter

1 ½ tablespoons all-purpose flour

Pinch of saffron threads

Pepper

¼ pound white mushrooms, thinly sliced

1 tablespoon crème fraîche

1. Add the mussels to a large pot and season with salt and pepper. Cover and cook over high heat, stirring once or twice, just until they open, 3 to 5 minutes. Remove the pot from the heat. Remove the mussel meat from the shells and reserve. Discard the shells and any unopened mussels. Pour the broth through a fine strainer lined with a moistened paper towel into a glass measuring cup.

2. In a medium saucepan, melt the butter over medium-low heat. Add the onion and cook until softened. Stir in the rice. Add the chicken broth and season with salt and pepper. Bring to a boil, then reduce the heat to low, cover, and cook until the rice is tender and the water is absorbed, 17 to 20 minutes.

3. Meanwhile, make the sauce: In a large saucepan, melt the butter over medium heat. Whisk in the flour until it starts foaming. Whisk in the saffron and reserved mussel broth with enough water to make 1 cup. Season with pepper. Bring to a boil, whisking, then add the mushrooms, reduce the heat to very low, and cook for 10 minutes.

4. Remove the pan from the heat and stir in the mussels, crab, and crème fraîche.

5. Brush a ring mold with butter and pack in the hot rice. Invert a round platter over the mold. Holding the mold and platter together, quickly invert the rice onto the platter. Pour the sauce in the center of the rice ring and serve.

BOILED RICE

- *Riz nature* -

❖ EASY   ❖ INEXPENSIVE   ❖ 20 MINUTES   ❖ SERVES 4

Salt

2 ¼ cups long-grain rice

❖   ❖   ❖   ❖   ❖

1. Bring a medium saucepan of salted water to a boil.

2. Rinse the rice under cold running water, then drain. Add to the boiling water and cook, uncovered, until tender, 17 to 20 minutes.

3. Drain the rice in a colander under cold running water, then drain again well. Transfer to a warmed serving dish and serve.

From Françoise:

• Taste the rice as it cooks to see if it's tender. It can take more or less time depending on the quality.

• If needed, reheat the rice in a low oven or in a skillet, fluffing it with a fork.

• The secret to rice that's very white: Add a little lemon juice to the cooking water. Boiled rice that's snowy white is more appetizing.

PASTA & RICE

RICE PILAF
- *Riz pilaf* -

❖ EASY   ❖ INEXPENSIVE   ❖ 25 MINUTES   ❖ SERVES 4

2 tablespoons butter
1 onion, finely chopped
1 ¼ cups long-grain or basmati rice
2 ½ cups water or broth

1 bouquet garni made with parsley, thyme,
  and bay leaf
Salt and pepper

❖ ❖ ❖ ❖ ❖

1. In a medium saucepan, melt the butter over medium-low heat. Add the onion and cook until softened. Stir in the rice. Add the water or broth and the bouquet garni. Season with salt and pepper. Bring to a boil, then reduce the heat to low, cover, and cook until the rice is tender and the water is absorbed, 17 to 20 minutes.

2. Remove the bouquet garni. Fluff the rice, transfer to a warmed serving dish, and serve.

From Françoise:

• Check the cooking time on the package of rice.

• Before cooking the rice, rinse it under cold running water, then drain well and dry in a clean kitchen towel.

• Your pilaf will be better if instead of water you moisten it with meat or vegetable broth or, if it's to serve with seafood, the court-bouillon that's been used to poach the fish.

RICE PILAF WITH MUSHROOMS, TOMATOES, AND BELL PEPPER

- *Pilaf à la créole* -

❖ EASY   ❖ INEXPENSIVE   ❖ 25 MINUTES   ❖ SERVES 4

4 tablespoons butter or oil

1 onion, finely chopped

1 ¼ cups long-grain or basmati rice

2 ½ cups water or broth

1 bouquet garni made with parsley, thyme,
   and bay leaf

Salt and pepper

¼ pound white mushrooms, cut into ½-inch dice

2 tomatoes, peeled, seeded, and chopped

1 bell pepper, cut into ½-inch dice

❖ ❖ ❖ ❖ ❖

1. In a medium saucepan, melt 2 tablespoons of the butter or heat the oil over medium-low heat. Add the onion and cook until softened. Stir in the rice. Add the water or broth and the bouquet garni. Season with salt and pepper. Bring to a boil, then reduce the heat to low, cover, and cook until the rice is tender and the water is absorbed, 17 to 20 minutes.

2. In a large skillet, melt the remaining 2 tablespoons of butter or heat the remaining oil over medium-low heat. Add the mushrooms, tomatoes, and bell pepper and cook until softened. Reduce the heat to low, cover, and cook for 10 minutes.

3. Fluff the rice and transfer to a warmed serving dish. Spoon the vegetables over the top and serve.

From Françoise:

• All kinds of mushrooms can be used here; for instance, oyster mushrooms or the wild mushroom mix available at most markets.

PASTA
& RICE

CURRIED RICE WITH POACHED EGGS

- *Riz curry aux oeufs pochés* -

❖ INTERMEDIATE   ❖ INEXPENSIVE   ❖ 30 MINUTES   ❖ SERVES 4

2 tablespoons butter

1 onion, finely chopped

1 ¼ cups long-grain or basmati rice

2 teaspoons curry powder

Salt and pepper

3 tablespoons white vinegar

4 large eggs

❖ ❖ ❖ ❖ ❖

1. In a medium saucepan, melt the butter over medium-low heat. Add the onion and cook until softened. Stir in the rice and curry powder. Add 2 ½ cups of water. Season with salt and pepper. Raise the heat, bring to a boil, then reduce the heat to low and cook until the rice is tender and the water is absorbed, 17 to 20 minutes.

2. In a sauté pan or large saucepan, bring 2 quarts of water to a boil with the vinegar. Reduce the heat to medium and keep it at a gentle boil.

3. Break 1 egg at a time into a cup. Holding the cup close to the water, carefully slide the egg into the pan. Using a spoon, coax the white around the yolk. Poach the eggs over medium heat until the white is set and the yolk is still soft, 3 to 4 minutes. Using a slotted spoon, transfer the eggs to paper towels and keep warm.

4. Fluff the rice and transfer it to a warmed serving dish. Set the poached eggs on top and serve.

From Françoise:

• You can make this into a beginner's recipe by substituting hard-boiled eggs for the poached eggs.

• Chicken broth can replace the water in this pilaf. It's better. But salt carefully, as prepared broth usually is already seasoned.

• I heartily recommend that you add a dollop of crème fraîche over each egg just before serving.

• The heat in curry powder varies, so start out adding a little and add more later, even if it's at the end of cooking.

SPANISH RICE PILAF WITH SAUSAGES, HAM, AND RED PEPPER

- *Riz à la valencienne* -

❖ EASY   ❖ MODERATE   ❖ 25 MINUTES   ❖ SERVES 4

2 tablespoons olive oil

1 onion, finely chopped

1 ¼ cups long-grain or basmati rice

1 tomato, peeled, seeded, and coarsely chopped

1 peeled roasted red bell pepper,
   cut into thin strips

2 artichoke hearts, coarsely chopped

3 ½ ounces dry-cured ham, cut into ¼-inch dice

4 small pork sausages, cut into 1-inch lengths

Salt and pepper

½ cup fresh or frozen petit pois peas

❖ ❖ ❖ ❖ ❖

1. In a flameproof casserole, heat the oil over medium-low heat. Add the onion and cook until softened. Stir in the rice. Add 2 ½ cups of water, the tomato, roasted pepper, artichoke hearts, ham, and sausages. Season with salt and pepper. Bring to a boil, then reduce the heat to low, cover, and cook for 10 minutes.

2. Add the peas and cook until the rice is tender and the water is absorbed, 7 to 10 minutes. Serve in the casserole.

From Françoise:
• You could replace the black pepper with *piment d'Espelette*, the mildly hot ground Basque red pepper.

• For a slightly smoky taste, try Spanish *pimenton de la Vera* or substitute a piquillo pepper for the regular roasted red bell pepper.

• I also like to add a pinch of saffron threads.

• This is a quick recipe to pull together with whatever you have on hand. You can use leftover chicken, vegetables, ham, sausage, and/or olives.

• If you don't want to open a bottle of roasted red peppers just to use one, sometimes you can buy them individually at Italian specialty shops.

PASTA
& RICE

FRENCH PAELLA

- *Paella* -

❖ INTERMEDIATE   ❖ MODERATE   ❖ 2 HOURS   ❖ SERVES 6 TO 8

1 pound mussels, scrubbed and debearded

3 tablespoons butter

1 tablespoon oil

3 ½-pound chicken, cut into 8 serving pieces

5 ounces boneless bottom round veal roast,
    cut into ½-inch dice

5 ounces boneless shoulder end pork loin,
    cut into ½-inch dice

2 onions, chopped

1 red bell pepper, thinly sliced

Salt and pepper

1 or 2 zucchini, halved lengthwise and
    cut into 1-inch pieces

3 tomatoes, peeled, seeded, and coarsely
    chopped

3 ½ ounces chorizo, sliced crosswise

2 garlic cloves, crushed

2 cups rice

Pinch of saffron threads

1 cup fresh or frozen petit pois peas

1 can artichoke bottoms, drained and quartered

1 ½ pounds langoustines

❖ ❖ ❖ ❖ ❖

1. Add the mussels to a large pot, cover, and cook over high heat, stirring once or twice, just until they open, 3 to 5 minutes. Using a slotted spoon, transfer the mussels to a bowl and remove 1 shell from each. Pour the broth through a fine strainer lined with a moistened paper towel into a glass measuring cup.

2. In a very large flameproof casserole, melt the butter in the oil over medium-high heat. Add the chicken, veal, and pork and cook until nicely browned. Add the onions and bell pepper and season with salt and pepper. Reduce the heat to medium, cover, and cook for 10 minutes.

3. Stir in the zucchini, tomatoes, chorizo, garlic, and reserved mussel broth. Reduce the heat to low, cover, and cook for 20 minutes.

4. Add the rice, saffron, and enough water to barely cover the rice. Raise the heat to medium-high and bring to a simmer. Reduce the heat to low, cover, and cook for 10 minutes. Add the peas and artichokes and cook until the rice is tender and the water is absorbed, 10 to 20 minutes. Add the langoustines and mussels in the half shell just long enough to cook the langoustines. Transfer to a large serving dish or a large skillet and serve.

From Françoise:

• Serve sangria as an aperitif, but no hors d'oeuvre. After the paella you can serve a salad if you like and a light dessert such as fruit or ice cream. For wine, pour a chilled rosé or light red wine.

• Paella takes long to make, but it can be prepared through Step 3 a day ahead.

COUSCOUS SALAD WITH TOMATOES, CUCUMBERS, AND HERBS

- *Taboulé* -

❖ EASY   ❖ INEXPENSIVE   ❖ 10 MINUTES, PLUS 2 HOURS CHILLING   ❖ SERVES 4

2 ripe tomatoes (10 ounces), quartered

½ cucumber, quartered

1 small spring onion, quartered

Juice of 1 lemon

2 to 3 tablespoons olive oil, to taste

1 cup mixed chopped mint, parsley, and chives

1 teaspoon salt

Pepper

1 ⅓ cups couscous

Boston lettuce leaves for decorating

❖   ❖   ❖   ❖   ❖

1. In a food processor, finely chop the tomatoes with the cucumber, onion, lemon juice, olive oil, herbs, salt, and pepper.

2. In a medium bowl, toss the couscous with the tomato salad. Cover and refrigerate at least 2 hours or overnight, stirring occasionally.

3. Line a salad bowl with the lettuce. Mound the couscous salad on top and serve.

From Françoise:

• It is sometimes recommended to cover the couscous first with water and let it soak until the liquid is absorbed. The couscous salad will be moister that way. But it's really a matter of taste.

• If you use a seedless cucumber or a small Lebanese cucumber, you do not need to peel it.

PASTA
& RICE

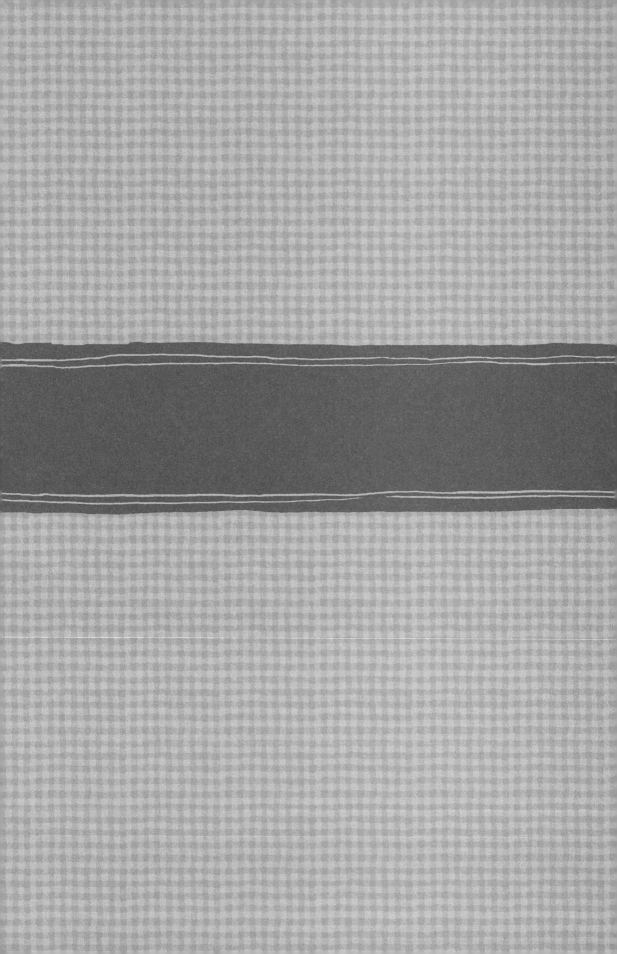

SAUCES

HOMEMADE MAYONNAISE

- *Sauce mayonnaise* -

❖ INTERMEDIATE ❖ INEXPENSIVE ❖ 10 MINUTES ❖ SERVES 4

1 large egg yolk
1 teaspoon Dijon mustard
¾ cup oil

1 teaspoon to 1 tablespoon vinegar
Salt and pepper

❖ ❖ ❖ ❖ ❖

1. In a small bowl, whisk the egg yolk with the mustard. Blend in the oil a few drops at a time to begin, then in a steady stream. Beat in the vinegar, to taste, and season with salt and pepper.

From Françoise:
• Please note that the finished dish contains raw egg.

• Just before serving, beat in 1 teaspoon of boiling water. The sauce will be lighter and will hold better.

• All the ingredients for mayonnaise must be at room temperature.

• If your mayonnaise separates, it may be because the ingredients weren't all at the same temperature; the oil was added too quickly at the beginning; or you added too much oil in proportion to the egg yolk.

• Mayonnaise prepared with an electric mixer uses a whole egg—the white as well as the yolk—but otherwise the same quantities as in this recipe. However, you add everything to the bowl at the same time, even the oil, then beat a few seconds until emulsified.

• Mayonnaise can be used to coat a cold dish, such as fish, chicken, vegetables, or hard-boiled eggs. All you need to do is beat in a little plain powdered gelatin that has been melted in warm water and then allowed to cool but is still liquid.

• To make a lemon mayonnaise, simply use fresh lemon juice in place of the vinegar.

EVAPORATED MILK MAYONNAISE

- *Sauce mayonnaise au lait condensé* -

❖ EASY   ❖ INEXPENSIVE   ❖ 10 MINUTES   ❖ SERVES 4

1 tablespoon evaporated milk

¾ cup oil

1 teaspoon Dijon mustard

1 teaspoon to 1 tablespoon vinegar or
   fresh lemon juice

Salt and pepper

❖ ❖ ❖ ❖ ❖

1. In a small bowl, whisk the evaporated milk until frothy. Gradually add the oil, whisking until incorporated. Beat in the mustard and vinegar or lemon juice and season with salt and pepper.

From Françoise:

• This recipe allows you to make mayonnaise without using a raw egg yolk.

• The mustard and the pepper can be replaced with chopped herbs, 1 or 2 finely chopped garlic cloves or shallots, or anchovy puree.

• All the ingredients must be at room temperature.

• Using lemon juice instead of vinegar will make the mayonnaise whiter.

GREEN MAYONNAISE

- *Sauce verte* -

❖ INTERMEDIATE   ❖ INEXPENSIVE   ❖ 30 MINUTES   ❖ SERVES 4

2 ounces baby spinach

2 ounces watercress leaves

1 teaspoon mixed parsley, chervil, chives,
   and tarragon leaves

1 large egg yolk

1 teaspoon Dijon mustard

¾ cup oil

1 teaspoon to 1 tablespoon vinegar or
   fresh lemon juice

Salt and pepper

❖ ❖ ❖ ❖ ❖

1. Bring a large saucepan of water to a boil. Add the spinach, watercress, and herbs and cook for 5 minutes. Drain and squeeze out as much water as possible. Using the back of a spoon, press the greens through a fine sieve into a bowl. Refrigerate until chilled.

continued

2. In a small bowl, whisk the egg yolk with the mustard. Blend in the oil a few drops at a time to begin, then in a steady stream. Beat in the vinegar or lemon juice and season with salt and pepper.

3. Stir the chilled herb puree into the mayonnaise.

From Françoise:
• Please note that the finished dish contains raw egg.

• Since this is a kind of mayonnaise, the same precautions apply. All the ingredients need to be at the same temperature, whether room temperature or cold. Just take them out of the refrigerator 15 minutes before beginning the recipe and you won't have any problem.

• This is a great sauce for simple dishes like poached fish fillets or hard-boiled eggs.

TARTAR SAUCE

- Sauce tartare -

❖ INTERMEDIATE ❖ INEXPENSIVE ❖ 15 MINUTES ❖ SERVES 4

1 large egg yolk
1 teaspoon Dijon mustard
¾ cup oil
1 teaspoon to 1 tablespoon vinegar
4 or 5 cornichons, thinly sliced

1 small onion, finely chopped
1 to 2 teaspoons capers, chopped
1 tablespoon mixed finely chopped parsley, chervil, tarragon, and chives
Salt and pepper

❖ ❖ ❖ ❖ ❖

1. In a small bowl, whisk the egg yolk with the mustard. Blend in the oil a few drops at a time to begin, then in a steady stream. Beat in the vinegar, cornichons, onion, capers, and herbs. Season with pepper and, lightly, with salt.

From Françoise:
• Please note that the finished dish contains raw egg.

• Tartar sauce is typically made with a hard-boiled egg yolk, but I like to use a raw egg yolk because the sauce is easier to make and holds up better.

• Serve with cold meats or fish.

MAYONNAISE WITH CORNICHONS, CAPERS, AND FINES HERBES

- *Sauce gribiche* -

❖ INTERMEDIATE   ❖ INEXPENSIVE   ❖ 15 MINUTES   ❖ SERVES 4

1 large hard-boiled egg yolk

1 teaspoon Dijon mustard

¾ cup oil

1 teaspoon to 1 tablespoon vinegar

4 or 5 cornichons, finely chopped

4 or 5 capers, chopped

1 tablespoon mixed finely chopped parsley, chervil, tarragon, and chives

Salt and pepper

❖ ❖ ❖ ❖ ❖

1. In a small bowl, mash the egg yolk with the mustard. Blend in the oil a few drops at a time to begin, then in a steady stream. Beat in the vinegar, cornichons, capers, and herbs. Season with pepper and, lightly, with salt.

From Françoise:

• For the chopped herbs, you can use all of them or only one, depending on what's available.

• You could also add capers and the hard-boiled egg white, finely chopped, at the same time as the cornichons, as well as a squeeze of lemon juice.

• Serve with cold fish, or calf's head or feet.

ROQUEFORT MAYONNAISE

- *Mayonnaise-mousseline au roquefort* -

❖ INTERMEDIATE   ❖ INEXPENSIVE   ❖ 15 MINUTES   ❖ SERVES 4

6 tablespoons crumbled Roquefort cheese (about 1 ½ ounces)

3 tablespoons thick fromage blanc or yogurt

1 large egg yolk

1 teaspoon Dijon mustard

¾ cup oil

Salt and pepper

Cayenne pepper (optional)

SAUCES

continued

1. Using the back of a spoon, press the cheese through a sieve into a bowl. Beat in the fromage blanc or yogurt.

2. In a small bowl, whisk the egg yolk with the mustard. Blend in the oil a few drops at a time to begin, then in a steady stream. Season with salt, pepper, and cayenne, if using.

3. Stir the cheese mixture into the mayonnaise. Taste for seasoning.

From Françoise:

• Please note that the finished dish contains raw egg.

• This mayonnaise would be a good partner to hard-boiled eggs, cold boiled asparagus, artichoke bottoms, or cold poached fish. You could even serve it as a dipping sauce for vegetables like celery sticks, tomatoes, and crunchy romaine lettuce leaves.

• For a more pungent flavor, use Stilton cheese in place of the Roquefort.

SPICY MAYONNAISE
- *Rouille* -

❖ INTERMEDIATE ❖ INEXPENSIVE ❖ 15 MINUTES ❖ SERVES 4

¼ cup fresh bread crumbs
¾ cup milk
1 or 2 garlic cloves

1 small red chile or cayenne pepper to taste
Salt
6 tablespoons olive oil

❖ ❖ ❖ ❖ ❖

1. In a bowl, soak the bread crumbs in the milk, then squeeze out as much milk as possible, discarding the milk. Using a mortar or small food processor, grind the garlic and chile, if using, to a paste. Add the bread crumbs, salt, and cayenne pepper, if using, and puree. Blend in the olive oil a few drops at a time to begin, then in a steady stream.

From Françoise:

• I often flavor my rouille with saffron, which also gives the sauce a golden color.

• Serve with bouillabaisse or fish soup. You can also spread it on toasts to serve with drinks, preferably pastis.

GARLICKY MAYONNAISE

- *Sauce aïoli* -

❖ INTERMEDIATE ❖ INEXPENSIVE ❖ 15 MINUTES ❖ SERVES 8

5 to 7 garlic cloves
1 large egg yolk
Salt and pepper

1 ½ cups olive oil
1 tablespoon fresh lemon juice

❖ ❖ ❖ ❖ ❖

1. Using a mortar or small food processor, grind the garlic to a paste. Add the egg yolk, salt, and pepper and puree. Blend in the olive oil a few drops at a time to begin, then in a steady stream. Beat in 1 tablespoon of boiling water and the lemon juice.

From Françoise:
• Please note that the finished dish contains raw egg.

• Since this is a kind of mayonnaise, the same precautions apply. All the ingredients need to be at the same temperature.

• You can use more or less garlic to taste.

• Aïoli sauce is traditionally served as part of a "grand aïoli," a special-occasion dish with boiled cauliflower florets, new potatoes, carrots, green beans, and more.

• Serve with all cold meats, cold poached fish, hard-boiled eggs, cod, boiled beef, or vegetables.

CLASSIC PESTO

- *Sauce pesto* -

❖ EASY ❖ INEXPENSIVE ❖ 15 MINUTES ❖ SERVES 4

4 or 5 garlic cloves
Salt and pepper
1 large bunch of basil, stems removed
1 tablespoon pine nuts

2 tablespoons grated Parmesan cheese
7 tablespoons olive oil

continued

SAUCES

1. In a mortar or mini food processor, puree the garlic. Season with salt and pepper. Gradually add the basil leaves and pine nuts, working the ingredients to a paste. Add the cheese. Gradually blend in the olive oil as for a mayonnaise.

From Françoise:

• Serve with pasta, salads, soups, or meat.

• You can also add peeled, seed, and chopped tomatoes to the mix with the basil.

SHALLOT, HERB, AND CAPER VINAIGRETTE
- *Sauce ravigote* -

❖ EASY ❖ INEXPENSIVE ❖ 10 MINUTES ❖ SERVES 4

1 tablespoon vinegar
3 tablespoons oil
Salt and pepper
1 shallot or small onion, finely chopped

1 to 2 tablespoons mixed chopped chervil,
 tarragon, and chives
1 teaspoon small capers

❖ ❖ ❖ ❖ ❖

1. In a medium bowl, whisk the vinegar with the oil and season with salt and pepper. Beat in the shallot or onion, herbs, and capers.

From Françoise:

• Serve this pungent vinaigrette with calf's head or feet, cold meats, or fish.

• Cut the herbs into a glass using scissors. It's simple and the herbs stay fresh longer.

CLASSIC HOLLANDAISE SAUCE
- *Sauce hollandaise* -

❖ ADVANCED ❖ INEXPENSIVE ❖ 15 MINUTES ❖ SERVES 4

2 large egg yolks
Salt and pepper

A few drops of fresh lemon juice
7 tablespoons butter, cut into pieces

1. In a small, heavy saucepan, whisk the egg yolks with 2 tablespoons of cold water until light, about 30 seconds. Season with salt, pepper, and lemon juice. Set the pan over very low heat and whisk constantly until the mixture thickens and becomes fluffy. Remove the pan from the heat and gradually add the butter, whisking so it melts creamily. Keep the sauce warm in a water bath.

From Françoise:
• Some cooks wait to add the lemon juice until just before serving. After much experience, I learned to do just the opposite. I've found that if I add the lemon juice at the beginning, the sauce seems to emulsify much more easily.

• You can make a hollandaise sauce by setting the saucepan in a hot water bath instead of directly over the heat. It takes longer for the sauce to emulsify, but it's less likely to curdle.

• A hollandaise sauce cannot be reheated. If you can't serve it at once, keep it warm in a tepid water bath—you should be able to put your finger in the water without burning yourself. If the water bath is too hot, the sauce will separate.

• Serve with poached fish, asparagus, or artichoke bottoms.

ORANGE HOLLANDAISE SAUCE

- *Sauce maltaise* -

❖ ADVANCED   ❖ INEXPENSIVE   ❖ 15 MINUTES   ❖ SERVES 4

2 large egg yolks
Salt and pepper
A few drops of fresh lemon juice

7 tablespoons butter, cut into pieces
2 tablespoons fresh orange juice
Finely grated orange zest

❖ ❖ ❖ ❖ ❖

1. In a small, heavy saucepan, whisk the egg yolks with 2 tablespoons of cold water until light, about 30 seconds. Season with salt, pepper, and lemon juice. Set the pan over very low heat and whisk constantly until the mixture thickens and becomes fluffy. Remove the pan from the heat and gradually add the butter, whisking so it melts creamily. Whisk in the orange juice and zest. Keep the sauce warm in a water bath.

From Françoise:
• Serve with asparagus.

• If you use a blood orange, you'll get a beautiful rosy sauce.

• This sauce cannot be reheated. If you can't serve it at once, keep it warm in a tepid—not hot—water bath.

SAUCES

CREAMY HOLLANDAISE SAUCE

- *Sauce mousseline* -

❖ ADVANCED ❖ INEXPENSIVE ❖ 15 MINUTES ❖ SERVES 4

2 large egg yolks
Salt and pepper
A few drops of fresh lemon juice

7 tablespoons butter, cut into pieces
2 or 3 tablespoons crème fraîche

❖ ❖ ❖ ❖ ❖

1. In a small, heavy saucepan, whisk the egg yolks with 2 tablespoons of cold water until light, about 30 seconds. Season with salt, pepper, and lemon juice. Set the pan over very low heat and whisk constantly until the mixture thickens and becomes fluffy. Remove the pan from the heat and gradually add the butter, whisking so it melts creamily. Whisk in the crème fraîche. Keep the sauce warm in a water bath.

From Françoise:

• The sauce is even better if you whip the crème fraîche to soft peaks before folding it in.

• Serve with poached fish or asparagus.

• Mousseline sauce is sometimes the name used for a béchamel or white sauce enriched with crème fraîche. It's also very good and much easier to make.

CLASSIC BÉARNAISE SAUCE

- *Sauce béarnaise* -

❖ ADVANCED ❖ INEXPENSIVE ❖ 30 MINUTES ❖ SERVES 4

3 tablespoons vinegar
2 shallots, finely chopped
1 teaspoon chopped tarragon leaves

2 large egg yolks
Salt and pepper
7 tablespoons butter, cut into pieces

❖ ❖ ❖ ❖ ❖

1. In a small, heavy saucepan, simmer the vinegar with the shallots and tarragon until the liquid evaporates.

2. Remove the pan from the heat and let cool slightly. Whisk in the egg yolks with 2 tablespoons of cold water until light, about

30 seconds. Season with salt and pepper. Set the pan over very low heat and whisk constantly until the mixture thickens and becomes fluffy. Remove the pan from the heat and gradually add the butter, whisking so it melts creamily. Keep the sauce warm in a water bath.

From Françoise:
• Make this sauce just before serving because it cannot be reheated.

• The secrets to a successful béarnaise sauce: Use a whisk and use a saucepan with a heavy bottom, such as enameled cast iron.

• If you don't have fresh tarragon, use tarragon vinegar.

• You can make a béarnaise sauce by setting the saucepan in a hot water bath instead of directly over the heat. It takes longer for the sauce to emulsify, but it's less likely to curdle.

• Serve with sautéed or grilled steak, poached or hard-boiled eggs, or grilled or fried fish.

SPICY SHALLOT SAUCE
- *Sauce diable* -

❖ EASY   ❖ INEXPENSIVE   ❖ 15 MINUTES   ❖ SERVES 4

1 ½ cups dry white wine
2 shallots, finely chopped
½ cup concentrated beef broth
Pepper

Pinch of cayenne pepper
1 teaspoon flavored Dijon mustard
2 tablespoons ketchup (optional)

❖ ❖ ❖ ❖ ❖

1. In a medium saucepan, boil the wine with the shallots until the liquid is reduced by half, about 10 minutes. Add the broth, pepper, and cayenne and boil for 3 minutes. Remove the pan from the heat and whisk in the mustard and, if using, the ketchup.

From Françoise:
• To get ½ cup of concentrated beef broth, simmer the broth until reduced by one-third or half.

• Make this sauce just before serving.

• Serve with crusty mustard-grilled chicken or squab, breaded meat or chicken cutlets, breaded pig's feet, grilled fish.

• Adding mixed chopped herbs (parsley, chives, tarragon, chervil) at the last minute gives this pungent sauce even more flavor.

SAUCES

CLASSIC BÉCHAMEL SAUCE
- *Sauce Béchamel* -

❖ EASY ❖ INEXPENSIVE ❖ 15 MINUTES ❖ SERVES 4

3 tablespoons butter
3 tablespoons all-purpose flour

2 cups milk
Salt and pepper

❖ ❖ ❖ ❖ ❖

1. In a medium saucepan, melt the butter over medium heat. Whisk in the flour until it starts foaming. Whisk in the milk. Season with salt and pepper. Bring to a boil, whisking, then reduce the heat to very low and cook for 10 minutes.

From Françoise:
• A pinch of freshly grated nutmeg adds a delicate flavor to mild béchamel sauce.

• To make a creamy béchamel sauce, whisk in 2 or 3 tablespoons of crème fraîche at the very end and, if you like, a little fresh lemon juice.

• Serve béchamel sauce with poached or hard-boiled eggs, white meats, poached fish, or most boiled vegetables.

• It's much better to mix the sauce with a whisk than a wooden spoon because it's quicker and helps prevent lumps.

ROSY BÉCHAMEL SAUCE
- *Sauce Aurore* -

❖ EASY ❖ INEXPENSIVE ❖ 15 MINUTES ❖ SERVES 4

3 tablespoons butter
3 tablespoons all-purpose flour
2 cups milk

Salt and pepper
1 teaspoon tomato paste

❖ ❖ ❖ ❖ ❖

1. In a medium saucepan, melt the butter over medium heat. Whisk in the flour until it starts foaming. Whisk in the milk. Season with salt and pepper. Bring to a boil, whisking, then reduce the heat to very low and cook for 10 minutes. Beat in the tomato paste and serve.

From Françoise:
• Serve with poached or hard-boiled eggs, poached fish, white meats, or some boiled vegetables like cauliflower.

CLASSIC MORNAY SAUCE
- *Sauce Mornay* -

❖ EASY ❖ INEXPENSIVE ❖ 15 MINUTES ❖ SERVES 4

3 tablespoons butter
3 tablespoons all-purpose flour
2 cups milk

½ cup shredded Gruyère cheese
Pepper

❖ ❖ ❖ ❖ ❖

1. In a medium saucepan, melt the butter over medium heat. Whisk in the flour until it starts foaming. Whisk in the milk. Season with pepper. Bring to a boil, whisking, then reduce the heat to very low and cook for 5 to 10 minutes. Remove the pan from the heat and beat in the cheese. Season carefully with salt.

From Françoise:
• Once the cheese is added, do not return the sauce to the heat.

• Serve with white meats or, especially, poached or hard-boiled eggs, poached fish, or some boiled vegetables, including potatoes, cauliflower florets, boiled salad greens, spinach, or carrots.

• Since the cheese has salt in it, taste the sauce after the cheese has been added before seasoning to see if additional salt is needed.

CREAMY ONION SAUCE
- *Sauce Soubise* -

❖ EASY ❖ INEXPENSIVE ❖ 45 MINUTES ❖ SERVES 4

½ pound onions, thinly sliced
4 tablespoons (½ stick) butter
3 tablespoons all-purpose flour

2 cups milk
Salt and pepper

❖ ❖ ❖ ❖ ❖

1. Bring a large saucepan of water to a boil. Add the onions and cook for 10 minutes. Drain well. In a medium saucepan, melt 1 tablespoon of the butter over low heat. Add the onions, cover, and cook for 10 minutes.

2. In another medium saucepan, melt the remaining 3 tablespoons of butter over medium heat. Whisk in the flour until it starts foaming.

continued

Whisk in the milk. Season with salt and pepper. Bring to a boil, whisking. Add the onions, reduce the heat to very low, and cook for 10 minutes.

From Françoise:
• The onions should remain perfectly white. You might add a tablespoon or two of water to the pan with the onions and butter in Step 1 to keep them from coloring.

• Sweet onions do not need to be blanched first. Add them directly to the butter in Step 1.

• For a smooth sauce, press it through a sieve.

• Serve with hard-boiled or poached eggs, veal cutlets or chops, poultry, and vegetables such as potatoes or artichoke bottoms.

• I like to add crème fraîche to my Soubise sauce just before serving.

• To make a tomato-onion sauce, whisk a tablespoon of tomato paste into the sauce at the end.

VELVETY SAUCE
- *Sauce ivoire* -

❖ EASY   ❖ INEXPENSIVE   ❖ 15 MINUTES   ❖ SERVES 4

3 tablespoons butter
3 tablespoons all-purpose flour
2 cups chicken broth

Pepper
2 large egg yolks
2 tablespoons crème fraîche

❖ ❖ ❖ ❖ ❖

1. In a medium saucepan, melt the butter over medium heat. Whisk in the flour until it starts foaming. Whisk in the broth. Season with pepper. Bring to a boil, whisking, then reduce the heat to very low and cook for 10 minutes.

2. In a cup, blend the egg yolks with the crème fraîche. Remove the pan from the heat and whisk in the yolk mixture.

From Françoise:
• Do not add salt without tasting the finished sauce first because chicken broth is usually already salted.

• Serve with poultry.

SILKY MUSTARD SAUCE

- *Sauce moutarde* -

❖ EASY ❖ INEXPENSIVE ❖ 15 MINUTES ❖ SERVES 4

4 tablespoons (½ stick) butter

3 tablespoons all-purpose flour

2 cups meat broth or water

Salt and pepper

1 tablespoon Dijon mustard

Chopped parsley leaves

❖ ❖ ❖ ❖ ❖

1. In a medium saucepan, melt 3 tablespoons of the butter over medium heat. Whisk in the flour until it starts foaming. Whisk in the broth or water. Season with salt and pepper. Bring to a boil, whisking, then reduce the heat to very low and cook for 10 minutes.

2. Remove the pan from the heat and whisk in the mustard, the remaining 1 tablespoon of butter, and the parsley.

From Françoise:

• To make a really simple mustard sauce, whisk mustard with salt, pepper, and lemon juice, then gradually blend in crème fraîche as for a mayonnaise.

• Serve with fish.

BASIC WHITE SAUCE

- *Sauce blanche* -

❖ EASY ❖ INEXPENSIVE ❖ 15 MINUTES ❖ SERVES 4

3 tablespoons butter

3 tablespoons all-purpose flour

2 cups meat broth

Salt and pepper

❖ ❖ ❖ ❖ ❖

1. In a medium saucepan, melt the butter over medium heat. Whisk in the flour until it starts foaming. Whisk in the broth. Season with salt and pepper. Bring to a boil, whisking, then reduce the heat to very low and cook for 10 minutes.

SAUCES

continued

• Either beat the broth, cold, into the hot butter-and-flour roux or, alternatively, beat hot broth into a cooled roux and you'll never have lumps.

• If you serve this white sauce with poached fish, replace the meat broth with fish broth. You won't need to add salt since the fish broth is already seasoned.

RICH CURRY SAUCE

- *Sauce au curry* -

❖ EASY   ❖ INEXPENSIVE   ❖ 15 MINUTES   ❖ SERVES 4

3 tablespoons butter

3 tablespoons all-purpose flour

1 to 2 teaspoons curry powder

2 cups broth or water

Salt and pepper

1 or 2 tablespoons crème fraîche

❖ ❖ ❖ ❖ ❖

1. In a medium saucepan, melt the butter over medium heat. Whisk in the flour and curry powder until it starts foaming. Whisk in the broth or water. Season with salt and pepper. Bring to a boil, whisking, then reduce the heat to very low and cook for 10 minutes. Beat in the crème fraîche, bring to a simmer, and serve.

From Françoise:

• Curry powders can vary in heat, so add it gradually to taste. The crème fraîche mellows its pungency.

• Serve with white meats like veal or boiled hen, poached or hard-boiled eggs, poached fish, or, especially, rice.

CREAMY CAPER SAUCE

- *Sauce aux câpres* -

❖ EASY   ❖ INEXPENSIVE   ❖ 15 MINUTES   ❖ SERVES 4

5 tablespoons butter

3 tablespoons all-purpose flour

2 cups fish broth

Pepper

1 large egg yolk

1 or 2 tablespoons small capers

1. In a medium saucepan, melt 3 tablespoons of the butter over medium heat. Whisk in the flour until it starts foaming. Whisk in the broth. Season with pepper. Bring to a boil, whisking, then reduce the heat to very low and cook for 10 minutes.

2. Meanwhile, in a cup, whisk the egg yolk with the capers. Whisk in a little of the hot sauce, then whisk this mixture into the remaining sauce. Do not let it boil.

3. Remove the pan from the heat and whisk in the remaining 2 tablespoons of butter until it melts creamily. Serve at once.

From Françoise:
• Some cooks like to enrich this caper sauce with a little milk. Personally, I prefer to whisk in crème fraîche. It's not essential, though, if you don't like it.

• Serve with poached fish.

CLASSIC POULETTE SAUCE
- *Sauce poulette* -

❖ EASY ❖ INEXPENSIVE ❖ 20 MINUTES ❖ SERVES 4

3 tablespoons butter
¼ pound mushrooms, thinly sliced
3 tablespoons all-purpose flour
2 cups chicken, beef, or fish broth

Salt and pepper
1 or 2 large egg yolks
Juice of ½ lemon

❖ ❖ ❖ ❖ ❖

1. In a medium saucepan, melt the butter over medium heat. Add the mushrooms and cook until tender. Whisk in the flour and cook until it starts foaming. Whisk in the broth and season with salt and pepper. Bring to a boil, whisking, then reduce the heat to very low and cook for 10 minutes.

2. In a small bowl, blend the egg yolks with the lemon juice. Whisk 2 or 3 tablespoons of the hot sauce into the yolk mixture. Remove the pan from the heat and whisk in the yolk mixture. Serve at once.

From Françoise:
• If you have leftover meat pan juices or beef, chicken, or seafood broth, use it to make this sauce, depending on what you're serving it with.

• You can add chopped parsley leaves just before serving.

• Serve with off-cuts like calf's head or lamb's feet or boiled chicken, mussels, or cockles.

RICH SAUCE

- *Sauce bâtarde* -

❖ EASY   ❖ INEXPENSIVE   ❖ 15 MINUTES   ❖ SERVES 4

5 tablespoons butter
3 tablespoons all-purpose flour
Salt and pepper

1 or 2 large egg yolks
1 tablespoon crème fraîche
1 tablespoon fresh lemon juice

❖ ❖ ❖ ❖ ❖

1. In a medium saucepan, melt 3 tablespoons of the butter over medium heat. Whisk in the flour until it starts foaming. Whisk in 2 cups of water. Season with salt and pepper. Bring to a boil, whisking, then reduce the heat to very low and cook for 10 minutes.

2. In a bowl, whisk the egg yolks with the crème fraîche and lemon juice. Whisk in a little of the hot sauce, then whisk this mixture into the remaining sauce until it thickens slightly. Do not let it boil. Remove the pan from the heat and whisk in the remaining 2 tablespoons of butter until it melts creamily.

From Françoise:

• You can make this sauce more or less rich by adding or cutting back on the egg yolks and crème fraîche.

• The long, slow cooking in Step 1 makes the sauce more refined, but beyond 15 minutes the sauce may separate.

• Do not return the sauce to the heat once the butter has been added in Step 2.

• Serve with poached fish or some vegetables such as cauliflower, potatoes, or celery.

MADEIRA SAUCE

- *Sauce madère* -

❖ EASY   ❖ MODERATE   ❖ 25 MINUTES   ❖ SERVES 4

5 tablespoons butter
¼ pound small white mushrooms,
  quartered lengthwise
1 onion, finely chopped

¼ cup all-purpose flour
1 cup dry white wine
Salt and pepper
¼ cup Madeira

1. In a medium saucepan, melt 4 tablespoons of the butter over medium heat. Add the mushrooms and onion and cook until softened. Whisk in the flour and cook until it starts foaming. Whisk in the wine and 2 cups of water and season with salt and pepper. Bring to a boil, whisking, then reduce the heat to very low and cook for 15 minutes.

2. Remove the pan from the heat. Whisk in the Madeira, then whisk in the remaining 1 tablespoon of butter until it melts creamily.

From Françoise:

• Since not everyone likes the taste of Madeira, you could substitute another fortified wine like port or sherry.

• The sauce should be fairly thick at the end of Step 1. The addition of Madeira in Step 2 thins it out and adds flavor.

• Serve with beef tenderloin or roast beef or with reheated ham, veal, beef tongue, or sweetbreads.

RED WINE SAUCE WITH MUSHROOMS
- *Sauce bourguignonne* -

❖ EASY　　　　❖ INEXPENSIVE　　　　❖ 30 MINUTES　　　　❖ SERVES 4

2 ½ cups full-bodied red wine

2 shallots, chopped

1 bouquet garni made with parsley, thyme,
  and bay leaf

3 tablespoons butter

3 tablespoons all-purpose flour

Salt and pepper

Cayenne pepper

4 or 5 white mushrooms, thinly sliced

❖　❖　❖　❖　❖

1. In a medium saucepan, combine the wine with the shallots and bouquet garni. Bring to a simmer over medium heat and cook at a gentle boil, uncovered, until reduced to 2 cups, about 10 minutes.

2. In another medium saucepan, melt the butter over medium heat. Whisk in the flour until it starts foaming. Strain in the 2 cups of wine, whisking. Season with salt, pepper, and cayenne. Bring to a boil, whisking, then reduce the heat to very low and cook for 15 minutes. Add the mushrooms and cook for 5 minutes. Serve.

From Françoise:

• This sauce is also called "matelote."

• Boiling the wine with the shallots and bouquet garni concentrates the flavor and adds complexity.

• Serve with poached or hard-boiled eggs or river fish.

SAUCES

ZESTY TOMATO SAUCE

- *Sauce piquante* -

❖ EASY   ❖ INEXPENSIVE   ❖ 35 MINUTES   ❖ SERVES 4

4 tablespoons (½ stick) butter

3 tablespoons all-purpose flour

1 tablespoon tomato paste

1 tomato, chopped

2 cups concentrated meat broth

1 shallot, finely chopped

6 tablespoons dry white wine

6 tablespoons vinegar

Black peppercorns

3 cornichons, thinly sliced

1 tablespoon mixed chopped parsley and
  tarragon leaves

❖ ❖ ❖ ❖ ❖

1. In a medium saucepan, melt 3 tablespoons of the butter over medium heat. Whisk in the flour until it starts foaming. Whisk in the tomato paste, tomato, and broth. Bring to a boil, whisking, then reduce the heat to very low, partly cover, and cook for 20 minutes.

2. In a small saucepan, combine the shallot with the wine, vinegar, and peppercorns. Cook over medium heat until reduced by half. Stir into the sauce and cook for 10 minutes. Press the sauce through a fine strainer. Just before serving, stir in the cornichons, herbs, and remaining 1 tablespoon of butter.

From Françoise:

• To get 2 cups of concentrated beef broth, simmer the broth until reduced by one-third or half.

• If you don't have any fresh tarragon, use tarragon-infused vinegar.

• Serve with off-cuts or organ meats like tongue, calf's head, or grilled pig's feet or with pork chops or boiled beef.

TOMATO-MUSHROOM SAUCE

- Sauce chasseur -

❖ EASY   ❖ INEXPENSIVE   ❖ 25 MINUTES   ❖ SERVES 4

3 tablespoons butter

¼ pound white mushrooms, thinly sliced

2 shallots, finely chopped

3 tablespoons all-purpose flour

1 cup dry white wine

1½ cups broth or water

1 tablespoon tomato paste

1 bouquet garni made with parsley, thyme, and bay leaf

Salt and pepper

Chopped parsley, chervil, or tarragon leaves for sprinkling

❖ ❖ ❖ ❖ ❖

1. In a medium saucepan, melt the butter over medium heat. Add the mushrooms and cook until tender. Stir in the shallots. Stir in the flour and cook until it starts foaming. Add the wine, broth or water, tomato paste, and bouquet garni. Season with salt and pepper. Cover and bring to a simmer, then reduce the heat to low and cook for 15 minutes.

2. Remove the bouquet garni. Sprinkle with the herbs and serve.

From Françoise:

• For a more deeply flavored sauce, it's always better to add chicken or meat broth instead of water.

• Serve with pan-seared meats such as beef tenderloin, cutlets, pot-roasted chicken, or rabbit.

EASY TOMATO SAUCE

- Sauce tomate italienne -

❖ EASY   ❖ INEXPENSIVE   ❖ 30 MINUTES   ❖ SERVES 4

1 tablespoon plus 1 teaspoon butter

1 garlic clove, finely chopped

2 shallots, finely chopped

2 ounces pancetta, finely chopped

1 cup dry white wine

6-ounce can tomato paste

1 bouquet garni made with parsley, thyme, and bay leaf

Salt and pepper

1 teaspoon all-purpose flour

continued

1. In a medium saucepan, melt the 1 tablespoon of butter over medium heat. Add the garlic, shallots, and pancetta and cook until just beginning to brown. Add the wine, 1 ½ cups water, the tomato paste, and bouquet garni. Season with salt and pepper. Reduce the heat to medium-low and cook, uncovered, for 20 minutes.

2. In a cup, mash the flour with the remaining 1 teaspoon of butter. Gradually whisk this paste into the simmering sauce until it thickens slightly. Remove the bouquet garni and serve.

From Françoise:

• If the sauce seems a little acidic, add a teaspoon of sugar.

• Serve with boiled beef, meatballs, or grilled pork chops; tongue, liver, brains, or grilled feet; fried or poached fish or salt cod; poached or hard-boiled eggs; pasta, rice, or polenta.

FRESH TOMATO SAUCE

- Sauce aux tomates fraîches -

❖ EASY ❖ INEXPENSIVE ❖ 1 HOUR, 10 MINUTES ❖ SERVES 4

1 ½ pounds tomatoes, quartered
2 onions, chopped
½ carrot, peeled and chopped
1 garlic clove, crushed
1 bouquet garni made with parsley, thyme,
   and bay leaf

Salt and pepper
1 teaspoon all-purpose flour
1 tablespoon butter, softened
Chopped parsley leaves for sprinkling

❖ ❖ ❖ ❖ ❖

1. In a large saucepan, combine the tomatoes with the onions, carrot, garlic, and bouquet garni. Season with salt and pepper. Cook over medium heat, uncovered, for 45 minutes to 1 hour.

2. Remove the bouquet garni. Puree the sauce using a food mill or food processor. Return the sauce to medium heat. In a cup, mash the flour with the butter. Gradually whisk this paste into the simmering sauce until it thickens slightly. Sprinkle with parsley and serve.

From Françoise:

• The advantage of a food mill is that it strains out the tomato skins and seeds. If you use a food processor to puree the sauce, you might want to peel and seed the tomatoes first to get a smooth texture.

• If the tomato sauce still looks watery after an hour of cooking, boil it for a few minutes until it thickens. On the other hand, if it looks plenty thick, do not add the butter-and-flour paste.

• Serve with roasted meats, hard-boiled eggs or omelets, pasta, rice, or green beans.

BOLOGNESE SAUCE

- *Sauce bolognaise* -

❖ EASY   ❖ INEXPENSIVE   ❖ 50 MINUTES   ❖ SERVES 4

2 tablespoons butter

1 carrot, peeled and cut into ¼-inch dice

1 onion, cut into ¼-inch dice

1½ tablespoons all-purpose flour

2 cups meat broth or water

1 teaspoon tomato paste

2 tomatoes, chopped

Salt and pepper

2 ounces white mushrooms, finely chopped

1 thin slice baked ham, finely chopped

Mixed chopped parsley, chervil, and tarragon
   leaves for sprinkling

❖ ❖ ❖ ❖ ❖

1. In a large saucepan, melt the butter over medium heat. Add the carrot and onion and cook until lightly browned. Stir in the flour and cook until lightly browned. Add the broth or water, tomato paste, and tomatoes. Season with salt and pepper. Cook, stirring, until slightly thickened, then cook at a gentle boil until reduced by half, about 30 minutes.

2. Strain the sauce and return it to the pan. Stir in the mushrooms and ham and cook for 10 minutes. Sprinkle with the herbs just before serving.

From Françoise:

• Parsley alone is fine if that's all you have, but a mix of herbs is even better.

• Serve with pasta, rice, or some boiled vegetables, including celery, fennel, or Swiss chard.

SAUCES

AROMATIC SHELLFISH SAUCE
- *Sauce américaine* -

FISH STOCK
1 pound fish heads, bones, and shellfish shells,
   rinsed
2 onions, each stuck with 1 whole clove
1 garlic clove, crushed
1 bouquet garni made with parsley, thyme,
   and bay leaf
Salt
Black peppercorns

2 tablespoons butter
1 onion, finely chopped

2 shallots, finely chopped
Mixed, finely chopped parsley and
   tarragon leaves
¼ cup Cognac
¾ cup dry white wine
2 tablespoons tomato paste
1 garlic clove, crushed
1 or 2 pinches of cayenne pepper
Pepper
2 tablespoons crème fraîche
1 tablespoon all-purpose flour

❖ ❖ ❖ ❖ ❖

1. Make the fish stock: In a large pot, combine the fish heads, bones, and shells with the onions, garlic, bouquet garni, salt, peppercorns, and 4 cups of water. Bring to a simmer over medium heat, then reduce the heat to low and cook at a bare simmer, uncovered, for 1 hour. Strain into a large glass measuring cup.

2. In a large saucepan, melt the butter over medium heat. Add the onion, shallots, parsley, and tarragon, reduce the heat to medium-low, and cook until softened. Add the Cognac and bring to a boil, then tilt the pan and carefully ignite. When the flames subside, add the wine, 2 cups of the fish stock, the tomato paste, and garlic. Season with cayenne and pepper. Increase the heat to medium, bring to a simmer, and cook at a gentle boil, uncovered, for 15 minutes.

3. In a cup, blend the crème fraîche with the flour. Remove the pan from the heat and gradually whisk in the paste. Return the pan to the heat and bring to a simmer, whisking. Serve.

From Françoise:

• Sauce américaine is not a recipe for novices or cooks in a rush. Here it is anyway, with this caveat. When you make it for the first time, pick a day when you're not having company or you may get frustrated.

• Ask your fishmonger for fish heads, bones, and lobster shells. Pick up a few blue crabs, too, which will deepen the flavor of your stock enormously.

• Serve with firm-fleshed fish such as monkfish or with squid or shellfish.

CREAMY GUACAMOLE

- *Sauce épicée à l'avocat* -

❖ EASY　　　❖ INEXPENSIVE　　　❖ 15 MINUTES　　　❖ SERVES 4 TO 6

1 tomato, peeled, seeded, and coarsely chopped
1 avocado, peeled, pitted, and coarsely chopped
Juice of 1 lemon
1 small spring onion, coarsely chopped

Salt
1 pinch of cayenne pepper or a dash of hot sauce
½ cup crème fraîche

❖　❖　❖　❖　❖

1. In a food processor, puree the tomato with the avocado, lemon juice, onion, salt, cayenne or hot sauce, and crème fraîche.

From Françoise:
• Spread on toasts or in artichoke bottoms. Or scrape into a bowl and serve as a dip for raw vegetables like celery ribs and even more avocado.

• Prepare this sauce just before serving because the avocado darkens on standing.

WHIPPED CREAM

- *Crème chantilly* -

❖ EASY　　　❖ INEXPENSIVE　　　❖ 10 MINUTES　　　❖ SERVES 4

¾ cup heavy cream

2 to 3 tablespoons vanilla sugar

❖　❖　❖　❖　❖

1. In a chilled bowl and using a chilled whisk or an electric mixer with chilled beaters, whip the cream until it starts to thicken. Add the vanilla sugar and beat until soft peaks form.

From Françoise:
• Be careful not to overbeat the heavy cream or it will turn to butter.

• The whipped cream can be covered and refrigerated for up to 2 hours. Whisk it before using.

• The heavy cream, the bowl, and the beaters must be very cold when you whip cream. It's even a good idea to set the bowl of cream in a slightly larger bowl of iced water when beating.

SAUCES

CLASSIC BUTTERCREAM FROSTING
- Crème au beurre -

❖ INTERMEDIATE   ❖ MODERATE   ❖ 20 MINUTES   ❖ FROSTS 1 CAKE TO SERVE 6 TO 8

3 large egg yolks
¾ cup confectioners' sugar or ½ cup
  granulated sugar

12 tablespoons (1 ½ sticks) butter, softened

❖ ❖ ❖ ❖ ❖

1. In a medium bowl set over a pan of hot water, combine the egg yolks and sugar. Using an electric mixer or whisk, beat the mixture until it is very smooth and thick. Remove the pan from the heat and let cool completely, about 15 minutes.

2. Gradually beat in the softened butter until smooth.

From Françoise:

• Take the butter out of the refrigerator 1 or 2 hours before you plan to make the frosting.

• Confectioners' sugar is better for making buttercream because it blends more smoothly into the softened butter than granulated sugar.

• Use the buttercream while it's soft. If it does get firm, beat it again until soft.

• If you would like fluffier buttercream, fold in 1 or 2 egg whites beaten with sugar until stiff just before using.

• To make praline buttercream, fold in ¾ cup of Praline (page 680) ground to a powder in a food processor just before using. Add less sugar when making the buttercream.

MOCHA BUTTERCREAM FROSTING
- *Crème moka* -

❖ INTERMEDIATE   ❖ MODERATE   ❖ 20 MINUTES   ❖ FROSTS 1 CAKE TO SERVE 6 TO 8

1 tablespoon instant coffee

3 large egg yolks

¾ cup confectioners' sugar or ½ cup
  granulated sugar

12 tablespoons (1 ½ sticks) butter, softened

❖ ❖ ❖ ❖ ❖

1. In a cup, dissolve the coffee in 1 tablespoon of hot water. Let cool.

2. In a medium bowl set over a pan of hot water, combine the coffee with the egg yolks and sugar. Using an electric mixer or whisk, beat the mixture until it is very smooth and thick. Remove the pan from the heat and let cool completely, about 15 minutes.

3. Gradually beat in the softened butter until smooth.

From Françoise:

• This method of making mocha buttercream is my own invention. Having often had my buttercream curdle when beating the coffee into the finished cream, I found a trick that always seems to work. I beat the coffee with the eggs and sugar before beating in the butter.

• If you don't use all the buttercream on the day you make it, cover it before refrigerating so it doesn't absorb any odors. Remove it from the refrigerator and let it soften slightly, then beat briefly before using.

SAUCES

CLASSIC CHOCOLATE GANACHE

- Crème ganache au chocolat -

❖ EASY   ❖ MODERATE   ❖ 10 MINUTES   ❖ MAKES ENOUGH FOR 1 CAKE OR 3 DOZEN SMALL MERINGUES

¾ cup crème fraîche

2 ½ ounces bittersweet chocolate, chopped

❖ ❖ ❖ ❖ ❖

1. In a small saucepan, combine the crème fraîche with the chocolate and melt over low heat, without stirring, until barely simmering. Remove the pan from the heat and stir with a wooden spoon; let cool slightly. Using an electric mixer, beat the ganache until doubled in volume.

From Françoise:
• Use the ganache immediately without waiting for it to get firm.

• I sometimes flavor my ganache with 1 or 2 tablespoons of liqueur or spirits such as curaçao, Cointreau, rum, kirsch, or whisky.

CHOCOLATE FROSTING

- Glaçage au chocolat -

❖ EASY   ❖ MODERATE   ❖ 10 MINUTES   ❖ FROSTS 1 CAKE TO SERVE 5 TO 6

¼ pound bittersweet chocolate, chopped
½ cup confectioners' sugar

4 tablespoons (½ stick) butter, softened

❖ ❖ ❖ ❖ ❖

1. In a double boiler, melt the chocolate over medium heat without stirring. Sift the confectioners' sugar into the melted chocolate. Using a wooden spoon, mix well to blend. Remove the pan from the heat. Beat in the softened butter until smooth. Beat in 3 or 4 tablespoons of cold water to achieve the desired texture. Let cool slightly before using.

From Françoise:
• Do not let the frosting cool completely before using.

• Do not heat the chocolate too much when melting it or it won't have an even color when you spread it.

CLASSIC PASTRY CREAM

- *Crème pâtissière* -

❖ INTERMEDIATE   ❖ INEXPENSIVE   ❖ 15 MINUTES   ❖ SERVES 4

2 cups milk
Pinch of salt
½ cup sugar

2 tablespoons vanilla sugar
4 large eggs
¼ cup all-purpose flour

❖ ❖ ❖ ❖ ❖

1. In a large saucepan, bring the milk to a bare simmer with the salt.

2. In a bowl, beat the sugar with the vanilla sugar and the eggs until thick and light, 2 to 3 minutes. Beat in the flour. Gradually whisk in the hot milk.

3. Return the mixture to the pan and bring to a boil over medium heat, whisking constantly, then reduce the heat to low and cook, whisking, for 2 minutes.

From Françoise:
• Cooled pastry cream is often spread in baked tart shells and then covered with fresh fruit or piped into choux puffs or éclairs. Or, you may serve pastry cream warm, as a dessert sauce.

• Pastry cream is traditionally flavored with kirsch, rum, or vanilla. You can use vanilla seeds scraped from a vanilla bean instead of vanilla sugar. Add them to the milk in Step 1; then rinse the bean and reuse for another recipe.

• When the pastry cream is made, rub a pat of butter over the surface to prevent a skin from forming. Cover it only after it has cooled.

• To turn pastry cream into almond cream, whisk in 2 tablespoons of ground almonds or 3 or 4 crushed amaretto cookies. Almond cream is delicious spread in a tart shell and covered with sliced fruit.

SAUCES

BÉCHAMEL-STYLE PASTRY CREAM

- Crème pâtissière béchamel -

❖ INTERMEDIATE ❖ INEXPENSIVE ❖ 15 MINUTES ❖ SERVES 4

4 tablespoons (½ stick) butter
¼ cup all-purpose flour
2 cups milk
½ cup sugar

1 tablespoon vanilla sugar or 1 vanilla bean,
  seeds scraped
Pinch of salt
2 large egg yolks

❖ ❖ ❖ ❖ ❖

1. In a large saucepan, melt the butter over medium heat. Whisk in the flour until it starts foaming. Add the milk, sugar, vanilla sugar or vanilla seeds, and salt and bring to a boil, whisking constantly, then reduce the heat to very low and cook, whisking, for 2 to 3 minutes. Remove the pan from the heat and whisk in the egg yolks.

From Françoise:

• Instead of vanilla, you can flavor the pastry cream with orange flower water, finely grated lemon zest, coffee, rum, or another spirit.

• If you let the butter and flour cook until the paste turns a light brown color, the pastry cream will not be as thick but it will have a lovely hazelnut taste.

• This pastry cream may be served chilled, in custard cups, or it may be used as a topping for tarts, crêpes, or other pastries.

CLASSIC VANILLA CUSTARD SAUCE

- Crème anglaise -

❖ INTERMEDIATE ❖ MODERATE ❖ 20 MINUTES, PLUS 2 TO 3 HOURS CHILLING ❖ SERVES 4

2 cups milk
1 tablespoon vanilla sugar or 1 vanilla bean,
  seeds scraped

Pinch of salt
4 or 5 large egg yolks
½ cup sugar

1. In a large saucepan, bring the milk to a bare simmer with the vanilla sugar or vanilla seeds and salt.

2. Meanwhile, in a bowl, beat the egg yolks with the sugar until thick and light. Whisk in half the hot milk, then whisk the mixture back into the remaining milk. Cook over low heat, stirring constantly with a wooden spoon, until the custard thickens slightly. Remove the pan from the heat and let the custard cool slightly. Scrape into a bowl, cover, and refrigerate until cold, 2 to 3 hours. Serve very cold.

From Françoise:
• A tip for beginners: If you whisk a teaspoon of potato starch into the milk in Step 1, your sauce won't curdle.

• Your custard is perfectly cooked when you can draw a finger across the back of the spoon and it leaves a clear trail.

• You can get away with adding only 2 or 3 egg yolks. Instead, push the flavoring a little, adding more vanilla or finely grated lemon zest.

• Do not let the custard boil or it will curdle. If it does curdle, try removing the pan from the heat immediately and beating it with a whisk.

• For more vanilla flavor, add a vanilla bean and the seeds to the milk in Step 1. Remove the vanilla bean before serving.

• Custard sauce can be flavored many ways: with finely grated lemon zest, caramel sauce, or 1 teaspoon instant coffee, for example.

• The sauce can be chilled more quickly: Set the bowl in a larger bowl of ice water. Cover and refrigerate.

FRUIT COULIS
- Coulis de fruits -

❖ VERY EASY　　　❖ MODERATE　　　❖ 10 MINUTES　　　❖ SERVES 4

½ pound strawberries, raspberries, apricots, or peaches, pitted and cut into chunks if large

¾ cup sugar
Juice of 1 lemon

❖　❖　❖　❖　❖

1. In a food processor, puree the fruit with the sugar and lemon juice until smooth. If needed, work the puree through a food mill or sieve to remove any seeds.

From Françoise:
• This coulis can be refrigerated for 3 or 4 days.

• Frozen fruit or fruit in syrup can also be used to make a coulis. Reduce the amount of added sugar if you use sweetened fruit.

• If the puree is too thick, thin it with a little cold mineral water.

• This coulis can be poured as a topping with so many desserts: ice cream, pound cake, rice pudding, panna cotta, poached meringue, soufflés, and apple charlotte, to name a few.

SAUCES

DESSERTS

ICY KIRSCH-MARINATED PINEAPPLE
- *Ananas au kirsch* -

❖ EASY ❖ INEXPENSIVE ❖ 10 MINUTES ❖ SERVES 4

4 slices pineapple
4 macerated cherries

¼ cup kirsch

❖ ❖ ❖ ❖ ❖

1. On each dessert plate, arrange 1 slice of pineapple, top with 1 cherry, and sprinkle with kirsch. Serve very cold.

From Françoise:
• Rum or Cognac can replace the kirsch, according to your taste and what's available.

• A pineapple is usually ripe when the skin is an orangish color, though sometimes a pineapple with a little green is very good. You can tell how fresh it is by looking at the green leaves on top. Most of all, it will smell ripe. A pineapple that is spotted with brown might be past its prime.

MARINATED PINEAPPLE SALAD IN THE SHELL
- *Ananas à la Belle-de-Meaux* -

❖ ADVANCED ❖ INEXPENSIVE ❖ 20 MINUTES, PLUS 30 MINUTES CHILLING ❖ SERVES 4

1 pineapple, sliced in half lengthwise
½ cup sugar
¼ cup kirsch
½ pound strawberries, hulled and halved
  or quartered

WHIPPED CREAM
½ cup heavy cream
1 tablespoon vanilla sugar

❖ ❖ ❖ ❖ ❖

1. Using a grapefruit knife, cut out the flesh from each pineapple half in one piece, leaving the shells intact. Cut the flesh into ½-inch dice, discarding the woody core.

2. In a bowl, combine the pineapple dice with the sugar and kirsch and toss to coat. Cover and refrigerate for 30 minutes.

3. Make the whipped cream: In a chilled bowl and using a chilled whisk, beat the cream until it starts to thicken. Add the vanilla sugar and beat until soft peaks form.

4. Fold the strawberries into the pineapple dice. Mound the fruit salad in the pineapple

shells and pipe or dollop the whipped cream on top. Refrigerate until serving.

From Françoise:
• Be careful not to overbeat the heavy cream or it will turn to butter.

• The whipped cream can be covered and refrigerated for up to 2 hours. Whisk it before using.

• You can buy vanilla sugar in certain supermarkets, but it is easy to make your own: Split one vanilla bean and scrape out the seeds, reserving them for another use. Place the scraped bean in a glass jar and cover it with 1 to 2 cups of sugar. Shake it occasionally and leave it in your pantry. After a week or two, your sugar will be perfumed with the vanilla.

MARINATED PINEAPPLE SUNDAE IN THE SHELL
- *Ananas en gondole* -

❖ ADVANCED   ❖ INEXPENSIVE   ❖ 30 MINUTES   ❖ SERVES 4

1 pineapple, sliced in half lengthwise
½ cup sugar
¼ cup kirsch or rum
½ pint vanilla ice cream

A few strawberries, hulled and halved or quartered, raspberries, or macerated cherries for decorating

❖ ❖ ❖ ❖ ❖

1. Using a grapefruit knife, cut out the flesh from each pineapple half in one piece, leaving the shells intact. Cut the flesh into ½-inch dice, discarding the woody core.

2. In a bowl, combine the pineapple dice with the sugar and kirsch or rum and toss to coat.

3. Mound the pineapple salad in the shells. Using a melon baller, top with small scoops of ice cream. Decorate with the strawberries, raspberries, or cherries and serve.

From Françoise:
• If you toss the pineapple with 2 or 3 sliced bananas in Step 2, this sundae will serve 6. Then add the rum instead of kirsch.

ORANGE SALAD WITH RUM
- *Salade d'oranges* -

❖ EASY   ❖ INEXPENSIVE   ❖ 20 MINUTES, PLUS 2 HOURS CHILLING   ❖ SERVES 4

4 very firm oranges
Shredded mint

½ cup sugar
2 tablespoons rum

❖ ❖ ❖ ❖ ❖

1. Using a sharp knife, peel 3 of the oranges, removing all the white pith. Scrub the remaining orange well. Thinly slice all the oranges crosswise, removing any seeds.

2. In a bowl, combine the oranges with the mint, sugar, and rum and toss to coat. Cover and refrigerate for 2 hours before serving.

From Françoise:
• For children, omit the rum.

• If you don't like the orange peel in the salad, peel all the oranges, but finely grate the zest of 1 orange and add it to the salad.

• You can vary the recipe by tossing sliced grapefruit into the mix and adding a little more sugar.

• To serve, decorate with a mint sprig and set a macerated cherry in the center of the top orange slices.

FRENCH BANANA SPLIT
- *Banana split* -

❖ EASY   ❖ INEXPENSIVE   ❖ 10 MINUTES   ❖ SERVES 4

Mixed fresh fruit, halved or quartered if large
Candied fruit, chopped (optional)
Fruit jam
1 pint ice cream

4 bananas, halved lengthwise
¼ cup crème fraîche
4 baked meringues or butter cookies

❖ ❖ ❖ ❖ ❖

1. In each dessert dish, spread a little fruit, sprinkle with the candied fruit, if using, and dot with the jam. Scoop ice cream on top and arrange 2 banana halves in the dish. Dot with more jam and dollop with the crème fraîche. Garnish with a meringue or cookie and serve.

From Françoise:
• Start with ice cream and bananas, the only two required ingredients, then experiment from there.

RUM-FLAMBÉED BANANAS

- Bananes flambées au rhum -

❖ EASY ❖ INEXPENSIVE ❖ 15 MINUTES ❖ SERVES 4

2 tablespoons unsalted butter
4 bananas, halved lengthwise
Juice of ½ lemon

6 tablespoons sugar
½ to ¾ cup rum

❖ ❖ ❖ ❖ ❖

1. In a large skillet, melt the butter over medium heat. Add the bananas and squeeze in the lemon juice. Cook until nicely browned, 3 to 4 minutes per side.

2. Transfer the bananas to a warmed serving dish. Sprinkle with 3 tablespoons of the sugar. In a small saucepan, bring the rum and remaining 3 tablespoons of sugar to a boil, then tilt the pan and carefully ignite. Pour the flaming rum over the bananas and serve.

From Françoise:
• Select bananas that are ripe but still firm, with skin that is yellow with no brown spots. They are less likely to fall apart during cooking.

• The serving dish should be nice and hot because the rum will stop flaming when it hits a cold dish.

• For a simple Martinique-style variation, add orange juice, raisins, and 1 whole clove to the saucepan with the rum. Remove the clove before serving.

• If serving children, replace the rum with orange juice and do not flame the dish.

DESSERTS

BANANA-STUFFED CRÊPES WITH RUM

- Bananes en chemise -

❖ EASY ❖ INEXPENSIVE ❖ 30 MINUTES, PLUS 1 HOUR RESTING ❖ SERVES 4

CRÊPES
¾ cup all-purpose flour
1 cup water or milk
1 large egg, lightly beaten
2 tablespoons unsalted butter, melted,
   plus more for brushing
¼ teaspoon salt
Sugar for sprinkling

2 tablespoons unsalted butter
4 bananas, halved lengthwise
Juice of ½ lemon
6 tablespoons sugar
½ to ¾ cup rum

❖ ❖ ❖ ❖ ❖

1. Make the crêpes: In a medium bowl, whisk the flour with the water or milk, egg, the 2 tablespoons of melted butter, and the salt. Cover and let stand for at least 1 hour at room temperature, or for up to 1 day refrigerated.

2. Meanwhile, in a large skillet, melt the butter over medium heat. Add the bananas and squeeze in the lemon juice. Cook until nicely browned, 3 to 4 minutes per side.

3. Lightly brush an 8-inch skillet with melted butter and heat over medium heat. Whisk the batter and add 2 to 3 tablespoons to the skillet, swirling to coat the bottom. Cook until the edges begin to brown, about 30 seconds. Flip using a thin-bladed spatula and cook for 20 seconds. Slide onto a plate, sprinkle with sugar, and repeat with the remaining batter, stacking the crêpes as they're cooked.

4. Set 1 banana half on each crêpe, sprinkle with some of 3 tablespoons of sugar, and roll up. Arrange the stuffed crêpes in a gratin dish. In a small saucepan, bring the rum and remaining 3 tablespoons of sugar to a boil, then tilt the pan and carefully ignite. Pour the flaming rum over the crêpes and serve.

From Françoise:
• For a really dramatic presentation, bring the stuffed crêpes to the table and pour the flaming rum over them at the table.

SAUTÉED BANANAS WITH SPICED RED WINE SYRUP

- Bananes Bacchus au sirop de vin rouge -

❖ EASY   ❖ INEXPENSIVE   ❖ 15 MINUTES   ❖ SERVES 4

2 tablespoons unsalted butter

4 bananas, peeled

1 cup red wine

4 to 5 tablespoons sugar

1 whole clove

1 tablespoon vanilla sugar or 1 vanilla bean, scraped

Peel of ½ orange

❖ ❖ ❖ ❖ ❖

1. In a large skillet, melt the butter over medium heat. Add the bananas and cook until nicely browned, 3 to 4 minutes per side. Transfer to a paper towel–lined plate.

2. In the same skillet, combine the wine with the sugar, whole clove, vanilla sugar or vanilla seeds, and orange peel. Bring to a boil, then reduce the heat to medium-low and simmer for 2 minutes. Return the bananas to the skillet. Reduce the heat to low, cover, and cook for 5 minutes.

3. Remove the whole clove and orange peel. Transfer the bananas to a warmed serving dish. Pour the wine syrup over the bananas and serve.

From Françoise:

• Scrub the orange under cold running water before cutting off the peel to remove any chemicals.

FRESH STRAWBERRIES WITH WHIPPED CREAM

- Fraises à la chantilly -

❖ EASY   ❖ INEXPENSIVE   ❖ 30 MINUTES   ❖ SERVES 4

WHIPPED CREAM

½ cup heavy cream

1 tablespoon vanilla sugar

1 pound strawberries, hulled and halved or quartered if large

Sugar for serving

DESSERTS

continued

1. Make the whipped cream: In a chilled bowl and using a chilled whisk, beat the cream until it starts to thicken. Add the vanilla sugar and beat until soft peaks form.

2. Mound the strawberries in a serving dish and serve with the whipped cream.

From Françoise:

• Raspberries can replace the strawberries.

• I like to drizzle the fruit with fresh lemon juice, as it brings out their flavor.

• The whipped cream can be flavored with shredded coconut, grated lime zest, or finely grated fresh ginger.

• You might also omit the whipped cream and instead serve the berries with crème fraîche sprinkled with vanilla sugar and shaved chocolate.

• If you are dolloping the whipped cream on the berries, do it just before serving.

ORANGE-MARINATED STRAWBERRIES WITH WHIPPED CREAM
- Fraises Romanoff -

❖ EASY ❖ INEXPENSIVE ❖ 30 MINUTES, PLUS 2 HOURS CHILLING ❖ SERVES 4

1 pound strawberries, hulled and halved
  or quartered if large
3 tablespoons curaçao
Juice of 1 orange
Juice of 1 lemon
2 tablespoons sugar

WHIPPED CREAM
½ cup heavy cream
1 tablespoon vanilla sugar

❖ ❖ ❖ ❖ ❖

1. In a serving dish, combine the strawberries with the curaçao, orange juice, lemon juice, and sugar and toss gently to coat. Refrigerate for 2 hours.

2. Make the whipped cream: In a chilled bowl and using a chilled whisk, beat the cream until it starts to thicken. Add the vanilla sugar and beat until soft peaks form.

3. Just before serving, dollop the whipped cream on the strawberries and serve.

RASPBERRIES WITH SUGAR

- *Framboises au sucre* -

❖ EASY   ❖ MODERATE   ❖ 10 MINUTES   ❖ SERVES 4

1 pound raspberries

Sugar for serving

❖ ❖ ❖ ❖ ❖

1. Mound the raspberries in a serving dish and refrigerate. Serve, passing the sugar separately.

From Françoise:

• Strawberries can also be served this way. Hull them and halve and quarter them if they're large.

• If you like, pass a bowl of crème fraîche or whipped cream with the berries.

RASPBERRIES WITH ICE CREAM AND ALMONDS

- *Framboise Melba* -

❖ EASY   ❖ INEXPENSIVE   ❖ 15 MINUTES   ❖ SERVES 4

2 tablespoons raspberry or red currant jelly
1 pint vanilla ice cream

½ pound raspberries
1 tablespoon sliced or chopped blanched almonds

❖ ❖ ❖ ❖ ❖

1. In a small saucepan, melt the jelly in 1 tablespoon of water.

2. Scoop the ice cream into chilled dessert bowls. Mound the raspberries on top. Drizzle with the melted jelly, sprinkle with the almonds, and serve.

From Françoise:

• Instead of water, you could melt the jelly in 1 tablespoon of kirsch or Cognac.

• This dessert can also be made with strawberries or mixed fruit. Peaches are, of course, the classic fruit for Melba (page 664).

DESSERTS

RED CURRANTS WITH SUGAR

- *Groseilles au sucre* -

❖ EASY ❖ MODERATE ❖ 10 MINUTES, PLUS 2 HOURS CHILLING ❖ SERVES 4

1 pound red or white currants, stems removed
Sugar to taste

Juice of 1 lemon

❖ ❖ ❖ ❖ ❖

1. In a serving dish, combine the currants with the sugar and lemon juice and refrigerate for 2 hours. Toss gently just before serving.

From Françoise:
• Fresh currants are very tart and definitely need to be sweetened.

• A mix of red and white currants would be very nice. White currants are a little sweeter than the red berries.

• If you like, sprinkle the currants with kirsch before refrigerating.

PEACHES WITH ICE CREAM AND ALMONDS

- *Pêches Melba* -

❖ EASY ❖ INEXPENSIVE ❖ 15 MINUTES ❖ SERVES 4

2 tablespoons raspberry or red currant jelly
2 tablespoons kirsch
1 pint vanilla ice cream

4 peaches, peeled, halved, and pitted
1 tablespoon sliced blanched almonds

❖ ❖ ❖ ❖ ❖

1. In a small saucepan, melt the jelly in the kirsch.

2. Scoop the ice cream into chilled dessert bowls. Top with the peaches. Drizzle with the melted jelly, sprinkle with the almonds, and serve.

From Françoise:
• To peel the peaches easily, score the bottoms lightly and drop in boiling water for a few seconds, then drain.

• If you would like to embellish this already refined dish, whip a little crème fraîche and dollop it over the peaches just before serving.

• To vary the dish and give it more color, sprinkle chopped, unsalted pistachios, chopped praline, or shredded mint or verbena leaves over the top.

POACHED PEARS WITH WARM CHOCOLATE SAUCE
- *Poires Belle-Hélène* -

❖ EASY   ❖ INEXPENSIVE   ❖ 40 MINUTES, PLUS 2 TO 3 HOURS CHILLING   ❖ SERVES 4

¾ cup sugar

4 large or 8 small firm pears, peeled, halved lengthwise, and cored

½ lemon

¼ pound bittersweet chocolate, finely chopped

1 tablespoon unsalted butter

❖ ❖ ❖ ❖ ❖

1. In a medium saucepan, combine 2 cups of water with the sugar. Place over medium-low heat and cook until large bubbles form. Immediately remove the pan from the heat. Rub the pear halves with the lemon to discourage browning. Add the pears to the sugar syrup and cook over medium heat until tender, 15 to 25 minutes. Let the pears cool slightly in the syrup, then refrigerate until cold, 2 to 3 hours.

2. If needed, remove the pears from the poaching liquid and simmer the liquid until it thickens slightly.

3. In a medium saucepan, melt the chocolate with the butter over low heat. Stir with a wooden spoon until smooth. Stir in 2 to 3 tablespoons of the pear poaching liquid.

4. Spoon the pears into dessert bowls, pour the warm chocolate sauce over the top, and serve.

From Françoise:

• If you're in a rush, store-bought pears in syrup are also very good. Then you'll only have the chocolate sauce to make, and the whole recipe will take you barely 10 minutes. When you have a day off, you can poach the pears in syrup yourself, then they'll be ready to serve when you're busy.

• Select pears that are still firm. They can take more or less time to cook until tender depending on the variety and ripeness.

• Pears Belle-Hélène are often served with scoops of vanilla ice cream. For another exquisite variation, pour a little crème de cassis over the pears instead of chocolate sauce.

• I probably don't need to tell you how delicious this is with whipped cream.

DESSERTS

BUTTERY BAKED APPLES

- *Pommes bonne femme* -

❖ EASY ❖ INEXPENSIVE ❖ 35 MINUTES ❖ SERVES 4

4 large apples
4 tablespoons (½ stick) unsalted butter, softened

2 to 3 tablespoons sugar

❖ ❖ ❖ ❖ ❖

1. Preheat the oven to 400 degrees.

2. Using a sharp knife, cut a thin slice from the top and bottom of each apple. Working from the stem end and using a melon baller, apple corer, or sharp knife, remove the interior core and seeds to within ½ inch of the bottom.

3. Set the apples in a gratin dish. Add 1 table-spoon of butter to each apple and sprinkle with sugar. Transfer to the oven and bake until tender, 20 to 30 minutes. Serve warm or at room temperature.

From Françoise:

• Apples often burst during baking. To help prevent this, using a knife, score the apple skin with a spiral working from top to bottom.

• These baked apples have so many variations: You can add a teaspoon of red currant jelly or honey to each apple before adding the butter. Or dollop the top with finely chopped dried fruit, mixed with chopped apple and crème fraîche.

SKILLET-CARAMELIZED APPLES

- *Pommes caramélisées à la poêle* -

❖ EASY ❖ INEXPENSIVE ❖ 15 MINUTES ❖ SERVES 4

2 tablespoons unsalted butter
3 apples, peeled, cored, quartered, and
  thinly sliced

¼ cup sugar
¼ cup rum

❖ ❖ ❖ ❖ ❖

1. In a large skillet, melt the butter over me-dium heat. Add the apples and cook, stirring occasionally, for 10 minutes. Sprinkle with the sugar.

2. Add the rum and bring to a simmer, then tilt the skillet and carefully ignite. Serve immediately.

From Françoise:
• Stir the apples delicately while they are cooking so they don't break.

• This is a good dish for beginners. It's easy
and fast.

• I like to add rum-plumped raisins to my
sautéed apples just before serving.

LAYERED CINNAMON-APPLE AND RAISIN MOLD

- *Pommes en charlotte* -

❖ EASY   ❖ INEXPENSIVE   ❖ 1 HOUR, 15 MINUTES, PLUS OVERNIGHT SETTING   ❖ SERVES 4

Butter for brushing
2 pounds apples, peeled, cored, quartered,
  and thinly sliced
¾ cup sugar

⅔ cup raisins
3 tablespoons butter, cut into ¼-inch dice
½ teaspoon cinnamon
Juice of ½ lemon

❖ ❖ ❖ ❖ ❖

1. Preheat the oven to 400 degrees. Brush a
charlotte mold or soufflé dish with butter.

2. Layer one-third of the apples in the mold,
then sprinkle with ¼ cup of the sugar, ⅓ cup
of the raisins, 1 tablespoon of the butter, and
¼ teaspoon of cinnamon. Repeat the layering,
finishing with a layer of apples. Sprinkle with
the remaining ¼ cup of sugar and 1 tablespoon
of butter and drizzle with the lemon juice.

3. Cover, transfer to the oven, and bake for
1 hour, packing down the ingredients with a
wooden spoon halfway through cooking. Let
cool completely at room temperature in the
mold overnight.

4. To serve, run a knife around the mold. Invert
a round platter over the dish. Holding the
mold and platter together, quickly invert the
apple mold onto the platter.

From Françoise:
• Choose slightly acidic, pectin-rich apples like
Granny Smiths to make this dessert. They set
up better than sweet, ripe apples.

DESSERTS

HOMEMADE APPLESAUCE
- *Compote de pommes* -

❖ EASY   ❖ INEXPENSIVE   ❖ 40 MINUTES   ❖ SERVES 4

2 pounds apples, peeled, cored, and quartered   **½ cup sugar**

❖ ❖ ❖ ❖ ❖

1. In a flameproof casserole, cook the apples, covered, over low heat until very soft, about 30 minutes. Add the sugar and beat with a wooden spoon until the sugar melts and the apples fall apart into a puree.

From Françoise:
• The cooking time can vary according to the type of apple. You may need to add a little water if the cooking time is very long.

• I like to beat in 1 tablespoon of butter and a little ground cinnamon just before serving. Not everyone likes cinnamon, though, so sometimes I add vanilla sugar instead.

• Some people like to cook the apples with whole cloves. Not bad so long as you remember to remove them before serving.

• For a silky texture, puree the applesauce in a food processor or food mill.

CALVADOS-FLAMBÉED APPLES
- *Compote chaude flambée au calvados* -

❖ EASY   ❖ INEXPENSIVE   ❖ 35 MINUTES   ❖ SERVES 4

3 tablespoons unsalted butter
¾ pound apples, peeled, cored, quartered,
**   and sliced ½ inch thick**

¼ cup sugar
¼ cup Calvados
¾ cup crème fraîche

❖ ❖ ❖ ❖ ❖

1. In a large skillet, melt the butter over medium heat. Add the apples and cook, shaking the pan occasionally, until lightly browned. Reduce the heat to low, cover, and cook until tender, 15 to 20 minutes, depending on the variety.

2. Add the sugar and shake the skillet to mix. Pour in the Calvados and bring to a simmer, then tilt the skillet and carefully ignite. Transfer to a warmed serving dish and serve, passing the crème fraîche separately.

From Françoise:
• Do not stir the apples; they should not turn into applesauce.

• Calvados, like all alcohol, does not burn easily unless it's poured over hot food. If the food is lukewarm, ignite the alcohol separately in a small pan, then pour it over the food.

APPLE-PEAR CRUMBLE
- *Crumble aux pommes-poires* -

❖ EASY   ❖ INEXPENSIVE   ❖ 45 MINUTES   ❖ SERVES 4

4 tablespoons (½ stick) unsalted butter,
   cut into ¼-inch dice, plus more for brushing
2 apples, peeled, cored, and cut into chunks
2 pears, peeled, cored, and cut into chunks

6 tablespoons all-purpose flour
6 tablespoons sugar
½ teaspoon salt

❖ ❖ ❖ ❖ ❖

1. Preheat the oven to 400 degrees. Brush a gratin dish with butter. Spread the apples and pears in the dish.

2. In a bowl, rub the butter into the flour. Add the sugar and salt and toss to make a sandy mixture. Sprinkle over the fruit. Transfer to the oven and bake for about 30 minutes.

3. Remove from the oven and serve warm or at room temperature.

From Françoise:
• If you are intimidated by making pastry dough or put off by the prospect of a sink full of dishes, this is the dessert for you. It's very simple and though not as dramatic as a fruit tart, it's just as delicious.

• Try other fruits in this crumble: apricots, plums, peaches, rhubarb, or dried apricots, or just plain rhubarb, adding extra sugar.

DESSERTS

RHUBARB COMPOTE
- Compote de rhubarbe -

❖ EASY   ❖ INEXPENSIVE   ❖ 1 HOUR, 20 MINUTES   ❖ SERVES 4

2 pounds rhubarb

¾ cup sugar

❖   ❖   ❖   ❖   ❖

1. Remove any leaves completely from the rhubarb. Peel away any tough parts of the stems. You may need to cut off a small piece from the bottom of each stalk to remove as much of the stringy part as possible. Then slice the stalks in ½-inch pieces crosswise.

2. In a large saucepan, combine the rhubarb with the sugar and ¼ cup of water and bring to a boil. Reduce the heat to medium, partly cover, and cook, stirring occasionally, until the rhubarb breaks down, about 10 minutes. Uncover and cook, stirring frequently, until the liquid has evaporated and the rhubarb is thick and jammy, 15 minutes to 1 hour.

From Françoise:

• This compote should have the texture of a puree. Boil it for a few minutes over high heat if it's too watery.

• Cooking a few sliced apples or dried apricots with the rhubarb will make the compote less acidic.

• Don't leave the compote in the saucepan unless it's a nonreactive pan. Transfer the rhubarb to a bowl as soon as it's cooked.

FRESH FRUIT SALAD
- Salade de fruits frais -

❖ EASY   ❖ INEXPENSIVE   ❖ 20 MINUTES, PLUS 2 HOURS CHILLING   ❖ SERVES 4

2 oranges
2 bananas, thickly sliced
Juice of ½ lemon
**2 apples, peeled, cored, quartered, and
   thinly sliced**

⅓ cup sugar
**3 tablespoons kirsch, rum, or Cognac
   (optional)**

1. Using a sharp knife, peel 1 of the oranges, removing all the white pith. Scrub the remaining orange well. Thinly slice both the oranges crosswise, removing any seeds. Add to a bowl.

2. Add the bananas, lemon juice, apples, sugar, and kirsch, if using, and toss to combine. Cover and refrigerate for 2 hours before serving.

From Françoise:

• For children, omit the alcohol. Flavor the salad instead with vanilla sugar and finely grated orange zest.

• Adapt the fruits to the season. Oranges and bananas are available year-round, though, and can serve as the base for other fruits.

FRUIT SALAD IN A MELON SHELL
- *Melon surprise* -

❖ EASY   ❖ MODERATE   ❖ 20 MINUTES, PLUS 1 HOUR CHILLING   ❖ SERVES 4

7 ounces wild strawberries or regular
  strawberries, halved or quartered if large
¾ cup sweet white wine
¼ cup sugar
¼ cup kirsch

20 cherries, pitted, or grapes, peeled
1 apple, peeled and cut into 1-inch cubes
1 pear, peeled and cut into 1-inch cubes
4 slices pineapple, cut into 1-inch cubes
1 cantaloupe

❖ ❖ ❖ ❖ ❖

1. In a bowl, combine the strawberries with the wine. Cover and refrigerate for 1 hour.

2. Strain the berries, reserving the wine. Puree the berries using a food mill or food processor. Combine the puree with the reserved wine, the sugar, and kirsch and refrigerate.

3. In a bowl, combine the cherries with the apple, pear, and pineapple. Refrigerate.

4. Using a sharp knife, cut a thin slice from the top and bottom of the melon. Cut the melon in half horizontally. Discard the seeds. Using a melon baller, scoop out the flesh, leaving a sturdy shell, and add to the other fruits. Add the berry puree to the fruits and toss gently to coat. Cover the fruit and melon shells separately and refrigerate until serving.

5. To serve, mound the fruit in the melon shells and serve chilled.

DESSERTS

FRENCH FRUIT GELATIN MOLD

- *Aspic de fruits au riesling en gelée* -

❖ INTERMEDIATE ❖ MODERATE ❖ 1 HOUR, 30 MINUTES, PLUS OVERNIGHT CHILLING ❖ SERVES 4 TO 6

10 tablespoons sugar

1 tablespoon fresh lemon juice

3 cups Riesling wine

1 ½ envelopes (1 ½ tablespoons) unflavored
  powdered gelatin

2 cups mixed fruits, such as cherries,
  strawberries, raspberries, grapes, plums,
  pineapple chunks, pitted and halved or
  quartered if large

Sweetened whipped cream for serving (optional)

❖ ❖ ❖ ❖ ❖

1. In a medium saucepan, combine the sugar with the lemon juice and 2 ¾ cups of the wine. Place over medium heat and bring to a bare simmer, stirring to dissolve the sugar.

2. In a small saucepan, sprinkle the gelatin over the remaining ¼ cup of wine. Let stand until spongy, about 3 minutes. Set the saucepan over medium heat and heat until the wine is warm and the gelatin melts, about 1 minute. Stir in the remaining wine syrup.

3. Pour ½ inch of the gelatin mixture into a deep 6- to 7-inch dish, turning to coat the sides, and refrigerate until set, about 30 minutes. Spoon one-third of the fruit into the dish and cover with more of the liquid gelatin.

Refrigerate until firm, about 10 minutes. Continue layering and chilling the fruit and gelatin. Refrigerate overnight until firm.

4. To unmold the fruit, dip the dish briefly in hot water. Run a knife around the dish. Invert a round platter over the dish. Holding the dish and platter together, quickly invert the fruit mold onto the platter. Serve with the whipped cream, if using.

From Françoise:

• A charlotte mold or small soufflé dish would be perfect here.

• The fruit mold can be prepared through Step 3 and refrigerated for up to a day ahead.

FRESH FRUIT COMPOTE

- *Compote de fruits frais* -

❖ EASY   ❖ INEXPENSIVE   ❖ 45 MINUTES   ❖ SERVES 4

**2 pounds mixed fruits, peeled, pitted, and
 cut into chunks**

¾ cup sugar, or to taste
2 tablespoons vanilla sugar (optional)

❖ ❖ ❖ ❖ ❖

1. In a large saucepan, combine the fruits with
the sugar and vanilla sugar, if using. Place over
medium heat and cook, uncovered, until the
fruits can be crushed easily, 30 to 45 minutes.

From Françoise:
• Try a mix of apples, pears, and plums.

• Don't let the fruits cook longer than necessary
so they keep as much of their flavor as possible.

• You can use less-than-perfect fruit or fruit
that's past its peak here.

DRIED APRICOT COMPOTE

- *Compote d'abricots secs* -

❖ EASY   ❖ INEXPENSIVE   ❖ 30 MINUTES, PLUS OVERNIGHT SOAKING   ❖ SERVES 4

½ pound dried apricots

⅓ cup sugar, or to taste

❖ ❖ ❖ ❖ ❖

1. In a bowl, cover the apricots generously with
water. Let soak overnight.

2. In a medium saucepan, combine the apricots
with their soaking liquid. Add the sugar. Place
over low heat and cook until tender, about 30
minutes. Serve warm or at room temperature.

From Françoise:
• You can add a few blanched almonds to the
apricots as they cook. I also like to add vanilla

sugar or a split vanilla bean to the pan. Or
pour a splash of kirsch into the apricots at
room temperature.

• Serve the compote in glasses with butter
cookies.

• You might sprinkle shredded verbena leaves
over the top.

DESSERTS

PRUNE COMPOTE
- *Compote de pruneaux* -

❖ EASY   ❖ INEXPENSIVE   ❖ 30 MINUTES, PLUS 2 TO 3 HOURS SOAKING   ❖ SERVES 4

½ pound pitted prunes

⅓ cup sugar, or to taste

❖ ❖ ❖ ❖ ❖

1. In a bowl, generously cover the prunes with water and let soak for 2 to 3 hours or overnight.

2. Transfer the prunes to a large saucepan with 1 ½ cups of the soaking liquid. Add the sugar, place over very low heat, and cook until tender, 20 to 30 minutes.

From Françoise:
• You can also serve the prunes plumped and drained without cooking them and minus the sugar. Simply soak them in water or tea for 10 hours. That's how I like to eat them.

WINE-POACHED PRUNES WITH VANILLA ICE CREAM
- *Pruneaux en chaud-froid* -

❖ EASY   ❖ INEXPENSIVE   ❖ 30 MINUTES, PLUS 2 HOURS SOAKING   ❖ SERVES 4

½ pound pitted prunes
1 ½ cups red wine
⅓ cup sugar

1 tablespoon vanilla sugar or 1 vanilla bean, seeds scraped
1 pint vanilla ice cream

❖ ❖ ❖ ❖ ❖

1. In a bowl, cover the prunes generously with warm water and let soak for 2 hours. Drain, reserving the soaking liquid.

2. In a large saucepan, combine the wine with 1 ½ cups of the prune soaking liquid, the sugar, and vanilla sugar or vanilla seeds. Place over medium heat and bring to a simmer, then reduce the heat to low and cook for 30 minutes.

3. To serve, spoon the prunes into dessert bowls. Scoop the ice cream on top and drizzle with the prune cooking liquid.

From Françoise:
• To make the prunes and their cooking liquid more aromatic, you can add cinnamon, orange peel, or 2 or 3 whole cloves. Remove the peel and cloves before serving.

• You might decorate the bowls with a cinnamon stick, a strip of orange peel, or a mint sprig.

• You can buy vanilla sugar in certain supermarkets, but it is easy to make your own: Split one vanilla bean and scrape out the seeds, reserving them for another use. Place the scraped bean in a glass jar and cover it with 1 to 2 cups of sugar. Shake it occasionally and leave it in your pantry. After a week or two, your sugar will be perfumed with the vanilla.

APRICOT JAM

- Marmelade d'abricots -

❖ EASY   ❖ MODERATE   ❖ 20 MINUTES, PLUS 12 HOURS MACERATING   ❖ MAKES ABOUT 5 CUPS

2 pounds apricots, halved, pits reserved
2 pounds sugar

Juice of ½ lemon

❖ ❖ ❖ ❖ ❖

1. In a bowl, combine the apricots with the sugar and toss to combine. Cover and refrigerate for 12 hours.

2. Transfer the apricot mixture to a large saucepan. Place over medium heat and bring to a boil, then reduce the heat to medium-low and cook for 10 minutes. Add the lemon juice and reserved pits and cook for 5 minutes. Skim off any scum that rises to the surface of the jam.

3. Using a slotted spoon, remove the pits. Transfer the jam to jars, leaving ¼ inch of space at the top. Close the jars and let the jam cool to room temperature. Store the jam in the refrigerator for up to 3 months.

From Françoise:
• If you have a candy thermometer, remove the pan from the heat when the mixture reaches 219 to 220 degrees.

DESSERTS

QUINCE JELLY
- Gelée de coings -

❖ EASY	❖ MODERATE	❖ 50 MINUTES	❖ MAKES ABOUT 5 CUPS

2 pounds quinces, cut into chunks with skin
   and seeds
1 vanilla bean, seeds scraped (optional)

Sugar
Juice of 1 lemon

❖ ❖ ❖ ❖ ❖

1. In a large saucepan, barely cover the quinces with water. Place over medium heat, bring to a boil, and cook until tender, about 30 minutes. Strain the liquid into a large glass measuring cup, pressing lightly on the fruit.

2. Pour the liquid back into the saucepan and add the vanilla seeds, if using, and 2 pounds of sugar per quart of liquid. Place over medium heat, bring to a boil, and cook for about 20 minutes, adding the lemon juice toward the end of cooking. Pour a little of the jelly on a plate and refrigerate; it should set fairly quickly. If not, cook a few minutes longer.

3. Pour the jelly into jars, leaving ¼ inch of space at the top. Close the jars and let the jelly cool to room temperature. Store the jelly in the refrigerator for up to 3 months.

From Françoise:
• Do not wash the quinces unless they are very dirty. Wipe them off instead.

• You can replace half the quinces with the same amount of apples.

FROMAGE BLANC PARFAIT WITH RAISINS AND SLICED ALMONDS
- Fromage blanc aux raisins secs et aux amandes -

❖ EASY	❖ INEXPENSIVE	❖ 15 MINUTES, PLUS 1 HOUR SOAKING	❖ SERVES 4

⅓ cup raisins
¼ cup rum
1 cup fromage blanc

2 to 3 tablespoons milk
¼ cup to ⅓ cup sugar
½ cup sliced almonds

1. In a bowl, combine the raisins with the rum and refrigerate until plump, about 1 hour.

2. In a bowl, combine the fromage blanc with the milk. Using an electric mixer or a whisk, beat the mixture for a few minutes until pillowy. Fold in the raisins, rum, sugar, and almonds. Scrape into chilled bowls and serve very cold.

From Françoise:
• Yogurt can be substituted for the fromage blanc.

• Make sure all the ingredients are very cold so the mixture doesn't need to be chilled before serving.

CREAMY COFFEE FROMAGE BLANC

- Fromage blanc à la crème et au café -

❖ EASY ❖ INEXPENSIVE ❖ 10 MINUTES ❖ SERVES 4

1 teaspoon instant coffee
¾ cup fromage blanc

¼ cup crème fraîche
3 to 4 tablespoons sugar

❖ ❖ ❖ ❖ ❖

1. In a cup, dissolve the coffee in 1 tablespoon of cold water.

2. In a bowl, combine the fromage blanc with the crème fraîche and coffee. Using an electric mixer or a whisk, beat the mixture for a few minutes until pillowy. Beat in the sugar at the very end. Scrape into chilled bowls and serve very cold.

From Françoise:
• Serve with delicate buttery cookies like tuiles, vanilla wafers, or crispy crêpes dentelles.

• The fromage blanc and crème fraîche must be very cold when you beat them.

• Try this with yogurt, too.

COFFEE CUSTARD

- Crème au café -

❖ EASY   ❖ INEXPENSIVE   ❖ 15 MINUTES, PLUS 2 TO 3 HOURS CHILLING   ❖ SERVES 4

2 cups milk

1 tablespoon instant coffee

Pinch of salt

2 large egg yolks

½ cup sugar

1 ½ tablespoons potato starch

❖ ❖ ❖ ❖ ❖

1. In a large saucepan, bring the milk to a bare simmer with the coffee and salt.

2. In a bowl, beat the egg yolks with the sugar until thick and light. Whisk in half the hot coffee milk, then whisk the mixture back into the remaining milk. Place over low heat and cook, stirring constantly with a wooden spoon, until the custard thickens slightly. Remove the pan from the heat and let the custard cool completely. Scrape into a serving dish or ramekins, cover, and refrigerate until cold, 2 to 3 hours. Serve very cold.

From Françoise:
• You can make this custard more delicate (but it's also trickier) by increasing the egg yolks to 5 or 6 and omitting the potato starch thickener.

CHOCOLATE CUSTARD

- Crème au chocolat -

❖ INTERMEDIATE   ❖ MODERATE   ❖ 20 MINUTES, PLUS 2 TO 3 HOURS CHILLING   ❖ SERVES 4

2 cups milk

3 ½ ounces bittersweet chocolate, chopped

Pinch of salt

4 or 5 large egg yolks

⅓ to ½ cup sugar

❖ ❖ ❖ ❖ ❖

1. In a large saucepan, bring the milk to a bare simmer with the chocolate and salt. Stir until smooth.

2. In a bowl, beat the egg yolks with the sugar until thick and light. Whisk in half the hot chocolate milk, then whisk the mixture back into the remaining milk. Place over low heat

and cook, stirring constantly with a wooden spoon, until the custard thickens slightly.

3. Remove the pan from the heat and let the custard cool completely. Scrape into dessert bowls or ramekins, cover, and refrigerate until cold, 2 to 3 hours. Serve very cold.

From Françoise:
• Serve with ladyfingers or buttery cookies.

PRALINE CREAM
- *Crème pralinée* -

❖ INTERMEDIATE   ❖ MODERATE   ❖ 15 MINUTES, PLUS 2 TO 3 HOURS CHILLING   ❖ SERVES 4

2 cups milk
1 tablespoon vanilla sugar
Pinch of salt
4 or 5 large egg yolks

⅓ cup sugar
½ to ¾ cup praline powder
Butter cookies for serving

❖   ❖   ❖   ❖   ❖

1. In a large saucepan, bring the milk to a bare simmer with the vanilla sugar and salt.

2. In a bowl, beat the egg yolks with the sugar until thick and light. Whisk in half the hot milk, then whisk the mixture back into the remaining milk. Place over low heat and cook, stirring constantly with a wooden spoon, until the custard thickens slightly. Stir in the praline powder.

3. Remove the pan from the heat and let the custard cool completely. Scrape into dessert bowls or ramekins, cover, and refrigerate until cold, 2 to 3 hours. Serve very cold with cookies.

From Françoise:
• Make your own Praline (page 680) and grind it in the food processor more or less finely to taste.

• Traditionally, delicate cookies like tuiles, vanilla wafers, or crispy crêpes dentelles are served with custards.

• The leftover egg whites can be frozen, then defrosted for later use.

DESSERTS

CRUNCHY ALMOND PRALINE

- *Amandes pralines* -

❖ INTERMEDIATE   ❖ MODERATE   ❖ 35 MINUTES   ❖ SERVES 4 TO 6

Oil for brushing
1 ¼ cups sugar

½ pound raw almonds
¼ teaspoon cinnamon

❖ ❖ ❖ ❖ ❖

1. Preheat the oven to 200 degrees. Generously brush a rimmed baking sheet with oil.

2. In a medium saucepan, combine the sugar with ½ cup of water, place over medium-low heat, and cook until large bubbles form. Add the almonds and cinnamon and cook, stirring often with a wooden spoon, until a deep amber caramel forms, about 15 minutes.

3. Quickly remove the pan from the heat. Wait 1 minute, then stir in 1 tablespoon of cold water. Return the pan to the heat and continue stirring to dissolve any lumps of caramel, about 2 minutes. Pour the almond mixture into the baking sheet. Transfer to the oven and bake for 5 minutes.

4. Let the praline cool slightly, then break it into pieces. Serve warm or at room temperature.

From Françoise:

• This excellent recipe is not difficult, but it does require your laserlike attention for 15 minutes in Step 2 while making the caramel. This can be tricky because the caramel can smoke and burn easily if not carefully watched.

• Hazelnut praline can be made in the same way.

• Praline can be stored for a week in an airtight container.

• Praline can also be ground to a powder in a food processor and used as a topping or flavoring.

OLD-FASHIONED VANILLA CUSTARD

- *Oeufs au lait* -

❖ EASY ❖ INEXPENSIVE ❖ 30 MINUTES, PLUS 2 TO 3 HOURS CHILLING ❖ SERVES 4

2 cups milk
⅓ cup sugar
1 tablespoon vanilla sugar

Pinch of salt
3 large eggs

❖ ❖ ❖ ❖ ❖

1. Preheat the oven to 400 degrees. In a large saucepan, bring the milk to a bare simmer with the sugar, vanilla sugar, and salt.

2. In a bowl, lightly beat the eggs to mix. Gradually whisk in the hot milk. Pour the custard into a small baking dish. Set the dish in a roasting pan and pour in hot water to reach halfway up the sides of the dish. Transfer to the oven and bake until just set, about 20 minutes. Remove the dish from the pan and let the custard cool completely. Cover and refrigerate until cold, 2 to 3 hours.

3. Serve cold in the baking dish.

From Françoise:

• Check the custard during cooking; if small bubbles appear, reduce the oven temperature.

• If you have a leftover egg white, you can use it here. Beat 2 whole eggs with your extra egg white and you have a very economical custard.

• This custard can also be baked in individual ramekins.

• When a pale blond skin appears on the surface of the custard, it's cooked.

DESSERTS

CLASSIC CRÈME CARAMEL
- *Crème renversée au caramel* -

❖ INTERMEDIATE   ❖ INEXPENSIVE   ❖ 1 HOUR, PLUS 2 TO 3 HOURS CHILLING   ❖ SERVES 4

¾ cup sugar

2 cups milk

1 tablespoon vanilla sugar

3 or 4 large eggs

❖ ❖ ❖ ❖ ❖

1. Preheat the oven to 400 degrees. In a small saucepan, combine ¼ cup of the sugar with 2 tablespoons of water. Place over medium-high heat, bring to a simmer, and cook, stirring often, until the sugar dissolves. Partly cover the pan and continue cooking until the sugar turns medium amber. Immediately pour the caramel into a small soufflé dish or other deep baking dish and quickly turn to coat the bottom and sides.

2. In a large saucepan, bring the milk to a bare simmer with the remaining ½ cup of sugar and the vanilla sugar.

3. In a bowl, lightly beat the eggs to mix. Gradually whisk in the hot milk. Pour the custard into the soufflé dish. Set the dish in a roasting pan and pour in hot water to reach halfway up the sides of the dish. Transfer to the oven and bake until just set, 30 to 45 minutes. Remove the soufflé dish from the pan and let the cream cool completely. Cover and refrigerate until cold, 2 to 3 hours.

4. To serve, run a knife around the dish. Invert a round platter over the dish. Holding the dish and platter together, quickly invert the cream onto the platter; the caramel sauce will spill out.

From Françoise:
• Check the custard during cooking; if small bubbles appear, reduce the oven temperature.

• The caramel is burning hot when you pour it into the soufflé dish, so you might want to wear oven mitts when turning the dish to coat.

CARAMEL PUDDING
- *Crème caramel* -

❖ INTERMEDIATE   ❖ INEXPENSIVE   ❖ 20 MINUTES, PLUS 2 TO 3 HOURS CHILLING   ❖ SERVES 4

½ cup sugar

1 ½ tablespoons potato starch

2 pinches of salt

2 large eggs

2 cups milk

1. In a small saucepan, combine ¼ cup of the sugar with 2 tablespoons of water. Place over medium-high heat, bring to a simmer, and cook, stirring often, until the sugar dissolves. Partly cover the pan and continue cooking until the sugar turns medium amber. Immediately remove the pan from the heat and let cool slightly. Add 3 tablespoons of water and return the caramel to medium-low heat, stirring to melt the caramel.

2. In a bowl, whisk the potato starch with the remaining ¼ cup of sugar, the salt, eggs, and milk. Pour into a medium saucepan, place over medium heat, and cook, stirring constantly with a wooden spoon, until the cream thickens. When the pudding barely simmers, remove the pan from the heat.

3. Stir the caramel into the pudding. Scrape into dessert bowls or ramekins, cover, and refrigerate until cold, 2 to 3 hours. Serve very cold.

From Françoise:
• Caramel custard can also be made by stirring caramel into custard sauce. It is a more delicate dessert, but it's also more expensive and trickier to prepare.

CARAMELIZED RUM-RAISIN PUDDING
- Crème meunière -

❖ INTERMEDIATE   ❖ INEXPENSIVE   ❖ 1 HOUR, PLUS 2 TO 3 HOURS COOLING   ❖ SERVES 4

⅔ cup raisins

2 tablespoons rum

¾ cup sugar

4 tablespoons (½ stick) unsalted butter

¼ cup all-purpose flour

2 cups milk

Pinch of salt

3 large eggs

1 teaspoon fresh lemon juice (optional)

❖ ❖ ❖ ❖ ❖

1. In a sieve, rinse the raisins with warm water to soften them. Pat dry and add to a bowl with the rum.

2. In a small saucepan, combine ¼ cup of the sugar with 2 tablespoons of water. Place over medium-high heat, bring to a simmer, and cook, stirring often, until the sugar dissolves. Partly cover the pan and continue cooking until the sugar turns medium amber. Immediately pour the caramel into a small soufflé dish or other deep baking dish and quickly turn to coat the bottom and sides.

3. Preheat the oven to 350 degrees. In a large saucepan, melt the butter over medium heat. Whisk in the flour until it starts foaming. Add the milk, the remaining ½ cup of sugar, and the salt and bring to a boil, whisking constantly, then reduce the heat to very low and cook, whisking, for 2 to 3 minutes.

4. In a bowl, whisk the eggs with the raisins, rum, lemon juice, if using, and a few tablespoons of the pastry cream. Whisk this mixture

continued

back into the remaining cream and cook over low heat for 1 to 2 minutes.

5. Scrape the mixture into the soufflé dish. Set the dish in a roasting pan and pour in hot water to reach halfway up the sides of the dish. Transfer to the oven and bake for about 30 minutes. Remove the soufflé dish from the pan and let the pudding cool completely.

6. To serve, run a knife around the dish. Invert a round platter over the dish. Holding the dish and platter together, quickly invert the pudding onto the platter; the caramel sauce will spill out.

From Françoise:
• To make this dish easier, don't bake it. Cover the dish and refrigerate it for 3 or 4 hours. If the pudding is thick enough, you can unmold it as directed in Step 5.

• If you have a spare egg white, beat it into the cream with the whole eggs in Step 4. It will make the pudding firmer.

SIMPLE SUMMER BERRY PUDDING
- Crème simple aux fruits rouges -

❖ EASY   ❖ MODERATE   ❖ 20 MINUTES, PLUS 2 TO 3 HOURS CHILLING   ❖ SERVES 6 TO 8

2 pounds mixed berries
⅓ cup potato starch
¾ cup sugar, plus more for sprinkling

1 tablespoon sliced almonds
1 cup crème fraîche

❖ ❖ ❖ ❖ ❖

1. In a large saucepan, barely cover the berries with water. Bring to a boil over medium-high heat, then remove from the heat. Working quickly, transfer to a food processor and puree. Blend in the potato starch and the ¾ cup of sugar. Scrape into a serving dish, dessert bowls, or ramekins. Cover and refrigerate until chilled, 2 to 3 hours.

2. Sprinkle with more sugar and the almonds, and serve, passing the crème fraîche separately.

From Françoise:
• This pudding should have a texture similar to pastry cream.

FROZEN CARAMEL PARFAIT

- *Plus-que-parfait au caramel* -

❖ INTERMEDIATE   ❖ INEXPENSIVE   ❖ 15 MINUTES, PLUS 2 HOURS FREEZING   ❖ SERVES 4

½ cup heavy cream, chilled
2 large eggs, separated

3 tablespoons sugar
1 tablespoon caramel sauce

❖ ❖ ❖ ❖ ❖

1. In a large chilled bowl, using an electric mixer with chilled beaters, whip the cream until soft peaks form. Cover and refrigerate.

2. In another bowl, using the electric mixer, beat the egg yolks with 2 tablespoons of the sugar and the caramel sauce until thick and light and the mixture leaves a thick ribbon trail when the beaters are lifted. Scrape onto the whipped cream, but do not mix.

3. In a medium bowl, beat the egg whites until soft peaks form. Add the remaining 1 tablespoon of sugar and beat at high speed until stiff and glossy.

4. Gently fold the egg whites into the caramel mixture. Scrape this mixture into parfait glasses, dessert bowls, or ramekins. Cover and freeze for 2 hours. Serve without unmolding.

From Françoise:
• Please note that the finished dish contains raw egg.

• If you make this dessert ahead of time, take it out of the freezer at the beginning of the meal and let it soften slightly in the refrigerator.

DESSERTS

FROZEN STRAWBERRY MOUSSE
- *Mousse aux fraises* -

❖ EASY   ❖ MODERATE   ❖ 10 MINUTES, PLUS 3 HOURS FREEZING   ❖ SERVES 4 TO 6

1 pound strawberries, hulled
½ cup sugar
Juice of ½ lemon

1 cup heavy cream
1 tablespoon vanilla sugar

❖ ❖ ❖ ❖ ❖

1. In a food processor, puree the strawberries with the sugar and lemon juice until smooth.

2. In a chilled bowl and using a chilled whisk, beat the cream until it starts to thicken. Add the vanilla sugar and beat until soft peaks form.

3. Gently fold the strawberry puree into the whipped cream. Scrape the mousse into a bowl, cover, and freeze for 3 hours.

4. To serve, using a soup spoon, scoop the mousse into chilled dessert bowls and serve.

From Françoise:
• The mousse can also be made with frozen strawberries.

CLASSIC CHOCOLATE MOUSSE
- *Mousse au chocolat* -

❖ EASY   ❖ MODERATE   ❖ 15 MINUTES, PLUS 2 TO 3 HOURS CHILLING   ❖ SERVES 4

¼ pound bittersweet chocolate,
  maximum 50 percent cocoa, chopped
1 tablespoon butter

4 large eggs, separated
Pinch of salt

❖ ❖ ❖ ❖ ❖

1. In a small saucepan or double boiler, melt the chocolate with the butter over low heat. Stir until smooth. Remove the pan from the heat and beat in the egg yolks using a wooden spoon.

2. In a bowl, combine the egg whites and the salt and beat until stiff. Beat one-quarter of the egg whites into the chocolate mixture, then gently fold this lightened mixture into the remaining egg whites.

3. Scrape the mousse into a serving dish or dessert bowls. Cover and refrigerate until cold, 2 to 3 hours.

From Françoise:
• Please note that the finished recipe contains raw egg.

• The whipped egg whites beaten into the chocolate mixture do lose volume, but they also lighten the chocolate, making it easier to fold the chocolate into the remaining egg whites.

• When folding the lightened chocolate mixture into the remaining whipped egg whites, use a rubber spatula or a wooden spoon, not a whisk.

• Egg whites that are too cold do not whip as well as whites at room temperature.

• If liquid collects under the mousse, it's because either the egg whites were not beaten until stiff or the mousse was not served quickly enough and the egg whites liquefied.

• You can add a little finely grated lemon or orange zest to the mousse, or even ½ teaspoon of instant coffee.

CHOCOLATE MARQUISE
- *Marquise au chocolat* -

❖ EASY   ❖ MODERATE   ❖ 20 MINUTES, PLUS 12 HOURS CHILLING   ❖ SERVES 4 TO 6

7 tablespoons unsalted butter, cut into
  ¼-inch dice, plus more for brushing
5 ounces bittersweet chocolate, chopped
2 large eggs, separated

⅔ cup confectioners' sugar, sifted,
  plus more for dusting
Pinch of salt

❖ ❖ ❖ ❖ ❖

1. Brush a small soufflé dish or other deep baking dish with butter. In a double boiler, melt the chocolate without stirring. Gradually beat in the diced butter, removing the pan from the heat so the butter melts creamily. Beat in the egg yolks and ⅓ cup of the confectioners' sugar.

2. In a bowl, beat the egg whites with the salt until foamy, then beat at high speed until stiff. Add in the remaining ⅓ cup of confectioners' sugar until glossy.

3. Gently fold the chocolate mixture into the beaten egg whites. Scrape the mixture into the soufflé dish. Cover and refrigerate for 12 hours.

4. To unmold, dip the bottom of the dish briefly in hot water. Run a knife around the marquise. Invert a round platter over the dish. Holding the dish and platter together, quickly invert the marquise onto the platter. Refrigerate until serving. Dust with confectioners' sugar and serve.

From Françoise:
• Please note that the finished recipe contains raw egg.

• Serve with Vanilla Custard Sauce (page 652).

DESSERTS

BANANA MOUSSE
- *Mousse de banane* -

❖ EASY ❖ INEXPENSIVE ❖ 15 MINUTES, PLUS 30 MINUTES CHILLING ❖ SERVES 4

2 ripe bananas
3 tablespoons sugar

2 large eggs, separated
Pinch of salt

❖ ❖ ❖ ❖ ❖

1. In a small saucepan, mash the bananas. Beat in the sugar and egg yolks. Warm over very low heat or in a double boiler, beating constantly, until the mixture thickens slightly, 2 to 3 minutes. Remove the pan from the heat and let cool slightly.

2. In a medium bowl, beat the egg whites with the salt until stiff. Gently fold the banana mixture into the beaten egg whites. Scrape the mousse into dessert bowls or glasses, cover, and refrigerate for 30 minutes.

From Françoise:
• Please note that the finished dish contains raw egg.

• The secret to a firm mousse: Make it at the last minute, because the egg whites will liquefy if held too long.

TANGY LEMON MOUSSE
- *Crème mousseuse au citron* -

❖ EASY ❖ INEXPENSIVE ❖ 20 MINUTES, PLUS 1 TO 2 HOURS CHILLING ❖ SERVES 4

½ cup sugar
2 pinches of salt
1 ½ tablespoons potato starch

2 lemons, scrubbed
2 large eggs, separated
2 tablespoons unsalted butter

❖ ❖ ❖ ❖ ❖

1. In a large saucepan, bring ¼ cup of the sugar to a bare simmer with ¾ cup of water and 1 pinch of the salt.

2. In a small bowl, beat the potato starch with 3 tablespoons of cold water. Beat into the sugar syrup and cook, stirring constantly, until just before it simmers; remove from the heat.

3. Finely grate ½ teaspoon of zest from the lemons. In a bowl, beat the lemon zest with ¼ cup lemon juice and the egg yolks. Add to

the sugar syrup and set over low heat, beating constantly until the mixture thickens slightly; do not let it boil. Remove the pan from the heat and stir in the butter. Set the pan in a bowl of ice water to cool the lemon curd to lukewarm.

4. Meanwhile, in a bowl, beat the egg whites with the remaining 1 pinch of salt until foamy. Gradually add the remaining ¼ cup of sugar and beat at high speed until stiff and glossy.

5. Carefully fold the beaten whites into the cooled lemon curd. Spoon this mousse into dessert bowls or ramekins. Cover and refrigerate until cold, 1 to 2 hours, before serving.

From Françoise:
• Please note that the finished dish contains raw egg.

• Egg whites that are too cold do not whip as well as whites at room temperature. Remove them from the refrigerator ahead of time and let them warm up slightly.

MERINGUE SNOW EGGS WITH CUSTARD SAUCE
- Oeufs à la neige -

❖ INTERMEDIATE   ❖ MODERATE   ❖ 40 MINUTES, PLUS 30 MINUTES CHILLING   ❖ SERVES 4

2 cups milk
1 tablespoon vanilla sugar or 1 vanilla bean,
  seeds scraped

Pinch of salt
4 large eggs, separated
1 cup sugar

❖ ❖ ❖ ❖ ❖

1. In a large saucepan, bring the milk to a bare simmer with the vanilla sugar or vanilla seeds and salt.

2. In a bowl, beat the egg yolks with ½ cup of the sugar until thick and light. Whisk in half the hot milk, then whisk the mixture back into the remaining milk. Place over low heat and cook, stirring constantly with a wooden spoon, until the custard thickens slightly. Remove the pan from the heat and let the custard cool completely. Scrape into a bowl and set in a larger bowl of ice water. Cover and refrigerate for 30 minutes.

3. Beat the egg whites until foamy. Gradually add the remaining ½ cup of sugar and beat at high speed until stiff and glossy.

4. Fill a large, deep skillet with 1 ½ inches of water, place over medium heat, and bring to a simmer. Using a large spoon, dollop 4 mounds of the meringue into the simmering water and cook until just set on the bottom, about 2 minutes. Gently flip the meringues and cook for 2 minutes longer; do not let the water boil.

continued

DESSERTS

5. Pour the custard sauce into 4 shallow bowls. Using a slotted spoon, transfer the meringues to the bowls and serve.

From Françoise:
• Meringue poached in water stays whiter than if cooked in milk. In addition, water won't boil over the way milk does.

• Whipped egg whites that are cooked even a few seconds too long tend to shrink. It's hard to tell you exactly how long to poach them, but try it and you will quickly get the hang of it.

FLOATING ISLAND WITH PRALINE
- Île flottante pralinée -

❖ INTERMEDIATE   ❖ MODERATE   ❖ 45 MINUTES, PLUS 30 MINUTES CHILLING   ❖ SERVES 4

CARAMEL
⅓ cup sugar
Juice of ½ lemon

VANILLA CUSTARD SAUCE
2 cups milk
1 tablespoon vanilla sugar or 1 vanilla bean, seeds scraped
Pinch of salt

4 or 5 large egg yolks
½ cup sugar

MERINGUE
4 large egg whites
Pinch of salt
6 tablespoons sugar
¼ cup chopped Almond Praline (page 680)

❖ ❖ ❖ ❖ ❖

1. Make the caramel: In a small saucepan, combine the sugar with the lemon juice and 2 tablespoons of water. Place over medium-high heat, bring to a simmer, and cook, stirring often, until the sugar dissolves. Reduce the heat to medium, partly cover the pan, and continue cooking until the sugar turns medium amber. Immediately pour the caramel into a 6- to 7-inch soufflé dish or other deep baking dish and quickly turn to coat the bottom and sides.

2. Make the vanilla custard sauce: In a large saucepan, bring the milk to a bare simmer with the vanilla sugar or vanilla seeds and salt.

3. In a bowl, beat the egg yolks with the sugar until thick and light. Whisk in half the hot milk, then whisk the mixture back into the remaining milk. Place over low heat and cook, stirring constantly with a wooden spoon, until the custard thickens slightly. Remove the pan from the heat and let the custard cool completely. Scrape into a bowl and set in a larger bowl of ice water. Cover and refrigerate.

4. Preheat the oven to 275 degrees. Make the meringue: Beat the egg whites with the salt until foamy. Gradually add the sugar and beat at high speed until stiff and glossy. Gently fold in the praline.

5. Spread the meringue in the soufflé dish. Set the dish in a roasting pan and pour in cold water to come halfway up the sides of the dish. Transfer to the oven and bake until just set, about 20 minutes. Let cool completely in the dish, then refrigerate until cold.

6. Pour the vanilla custard sauce into a large, shallow bowl. Dip the soufflé dish briefly in hot water. Carefully turn out the meringue into the custard. Serve immediately.

From Françoise:
• Take care to coat the bottom and sides of the soufflé dish well with caramel. It helps keep the meringue from slipping down during baking and chilling. For that reason, store-bought caramel and a nonstick baking dish will not work here.

• Don't forget to add the lemon juice when making the caramel; it helps keep the sugar from crystallizing. If crystals do form, you'll need to make another batch.

• The recipe can be prepared through Step 5 and refrigerated overnight, but do not unmold the meringue until just before serving.

• The praline can be omitted. Or sprinkle the praline over the meringue just before serving.

CLASSIC MERINGUES
- Meringues -

❖ INTERMEDIATE ❖ INEXPENSIVE ❖ 1 HOUR, 30 MINUTES ❖ SERVES 4

Butter for brushing
All-purpose flour for dusting
2 large egg whites

Pinch of salt
1 teaspoon fresh lemon juice
½ cup sugar

❖ ❖ ❖ ❖ ❖

1. Preheat the oven to 225 degrees. Brush a baking sheet with butter and dust lightly with flour, tapping off the excess.

2. In a medium bowl, beat the whites with the salt and lemon juice at low speed until foamy, then beat at high speed until firm peaks form when the beaters are lifted. Beat in the sugar 2 tablespoons at a time until shiny.

3. Spoon or pipe the meringue onto the baking sheet in 1 ½-inch mounds. Transfer to the oven and bake until firm, about 1 hour and 15 minutes. Let cool completely before serving.

From Françoise:
• Instead of buttering and flouring the baking sheet, you can line it with parchment paper or foil.

• Pastry chefs sometimes leave their meringues in a barely warm oven overnight, so be patient

DESSERTS

continued

until your meringues are completely dry if you don't want them to collapse when removed from the oven.

• Egg whites that are too cold do not whip as well as whites at room temperature. Remove them from the refrigerator half an hour ahead of time and let them warm up slightly.

• The meringues are cooked when they are firm and slightly browned.

• Baked meringues can be stored in an airtight container for up to 2 weeks.

CHOCOLATE GANACHE–STUFFED MERINGUES

- *Meringues à la ganache de chocolat* -

❖ INTERMEDIATE   ❖ INEXPENSIVE   ❖ 1 HOUR, 30 MINUTES   ❖ MAKES 2 TO 3 DOZEN MERINGUES

MERINGUES
2 large egg whites
Pinch of salt
1 teaspoon fresh lemon juice
½ cup sugar

CHOCOLATE GANACHE
¾ cup crème fraîche
2 ½ ounces bittersweet chocolate, chopped

❖ ❖ ❖ ❖ ❖

1. Preheat the oven to 225 degrees. Line a baking sheet with foil.

2. In a medium bowl, beat the egg whites with the salt and lemon juice at low speed until foamy, then beat at high speed until firm peaks form when the beaters are lifted. Beat in the sugar 2 tablespoons at a time until glossy.

3. Spoon or pipe the meringue onto the baking sheet in 1 ½-inch mounds. Transfer to the oven and bake until firm, about 1 hour and 15 minutes. Let cool completely before using.

4. Meanwhile, make the chocolate ganache: In a small saucepan, combine the crème fraîche with the chocolate and melt over low heat,

without stirring, until barely simmering. Remove the pan from the heat and stir with a wooden spoon; let cool slightly. Using an electric mixer, beat the ganache until doubled in volume.

5. Sandwich a little ganache between each pair of meringues and transfer to little foil cups. Arrange on a platter and refrigerate until slightly chilled, but not too long or the meringues will soften.

From Françoise:
• If you really want to make these ahead of time, they can be stored, stuffed or not, in an airtight container in the refrigerator for 1 to 2 days.

FRENCH BAKED ALASKA

- *Omelette glacée, meringuée et dorée au four* -

❖ INTERMEDIATE   ❖ MODERATE   ❖ 30 MINUTES   ❖ SERVES 6 TO 8

COOKED MERINGUE
4 large egg whites
Pinch of salt
1 ¼ cups sugar, plus more for sprinkling

Génoise (page 757) or yellow layer cake
¼ cup liqueur (see note below)
1 pint vanilla ice cream, softened

❖ ❖ ❖ ❖ ❖

1. Make the cooked meringue: In a medium bowl, beat the egg whites with the salt at low speed until foamy. Beat in the sugar 2 tablespoons at a time. Set the bowl over a saucepan of hot water and beat at high speed until tall peaks form when the beaters are lifted. Remove the bowl from the heat and continue beating until the meringue is cool. Cover and refrigerate.

2. Set the cake on a cardboard round. Using a serrated knife, split the cake in half horizontally. Brush the cut sides with the liqueur. Spread half of the ice cream over the bottom layer. Cover with the top layer and spread the remaining ice cream around the sides of the cake. Cover and freeze until the ice cream is firm.

3. Preheat the oven to 450 degrees.

4. Using a thin spatula, roughly spread the cooked meringue all over the top and sides of the cake; it shouldn't be too smooth. Sprinkle with sugar. Transfer to an ovenproof platter and bake just until the top is golden. Serve immediately.

From Françoise:

• For the liqueur, you could use Grand Marnier, Bénédictine, or another orange-flavored liqueur.

• If you're making the Génoise on page 757, omit the rum and lemon.

• Several steps in the Baked Alaska can be done in advance. The cooked meringue can be refrigerated for up to a week. Or the recipe can be prepared through Step 2 and frozen for several hours. Frost the cake and brown it in the oven just before serving.

• Variation: Soak chopped candied fruit in liqueur and scatter it over the bottom cake layer before spreading the ice cream on top.

• If you don't have an ovenproof platter, set the cake (on its cardboard round) on a baking sheet, then carefully transfer it to a platter to serve.

• If your meringue is spread thickly all over the cake and your oven is hot enough, the meringue will brown quickly—before the ice cream has time to melt.

DESSERTS

CREAMY RED CURRANT ICEBOX CAKE

- *Pudding délicieux à la crème* -

❖ INTERMEDIATE   ❖ MODERATE   ❖ 30 MINUTES, PLUS 30 MINUTES CHILLING   ❖ SERVES 4

VANILLA CUSTARD SAUCE

2 cups milk

1 tablespoon vanilla sugar or 1 vanilla bean,
  seeds scraped

Pinch of salt

4 or 5 large egg yolks

2 to 3 tablespoons sugar

KIRSCH SYRUP

¼ cup sugar

2 tablespoons kirsch or rum

⅓ cup red currant jelly

14 to 18 ladyfingers

❖ ❖ ❖ ❖ ❖

1. Make the vanilla custard sauce: In a large saucepan, bring the milk to a bare simmer with the vanilla sugar or vanilla seeds and salt.

2. In a bowl, beat the egg yolks with the sugar until thick and light. Whisk in half the hot milk, then whisk the mixture back into the remaining milk. Place over low heat and cook, stirring constantly with a wooden spoon, until the custard thickens slightly. Remove the pan from the heat.

3. Make the kirsch syrup: In a small saucepan, heat the sugar with ¾ cup of water, stirring, until the sugar dissolves. Remove the pan from the heat and stir in the kirsch or rum. Pour into a shallow bowl and let cool.

4. Sandwich a little red currant jelly between each pair of ladyfingers. Dip both sides of the ladyfinger sandwiches in the kirsch syrup and use them to line the bottom of a shallow glass

or ceramic baking dish. Pour the warm custard sauce over the ladyfingers. Cover and refrigerate until cold, 30 minutes or overnight. Serve straight from the dish.

From Françoise:

• For the baking dish, you just need something shallow and large enough to fit the ladyfingers snugly. And since it's not going into the oven, it can be a little fragile.

• The custard sauce should be sweetened less than usual because the ladyfingers, jelly, and syrup are all sugary.

• If your sauce curdles, try removing the pan from the heat immediately and beating it with a whisk or electric mixer.

• Don't add too much custard to the baking dish. The sauce should barely cover the ladyfingers; they shouldn't float in it.

RED CURRANT ICEBOX CAKE

- *Diplomate* -

❖ EASY ❖ MODERATE ❖ 40 MINUTES, PLUS 2 TO 3 HOURS CHILLING ❖ SERVES 6

¼ cup kirsch or rum
1 pound ladyfingers
Red currant jelly, melted

VANILLA CUSTARD SAUCE
2 cups milk

1 tablespoon vanilla sugar or 1 vanilla bean,
  seeds scraped
Pinch of salt
4 or 5 large egg yolks
2 to 3 tablespoons sugar

❖ ❖ ❖ ❖ ❖

1. Pour the kirsch or rum into a shallow bowl and dip in the ladyfingers. In a soufflé dish or other deep baking dish, arrange a layer of the ladyfingers in the bottom. Brush with the jelly. Continue layering ladyfingers and jelly, finishing with a layer of lady fingers. Cover with plastic and weight down with cans of food. Refrigerate for 2 to 3 hours.

2. Meanwhile, make the vanilla custard sauce: In a large saucepan, bring the milk to a bare simmer with the vanilla sugar or vanilla seeds and salt.

3. In a bowl, beat the egg yolks with the sugar until thick and light. Whisk in half the hot milk, then whisk the mixture back into the remaining milk. Place over low heat and cook,

stirring constantly with a wooden spoon, until the custard thickens slightly. Remove the pan from the heat. Let cool slightly, then refrigerate until cold.

4. To serve, run a knife around the dish. Invert a round platter over the dish. Holding the dish and platter together, quickly invert the cake onto the platter. Serve with the custard sauce.

From Françoise:
• You might decorate the top with crushed Praline (page 680).

• For a more elegant presentation, line the sides and bottom of the dish with some of the ladyfingers, flat sides facing inward and trimming the bottom ones to fit snugly.

DESSERTS

CINNAMON-APPLE BREAD PUDDING

- *Pudding aux pommes et fruits secs* -

❖ EASY   ❖ INEXPENSIVE   ❖ 1 HOUR   ❖ SERVES 6 TO 8

5 tablespoons unsalted butter, cut into
  ¼-inch dice, plus more for brushing
7 ounces stale bread, cut into 1-inch cubes
2 cups milk
3 large eggs, separated
6 tablespoons sugar
½ tablespoon vanilla sugar

1 ½ ounces candied orange peel, chopped
2 tablespoons rum
1 ½ pounds Golden Delicious apples, peeled,
  quartered, and thinly sliced
Pinch of salt
2 tablespoons stale bread crumbs
1 to 2 teaspoons cinnamon

❖ ❖ ❖ ❖ ❖

1. Preheat the oven to 425 degrees. Brush a baking dish with butter.

2. In a large bowl, combine the bread cubes with the milk and let soak. Beat in the egg yolks, sugar, vanilla sugar, orange peel, and rum. Fold in the apples.

3. In a bowl, beat the egg whites with the salt until foamy, then beat at high speed until stiff. Fold the beaten whites into the bread mixture.

4. Spread the bread pudding into the baking dish. Sprinkle with the bread crumbs and cinnamon and dot with the butter. Transfer to the oven and bake for 30 to 35 minutes. Serve warm or at room temperature.

From Françoise:
• You can add rum-soaked raisins or chopped almonds to the pudding. And grated orange zest can replace the candied orange peel.

• Also, fresh or canned cherries can be substituted for the apples. Since cherries are juicier than apples, add a little less milk. If you do use cherries, add kirsch instead of rum.

• You can buy vanilla sugar in certain supermarkets, but it is easy to make your own: Split one vanilla bean and scrape out the seeds, reserving them for another use. Place the scraped bean in a glass jar and cover it with 1 to 2 cups of sugar. Shake it occasionally and leave it in your pantry. After a week or two, your sugar will be perfumed with the vanilla.

RAISIN BREAD PUDDING
WITH CANDIED ORANGE PEEL
- *Pudding au pain et à l'écorce d'orange* -

❖ EASY ❖ INEXPENSIVE ❖ 1 HOUR, 30 MINUTES, PLUS 2 TO 3 HOURS CHILLING ❖ SERVES 4

⅔ cup raisins

1 cup sugar

Squeeze of lemon juice

7 ounces stale bread, cut into 1-inch cubes

2 cups milk

3 large eggs

½ teaspoon cinnamon

1½ ounces candied orange peel, chopped

❖ ❖ ❖ ❖ ❖

1. In a sieve, rinse the raisins in warm water. In a bowl, soak them in hot water for at least 15 minutes or until they have swollen to at least twice their size. Drain.

2. Preheat the oven to 350 degrees. In a small saucepan, combine ¼ cup of the sugar with 2 tablespoons of water and the lemon juice. Place over medium-high heat, bring to a simmer, and cook, stirring often, until the sugar dissolves. Partly cover the pan and continue cooking until the sugar turns medium amber. Immediately pour the caramel into a loaf pan and quickly turn to coat the bottom and sides.

3. In a large bowl, combine the bread cubes with the milk and let soak until very soft. Transfer to a food processor and pulse in the eggs, the remaining ¾ cup of sugar, and the cinnamon. Pour back into the bowl and stir in the raisins and candied orange.

4. Spread the bread pudding in the loaf pan. Transfer to the oven and bake for about 1 hour. Let cool completely, then cover and refrigerate until cold, 2 to 3 hours.

5. To serve, run a knife around the pan. Invert a platter over the pan. Holding the pan and platter together, quickly invert the pudding onto the platter; the caramel sauce will spill out.

From Françoise:

• If you have an extra egg white, you can pulse it in with the whole eggs in Step 3.

• Look for artisanal, small-batch candied fruit instead of the industrial variety, which doesn't have much flavor.

DESSERTS

CLASSIC APPLE TART

- *Tarte aux pommes* -

❖ INTERMEDIATE   ❖ INEXPENSIVE   ❖ 1 HOUR, PLUS 20 MINUTES RESTING   ❖ SERVES 6

PÂTE BRISÉE
1 ¼ cups all-purpose flour
½ teaspoon salt
5 tablespoons unsalted butter, cut into pieces

2 pounds apples, peeled, cored, quartered,
  and thinly sliced
Sugar for sprinkling

❖ ❖ ❖ ❖ ❖

1. Make the pâte brisée: In a bowl, combine the flour with the salt and butter. Rub the butter into the flour between your palms. Sprinkle in ¼ cup of water and knead briefly until large crumbs form. Press into a disk. On a lightly floured work surface, scrape the dough away from you with the heel of your hand in a long sliding motion, then press into a disk; repeat 3 times. Press into a disk, wrap, and refrigerate until firm, 15 to 20 minutes.

2. Preheat the oven to 400 degrees. On a lightly floured work surface, roll the dough into a round about ⅛ inch thick. Wrap the dough around the rolling pin and fit it into an 8- to 9-inch tart pan with a removable bottom. Trim off any excess. Use the scraps to patch any cracks. Prick holes all over the bottom of the tart shell with a fork.

3. Arrange the apple slices, overlapping them, in the tart shell. Transfer to the oven and bake for about 30 minutes. Unmold and set on a rack to cool. Sprinkle with sugar before serving.

From Françoise:

• If your pâte brisée is tough, it's because you worked the dough too much or you added too much water.

• If your dough doesn't roll out smoothly or breaks easily, it's because you didn't add enough water. Sprinkle it with a few drops, but do it quickly so the dough doesn't toughen.

• If the sides of the shell collapse, it's because the dough was too soft (too much water or the butter is too soft), the oven wasn't hot enough, or you didn't press the dough well against the sides.

• Check to see that the bottom of the tart shell is slightly browned. I think nothing is more disappointing when you're making a tart than a pastry crust that's not cooked through. It should be crunchy.

APPLE PIE

- Tourte aux pommes et aux épices -

❖ INTERMEDIATE   ❖ MODERATE   ❖ 1 HOUR, PLUS 30 MINUTES RESTING   ❖ SERVES 6 TO 8

PIE DOUGH

2 cups all-purpose flour

1 teaspoon salt

1 cup (2 sticks) unsalted butter, cubed

4 to 6 tablespoons ice water

1¼ to 1½ pounds apples, peeled, cored,
   quartered, and thinly sliced

¼ cup sugar

1 teaspoon cinnamon

½ teaspoon ground ginger

½ teaspoon freshly grated nutmeg

3 tablespoons unsalted butter,
   cut into ¼-inch dice

Egg yolk beaten with a little milk

❖   ❖   ❖   ❖   ❖

1. Make the pie dough: In a food processor, pulse the flour with the salt. Add the butter and pulse until the size of peas. Drizzle in the water and pulse until the crumbs are moistened; turn out onto a work surface. Gather into a ball, flatten, wrap in plastic, and refrigerate for 30 minutes.

2. Preheat the oven to 425 degrees. In a bowl, combine the apples with the sugar, cinnamon, ginger, and nutmeg and toss to coat. Spread the apple mixture in an 8- to 10-inch pie dish and dot with the butter.

3. On a lightly floured work surface, roll out the dough to a 10- to 12-inch round and center it over the filling. Trim the overhang to 1 inch and brush with water. Fold the overhang under itself and crimp to seal. Brush the top with beaten egg yolk mixture. Poke a hole in the center of the pie and insert a foil "chimney" to allow steam to escape.

4. Transfer the pie to the oven and bake until the crust is golden, 35 to 40 minutes, reducing the oven temperature to 400 degrees halfway through. Cover the edge of the pie if it begins to darken. Serve warm or at room temperature.

From Françoise:

• Apple pie can also be made double-crusted; simply double the amount of dough.

• The "chimney" cut in the top crust keeps the pie juices from boiling over.

DESSERTS

WHOLE APPLES IN FLAKY PASTRY

- *Bourdelots normands* -

❖ INTERMEDIATE ❖ INEXPENSIVE ❖ 1 HOUR, PLUS 20 MINUTES RESTING ❖ SERVES 4

PÂTE BRISÉE

2 cups all-purpose flour

1 teaspoon salt

½ cup (1 stick) unsalted butter,
  cut into pieces

4 tablespoons (½ stick) unsalted butter,
  plus more for brushing

4 medium apples, such as Golden Delicious

4 teaspoons apricot jam

¼ cup Calvados (optional)

1 large egg, lightly beaten

❖ ❖ ❖ ❖ ❖

1. Make the pâte brisée: In a bowl, combine the flour with the salt and butter. Rub the butter into the flour between your palms. Sprinkle in ¼ cup of water and knead briefly until large crumbs form. Press into a disk. On a lightly floured work surface, scrape the dough away from you with the heel of your hand in a long sliding motion, then press into a disk; repeat 3 times. Press into a disk, wrap, and refrigerate until firm, 15 to 20 minutes.

2. Preheat the oven to 425 degrees. Brush a baking sheet with butter.

3. Peel the apples. Working from the stem end and using a melon baller, apple corer, or sharp knife, remove the interior core and seeds to within ½ inch of the bottom. Add 1 teaspoon

of jam, 1 tablespoon of butter, and 1 tablespoon of Calvados, if using, to each apple.

4. On a lightly floured work surface, roll the dough into a square about ⅛ inch thick. Cut it into quarters. Set each stuffed apple on a square of dough and wrap, pressing on the seams to seal. Brush with the beaten egg.

5. Set the pastries on the baking sheet, transfer to the oven, and bake for 35 to 40 minutes. Serve warm.

From Françoise:

• If you have extra dough, stamp out 4 small rounds and set 1 on top of each wrapped apple before baking. Brush the dough round with more beaten egg.

FROMAGE BLANC TART

- *Tarte au fromage blanc* -

❖ INTERMEDIATE   ❖ INEXPENSIVE   ❖ 1 HOUR, PLUS 20 MINUTES RESTING   ❖ SERVES 6

PÂTE BRISÉE

1 ¼ cups all-purpose flour

½ teaspoon salt

5 tablespoons unsalted butter, cut into pieces

FILLING

¾ cup fromage blanc

⅓ cup crème fraîche

2 large eggs

3 tablespoons sugar

⅓ cup raisins, rinsed in warm water

2 tablespoons potato starch or cornstarch

6 tablespoons milk

❖ ❖ ❖ ❖ ❖

1. Make the pâte brisée: In a bowl, combine the flour with the salt and butter. Rub the butter into the flour between your palms. Sprinkle in ¼ cup of water and knead briefly until large crumbs form. Press into a disk. On a lightly floured work surface, scrape the dough away from you with the heel of your hand in a long sliding motion, then press into a disk; repeat 3 times. Press into a disk, wrap, and refrigerate until firm, 15 to 20 minutes.

2. Preheat the oven to 400 degrees. On a lightly floured work surface, roll the dough into a round about ⅛ inch thick. Wrap the dough around the rolling pin and fit it into an 8- to 9-inch tart pan with a removable bottom. Trim off any excess. Use the scraps to patch any cracks. Prick holes all over the bottom of the tart shell with a fork. Cut a round of foil slightly larger than the tart pan and roll up the edge. Fit it inside the tart shell. Bake for 5 to 10 minutes only; remove the foil.

3. Meanwhile, make the filling: In a bowl, beat the fromage blanc with the crème fraîche, eggs, sugar, and raisins. In a cup, blend the potato starch or cornstarch with the milk. Beat into the fromage blanc mixture.

4. Spread the filling in the partially baked shell. Transfer to the oven and bake until set, about 30 minutes.

From Françoise:

• Even though this tart is a dessert, it can be served as an entrée because it's not supersweet. Serve it warm in the winter or chilled in the summer.

• For the pâte brisée, the butter should be cold. As soon as water or eggs are added to the dough, it must be worked quickly or it toughens. However, it can be made in advance or doubled, with the extra dough reserved for another tart. Store it, wrapped in plastic, in the refrigerator for 1 to 2 days, or freeze it.

• You can flavor the dough with finely grated lemon or orange zest, cinnamon, or vanilla.

• It is essential to partially bake the tart shell or it will be soggy when the filling is added.

• If you like, dust the tart with confectioners' sugar just before serving.

DESSERTS

701

LATTICE-TOPPED SWEET SPINACH TART WITH CANDIED FRUIT

- *Tarte sucrée aux épinards* -

❖ INTERMEDIATE　　❖ MODERATE　　❖ 1 HOUR, PLUS 20 MINUTES RESTING　　❖ SERVES 8

PÂTE BRISÉE

1 ½ cups all-purpose flour

¾ teaspoon salt

7 tablespoons unsalted butter, cut into pieces

2 pounds spinach, tough stems removed

1 ounce candied orange peel, chopped

1 ounce candied melon peel, chopped

1 large egg yolk, mixed with 1 tablespoon water

PASTRY CREAM

2 tablespoons unsalted butter

2 tablespoons all-purpose flour

1 cup milk

½ cup sugar

1 tablespoon vanilla sugar

Pinch of salt

Finely grated zest of 1 lemon

3 large egg yolks

❖ ❖ ❖ ❖ ❖

1. Make the pâte brisée: In a bowl, combine the flour with the salt and butter. Rub the butter into the flour between your palms. Sprinkle in 5 or 6 tablespoons of water and knead briefly until large crumbs form. Press into a disk. On a lightly floured surface, scrape the dough away from you with the heel of your hand in a long sliding motion, then press into a disk; repeat 3 times. Press into a disk, wrap, and refrigerate until firm, 15 to 20 minutes.

2. Meanwhile, bring a large pot of water to a boil. Add the spinach and cook for 5 minutes. Drain and squeeze out as much water as possible. Puree the spinach using a food mill or food processor.

3. Make the pastry cream: In a large saucepan, melt the butter over medium heat. Whisk in the flour until it starts foaming. Whisk in the milk until the cream thickens, then reduce the heat to very low and cook for 2 minutes. Whisk in the sugar, vanilla sugar, and salt. Remove

the pan from the heat and whisk in the lemon zest and egg yolks. Beat in the spinach.

4. Preheat the oven to 400 degrees. On a lightly floured work surface, roll the disk into a round about ⅛ inch thick. Wrap the dough around the rolling pin and fit it into a 9- to 10-inch tart pan with a removable bottom. Trim off any excess. Spread half the spinach in the tart shell. Scatter the candied fruit over the top and spread the remaining spinach in the shell. Roll the scraps into a round. Using a pastry wheel, cut the round into ¾-inch-wide strips. Arrange the strips over the filling in a lattice pattern, pressing the ends onto the dough rim. Trim any excess. Brush the lattice with the egg yolk mixture.

5. Set the tart on a baking sheet, transfer to the oven, and bake for 25 to 30 minutes. Let cool completely. Serve at room temperature.

• The secret to weaving a lattice top like a basket: Alternate the direction of the dough strips as you lay them across the filling, arranging 1 lengthwise, then 1 crosswise, and so forth.

ALSATIAN FRUIT TART
- Tarte aux fruits à l'alsacienne -

❖ INTERMEDIATE ❖ MODERATE ❖ 1 HOUR, PLUS 1 HOUR RESTING ❖ SERVES 6

PÂTE SUCRÉE
1 ¼ cups all-purpose flour
5 tablespoons unsalted butter, softened
3 tablespoons sugar
½ teaspoon salt
1 small egg

1 ¼ pounds fruit, pitted, cored, and sliced
  as appropriate
1 large egg
¾ cup milk
¼ cup sugar

❖ ❖ ❖ ❖ ❖

1. Make the pâte sucrée: Mound the flour on a work surface. Make a well in the middle of the flour and add the butter, sugar, and salt and mix with your fingers. Add the egg and quickly work it with the other ingredients until partially mixed. Gradually incorporate the flour. Press into a disk. On a lightly floured work surface, scrape the dough away from you with the heel of your hand in a long sliding motion. Press into a disk, wrap, and refrigerate until firm, about 1 hour.

2. Preheat the oven to 400 degrees. On a lightly floured work surface, roll the dough into a round ⅛ to ¼ inch thick. Wrap the dough around the rolling pin and fit it into an 8- to 9-inch tart pan with a removable bottom. Trim off any excess. Use the scraps to patch any cracks. Prick holes all over the bottom of the tart shell with a fork.

3. Arrange the fruit in the tart shell. Transfer to the oven and bake for 20 minutes. In a bowl, beat the egg with the milk and sugar and pour over the fruit. Reduce the oven temperature to 350 degrees and bake until the filling is set, about 15 minutes.

DESSERTS

PINEAPPLE TART

- *Tarte aux ananas* -

❖ INTERMEDIATE　　❖ MODERATE　　❖ 45 MINUTES, PLUS 1 HOUR RESTING　　❖ SERVES 6

PÂTE SABLÉE

1 ¼ cups all-purpose flour

5 tablespoons unsalted butter, softened

6 tablespoons sugar

½ teaspoon salt

1 large egg yolk

PASTRY CREAM

1 cup milk

Pinch of salt

¼ cup sugar

2 large egg yolks

2 tablespoons all-purpose flour

1 tablespoon kirsch

5 pineapple slices, cut into chunks

Red currant jelly or apricot jam, melted

❖　❖　❖　❖　❖

1. Make the pâte sablée: Mound the flour on a work surface. Make a well in the middle of the flour and add the butter, sugar, and salt and mix with your fingers. Add the egg yolk and quickly work it with the other ingredients until partially mixed. Gradually incorporate the flour. Quickly crumble the mixture between your palms. Press into a disk, wrap, and refrigerate until firm, about 1 hour.

2. Preheat the oven to 350 degrees. On a lightly floured work surface, roll the dough into a round about ¼ inch thick. Wrap the dough around the rolling pin and fit it into an 8-inch tart pan with a removable bottom. Trim off any excess. Use the scraps to patch any cracks. Prick holes all over the bottom of the tart shell with a fork. Cut a round of foil slightly larger than the tart pan and roll up the edge. Fit it inside the tart shell. Bake until the crust is lightly browned and cooked through, 15 to 20 minutes; remove the foil. Transfer to a rack to cool completely, then unmold.

3. Meanwhile, make the pastry cream: In a large saucepan, bring the milk to a bare simmer with the salt. In a bowl, beat the sugar with the egg yolks until thick and light, 2 to 3 minutes. Beat in the flour. Gradually whisk in the hot milk.

4. Return the mixture to the pan and bring to a boil, whisking constantly, then reduce the heat to low and cook, whisking, for 2 minutes. Remove the pan from the heat and mix in the kirsch. Let cool slightly

5. Spread the pastry cream in the tart shell. Arrange the pineapple on top. Brush the pineapple lightly with the jelly or jam.

From Françoise:

• It is not critical to flavor the pastry cream with kirsch. Instead, you can add vanilla sugar or vanilla seeds at the same time as the regular sugar.

HONEY-WALNUT TART

- *Tarte aux noix et crème fouettée* -

❖ INTERMEDIATE ❖ MODERATE ❖ 1 HOUR, PLUS 30 MINUTES COOLING ❖ SERVES 6

Pâte Brisée (page 92)

5 tablespoons unsalted butter, softened

6 tablespoons sugar

3 large eggs

½ cup acacia honey

½ pound walnut halves, 10 of the nicest halves
   reserved, the rest chopped

WHIPPED CREAM

¾ cup heavy cream

1 tablespoon sugar

½ tablespoon vanilla sugar

❖ ❖ ❖ ❖ ❖

1. Preheat the oven to 400 degrees. On a lightly floured work surface, roll the dough into a round about ⅛ inch thick. Wrap the dough around the rolling pin and fit it into an 8- to 9-inch tart pan with a removable bottom. Trim off any excess. Use the scraps to patch any cracks. Prick holes all over the bottom of the tart shell with a fork. Cover and refrigerate.

2. In a bowl, using an electric mixer, beat the butter with the sugar. Add the eggs and honey and beat for 2 minutes. Beat in the chopped walnuts.

3. Spread the filling in the tart shell. Arrange the reserved walnut halves on top. Transfer to the oven and bake until a knife inserted in the filling comes out clean, 30 to 40 minutes.

4. Make the whipped cream: In a chilled bowl and using a chilled whisk, beat the cream until it starts to thicken. Add the sugar and vanilla sugar and beat until soft peaks form.

5. Let the tart cool completely. Serve with the whipped cream.

From Françoise:

• You can use a store-bought rolled piecrust here.

• If you are making the dough yourself, you might prepare it a day ahead. The next day, roll it out and line the tart pan with it, then refrigerate for 1 to 2 hours.

• Try pecans instead of walnuts.

DESSERTS

CINNAMON-WALNUT TART

- *Tarte aux noix et à la cannelle* -

❖ INTERMEDIATE   ❖ MODERATE   ❖ 1 HOUR, PLUS 1 HOUR RESTING   ❖ SERVES 6

PÂTE SABLÉE

1 ¼ cups all–purpose flour

½ teaspoon cinnamon

5 tablespoons unsalted butter, softened

6 tablespoons sugar

½ teaspoon salt

2 large egg yolks or 1 whole large egg

Butter for brushing

½ cup crème fraîche

¼ cup sugar

½ pound walnut halves, 10 of the nicest halves
   reserved, the rest chopped

1 teaspoon cinnamon

1 large egg white

⅓ cup confectioners' sugar

2 tablespoons kirsch (optional)

❖   ❖   ❖   ❖   ❖

1. Make the pâte sablée: Sift or whisk the flour with the cinnamon and mound on a work surface. Make a well in the middle of the flour and add the butter, sugar, and salt and mix with your fingers. Add the egg yolks or whole egg and quickly work them with the other ingredients until partially mixed. Gradually incorporate the flour. Quickly crumble the mixture between your palms. Press into a disk, wrap, and refrigerate until firm, about 1 hour.

2. Preheat the oven to 400 degrees. Brush an 8-inch tart pan with a removable bottom with butter. On a lightly floured work surface, roll the dough into a round about ¼ inch thick. Wrap the dough around the rolling pin and fit it into the tart pan. Trim off any excess. Use the scraps to patch any cracks. Prick holes all over the bottom of the tart shell with a fork. Cover and refrigerate.

3. Meanwhile, in a bowl, beat the crème fraîche with the sugar, chopped walnuts, and cinnamon. Spread the filling in the tart shell. Transfer to the oven and bake for 35 to 40 minutes. Remove the tart from the oven.

4. In a bowl, whisk the egg white with the confectioners' sugar and kirsch, if using. Arrange the reserved walnuts halves over the tart. Pour the glaze over the top and let cool completely before serving.

From Françoise:

• Please note that the finished dish contains raw egg.

CHOCOLATE ALMOND TART

- *Tarte croquante au chocolat* -

ALMOND CRUST

1 ¾ cups ground almonds

½ cup sugar

1 large egg yolk

5 tablespoons unsalted butter, softened,
  plus more for brushing

All-purpose flour for dusting

5 ounces bittersweet chocolate, chopped

3 large eggs, separated

5 tablespoons sugar

WHIPPED CREAM

¾ cup heavy cream

1 tablespoon vanilla sugar

❖ ❖ ❖ ❖ ❖

1. Make the almond crust: In a bowl, knead the ground almonds with the sugar and egg yolk until the crumbly mixture holds together. Press into a disk, wrap, and refrigerate until firm, about 30 minutes.

2. Preheat the oven to 300 degrees. Generously butter a 9- to 10-inch tart pan with a removable bottom. Dust with flour, shaking out the excess. Pat the dough over the bottom and up the sides of the tart pan. Transfer to the oven and bake for 30 to 35 minutes. Set on a rack in the pan and let cool completely. Carefully unmold the tart shell and set on a flat platter.

3. In a double boiler, melt the chocolate without stirring. Remove from the heat and beat in the 5 tablespoons of butter, then add the egg yolks and 4 tablespoons of the sugar and beat vigorously. Cover and refrigerate.

4. In a bowl, beat the egg whites at low speed until foamy, then beat at high speed until firm peaks form when the beaters are lifted. Beat in the remaining 1 tablespoon of sugar until glossy. Gently fold the beaten egg whites into the chilled chocolate mixture. Spread in the cooled tart shell and return to the refrigerator.

5. Make the whipped cream: In a chilled bowl and using a chilled whisk, beat the cream until it starts to thicken. Add the vanilla sugar and beat until soft peaks form. Dollop the whipped cream around the edge of the tart or spread it over the tart just before serving.

From Françoise:

• It is crucial to use a tart pan with a removable bottom to make this dessert and to butter it and flour it well—the sides, too.

• Please note that the finished dish contains raw egg.

APRICOT PUFF PASTRY TART

- Tarte feuilletée aux abricots frais -

❖ ADVANCED   ❖ MODERATE   ❖ 2 HOURS, PLUS RESTING TIME   ❖ SERVES 6

PUFF PASTRY

2 cups all-purpose flour

½ teaspoon salt

¾ cup (1 ½ sticks) unsalted butter

1 pound apricots, halved and pitted

1 to 2 tablespoons sugar

❖ ❖ ❖ ❖ ❖

1. Make the puff pastry: Mound the flour on a work surface. Make a well in the middle of the flour and add the salt and ½ cup of cold water. Gradually incorporate the flour. Cut the dough several times with a dough scraper to blend the ingredients but do not knead it. Press into a disk, wrap, and refrigerate for 15 minutes.

2. Pound the butter to make a pliable, 6-inch square; it should have the same firmness as the chilled dough. On a lightly floured work surface, using a lightly floured rolling pin, roll out the dough to a 12-inch round. Set the butter in the center of the dough, fold the dough over the butter, and press to seal. Turn the package over and roll into a rectangle. Fold over itself into thirds. Turn the dough so the folded edges are to the left and right. Roll out and fold the dough a second time; wrap and refrigerate for 10 to 15 minutes. Repeat the rolling, folding, and turning 2 more times and refrigerate. Repeat for a total of 6 times.

3. Preheat the oven to 425 degrees. On a lightly floured work surface, roll out the dough to fit an 8- to 9-inch tart pan with a removable bottom. Wrap the dough around the rolling pin and fit it into the pan. Trim off any excess.

4. Arrange the apricots in the tart shell. Transfer to the oven and bake for about 30 minutes. Sprinkle with the sugar. Carefully unmold the tart onto a cake rack.

From Françoise:

• This tart is really easy to do with store-bought all-butter puff pastry dough.

• If possible, refrigerate the tart shell for an hour before baking.

• Puff pastry is good for baking juicy fruits like apricots because it doesn't get soggy.

BUTTERY ALMOND PUFF PASTRY TART
- *Galette des rois* -

❖ INTERMEDIATE ❖ MODERATE ❖ 2 HOURS ❖ SERVES 6

1 pound all-butter Puff Pastry dough (page 738)
  or store-bought, cut in half
1 large egg white, lightly beaten
Confectioners' sugar for dusting

ALMOND FILLING
¼ cup sugar
2 tablespoons unsalted butter, softened
1 large egg yolk
⅓ cup ground almonds
2 tablespoons rum

❖ ❖ ❖ ❖ ❖

1. Sprinkle a baking sheet with water. On a lightly floured work surface, roll out one half of the dough to a round slightly thinner than ¼ inch. Using a pan lid as a guide, cut out a round with a sharp knife. Wrap the dough around the rolling pin and transfer to the baking sheet. Cover and refrigerate.

2. Make the almond filling: In a bowl, beat the sugar with the softened butter, egg yolk, ground almonds, and rum until smooth. Dollop the filling evenly over the dough round, leaving a 1-inch border. Refrigerate.

3. Preheat the oven to 425 degrees.

4. Roll out the second piece of dough to a round and cut to the same size as the first. Brush the border of the bottom round of dough with water. Wrap the second round of dough around the rolling pin and set on top. Press the edges together firmly. Scallop the edges slightly using the back of a knife. Brush the top with beaten egg white, making sure not to touch the sides.

5. Transfer to the oven and bake until lightly browned, 25 to 30 minutes. Just before it's done, dust the top with confectioners' sugar, return the tart to the top shelf of the oven and bake until caramelized. Watch carefully because the sugar can burn quickly. Serve warm or reheated.

From Françoise:
• This tart is traditionally eaten for Epiphany on January 6. A dried bean or small porcelain bean (a *fève*) is usually added to the tart at the same time as the filling. The guest who finds the *fève* in his slice is the king. If this tart is served at another time (no bean), it's often called *gâteau pithiviers*.

• If you like, using a sharp knife, score the top decoratively.

• A small, fine sieve is very handy for dusting the confectioners' sugar evenly over the top.

DESSERTS

CLASSIC MILLEFEUILLE

- *Mille-feuille à la crème* -

❖ INTERMEDIATE   ❖ MODERATE   ❖ 1 HOUR   ❖ SERVES 6

PASTRY CREAM
1 cup milk
Pinch of salt
¼ cup sugar
1 tablespoon vanilla sugar
2 large egg yolks

2 tablespoons all-purpose flour
1 tablespoon kirsch or rum (optional)

1 pound all-butter Puff Pastry dough (page 738)
  or store-bought, cut in half
Confectioners' sugar for dusting

❖ ❖ ❖ ❖ ❖

1. Make the pastry cream: In a large saucepan, bring the milk to a bare simmer with the salt. In a bowl, beat the sugar with the vanilla sugar and the egg yolks until thick and light, 2 to 3 minutes. Beat in the flour. Gradually whisk in the hot milk.

2. Return the mixture to the pan, place over medium heat, and bring to a boil, whisking constantly, then reduce the heat to low and cook, whisking, for 2 minutes. Remove the pan from the heat and mix in the kirsch or rum, if using. Let cool completely.

3. Preheat the oven to 425 degrees. Sprinkle a baking sheet with water.

4. On a lightly floured work surface, roll out each puff pastry half to a rectangle about ⅛ inch thick. Trim the edges. Wrap each rectangle around the rolling pin and transfer to the baking sheet, laying them side by side. Prick all over with a fork. Bake in the oven for 15 to 20 minutes. Let cool on a rack.

5. Turn one of the pastry rectangles upside down and dust with confectioners' sugar. Set on the baking sheet and bake on the top shelf of the oven until caramelized, about 1 minute. Watch carefully because the sugar burns easily.

6. Set the second pastry rectangle on a serving platter. Pipe or spread the pastry cream over the pastry, top with the caramelized rectangle, and press lightly to adhere.

From Françoise:
• If you prefer individual millefeuilles, cut each dough rectangle into 6 pieces before baking.

LEMON MERINGUE TART

- *Tarte meringuée au citron* -

❖ INTERMEDIATE   ❖ MODERATE   ❖ 1 HOUR, 30 MINUTES, PLUS 20 MINUTES RESTING   ❖ SERVES 6

PÂTE BRISÉE
1 ¼ cups all-purpose flour
Finely grated zest of ½ lemon
½ teaspoon salt
5 tablespoons unsalted butter, cut into pieces

FILLING
1 large egg
Pinch of salt

½ cup sugar
Finely grated zest of ½ lemon
Juice of 1 lemon
3 tablespoons unsalted butter, softened

MERINGUE
2 large egg whites
Pinch of salt
⅓ cup sugar

❖ ❖ ❖ ❖ ❖

1. Make the pâte brisée: In a bowl, combine the flour with the lemon zest, salt, and butter. Rub the butter into the flour between your palms. Sprinkle in ¼ cup of water and knead briefly until large crumbs form. Press into a disk. On a lightly floured work surface, scrape the dough away from you with the heel of your hand in a long sliding motion, then press into a disk; repeat 3 times. Press into a disk, wrap, and refrigerate until firm, 15 to 20 minutes.

2. Preheat the oven to 400 degrees. On a lightly floured work surface, roll the dough into a round about ⅛ inch thick. Wrap the dough around the rolling pin and fit it into an 8- to 9-inch tart pan with a removable bottom. Trim off any excess. Use the scraps to patch any cracks. Prick holes all over the bottom of the tart shell with a fork. Cover and refrigerate.

3. Make the filling: Using an electric mixer, beat the egg with the salt and sugar for 5 minutes. Beat in the lemon zest, lemon juice, and softened butter. Spread the filling in the tart

shell. Transfer to the oven and bake for 25 to 30 minutes. Let cool to room temperature. Reduce the oven temperature to 300 degrees.

4. Make the meringue: In a medium bowl, beat the egg whites with the salt until soft peaks form. Gradually add the sugar and beat until stiff and glossy peaks form.

5. Spread the meringue evenly over the filling, swirling it decoratively. Bake the tart on the top rack of the oven until the meringue is deep golden and set, 10 to 15 minutes.

From Françoise:
• Citrus zest is the thin, shiny, colorful layer of the peel. Take care not to include any of the bitter white pith underneath.

• Remember to bring your egg whites to room temperature before beating them. They whip better when they're not cold.

DESSERTS

CARAMELIZED APPLE UPSIDE-DOWN TART
- *Tarte tatin* -

❖ INTERMEDIATE   ❖ MODERATE   ❖ 45 MINUTES   ❖ SERVES 6

6 tablespoons sugar

3 tablespoons unsalted butter, cut into ¼-inch dice

7 firm medium apples, peeled, halved, and cored

Pâte Brisée (page 92) or Pâte Feuilletée
 (page 708)

Crème fraîche for serving

❖ ❖ ❖ ❖ ❖

1. Spread the sugar evenly in the bottom of an 8-inch tarte tatin pan or deep ovenproof skillet. Scatter the butter over the sugar. Arrange the apple halves on their sides in the pan in concentric circles with all the apples facing the same direction. Pack the apples close together.

2. Set the pan over low heat and cook the apples until the butter melts. Increase the heat to medium and cook until the syrup becomes a thick, golden brown, about 20 minutes. Baste the apples regularly with the syrup and press down slightly on the apples. Be careful not to let the caramel burn; adjust the heat if needed. Remove the pan from the heat and let cool slightly or completely.

3. Preheat the oven to 425 degrees. On a lightly floured work surface, roll the dough into a round about ⅛ inch thick about 2 inches larger than the pan. Wrap the dough around the rolling pin and set it on top of the apples. Carefully push the edge down inside the pan. Refrigerate until ready to bake.

4. Transfer the pan to the oven and bake until the pastry is golden, about 15 minutes. Remove the tart from the oven. Immediately invert a round platter over the pan. Holding the pan and platter together, quickly invert the tart onto the platter. Serve warm or at room temperature, with the crème fraîche.

From Françoise:
• Examples of firm apples are Golden Delicious, Fuji, Jonagold, and Northern Spy.

• If the apples aren't tender at the end of Step 2, transfer the pan to the oven and bake until the apples soften—before adding the dough.

RASPBERRY TARTLETS

- *Tartelettes aux framboises* -

❖ INTERMEDIATE   ❖ MODERATE   ❖ 1 HOUR, PLUS 1 HOUR RESTING   ❖ MAKES 6 TO 8 TARTLETS

PÂTE SABLÉE

1 ¼ cups all-purpose flour

5 tablespoons unsalted butter, softened

6 tablespoons sugar

½ teaspoon salt

1 large egg yolk

¾ pound raspberries

3 to 4 tablespoons red currant jelly

❖   ❖   ❖   ❖   ❖

1. Make the pâte sablée: Mound the flour on a work surface. Make a well in the middle of the flour and add the butter, sugar, and salt and mix with your fingers. Add the egg yolk and quickly work it with the other ingredients until partially mixed. Gradually incorporate the flour. Quickly crumble the mixture between your palms. Press into a disk, wrap, and refrigerate until firm, about 1 hour.

2. Preheat the oven to 350 degrees. On a lightly floured work surface, roll the dough until about ¼ inch thick. Using a pastry wheel or biscuit cutter, cut out 6 to 8 rounds to fit into 6 to 8 tartlet pans. Trim off any excess. Use the scraps to patch any cracks. Prick holes all over the bottom of the tart shells with a fork. Bake until the shells are lightly browned and cooked through, 10 to 15 minutes. Transfer to a rack to cool completely, then unmold.

3. Pack the raspberries in the tartlet shells. In a small saucepan, melt the jelly in 1 tablespoon of water. Brush the raspberries with the jelly.

From Françoise:

• These tartlets can also be filled with strawberries.

• Pâte sablée is easy to make. The more quickly you work, the better the crust will be. Take care to follow the order in which the ingredients are added.

• To keep the tartlet shells from sliding down in the pans as they bake, set a second tartlet pan inside each one. Or gently press a round of foil in the shells.

• Don't fill the shells with fruit until just before serving to keep them crisp.

• I often spread a little crème fraîche in the tartlet shells just before adding the fruit.

DESSERTS

FRUIT TARTLETS
- *Tartelettes aux fruits* -

❖ EASY   ❖ MODERATE   ❖ 25 MINUTES   ❖ MAKES 10 TARTLETS

PASTRY CREAM

1 cup milk

Pinch of salt

3 tablespoons sugar

½ tablespoon vanilla sugar

2 large egg yolks

2 tablespoons all-purpose flour

10 baked tartlet shells (page 713)

Fruit, peeled, pitted, and sliced as needed

❖ ❖ ❖ ❖ ❖

1. Make the pastry cream: In a large saucepan, bring the milk to a bare simmer with the salt. In a bowl, beat the sugar and vanilla sugar with the egg yolks until thick and light, 2 to 3 minutes. Beat in the flour. Gradually whisk in the hot milk.

2. Return the mixture to the pan, place over medium heat, and bring to a boil, whisking constantly, then reduce the heat to low and cook, whisking, for 2 minutes. Remove the pan from the heat and let cool.

3. Spread 1 tablespoon of the pastry cream in the tartlet shells. Arrange the fruit on top.

From Françoise:

• To give the pastry cream more vanilla flavor, add a scraped vanilla bean or vanilla seeds or both to the milk in Step 1. Remove and rinse the bean and save it for another use, like adding it to the sugar jar to make your own vanilla sugar.

OLD-FASHIONED RICE PUDDING
- *Riz au lait* -

❖ EASY   ❖ INEXPENSIVE   ❖ 45 MINUTES, PLUS 2 TO 3 HOURS CHILLING   ❖ SERVES 4

1 cup rice, rinsed

3 cups milk

1 tablespoon vanilla sugar

Pinch of salt

¾ cup sugar

1 tablespoon butter

1. Bring a large saucepan of water to a boil. Add the rice and cook for 5 minutes. Drain. Return the rice to the saucepan with the milk, vanilla sugar, and salt. Place over low heat, partly cover, and cook until the milk is absorbed, 30 to 35 minutes. Remove the pan from the heat and mix in the sugar and butter. Refrigerate until cold, 2 to 3 hours. Serve chilled.

From Françoise:
• Serve with jam, if you like.

• The rice is less likely to stick to the bottom of the saucepan if you don't add too much sugar at the beginning of cooking. One tablespoon of vanilla sugar or granulated sugar is plenty. Stir in the rest of the sugar when the milk has been absorbed.

• There's no need to stir the rice while it cooks. Mix only when you add the sugar and butter at the end.

• To vary the recipe, I sometimes add finely grated orange or lemon zest. Or I sauté sliced apples in butter and serve them alongside.

APPLE MERINGUE RICE PUDDING
- *Riz aux pommes meringuées* -

❖ EASY ❖ INEXPENSIVE ❖ 1 HOUR, PLUS 2 TO 3 HOURS CHILLING ❖ SERVES 4

1 cup rice, rinsed

3 cups milk

1 tablespoon vanilla sugar

2 pinches of salt

3 tablespoons unsalted butter, plus more
   for brushing

3 apples, peeled, cored, quartered,
   and thinly sliced

¾ cup sugar

2 tablespoons Cognac

2 large eggs, separated

❖ ❖ ❖ ❖ ❖

1. Bring a large saucepan of water to a boil. Add the rice and cook for 5 minutes. Drain. Return the rice to the saucepan with the milk, vanilla sugar, and 1 pinch of salt. Place over low heat, partly cover, and cook until the milk is absorbed, 30 to 35 minutes.

2. In a large skillet, melt 2 tablespoons of the butter over medium heat. Add the apples and 2 tablespoons of the sugar and cook for 10 minutes. Remove from the heat and sprinkle with the Cognac.

3. Brush a gratin dish with butter. Remove the rice from the heat and mix in ½ cup of the sugar, the remaining 1 tablespoon of butter, and 2 egg yolks. Spread the rice pudding in the gratin dish. Cover with the apples.

4. Beat the 2 egg whites with the remaining pinch of salt until they hold soft peaks. Beat in the remaining 2 tablespoons of sugar at high speed until stiff and glossy. Cover the

continued

apples and rice pudding completely with this meringue, spreading it all the way to the edges.

5. Preheat the broiler. Slide the gratin dish onto the top rack in the oven and bake until nicely browned, 3 to 5 minutes.

From Françoise:
• Pears or bananas can replace the apples.

• The Cognac can be omitted, especially if you're serving children.

• Sprinkle the apples with sugar when they begin to cook so they caramelize slightly.

• If you add an extra egg white or two (left over from another recipe), your meringue will be fluffier.

RICE PUDDING WITH MANDARIN ORANGES

- *Gâteau de riz aux mandarines* -

❖ EASY   ❖ INEXPENSIVE   ❖ 50 MINUTES, PLUS 2 TO 3 HOURS CHILLING   ❖ SERVES 4

¾ cup rice, rinsed

2 cups milk

1 tablespoon vanilla sugar

Pinch of salt

6 tablespoons sugar

1 tablespoon unsalted butter

2 mandarin oranges

I large egg, lightly beaten

❖   ❖   ❖   ❖   ❖

1. Bring a large saucepan of water to a boil. Add the rice and cook for 5 minutes. Drain. Return the rice to the saucepan with the milk, vanilla sugar, and salt. Place over low heat, partly cover, and cook until the milk is absorbed, 30 to 35 minutes.

2. Remove the pan from the heat and beat in the sugar and butter. Let cool slightly. Finely grate the zest of both oranges and mix into the rice with the egg. Cover and refrigerate until cold, 2 to 3 hours.

3. Peel the oranges and divide into segments. Serve the rice pudding very cold with the oranges.

From Françoise:
• To dress up the rice pudding, serve it with Vanilla Custard Sauce (page 652).

• If you'd like to present the pudding as a cake, pack it into a buttered soufflé dish or other deep baking dish before chilling. Then dip it in hot water to melt the butter and the cake will slide out onto a platter.

• You can buy vanilla sugar in certain supermarkets, but it is easy to make your own: Split one vanilla bean and scrape out the seeds, reserving them for another use. Place the scraped bean in a glass jar and cover it with 1 to 2 cups of sugar. Shake it occasionally and leave it in your pantry. After a week or two, your sugar will be perfumed with the vanilla.

RUM RICE PUDDING CAKE

- *Gâteau de riz martiniquais* -

❖ EASY   ❖ INEXPENSIVE   ❖ 35 MINUTES, PLUS 2 TO 3 HOURS CHILLING   ❖ SERVES 4

1 cup rice, rinsed

3 cups milk

1 tablespoon vanilla sugar

Pinch of salt

¾ cup sugar

1 tablespoon unsalted butter, plus more
   for brushing

2 tablespoons rum

1 large egg yolk

❖   ❖   ❖   ❖   ❖

1. Bring a large saucepan of water to a boil. Add the rice and cook for 5 minutes. Drain. Return the rice to the saucepan with the milk, vanilla sugar, and salt. Place over low heat, partly cover, and cook until the milk is absorbed, 30 to 35 minutes. Remove the pan from the heat and beat in the sugar and the 1 tablespoon of butter.

2. Let cool slightly. Beat in the rum and egg yolk. Brush a soufflé dish or other deep baking dish with butter. Pack the rice into the soufflé dish. Cover and refrigerate until cold, 2 to 3 hours.

3. To unmold the pudding, dip the dish briefly in hot water. Run a knife around the dish. Invert a round platter over the dish. Holding the dish and platter together, quickly invert the pudding onto the platter.

From Françoise:

• Serve the pudding with jam or fruit in syrup; pineapple is the natural choice.

• You might also pass a sauceboat of Vanilla Custard Sauce (page 652), flavored with 1 tablespoon of rum and the finely grated zest of ½ orange.

• If the rice isn't quite tender when all the milk has been absorbed, add a little more milk and cook until soft.

• The egg yolk makes the pudding richer, but can be omitted.

DESSERTS

CARAMELIZED RICE PUDDING

- *Gâteau de riz au caramel* -

❖ INTERMEDIATE ❖ INEXPENSIVE ❖ 1 HOUR, 30 MINUTES, PLUS COOLING ❖ SERVES 4

1 cup rice, rinsed

3 cups milk

1 tablespoon vanilla sugar

Pinch of salt

1 cup sugar

1 tablespoon unsalted butter

2 large eggs, lightly beaten

❖ ❖ ❖ ❖ ❖

1. Bring a large saucepan of water to a boil. Add the rice and cook for 5 minutes. Drain. Return the rice to the saucepan with the milk, vanilla sugar, and salt. Place over low heat, partly cover, and cook until the milk is absorbed, 30 to 35 minutes.

2. Meanwhile, preheat the oven to 350 degrees. In a small saucepan, combine ¼ cup of the sugar with 2 tablespoons of water. Place over medium-high heat, bring to a simmer, and cook, stirring often, until the sugar dissolves. Partly cover the pan and continue cooking until the sugar turns medium amber. Immediately pour the caramel into a soufflé dish or other deep baking dish and quickly turn to coat the bottom and sides.

3. Remove the rice pudding from the heat and beat in the remaining ¾ cup of sugar and the butter. Let cool slightly and beat in the eggs. Scrape the pudding into the soufflé dish. Transfer to the oven and bake for 30 to 45 minutes. Let cool in the dish.

From Françoise:

• I like to add a small handful of raisins that have been rinsed in warm water to the rice pudding at the same time as the eggs. You don't need to soak them first because they will get plump in the baking.

• You can omit the caramel and simply brush the soufflé dish with butter.

• The quantity of milk can vary according to the rice, which may absorb more or less, depending on the variety and age. The rice should be very moist before baking.

RICE PUDDING WITH POACHED PEARS

- *Poires à la Condé* -

❖ EASY   ❖ INEXPENSIVE   ❖ 1 HOUR, PLUS 2 TO 3 HOURS CHILLING   ❖ SERVES 4

---

1 cup rice, rinsed

3 cups milk

1 tablespoon vanilla sugar

Pinch of salt

1 ½ cups sugar

4 large or 8 small firm pears, peeled,
   halved lengthwise, and cored

½ lemon

Butter for brushing

2 large eggs, lightly beaten

❖ ❖ ❖ ❖ ❖

1. Bring a large saucepan of water to a boil. Add the rice and cook for 5 minutes. Drain. In the same saucepan, heat the milk over medium heat until barely simmering. Add the rice, vanilla sugar, and salt. Reduce the heat to low, partly cover, and cook until the milk is absorbed, 30 to 35 minutes.

2. Meanwhile, in a medium saucepan, combine 2 cups of water with ¾ cup of the sugar. Place over medium-low heat and cook until large bubbles form. Immediately remove the pan from the heat. Rub the pear halves with the lemon to discourage browning. Add the pears to the sugar syrup and cook over medium heat until tender, 15 to 25 minutes. Let the pears cool slightly in the syrup, then refrigerate until cold, 2 to 3 hours.

3. Brush a soufflé dish or other deep baking dish with butter. Remove the rice from the heat and beat in the remaining ¾ cup of sugar and the eggs. Pack the rice into the soufflé dish. Cover and refrigerate until cold, 2 to 3 hours.

4. To unmold the rice, dip the dish briefly in hot water. Run a knife around the dish. Invert a round platter over the dish. Holding the dish and platter together, quickly invert the rice onto the platter. Serve with the poached pears and syrup.

From Françoise:

• Select pears that are still firm. They can take more or less time to cook until tender depending on the variety and ripeness.

• Store-bought pears in syrup are also an option. They save a lot of time.

• If you like, flavor the pear syrup: In a small saucepan, combine the syrup with a little apricot jam and cook, stirring, just until the jam melts. Serve with the pears and rice pudding.

• Short-grain rice is the best choice for milky desserts; it's moister than the long-grain variety.

• Instead of regular milk, you might substitute almond milk. Reduce the sugar in the recipe, however, if the almond milk is sweetened.

DESSERTS

PINEAPPLE MERINGUE RICE PUDDING

- *Ananas meringué au riz* -

❖ INTERMEDIATE   ❖ INEXPENSIVE   ❖ 1 HOUR   ❖ SERVES 4

5 ounces pineapple chunks

2 tablespoons rum

2 large eggs, separated

Pinch of salt

3 tablespoons sugar

RICE PUDDING

1 cup rice, rinsed

3 cups milk

Pinch of salt

½ cup sugar

1 tablespoon vanilla sugar

❖ ❖ ❖ ❖ ❖

1. In a bowl, combine the pineapple with the rum. Cover and refrigerate.

2. Make the rice pudding: Bring a large saucepan of water to a boil. Add the rice and cook for 5 minutes. Drain. Return the rice to the saucepan with the milk and salt. Place over low heat, partly cover, and cook until the milk is absorbed, 30 to 35 minutes, adding the sugar and vanilla sugar halfway through.

3. Remove the pan from the heat. Beat in the egg yolks. Spread the rice pudding in a gratin dish. Cover with the marinated pineapple.

4. Beat the egg whites with the salt until they hold soft peaks. Beat in the 3 tablespoons of sugar at high speed until stiff and glossy. Cover the pineapple and rice pudding completely with this meringue.

5. Preheat the broiler. Slide the gratin dish onto the top rack in the oven and bake until nicely browned, 3 to 5 minutes.

From Françoise:

• You can also assemble these ingredients in individual ramekins.

• If you spread the meringue all the way to the edges of the gratin dish, it won't shrink during broiling.

CHOCOLATE SEMOLINA PUDDING CAKE

- *Semoule au chocolat sans façon* -

❖ EASY   ❖ INEXPENSIVE   .   ❖ 20 MINUTES, PLUS 2 TO 3 HOURS CHILLING   ❖ SERVES 4

2 cups milk

¼ cup sugar

2 ounces bittersweet chocolate, chopped

Pinch of salt

½ cup semolina

3 tablespoons unsalted butter

2 large eggs, lightly beaten

❖ ❖ ❖ ❖ ❖

1. In a medium saucepan, bring the milk to a bare simmer with the sugar, chocolate, and salt. Gradually add the semolina and cook, stirring often, until thickened, about 10 minutes. Remove the pan from the heat and beat in the butter and eggs.

2. Rinse a 6- to 7-inch charlotte mold or soufflé dish to moisten for easier unmolding. Scrape the pudding into the mold or dish. Let cool slightly, then refrigerate until cold, 2 to 3 hours.

3. To unmold the pudding, invert a round platter over the dish. Holding the dish and platter together, quickly invert the pudding onto the platter.

From Françoise:

• To vary the pudding, the chocolate can be replaced with raisins, diced pitted prunes, chopped candied fruit, or finely grated orange or lemon zest.

• Try this recipe with polenta, too. The flavor will be slightly different but also very good.

• Follow the proportions of semolina to milk here and do not cook the mixture longer than 10 minutes. That way you'll be sure the cake is very moist.

DESSERTS

CARAMELIZED SEMOLINA PUDDING CAKE

- *Gâteau de semoule au caramel* -

❖ INTERMEDIATE   ❖ INEXPENSIVE   ❖ 1 HOUR, PLUS 2 TO 3 HOURS CHILLING   ❖ SERVES 4

⅔ cup raisins

⅓ cup plus ¼ cup sugar

2 cups milk

1 tablespoon vanilla sugar

¼ teaspoon salt

⅔ cup semolina

2 large eggs, lightly beaten

❖　❖　❖　❖　❖

1. In a bowl, soak the raisins in hot water for at least 15 minutes. Drain.

2. Preheat the oven to 350 degrees. In a small saucepan, combine ¼ cup of the sugar with 2 tablespoons of water. Place over medium-high heat, bring to a simmer, and cook, stirring often, until the sugar dissolves. Partly cover the pan and continue cooking until the sugar turns medium amber. Immediately pour the caramel into a small soufflé dish or other deep baking dish and quickly turn to coat the bottom and sides.

3. In a medium saucepan over medium heat, bring the milk to a bare simmer with the vanilla sugar and salt. Gradually add the semolina and cook, stirring often, until thickened, about 10 minutes. Remove the pan from the heat and beat in the remaining ⅓ cup of sugar, the raisins, and eggs.

4. Scrape the pudding into the soufflé dish. Transfer to the oven and bake for about 30 minutes. Let cool to warm, then refrigerate until cold, 2 to 3 hours.

5. To unmold the pudding, invert a round platter over the dish. Holding the dish and platter together, quickly invert the pudding onto the platter; the caramel will spill out.

From Françoise:

• The raisins are not indispensable, but they are nice. You can replace them with finely grated lemon or orange zest.

• If you like, serve the pudding with Vanilla Custard Sauce (page 652) or jam.

YOGURT CAKE

- *Gâteau au yaourt* -

❖ EASY ❖ INEXPENSIVE ❖ 1 HOUR, PLUS 30 MINUTES COOLING ❖ SERVES 6

4 tablespoons (½ stick) unsalted butter
½ cup plain yogurt
1 cup sugar
1 ½ cups all-purpose flour

½ tablespoon baking powder
2 large eggs
1 tablespoon vanilla sugar
2 pinches of salt

❖ ❖ ❖ ❖ ❖

1. Preheat the oven to 350 degrees. Add the butter to a 7-inch soufflé dish or other deep baking dish and melt in the oven. Remove and turn the dish to coat.

2. In a bowl, using an electric mixer, beat the yogurt with the sugar. One at a time, add the flour, baking powder, eggs, vanilla sugar, salt, and melted butter, beating after each addition.

3. Scrape the batter into the soufflé dish. Transfer to the oven and bake for 40 to 50 minutes. Turn the cake out on a cake rack and cool completely before serving.

From Françoise:

• It's popular to make this cake with oil, but personally I prefer the taste of butter.

• Do not open the oven door during baking or the cake may fall.

• To give the cake a slightly different flavor, make it with brown butter.

CHOCOLATE MARBLE POUND CAKE

- *Gâteau marbré au chocolat* -

❖ EASY ❖ INEXPENSIVE ❖ 1 HOUR ❖ MAKES ONE 9- TO 10-INCH CAKE

¾ cup (1 ½ sticks) unsalted butter, melted,
  plus more for brushing
1 ¾ cups all-purpose flour, plus more for dusting
4 large eggs, separated
1 cup sugar

3 ½ ounces bittersweet chocolate, chopped
Pinch of salt

continued

DESSERTS

723

1. Preheat the oven to 375 degrees. Brush a 9- to 10-inch round cake pan or a loaf pan with butter. Dust with flour, tapping out the excess.

2. In a bowl, beat the egg yolks with the sugar. Beat in the melted butter and flour.

3. In a double boiler, melt the chocolate without stirring. Remove from the heat, stir, and let cool slightly.

4. In a bowl, whisk the egg whites with the salt until stiff. Gently fold the beaten whites into the egg yolk mixture.

5. Scrape half the batter into the bowl used to beat the egg whites. Gently fold in the melted chocolate until smooth.

6. Scrape half the plain batter into the cake pan. Spread the chocolate batter on top, then cover with the remaining plain batter. Using a table knife, cut swirls in the batter.

7. Transfer to the oven and bake for 20 minutes. Reduce the temperature to 350 degrees and bake until a toothpick inserted in the center comes out with moist crumbs attached, about 25 minutes.

8. Let the pound cake cool in the pan for 10 minutes, then unmold and let cool completely on a rack.

From Françoise:
• You are looking to create an irregular effect when you cut swirls into the batter; don't worry about creating any kind of perfect pattern.

BITTERSWEET CHOCOLATE CAKE
- *Reine de Saba* -

❖ INTERMEDIATE   ❖ INEXPENSIVE   ❖ 1 HOUR   ❖ SERVES 4

½ cup (1 stick) unsalted butter, barely melted, plus more for brushing
⅔ cup all-purpose flour, plus more for dusting
¼ pound bittersweet chocolate, grated
⅔ cup sugar

3 large eggs, separated
Pinch of salt

WHIPPED CREAM
½ cup heavy cream
1 tablespoon vanilla sugar

❖ ❖ ❖ ❖ ❖

1. Preheat the oven to 350 degrees. Brush a 7-inch tube pan with butter and dust with flour, tapping out the excess.

2. In a large bowl, beat the chocolate with the flour, sugar, barely melted butter, and egg yolks.

3. In a medium bowl, beat the egg whites with the salt until foamy, then beat at high speed until stiff. Gently fold the beaten whites into the chocolate mixture.

4. Scrape the batter into the tube pan, transfer to the oven, and bake for about 25 minutes; it

should be very moist. Turn out on a cake rack and let cool completely.

5. Make the whipped cream: In a chilled bowl and using a chilled whisk, beat the cream until it starts to thicken. Add the vanilla sugar and beat until soft peaks form. Cover and refrigerate.

6. Set the cake on a plate. Spoon or pipe the whipped cream into the center, and serve.

From Françoise:
• It's always a good idea to unmold a cake on a rack so it can cool without getting soft. The rack lets steam escape.

• You can also serve this cake with pastry cream.

TENDER HEART CHOCOLATE CAKE
- Coeur tendre en chocolat -

❖ EASY   ❖ INEXPENSIVE   ❖ 1 HOUR, 45 MINUTES, PLUS OVERNIGHT CHILLING   ❖ SERVES 4 TO 6

½ cup (1 stick) unsalted butter, softened,
  plus more for brushing
¼ pound bittersweet chocolate, chopped

3 large eggs, separated
3 tablespoons all-purpose flour
½ cup sugar

❖ ❖ ❖ ❖ ❖

1. Preheat the oven to 275 degrees. Brush a 6- to 7-inch springform pan or soufflé dish with butter.

2. In a double boiler, melt the chocolate without stirring. Remove from the heat and stir. Add the egg yolks and 4 tablespoons of the softened butter and beat well.

3. In a small bowl, mash the flour with the remaining 4 tablespoons of butter. Beat into the chocolate mixture.

4. In a bowl, beat the egg whites until foamy, then beat at high speed until stiff, beating in 1 tablespoon of the sugar halfway through. Add the remaining 7 tablespoons of sugar and beat until shiny.

5. Gently fold the beaten whites into the chocolate mixture. Scrape the batter into the springform pan or soufflé dish. Set in a roasting pan and pour in hot water to come halfway up the sides of the pan. Transfer to the oven and bake for 1 hour and 15 minutes. Let cool completely, then unmold. Cover and refrigerate overnight. Serve very cold.

From Françoise:
• This cake's crackly crust surrounds a very soft chocolate core. Take care not to bake it at too high a temperature or for too long or it will dry out.

• Select the best chocolate you can find for this recipe.

• Using a heart-shaped pan would make this cake a "coeur tendre" (tender heart).

DESSERTS

SUPER-MOIST CHOCOLATE CAKE
- *Moelleux au chocolat* -

❖ EASY   ❖ INEXPENSIVE   ❖ 2 HOURS, PLUS OVERNIGHT CHILLING   ❖ SERVES 4 TO 6

½ cup (1 stick) unsalted butter, cut into
  ¼-inch dice, plus more for brushing
½ cup sugar
¼ pound bittersweet chocolate, chopped

2 tablespoons Grand Marnier liqueur
3 tablespoons all-purpose flour
3 large eggs, separated

❖ ❖ ❖ ❖ ❖

1. Preheat the oven to 275 degrees. Brush a 6-inch soufflé dish or other deep baking dish with butter.

2. In a medium saucepan, bring ½ cup of water to a boil with the sugar. Remove the pan from the heat. Using a wooden spoon, stir in the chocolate, then the butter and liqueur until smooth. If needed, reheat gently in a double boiler.

3. In a bowl, beat the flour with the egg yolks; it will be stiff and hard to beat. When relatively smooth, gradually add it to the chocolate mixture, beating well.

4. In a bowl, beat the egg whites until foamy, then beat at high speed until stiff.

5. Gently fold the beaten whites into the chocolate mixture. Scrape the batter into the soufflé dish. Set in a roasting pan and pour in hot water to come halfway up the sides of the dish. Transfer to the oven and bake for about 1 hour and 15 minutes. Let cool completely, then unmold. Cover and refrigerate overnight. Serve very cold.

From Françoise:

• This cake puffs up during baking, but with chilling the soft interior sinks, which you'll notice when you unmold the cake. Not to worry. Run a knife around the cake. Invert a round platter over the dish. Holding the dish and platter together, quickly invert the cake onto the platter.

• If you like, serve the cake with whipped cream, flavored or not with vanilla. But don't add sugar. Its slight acidity will be a nice foil for the sweet cake.

CHOCOLATE AND MOCHA-CREAM LAYER CAKE

- *Samba aux crèmes ganache et moka* -

❖ INTERMEDIATE   ❖ MODERATE   ❖ 45 MINUTES   ❖ SERVES 6 TO 8

MOCHA BUTTERCREAM
1 tablespoon instant coffee
3 large egg yolks
¾ cup confectioners' sugar or ½ cup
   granulated sugar
¾ cup (1 ½ sticks) unsalted butter, softened

CHOCOLATE GANACHE
¾ cup crème fraîche
2 ½ ounces bittersweet chocolate, chopped

Génoise (page 757) or yellow layer cake
Bittersweet chocolate shavings or sprinkles
Confectioners' sugar for dusting (optional)

❖ ❖ ❖ ❖ ❖

1. Make the mocha buttercream: In a cup, dissolve the coffee in 1 tablespoon of hot water. Let cool.

2. In a medium bowl set over a pan of hot water, combine the coffee with the egg yolks and confectioners' or granulated sugar. Using an electric mixer or whisk, beat the mixture until it is very smooth and thick. Remove the pan from the heat and let cool completely, about 15 minutes.

3. Gradually beat in the softened butter until smooth.

4. Make the chocolate ganache: In a small saucepan, combine the crème fraîche with the chocolate and cook over low heat, without stirring, until barely simmering. Remove the pan from the heat and stir with a wooden spoon; let cool slightly. Using an electric mixer, beat the ganache until doubled in volume.

5. Set the cake on a cardboard round. Using a serrated knife, cut the cake in thirds horizontally. Spread two-thirds of the mocha buttercream over the tops of the 2 bottom layers. Reassemble the cake. Spread the remaining mocha buttercream over the sides of the cake. Pat on the chocolate shavings. Spread the chocolate ganache over the top of the cake. Dust with confectioners' sugar, if you like. Transfer the cake to a doily-lined cake plate.

From Françoise:
• If you are making the Génoise or yellow cake yourself, prepare it a day ahead so it will be easier to cut neatly. Omit the rum and lemon from the Génoise.

DESSERTS

POUND CAKE

- *Quatre-quarts* -

❖ EASY ❖ MODERATE ❖ 1 HOUR, PLUS CHILLING ❖ SERVES 4

5 tablespoons unsalted butter, barely melted,
  plus more for brushing
⅔ cup all-purpose flour, plus more for dusting
2 large eggs

6 tablespoons sugar
½ tablespoon vanilla sugar
½ teaspoon baking powder
2 pinches of salt

❖ ❖ ❖ ❖ ❖

1. Preheat the oven to 400 degrees. Butter a
7- to 8-inch springform pan or 8-inch loaf pan
and dust with flour, tapping out the excess.

2. In a medium bowl, beat the eggs and sugar
with an electric mixer until the mixture falls
from the beaters in a thick ribbon, beating in
the barely melted butter at the end.

3. In another bowl, whisk the flour with the
vanilla sugar, baking powder, and salt. Gently
fold into the egg mixture. Scrape into the pan,
transfer to the oven, and bake until the pound
cake is golden and a toothpick inserted in the
center comes out clean, 40 to 45 minutes. Let
cool for 5 minutes, then turn out onto a cake
rack to cool completely. Cover with foil if the
top begins to brown.

From Françoise:
• Instead of vanilla sugar, you can flavor
the pound cake with the finely grated zest of
1 lemon or orange.

• Your cake will be lighter if you sift the flour
with the baking powder. You can sift it directly
over the beaten egg mixture.

• Add the ingredients in the order listed in the
method for best results.

• When the pound cake is completely cooled,
wrap it in foil or plastic and refrigerate until
serving. It stays moist for several days.

KUGELHOPF

Kougloff

❖ ADVANCED   ❖ MODERATE   ❖ 1 HOUR, PLUS ABOUT 2 HOURS RISING   ❖ SERVES 4 TO 6

¾ cup raisins, rinsed in warm water

¼ cup rum

7 tablespoons lukewarm milk

⅓ cup sugar

1 tablespoon dry yeast

2 cups all-purpose flour

½ teaspoon salt

5 tablespoons unsalted butter, softened,
  plus more for brushing

12 whole almonds

1 large egg, lightly beaten

Confectioners' sugar for dusting

❖ ❖ ❖ ❖ ❖

1. In a small bowl, combine the raisins with the rum.

2. In a large bowl, combine the milk with the sugar and yeast and let stand for 5 minutes. Add ½ cup of the flour and the salt and beat with a wooden spoon until blended. Sprinkle the remaining 1 ½ cups of flour over the top; do not knead. Cover the bowl with plastic wrap and let rise at warm room temperature until the dough lifts the flour, about 1 hour.

3. Generously brush an 8-inch kugelhopf mold or tube pan with butter. Arrange the almonds in the bottom.

4. Add the softened butter, egg, raisins, and rum to the dough and knead until smooth and elastic. Shape the dough into a ball and make a hole in the middle. Set the ring of dough in the mold; it should fill the mold only halfway. Cover and let rise until doubled in bulk, about 1 hour.

5. Preheat the oven to 400 degrees. Transfer the kugelhopf to the oven and bake until golden brown, 35 to 40 minutes. Transfer to a cake rack and let stand for 10 minutes, then unmold. Dust with confectioners' sugar before serving.

From Françoise:

• In the 2 hour rising time, the kugelhopf develops its flavor and texture.

DESSERTS

729

PEAR UPSIDE-DOWN CUSTARD CAKE

- *Délicieux aux poires* -

❖ EASY   ❖ INEXPENSIVE   ❖ 1 HOUR, PLUS 2 TO 3 HOURS CHILLING   ❖ SERVES 6 TO 8

2 tablespoons unsalted butter, cut into
  ¼-inch dice, plus more for brushing
6 to 8 pear halves in syrup, drained and patted dry
¼ cup pear liqueur, Bénédictine, or Cointreau
10 ladyfingers

4 large eggs
2 cups milk
2 pinches of salt
⅔ cup sugar
1 tablespoon vanilla sugar

❖ ❖ ❖ ❖ ❖

1. Preheat the oven to 425 degrees. Brush a 9-inch soufflé dish or springform pan with butter. Arrange the pear halves in the dish, cut sides up and stems pointing to the center.

2. Pour the liqueur into a shallow bowl and dip in both sides of the ladyfingers. Arrange them in a layer on the pears.

3. In a medium bowl, lightly beat the eggs. In a medium saucepan, bring the milk to a bare simmer with the salt, sugar, and vanilla sugar. Remove the pan from the heat and gradually whisk it into the eggs.

4. Pour half of the custard over the ladyfingers and let it soak in, then add the remaining custard. Dot with the butter. Set in a roasting pan and fill with hot water to come halfway up the sides of the soufflé dish.

5. Transfer to the oven and bake until set, about 45 minutes. If the top browns too quickly, cover it with foil. Let cool slightly, then refrigerate until cold, 2 to 3 hours. Unmold before serving.

From Françoise:

• Make sure to use pears in syrup to make this recipe; fresh pears release too much liquid.

• Use liqueur in desserts that require cooking, not brandy or spirits with a perfume that quickly dissipates. Save spirits for fruit salads or to flambé crêpes.

• You can buy vanilla sugar in certain supermarkets, but it is easy to make your own: Split one vanilla bean and scrape out the seeds, reserving them for another use. Place the scraped bean in a glass jar and cover it with 1 to 2 cups of sugar. Shake it occasionally and leave it in your pantry. After a week or two, your sugar will be perfumed with the vanilla.

CARAMELIZED PINEAPPLE UPSIDE-DOWN CAKE
- *Gâteau caramelisé à l'ananas* -

❖ EASY   ❖ MODERATE   ❖ 1 HOUR, PLUS 1 HOUR COOLING   ❖ SERVES 6 TO 8

1 cup sugar

½ pound sliced pineapple in syrup,
  syrup reserved

1 ½ teaspoons vanilla sugar

2 large eggs

½ cup (1 stick) unsalted butter, cut into ¼-inch
  dice and softened

⅔ cup all-purpose flour

1 teaspoon baking powder

¼ teaspoon salt

❖ ❖ ❖ ❖ ❖

1. In a small saucepan, combine ½ cup of the sugar with ¼ cup of pineapple syrup. Place over medium-high heat, bring to a simmer, and cook, stirring often, until the sugar dissolves. Partly cover the pan and continue cooking until the sugar turns medium amber. Immediately pour the caramel into an 8- to 9-inch cake pan and quickly turn to coat the bottom and sides.

2. Preheat the oven to 400 degrees. In a bowl, using an electric mixer, beat the remaining ½ cup of sugar with the vanilla sugar and eggs until smooth. Beat in the butter, then the

flour, baking powder, and salt until smooth and dense.

3. Arrange the pineapple slices in the bottom of the caramelized pan. Cover with the batter evenly. Transfer to the oven and bake for 45 to 50 minutes. Let cool slightly in the pan, then unmold on a cake rack and let cool completely.

From Françoise:

• If you prefer not to caramelize the pan, brush it generously with butter and sprinkle with sugar, tapping out the excess.

CLASSIC MADELEINES
- *Madeleines* -

❖ EASY   ❖ MODERATE   ❖ 20 MINUTES   ❖ MAKES 12

4 tablespoons (½ stick) unsalted butter, softened,
  plus melted butter for brushing

½ cup all-purpose flour, plus more for dusting

1 large egg

5 tablespoons sugar

1 tablespoon vanilla sugar

Pinch of salt

¼ teaspoon baking powder

continued

1. Preheat the oven to 425 degrees. Brush a madeleine pan with melted butter and dust with flour, tapping out the excess.

2. In a bowl, using an electric mixer, beat the egg with the sugar, vanilla sugar, and salt until thick and light. Using a wooden spoon, beat in the flour and baking powder, then the softened butter.

3. Spoon about 1 tablespoon of batter into each mold. Transfer the pan to the oven and bake until golden around the edges and a toothpick inserted into the center of a madeleine comes out clean, 10 to 12 minutes. Turn out the madeleines on a cake rack to cool.

From Françoise:

• The madeleines can also be flavored with finely grated lemon zest or orange flower water.

• These little cakes can be stored in an airtight container for up to a week.

• Do not beat the batter with a whisk or the cakes will be too crumbly.

• Use a brush when buttering the madeleines so every crevice is coated.

SLICE-AND-BAKE ALMOND COOKIES
- *Pains d'amandes* -

❖ EASY   ❖ MODERATE   ❖ 40 MINUTES, PLUS OVERNIGHT CHILLING   ❖ MAKES ABOUT 60 COOKIES

4 cups all-purpose flour
1 ⅔ cups sugar
1 cup finely chopped almonds
2 large eggs
½ teaspoon salt

10 tablespoons unsalted butter, barely melted,
  plus more for brushing
¼ cup rum
2 teaspoons baking powder
1 teaspoon cinnamon

❖ ❖ ❖ ❖ ❖

1. In a bowl, beat the flour with the sugar, almonds, eggs, salt, barely melted butter, rum, baking powder, and cinnamon until a firm dough forms. Gather the dough into a ball and shape it into 2 logs, each about 1 ½ to 2 inches in diameter. Wrap in plastic and refrigerate overnight until very firm.

2. Preheat the oven to 400 degrees. Brush 2 large baking sheets with butter.

3. Using a thin, sharp knife, slice the logs ¼ inch thick. Arrange the slices on the baking sheets. Transfer to the oven and bake the cookies on the upper and lower racks until golden around the edges and on the bottom, 5 to 6 minutes. Let the cookies cool for 10 minutes on the baking sheets, then transfer them to cake racks to cool completely.

• I still remember these cookies from when I was a girl. My family from the north sent them every Christmas, along with waffles. My Aunt Blanche's were so delicious I begged for the recipe. Here it is, and it's golden. These proportions will yield about 60 cookies.

• These cookies can be stored in an airtight container.

• Do not use ground almonds here; the result won't be nearly as good.

• Vanilla sugar can replace the cinnamon.

• This dough, which is stiff and hard to work, must be refrigerated for about 12 hours before being sliced and baked.

• If you need to reuse your baking sheets to bake all the cookies, it's not necessary to butter them more than once.

BUTTERY MINI ALMOND CAKES
- *Friands aux amandes* -

❖ EASY   ❖ INEXPENSIVE   ❖ 30 MINUTES   ❖ MAKES ABOUT 10 MEDIUM CAKES

4 tablespoons (½ stick) unsalted butter,
  plus melted butter for brushing
3 large egg whites
⅔ cup confectioners' sugar

½ cup ground almonds
3 tablespoons all-purpose flour
Pinch of salt

❖ ❖ ❖ ❖ ❖

1. Preheat the oven to 450 degrees. Brush the cups of a muffin pan with butter.

2. In a bowl, using a wooden spoon, beat the egg whites with the confectioners' sugar, ground almonds, flour, and salt until smooth.

3. In a small saucepan, melt the butter until it foams and smells nutty. Remove the pan from the heat and gradually beat the butter into the batter.

4. Spoon the batter into the muffin cups. Transfer to the oven and bake the cakes for 5 minutes, then reduce the oven temperature to 400 degrees and bake until golden brown, about 10 minutes. Let cool slightly, then run a knife around each cake and transfer them to a cake rack to cool.

From Françoise:
• Do not use a whisk to beat the batter or it will be too frothy.

• You can also make mini cakes using a mini muffin pan. Bake the cakes for 5 minutes less.

• Buy European-style butter to make these buttery cakes.

DESSERTS

ALMOND PUFF PASTRY COOKIES

- *Petits feuilletés aux amandes* -

❖ EASY   ❖ MODERATE   ❖ 1 HOUR   ❖ MAKES ABOUT 40 COOKIES

1 pound all-butter Puff Pastry dough (page 708)
  or store-bought
1 large egg, lightly beaten

⅔ cup decorating sugar
1 cup finely chopped almonds

❖ ❖ ❖ ❖ ❖

1. Cover a baking sheet with foil and sprinkle with water.

2. On a lightly floured work surface, roll out the dough to an 8-inch square ⅛ inch thick. Brush the dough with the beaten egg. Sprinkle with ⅓ cup of the sugar and ½ cup of the chopped almonds. Roll a rolling pin lightly over the top to make the sugar and nuts adhere.

3. Wrap the dough around the rolling pin and turn it over. Brush the other side with beaten egg and sprinkle with the remaining almonds and sugar. Pat lightly. Cut the dough into four 2-inch strips, then crosswise about 1 inch wide. Pick up each one and twist it at both ends. Transfer the cookies to the baking sheet as they are shaped. Cover and refrigerate for 15 minutes. Preheat the oven to 400 degrees.

4. Transfer the cookies to the oven and bake until puffed and brown, 20 to 25 minutes, reducing the oven temperature to 350 halfway through baking.

QUICK RUM BABA

- *Baba-minute* -

❖ EASY   ❖ INEXPENSIVE   ❖ 45 MINUTES   ❖ SERVES 6

Butter for brushing
1 ⅓ cups sugar
3 large eggs, separated
1 tablespoon milk

1 cup all-purpose flour
1 tablespoon baking powder
2 pinches of salt
¼ cup rum

❖ ❖ ❖ ❖ ❖

1. Preheat the oven to 350 degrees. Brush a ring mold with butter.

2. In a medium bowl, using an electric mixer, beat ⅓ cup of the sugar with the egg yolks

until light. Beat in the milk. Then sift the flour with the baking powder over the mixture and beat in.

3. In another bowl, beat the egg whites with the salt until foamy, then beat at high speed until stiff. Gently fold the beaten whites into the egg yolk mixture.

4. Scrape the batter into the ring mold, filling it three-quarters full. Transfer to the oven and bake for about 20 minutes.

5. Meanwhile, in a small saucepan, bring 1 cup of water to a simmer with the remaining 1 cup of sugar, stirring to dissolve the sugar. Remove

the pan from the heat and let cool slightly, then add the rum.

6. Turn out the cake on a platter. Pour some of the hot rum syrup over the cake and let absorb. Repeat, using all the syrup.

From Françoise:
• This cake can be prepared for children by replacing the rum with another flavoring.

• This spongy cake absorbs the sugar syrup better when it is warm than at room temperature.

• To make the cake shiny, brush it with apricot jam that has been melted in a little water.

MINI RUM-SOAKED CAKES
- *Petites brioches au rhum* -

❖ EASY   ❖ INEXPENSIVE   ❖ 50 MINUTES   ❖ MAKES 6 CAKES

Butter for brushing
1 ⅓ cups sugar
3 large eggs, separated
1 tablespoon milk
1 cup all-purpose flour

1 tablespoon baking powder
2 pinches of salt
¼ cup rum
2 tablespoons apricot jam

❖ ❖ ❖ ❖ ❖

1. Preheat the oven to 350 degrees. Brush the cups of a muffin pan with butter.

2. In a medium bowl, using an electric mixer, beat ⅓ cup of the sugar with the egg yolks until light. Beat in the milk. Then sift the flour with the baking powder over the mixture and beat in.

3. In another bowl, beat the egg whites with the salt until foamy, then beat at high speed

until stiff. Gently fold the beaten whites into the egg yolk mixture.

4. Spoon the batter into the muffin cups, filling them three-quarters full. Transfer to the oven and bake for 15 minutes.

5. Meanwhile, in a small saucepan, bring 1 cup of water to a simmer with the remaining 1 cup

DESSERTS

continued

of sugar, stirring to dissolve the sugar. Remove the pan from the heat and let cool slightly, then add the rum.

6. Remove the cakes from the cups, then replace them. Pour some of the hot rum syrup over the cakes and let absorb. Repeat, using all the syrup. Transfer the soaked cakes to a platter.

7. In a small saucepan, melt the jam in 1 tablespoon of water, then simmer until slightly thickened, 1 to 2 minutes. Brush the jam on the tops of the cakes.

From Françoise:

• If you like, decorate the cakes with candied cherries and Angelica.

• These cakes are pretty spectacular served as is, but they're even better with whipped cream.

RUM-MARINATED DRIED FRUIT
- *Mendiants au rhum* -

❖ EASY   ❖ MODERATE   ❖ 30 MINUTES, PLUS CHILLING AND MACERATING   ❖ MAKES 2 QUARTS

---

1 ½ pounds large pitted prunes

1 pound dried apricots

4 cups strong tea

¾ cup sugar

1 pound dried figs, rinsed in warm water
  and patted dry

¼ pound raisins, rinsed in warm water
  and patted dry

¼ pound walnut halves

3 cups white rum

❖　❖　❖　❖　❖

1. In a bowl, combine the prunes with the apricots and tea and refrigerate overnight. Drain.

2. In a small saucepan, bring ¾ cup of water to a simmer with the sugar, stirring to dissolve the sugar. Remove the pan from the heat and let cool completely.

3. Divide all the dried fruits and the sugar syrup between two 1-quart canning jars, spacing the walnut halves among the fruits. Fill the jars with the rum. Close the jars and store for 1 month before serving.

JAM THUMBPRINTS

Petits-fours à la confiture

❖ EASY ❖ INEXPENSIVE ❖ 40 MINUTES ❖ MAKES 15 TO 20 COOKIES

4 tablespoons (½ stick) unsalted butter, softened,
  plus more for brushing
1 cup all-purpose flour, plus more for dusting
6 tablespoons sugar

1 large egg, separated
Pinch of salt
½ cup jam

❖ ❖ ❖ ❖ ❖

1. Preheat the oven to 350 degrees. Brush a baking sheet with butter and dust with flour, tapping off the excess.

2. In a medium bowl, beat the softened butter with the sugar until light and fluffy using a wooden spoon. Beat in the egg yolk, then the flour and salt. When the dough becomes too stiff to beat, knead it by hand.

3. Roll the dough into 1-inch balls and set on the baking sheet. Make a dent in the cookies using your thumb and fill with jam. Beat the egg white lightly with a fork. Brush the cookies with the beaten white.

4. Transfer to the oven and bake for 20 to 25 minutes. Let the cookies cool on the sheets for 5 minutes, then transfer to racks to cool completely.

From Françoise:

• The beaten egg white brushed on the cookies helps them brown nicely.

• These cookies keep very well for a few days in an airtight container.

• You can dust the cookies with confectioners' sugar before serving if you like.

CLASSIC GRAND MARNIER SOUFFLÉ

Soufflé à la liqueur

❖ INTERMEDIATE ❖ MODERATE ❖ 50 MINUTES ❖ SERVES 4

2 tablespoons unsalted butter, plus more
  for brushing
2 ½ tablespoons all-purpose flour
1 cup milk
6 tablespoons sugar

4 large eggs, separated
¼ cup Grand Marnier
Pinch of salt

continued

1. Preheat the oven to 350 degrees. Brush a soufflé dish with butter.

2. In a large saucepan, melt the 2 tablespoons of butter over medium heat. Whisk in the flour until it starts foaming. Add the milk and sugar and bring to a boil, whisking constantly, then reduce the heat to very low and cook, whisking, for 2 to 3 minutes. Remove the pan from the heat and whisk in the egg yolks and Grand Marnier.

3. In a bowl, beat the egg whites with the salt until foamy, then beat at high speed until stiff. Beat one-quarter of the beaten whites into the soufflé base, then fold this lightened mixture into the remaining whites.

4. Scrape the soufflé mixture into the soufflé dish, filling it three-quarters full. Transfer to the oven and bake until puffed and browned, about 30 minutes. Serve immediately.

From Françoise:

• You can use any favorite liqueur to flavor this soufflé.

• If you'd like the soufflé to rise evenly, run a table knife around the edge to make a groove.

• Everybody knows the trick to making a soufflé is getting organized. If it waits in the oven 15 minutes too long, it will fall. A good tip: Scrape the soufflé into the dish and refrigerate just before the meal, then heat the oven just before sitting down. When you've served the main course, that is half an hour before dessert, bake the soufflé in the oven.

CLASSIC PASTRY CREAM PUFFS
- *Choux à la crème* -

❖ ADVANCED ❖ MODERATE ❖ 1 HOUR ❖ MAKES ABOUT 12 MEDIUM PUFFS

Butter for brushing

CHOUX PASTRY
5 tablespoons unsalted butter
½ teaspoon salt
1 cup all-purpose flour
4 large eggs

PASTRY CREAM
2 cups milk
Pinch of salt

½ cup sugar
2 tablespoons vanilla sugar
4 large egg yolks
¼ cup all-purpose flour
1 tablespoon kirsch or rum (optional)
7 tablespoons unsalted butter, softened

CARAMEL
1 cup sugar
½ teaspoon fresh lemon juice

❖ ❖ ❖ ❖ ❖

1. Preheat the oven to 400 degrees. Brush 2 baking sheets with butter.

2. Make the choux pastry: In a saucepan, bring 1 cup of water, the butter, and salt to a boil. When the butter melts, remove the pan from

the heat, add all the flour at once, and beat well using a wooden spoon. Return the pan to low heat and beat until the dough is smooth and pulls away from the pan to form a ball. Off the heat, add the eggs, 1 at a time, beating well after each addition.

3. Drop tablespoons of the batter onto the baking sheets, spacing them well apart. Transfer to the oven and bake until puffed and golden, 20 to 30 minutes, reducing the oven temperature to 350 degrees after 20 minutes. Transfer to a rack to cool slightly.

4. Meanwhile, make the pastry cream: In a large saucepan, bring the milk to a bare simmer with the salt. In a bowl, beat the sugar with the vanilla sugar and the egg yolks until thick and light, 2 to 3 minutes. Beat in the flour. Gradually whisk in the hot milk.

5. Return the mixture to the pan, place over medium heat, and bring to a boil, whisking constantly, then reduce the heat to low and cook, whisking, for 2 minutes. Remove the pan from the heat and beat in the kirsch or rum, if using. Let cool to tepid and gradually beat in the softened butter. Let cool completely.

6. Make the caramel: In a medium saucepan, combine the sugar with 6 tablespoons of water and the lemon juice. Place over medium-high heat, bring to a simmer, and cook, stirring often, until the sugar dissolves. Partly cover the pan and continue cooking until the sugar turns light amber. Immediately remove the pan from the heat. Quickly dip the tops of the choux puffs in the caramel and transfer to a lightly oiled baking sheet to let harden.

7. Cut a thin lid in the top of each puff without completely detaching it. Carefully spoon or pipe the pastry cream in the puffs.

From Françoise:
• For choux pastry, it's important to follow the proportions.

RUM-SCENTED FRENCH TOAST

- *Pain perdu* -

❖ EASY   ❖ INEXPENSIVE   ❖ 30 MINUTES   ❖ SERVES 4

1 cup milk

½ cup sugar

2 tablespoons rum

2 large eggs

4 to 8 slices of stale bread or brioche

3 tablespoons unsalted butter

1 tablespoon oil

❖ ❖ ❖ ❖ ❖

1. In a shallow bowl, beat the milk with 2 tablespoons of the sugar and the rum. In another shallow bowl, lightly beat the eggs.

2. Soak the bread in the sweet milk for at least 2 minutes, then dip in the beaten eggs.

DESSERTS

continued

3. In a large skillet, melt the butter in the oil over medium heat. Add the soaked bread without crowding and cook until nicely browned, 1 to 2 minutes per side. Transfer to a warmed platter, sprinkle generously with the remaining sugar, and serve.

From Françoise:
• Bread that's a little stale makes the best French toast.

• This French toast is fantastic served with cherries that have been sautéed in butter with a little sugar and shredded verbena leaves.

• If serving the French toast for breakfast or to children, replace the rum with vanilla sugar.

• You can use challah instead of brioche.

CHESTNUT-CHOCOLATE MOLD

- Turinois -

❖ EASY   ❖ MODERATE   ❖ 40 MINUTES, PLUS 12 HOURS CHILLING   ❖ SERVES 6 TO 8

1 pound unsweetened chestnut puree
3 ½ ounces bittersweet chocolate, grated
6 tablespoons sugar
½ tablespoon vanilla sugar

7 tablespoons unsalted butter, softened
Walnut halves, hazelnuts, sugar flowers, or
   unsweetened cocoa powder for decorating

❖ ❖ ❖ ❖ ❖

1. In a large saucepan, warm the chestnut puree over very low heat, stirring and crushing it with a wooden spoon so it doesn't stick. Transfer to a bowl of a standing mixer with a paddle, then beat in the chocolate, sugar, and vanilla sugar until smooth. Let cool slightly.

2. Beat in the softened butter until smooth and light.

3. Cut a round of parchment paper to fit in the bottom of a 5- to 6-inch soufflé dish or other round mold. Pack the chestnut mixture into the dish and smooth the top. Cover and refrigerate for 12 hours.

4. Unmold onto a round platter and remove the paper. Decorate with nuts or flowers, or dust with cocoa, and serve.

From Françoise:
• You might serve this dessert with unsweetened whipped cream, which brings out the flavor of the chestnut and chocolate.

• Don't try to make this dessert with melted chocolate. The result won't be the same. Grate the chocolate on a box grater or shave it using a vegetable peeler.

• The smooth texture of the chestnut-chocolate mixture depends on the vigorous beating of the different ingredients. Since nothing is melted, this requires some elbow grease. If you have a standing mixer with a paddle, use it.

HONEY-ANISE CAKE

- *Pain d'épice* -

❖ EASY   ❖ INEXPENSIVE   ❖ 2 HOURS   ❖ MAKES 12 TO 15 SLICES

⅔ cup acacia honey

5 tablespoons sugar

3 tablespoons unsalted butter, plus more
  for brushing

2 large egg yolks

2 ½ cups all-purpose flour

1 tablespoon baking powder

Pinch of salt

2 tablespoons pastis or 1 teaspoon anise seeds

❖ ❖ ❖ ❖ ❖

1. In a small saucepan, melt the honey with
the sugar, 2 tablespoons of water, and the 3
tablespoons of butter without letting it boil.
Remove from the heat.

2. In a medium bowl, beat the egg yolks with
2 tablespoons of the honey mixture, then add
this mixture to the remaining honey, beating
vigorously.

3. In another bowl, whisk the flour with the
baking powder and salt. Using a wooden
spoon, gradually beat in the honey mixture
and the pastis or anise seeds until smooth and
compact, about 15 minutes.

4. Preheat the oven to 350 degrees. Line the
bottom and sides of a 9- to 10-inch loaf pan

with foil or parchment paper and brush it
with butter. Scrape the batter into the pan and
smooth the top. Transfer to the oven and bake
for about 1 hour and 15 minutes, covering
the pan with foil halfway through baking and
reducing the oven temperature to 325 degrees.
Unmold on a cake rack, peel off the foil or
parchment, and let cool.

From Françoise:

• Wrapped in foil, this cake will keep for up to
2 weeks in the refrigerator.

• I recommend a nonstick pan for baking the
cake because the sugary batter sticks easily.

DESSERTS

CHOCOLATE-CHESTNUT YULE LOG
- Bûche de Noël aux marrons -

❖ EASY   ❖ INEXPENSIVE   ❖ 30 MINUTES   ❖ SERVES 4

¼ **pound bittersweet chocolate, chopped**
¾ **cup confectioners' sugar**

7 **tablespoons unsalted butter, softened**
1 **pound unsweetened chestnut puree**

❖ ❖ ❖ ❖ ❖

1. In a large nonstick saucepan, melt the chocolate over low heat. Using a wooden spoon, beat in ½ cup of the confectioners' sugar, the softened butter, and the chestnut puree until smooth.

2. Scrape this mixture onto a sheet of parchment paper or foil. Shape it into a log. Wrap it and refrigerate, or even freeze it, until firm.

3. Unwrap and transfer to a platter. Using the tines of a fork, decorate the log to look like rough bark, then smooth slightly with a table knife dipped in warm water. Dust with confectioners' sugar to resemble snow.

From Françoise:

• If you warm the chestnut puree separately, it will be easier to incorporate into the rest of the mixture.

• Carefully melting the chocolate in the microwave oven works very well.

• Confectioners' sugar makes a smoother texture than granulated sugar.

• For year-end parties, you can embellish the log with holiday decorations.

• This is a great recipe for beginners. There's nothing tricky about it, it's not expensive, it's quick, and there's no cooking involved. What's more, it's excellent.

CHOCOLATE-CHESTNUT "POTATOES"
- *Pommes de terre de carnaval déguisées au chocolat* -

❖ EASY ❖ MODERATE ❖ 20 MINUTES, PLUS 12 HOURS CHILLING ❖ MAKES ABOUT 20 "POTATOES"

1 pound unsweetened chestnut puree
3 ½ ounces bittersweet chocolate, grated
¾ cup sugar

½ tablespoon vanilla sugar
7 tablespoons unsalted butter, softened
Unsweetened cocoa powder for dusting

❖ ❖ ❖ ❖ ❖

1. In a large saucepan, warm the chestnut puree over very low heat, stirring and crushing it with a wooden spoon so it doesn't stick. Transfer to a bowl of a standing mixer with a paddle and beat in the chocolate, sugar, and vanilla sugar until smooth. Let cool slightly.

2. Beat in the softened butter until smooth and light. Cover and refrigerate for 12 hours.

3. Shape tablespoons of the mixture into irregular potato shapes. Dust with cocoa and serve.

BITTERSWEET CHOCOLATE TRUFFLES
- *Truffes au chocolat* -

❖ EASY ❖ MODERATE ❖ 30 MINUTES, PLUS OVERNIGHT CHILLING ❖ MAKES ABOUT 20 TRUFFLES

¼ pound bittersweet chocolate, chopped
1 large egg yolk
5 tablespoons unsalted butter, softened
1 tablespoon crème fraîche

¼ cup confectioners' sugar
2 tablespoons whisky, rum, or Cointreau
  (optional)
2 tablespoons unsweetened cocoa powder

❖ ❖ ❖ ❖ ❖

1. In a double boiler, melt the chocolate without stirring. Remove from the heat and using a wooden spoon, beat in the egg yolk, then gradually the softened butter. Beat in the crème fraîche, confectioners' sugar, and alcohol, if using.

2. Transfer to the refrigerator and chill until firm, at least 3 hours or overnight.

continued

3. Spread the cocoa in a shallow bowl. Roll teaspoons of the chocolate mixture in the cocoa and remove using a fork to a platter. Cover and refrigerate overnight before serving.

From Françoise:
• These truffles can be refrigerated for up to 2 weeks.

• You can add chopped almonds or hazelnuts to the mixture in Step 1. Or roll the truffles in chocolate sprinkles instead of cocoa powder.

• Sift the confectioners' sugar to remove any lumps.

• Using the finest chocolate and butter available will make the best truffles.

• Do not increase the amount of crème fraîche, assuming more is better. In fact, the truffles will be tasty—but too soft when they're not chilled.

CHOCOLATE-CARAMEL CANDIES
- *Caramels au chocolat* -

❖ EASY ❖ MODERATE ❖ 15 MINUTES, PLUS 30 MINUTES COOLING ❖ MAKES 40 TO 50 CANDIES

3 ½ ounces bittersweet chocolate, chopped
½ cup sugar
⅓ cup acacia honey

3 tablespoons unsalted butter
Oil for brushing

❖ ❖ ❖ ❖ ❖

1. In a medium saucepan, preferably nonstick, melt the chocolate with the sugar, honey, and butter over low heat for 10 minutes, stirring occasionally.

2. Brush a nonstick cake pan with oil. Pour in the hot caramel and let cool to lukewarm, about 30 minutes.

3. Turn out the soft caramel onto a work surface, preferably marble. Using a chef's knife, score the caramel, indicating where you will

cut it into squares. Let the caramel firm up completely before cutting all the way through. Wrap in squares of parchment paper.

From Françoise:
• Do not wrap the caramels in foil, which tends to stick.

• If you're afraid of the caramel sticking to anything, use nonstick utensils, from the saucepan to the spoon.

VANILLA BAVARIAN CREAM
- *Bavarois à la vanille* -

❖ ADVANCED   ❖ MODERATE   ❖ 40 MINUTES, PLUS 12 HOURS CHILLING   ❖ SERVES 6 TO 8

BAVARIAN CREAM
¼ ounce plain gelatin powder
2 cups milk
2 tablespoons vanilla sugar or 1 vanilla bean,
  seeds scraped
Pinch of salt

6 large egg yolks
⅓ cup sugar, plus more for sprinkling

WHIPPED CREAM
1½ cups heavy cream
Pinch of salt

❖ ❖ ❖ ❖ ❖

1. Make the Bavarian cream: Sprinkle the gelatin over ¼ cup of water and leave until spongy, about 5 minutes.

2. In a large saucepan, bring the milk to a bare simmer with the vanilla sugar or vanilla seeds and salt.

3. In a bowl, beat the egg yolks with the sugar until thick and light. Whisk in half the hot milk, then whisk the mixture back into the remaining milk. Place over low heat and cook, stirring constantly with a wooden spoon, until the custard thickens slightly. Remove the pan from the heat.

4. Melt the gelatin in a water bath over low heat and stir into the hot custard. Cover and refrigerate until it starts to thicken.

5. Meanwhile, make the whipped cream: In a chilled bowl and using a chilled whisk or an electric mixer with chilled beaters, whip the

cream until it starts to thicken. Add the salt and beat until lightly whipped. Gently fold the whipped cream into the custard.

6. Rinse an 8- to 9-inch soufflé dish or other deep baking dish with water and sprinkle it with sugar. Scrape the Bavarian cream into the dish and smooth the top. Cover and refrigerate for at least 12 hours and up to 48 hours.

7. Dip the mold into hot water and unmold on a round platter.

From Françoise:
• The Bavarian cream can be served as is, with the whipped cream or with Fruit Coulis (page 653).

• If you like, it can be flavored with 2 tablespoons of the spirit or liqueur of your choice: kirsch, Grand Marnier, Cointreau. Increase the amount of gelatin slightly.

DESSERTS

745

CHARLOTTE WITH VANILLA BAVARIAN CREAM

- Charlotte russe à la crème de bavarois -

❖ ADVANCED   ❖ MODERATE   ❖ 1 HOUR, PLUS 12 HOURS CHILLING   ❖ SERVES 6 TO 8

BAVARIAN CREAM

¼ ounce plain gelatin powder

2 cups milk

2 tablespoons vanilla sugar or 1 vanilla bean,
  seeds scraped

Pinch of salt

6 large egg yolks

½ cup sugar

WHIPPED CREAM

1 ½ cups heavy cream

Pinch of salt

Butter for brushing

Sugar for sprinkling

2 tablespoons eau-de-vie

20 ladyfingers

❖ ❖ ❖ ❖ ❖

1. Make the Bavarian cream: Sprinkle the gelatin over ¼ cup of water and leave until spongy, about 5 minutes.

2. In a large saucepan, bring the milk to a bare simmer with the vanilla sugar or vanilla seeds and salt.

3. In a bowl, beat the egg yolks with the sugar until thick and light. Whisk in half the hot milk, then whisk the mixture back into the remaining milk. Place over low heat and cook, stirring constantly with a wooden spoon, until the custard thickens slightly. Remove the pan from the heat.

4. Melt the gelatin in a water bath over low heat and stir into the hot custard. Cover and refrigerate until it starts to thicken.

5. Meanwhile, make the whipped cream: In a chilled bowl and using a chilled whisk or an electric mixer with chilled beaters, whip the cream until it starts to thicken. Add the salt and beat until lightly whipped. Gently fold the whipped cream into the custard.

6. Brush a 9- to 10-inch soufflé dish or other deep baking dish with butter and sprinkle with sugar, tapping out the excess. In a shallow bowl, combine the eau-de-vie with 2 tablespoons of water. Dip the ladyfingers in the eau-de-vie. Line the sides and bottom of the soufflé dish with the moistened ladyfingers, flat sides facing inward and trimming the bottom ones to fit snugly. Scrape the Bavarian cream into the dish and smooth the top. Cover and refrigerate for at least 12 hours and up to 48.

7. Dip the mold into hot water and unmold on a round platter.

From Françoise:

• The Bavarian cream needs to be on the point of setting when you add it to the soufflé dish so the ladyfingers stay in place.

• If you add alcohol to the Bavarian cream, increase the amount of gelatin in the mixture.

CHOCOLATE-CHESTNUT CHARLOTTE

- *Charlotte au chocolat* -

❖ EASY ❖ MODERATE ❖ 30 MINUTES, PLUS OVERNIGHT CHILLING ❖ SERVES 4

5 tablespoons unsalted butter, plus more
  for brushing
Sugar for sprinkling
¼ cup orange liqueur or rum
¼ pound ladyfingers

6 ounces bittersweet chocolate, chopped
½ pound unsweetened chestnut puree
4 large eggs, separated
Pinch of salt

❖ ❖ ❖ ❖ ❖

1. Brush a charlotte mold or other deep baking dish with butter and sprinkle with sugar, tapping out the excess. Pour the orange liqueur or rum in a shallow bowl. Dip in the ladyfingers; reserve 6. Line the sides and bottom of the mold with the remaining moistened ladyfingers, flat sides facing inward and trimming the bottom ones to fit snugly.

2. In a medium saucepan, melt the chocolate over low heat with 1 tablespoon of the butter. Beat in the remaining 4 tablespoons of butter and the chestnut puree until smooth. Remove the pan from the heat and beat in the egg yolks.

3. In a bowl, beat the egg whites with the salt until foamy, then beat at high speed until stiff. Beat one-quarter of the egg whites into the chocolate mixture, then gently fold this lightened mixture into the remaining beaten whites.

4. Scrape one-half of the chocolate mixture into the mold. Lay 3 of the reserved ladyfingers on top. Fill with the remaining chocolate mixture and cover with the 3 remaining ladyfingers. Cover and refrigerate for at least 12 hours and up to 48.

5. Dip the mold into hot water and unmold on a round platter.

From Françoise:

• Please note that the finished dish contains raw egg. It's basically a no-cook dessert.

• If you like, you can decorate the charlotte with whipped cream or candied fruit.

DESSERTS

SUMMER BERRY CHARLOTTE

- *Charlotte aux fruits rouges* -

❖ ADVANCED   ❖ EXPENSIVE   ❖ 1 HOUR, PLUS 12 HOURS CHILLING   ❖ SERVES 6 TO 8

BAVARIAN CREAM
⅛ ounce plain gelatin powder
1 cup milk
1 tablespoon vanilla sugar or 1 vanilla bean,
   seeds scraped
Pinch of salt
3 large egg yolks
¼ cup sugar

½ pound strawberries, hulled, or raspberries
1 to 2 tablespoons sugar, or to taste

Butter for brushing
15 ladyfingers

WHIPPED CREAM
1 ½ cups heavy cream
Pinch of salt

BERRY PUREE
1 pound strawberries, hulled, or raspberries
1 cup sugar
Juice of 2 lemons

❖ ❖ ❖ ❖ ❖

1. Make the Bavarian cream: Sprinkle the gelatin over 2 tablespoons of water and leave until spongy, about 5 minutes.

2. In a large saucepan, bring the milk to a bare simmer with the vanilla sugar or vanilla seeds and salt.

3. In a bowl, beat the egg yolks with the sugar until thick and light. Whisk in half the hot milk, then whisk the mixture back into the remaining milk. Place over low heat and cook, stirring constantly with a wooden spoon, until the custard thickens slightly. Remove the pan from the heat.

4. Melt the gelatin in a water bath over low heat and stir into the hot custard. Cover and refrigerate until it starts to thicken.

5. Reserve 20 of the nicest berries for decorating. In a bowl, toss the remaining berries with the 1 to 2 tablespoons sugar.

6. Meanwhile, make the whipped cream: In a chilled bowl and using a chilled whisk or an electric mixer with chilled beaters, whip the cream until it starts to thicken. Add the salt and beat until lightly whipped. Gently fold the whipped cream into the custard.

7. Brush a 9- to 10-inch soufflé dish or other deep baking dish with butter and sprinkle with sugar, tapping out the excess. Line the sides and bottom of the soufflé dish with some of the ladyfingers, flat sides facing inward and trimming the bottom ones to fit snugly. Scrape one-third of the Bavarian cream into the dish and smooth the top. Add half the berries. Layer with the cream and berries, finishing with a layer of cream. Cover with 3 of the remaining ladyfingers. Cover and refrigerate for at least 12 hours and up to 48.

8. Meanwhile, make the berry puree: In a food processor, puree the fruit with the sugar and lemon juice until smooth. If needed, work the

puree through a food mill or sieve to remove any seeds. Refrigerate.

9. Dip the mold into hot water and unmold on a round platter. Pour some of the berry puree over the top and serve the charlotte, passing the remaining berry puree separately.

From Françoise:
• You can make the berry puree using frozen strawberries or raspberries. If they are sweetened, puree them without additional sugar. Don't use frozen berries inside the charlotte, though.

• Charlottes can be frozen. Defrost them slowly in the refrigerator, not at room temperature.

CLASSIC LADYFINGERS
- *Biscuits à la cuiller* -

❖ ADVANCED ❖ INEXPENSIVE ❖ 40 MINUTES ❖ MAKES 50

Butter for brushing
½ cup all-purpose flour, plus more for sprinkling
5 large eggs, separated
⅔ cup sugar

½ cup potato starch
Pinch of salt
Confectioners' sugar for dusting

❖ ❖ ❖ ❖ ❖

1. Preheat the oven to 275 degrees. Position the racks in the upper and lower thirds of the oven. Brush 2 baking sheets with butter and sprinkle with flour, tapping off the excess.

2. In a bowl, using an electric mixer, beat the egg yolks with the sugar until light and thick enough to leave a ribbon trail.

3. Sift the flour with the potato starch over the egg yolk mixture and gently fold in.

4. In a bowl, beat the egg whites with the salt until foamy, then beat at high speed until stiff. Gently fold the beaten whites into the egg yolk mixture.

5. Pipe or spoon the batter onto the baking sheets in fingers, spacing them well apart. Transfer to the oven and bake until lightly browned, 18 to 20 minutes, shifting the pans from top to bottom and front to back halfway through baking. Let the ladyfingers cool slightly on the sheets, then transfer to racks to cool completely. Dust with confectioners' sugar before serving.

From Françoise:
• If you don't have more than one baking sheet, you can use the bottom of a broiler pan. Butter and flour it, too.

• This batter is very delicate because it doesn't have any baking powder; beaten egg whites give it lift. Get the batter in the oven as soon as it's made, or it will deflate.

• Ladyfingers can be stored in an airtight container for up to 1 week.

DESSERTS

JAM-FILLED ROULADE

- *Biscuit roulé à la confiture* -

❖ ADVANCED   ❖ INEXPENSIVE   ❖ 30 MINUTES, PLUS 30 MINUTES CHILLING   ❖ SERVES 4 TO 6

3 large eggs, separated
½ cup sugar
1 tablespoon vanilla sugar
Pinch of salt

½ cup all-purpose flour
¾ cup strawberry or raspberry jam
Decorating sugar or confectioners' sugar
   for sprinkling

❖ ❖ ❖ ❖ ❖

1. Preheat the oven to 450 degrees. Line an 8-by-12-inch sheet pan with foil.

2. In a bowl, using an electric mixer, beat the egg yolks with the sugar and vanilla sugar until light and thick enough to leave a ribbon trail.

3. In another bowl, beat the egg whites with the salt until foamy, then beat at high speed until stiff.

4. Sift ¼ cup of the flour over the egg yolk mixture and gently fold in. Then gently fold in half the beaten whites. Repeat, folding in the remaining flour and whites.

5. Spread the batter on the sheet pan. Transfer to the oven and bake until lightly browned, 8 to 10 minutes.

6. Invert the cake onto a clean, damp kitchen towel; wait 1 minute for the cake to soften slightly. Gently peel off the foil but leave it on top of the cake. Turn the cake over onto the foil.

7. Spread a thin layer of jam on the warm cake, leaving a ½-inch border. Roll up the cake, using the foil as a guide, then wrap in the foil and refrigerate until chilled.

8. Remove the foil. Sprinkle with decorating sugar or confectioners' sugar before serving.

From Françoise:

• You can buy vanilla sugar in certain supermarkets, but it is easy to make your own: Split one vanilla bean and scrape out the seeds, reserving them for another use. Place the scraped bean in a glass jar and cover it with 1 to 2 cups of sugar. Shake it occasionally and leave it in your pantry. After a week or two, your sugar will be perfumed with the vanilla.

COCONUT ROULADE

- *Biscuit roulé à la noix de coco* -

❖ ADVANCED   ❖ MODERATE   ❖ 30 MINUTES, PLUS 30 MINUTES CHILLING   ❖ SERVES 4 TO 6

COCONUT SYRUP

⅔ cup sugar

Juice of ½ lemon

4 to 6 tablespoons rum

1 cup sweetened shredded coconut,
   1 tablespoon reserved

1 pint passion fruit, mango, or lime sorbet
   (optional)

CAKE

3 large eggs, separated

½ cup sugar

1 tablespoon vanilla sugar

Pinch of salt

½ cup all-purpose flour

❖　❖　❖　❖　❖

1. Preheat the oven to 450 degrees. Line an 8-by-12-inch sheet pan with foil.

2. Make the coconut syrup: In a small saucepan, bring the sugar to a simmer with ⅔ cup of water, stirring to dissolve the sugar. Boil for 1 minute, then remove the pan from the heat and stir in the lemon juice, rum, and coconut.

3. Make the cake: In a bowl, using an electric mixer, beat the egg yolks with the sugar and vanilla sugar until light and thick enough to leave a ribbon trail.

4. In another bowl, beat the egg whites with the salt until foamy, then beat at high speed until stiff.

5. Sift ¼ cup of the flour over the egg yolk mixture and gently fold in. Then gently fold in half the beaten whites. Repeat, folding in the remaining flour and whites.

6. Spread the batter on the sheet pan. Transfer to the oven and bake until lightly browned, 8 to 10 minutes.

7. Invert the cake onto a clean, damp kitchen towel; wait 1 minute for the cake to soften slightly. Gently peel off the foil but leave it on top of the cake. Turn the cake over onto the foil.

8. Brush the coconut syrup on the warm cake, leaving a ½-inch border. Roll up the cake, using the foil as a guide, then wrap in the foil and refrigerate until chilled.

9. Remove the foil. Sprinkle with the reserved coconut before serving. Serve with the sorbet, if desired.

From Françoise:

• The cake must cook quickly. Bake it when the oven is at the correct temperature and don't cook it for more than 10 minutes; the top should be barely brown.

• If you work quickly to unmold and roll the roulade while it's still moist—and supple—it won't break. It's as simple as that.

DESSERTS

APPLE FRITTERS

- Beignets aux pommes -

❖ INTERMEDIATE   ❖ MODERATE   ❖ 30 MINUTES, PLUS 1 HOUR RESTING   ❖ SERVES 4

FRITTER BATTER

1 cup all-purpose flour

Salt

1 large whole egg, plus 2 large egg whites

1 tablespoon oil

½ to ⅔ cup beer or water

1 pound apples, peeled, cored, and sliced
   crosswise ¼ inch thick

4 cups oil for frying

Sugar for sprinkling

❖ ❖ ❖ ❖ ❖

1. Make the fritter batter: In a large bowl, whisk the flour with ¼ teaspoon of salt, the whole egg, and oil. Gradually whisk in the ½ cup of beer or water. The mixture should be thicker than crêpe batter. Cover and let stand for 1 hour.

2. Just before using, beat the egg whites with a pinch of salt until foamy, then beat at high speed until stiff. Fold into the batter.

3. In a large skillet, heat the oil to 375 degrees. Using a fork, dip the apple slices one at a time in the batter. Gently drop them into the oil without crowding. Fry the apples, turning them once, until puffed and golden, 1 to 3 minutes total. Using a slotted spoon, transfer the fritters to paper towels to drain. Keep warm in a low oven while frying the remaining apples. Sprinkle with sugar and serve very hot.

From Françoise:

• Traditionally, fritter batter is made with beer, but you can add milk or even water. You can also replace one-quarter of the flour with potato starch. I often flavor my batter with a little rum.

• The beaten eggs whites make a lighter fritter.

• You can also make pear, apricot, and banana fritters.

BANANA FRITTERS

- *Beignets de bananes* -

❖ INTERMEDIATE   ❖ MODERATE   ❖ 25 MINUTES, PLUS 1 HOUR MACERATING   ❖ SERVES 4

4 firm bananas, peeled and sliced lengthwise

¾ cup rum

1 tablespoon sugar, plus more for sprinkling

4 cups oil for frying

QUICK FRITTER BATTER

2 large egg whites

Pinch of salt

A few drops of fresh lemon juice

1½ tablespoons potato starch

❖ ❖ ❖ ❖ ❖

1. In a bowl, combine the bananas with the rum and 1 tablespoon of sugar.

2. In a large skillet, heat the oil to 375 degrees.

3. Make the quick fritter batter: In a large bowl, beat the egg whites with the salt and lemon juice until foamy, then beat at high speed until stiff. Gradually fold in the potato starch.

4. Using a fork, dip the bananas one at a time in the batter. Gently drop them into the oil without crowding. Fry the bananas, turning them once, until puffed and golden, 1 to 3 minutes total. Using a slotted spoon, transfer the fritters to paper towels to drain. Keep warm in a low oven while frying the remaining bananas. Sprinkle with sugar and serve very hot.

SWEET DEEP-FRIED PUFFS

- *Beignets soufflés* -

❖ ADVANCED   ❖ MODERATE   ❖ 45 MINUTES   ❖ SERVES 4

5 tablespoons unsalted butter

½ teaspoon salt

1 cup all-purpose flour

4 large eggs

4 cups oil for frying

Sugar for sprinkling

❖ ❖ ❖ ❖ ❖

1. In a saucepan, bring 1 cup of water, the butter, and salt to a boil. When the butter melts, remove the pan from the heat, add all the flour at once, and beat well using a wooden spoon.

Return the pan to low heat and beat until the dough is smooth and pulls away from the pan

continued

to form a ball. Off the heat, add the eggs, one at a time, beating well after each addition.

2. In a large skillet, heat the oil to 375 degrees.

3. Pushing the batter off a small spoon with a finger, gently drop the dough into the oil without crowding. Fry the dough, turning once, until puffed and golden, 1 to 3 minutes total. Using a slotted spoon, transfer the puffs to paper towels to drain. Keep warm in a low oven while frying the remaining batter. Sprinkle with sugar and serve very hot.

From Françoise:
• Don't add too many spoonfuls of the batter to the oil at the same time. They need plenty of room to fry properly.

• The choux pastry can be made several hours in advance. Cover it and refrigerate.

• These are also called "pets-de-nonne" (nuns' farts, sometimes translated at nuns' sighs).

CANDIED FRUITCAKE
- *Cake aux fruits confits* -

❖ EASY   ❖ MODERATE   ❖ 1 HOUR, 30 MINUTES   ❖ SERVES 4 TO 6

½ cup (1 stick) unsalted butter, softened, plus more for brushing
⅔ cup sugar
3 large eggs
1 ⅔ cups all-purpose flour

½ tablespoon baking powder
Pinch of salt
1 tablespoon rum
⅔ cup raisins
⅔ cup chopped candied fruit

❖ ❖ ❖ ❖ ❖

1. Preheat the oven to 400 degrees. Brush a 9- to 10-inch loaf pan with butter, then line with parchment paper. Brush the paper with butter.

2. In a bowl, beat the softened butter with the sugar until creamy and light. Beat in the eggs, one at a time. Don't worry if the batter is lumpy. Quickly beat in the flour, baking powder, salt, rum, raisins, and candied fruit just until smooth; do not overbeat.

3. Scrape the batter into the pan. Transfer to the oven and bake for 20 minutes. Reduce the oven temperature to 225 degrees. Using a sharp knife, score the cake batter lengthwise, then bake until a knife inserted in the center comes out clean, about 40 minutes.

From Françoise:
• Sprinkle the top with confectioners' sugar before serving, if you like.

• The fruits won't fall to the bottom of the cake if the batter is firm, the oven is hot when you slide the cake in the oven (the temperature is reduced after 20 minutes), and you take the precaution—nice but not crucial—of tossing the fruits in flour before adding them to the batter.

SIMPLE ALMOND CAKE

- *Cake aux amandes* -

❖ EASY   ❖ MODERATE   ❖ 1 HOUR, 15 MINUTES, PLUS 30 MINUTES COOLING   ❖ MAKES 14 TO 16 SLICES

10 tablespoons unsalted butter, softened,
  plus more for brushing
2 cups all-purpose flour
⅔ cup sugar
¼ teaspoon salt

½ tablespoon baking powder
3 large eggs
1 cup whole almonds, coarsely chopped
¼ cup rum

❖   ❖   ❖   ❖   ❖

1. Preheat the oven to 400 degrees. Brush a 9- to 10-inch loaf pan with butter, then line with parchment paper. Brush the paper with butter.

2. In a large bowl, using an electric mixer, beat the flour with the sugar, salt, and baking powder. Beat in the butter until crumbly. Beat in the eggs, then the chopped almonds and rum just until smooth; do not overbeat.

3. Scrape the batter into the loaf pan. Transfer to the oven and bake for 30 minutes. Reduce the oven temperature to 350 degrees and bake for 30 minutes. Turn out on a cake rack and let cool completely before slicing.

From Françoise:
• Your cake will be heavy if you use ground almonds instead of chopped almonds. Chop them coarsely using a large chef's knife or food processor.

LIGHT LEMON CAKE

- *Cake mousseline au citron* -

❖ EASY   ❖ MODERATE   ❖ 1 HOUR, 15 MINUTES, PLUS 30 MINUTES COOLING   ❖ MAKES 14 TO 16 SLICES

7 tablespoons unsalted butter, softened,
  plus more for brushing
1 ¾ cups all-purpose flour
1 cup sugar
¼ teaspoon salt
½ tablespoon baking powder

Juice and finely grated zest of ½ lemon
2 large eggs
½ cup milk
1 cup whole almonds, coarsely chopped

DESSERTS

continued

1. Preheat the oven to 400 degrees. Brush a 9- to 10-inch loaf pan with butter, then line with parchment paper. Brush the paper with butter.

2. In a large bowl, using an electric mixer, beat the flour with the sugar, salt, and baking powder. Beat in the butter and lemon juice and zest for 2 to 3 minutes. Beat in the eggs and milk until smooth and light, about 2 minutes.

3. Scrape the batter into the loaf pan. Transfer to the oven and bake for 25 minutes. Reduce the oven temperature to 350 degrees and bake for 20 to 25 minutes. Turn out on a cake rack and let cool completely before slicing.

From Françoise:

• The zest from an orange or clementine can replace the lemon zest. It's always a good idea to scrub the peel of any citrus fruit before using the zest. Using untreated fruit is also smart.

• It's important to take the eggs, butter, and milk out of the refrigerator ahead of time because they should all be at room temperature.

• An electric mixer is especially good in this recipe because the batter benefits from the whipping.

GLAZED LEMON CAKE
- *Manqué au citron* -

❖ EASY   ❖ INEXPENSIVE   ❖ 1 HOUR   ❖ SERVES 4 TO 6

4 tablespoons (½ stick) unsalted butter, melted,
  plus more for brushing
¾ cup all-purpose flour, plus more for dusting
4 large eggs, separated
Finely grated zest from ½ lemon
⅔ cup sugar
½ tablespoon vanilla sugar

½ teaspoon baking powder
Pinch of salt

LEMON GLAZE
1 cup confectioners' sugar
1 to 2 tablespoons fresh lemon juice

❖   ❖   ❖   ❖   ❖

1. Preheat the oven to 350 degrees. Brush an 8- to 9-inch springform pan with butter, then dust with flour, patting out the excess.

2. In a bowl, beat the egg yolks with the lemon zest, sugar, and vanilla sugar until foamy. Gradually add the melted butter, beating continuously, as for a mayonnaise. Sift the flour with the baking powder over the egg mixture and beat until creamy.

3. In another bowl, beat the egg whites with the salt until foamy, then beat at high speed until stiff. Gently fold the whites into the batter.

4. Scrape the batter into the springform pan. Transfer to the oven and bake for 40 minutes. Increase the oven temperature to 400 degrees and bake for 5 minutes. Turn out on a cake rack and let cool completely.

5. Make the lemon glaze: Using a wooden spoon, beat the confectioners' sugar with the lemon juice until creamy, 1 to 2 minutes. Using a thin spatula, spread the glaze over the cake.

From Françoise:
• If you have the time, return the glazed cake to the oven with the door open to dry out the glaze, but do not brown it.

LIGHT RUM AND LEMON CAKE
- *Biscuit génois* -

❖ INTERMEDIATE ❖ MODERATE ❖ 1 HOUR, PLUS 45 MINUTES COOLING ❖ SERVES 6 TO 8

5 tablespoons unsalted butter, melted, plus more
  for brushing
½ cup all-purpose flour, plus more for dusting
3 large eggs
½ cup sugar
1 tablespoon vanilla sugar

Pinch of salt
1 tablespoon rum
½ cup potato starch
1 teaspoon baking powder
Juice and finely grated zest of ½ lemon

❖ ❖ ❖ ❖ ❖

1. Preheat the oven to 400 degrees. Brush an 8-inch springform pan with butter and dust with flour, patting out the excess.

2. Warm a large bowl with hot water. Add the eggs and warm slightly. Pour out the water and dry the bowl.

3. In the warmed bowl, beat the eggs with the sugar, vanilla sugar, salt, and rum at high speed until thick and light. Continue beating for 2 to 3 minutes until cool. Sift the flour with the potato starch and baking powder over the egg mixture and fold in. Gently fold in the melted butter, lemon juice, and zest.

4. Scrape the batter into the springform pan. Transfer to the oven and bake for about 40 minutes. Turn out on a cake rack and let cool completely.

From Françoise:
• My way of making génoise is unconventional, but it's easier than the traditional method. For instance, I warm the bowl used to beat the eggs and the eggs in the shell instead of beating the egg-and-sugar mixture over a warm water bath.

• You can make a layer cake if you split the génoise horizontally into 2 or 3 layers and spread them with buttercream, chocolate ganache, or jam.

DESSERTS

CLASSIC CHERRY CLAFOUTIS
- *Clafoutis* -

❖ EASY   ❖ MODERATE   ❖ 55 MINUTES   ❖ SERVES 4

Butter for brushing
½ cup all-purpose flour
⅔ cup sugar, plus more for sprinkling
Pinch of salt

3 large eggs
1 ½ cups milk
1 pound cherries, unpitted

❖   ❖   ❖   ❖   ❖

1. Preheat the oven to 400 degrees. Brush a gratin dish with butter.

2. In a bowl, whisk the flour with the sugar and salt. Whisk in the eggs one at a time, then the milk until smooth.

3. Arrange the cherries in the gratin dish. Pour the batter over the top.

4. Transfer to the oven and bake for about 45 minutes. Sprinkle with sugar and serve warm or at room temperature.

From Françoise:

• Let your guests know that the cherries are unpitted. You can pit the cherries, but the pits help give this dessert its flavor, and also cherries with pits don't collapse.

• Clafoutis batter is just a thick crêpe batter.

• Traditionally, this dessert is made with sweet red cherries, but it's also good with tart cherries.

• You can use a variety of fruit: apricots, plums, apples, and pears, depending on the season and what's available.

• Try a scoop of cherry granita or sorbet with the clafoutis.

APPLE-RAISIN CLAFOUTIS

- *Clafoutis normand aux pommes* -

❖ EASY ❖ INEXPENSIVE ❖ 45 MINUTES ❖ SERVES 4

3 tablespoons unsalted butter, melted, plus more
  for brushing
¼ cup sugar
Pinch of salt
1 large egg
½ cup crème fraîche

1 ½ tablespoons all-purpose flour
2 or 3 apples, peeled, cored, quartered,
  and thinly sliced
Lemon juice for sprinkling
¼ cup raisins, rinsed in warm water

❖ ❖ ❖ ❖ ❖

1. Preheat the oven to 400 degrees. Brush a
round 8-inch gratin dish with butter.

2. In a bowl, beat the sugar with the salt and
egg until light. Beat in the crème fraîche and
flour. Reserve 3 tablespoons of the batter.

3. Fold the apples, lemon juice, and raisins into
the batter. Scrape into the gratin dish. Transfer
to the oven and bake for 15 minutes. Stir the
melted butter into the reserved batter and
pour this mixture into the gratin dish. Increase
the oven temperature to 425 degrees and
bake for 15 minutes. Serve warm or at room
temperature.

From Françoise:

• The clafoutis can be assembled and then slid
into the oven just before sitting down to eat.

• You can flame this clafoutis with Calvados.
Bring ¼ cup of Calvados to a simmer in a small
pan, then tilt and carefully ignite. Pour it flaming over the baked clafoutis.

DESSERTS

CRISPY DEEP-FRIED PASTRIES

- *Merveilles* -

❖ INTERMEDIATE   ❖ INEXPENSIVE   ❖ 45 MINUTES, PLUS 1 HOUR RESTING   ❖ MAKES 40 TO 50 PASTRIES

3 large eggs

¼ cup sugar, plus more for sprinkling

½ teaspoon salt

4 tablespoons (½ stick) unsalted butter, softened

1 tablespoon rum or orange flower water

2 cups all-purpose flour

4 cups oil for frying

❖ ❖ ❖ ❖ ❖

1. In a large bowl, using an electric mixer, beat the eggs with the sugar and salt. Beat in the softened butter and rum or orange flower water. Add the flour and knead until smooth, 2 to 3 minutes. Stretch the dough and press it into a ball 3 times. Wrap the dough in plastic and refrigerate for at least 1 hour.

2. Divide the dough in quarters. On a lightly floured work surface, roll out each quarter to as thin a sheet as possible. Using a pastry wheel or large chef's knife, cut the dough into 3-by-2-inch rectangles. Or cut the dough into 1-inch-wide strips and tie into loose knots. As the dough is cut, transfer it to a floured kitchen towel.

3. In a large skillet, heat the oil to 375 degrees. Gently drop a few of the pastries into the oil without crowding. Fry them, turning the pastries once, until golden, 1 to 3 minutes total. Using a slotted spoon, transfer the pastries to paper towels to drain. Keep warm in a low oven while frying the remaining pastries. Sprinkle with sugar and serve hot or at room temperature.

CRISPY VANILLA WAFERS

- *Langues de chat* -

❖ EASY   ❖ INEXPENSIVE   ❖ 30 MINUTES, PLUS 15 MINUTES COOLING   ❖ MAKES ABOUT 20 COOKIES

4 tablespoons (½ cup) butter, softened,
  plus more for brushing

½ cup all-purpose flour, plus more for dusting

2 large egg whites

⅓ cup sugar

1 tablespoon vanilla sugar

Pinch of salt

1. Preheat the oven to 425 degrees. Brush a baking sheet with butter and dust with flour, tapping off the excess.

2. In a hot but not boiling double boiler, warm the egg whites.

3. Meanwhile, using an electric mixer, beat the softened butter with the sugar, vanilla sugar, and salt until smooth and creamy. Lightly beat the warmed egg whites using a fork. Still using a fork, beat the egg whites into the butter mixture. Using a wooden spoon, stir in the flour just to mix.

4. Using a small spoon or a piping bag, spread the batter on the baking sheet in long ovals or rounds, spacing them 1 inch apart. Transfer to the oven and bake until set and lightly browned around the edges, 10 to 12 minutes. Using a metal spatula, immediately transfer them to a rack to cool.

From Françoise:

• Transfer the cookies to a rack while they're still warm. If they cool on the baking sheet, they may break when you try to remove them.

• The cookies can be stored for a day or two in an airtight container.

• Don't try to use your electric mixer instead of a fork or spoon trying to save time. The batter will turn foamy, and the cookies won't be anything like traditional langues de chats (cats' tongues).

• It is crucial to warm the egg whites so they blend properly with the other ingredients. But don't make the double boiler or water bath too hot or the whites will cook. That would be a catastrophe!

CRISPY CURRANT WAFERS

- *Palets aux raisins* -

❖ EASY   ❖ INEXPENSIVE   ❖ 30 MINUTES   ❖ MAKES ABOUT 3 DOZEN COOKIES

⅓ cup dried currants, rinsed in warm water
1 tablespoon rum
½ cup (1 stick) butter, softened,
   plus more for brushing

1 cup all-purpose flour, plus more for dusting
Pinch of salt
⅔ cup sugar
2 large eggs

❖ ❖ ❖ ❖ ❖

1. In a bowl, combine the currants with the rum.

2. Preheat the oven to 400 degrees. Brush a baking sheet with butter and dust with flour, tapping off the excess.

3. In a large bowl, using an electric mixer, beat the softened butter with the salt and sugar until smooth and creamy. Add the eggs, one at a time, beating after each addition. Beat in the

continued

DESSERTS

1 cup of flour, the currants, and rum to make a stiff batter.

4. Drop teaspoons of the batter on the baking sheet, spacing them 1 inch apart. Transfer to the oven and bake until set and lightly browned around the edges, 10 to 15 minutes. Using a metal spatula, immediately transfer them to a rack to cool when baking the second batch.

From Françoise:
• Take the butter out of the refrigerator well ahead of baking. It should be as soft as crème fraîche when you beat it with the sugar. Do not melt the butter to save time. You won't get at all the same result.

BUTTERY SANDIES
- *Sablés* -

❖ EASY   ❖ INEXPENSIVE   ❖ 30 MINUTES, PLUS 1 HOUR RESTING   ❖ MAKES 1 DOZEN

1 cup all-purpose flour
⅓ cup sugar, plus more for sprinkling
Pinch of salt

4 tablespoons (½ stick) unsalted butter, cut into pieces, plus more for brushing
1 large egg yolk

❖   ❖   ❖   ❖   ❖

1. In a food processor, whir the flour, sugar, and salt until mixed. Add the butter and pulse until the dough resembles coarse crumbs. Add the egg yolk and pulse until the dough holds together when pinched. Press into a ball, wrap in plastic, and refrigerate for at least 1 hour.

2. Preheat the oven to 350 degrees. Brush a baking sheet with butter.

3. On a lightly floured work surface, roll out the dough ¼ inch thick. Using a 3-inch round cookie cutter, stamp out the dough and transfer to the baking sheet. Prick all over with a fork. Reroll the scraps and cut out more cookies.

4. Transfer to the oven and bake the cookies until they are light brown around the edges, 10 to 12 minutes. Let the cookies cool on the baking sheets for about 5 minutes, then, using a metal spatula, carefully transfer them to a rack to cool completely. If you like, sprinkle with sugar before serving.

From Françoise:
• Regular sablés should be sand colored, while sablés nantais, which are brushed with egg yolk before baking, are golden and shiny.

BRITTANY SANDIES WITH ORANGE FLOWER WATER

- *Sablés bretons à la fleur d'oranger* -

❖ EASY   ❖ INEXPENSIVE   ❖ 30 MINUTES, PLUS 1 HOUR RESTING   ❖ MAKES ABOUT 2 DOZEN

1 ¼ cups all-purpose flour

6 tablespoons sugar, plus more for sprinkling

7 tablespoons salted butter, cut into pieces,
  plus more for brushing

1 whole large egg or 2 large egg yolks

1 tablespoon candied angelica

½ teaspoon orange flower water

❖ ❖ ❖ ❖ ❖

1. In a food processor, whir the flour and sugar until mixed. Add the butter and pulse until the dough resembles coarse crumbs. Add the egg or egg yolks, candied angelica, and orange flower water and pulse until the dough holds together when pinched. Press into a ball, wrap in plastic, and refrigerate for at least 1 hour.

2. Preheat the oven to 350 degrees. Brush a baking sheet with butter.

3. On a lightly floured work surface, roll out the dough ¼ inch thick. Using a 3-inch round cookie cutter, stamp out the dough and transfer to the baking sheet. Reroll the scraps and cut out more cookies.

4. Transfer to the oven and bake the cookies until they are light brown around the edges, 10 to 12 minutes. Let the sugar cookies cool on the baking sheets for about 5 minutes, then, using a metal spatula, carefully transfer them to a rack to cool completely. If you like, sprinkle with sugar before serving.

From Françoise:
• Using salted butter (beurre salé) is what makes these sablés Breton, since it's a regional specialty.

• The cookies can be stored in an airtight container.

• The cookie dough can be pressed into a disk, wrapped well in plastic, and frozen. Or if it's going to be frozen for only a short time, roll it into a sheet and freeze, ready for stamping.

DESSERTS

FRIED NORTH AFRICAN SEMOLINA COOKIES
- Makroutes -

❖ EASY   ❖ MODERATE   ❖ 30 MINUTES   ❖ SERVES 4

1 ½ cups semolina
15 tablespoons unsalted butter,
  10 tablespoons softened
½ cup ground almonds

2 tablespoons sugar
½ teaspoon cinnamon
Honey for serving (optional)

❖ ❖ ❖ ❖ ❖

1. In a medium bowl, moisten the semolina with 3 tablespoons of water. Beat in the 10 tablespoons of softened butter until smooth.

2. In a small bowl, mix the almonds with the sugar and cinnamon. Moisten with enough water to make a paste that holds together.

3. Roll the semolina dough into a cylinder. about 1 ½ inches in diameter. Make a deep groove in the cylinder and fill with the almond mixture. Press the semolina dough around the almond paste to seal. Roll again into a neat cylinder. Slice it crosswise ½ inch thick.

4. In a large skillet, melt the remaining 5 tablespoons of butter over medium heat. When it foams, add the semolina slices without crowding and fry until golden on both sides. Using a slotted spoon, transfer the cookies to paper towels to drain and continue frying.

5. Transfer to a plate, drizzle with the honey, if using, and serve.

BRIOCHE LOAF
- Gâteau brioché -

❖ ADVANCED   ❖ MODERATE   ❖ 55 MINUTES, PLUS 2 HOURS RESTING   ❖ MAKES ABOUT 20 SLICES

¼ cup warm milk
3 tablespoons sugar
1 tablespoon dry yeast
2 cups all-purpose flour, plus more
  for sprinkling

1 teaspoon salt
2 large eggs
7 tablespoons unsalted butter, softened,
  plus more for brushing

1. In a large bowl, combine the milk with 1 ½ tablespoons of the sugar and the yeast and let stand for 5 minutes. Gradually add the 2 cups of flour and salt and beat with a wooden spoon until blended. Beat in the eggs. Knead until smooth and elastic.

2. Pat out the dough and set one-third of the softened butter on top. Wrap the butter in the dough and knead until incorporated. Repeat 2 more times with the remaining butter, kneading well after each addition. Then knead for 5 to 7 minutes longer until the dough is nice and elastic. Sprinkle lightly with flour and shape into a ball.

3. Return the dough to the bowl, cover with plastic wrap, and let rise at warm room temperature until the dough doubles in bulk, about 1 hour.

4. Generously brush a 9- to 10-inch loaf pan with butter.

5. Punch down the dough. Add the remaining 1 ½ tablespoons of sugar. Transfer the dough to the loaf pan; it should fill the pan only halfway. Cover and let rise until doubled in bulk, about 1 hour.

6. Preheat the oven to 400 degrees and heat a baking sheet in the oven. Using scissors, snip the dough in 5 or 6 places. Transfer the pan to the hot baking sheet in the oven and bake until golden brown, 30 to 35 minutes. Transfer to a cake rack and let stand for 10 minutes, then unmold.

From Françoise:

• Instead of rising relatively quickly at a warm room temperature in Step 5, the dough can rise slowly in the refrigerator overnight. Then proceed with the recipe.

• Very important: All the ingredients, especially the butter, must be at room temperature. Remove them from the refrigerator well in advance, or warm the bowl in hot water and wipe dry before adding the ingredients. The cooler the temperature of the kitchen, the longer the dough will take to rise.

• If you are using a standing mixer, beat the dough at medium speed for 15 minutes in Step 1 before adding the butter. Then reduce the speed in Step 2 and knead for only 2 or 3 minutes.

• Adding too much sugar at the beginning reduces the lift of the yeast. Better to add only half at the start and the rest during the final kneading just before transferring the dough to the loaf pan.

• When you lift and pull the dough it should stretch like chewing gum without breaking.

• Add the specified amount of salt in the recipe or the brioche will taste bland.

• The bottom of the brioche must be set so the dough doesn't fall. That's why the loaf pan is set on a hot baking sheet in the oven and not on a rack.

• Dough that has risen for the second time can be frozen in the loaf pan. The day before baking, transfer the pan to the refrigerator several hours ahead of time to bring it slowly to the right temperature.

DESSERTS

SIMPLE VANILLA FLAN

- Flan à la vanille -

❖ EASY   ❖ INEXPENSIVE   ❖ 30 MINUTES, PLUS 45 MINUTES COOLING   ❖ SERVES 4 TO 6

Butter for brushing

2 cups milk

2 pinches of salt

1 tablespoon vanilla sugar or 1 vanilla bean,
   seeds scraped

½ cup sugar

3 large eggs

3 tablespoons all-purpose flour

❖ ❖ ❖ ❖ ❖

1. Preheat the oven to 425 degrees. Butter an 8- to 9-inch springform pan or soufflé dish.

2. In a medium saucepan, heat the milk with the salt and vanilla sugar or vanilla seeds until barely simmering. Remove from the heat.

3. Meanwhile, in a bowl, using an electric mixer, beat the sugar with the eggs until light. Beat in the flour in several batches. Then beat in ½ cup of the hot but not boiling milk. When the mixture is smooth with no lumps, beat in the remaining 1 ½ cups of milk.

4. Pour the custard into the springform pan or soufflé dish. Transfer to the oven and bake for 20 to 25 minutes. Let cool completely. Serve the flan in the pan or unmold once it's cooled.

From Françoise:

• Do not try to cut corners on this (already easy) recipe by adding all the milk at once. You'll get a floury deposit on the bottom.

• For a more delicate texture, use cornstarch instead of flour.

CARAMEL-PINEAPPLE FLAN

- Flan à l'ananas -

❖ EASY   ❖ MODERATE   ❖ 1 HOUR, 15 MINUTES, PLUS 45 MINUTES COOLING   ❖ SERVES 6 TO 8

CARAMEL

½ cup sugar

½ teaspoon fresh lemon juice

1 cup canned crushed pineapple, syrup reserved

1 cup sugar

6 large eggs

2 tablespoons potato starch

3 tablespoons kirsch or rum

1. Preheat the oven to 400 degrees.

2. Make the caramel: In a medium saucepan, combine the sugar with 3 tablespoons of water and the lemon juice. Bring to a simmer over medium-high heat and cook, stirring often, until the sugar dissolves. Partly cover the pan and continue cooking until the sugar turns medium amber. Immediately pour the caramel into a 6- to 7-inch springform pan or soufflé dish and quickly turn to coat the bottom and sides.

3. In a medium saucepan, combine the crushed pineapple with the reserved syrup and the sugar and simmer for 2 minutes.

4. In a large bowl, lightly beat the eggs to mix. In a cup, blend the potato starch with a little of the beaten egg, then beat this mixture into the remaining eggs. Beat in the pineapple and kirsch or rum.

5. Pour the custard into the springform pan or soufflé dish. Set in a roasting pan and pour in hot water to come halfway up the side of the pan. Transfer to the oven and bake for 45 minutes. Let cool completely. Unmold before serving.

From Françoise:

• Once unmolded, the flan can be decorated with half-rounds of pineapple and candied cherries to make it more colorful. Don't hesitate to use fresh pineapple.

• This flan can also be made with other fruit in syrup, such as apricots, peaches, and pears.

SUPER-EASY PRUNE FLAN

- *Flan aux pruneaux* -

❖ EASY   ❖ INEXPENSIVE   ❖ 1 HOUR, PLUS 45 MINUTES COOLING   ❖ SERVES 4 OR 5

Butter for brushing
2 tablespoons all-purpose flour
⅓ cup sugar
2 large eggs, lightly beaten

¾ cup milk
2 pinches of salt
½ pound pitted prunes

❖ ❖ ❖ ❖ ❖

1. Preheat the oven to 350 degrees. Brush a gratin dish with butter.

2. In a bowl, whisk the flour with the sugar, eggs, milk, and salt until smooth. Add the prunes.

3. Pour the mixture into the gratin dish. Transfer to the oven and bake for 40 to 45 minutes. Serve warm or at room temperature.

From Françoise:

• This recipe is very quick to prepare if you use moist prunes to start with, usually sold vacuum-packed. If your prunes are not especially soft, soak them for a few hours ahead of time in warm water.

DESSERTS

BRITTANY RAISIN FLAN
- *Far breton* -

❖ EASY ❖ INEXPENSIVE ❖ 1 HOUR, 30 MINUTES, PLUS 45 MINUTES COOLING ❖ SERVES 4

Butter for brushing
⅔ cup raisins
⅓ cup rum
1 cup all-purpose flour

½ cup sugar
3 large eggs, lightly beaten
2 cups milk

❖ ❖ ❖ ❖ ❖

1. Preheat the oven to 400 degrees. Butter a gratin dish. In a small bowl, soak the raisins in the rum.

2. In a large bowl, whisk the flour with the sugar and eggs. Gradually whisk in the milk, raisins, and rum.

3. Pour the mixture into the gratin dish. Transfer to the oven and bake for 15 minutes. Reduce the oven temperature to 350 degrees and bake for 1 hour. Serve at room temperature in the baking dish.

From Françoise:
• You can replace the raisins with pitted prunes, in which case you won't need to soak them in rum.

• If you like, dust the top with confectioners' sugar before serving.

CLASSIC CRÊPES
- *Crêpes* -

❖ EASY ❖ INEXPENSIVE ❖ 30 MINUTES, PLUS 1 HOUR RESTING ❖ SERVES 4; MAKES ABOUT 12 CRÊPES

1 cup all-purpose flour
1 ½ cups milk
2 large eggs, lightly beaten

3 tablespoons unsalted butter, melted
½ teaspoon salt
Sugar for sprinkling

1. In a medium bowl, whisk the flour with the milk, eggs, 2 tablespoons of the melted butter, and the salt. Cover and let stand for at least 1 hour.

2. Lightly brush a 6- or 7-inch skillet with a little of the melted butter and heat over medium heat. Whisk the batter and add about 2 tablespoons to the skillet, swirling to coat the bottom. Cook until the edge begins to brown, about 30 seconds. Flip using a thin-bladed spatula and cook for 20 seconds. Slide onto a plate and repeat with the remaining batter, stacking the crêpes as they're cooked and adding more butter to the pan as needed.

3. Sprinkle the crêpes with sugar and fold into quarters or roll up. Serve right away.

From Françoise:
• If you have any crêpes left over, use them to make a first course or a dessert another day. Wrapped in foil, they can be refrigerated for 2 or 3 days.

• If at all possible, let the batter rest for at least an hour before cooking.

ORANGE CRÊPES
- Crêpes à l'orange -

❖ EASY   ❖ INEXPENSIVE   ❖ 15 MINUTES   ❖ SERVES 4

3 tablespoons unsalted butter, melted
8 cold crêpes (page 768)

2 tablespoons sugar, plus more for sprinkling
Juice of 2 oranges

❖ ❖ ❖ ❖ ❖

1. Warm a skillet and brush it with a little of the melted butter. Add the crêpes one at a time or more, if the pan is large, and heat through, turning once. Sprinkle the crêpes with sugar. Fold them into quarters and transfer to a heat-proof serving dish. Repeat with the remaining crêpes, brushing the skillet with more butter and sprinkling the crêpes with sugar.

2. Add the orange juice to the skillet with 2 tablespoons of sugar. Bring to a boil, stirring, then pour over the crêpes and serve.

From Françoise:
• When there are no children at the table, I add a little rum to the orange juice. I can even flame the mixture—if enough rum is added—and pour it over the crêpes, which is fantastic.

• If you're making crêpe batter especially for this recipe, whisk in finely grated orange zest.

DESSERTS

CLASSIC CRÊPES SUZETTE
- *Crêpes Suzette* -

❖ EASY   ❖ MODERATE   ❖ 45 MINUTES, PLUS 1 HOUR RESTING   ❖ SERVES 4; MAKES ABOUT 12 CRÊPES

CRÊPES

1 cup all-purpose flour

1½ cups milk

2 large eggs, lightly beaten

3 tablespoons unsalted butter, melted

½ teaspoon salt

FILLING

10 tablespoons unsalted butter, softened

½ cup sugar

½ cup Grand Marnier liqueur, plus more
  for flambéing

2 tablespoons ground almonds

Finely grated zest of 1 orange

❖ ❖ ❖ ❖ ❖

1. Make the crêpes: In a medium bowl, whisk the flour with the milk, eggs, 2 tablespoons of the melted butter, and the salt. Cover and let stand at least 1 hour.

2. Lightly brush a 6- or 7-inch skillet with a little of the remaining melted butter and heat over medium heat. Whisk the batter and add about 2 tablespoons to the skillet, swirling to coat the bottom. Cook until the edges begin to brown, about 30 seconds. Flip using a thin-bladed spatula and cook for 20 seconds. Slide onto a plate and repeat with the remaining batter, stacking the crêpes as they're cooked and adding more butter to the pan as needed.

3. Make the filling: In a bowl, using an electric mixer, beat the softened butter with the sugar, ¼ cup of the liqueur, ground almonds, and orange zest. Spread some of the filling on each crêpe and roll up or fold into quarters. Transfer to a heatproof serving dish.

4. In a small saucepan, bring the remaining ¼ cup of liqueur to a simmer. Tilt the pan and carefully ignite. Pour the flaming liqueur over the crêpes and serve right away.

From Françoise:

• If you make the crêpes in advance (and you can refrigerate them, wrapped in foil, for 2 or 3 days), sprinkle sugar in between each one so they're easier to pull apart.

RUM-FLAMBÉED CRÊPES
- Crêpes flambées au rhum -

❖ EASY   ❖ MODERATE   ❖ 40 MINUTES, PLUS 1 HOUR RESTING   ❖ SERVES 4; MAKES ABOUT 12 CRÊPES

1 cup all-purpose flour

1 ½ cups milk

2 large eggs, lightly beaten

3 tablespoons unsalted butter, melted

½ teaspoon salt

2 to 3 tablespoons rum

❖ ❖ ❖ ❖ ❖

1. In a medium bowl, whisk the flour with the milk, eggs, 2 tablespoons of the melted butter, and the salt. Cover and let stand at least 1 hour.

2. Lightly brush a 6- or 7-inch skillet with a little of the remaining melted butter and heat over medium heat. Whisk the batter and add about 2 tablespoons to the skillet, swirling to coat the bottom. Cook until the edge begins to brown, about 30 seconds. Flip using a thin-bladed spatula and cook for 20 seconds. Slide onto a plate and repeat with the remaining batter, stacking the crêpes as they're cooked and adding more butter to the pan as needed. Fold the crêpes into quarters or roll up and transfer to a heatproof serving dish.

3. In a small saucepan, bring the rum to a simmer. Tilt the pan and carefully ignite. Pour the flaming rum over the crêpes and serve right away.

From Françoise:

• You can keep the crêpes warm in the oven with the door open or between 2 plates set over a pan of simmering water.

• The best way to serve this is to pour the flaming rum over the crêpes at the table. You can even flame the rum at the table if you have a small hot plate or burner.

DESSERTS

BELGIAN DESSERT WAFFLES

- *Gaufres bruxelloises chaudes* -

❖ EASY   ❖ MODERATE   ❖ 30 MINUTES   ❖ MAKES ABOUT 10 WAFFLES

1 cup milk

10 tablespoons unsalted butter

3 tablespoons sugar, plus more for serving

1 tablespoon vanilla sugar

¼ teaspoon salt

2 cups all-purpose flour

2 or 3 large eggs, separated

Oil for brushing

Whipped cream (page 647) for serving

❖ ❖ ❖ ❖ ❖

1. Preheat the oven to 225 degrees.

2. In a medium saucepan, combine the milk with the butter, sugar, vanilla sugar, and salt and bring to a bare simmer. Remove the pan from the heat and beat in the egg yolks.

3. In a bowl, beat the egg whites until stiff. Gently fold the beaten whites into the batter.

4. Heat and grease a waffle iron. Pour the batter into the iron and cook until the waffles are golden, 6 minutes. Transfer the waffles to the oven. Repeat with the remaining batter. Dust the waffles with sugar and serve with whipped cream.

From Françoise:

• The batter can be prepared and refrigerated just before the meal but no longer or the beaten egg whites will deflate.

• You can buy vanilla sugar in certain supermarkets, but it is easy to make your own: Split one vanilla bean and scrape out the seeds, reserving them for another use. Place the scraped bean in a glass jar and cover it with 1 to 2 cups of sugar. Shake it occasionally and leave it in your pantry. After a week or two, your sugar will be perfumed with the vanilla.

ICE CREAM WITH DARK CHOCOLATE SAUCE
- *Glace Armenonville* -

❖ EASY ❖ INEXPENSIVE ❖ 10 MINUTES ❖ SERVES 4

¼ pound bittersweet chocolate, chopped
2 tablespoons unsalted butter

½ pint ice cream

❖ ❖ ❖ ❖ ❖

1. In a small saucepan, combine the chocolate with the butter and 2 tablespoons of water and melt over low heat. Remove from the heat and stir with a wooden spoon. Scoop the ice cream into bowls, spoon the chocolate sauce over the top, and serve.

From Françoise:

• Try vanilla, vanilla-coffee, or vanilla-hazelnut ice cream here.

• Pass additional sauce in a warmed sauceboat at the table. You guests will definitely help themselves to more.

HOMEMADE VANILLA–CRÈME FRAÎCHE ICE CREAM
- *Glace à la vanille* -

❖ INTERMEDIATE ❖ EXPENSIVE ❖ 15 MINUTES, PLUS 3 HOURS CHILLING AND FREEZING ❖ SERVES 4

2 cups milk
1 to 2 tablespoons vanilla sugar
Pinch of salt
5 large egg yolks

1 ¼ cups sugar
1 teaspoon potato starch or cornstarch
½ cup crème fraîche

❖ ❖ ❖ ❖ ❖

1. In a medium saucepan, bring the milk to a bare simmer with the vanilla sugar and salt. Remove the pan from the heat.

2. In a bowl, whisk the egg yolks with the sugar and potato starch or cornstarch. Whisk in half the hot milk, then whisk the mixture back into the remaining milk. Place over low heat and

cook, stirring constantly with a wooden spoon, until the custard thickens slightly.

3. Remove the pan from the heat. Let the custard cool slightly, then refrigerate until cold.

continued

DESSERTS

4. Whisk in the crème fraîche. Pour the ice-cream base into an ice-cream maker and freeze according to the manufacturer's instructions. Pack the ice cream into a plastic container.

5. Press a sheet of plastic wrap directly onto the surface of the ice cream and close with an airtight lid. Freeze the vanilla ice cream until firm, at least 2 hours.

From Françoise:
• Do not let the custard come to a simmer in Step 2 or you'll cook the yolks. Your custard is perfectly cooked when you can draw a finger across the back of the spoon and it leaves a clear trail.

• This recipe is easy but requires time and attention. It's probably the kind of thing you'll make only once in a while since it's easy to find small-batch artisanal ice cream now.

• Freezing time can vary among refrigerators.

VIETNAMESE COFFEE ICE CREAM
- Glace au lait condensé au café -

❖ EASY   ❖ INEXPENSIVE   ❖ 10 MINUTES, PLUS 2 HOURS FREEZING   ❖ SERVES 4

1 large egg, separated
1 can (5 ounces) evaporated milk

3 tablespoons sugar
1 teaspoon instant coffee

❖ ❖ ❖ ❖ ❖

1. In a bowl, whisk the egg yolk with the evaporated milk, sugar, and instant coffee.

2. In a bowl, beat the egg whites until stiff. Gently fold the beaten whites into the egg yolk mixture.

3. Pour into a plastic container and close with an airtight lid. Freeze the ice cream until firm, at least 2 hours.

From Françoise:
• If you use an electric mixer, the ice cream will be lighter.

• Instead of instant coffee, you can use unsweetened cocoa powder.

CHOCOLATE ICE CREAM WITH VANILLA WHIPPED CREAM

- *Chocolat liégeois* -

❖ EASY   ❖ MODERATE   ❖ 25 MINUTES   ❖ SERVES 4

½ cup heavy cream
1 tablespoon vanilla sugar

½ pint chocolate ice cream

❖ ❖ ❖ ❖ ❖

1. In a chilled bowl and using a chilled whisk or an electric mixer with chilled beaters, whip the cream until it starts to thicken. Add the vanilla sugar and beat until soft peaks form.

2. Scoop the ice cream into bowls, dollop the whipped cream on top, and serve at once.

From Françoise:
• Melted chocolate is often spooned into the bowl before the ice cream and whipped cream are added.

• Coffee is another traditional flavor of ice cream served with vanilla whipped cream. Café liégeois is also made with a chilled blend of equal parts strong coffee, milk, and sugar, plus a half part crème fraîche.

DESSERTS

CLASSIC CHOCOLATE PROFITEROLES

- *Profiteroles au chocolat* -

❖ INTERMEDIATE ❖ MODERATE ❖ 1 HOUR ❖ SERVES 4

Butter for brushing
1 pint vanilla ice cream

1 cup all-purpose flour
4 large eggs

CHOUX PASTRY
5 tablespoons unsalted butter
½ teaspoon salt

CHOCOLATE SAUCE
¼ pound bittersweet chocolate, chopped
2 tablespoons unsalted butter

❖ ❖ ❖ ❖ ❖

1. Preheat the oven to 400 degrees. Brush 2 baking sheets with butter.

2. Make the choux pastry: In a saucepan, bring 1 cup of water, the butter, and salt to a boil. When the butter melts, remove the pan from the heat, add all the flour at once, and beat well using a wooden spoon. Return the pan to low heat and beat until the dough is smooth and pulls away from the pan to form a ball. Off the heat, add the eggs, one at a time, beating well after each addition.

3. Drop tablespoons of the batter onto the baking sheets, spacing them well apart. Transfer to the oven and bake until puffed and golden, 20 to 30 minutes, reducing the oven temperature to 350 degrees after 20 minutes. Transfer to a rack to cool completely.

4. Meanwhile, make the chocolate sauce: In a small saucepan, combine the chocolate with the butter and 2 tablespoons of water and melt over low heat. Remove from the heat and stir with a wooden spoon.

5. Cut each puff in half horizontally. Carefully spoon the ice cream in the puffs and close like a sandwich. Pour the chocolate sauce over the profiteroles and serve immediately.

From Françoise:
• The choux pastry can puff up without being fully cooked inside. The result: They collapse as soon as they're out of the oven. Make sure they are firm when you tap them.

• Keep your eye on the chocolate as it melts. If it's too hot or heated for too long, it can seize up and become lumpy.

HOMEMADE STRAWBERRY ICE CREAM
- *Glace aux fraises* -

❖ INTERMEDIATE   ❖ EXPENSIVE   ❖ 20 MINUTES, PLUS 3 HOURS CHILLING AND FREEZING   ❖ SERVES 4

2 cups milk

Pinch of salt

5 large egg yolks

1 ¼ cups sugar

1 teaspoon potato starch or cornstarch

½ pound strawberries, hulled

½ cup crème fraîche

❖ ❖ ❖ ❖ ❖

1. In a medium saucepan, bring the milk to a bare simmer with the salt. Remove the pan from the heat.

2. In a bowl, whisk the egg yolks with the sugar and potato starch or cornstarch. Whisk in half the hot milk, then whisk the mixture back into the remaining milk. Place over low heat and cook, stirring constantly with a wooden spoon, until the custard thickens slightly.

3. Remove the pan from the heat. Let the custard cool slightly, then refrigerate until cold.

4. In a food processor, puree the strawberries until smooth.

5. Whisk the strawberry puree and crème fraîche into the custard. Pour the ice-cream base into an ice-cream maker and freeze according to the manufacturer's instructions. Pack the ice cream into a plastic container.

6. Press a sheet of plastic wrap directly onto the surface of the ice cream and close with an airtight lid. Freeze the ice cream until firm, at least 2 hours.

From Françoise:

• Try raspberries instead of strawberries. You might want to strain out the seeds before adding the puree to the custard.

• You can reduce the number of egg yolks if you increase the amount of crème fraîche.

DESSERTS

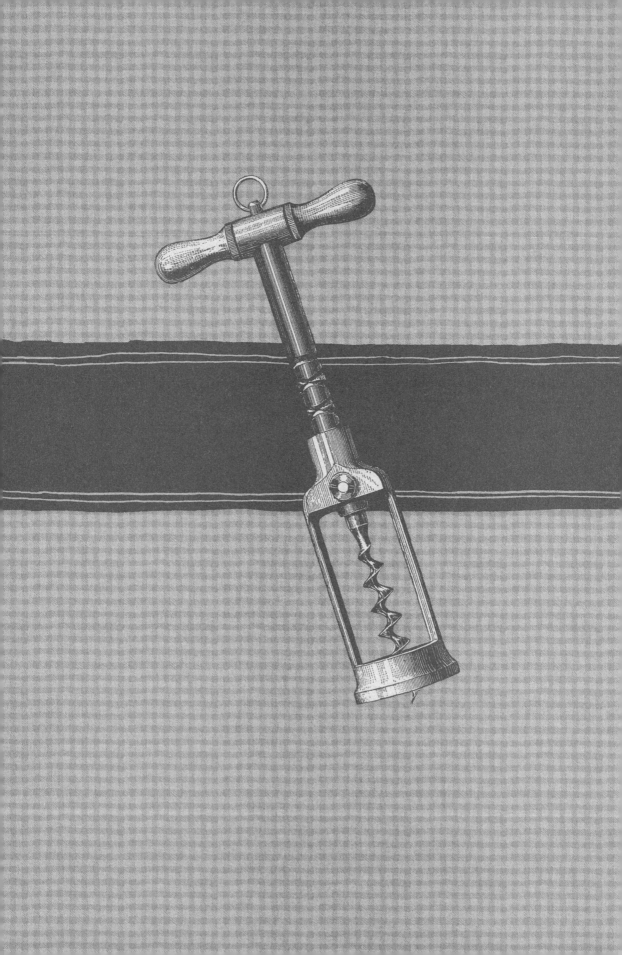

COCKTAILS & DRINKS

RICH VANILLA-BEAN HOT CHOCOLATE

- Chocolat chaud maison -

1 ¾ cups milk

1 cup heavy cream

¼ pound bittersweet chocolate, chopped

¼ cup sugar

1 vanilla bean, split and seeds scraped

❖ ❖ ❖ ❖ ❖

1. In a medium saucepan, combine the milk with the cream, chocolate, sugar, and vanilla seeds and cook over low heat until barely simmering. Remove the pan from the heat, cover, and let stand for 15 minutes, stirring occasionally, until smooth and flavorful. Serve hot.

From Françoise:

• For a frothy drink, whisk the hot chocolate or whir it in the blender just before serving.

• If you'd like a drink that's slightly bitter, add unsweetened cocoa powder.

MANGO-LYCHEE FRAPPÉ

- Cocktail exotique -

3 mangos, peeled and diced

10 ounces lychees, peeled and seeded

2 tablespoons sugar

Juice of 1 lemon

4 ice cubes

❖ ❖ ❖ ❖ ❖

1. In a blender, puree the mangoes with the lychees, sugar, and lemon juice until smooth. Add the ice cubes and blend until frothy.

SUMMER BERRY FIZZ

- *Cocktail de fruits rouges* -

½ pound strawberries, hulled

½ pound raspberries

½ lemon, peeled and diced

1 tablespoon cherry syrup

1 tablespoon cassis syrup

3 to 4 tablespoons sugar

Sparkling water

❖ ❖ ❖ ❖ ❖

1. In a blender, puree the strawberries with the raspberries, diced lemon, cherry syrup, cassis syrup, and sugar until smooth. Pour into a pitcher, top with sparkling water, and serve.

From Françoise:

• Serve in frosted mugs.

• You can use frozen strawberries and raspberries. Let them thaw slightly first.

BANANA SMOOTHIE

- *Lait à la banane* -

2 cups milk

2 bananas, thickly sliced

Pinch of cinnamon or dash of pure vanilla extract

4 ice cubes

❖ ❖ ❖ ❖ ❖

1. In a blender, puree ½ cup of the milk with the bananas until smooth. Add the remaining 1 ½ cups of milk, the cinnamon or vanilla, and ice cubes and blend. Serve in very cold glasses.

COCKTAILS & DRINKS

SPARKLING CITRUS-GAZPACHO COOLER
- *Sangrita* -

Juice of 1 orange

Juice of 2 limes

1 or 2 small spring onions or scallions

¼ bell pepper, coarsely chopped

3 ripe tomatoes, peeled, seeded, and chopped

Hot sauce

Salt and pepper

Sparkling water

6 ice cubes

❖ ❖ ❖ ❖ ❖

1. In a blender, puree the orange juice and lime juice with the onions or scallions, bell pepper, and tomatoes until smooth. Season with hot sauce, salt, and pepper. Pour into a pitcher and top with sparkling water. Serve in frosted mugs with an ice cube in each.

MILK AND HONEY REFRESHER
- *Lait du dragon* -

¾ cup milk

1 teaspoon honey

1 banana, thickly sliced

3 or 4 blanched almonds

1 teaspoon brewer's yeast

1 teaspoon wheat germ

Dash of pure vanilla extract

❖ ❖ ❖ ❖ ❖

1. In a blender, combine the milk and honey with the banana, almonds, brewer's yeast, wheat germ, and vanilla until frothy. Serve at once in a large mug.

PEACH MILKSHAKE

- *Milk-shake aux pêches* -

❖ SERVES 4

4 or 5 ripe peaches, peeled, halved, and pitted
½ lemon, peeled and diced
¾ cup milk

1 tablespoon sugar
2 or 3 scoops vanilla ice cream

❖ ❖ ❖ ❖ ❖

1. In a blender, puree the peaches and diced lemon with the milk and sugar until smooth. Add the ice cream and blend at low speed just until incorporated. Serve cold with straws.

From Françoise:
• Try this milkshake with other fruits: 8 to 10 apricots or plums; 4 or 5 peeled pears; 2 to 2 ½ cups raspberries, strawberries, or pitted cherries; or 4 bananas.

WHITE LADY

- *White Lady* -

❖ SERVES 1

2 ounces gin
1 ounce Cointreau

1 tablespoon fresh lemon juice
1 or 2 ice cubes

❖ ❖ ❖ ❖ ❖

1. In a blender, combine the gin with the Cointreau and lemon juice. Add the ice cubes and blend at low speed to start, then blend at high speed until frothy. Pour into a cocktail glass, iced or not, and serve.

COCKTAILS & DRINKS

GIN FIZZ

- Gin fizz -

1 large egg white (optional)

2 lemons, peeled and diced

2 tablespoons sugar

2 ounces gin

4 ice cubes

Sparkling water

❖ ❖ ❖ ❖ ❖

1. In a blender, combine the egg white, if using, with the diced lemons, sugar, and gin. Add the ice cubes and blend at low speed to start, then blend at high speed until frothy. Pour into a whisky glass, top with sparkling water, and serve with a straw.

FRESH TOMATO BLOODY MARY

- Bloody Mary -

2 ripe medium tomatoes, coarsely chopped

2 ounces vodka

1 lemon wedge, peeled and diced

A few dashes of Worcestershire sauce

2 or 3 drops hot sauce or a pinch of cayenne
 pepper

Salt and pepper

2 or 3 ice cubes

❖ ❖ ❖ ❖ ❖

1. In a blender, combine the tomatoes with the vodka, diced lemon, Worcestershire sauce, and hot sauce or cayenne. Season with salt and pepper. Blend for 15 to 20 seconds. Pour into a mug, add the ice cubes, and serve.

From Françoise:

• Instead of fresh tomatoes, you could use ¾ cup of tomato juice.

WHITE WINE PUNCH
- *Cup au vin blanc* -

❖ 1 HOUR CHILLING   ❖ SERVES 18 TO 20

1 lemon, thinly sliced

1 orange, thinly sliced

20 grapes, peeled

2 ripe peaches, peeled and thinly sliced

1 tender celery rib

4 to 5 tablespoons sugar

3 cups dry white wine

1 cucumber wedge, thinly sliced

2 ounces Cognac, or to taste

1 ounce Cointreau, or to taste (optional)

❖ ❖ ❖ ❖ ❖

1. In a punch bowl, combine all the ingredients. Cover and refrigerate until cold, at least 1 hour.

From Françoise:

• In warm weather, it's a good idea to mix the alcohol with a half-bottle of sparking water—or even an entire bottle.

RUM PUNCH
- *Punch guadeloupéen* -

❖ SERVES 1

1 part sugar syrup

2 parts white rum

Pinch of freshly grated nutmeg

1 thin strip of lemon zest

1 ice cube, crushed

❖ ❖ ❖ ❖ ❖

• In a glass, combine the sugar syrup with the rum and nutmeg. Add a twist of lemon and the ice. Serve with a straw or demitasse spoon.

From Françoise:

• For a variation, in a glass, combine the sugar syrup and rum with 1 whole ice cube and the twist of lemon.

COCKTAILS
& DRINKS

HOT TEA PUNCH
- Punch au thé -

❖ SERVES 12

1 ¾ cups sugar

2 to 3 teaspoons black tea

1 ½ cups white rum

12 thin lemon slices

❖ ❖ ❖ ❖ ❖

1. In a medium saucepan, bring 3 cups of water to a boil with the sugar, stirring to dissolve the sugar. Remove the pan from the heat, add the tea, and let steep for 2 to 3 minutes.

2. Meanwhile, in a large saucepan, warm the rum; do not let it boil. Strain in the tea and add the lemon slices. Bring to a simmer, tilt the pan, and carefully ignite. When the flames subside, serve the punch, adding 1 lemon slice to each glass.

PORTO FLIP
- Porto-flip -

❖ SERVES 1

2 ounces ruby port

1 large egg

1 teaspoon sugar

2 pinches freshly grated nutmeg

❖ ❖ ❖ ❖ ❖

1. In a blender, combine the port with the egg and sugar. Blend at low speed to start, then blend at high speed until frothy. Pour into a Bordeaux glass, dust with the nutmeg, and serve with a straw.

ORANGE SPARKLER

- *Marquise au champagne* -

3 cups champagne or sparkling white wine

1 ½ cups sparkling water

½ cup orange liqueur

2 small handfuls of strawberries,
   halved or quartered if large, or, preferably,
   wild strawberries

❖ ❖ ❖ ❖ ❖

1. In a chilled pitcher, combine the champagne or wine with the water and liqueur. Add the strawberries and serve.

From Françoise:
• Raspberries create a different effect but also are tasty in this drink.

SANGRIA

- *Sangria* -

4 cups full-bodied red wine

3 cups sweet wine

½ cup sugar

Freshly grated nutmeg

1 teaspoon cinnamon

3 oranges, thinly sliced

1 lemon, thinly sliced

6 peaches or other juicy fruit, chopped

Ice cubes

Sparkling water

❖ ❖ ❖ ❖ ❖

1. In a large bowl, combine the red and sweet wines with the sugar, nutmeg, and cinnamon and stir to dissolve the sugar. Add the oranges, lemon, and peaches. Cover and refrigerate until cold, 2 to 3 hours.

2. Add the ice cubes, top with the sparkling water, and serve.

From Françoise:
• For serving, you may need to divide the sangria into 2 large pitchers before adding the ice cubes and sparkling water.

COCKTAILS
& DRINKS

PINK COCKTAIL

- *Rose cocktail* -

1 ounce sweet vermouth

1 ounce dry vermouth

Splash of orange bitters

½ ounce kirsch

½ ounce cherry brandy

1 ounce gin

1 brandied cherry

1 thin strip of orange zest

❖ ❖ ❖ ❖ ❖

1. In a cocktail shaker, combine the sweet and dry vermouths with the orange bitters, kirsch, brandy, and gin. Shake well and pour into a cocktail glass. Add the brandied cherry and a twist of orange.

From Françoise:

• To make this drink less alcoholic, the cherry brandy can be replaced with cherry syrup and crushed ice can be added.

SHERRY COBBLER

- *Sherry cobler* -

1 ounce Cognac

½ ounce dry amontillado or oloroso sherry

1 ounce curaçao

1 ice cube

½ ounce cherry brandy

1 thin slice of lemon or orange

❖ ❖ ❖ ❖ ❖

1. In a blender, combine the Cognac with the sherry, curaçao, and ice cube. Blend at low speed to start, then blend at high speed until frothy. Stir in the brandy. Pour into a glass, decorate with the slice of lemon or orange, and serve.

CONVERSION CHART

ALL CONVERSIONS ARE APPROXIMATE.

❖ ❖ ❖ ❖ ❖

Liquid Conversions		Weight Conversions		Oven Temperatures		
U.S.	METRIC	U.S./U.K.	METRIC	ºF	GAS MARK	ºC
1 tsp	5 ml	½ oz	14 g	250	½	120
1 tbs	15 ml	1 oz	28 g	275	1	140
2 tbs	30 ml	1 ½ oz	43 g	300	2	150
3 tbs	45 ml	2 oz	57 g	325	3	165
¼ cup	60 ml	2 ½ oz	71 g	350	4	180
⅓ cup	75 ml	3 oz	85 g	375	5	190
⅓ cup + 1 tbs	90 ml	3 ½ oz	100 g	400	6	200
⅓ cup + 2 tbs	100 ml	4 oz	113 g	425	7	220
½ cup	120 ml	5 oz	142 g	450	8	230
⅔ cup	150 ml	6 oz	170 g	475	9	240
¾ cup	180 ml	7 oz	200 g	500	10	260
¾ cup + 2 tbs	200 ml	8 oz	227 g	550	Broil	290
1 cup	240 ml	9 oz	255 g			
1 cup + 2 tbs	275 ml	10 oz	284 g			
1 ¼ cups	300 ml	11 oz	312 g			
1 ⅓ cups	325 ml	12 oz	340 g			
1 ½ cups	350 ml	13 oz	368 g			
1 ⅔ cups	375 ml	14 oz	400 g			
1 ¾ cups	400 ml	15 oz	425 g			
1 ¾ cups + 2 tbs	450 ml	1 lb	454 g			
2 cups (1 pint)	475 ml					
2 ½ cups	600 ml					
3 cups	720 ml					
4 cups (1 quart)	945 ml					
	(1,000 ml is 1 liter)					

INDEX

❖ ❖ ❖ ❖ ❖

Caper sauce, creamy, 638–39
Caramel:
    chocolate-, candies, 744
    crème, 682
    parfait, frozen, 685
    pudding, 682–83
    rice pudding, 718
Carbonnade, 213
Carottes:
    braisées aux oignons, 508
    à la pompadour, 508–9
    râpées, 67
    en soufflé, 507
    Vichy, 506–7
Carré d'agneau persillade, 230–31
Carré de porc braisé à l'orange, 245
Carrelet meunière, 424
Carrelets frits, 423
Carrot(s):
    buttery glazed, 506–7
    diced potatoes and, with creamy
        sauce, 508–9
    shredded, with lemony vinaigrette,
        67
    slow-cooked, with pearl onions, 508
    soufflé, 507
Cassolettes duchesse, 588–89
Cassoulet, 224–25
Cauliflower:
    boiled, 550
    golden creamy, 549–50
    soufflé, 550–51
Celery:
    ribs with anchovy dipping sauce,
        524
    tomato-braised, 524–25
Celery root:
    and beet salad with walnuts, 29
    diced, simmered with tomato,
        mushroom, and ham sauce, 523
    golden gratin of, with Gruyère, 522
    julienne in mustard mayonnaise, 65
    and potato puree, 521–22
    and potato soup, pureed, with
        garlic, 14–15
    soup, silky, 11
Cèpes à la bordelaise, 561
Cervelle:
    grenobloise, 318
    maître-d'hôtel, 319
    meunière, 320
Champignons:
    citronette, 42
    farcis, 86
    à la grecque, 66
    sautés aux fines herbes, 562
    surprise, 42–43
Chanterelle mushrooms:
    creamy, 559
    garlicky pan-seared, 558–59
Charlotte de pâtes, 610–11
Charlottes, 746–49
    berry, summer, 748–49
    chocolate-chestnut, 747
    with vanilla Bavarian cream, 746

Chateaubriands aux pommes de terres,
    196–97
Cheese. *See also* Gruyère; Roquefort
    goat, toasts, salad with, 109
Chef's salad, French, 45
Cherry clafoutis, 758
Chestnut(s):
    chocolate charlotte, 747
    chocolate mold, 740
    chocolate "potatoes," 743
    chocolate Yule log, 742
    puree, velvety, 563
    slow-cooked, 563–64
Chicken, 260–76, 278–81. *See also* Hen;
    Liver(s); Rooster
    with bacon and thyme, 272
    Calvados-flamed, with creamy
        sauce, 273
    citrus-marinated, 265–66
    Cognac-flamed, with creamy
        tarragon sauce, 270
    with corn stuffing, 276
    crusty mustard-grilled, with shallot
        sauce, 266–67
    curried, brioches stuffed with, 98
    cutlets with creamy tarragon sauce,
        278–79
    with mushrooms and shallot, 268
    with mushrooms and tomatoes,
        269–70
    noodle soup with Gruyère, 23
    pilaf, spiced, 267
    with pork and tarragon stuffing,
        275
    pot pie with green olives, 280–81
    pot-roasted, with green olives,
        tomatoes, and golden potatoes,
        264
    pot-roasted, with spring vegetables,
        265
    with red peppers, currants, and
        spices, 268–69
    roast, classic, 260
    roast, rice-stuffed, 261
    roast, savory meat-stuffed, 263
    with rye bread and and beef
        marrow stuffing, 274–75
    salad with vegetable julienne, 44
    soup with angel hair pasta, 20–21
    soup with giblets, 20
    soup with Parmesan, bread crumbs,
        and egg, 6
    spit-roasted, 262
    stuffed, rich, 274
    -stuffed crêpes, crispy, 279–80
    with tomatoes, mushrooms, olives,
        and almonds, 271
    with velvety pepper stew, 272–73
Chinese artichokes, buttery sautéed,
    570
Chipolatas au chou, 353–54
Chive and horseradish sauce, 589
Chocolat:
    chaud maison, 780
    liégeois, 775

Chocolate:
    almond tart, 707
    bittersweet, truffles, 743–44
    caramel candies, 744
    chestnut charlotte, 747
    chestnut mold, 740
    chestnut "potatoes," 743
    custard, 678–79
    dark, sauce, ice cream with, 773
    frosting, 650
    ganache, 650, 727
    ganache-stuffed meringues, 692
    hot, rich vanilla-bean, 780
    ice cream with vanilla whipped
        cream, 775
    marquise, 687
    mousse, 686–87
    profiteroles, 776
    sauce, poached pears with, 665
    semolina pudding cake, 721
Chocolate cake, 724–25
    chestnut Yule log, 742
    marble pound, 723–24
    with mocha-cream layer, 727
    super-moist, 726
    tender heart, 725
Chorizo and monkfish skewers, 402
Chouchouka, 127
Choucroute, 354–55
Choux à la crème, 738–39
Choux pastries, 99–100, 585–86,
    738–39, 753–54, 776
Cinnamon-walnut tart, 706
Citrus-gazpacho cooler, sparkling,
    782
Civet de lièvre, 373–74
Clafoutis:
    apple-raisin, 759
    cherry, 758
Cobbler, sherry, 788
Cockles:
    and macaroni with creamy tomato
        sauce, 462
    molded rice pilaf with creamy sauce
        and, 463
    with shallots and crispy crumbs,
        461
Cocktails:
    de crevettes, 482–83
    exotique, 780
    de fruits de mer, 482
    de fruits rouges, 781
Cocktails and alcoholic beverages,
    783–88
    fresh tomato bloody mary, 784
    gin fizz, 784
    hot tea punch, 786
    orange sparkler, 787
    pink cocktail, 788
    porto flip, 786
    rum punch, 785
    sangria, 787
    white lady, 783
    white wine punch, 785
Coconut roulade, 750